1914: FIGHT THE GOOD FIGHT

www.transworldbooks.co.uk

1914: Fight the Good Fight

Britain, the Army and the Coming of the First World War

Allan Mallinson

BANTAM PRESS

LONDON · TORONTO · SYDNEY · AUCKLAND · JOHANNESBURG

TRANSWORLD PUBLISHERS
61–63 Uxbridge Road, London W5 5SA
A Random House Group Company
www.transworldbooks.co.uk

First published in Great Britain
in 2013 by Bantam Press
an imprint of Transworld Publishers

A CIP catalogue record for this book
is available from the British Library.

ISBNs 9780593067604 (cased)
9780593067611 (tpb)

Maps by Tom Coulson at Encompass Graphics

Addresses for Random House Group Ltd companies outside the UK
can be found at: www.randomhouse.co.uk
The Random House Group Ltd Reg. No. 954009

The Random House Group Limited supports the Forest Stewardship Council® (FSC®),
the leading international forest-certification organisation. Our books carrying the
FSC label are printed on FSC®-certified paper. FSC is the only forest-certification
scheme supported by the leading environmental organisations, including
Greenpeace. Our paper procurement policy can be found at
www.randomhouse.co.uk/environment

Typeset in 10/14.5pt Stone Serif by Falcon Oast Graphic Art Ltd.
Printed and bound in Great Britain by Clays Ltd, Bungay, Suffolk

2 4 6 8 10 9 7 5 3

MIX
Paper from
responsible sources
FSC® C016897

War is the ultimate resource of policy, by which the nation seeks to impose its will on its enemies in defence of its honour, its interests, and its existence.

Field Service Regulations 1909, with amendments 1914

CONTENTS

List of Maps — ix
List of Illustrations — x
Author's Note and Acknowledgements — xi
Preface — xvii

1 The Lamps Begin to Flicker — 1
2 Allies of the Old Century — 22
3 Lessons — 47
4 The Contemptible Little Army — 71
5 Plans — 99
6 Calculations — 121
7 The Sea and the Dry Land — 140
8 The Bones of Grenadiers — 169
9 A Deadly Quadrille — 179
10 The Great Question Answered — 189
11 The Call to Arms — 219
12 An Army with a Country Attached to It — 235
13 Fear God. Honour the King. — 259
14 The First Dusting — 274
15 Mons – the Stubborn Resistance — 296
16 Shrapnel Monday — 320
17 'Very well, gentlemen, we will fight' — 336
18 'A day will be written in story' — 355
19 'C'est la France qui vous supplie' — 374
20 'En avant!' — 402
21 The Race to the Sea; and What Might Have Been — 417

CONTENTS

Postscript: Desperate Appeals against the Decision of Fate   440

Appendix: The British Expeditionary Force, August 1914 –
    Order of Battle   465
Picture Acknowledgements   477
Index   481

MAPS

Europe 1914	xiv–xv
German unification, 1864–70	30–1
The Schlieffen concept	102–3
The armies line up – Western Front	238–9
The Schlieffen concept unfolds	270–1
Shoulder to shoulder	278–9
Le Cateau	360–1
The 'miracle on the Marne' and the 'race to the sea'	418–19
What might have been	434

ILLUSTRATIONS

Mobilization poster, 4 August 1914   14
The Entente Cordiale   57
His Majesty's Army Special Reserve   63
The Dreadnought Race   145
'Brave little Belgium'   185
Allies: Sir John French arrives in Paris   241
'The Triumph of "Culture"'   253
'India for the King!'   424

AUTHOR'S NOTE AND ACKNOWLEDGEMENTS

I was one of the last members of the (army) general staff, before it was eviscerated and subsumed within the new (tri-service) defence staff. Indeed, as a young major, 'general staff officer grade II' (GSO2), I worked in the Directorate of Military Operations, in the branch concerned with war in Europe – the branch that plays so central a part in this story. In our ancient safe were documents going back to the time of the most famous, or infamous, of directors, Major-General (later Field Marshal) Henry Wilson, who features equally prominently in this book. I was posted there after a year at the Staff College in Camberley (the college has since moved to Shrivenham and been tri-serviced out of all recognition), where Wilson had been commandant before returning to the War Office in 1910 to make the plans for mobilization, and where I was trained in the same discipline of 'staff writing' as Wilson's own GSO2s: what was, and occasionally still is, called 'minor staff duties', or 'minor SD'. As I delved in the great stash of War Office papers in the National Archives while researching for this book – the briefing notes, minutes, memoranda, lists and letters – it felt at times as if I were reading documents that had only just been filed. Where I have quoted from these, or from other unpublished sources, in what follows, I have not provided individual notes of attribution in every case as this would have imposed a cumbersome weight of annotation on the text. Nor have I included a separate bibliography, for it would have gone on for too many pages – especially the primary documents (and perhaps even more so the secondary, for I consulted virtually every regimental and corps history)

– and in the end would not have added very much, except for a monument to the capacity for making lists. Nor was I inclined, as I did in *The Making of the British Army*, a much broader work, to include a 'further reading' list; for how to be usefully selective? I have, however, footnoted specific references to published work in the usual way.

As always in writing a book there are many people to thank. I do not use researchers, but with *Fight the Good Fight* I discussed my thoughts with three people in particular. In the earliest stages I put my 'big ideas' to the late Sir John Keegan, who, bed-ridden even as he was, gave me the greatest encouragement. Professor John Röhl, Emeritus Professor of History at the University of Sussex, read the first draft and was unsparingly generous in his critical commentary, even as he was preparing for publication the third volume of his biography of the Kaiser. And my former branch colonel in the Ministry of Defence (and later Director of Infantry), Major-General Ray Pett, read the second draft, as he used to read my briefs and papers before they could be officially circulated at the 'War Office', and made many observations and suggestions. I am indebted to the three of them for the depth they have added. I am also particularly grateful to Professor Thomas Otte, Professor of Diplomatic History at the University of East Anglia, whose guidance in the maze of Belgian neutrality (particularly that of the Scheldt) was invaluable. Any mistakes are of course mine. But of mistakes I would plead the opinion of Edward Thomas, killed in France in 1917: 'Better a thousand errors so long as they are human than a thousand truths lying like broken snail-shells round the anvil of a thrush.'*

I am especially beholden to my wife for her support in what has been a longer and more intensive project than originally envisaged, and to many others who have contributed directly and indirectly. To General Sir Richard Shirreff, the Deputy Supreme Allied Commander Europe (NATO), whose familiarity with the initial clashes in 1914 near his present-day headquarters at Mons in Belgium was a very real inspiration in my early reconnaissances, and to Lady (Sarah-Jane) Shirreff for her hospitality. To Lady (Fiona) Fraser for all manner of help and advice. Likewise to Erica Wagner, former literary editor of *The Times*, and to Rose Wild, the *Times* archivist. To Sir Ivor Roberts,

* 'History and the Parish', from *The South Country* (1909).

Master of Trinity College, Oxford; Sir John Scarlett, formerly head of the Secret Intelligence Service; Patrick Rock, the Prime Minister's policy adviser; Lord Valentine Cecil, 'Once a Grenadier, always a Grenadier'; and Raymond Asquith, 3rd Earl of Oxford and Asquith, for kindness over a number of details. To Major Maurice French, late of the Royal Fusiliers, for his great generosity in lending me for so long the papers of his uncle, Lieutenant Maurice Dease VC. To the officers commanding regimental headquarters, and curators of military museums too numerous to mention, for their patience in answering questions, giving me access to documents of all kinds, and the loan of diaries, maps and photographs – especially the curators of the Weapons Collection of the Small-Arms School Corps at Warminster, and with particular affection for the smallest (and private) museum of all, the Wagoners' Special Reserve at Sledmere, and to Sir Tatton Sykes and his curator, Sandra Oakins. To the staff of the National Archives at Kew and of the German Historical Institute (London), and especially to the librarians of the Royal United Services Institute (Whitehall), the Prince Consort's Library (Aldershot) and the School of Infantry (Warminster). To Diane Lees, Director-General of the Imperial War Museum (and fellow trustee of the Ogilby Army Museums Trust), and Anthony Richards, the IWM's Head of Documents and Sound.

To my editor at Transworld, Simon Taylor, for striving indefatigably to make the book understandable to those who have not served on the General Staff; to my copy-editor, Gillian Somerscales, for being so diligent an assayer of the narrative and kindly *arbiter elegantiarum*; to Sheila Lee for her imaginative picture research, Tom Coulson of Encompass Graphics for the clarity of the maps, Phil Lord for his assured design, Auriol Griffith-Jones for her sedulous indexing, Claire Ward and Steve Mulcahey for a most striking cover, and Katrina Whone, managing editor, for pulling it all together.

And ultimately to St Paul (via the Reverend John Monsell) for a glorious title.

EUROPE 1914

- Central Powers
- Slavic allies of Russia
- Triple Entente

Baltic Sea

RUSSIAN EMPIRE

AUSTRIA-HUNGARY

ROMANIA

SERBIA

MONT.

BULGARIA

Black Sea

ALB.

OTTOMAN EMPIRE

GREECE

DODECANESE
(Italian)

CYPRUS
(British)

ARABIA

LIBYA
(invaded by
Italy, 1911)

EGYPT

Only a man harrowing clods
In a slow silent walk
With an old horse that stumbles and nods
Half asleep as they stalk.

Only thin smoke without flame
From the heaps of couch-grass;
Yet this will go onward the same
Though Dynasties pass.

Yonder a maid and her wight
Come whispering by:
War's annals will cloud into night
Ere their story die.

In Time of 'The Breaking of Nations'
Thomas Hardy, 1915

Preface

In Time of 'The Breaking of Nations'

War's annals – those at least of the British Expeditionary Force of August 1914 – have indeed clouded into night. Too often only the trenches stand clearly in the popular mind's eye, as if what preceded them in the First World War (and what followed, in late 1918) were all of a piece.

When the Serbian nationalist Gavrilo Princip fired two deadly shots into the Archduke Franz Ferdinand's car in Sarajevo on 28 June, the result was a diplomatic cat's cradle – statesmen, ambassadors and soldiers manoeuvring in a tangle of ambiguous treaties, ill-defined *ententes* and inflexible military plans, a snarl that pleased the warlike and confounded the peaceable. For a time, too, it paralysed the uncommitted, not least Britain. Never was St Paul more apt than in July 1914 – 'Evil communications corrupt good manners' – for the old 'Concert of Europe', the balance of power conceived at the Congress of Vienna a century earlier, now hardened into two armed camps, conducted its diplomacy by telegram at a slower speed than the armies mobilized by railway.

There had been other crises in the decade before, and the worst that had happened was local war in the Balkans; yet somehow Princip's two shots would propel the German army into neutral Belgium and on towards Paris. Britain had always taken a decidedly semi-detached position on continental affairs, even while desiring the balance of power in Europe; the foreign secretary, Sir Edward Grey, went abroad only once during his nine years in office (and only then, in April 1912, to accompany the King to Paris). And yet now, for the first time in a hundred years, Britain would send troops across the Channel – albeit with no very clear idea how they should be used. In 1914 there were 100,000 of them; by 1918 there would be over two million.

'No part of the Great War compares in interest with its opening,' wrote Churchill in his foreword to Lieutenant (later Major-General) Edward Spears' remarkable account of his time as a liaison officer with the French army:

> The measured, silent drawing together of gigantic forces, the uncertainty of their movements and positions, the number of unknown and unknowable facts made the first collision a drama never surpassed. Nor was there any other period in the War when the general battle was waged on so great a scale, when the slaughter was so swift or the stakes so high. Moreover, in the beginning our faculties of wonder, horror and excitement had not been cauterized and deadened by the furnace fires of years. In fact the War was decided in the first twenty days of fighting, and all that happened afterwards consisted in battles which, however formidable and devastating, were but desperate and vain appeals against the decision of fate.*

Fate – the power or principle that predetermines events – seems in the minds of many also to have been the bringer of that war. How but for some malign force could the assassination of an Austrian archduke in a place that few outside the Balkans had heard of, let alone could find on a map, send the Royal Navy to its battle stations and the British army to France? Fate made statesmen and officials purblind, unable to see the consequences of arms races, treaties and threats, so that they sleep-walked ('Half asleep as they stalked') into war.† A hundred years on, there is still no consensus on *die Kriegsschuldfrage* – the question of war guilt – or even the precise dynamics of the July

---

* Edward Spears, *Liaison 1914* (London, 1930). In August 1914 Churchill had been first lord of the Admiralty; in 1916 he commanded a battalion on the Western Front; he was subsequently minister of munitions; in 1919 he became secretary of state for war and for air, in 1921 secretary of state for the colonies, and from 1924 to 1929, chancellor of the exchequer. In 1940, as prime minister, he would appoint Spears his personal representative to the French PM.

† See, for example, the Cambridge historian Christopher Clark's *The Sleepwalkers: How Europe Went to War in 1914* (London, 2012). Churchill wrote to his wife on 28 July of Europe's being in 'a kind of dull cataleptic trance'.

crisis. Frequently in popular imagination and narrative the outbreak of war is a catastrophic inevitability, connected somehow with mobilization and railway timetables, as if some sorcerer's apprentice had lost control of his broom, unable to conjure the magic words that would stop its mindless exertions before unleashing the deluge. In an episode of *The West Wing*, Warner Brothers' fictional portrayal of the US presidency (Episode 88 – 'Twenty-Five'), the Speaker of the House of Representatives solemnly recounts the course of the July crisis to the President's staff as a warning that events have their own momentum. And in the 1974 TV docudrama on the Cuban crisis, *The Missiles of October*, President John F. Kennedy is haunted by his reading of Barbara Tuchman's 1962 Pulitzer-Prize-winning book *The Guns of August*, and the seeming inability of the statesmen of Europe to find the lever that would stop the machinery of mobilization and thereby the First World War – as if there were any such lever that could do so.* Yet the pre-war arrangements did not ultimately remove choice; they only made it harder. *Fight the Good Fight* is concerned principally with the *military* choices, and specifically Britain's.

'In fact the War was decided in the first twenty days of fighting.' But where? Although major battles were fought on the Eastern Front, between the Austrians and Russians in Galicia, and between the Germans and Russians in East Prussia, it was in Belgium and northern France that 'the decision of fate' was made. And the British army – the 'British Expeditionary Force' – small though it was, helped make that decision. The 'Schlieffen Plan', bold, cunning and ruthless, painstakingly crafted by the Prussian general staff over a decade and a half in order to gain rapid victory in the west so that German troops could then be switched east to deal with the real enemy, Russia, was wrecked by Belgian *jas* in Napoleonic shakos, by French *poilus* in red trousers – and by British 'Tommies' in khaki peaked caps, the 'Old Contemptibles', the name they adopted with characteristic irony after

---

* Barbara Tuchman (1912–89) was an American journalist and historian, a lecturer at Harvard and the US Navy War College. Kennedy had a high regard for *The Guns of August*, published in Britain with the title *August 1914*, which he sent to senior officers and Washington staff. It still has a powerful resonance, in the US especially: in August 2006 Richard Holbrooke, former ambassador to the UN (and later President Obama's special representative to Pakistan and Afghanistan), wrote a cautionary article in the *Washington Post* on the escalatory situation in Iraq and Lebanon under the headline 'The Guns of August'.

the Kaiser's supposed mockery of 'Britain's contemptible little army'.

The official *History of the Great War* describes the British Expeditionary Force (BEF) as 'incomparably the best trained, best organised and best equipped British Army that ever went forth to war',* but by midnight on 22 November, the end of the First Battle of Ypres and the close of the qualifying period for the medal known colloquially as the Mons Star, the army that had left England in the middle of August was the proverbial shadow of its former self, recognizable more in form than in substance, like the fast-flowing river which, though remaining the same stream, is not the same water. There were but a handful of officers, and a hundred or so men, left in each of the thousand-strong battalions that had marched out of barracks in Aldershot, Colchester, York, Edinburgh, Dublin and the other home garrisons of the old regular army. Casualties between 5 August and 30 November were 86,237. One in ten of those who had crossed to France in August had been killed.

Need the losses have been so great? Might the BEF have achieved more? Could Germany have been fought beyond just a standstill – to early capitulation indeed?

The BEF was without doubt the best trained, best organized and best equipped British army that had ever gone forth to war, but in truth this was only saying so much, for Britain had always sought to evade a continental commitment and its cost in blood and (especially) treasure. The accolade masked deficiencies both material and moral – grave deficiencies. Ironically, too, the strenuous efforts to reform the army after the débâcles of the Boer War had an unintended consequence: they brought the army to an unprecedented pitch of efficiency, but in August 1914 they also brought it to the wrong place, at the wrong time, and trusting in an ally – France – whose own army, in its obsession with the overwhelming moral power of the offensive, had put its trust in the wrong generals and the wrong strategy.

Much has been and continues to be written about the desperate attempts of statesmen and diplomats to find the right lever to pull after the assassination at Sarajevo. The obsession with this lever has tended to

---

* Brigadier-General J. E. Edmonds, *History of the Great War Based on Official Documents*, 29 vols (London, 1923–49), vol. 1. This massive work, usually known (and cited hereafter) simply as the *Official History*, was written as a technical history for military staff by the Historical Section of the Committee of Imperial Defence.

divert attention from Britain's failure to find the right military strategy – fundamentally a political failure, for strategy is first the product of policy. But even analyses of British military strategy too often betray a misunderstanding of how the War Office worked, especially the function of its directors. Nor have they examined, in the light of subsequent events, the alternative strategies for a continental engagement proposed beforehand by men such as the first lord of the Admiralty, the young Winston Churchill, and Douglas Haig, who in 1914 was a relatively junior corps commander in the BEF.

Fight the Good Fight is essentially an Anglocentric perspective of the BEF's first twenty days, and of what came before – specifically, Britain's wishful detachment from the affairs of continental Europe, notwithstanding the implied alliance of the Entente Cordiale. It was a full month after the shooting in Sarajevo before the cabinet properly discussed the situation in Europe; and even once the fighting began, a mood of semi-detachment persisted for weeks. *Fight the Good Fight* is not, however, another book about the causes of the First World War. It explains the grand strategic shift that came about in the century beforehand, which slowly eroded Britain's 'splendid isolation', but only to set the strategic context for the military plans and actions. It describes the army's Edwardian regeneration after its drubbings by the Boers, and recounts the BEF's almost calamitous experience of the first twenty days' fighting, until the 'Old Contemptibles' took up the pick and the spade in the middle of September 1914, when the war began to change from one of movement into the more familiar image of the trenches. There followed the arrival of the 'Terriers', the 'Pals' and, ultimately, the conscripts – and of course the poets; and with them the sense of pity, of futility.

There was no sense of pity or futility in the old BEF, for these men were professionals. Indeed, the Kaiser called them mercenaries – a jibe with which A. E. Housman made ironic play in his 'Epitaph on an Army of Mercenaries':

> These, in the day when heaven was falling,
> The hour when earth's foundations fled,
> Followed their mercenary calling
> And took their wages and are dead.

Their shoulders held the sky suspended;
They stood, and earth's foundations stay;
What God abandoned, these defended,
And saved the sum of things for pay. *

'In fact the War was decided in the first twenty days of fighting.' If so, need there have been the subsequent 'desperate and vain appeals against the decision of fate'? Could the first twenty days' fighting have been more immediately decisive, bringing the war to a prompt end – 'over by Christmas', as so many believed it would be; or at least by Christmas 1915?

As I try to show, if there had been a firmer political grasp on British military strategy in the decade before 1914, and greater vision at the War Office, the answer is – 'yes', just possibly. At the very least, the Western Front need not have looked as it did in the years that followed. This is not mere hindsight, as the counsels of Winston Churchill, the youngest member of the cabinet, and Douglas Haig, the most junior of the generals summoned to the 'war council' on 5 August that fateful year, show all too clearly. Had those counsels been taken, the whole course of the war – its length, its cost, its outcome – might have been radically different. And what a different century might then have followed.

As it was, the BEF 'took their wages and are dead'. *Fight the Good Fight* explains how and why.

* First published in *The Times*, 31 October 1917, with a commemorative article on the BEF at Ypres. Two days earlier, in a speech during Parliament's 'Vote of Thanks to the Forces', the then prime minister, David Lloyd George, said of the BEF: 'The old Army is the Army that gathered the spears of the Prussian legions into its breast, and in perishing saved Europe. No sacrifice in the history of the world has had greater results, and those seven [sic] divisions have a unique position in history and in the annals of the British Army.'

The lamps are going out all over Europe;
we shall not see them lit again in our lifetime.

Sir Edward Grey, August 1914

Chapter One

THE LAMPS BEGIN TO FLICKER

The lights were barely up to the job. Gladstone had had electricity put in at 10 Downing Street during his fourth and final administration, twenty years before, but the three brass chandeliers in the Cabinet Room were not meant to illuminate the meetings of great men. As a rule ministers met in the full light of day, which flooded through the big sash windows on two sides of the house in which history had been made for nearly two centuries. Now, just after nine o'clock on Tuesday, 4 August 1914, in the last evening of the hundred years' peace (peace, at least, between Britain and her continental neighbours), the place was dim, even dingy, adding to the atmosphere of impending doom. All day there had been telegrams and rumours, but no word from the German embassy in Carlton House Terrace just across The Mall, and nothing since mid-afternoon from the British ambassador in Berlin; nor anything from the new foreign section of the Secret Service Bureau (in time, the Secret Intelligence Service – MI6) and its agents in the Low Countries. The previous day Germany had declared war on France and German troops had invaded Belgium, whose neutrality Britain felt obliged to defend by a treaty of 1839. The ambassador in Berlin had been instructed to inform the Kaiser's government that unless an assurance was received by midnight that the German army would halt its advance, Britain would 'feel

1

bound to take all steps in [her] power to uphold the neutrality of Belgium'. Now, as the hour approached for the expiry of the ultimatum, the prime minister, 'H.H.' (Herbert Henry) Asquith, called his principal secretaries of state together. But what was there to do other than wait?

The easy-going Asquith, sixty-one years old and white-haired but distractedly in love with a girl less than half his age – Venetia Stanley, to whom he wrote daily, sometimes several times, and even during cabinet meetings – for once looked grave. His foreign secretary and fellow Balliol classicist, Sir Edward Grey, tall but stooping, looking pallid, worn-out and a good deal older than his fifty-two years, had the air of a defeated man. The lord chancellor and caretaker-minister at the War Office,* the 58-year-old Edinburgh- and Göttingen-educated philosopher, barrister and bachelor Richard Burdon (Viscount) Haldane, looked more than usually ponderous.

Only the chancellor of the exchequer, David Lloyd George, perhaps because he had not previously been one of the inner council, seemed undaunted: a handsome figure, not yet of the famous white locks (his hair merely curled over his collar in a slightly raffish way), the same age as Grey but with the vigour of a man half his years, he looked as bluff as the foreign secretary looked broken. A large crowd had gathered in Downing Street, and cheered each minister as he arrived.

One of the inner council who was not yet there to add spark to the lifeless gathering was the first lord of the Admiralty, the youngest member of the cabinet and the only one with first-hand military experience: the 39-year-old Winston Churchill.† He was still at his desk in Admiralty House the other side of Horse Guards Parade, sending signals to the far side of the world. The previous Thursday he had wired the commander-in-chief (C-in-C) Mediterranean, warning that war 'now

---

* The War Office was the department of the secretary of state for war, the cabinet minister responsible for the army – at this stage, Asquith himself, who held the position along with the premiership. The Admiralty was the corresponding department of state for the navy, whose minister was known as the first lord of the Admiralty, usually just 'first lord'. The professional head of the navy was (and is) known as the first sea lord (1SL).

† Churchill had been a regular officer in the army until just before the Boer War, in which he had then served as a volunteer after a brief but notable stint as a war correspondent. After the war he had joined the Yeomanry, the volunteer cavalry, and in August 1914 was a squadron leader in the Oxfordshire Hussars with the rank of major.

seems probable', that it looked as if Italy would not throw her lot in with Germany, and that the British fleet should be prepared to help the French navy to convoy troops from North Africa. That very morning the C-in-C, Admiral Sir Berkeley Milne, had replied *'Indomitable, Indefatigable* shadowing *Goeben* and *Breslau* [all battle-cruisers] 37° 44 North 7° 56 East', and at 5.30 in the afternoon Churchill had signalled to all ships: 'The war telegram will be issued at midnight authorizing you to commence hostilities against Germany, but in view of our ultimatum they may decide to open fire at any moment. You must be ready for this.'

Churchill himself was ready; he had been for a week and more. Others of the cabinet were still unwilling or unable to contemplate what was about to happen, as if there might yet be some deliverance even as the sand in the glass ran out.

At length came the home secretary, Reginald McKenna, tall, trim, a champion Cambridge oarsman, whom Churchill had supplanted at the Admiralty three years earlier. He had with him a piece of paper:

Time: 9.5 p.m.
Date: Aug. 4th, 1914.

The following message has been intercepted by the W.O. Censor:-
To German Ambassador from Berlin.
English Ambassador has just demanded his passport shortly after seven o'clock declaring war.

(Signed) Jagow

Asquith read it and passed it to the others. Gottlieb von Jagow was the German foreign minister: could there be any doubt of its authenticity or its meaning? But there was as yet no word from Sir Edward Goschen, the 'English' ambassador in Berlin. Why had he 'declared war' five hours early? There were still two hours before the ultimatum expired at midnight Central Europe Time, 11 p.m. in London; was the telegram – which was not in cipher – a trick? Did the Germans intend some *coup* against British ships, or even a landing somewhere? Should the telegram be treated as the commencement of hostilities? Asquith and his ministers were quite at a loss. Alert the fleet and the coastal defences, they decided.*

The first lord would need no urging. The Grand Fleet had been practising its mobilization† procedures when the pistol had been fired in Sarajevo, and at the end of the royal review at Portland a month later, on 28 July, instead of standing them down, Churchill, with some daring, had ordered the dreadnoughts and cruisers to steam 'at high speed, and without lights' through the Straits of Dover into the North Sea and onwards to their battle station, the lonely Orkney anchorage of Scapa Flow. But for the rest, the PM and his gathered few resolved to wait until eleven. There was just a chance, however remote, that a message might yet arrive from Berlin; and then something might be arranged to forestall the clash of nations that for a decade had haunted the capitals of Europe, yet somehow had hitherto been avoided by, in Lloyd George's words, 'goodwill and wise counsel'.

But no message came. As the hour approached, conversation in the Cabinet Room ceased, eyes glancing anxiously instead between clock and door. Then the deep notes of Big Ben broke the solemn silence: 'Doom!', 'Doom!', 'Doom!' – to the last stroke, as Lloyd George remembered it. Soon after, the telephones began ringing.

---

* Asking for one's passport (a diplomatic passport was used to travel to and from a post but was otherwise deposited with the foreign ministry on arrival) was the means of indicating a formal breach of diplomatic relations, the implication being that a diplomat would not be returning unless and until hostilities ceased. Up until the Second World War, 'the breaking of diplomatic relations was very often the prelude to war or to some form of military action' (Sir Ivor Roberts, ed., *Satow's Diplomatic Practice*, 6th edn, Oxford, 2009). For instance, on 2 September 1939 Sir Neville Henderson in Berlin was instructed to send a final warning to Hitler. Chamberlain announced this in the House of Commons, saying: 'Unless the German Government are prepared to give assurances that the German Government have suspended aggressive action against Poland and are prepared promptly to withdraw their forces from Polish territory, the Government in the United Kingdom will without hesitation fulfil their obligation to Poland . . . If the reply to this last warning is unfavourable, and I do not suggest it is likely to be otherwise, his Majesty's Ambassador is instructed to ask for his passports.' An ambassador today keeps his diplomatic passport throughout his tour, but, by the terms of the Vienna Convention (1961), when he is leaving the country for whatever cause informs the foreign ministry who will be in charge of the embassy in his stead (correspondence with Sir Ivor Roberts, former ambassador in Serbia and in Italy, President of Trinity College Oxford, editor of *Satow*, 6th edn). For an explanation of the 'English' ambassador's false start, see the note on pages 18–21.

† Mobilization was (and is) 'the process by which an armed force passes from a peace to a war footing, that is to say its completion to war establishment in personnel, transport and animals, and the provision of its war outfit' (*Field Service Regulations*, Part II: *Organization and Administration*, 1914).

4

In Government House, Aldershot, the Victorian villa that was the residence of the general officer commanding-in-chief (GOC-in-C) Aldershot Command, Lieutenant-General Sir Douglas Haig, it rang just before midnight. On the line was the headquarters duty officer, Captain John Harding-Newman.* The War Office had just wired, he told Haig: 'War has broken out with Germany,' and the GOC-in-C, who would command one of the two corps of the Expeditionary Force (later the *British* Expeditionary Force – BEF), was required at a 'war council' at 10 Downing Street the following afternoon.

Haig was entirely composed, relieved almost, now that a decision had come. That it was war came as no surprise at all: he, like many another senior officer, had seen the German army at its annual manoeuvres and was in no doubt of its restless, aggressive strength.† In any case, the War Office, anticipating the worst, had already ordered general mobilization: the telegram consisting of the single word 'Mobilize' and signed 'Troopers', the code name for the secretary of state for war, had arrived at Aldershot at 5.30 p.m., and Aldershot Command had in turn sent out its own telegrams to its subordinate headquarters. 'Everything had been so well thought out and foreseen,' wrote Haig in his diary, 'that I, as C-in-C Aldershot, was never called upon for a decision.' He promptly went to bed.‡

At about the same time, a young Foreign Office official, Harold Nicolson (who had married Vita Sackville-West the year before), home on leave from the embassy in Constantinople, rang long on the bell at the side entrance of the German embassy, on the steps leading from The Mall to the Duke of York's Column in Waterloo Place. Eventually a surly footman opened the door and said that the

---

* By 1918 Harding-Newman would be a major-general, so great had been the casualties among regular officers, and the expansion of the army.
† As early as 1897, G. W. Steevens, the *Daily Mail*'s war correspondent, had written: 'The German Army is the most perfectly adapted, perfectly running machine. Never can there have been a more signal triumph of organisation over complexity. The armies of other nations arc not so completely organised. The German Army is the finest thing of its kind in the world; it is the finest thing in Germany of any kind . . . The German Army is organised with a view to war, with the cold, hard, practical, business-like purpose of winning victories.' Churchill, Haldane and many senior officers, including Haig, had seen it for themselves.
‡ 'Precautionary Measures' had been ordered on 29 July, the day Germany declared war on Russia, activating the key levers of mobilization. These included the despatch of warning telegrams to some 98,000 reservists for the BEF, and to the Territorial Force. For more on the various groups of reservists and volunteers, see chapter 4 below.

ambassador had already gone to bed and was not to be disturbed.*

'You must tell the butler immediately that I must see His Excellency with an urgent message,' demanded Nicolson. This message was a substitute declaration of war. Shortly before ten o'clock a news agency had reported that Germany had declared war on Great Britain, and so the Foreign Office had torn up the preparatory draft referring to the expiry of the ultimatum and composed a new declaration, which was taken to the embassy after eleven o'clock by Lancelot Oliphant, a junior clerk in the Eastern Department. Soon afterwards it had been realized that the report was false, so a third declaration, reverting to the original wording, was drawn up. Nicolson, whose father was the permanent secretary at the Foreign Office, was sent to retrieve the version that Oliphant had taken and deliver instead one that made clear that a state of war existed because the ultimatum had expired without any response having been received from Berlin.

At length the butler appeared and led Nicolson up to the private apartments, where the ambassador, Karl Max Fürst (Prince) von Lichnowsky, lay on a brass bed in his pyjamas. Nicolson told him there had been a slight error in the document sent previously and he had come to substitute for it the correct version. Prince Lichnowsky pointed to the table, where an envelope was lying unattended: 'You will find it there,' he said, as if in a daze. It seemed he had not read it, but guessed its significance since the passports of the embassy staff were enclosed. Nicolson had been told to get a receipt, so he took the blotting pad, pen and ink-bottle across to the bed. While the ambassador was signing, shouting came from The Mall, and then singing – the 'Marseillaise' – as crowds streamed back from Buckingham Palace. Earlier in the day they had broken the embassy windows.

Lichnowsky took no notice. Without a word, having signed the receipt he turned out the pink lamp beside the bed – but then, perhaps feeling that he had been uncivil, turned it on again. 'Give my best regards to your father,' he said, sadly, with the pronounced 'r' and short 'a' of the accent of Silesia, his birthplace: 'I shall not in all probability see him before my departure.'†

* The following account draws on Harold Nicolson's *Portrait of a Diplomatist* (London, 1930).
† Lichnowsky was devastated by what the 'gangsters' and 'swine' (his words) in Berlin had done, as Walter Hines Page, the US ambassador in London, witnessed when he went to Carlton House Terrace the following day to take over Germany's affairs (Page

*

The next morning, 5 August, Douglas Haig motored to London and called on Field Marshal Sir John French at the Metropole Hotel off Trafalgar Square, where the senior staff of the BEF headquarters were gathering.* If things went as expected, French, his old friend and supporter, would be his commander-in-chief. Then he walked round the corner to the War Office, the Edwardian baroque *palazzo* (known as the Pepper Pot because of the domes on the roof) opposite the Horse Guards in Whitehall, for the customary medical examination. He was passed 'physically fit for active service at home or abroad' – no surprise, for at the age of fifty-three Haig was trim and active: he rode daily, played golf regularly and vigorously, and was no longer troubled by the liver complaints resulting from malaria a dozen years before, which had evidently been cured by spa treatments in Switzerland and Wales.†

Next he strode up the impressive double staircase to the second floor and into the dark-panelled office of the secretary of state, where the military members of the Army Council were assembled with Haldane for a preliminary meeting.‡ On the Adam chimneypiece opposite the secretary of state's desk stood a marble bust of the duke of Wellington – the Iron Duke presiding, as it were, once more over a council of generals for another war in Europe, a century on.

---

to President Wilson, 9 August 1914, *Papers of Woodrow Wilson*, Volume 20, Princeton, 1975). Next day the *Daily Mirror* would report that 'Absolute quiet prevailed at the German Embassy at 11.15 pm last night, though earlier in the evening there had been some booing. The Ambassador sat in his room on the lower floor writing dispatches. The window was open and the room was fully lighted. At 11.30 pm he finished and his butler came to close the window and put out the lights. As the clock struck twelve the few people still outside the Embassy began to suggest that the Ambassador had departed. In response to an enquiry by the *Daily Mirror* the butler smilingly replied, "The people are mistaken – the Ambassador has gone to bed."'

* The headquarters itself – a staff of several hundred officers and men – was assembling at the Polygon Hotel in Southampton, a huge Victorian pile at which many of the *Titanic*'s passengers had stayed before embarking, and which was demolished in 1999.

† How rigorous the War Office medicals were must be open to conjecture, however: two generals attending the war council that day would soon be dead of the strain of events, one of them – Haig's fellow corps commander, James Grierson – before the month was out.

‡ The seven-member Army Council had been established in 1904 to govern the army. At its head was the secretary of state for war. The four military members were the chief of the imperial general staff (the professional head of the British, Indian and colonial armies), the adjutant-general (responsible for personnel matters), the quartermaster-general (responsible for logistic and supply matters within the army), and the master-general of the ordnance (responsible for the procurement of materiel).

Haig was not encouraged by what he heard: the plans seemed inflexible. He spoke his mind, so far as the junior corps commander of the BEF could, and when the meeting broke up he drove to the Cavalry Club in Piccadilly for lunch.

At four o'clock the war council assembled in the Cabinet Room. It was hot and crowded. The 'frocks', as the men in uniform called the frock-coated politicians, sat facing the windows at the green-baize-covered table, and the 'brass hats' (brass wire decorated the hat-peaks of senior officers of both services), though not all were in uniform that afternoon, took the rest of the places, with the more junior of the Admiralty and War Office staff perched on chairs against the walls – 'rather a motley gathering', Asquith called it. There were in fact just four 'frocks' – the prime minister, the foreign secretary, the first lord of the Admiralty and Lord Haldane. Asquith had himself held the portfolio of secretary for war since March, when Jack Seely had had to resign over his mishandling of events connected with the Irish home rule bill – the so-called Curragh Mutiny. Haldane had preceded Seely at the War Office, and Asquith had realized – albeit belatedly – that it made sense to have him keep watch in his old department in addition to his duties as lord chancellor; for Haldane had one of the finest minds in Westminster and had been the leading political light in army reform in the decade following the Boer War. Asquith, on the other hand, notwithstanding his formidable cerebral powers, was not known for active vigour in using them at the best of times: 'wait and see' was a phrase he had once used, and it had stuck to him as a quasi-motto. His tenure at the War Office had been torpid. It could even have been called negligent. He might perhaps have recalled Seely, except that after the Curragh 'fiasco' he had a low opinion of the 'arch-colonel', as he called him.* Not that the former secretary for war was fretting, for Colonel Seely – he held a commission in the Yeomanry (the reserve cavalry) – was about to leave London for the Isle of Wight to pack his kit before reporting for duty as a liaison officer with the BEF.

The 'brass hats' were an eclectic group – upwards of a dozen in all. The most senior of them was the 81-year-old Field Marshal Lord Roberts, known affectionately to all ranks as 'Bobs'. As a field marshal he was

---

* He used both 'arch-colonel' and 'fiasco' in his letter to Venetia Stanley that evening (*Letters to Venetia Stanley*, ed. M and E. Brock, Oxford, 1982). The Curragh episode had caused him a great deal of political embarrassment.

technically still in service, but had left the active list in 1904, and was invited now as an 'elder statesman' – for the sake of form perhaps, or even of sentiment (Asquith thought him 'senile'). Next, and in a somewhat ambiguous position, was Lord Kitchener. As a field marshal he too was technically still in service, although he had retired from the active list in 1910 as C-in-C India, and was now the British agent and consul-general – effectively viceroy – in Egypt. He was also, as few were aware, about to be made secretary for war. Kitchener had happened to be in London for meetings at the Colonial Office (and to lobby for appointment as viceroy of India), and the morning before had left home at Broome in Kent for the Dover ferry, the train on to Marseilles and the packet thence to Cairo. However, Asquith managed to have him intercepted at Dover Harbour station, recalling him to attend the war council, after which he would be formally appointed secretary of state, with a place in the cabinet – the 'hazardous experiment', as he dubbed it.*

Also at the table were the military members of the Army Council and the senior officers of the BEF, along with General Sir Ian Hamilton, GOC Mediterranean and inspector-general of overseas forces (who would lose his name at Gallipoli the following year). The first sea lord, the German-born Prince Louis of Battenberg, was also present.† For all his admirable personal qualities, Prince Louis was not in the same league as his predecessor-but-one, Admiral of the Fleet Lord ('Jacky', sometimes 'Jackie') Fisher, who would soon be recalled to take his place. His military counterpart, the chief of the imperial

---

* It was hazardous in two respects. Kitchener's well-known taciturnity did not augur well for cabinet government in direction of the war; and, with the possible exception of General George Monck in the transitional years after the Restoration of 1660, it was constitutionally unprecedented for the post of secretary for war to go to a soldier (which, as a field marshal, Kitchener remained, strictly speaking). Notwithstanding these hazards, Asquith saw the attraction of having a man who undoubtedly knew his business, thereby giving the cabinet a more warlike appearance.

† Through the family connections of the Victorian court, Prince Louis had joined the Royal Navy in 1868, becoming a British citizen. Anti-German sentiment (August 1914 was a time when, reportedly, dachshunds were kicked in the street) would force his resignation in October, and in time a change of his surname to Mountbatten (he was also created marquess of Milford Haven). The other 'German' at the meeting was the master-general of the ordnance, Major-General Stanley von Donop. The relative obscurity of the appointment, and the fact that his branch of the family had been settled in England since the beginning of the previous century, saved him from too much trouble. Ironically, in 1917 the German high court threw out a petition by the prince of Lippe-Detmold for the forfeiture of Donop's rights to shares in the family estates in Lippe, ruling that in serving his country as a British officer in the war with Germany he merely did his 'civic duty . . . [and] acted in accordance with the law of honour'.

general staff (CIGS), General Sir Charles Douglas, would not last long, either. Previously inspector-general of the forces, he had been hurriedly appointed at the beginning of April when Sir John French resigned as CIGS in the wake of Seely's departure. Not in the best of health, he would die of the strain of office two months into the war ('Bobs' would be dead in four).*

Douglas had brought with him the director of military operations (DMO), the officer responsible for operational planning, Major-General Henry Wilson.† Wilson was as tall as Sir John French – 'the little field marshal' – was short, an Irishman of unbounded self-confidence and a penchant for intrigue. The wags said that he got sexually excited whenever he saw a politician (French's excitement, on the other hand, was just as prodigious, but occasioned entirely by the opposite sex). It did not matter to Wilson that Douglas was, to his mind, a dud, or that no one in the room knew a fraction of what he did about the French intentions or the secret plans for the employment of the BEF, for the plans had been made – the complex railway and shipping tables and movement orders; Wilson himself had made them, or cajoled the other departments responsible. And as far as he was concerned, that was really all there was to it.

However, the prime minister had called the meeting to decide what to do. The War Office – Wilson – may have made its plans, but the cabinet had made no decisions. Chief of these was what to do with the BEF. For the BEF was the army's cutting edge – six infantry divisions and one of cavalry (seventy-two infantry battalions and fourteen cavalry regiments‡), together with supporting arms and lines-of-

---

* French had been appointed inspector-general of the forces on 28 July, having been without a job for almost three months – although as a field marshal he remained nominally at duty ('a field marshal never retires'). His appointment as commander of the BEF was as near a foregone conclusion as makes no odds, except that French himself believed he was finished – and, indeed, throughout the summer had given that impression to all and sundry.

† The mobilization plan had him relinquishing his post as DMO (which would be filled by a reservist officer) to be deputy chief of staff of the BEF. At the meeting he wore, so to speak, two (brass) hats. He would end the war as CIGS.

‡ The terms 'battalion' and 'regiment' can sometimes be confusing. In the infantry, 'regiment' was the name – the 'brand': e.g. the Manchester Regiment, the Sherwood Foresters, the Gordon Highlanders. Each regiment comprised a number of regular (active) battalions, usually two, each about a thousand strong, and several part-time auxiliary battalions. All the battalions, whether regular or auxiliary, wore the same regimental cap-badge (with some arcane exceptions). In the cavalry the regiment was the active element, about 500 strong; there were no separate battalions. Infantry

communication troops. With its reservists recalled to the colours, it would number some 165,000 men. The BEF was, in effect, the regular army at home; the rest of the army was scattered in garrisons about the world, guarding the empire. Just as in 1808 the foreign secretary, Canning, had warned Sir John Moore as he took command of the expeditionary force in Spain that it was 'not merely a considerable part of the dispensable force of this country. It is in fact *the* British army . . . Another army it has not to send,' so too might Asquith warn his generals. Unlike the continental powers with their large conscript armies, Britain did not have a deep pool of reservist manpower to call up. Nor was the Territorial Army (strictly, at this time, the Territorial *Force*, TF) equipped or trained for continental warfare; War Office plans assumed a period of six months' training before the TF would be ready to take to the field – even for home defence (although, of course, if it had to it would oppose invasion as best it could). In any case, the law as it stood could not compel its members to serve abroad.

That a war council – in effect, an executive war cabinet with military advisers present – had assembled to decide the question, in Churchill's words, 'How should we wage the war that had just begun?' was only proper, for Britain, unlike Germany or Austria, was not ruled by its military. It was just rather late in the day to be discussing so fundamental an issue of strategy. Besides, what to do was conditioned, as ever, by what practicably could be done. And here the quarrel began – although, because the meeting was effectively unminuted, what was said can only, and only partially, be determined from diaries, letters and other recollections.*

The prime minister – 'Squiffy', as he was known from his habit of

---

battalions were subdivided into companies; cavalry regiments into squadrons (and, in turn, troops). The army's active strength on 1 August 1914 was 247,798, of which nearly half were serving overseas. The infantry comprised 148 regular battalions, half of them abroad (fifty-one in India), and the cavalry thirty-one regiments, of which a third were abroad (nine in India). Under the plans outlined in *Future Force 2020* (published in 2012), in 2015 the entire British army will have just thirty-one regular infantry battalions (including two of Gurkhas). The army overall will be significantly weaker numerically than the BEF of 1914: 82,000 regulars and 30,000 Territorial Army (renamed the 'Reserve').

* Cabinet meetings at that time were not formally minuted, but this would soon change, and one of the officers in the room that afternoon, Lieutenant-Colonel Maurice Hankey, secretary of the Committee of Imperial Defence (CID), would become the first cabinet secretary. His own notes on the 5 August meeting, however, are in Public Record Office (PRO) Cabinet (CAB) File 22/1.

swaying on his feet when speaking in the Commons – made his open-ing remarks. He had, he explained, 'summoned the great soldiers [sic] at the earliest possible moment': the Germans had crossed the frontier into Belgium early the day before, war had formally been declared between Britain and Germany, between Russia and Germany and between France and Germany, but as yet Austria was not technically at war with any country except Serbia. One advantageous factor in the situation was that Italy had not indeed thrown in her lot with Germany and Austria;* another was that – to the surprise of almost everyone – the Belgians were resisting the invasion vigorously. Asquith further believed – wrongly as it turned out – that the Germans had also violated Dutch territory, the 'Maastricht corridor'. Although he does not appear to have said so, the implication was that the problem of the territorial waters of the Scheldt, and therefore access to Antwerp, was no more.†

The floor was then given to Sir John French, who outlined the design for the deployment of the BEF. In anticipation of a German hook through neutral Belgium, Wilson had been working secretively for the past four years on a plan for the force to operate on the left of the French line against the German right flank along the Belgian border.‡ It involved first concentrating at Maubeuge, some 5 miles short of the border, which required a complicated movement plan by sea and rail, and it was this, as well as every detail of mobilization of

* Italy was a part of the so-called Triple Alliance, but her prime minister told the Germans and Austrians that his government regarded the alliance as defensive only. At a second war council, on 6 August, Grey would give a categorical assurance of Italian neutrality.
† The Treaty of London, 1839, by which the Dutch conceded independence to Belgium, and under which Britain as a signatory felt obliged to act when the Germans violated Belgian neutrality, allowed free passage of the Scheldt – Dutch territorial waters – to any ship heading for Antwerp for the purposes of commerce. As a neutral nation, the Dutch could not allow warships to use their territorial waters (except to make good repairs essential to staying afloat), but the Foreign Office had never been able to establish the precise status of the Scheldt in war, which appeared to rule out Antwerp as a point of entry each time the CID had examined the option of the BEF's going to the direct sup-port of the Belgians. Asquith was now wishfully assuming that, Dutch territory having (as he thought) been violated and the treaty therefore broken by the Germans, the Dutch would thenceforth be allies of Britain and open the Scheldt to British warships. The issue is discussed in more detail in chapter 7.
‡ So secretively, for example, that Haig for one may not have been familiar with it, writing in his diary: 'Sir John French gave in outline a [sic – not 'the'] pre-arranged plan . . . ' (*Douglas Haig: War Diaries and Letters 1914–18*, ed. Gary Sheffield and John Bourne, London, 2005).

men, horses and materiel, that the DMO and his staff had worked out (while Sir John French had been CIGS, indeed) with the French general staff. But Wilson, with the approval of three successive CIGSs, had made two critical assumptions in his plan: that it was what the politicians would approve, and that Britain would mobilize at the same time as the French.

Both assumptions were dubious. Since there was no formal alliance with France, Britain was not committed to action; the decision the day before, 4 August, to declare war on Germany – in the end on the ostensible principle of defending Belgian neutrality – was slow to come, and so, therefore, was the decision to mobilize. Paris had called up its reservists and gone onto a war footing on 1 August, London on the fourth; Wilson's movement tables were already therefore three days out of synchronization. When Sir John French finished outlining the plan (in effect, Wilson's) he gave his own opinion that because of late mobilization, Maubeuge would probably be no longer an option, but that the BEF should go to France anyway, to Amiens, a safer place to concentrate. Wilson, doubtless in an effort to help his future chief and move the discussion along, somewhat contradicted his own belief in the necessity of sticking to the existing deployment plans by mentioning 'the flexibility of [the] French railway system for switching'.* But then, to his dismay, French suggested that perhaps it would be best to go thence to Antwerp and operate with the Belgian and Dutch armies (to which no thought had been given since 1912, and no serious planning since 1906) – a 'ridiculous proposal', Wilson wrote in his diary, adding that 'Haig asked questions and this led to our discussing strategy like idiots'.†

In fact it is more likely that because Haig was the most junior general at the table (Wilson was seated behind the CIGS) he spoke last; certainly that is his own recollection. Even before Haig spoke, however, cold water was being poured on the Antwerp idea. Churchill stated that the Straits of Dover were already completely sealed but the navy could not with certainty protect the BEF's transports on the longer passage across the North Sea to the Scheldt, the enemy side of

---

* He had in fact sent four officers to Paris a month before to look at the alternative possibility of Amiens as the concentration area, in order to make full use of the railways in redeploying from there 'according as the situation might develop'.
† C. E. Callwell, *Field Marshal Sir Henry Wilson: His Life and Diaries* (London, 1927).

[Form to be used when the whole
of the Army Reserve is called out.]

Army Form D. 457.

GENERAL MOBILIZATION
Army Reserve
(REGULAR AND SPECIAL RESERVISTS).

HIS MAJESTY THE KING has been graciously pleased to direct by Proclamation that the Army Reserve be called out on permanent service.

ALL REGULAR RESERVISTS are required to report themselves at once at their place of joining in accordance with the instructions on their identity certificates for the purpose of joining the Army.

ALL SPECIAL RESERVISTS are required to report themselves on such date and at such places as they may be directed to attend for the purpose of joining the Army. If they have not received any such directions, or if they have changed their address since last attendance at drill or training, they will report themselves at once, by letter, to the Adjutant of their Unit or Depot.

The necessary instructions as to their joining will then be given.

The call-up of reservists began in earnest on 5 August, three days after the French, although with unrealistic optimism the War Office had based its plans on the two countries mobilizing simultaneously. Nothing illustrates better the disjointed strategic thinking of the military planners and their political masters than the delay in mobilization, which would cost the BEF dearly in its opening battles.

the Straits, nor could it support operations at Antwerp subsequently. Moreover, there were no spare warships, for the rest of the navy was needed for the 'imperial concentration': bringing troops back from the far side of the world. (French then said he would be prepared to land at Ostend and march the 70 miles to Antwerp – plucky, but not entirely practical.) The CIGS, Douglas, pointed out that the movement plans were to embark the BEF principally at Southampton, Queenstown (Ireland) and Glasgow and to disembark them variously at the Channel ports, and that the French had arranged the rolling stock and timetables accordingly; a change of destination at the last moment could have serious consequences.* Haig's questions, when they came, were very much to the point. Did we have enough troops, with the Belgians, to carry on a campaign independently of the French? What exactly did we know of the fighting power of the Belgian army? But first, others were asked their opinion, 'Bobs' included, and the general mood appeared to be for going to France as soon as possible, but further to the south than Maubeuge – probably to Amiens. Churchill then suggested that the BEF should concentrate well to the rear of the French army – further even than Amiens – to form a strategic reserve. It was a sensible proposal that would preserve freedom of action, which was his, and probably Asquith's, instinct, but it irritated Wilson, who had to all intents and purposes integrated the BEF in the French order of battle.† Kitchener asked that a senior officer of the *État-Major de l'Armée*, the French general staff, come to London at once to brief them on the situation as they saw it.

In raising Antwerp as an option, however, Sir John French had instinctively – he was an instinctive soldier – raised the question of strategic independence. British strategy was otherwise being dictated by the French army's campaign plan, and that plan contained a fatal assumption: that if the Germans did enter Belgium it would not be in overwhelming strength, that they would not cross the Meuse but 'hook in' tight to try to envelop the French about Metz, as they had

---

* Since 1909 the War Office and the director of [sea] transport at the Admiralty had been working on the advice of the director of naval intelligence that for safety all troop movement across the Channel should be west of a line from Dungeness to Cap Gris Nez. This ruled out Calais and Dunkirk, but not Boulogne.
† Usually abbreviated to 'orbat', the order of battle is the command structure, composition and disposition of formations and units of an armed force for operations, or for administration in peace.

done in 1870; and so the BEF would not be deploying on a major German axis of advance. In fact, of the 'brass hats' only Kitchener and Haig were thinking – or at least trying to think – truly strategically. For while the view of the general staff, as exemplified by Wilson, and of the French general staff, was that a continental war would be brief, along the lines of the Franco-Prussian War of 1870–1 (which had, in effect, been over in a month and a half), Kitchener's view, as yet unexpressed, was that it would be a long war, requiring the massive mobilization of national resources. And, indeed, as soon as he was appointed secretary of state he would waste no time in mobilizing those resources – famously by the 'Your Country Needs YOU!' posters.

Haig thought the same. Only the day before, he had written to Haldane (as well as to Major Philip Howell, one of his protégés, who as a brigadier-general would be killed on the Somme in 1916):

> I venture to hope that our only bolt (and that not a very big one) may not suddenly be shot on a project of which the success seems to me to be quite doubtful – I mean the checking of the advance into France. Would it not be better to begin at once to enlarge our Exped[itionar]y Force by amalgamating less regular forces with it? In three months time we should have quite a considerable army.

His reasoning was simple: the combatants would be fighting for their existence, and therefore none would acknowledge defeat after a short struggle; the war would last several years, and it would be necessary to have a strong and effective force at the eventual peace conference. In the letter he mentions a figure of 300,000 to be amassed over three months, 'so that when we do take the field we can act decisively'.* At the war council, Haig now reiterated his opinion that the war would be a long one and advocated a further target of a million men under arms; and in order to organize, train and lead them he urged that 'a considerable proportion of officers and NCOs should be withdrawn from the Expeditionary Force'. At the preliminary meeting in the War Office that morning he had already suggested that the BEF ought not to cross the water for two or three months, during which 'the immense resources of the Empire' could

---

* Churchill had advanced this idea at a key meeting of the CID three years earlier. See chapters 7 and 21 below.

be developed, but Wilson had pointed out that there were no material resources for a long war, and that the opinion of both the French and the British general staffs was that the contest would be a brief one (a view soon to be popularized as 'over by Christmas'). Irrespective of the war's likely length, Sir John French now strenuously objected to any substantial weakening of the BEF. His opinion, as the BEF's commander, was clearly going to carry the utmost weight in the matter, and in the end it was decided that only three officers per battalion would be kept back to help train reinforcements. As to where exactly the BEF would concentrate, there was a general feeling that 'we must help France in the way the French Staff thought would be most effective'.*

And so the war council – which Wilson in his diary called 'an historic meeting of men, mostly entirely ignorant of their subject' – resolved to send the BEF to France, in a strength to be decided, to a place to be determined, and to operate along lines as yet unspecified.† That it could have happened thus, after all the years of careful preparation, remains a cautionary tale for military planners and policy-makers alike.

Yet it was the coming of war itself – at least in the manner of its beginning – that seemed most inexplicable. The assassination of an Austrian archduke in a place few people had heard of, and an old, obscure and imprecise treaty on the independence of Belgium – 'a scrap of paper' the German chancellor, Bethmann Hollweg, called it when the British ambassador paid his final visit the day before – by what design and error had the great powers begun to march? In his war memoirs, Lloyd George, who would succeed Asquith as prime minister in December 1916, admits the political dereliction:

---

* Winston Churchill, *The World Crisis* (London, 1923–7).
† The recollections of this meeting by those attending are very varied. Sir John French, in his memoir *1914* (London, 1919), is so selective, with no word of Antwerp, as to cast early doubt on that narrative as a whole: 'The soldiers themselves were not agreed. Lord Kitchener thought that our position on the left of the French line at Maubeuge would be too exposed, and rather favoured a concentration farther back in the neighbourhood of Amiens. Sir Douglas Haig suggested postponing any landing till the campaign had actively opened and we should be able to judge in which direction our co-operation would be most effective. Personally, I was opposed to these ideas, and most anxious to adhere to our original plans. Any alteration in carrying out our concentration, particularly if this meant delay, would have upset the French plan of campaign and created much distrust in the minds of our Allies.'

During the eight years that preceded the war, the cabinet devoted a ridiculously small percentage of its time to a consideration of foreign affairs ... Education, Temperance, Land Taxation – culminating in the most serious constitutional crisis since the Reform Bill – the Parliament Act, Home Rule, and the Disestablishment of the Church in Wales: these subjects challenged an infinite variety of human interests, sentiment and emotion.*

He railed, too, against the 'stubborn miscalculation, muddle and lack of coordination' of military leaders, 'which resulted in mowing down the flower of the finest armies ever put in the field by France and England'. With 'goodwill and wise counsel' it could all have been avoided. But, then, he would also write: 'The last thing the vainglorious Kaiser wanted was a European War.' And that was a fatal misjudgement too.

But the question of 'war guilt' – *die Kriegsschuldfrage* – was a matter for later. From Berlin the seasoned correspondent of the *Daily News*, Henry Nevinson, wired the essential truth: 'as the herald who proclaimed the beginning of the long war between Athens and Sparta, *This day sees the beginning of many sorrows for the most civilised peoples of the world.*'

Yet they had once been famous allies.

NOTE
The intercepted German telegram of 4 August, and the departure of the ambassadors
In his official report on the breaking of diplomatic relations, the British ambassador in Berlin, Sir Edward Goschen (descended from

---

* David Lloyd George, *War Memoirs* (London, 1933–6). It would be easy to dismiss Lloyd George's memoirs as merely self-serving, but one contemporary reviewer – Churchill – was more circumspect: 'This book is quite characteristic of its author. It has native pith and eloquence; but there is no straining at literary effort ... Mr. Lloyd George has made no attempt to court popularity or conciliate contemporary opinion. His judgments are almost invariably severe and occasionally unduly patronizing, but always searching and worthy to be weighed.' Perhaps, however, Lloyd George was merely bewailing the perennial failing of democratic governments in time of peace. The marquess of Lansdowne (secretary for war and then foreign secretary in the Tory administrations between 1895 and 1905) had made the same complaint ten years earlier: questions of strategy facing the empire slid into the background, he complained, as he and his colleagues became 'busier and busier with Land Bills and suchlike rubbish' (letter to Sir John Ardagh, Director of Military Intelligence, 1896).

Leipzig merchants), explains that, as instructed, he called on the German foreign minister, Gottlieb von Jagow, twice on 4 August. On the first occasion, in the early afternoon, he asked for an undertaking that Germany would 'refrain from violating Belgian neutrality', and received at once the reply that troops had already crossed into Belgium and that it was quite impossible to halt the advance since Germany would thereby lose time in which the Russians could bring troops to the eastern border. The ambassador told Jagow that 'the violation of the Belgian frontier rendered . . . the situation exceedingly grave', and urged him to reconsider, but Jagow reiterated that it was quite impossible. The ambassador then withdrew and wired London. Receiving a further telegram later in the afternoon, 'in compliance with the instructions therein contained, I again proceeded to the Imperial Foreign Office and informed the Secretary of State that unless the Imperial Government could give the assurance by 12 o'clock that night that they would proceed no further with their violation of the Belgian frontier and stop their advance, I had been instructed to demand my passports and inform the Imperial Government that His Majesty's Government would have to take all steps in their power to uphold the neutrality of Belgium and the observance of a treaty to which Germany was as much a party as themselves'.

Jagow replied that he could give no other answer but that which he had given earlier. The ambassador then gave Jagow a written summary of the telegram, 'and, pointing out that you [the foreign secretary, Sir Edward Grey] had mentioned 12 o'clock as the time when His Majesty's Government would expect an answer, asked him whether, in view of the terrible consequences which would necessarily ensue, it were not possible even at the last moment that their answer should be reconsidered. He replied that if the time given were even twenty-four hours or more, his answer must be the same. I said that in that case I should have to demand my passports. This interview took place at about 7 o'clock.'

He then went to see the chancellor, Bethmann Hollweg, at which point the 'scrap of paper' remark was made.

Sir Edward Goschen then explains why London had heard nothing from him since the middle of the afternoon: 'After this somewhat painful interview I returned to the embassy and drew up a telegraphic report of what had passed. This telegram was handed in at the Central

Telegraph Office a little before 9 p.m. It was accepted by that office, but apparently never dispatched.'

This was probably because the German foreign office instructed the telegraph office not to send it (the telegram may have been in code, but not necessarily, as it was reporting established fact), being uncertain whether or not the two countries were now at war. For, in a meeting every bit as tragi-comical as Harold Nicolson's with the German ambassador in London, 'at about 9.30 p.m. Herr von Zimmermann, the Under-Secretary of State, came to see me,' continues Goschen. 'After expressing his deep regret that the very friendly official and personal relations between us were about to cease, he asked me casually whether a demand for passports was equivalent to a declaration of war. I said that such an authority on international law as he was known to be must know as well or better than I what was usual in such cases. I added that there were many cases where diplomatic relations had been broken off, and, nevertheless, war had not ensued; but that in this case he would have seen from my instructions, of which I had given Herr von Jagow a written summary, that His Majesty's Government expected an answer to a definite question by 12 o'clock that night and that in default of a satisfactory answer they would be forced to take such steps as their engagements required. Herr Zimmermann said that that was, in fact, a declaration of war, as the Imperial Government could not possibly give the assurance required either that night or any other night.'

The following day, 5 August, Prince Lichnowsky, the German ambassador, travelled by special train with his staff to Harwich to embark for neutral Holland and thence Berlin. 'The arrangements for our departure were perfectly dignified and calm,' he would write in his memoir of his time in London. 'The King had previously sent his equerry, Sir E. Ponsonby, to express his regrets at my departure and that he could not see me himself. Princess Louise wrote to me that the whole family were sorry we were leaving. Mrs. Asquith and other friends came to the Embassy to take leave.' Others of his staff had managed to leave on the same terms, despite some impromptu window-breaking. The consul-general, Robert von Ranke, placed his house in the care of his sister in Wimbledon, Amalie – mother of the poet Robert Graves. A guard of honour presented military compliments at Parkestone Quay: 'I was treated like a departing Sovereign,' Lichnowsky recalled.

In Berlin that day, Sir Edward Goschen left by side streets for a station outside the city; his German servants spat at him as he left. He travelled by train in company with the Belgian ambassador to the Dutch border, arriving in London eight days later. The Königlich Preußische und Großherzoglich Hessische Staatseisenbahn – the Prussian–Hessian state railway – raised a bill for the ambassadorial train. The British government paid it in full through Dutch intermediaries.

Chapter Two

ALLIES OF THE OLD CENTURY

We have no eternal allies, and we have no perpetual enemies. Our interests are eternal and perpetual, and those interests it is our duty to follow.

Lord Palmerston, 1848

British soldiers used to sing a lot, and sometimes aptly. A Royal Artillery captain recalled his battery's voice as their transport came into the mouth of the Seine ten days after mobilization: 'Then, to my astonishment, they burst into the "Marseillaise." How and where they had learned it I have no idea. But sing it they did, and very well too. They took that little curly bit in the middle, where a B flat comes when you least expect it, just like an old hunter clearing a stiff post-and-rails.'*

The 18th Hussars, one of the regiments of the 2nd Cavalry Brigade, also burst into song as their ship came into Boulogne on 16 August: 'Here we are, here we are, here we are again!' The officers were puzzled; the last time they had been 'here' was for the Battle of Waterloo, ninety-nine years earlier. Perhaps the regimental history lessons had been particularly vivid, or some of the old sweats had had grandfathers who stood with the duke of Wellington that day – might even have seen him shake hands with Prince Blücher by the aptly named inn La Belle Alliance as the Prussians arrived on the field at the

* A. Corbett-Smith, *The Retreat From Mons, By One Who Shared In It* (London, 1916).

22

eleventh hour: 'Lieber Kamerad!' old Blücher had hailed the duke. And indeed, if six days later the 18th Hussars had ridden for another 25 miles before running into the Germans, they would have arrived on that old battlefield.

The Kaiser himself was perfectly aware of the terrible reversal of fortunes since the climactic encounter of 18 June 1815. On the morning that the British ambassador left Berlin, he sent an aide-de-camp to the embassy with a message deploring 'the action of Great Britain in joining with other nations against her old allies at Waterloo'. Evidently a hundred years and all that had passed therein was nothing to the Imperial mind; but the Kaiser appeared to forget that *Belgian* troops had also stood with the allies at Waterloo.

Yet the battle was not just a romantic memory, to be recalled by statesman and trooper alike for their own purposes; it was the starting point (or at least a major waypoint) on the long road to 1914. The final act of the Congress of Vienna had been signed on 9 June 1815, just nine days before Napoleon Bonaparte's nemesis near the little Belgian village of which no one would otherwise have heard. His escape from Elba – 'the Hundred Days' – disturbed the Congress, but in the end did not change anything. Wellington's emphatic victory, however, underwrote Vienna's vision of the future: from now on, disputes would be settled by negotiation among the great powers.

The Congress had been convened by the first Treaty of Paris, in 1814 after Napoleon's abdication, to settle the national boundaries that had been drawn and redrawn during two decades of war, during which first the revolutionary government of France and then the 'Great Disturber' himself had torn up the map of Europe. Now representatives of European states, large and petty, that had legally existed before the wars gathered in the Austrian capital to distribute – or restore – the territories of the late French Empire and Napoleon's two remaining allies, the king of Denmark and the king of Saxony (the grand duke of Warsaw). There was no representative of the Ottoman Empire, however, for Turkey had been only indirectly engaged in the wars, and Russia objected to any meddling with the Ottoman Balkans, which the Tsar regarded as his own hunting ground.*

---

* The Ottoman Empire was certainly ailing by this time, but it would be four more decades before the phrase 'the sick man of Europe' became current.

For Britain especially, 'balance of power' was the determining principle. Her object was to curb the future ambitions of each of the four
great continental states (France, Prussia, Austria and Russia), which
together with Britain would henceforth arbitrate in disputes among
the lesser powers. This joint authority was somewhat lyrically
expressed as the 'Concert of Europe', or more prosaically the
'Congress System'; what it amounted to was ad hoc sessions of
the original Vienna conference. The underlying assumption,
enshrined in the final act of the treaty, was that the boundaries
established in 1815 could not be altered without the consent of the
eight signatories to the act, and, by extension, that the great powers
held rights to intervene in states threatened by internal rebellion (a
concept eventually formally enshrined in the UN Charter in 1945).*
One of the most significant boundary extensions saw Prussia gain half
of Saxony, part of the Duchy of Warsaw and the lion's share of the
Rhineland, as well as a large portion of Westphalia, making her a
power in the continental west as well as in the east.

Reasonable as it sounds, and sounded, especially after a century of
continual dynastic war, 'balance of power' was a doctrine soon being
described by British ultra-liberals as a 'Moloch' – a god requiring
human sacrifice. Forty years on, as the Crimean War broke Britain's
long peace, the radical MP John Bright was railing at it as 'a foul idol',
arguing in the House of Commons in March 1854 that 'if this phrase
of the "balance of power" is to be always an argument for war, the pretext for war will never be wanting, and peace can never be secure'.†

Of all the articles of the act, however, none was to herald misfor-
tune more than number 65: 'The ancient United Provinces of the
Netherlands and the late Belgic provinces . . . shall form, together
with the countries and territories designated in the same article,
under the sovereignty of his Royal Highness the Prince of Orange-

---

* Spain, Portugal and Sweden were the other three of the eight signatories known
collectively as the 'European powers', although they were not classified as *great* powers.
The 'Congress System' was formally established by a separate treaty signed in
November.
† The United States was not represented at the Congress. It is tempting to speculate on
the course of history had she been so, for by the 'Monroe Doctrine' of 1823 she
effectively repudiated her interest in the balance of power in Europe (although she
would certainly profit by it); had the US been a partner in Vienna, the doctrine might
not have been declared so restrictively, and US engagement in Europe a century later
might have been more decisive. A big 'if', but an intriguing one nonetheless.

Nassau, sovereign prince of the United Provinces, the kingdom of the Netherlands . . .' With these congressional draftsman's words, the former predominantly Catholic and French-speaking Austrian Netherlands (more or less the present-day Belgium), which had been incorporated in the French republic in 1795 and then in 1804 the empire, were to be united with the former almost exclusively Protestant Dutch republic, and later the puppet kingdom of Holland (the puppet king being Napoleon's brother Louis), annexed in 1810. The creation of this artificial polity, to limit French control of the North Sea coast, was a triumph for Lord Castlereagh, Britain's foreign secretary and chief negotiator, anxious, as every Englishman since Queen Elizabeth's day had been, lest winds and tides allow a Catholic fleet to bear down from the Scheldt on the ancient Saxon shore (and keen, also, to have a strong buffer state between France and Prussia).* However, article 65 lit a slow fuse in the 'cockpit of Europe' – a description used of the 'Belgic provinces' as early as 1640 – that would burn right through to the powder keg a century later.

In fact the fuse first began to give off smoke after only fifteen years, when the Belgians suddenly declared independence. Russia, Prussia and Austria were all for enforcing the terms of the Vienna treaty. However, France, by now pretty well rehabilitated as a member of the Concert, and certainly recovering as a self-confident great power, saw an opportunity to reincorporate Belgium in the French state. Britain, notably her new foreign secretary, Lord Palmerston, was alarmed both at the breakup of the buffer state and at 40 miles of Belgian sand dunes falling into the hands of a potentially hostile power. For although of late London and Paris had been enjoying cordial relations, this unusual state of affairs was put in jeopardy by a sudden and simultaneous French revolution – if a comparatively bloodless one. In July 1830 the Bourbon king was ousted in favour of his cousin the duc d'Orléans, enthroned as King Louis Philippe, and for a while French revanchism looked a distinct threat.

The course of history now took one of its most lethal turns when the Concert failed to act to maintain the Dutch–Belgian union, mongrel though it might be, distracted by yet another revolution – in

---

* It also served to mollify the Dutch over Britain's insistence on keeping the Cape Colony and Ceylon, taken from them when they had succumbed to Napoleon.

that other troublesome nation without a state, Poland (most of which Vienna had given to the Tsar). Russia was hard put to contain the uprising, and Austria watched anxiously for any contagion; in the circumstances there was no question of either country sending troops to the Low Countries. Palmerston, his overriding priority now being to keep France out of the Netherlands rather than to keep the kingdom together, reckoned that the best he could achieve was an independent and neutral Belgium. Arguing that Vienna had been overtaken by events, he succeeded in brokering another treaty whereby the Dutch conceded Belgian independence, and the great powers guaranteed the new nation's neutrality. It was an entangling treaty the like of which Britain had never before contracted; not even the ancient Anglo-Portuguese alliance had committed her to such unlimited liability.*

But Palmerston reckoned it was a price worth paying, for Francophobia, or at least the suspicion of French designs, was strong in England, where the Scheldt was seen as the barrel of a huge gun pointing at the English Channel. And the policy of maintaining a balance of power left Britain free to pursue her colonial expansion. Besides, there would soon come a thaw in relations with France (the term 'Entente Cordiale', although usually associated with the agreement concluded under Edward VII, was in fact first heard in the 1840s), reducing the fear of a hostile coast, and the Belgian liability seemed to diminish. Britain even agreed to demolish the forts on the frontier with France, whose construction the duke of Wellington had overseen under the terms of the Vienna treaty. And although this midwinter spring of the Entente would be followed by a cold snap in 1851 when yet another coup in Paris brought Bonaparte's nephew Louis to the imperial throne as 'Napoleon III' (he had first taken the presidency of the new republic after the ejection of King Louis

---

* As expressed in article VII of the Treaty of London, 1839 (the formalities took far longer to conclude than the actual separation): 'Belgium, within the limits specified in Articles I, II, and IV, shall form an independent and perpetually neutral State. It shall be bound to observe such neutrality towards all other States.' The preamble to the treaty states that its provisions 'are thus placed under the guarantee of their said Majesties [of Britain, Austria, France, Prussia, Russia and the Netherlands]'. Whether this obliged the signatories to intervene, or merely enabled them to, was never definitively established in the seventy-five years prior to the First World War – another monument to imprecise drafting to set alongside the question of navigability of the Scheldt in wartime, the subject of one of the treaty's sub-clauses.

Philippe in 1848, the year of upheavals across Europe), it developed thereafter into unprecedented Anglo-French military cooperation, with troops fighting side by side in the Crimean War (1854–6) and in China in the Second Opium War (1856–60).*

However, such were the older habits of Anglo-French military conflict that even while British and French troops were fighting as one on the far side of the world, there was an invasion scare at home. It was as if Britain needed the old familiar threat to define her own security policy. As Sir Hew Strachan, the pre-eminent British historian of the First World War, has put it, 'Britain continued to use the threat of France as its antidote to complacency,' adding that one of the more surprising outcomes of the nineteenth century was that there *was* no war between Britain and France after 1815, thereby proving 'that arms races do not invariably cause conflict – and indeed that they might even deter it'.[†]

On the other hand, arms races can create perceptions of hostility, and France had been modernizing her fleet, which was bound to set the Whitehall dovecots aflutter. She had built no wooden warships for a decade: her new ironclads with their breech-loading cannon gave La Royale a decisive edge.[‡] The French were also strengthening

---

* There had been naval cooperation against the Turks in 1827, and, indeed, during the brief fighting in the Belgian war of independence, but so novel was the experience of an allied army in the Crimea that the British commander, Lord Raglan, who had lost an arm at Waterloo, referred more than once to the French as 'the enemy', before correcting himself. The war itself was an early manifestation of Russian miscalculation in Balkan affairs. The pretext for the Tsar's interference was the guardianship of the 'holy places' in Palestine, a three-way tussle between Islam (Palestine was a dominion of the Ottoman Turkish Empire), Catholicism (France – Napoleon III – was a self-appointed guardian), and Greek Orthodoxy (and hence the Russian Orthodox Tsar Nicholas I). This religious appendix grumbled for several years but seemed to have subsided when Nicholas resolved to settle the 'sick man of Europe' once and for all. Expecting support from Britain, Prussia and Austria, he planned to dismember what remained of European Turkey. However, neither Britain nor Austria wanted to see Russia in control of the Dardanelles. War followed in 1854, with Britain, France and Turkey laying siege to Sevastopol, the great naval fortress in the Crimea, though neither Prussia nor Austria took part. Nicholas died of pneumonia early the next year, brought on by exertion and foul weather, and was succeeded by his son, Alexander II, who in January 1856 took Russia out of the war on very unfavourable terms, including the loss of a battle fleet on the Black Sea.
† Hew Strachan, Chichele Professor of the History of War, Oxford, 'Entente Cordiale: War and Empire', in the *Royal United Services Institute Journal*, April 2004.
‡ La Marine Nationale (La Royale, as the French navy was and still is popularly known, for reasons variously ascribed) had introduced the first true steam-screw warship into service (1850), followed by the first ironclad (1859), named respectively *Le Napoléon* and *La Gloire* – neither of them names calculated to promote *entente*.

Cherbourg as a fortress-port, with no other apparent rationale than as a base for invasion. And it seemed they might have cause, too: in 1858 a bomb thrown at Napoleon III by the Italian nationalist Felice Orsini was found to have been made in England.*

The assassination attempt, besides being diplomatically embarrassing, was extraordinarily futile. Not only did it fail, but Napoleon III would anyway prove to be an ally of Italian nationalism: the following year he sent 130,000 troops to help Piedmont–Sardinia expel the Austrians from northern Italy (partly in recognition of their active support in the Crimean War†). But although Napoleon III showed no lasting animus over the bomb-testing, Palmerston, once back in office as prime minister (the Orsini incident had briefly cost him the premiership), began a huge programme of fort-building to protect the Royal Navy's bases. And in case the French were able to do what they had never before succeeded in doing (at least, not since 1066) – landing a sizeable invasion force – he promoted an equally ambitious home defence movement, the 'rifle volunteers'. For war between France and Austria, even in Italy, somehow seemed to expose the island nation's vulnerability, though the chickens of neglect in the years since Waterloo had already come home noisily to roost in the Crimea. The poet laureate, Alfred, Lord Tennyson, caught the mood in his call-to-arms 'The War', the first stanza of which ran memorably:

> There is a sound of thunder afar,
> Storm in the south that darkens the day,
> Storm of battle and thunder of war,
> Well, if it do not roll our way.
> Form! form! Riflemen form!
> Ready, be ready to meet the storm!
> Riflemen, riflemen, riflemen form!‡

---

* At the end of 1857 Orsini briefly visited England, where he contacted the gunsmith Joseph Taylor and asked him to make six bombs to one of his own designs, testing them in Sheffield and Devon with the aid of French radicals and English sympathizers.
† The Kingdom of Sardinia sent 15,000 experienced and well-equipped troops to the war. They fought with dash and skill: the war correspondent of *The Times*, William Howard Russell, reckoned them to have the best artillery in the Crimea, and was equally impressed by the fire and movement of the *Bersaglieri* (riflemen).
‡ Published in *The Times*, 9 May 1859.

Gladstone, as chancellor of the exchequer, was deeply opposed to spending on forts. Writing to Lord John Russell (who would succeed Palmerston in 1865, before Gladstone himself became prime minister three years later), he urged an alliance with France 'as the true basis of peace in Europe, for England and France never will unite in any European purpose which is radically unjust'. The Concert of Europe was demonstrably failing; here instead was the alternative vision – a treaty of military cooperation with the old enemy. And it was being proposed by the man who, with his political arch-enemy Disraeli, would dominate British politics for three decades – until 1895, when Lord Salisbury would take the reins of government once more to continue Disraeli's preference for 'splendid isolation'.*

Soon, however, Tennyson's 'sound of thunder afar' would be coming not just from 'storm in the south' but from storm in the east and north too, with echoes much closer to home. In June 1862 the Prussian ambassador to St Petersburg, Otto von Bismarck, visited London. At a reception at the Russian ambassador's he told Disraeli, then in opposition:

I shall soon be compelled to undertake the conduct of the Prussian government. My first care will be to re-organise the army, with or without the help of the Landtag [diet, or parliament] . . . As soon as the army shall have been brought into such a condition as to inspire respect, I shall seize the first best pretext to declare war against Austria, dissolve the German [Confederation] Diet, subdue the minor states and give national unity to Germany under Prussian leadership. I have come here to say this to the Queen's ministers.[†]

Within ten years he had accomplished this ambitious plan, principally by the sword – or, as he famously put it in a speech to the Landtag's budget committee the year after his London visit, by 'blood and iron' (though, in German, rendered the other way round): 'Prussia's borders according to the Vienna Treaties [of 1814–15] are not favourable for a healthy, vital state; it is not by speeches and majority resolutions that the great questions of the time are decided

* Although neither Disraeli nor indeed Lord Salisbury (who even argued against the use of it) seems to have used the term, it popularly and aptly described their foreign policy.
† Jonathan Steinberg, *Bismarck: A Life* (Oxford, 2011).

Baltic Sea

POMERANIA

WEST
PRUSSIA

EAST
PRUSSIA

POSEN

RUSSIAN
EMPIRE

SILESIA

AUSTRIA- HUNGARY

GERMAN UNIFICATION
1864–70

Prussia   Other German states

– that was the big mistake of 1848 and 1849 [the widespread European revolutionary movements] – *sondern durch Eisen und Blut.'*

One of Bismarck's 'great questions of the time' was that of Schleswig and Holstein, which many years later Palmerston would say that only three people had ever understood: 'Prince Albert, and he is dead; a German professor who has since gone mad; and myself – and I have forgotten it.' These two independent states at the foot of the Jutland peninsula were in personal union with Denmark, the Danish king being also duke of Schleswig and of Holstein. In effect they were one state, the 'grand duchy' of Schleswig-Holstein; but Holstein, almost wholly German-speaking, was a member of the German Confederation (Deutscher Bund), an association of the German-speaking states of Europe, created in 1815,[†] while Schleswig, with more Danish than German speakers, was not. And while Holstein, as a German state, was subject to the Salic Law,[‡] in particular that of 'agnatic succession' which precluded inheritance by or even through the female line, in practice Schleswig was not. For centuries this had not mattered, but by the middle of the nineteenth it did. At this point Frederick VII of Denmark had no heir: he was twice divorced and had contracted a third, but morganatic, marriage.[§] German nationalist feeling within the grand duchy, growing since 1815, favoured the incorporation of the whole of Schleswig-Holstein in the Deutscher

---

* 'but through iron and blood' (speech to the Landtag's budget committee, 1863), an allusion to the 'liberation poet' Max von Schenckendorf's 1813 exhortation:

Denn nur Eisen kann uns retten	Then only iron can rescue us,
Uns erlösen kann nur Blut	And only blood can save
von der Sünde schweren Ketten,	From the heavy chains of sin,
Von des Bösen Übermut.	From the malignant spirits.

The insistence on 'blood and iron' was not purely, or perhaps even primarily, a reference to the capacity of the Prussian army, but rather to two related factors: first, the ability of the various German states to produce the iron (and related war materials); secondly, the willingness to use them if, and when, necessary.
† The Confederation, in many respects heir to the Holy Roman Empire, was really little more than an economic cooperation zone (most states other than Austria were separate members of the Zollverein, the customs union). In 1848 a general assembly (the 'Confederation Diet') met for the first time in Frankfurt and appointed an executive, but this executive could exercise only those powers ceded to it by individual member states.
‡ So called because it was derived from the law codified by the Salian Franks under Clovis I in the sixth century.
§ A form of marriage by which the husband's titles and privileges do not pass to the wife, nor to any children born of the marriage.

32

Bund, thereby detaching Schleswig from Denmark. Conversely, with no prospect of a male heir and in order to keep his ducal possessions in the family, Frederick and the Danish nationalists sought to re-incorporate Schleswig within Denmark (the duchy having once been a dependency), in the process detaching it from Holstein.

In the heightened state of nationalism prevailing throughout Europe in 1848 this tug-of-war had come to fighting, which con-tinued in fits and starts for three years, initially between Danish and Schleswig-Holstein (German) troops, but later involving also Prussian and Saxon troops and those of the lesser states of the Confederation. The strong Danish navy blockaded Prussian ports, and after initially withdrawing in Jutland, the Danish army gained some significant if inconclusive victories. Palmerston returned to the diplomatic fray, and a negotiated peace in 1851 was followed by another Treaty of London. In essence, this joined both Schleswig and Holstein (and the smaller duchy of Saxe-Lauenburg abutting Holstein) in personal union with the king of Denmark, and set aside the Salic Law; but the states were to remain as independent entities, with Schleswig having no closer constitutional tie with Denmark than had Holstein.

This compromise did not prevent secessionist feelings intensifying throughout the following decade, with Holstein and the Schleswig Germans pressing for incorporation in a 'Greater Germany', the Schleswig Danes for integration with Denmark. Bismarck saw the opportunity to expand those borders of Prussia which he considered 'not favourable for a healthy, vital state' (he was especially taken by the prospect of a ship canal between the Baltic, at Kiel, and the North Sea to avoid incurring tolls on passage through Danish waters).* Unfortunately for themselves, the Danes, probably believing they would be supported by Britain, obliged him with a *casus belli*.† The London peace treaty stipulated that Schleswig should not be treated any differently from Holstein in its relations with Denmark, but when Holstein refused to ratify the liberal constitutional reforms of the

---

* Although the Prussian navy was a small affair and there was no immediate military implication in building such a canal, its potential strategic significance would have been apparent to all – not least Britain.
† The Prince of Wales had just married Alexandra, daughter of the Danish heir pre-sumptive, soon to be King Christian IX, and Palmerston had made a number of ambiguous speeches that could have been taken to imply that Britain would not be able to sit idly by while Danish sovereignty was threatened.

1850s and early 1860s, the parliament in Copenhagen went ahead and ratified the revisions for Schleswig. It was nothing that 'goodwill and wise counsel' (which London, unlike Bismarck, had a tendency to equate with diplomacy) could not have sorted out, but with the death of Frederick and the disputed accession of the new king, Christian IX, Bismarck was able to call for occupation of Holstein by forces of the German Confederation. The Danish government abandoned Holstein and pulled the Danish army back to the Schleswig border.

In the depths of winter 1864, Prussian, Austrian and other Confederation troops moved through Holstein and into Schleswig. Danish resistance was ill-conceived and patchy, and Schleswig was quickly over-run. Indeed, both Prussian and Austrian troops crossed into Denmark proper. By midsummer 1865 the fighting was over, and in the peace treaty that followed Schleswig-Holstein was incorporated in the Confederation, with Schleswig and Lauenburg under Prussian control and Holstein under Austrian. Some 200,000 Danes were now subject to German rule, and as a result Danish-speaking conscripts would die in Belgium and northern France in August 1914 – and many more thereafter on the Western Front.* From now on in Copenhagen it was *La perfide Albion*, while to Berlin, Britain was full of bluster. Bismarck in any case had such a low opinion of her military capability, especially after the débâcles of the Crimean War, that he had vividly expressed his contempt when a nervous official asked what he would do if a British army were to land on the coast of Prussia: 'I should send a policeman to arrest it.'

For Bismarck, however, this episode was no more than a satisfactory beginning. 'As soon as the army shall have been brought into such a condition as to inspire respect,' he had told Disraeli, 'I shall seize the first best pretext to declare war against Austria.' The Prussian army had certainly earned the grudging respect of the Danes (the defeats it had inflicted on them would paralyse Copenhagen in the two world

---

* The 17th and 18th Divisions, which in 1914 formed IX Corps, were predominantly Schleswig-Holstein troops (with a whole brigade of 18 Div which was Schleswig-raised). They were some of the first in action against the BEF at Mons, and were in the thick of the fighting up to the Aisne. Northern (Danish-speaking) Schleswig would be restored to Denmark by the Treaty of Versailles in 1919.

wars*), the lesser German states and, not least, the Prussian people themselves, though Austria had somehow failed to take the true measure of the revitalized Prussian army – in particular the superior breech-loading Dreyse rifle, or 'needle gun', which allowed their infantrymen to fire five rounds from a prone position for every one from the standing position necessary with the Danes' (and Austrians') muzzle-loaders. Nor had Vienna yet appreciated the emerging strategic genius of Helmuth von Moltke (ironically, born and brought up in the Danish service), who had been appointed chief of the Prussian *Grosser Generalstab* (literally, 'great general staff') in 1857 and who would remain in post for thirty years – whose memory, indeed, would be invoked by the Kaiser on the very eve of war in 1914.†

No, Bismarck was not finished, certainly not with Austria. And Tennyson's 'storm in the south' would serve his purpose well, for although the storm seemed largely past, Austria having been driven out of the greater part of northern Italy in 1859 with the help of France, there remained 'Italia Irredenta' (literally 'unredeemed Italy', a religio-romantic label characteristic of the Risorgimento) – those Italian-speaking provinces yet to be incorporated in the new Italian state, notably the Tyrol and Venetia. Bismarck therefore decided to make friends in the south who would distract the Austrians, allowing him to reshape the German Confederation to Prussia's advantage. In April 1866 the Prussian envoy in Florence (the new Italian capital) signed a secret agreement committing the two states to assist each other in a war against Austria, and Bismarck contrived a crisis over the administration of Schleswig-Holstein to bring the war about. Obligingly, Austria brought the dispute before the Confederation diet,

---

* Danish forces would not make war outside their frontiers again until the 1999 air campaign against Serbia (in the former Federal Republic of Yugoslavia). Swedish support having been withheld in 1863–4, it was clear that Denmark could not rely on 'Scandinavianism', and that she could not stand against the might of Germany; hence the so-called 'favourable neutrality' of 1914–18, and the 'adjustment policy' and later 'cooperation policy' during the Nazi occupation in the Second World War – to the immense chagrin of large parts of her military, even today. The author recalls the pride with which the Danish Guard Hussars, to which he was briefly attached in the late 1980s, related their bloody resistance to forced disarmament in 1943 – and the preservation of the retributive German bullet holes in the portrait of (the British) King Edward VII, a former colonel-in-chief.

† Helmuth Karl von Moltke, 1800–91, known as Moltke the Elder (or the Elder Moltke) to distinguish him from his nephew and future chief of the *Grosser Generalstab*, Helmuth Johann von Moltke (the Younger Moltke), 1848–1916.

and convened the Holstein assembly. Prussia – that is, Bismarck; the king himself took fright at the prospect of war, fearing the army would be outnumbered – declared that the Gastein Convention, which governed the administration of the duchies, had been nullified by Austria's action, and promptly invaded Holstein. The Confederation diet responded by backing Austria; and Bavaria, Württemberg, Saxony, Hanover, Baden and several of the smaller states began mobilizing. At once Bismarck pronounced the Confederation at an end and sent Moltke into Austrian Bohemia, where on 3 July at Sadowa (Königgrätz) Prussian troops defeated a numerically superior army. Austria sued for peace, which left the German states isolated, and these in turn Moltke defeated or obliged to seek terms.

It was all over in seven weeks. Prussia annexed Hanover, Hesse, Nassau, Frankfurt and Schleswig-Holstein (Saxony was spared because she had stood only on the defensive in Bohemia, with Austria, although her military administration would be thoroughly Prussianized). The Confederation, the Deutscher Bund, was now replaced by the Prussian-led Norddeutscher Bund, which, as its name suggests, did not include Bavaria, Württemberg and Baden. It also, of course, excluded Austria, on whom Bismarck shrewdly imposed only moderate peace terms, a decision that would serve him well when he came to formalize an Austro-German alliance in 1879.

Historians dispute just how much of a master plan for the enlargement of Prussia Bismarck really had, stressing instead his opportunism (perhaps like Hitler's in the 1930s). However, to elevate luck to such a position of pre-eminence in policy seems, even with hindsight, unfeasible: Bismarck could scarcely have recognized or made the opportunities so consummately well without a clear concept of what was both possible and desirable – the sort of grand design of which he had spoken to Disraeli. As ever, though, there were alternatives: first, the so-called *Kleindeutsche Lösung* (Little German Solution), which would stop at the Austrian border; secondly, the *Grossdeutsche Lösung* (Greater German Solution), which would incorporate Austria in the German state. But *klein* or *gross*, Bismarck's Prussia–Germany of 1866 was no longer the nation of 1815 and the Congress of Vienna. Neither was Austria, whose territory had shrunk almost in proportion to Prussia's gain (the war with Italy had cost her Venetia). Yet neither Britain nor France felt able – or perhaps saw the need – formally to revisit the Vienna treaty's assumptions and terms, and its subsequent protocols; not even the 1839 Treaty of London and its guarantee of Belgian neutrality.

Prussia – Bismarck – certainly would not have wanted international scrutiny of a treaty (London) whose very vagueness allowed him latitude. And what interest would that other signatory, Austria, have in re-examining it? Her dominance of the German states, the old Confederation, was finished; she had no territorial interest in the Netherlands any longer, and Baden, Württemberg and Bavaria stood solidly between her and the French border. Instead, both faces of the double-headed eagle now turned east, to the Balkans. In the wake of Austria's defeat by Prussia, Hungary began calls for separation, which the Emperor Franz Joseph headed off by giving his Hungarian domains equal status with his Austrian, creating the Dual Monarchy of Austria-Hungary.* Ten years later, in 1878, with the further dis-integration of the Ottoman Empire, the Dual Monarchy would acquire Bosnia (and Herzegovina) – whose capital was Sarajevo.

Still Bismarck was not finished. And if wresting the neck of Jutland from the Danes, and delivering a knock-out blow to the Austrians in seven weeks, looked like genius, then the final act of the three-part drama which was the unification of Germany was dazzling in its cunning and execution. The attraction of a war with France was perhaps obvious only to a statesman like Bismarck, and the defeat of the apparently formidable French army conceivable only to a soldier like Moltke. France posed no active threat to Prussia or the German states; her enmity with Austria over Italian unification had even been propitious. Yet Paris's attempts at a *rapprochement* with Vienna after the defeats of 1866 reinforced Bismarck's conviction that humiliating France would serve a wider strategic purpose: for he was already convinced that war with the old enemy – whose liberal ideas under Napoleon III were offensive to him, the king and the entire *Junker* caste† – would bind the north German states to Prussia and, if he

---

* Hungary had been a Habsburg dominion since the end of the seventeenth century, when the 'Holy League' had recaptured the capital, Buda, from the Ottoman Turks. Hungarian nationalism had always made for periodic turmoil, however, most recently in the 'Spring of Nations', 1848.

†Literally 'young lords': the Teutonic landowning gentry from which the great bulk of the officer and administrative class was drawn, elevated by Bismarck into an almost quasi-religious order, the repository of Prussian values and Spartan, self-sacrificing strength.

played his cards right, bring in those of the south too.

The problem was that the 'Second Empire', as Napoleon III's polity was known, had an impressive military reputation: on the face of it, fifteen years of victory – in the Crimea, Italy, Mexico and Algeria – represented a formidable and varied capability. The French army's rifles – first the Minié, which the British army had hastily purchased during the Crimean War, and by 1870 the Chassepot, in most ways superior even to the Dreyse – had seen off the armies of two of the great powers of the Congress (Russia and, in Italy, Austria); there seemed no reason why it should not see off a third. The basis of French success was, however, brittle. The army was conscript, like the Prussian, but until 1866, the year of Prussia's victory over Austria, it was based on seven-year conscription, which (not unlike the British terms of enlistment) produced an army with a strong military *esprit* well suited to colonial and overseas wars, but without the capacity to generate ready reserves, for there was not the turnover of recruits.*
While there was no external threat to the state, and with strong border forts behind which new armies could be built, this was all very well, but Bismarck's new Prussia was a threat of quite another order. In response to the stunning victory at Sadowa, France had reorganized her conscription on more nearly universal but still short-term lines, including a reserve akin to the later British 'Territorials' – the Garde Nationale Mobile – but in 1870 these reforms had hardly begun to take effect. In addition, French officers (the whole system, indeed), while experienced and Gallically brave, still relied on strong Napoleonic top-down leadership, which the Napoleonic nephew was incapable of providing. By contrast, and perhaps surprisingly given

---

* Conscripts were selected by lot: half of those chosen then formed an untrained reserve, from which substitutes could be paid for service with the colours (i.e. with a unit). It may have looked impressive on paper, but in practice it meant that the theoretical 'reserve' was full of middle-aged 'semi-conscripts' each filling several substitute places in different units – a military pluralism akin to the Church of England's practice of clergy holding several benefices at once, paying curates to turn up on parade in their stead. The Prussians, on the other hand, had several tiers of reserves within two broad categories – *Landsturm* and *Landwehr* – through which reservists passed as they grew older. A man of military age (seventeen), if fit, was drafted into the *Landsturm*; at twenty he would then serve for two or three years with the colours (i.e. the active army), passing then into the active reserve (*Ersatztruppen* – battle-casualty replacement troops); after four or five years he would be transferred to the *Landwehr*, a home defence corps, until at the age of about 45 he would return to the *Landsturm* for five years, liable for general duties.

the stereotypical image of German rigidity, Prussian officers were stimulated by Moltke to an impressive degree of improvisation and initiative. Strategy, they were taught, was a system of expedients only: a plan for the whole course of a campaign was impossible. An understanding of the military objectives necessary for achieving the political goal was all that could be computed, for no plan could survive first contact with the enemy.* Moltke therefore created a body of doctrine within the general staff so that junior officers encountering the problems of first contact would find their own solutions that would nevertheless conform to his general ideas – what a century later would be known as *Auftragstaktik* (literally, 'task tactics'), and a century earlier would have been recognized by Nelson's 'band of brothers' as the way to run a fleet. Crucially, combined with technological advances in communications, principally the railways and the electric telegraph, this meant that the Prussian general staff would not now need to *mass* the various armies in the course of mobilization – always the bane of planners and a giveaway to the opposing side as far as intentions were concerned; they had only to ensure that the armies could converge on the battlefield itself. It made for the greater concentration of troops at the decisive point, and favoured the tactics of envelopment. Ironically, in this, Moltke was only applying Napoleonic principles – of holding armies *désunis*,† with the capability of their rapidly becoming *réunis* – which the French themselves seemed to have forgotten.

Second Empire France was a prickly country. The very name 'Napoleon', even attached to Napoleon III, promised – threatened – turmoil. Bonaparte's nephew had come to power by *coup d'état*: he stood for the destruction of the 'anti-French' settlement of 1815, and he had used his armies not just against Russia in the Crimea but against the nation he perceived as the greatest prop to the old Vienna settlement – Austria. By 1870 even Gladstone, prime minister in the first of his four administrations, was concerned that *L'Empereur* had designs on Belgium. Yet despite the recent string of victories, France

---

* 'Therefore no plan of operations goes with any degree of certainty beyond the first contact with the hostile main force': Moltke, *Military Works*, Volume IV, *Operative Preparations for Battle* (Newport, RI, US Naval War College, 1935).
† Literally, 'disunited', but in the Napoleonic sense of 'loosely', to make the best use of space and resources, but able to combine quickly for concerted action – *réunis*.

was conscious of her waning military power compared with Prussia (and, colonially, with Britain). Circumspection should therefore have been the order of the day in Paris; but in fact Bismarck would find it easy to provoke *le coq gaulois* into war, and over a dynastic question that would have been at once familiar to the despised *ancien régime*: the succession to the throne of Spain.

Napoleon III had been trying to persuade King Wilhelm I of Prussia to oppose the candidacy of a German prince, Leopold of Hohenzollern-Sigmaringen. By great and devious adroitness – including making public the famous 'Ems Telegram' – on 15 July 1870 Bismarck manoeuvred the French into declaring war, without allies. Not only did this mean that France would fight alone, the French declaration of war would bring Prussia allies aplenty – the North German Confederation *and* the south German states. Exactly as Bismarck had calculated.

The affair of the Ems Telegram is worth a closer look, since it reveals a great deal about the nature of the Prussian state – the dominating polity of the Greater Germany that would emerge from the war. For it is easy to be seduced by the evident civilization and high culture that at this time were such an inspiration for intellectual Europe, the impressive social welfare system in particular standing in curious contrast with the authoritarianism of Prussian government and institutions (as culture and welfare did in 1930s Germany too).* On

---

* And this notwithstanding Bismarck's heavy-handed secularization policy, about to get under way – the Kulturkampf (literally, 'culture struggle'). In 1871, 38% of the population of the new German Empire was Catholic. Bismarck perceived a threat: an external point of allegiance (the Pope) and the potential for sympathy with Catholic nations such as France and Austria. On the other hand, he saw that he could increase his appeal to liberals and Protestants (61% of the population) by reducing the political and social influence of the Church of Rome. Bismarck's series of legislative measures to bring education (the 'Falk Laws'), marriage and some clergy appointments fully under state control saw the arrest, or removal from their cures, of priests and bishops who resisted. At the height of the Kulturkampf, half the Prussian bishops were in prison or in exile, a quarter of parishes had no priest, half the monks and nuns had left the country, a third of the monasteries and convents were closed, and nearly two thousand parish priests were imprisoned (as were thousands more laymen) or exiled. Gerard Manley Hopkins's celebrated poem 'The Wreck of the *Deutschland*' was composed in memory of five Franciscan nuns who, forced to leave Westphalia under the Falk Laws, drowned when the SS *Deutschland* foundered off Harwich. Bismarck's policies eventually backfired, however, energizing Catholics to become a political force in the Centre party. With the election in 1878 of a new pope, the more modern-minded Leo XIII, there was some *détente*, and with the departure of the anti-Catholic liberals from his coalition, and by judicious trimming, Bismarck was able to win over the Centre party on most of his policies, especially his attacks on the growing menace of socialism.

13 July the Prussian king, on holiday at Bad Ems, was taking his morning stroll when the French ambassador, Count Vincent Benedetti, approached him to present with the appropriate politeness and discretion the French demand that Wilhelm never again permit the candidacy of a Hohenzollern prince to the Spanish throne. Equally politely the king refused to bind himself to any course of action in the future. The king's secretary sent a telegram to Bismarck reporting the exchange, with permission to release an account of the events. Bismarck, in today's familiar phrase, 'sexed up' the account, omitting the conciliatory words so that it read as if Benedetti had made demands under threat of war, and Wilhelm had refused them outright.

The fire began to smoulder. Bismarck then fanned the flames by editing the telegram itself and releasing it to the press and foreign embassies that evening, giving an even starker impression of the encounter between the king and the envoy, in which Benedetti had been yet more demanding, and the king abrupt to the point of curtness. Further provoked by the clumsy translating of the French news agency Havas, French public opinion was outraged: the Prussian king had insulted the ambassador, and by extension the emperor – and therefore France herself. Nor could the timing have been better from Bismarck's point of view: a French public holiday fuelled the sense of outrage while at the same time hindering efforts by Benedetti to damp down the flames in a fuller report. Meanwhile in Prussia, indeed Germany as a whole, the king's curtness paled into insignificance when compared with the French demand that he should not advance the cause of a German candidate: this was an unmitigated insult to King Wilhelm – and therefore to Prussia herself. With great satisfaction, Bismarck told colleagues that the telegram 'would have the effect of a red rag on the Gallic bull'.

It did indeed. Benedetti was recalled, and on 19 July the French *chargé d'affaires* delivered the emperor's declaration of war – on Prussia alone, but the other states of the Norddeutscher Bund at once came in behind Berlin. The armies mobilized and moved to their concentration areas. The French tried both to mobilize and to concentrate simultaneously, with at times chaotic results. On the other hand, Moltke's plans – worked on since the victory in 1866 by the Prussian general staff with the cooperation of the staffs of the other armies of the Bund – had the two distinct functions completed sequentially and therefore more quickly (the model that the new British general staff would adopt when making their own plans in the decade before the First World War). In the *Grosser Generalstab*'s bible of the transition to war, railway timetables were the chapter and verse. By the end of July Moltke would have 300,000 men, in three armies, in place along the frontier – 50,000 more than the French under the personal command of Napoleon III; and the balance would weigh increasingly in German favour in the weeks that followed as the second-line reserves were embodied.

When fighting began in early August the excellent Chassepot rifle stopped the Prussians in their various tracks for a while. But across the board the far superior Krupp artillery* was able to pound the French infantry into retreat, while German cavalry and infantry felt for the flanks in accordance with Moltke's doctrine. French cavalry made heroic and utterly futile charges by return – not so much 'death or glory' as simply death. French generals vacillated; their staffs mis-calculated. German generals almost over-reached themselves, but fortune aided by Moltke's *Auftragstaktik* smiled on them, and soon the French found themselves enveloped, besieged and blockaded – unable to counter-attack with their famed *élan*. On 1 September Napoleon III himself was hopelessly surrounded at Sedan, on the Meuse near the Belgian border, and captured along with the bulk of four army corps. The government in Paris fell, and with it the Second Empire, replaced by *le gouvernement de la défense nationale* and the Third Republic. Napoleonic exile beckoned – this time not to St Helena but, of all places, Chislehurst in Kent (the Empress Eugénie smuggled out of Paris by her American dentist). The campaign of manoeuvre was all but over: at the end of the month Paris was besieged, and Bismarck and Moltke took quarters at Versailles. The city held out, under bombardment and close to starvation, until late January, when an armistice was signed.†

* Breech-loading field guns, therefore quicker firing than the French muzzle-loaders, made of steel strong enough to contain a greater charge and thus project to longer range (rather than the bronze of the 'Napoleonic' cannon), and with impact-fused ammunition which scattered zinc balls by explosive charge.
† The defence of Paris was undeniably heroic, and the privations dire. Even allowing for the broad French interpretation of edibility, rats, dogs and cats on restaurant menus (though suitably disguised with *noms de cuisine*) were desperate fare. Nor were Castor and Pollux, the only pair of elephants in the *jardin zoologique* (opened ten years before by the emperor), spared.

Not a single German soldier had set foot in Belgium, however. Bismarck may have been dismissive of the British army, and would have had no great opinion of the Belgian army either, but Moltke had no need of more troops opposing him than was necessary. Gladstone had made clear that violation of Belgian neutrality might lead to intervention. Indeed, the year before, fearing a pre-emptive French move through Belgium, he had seriously considered sending a force to Antwerp. As soon as war was declared the prime minister pressed for, and received, undertakings from both Germany and France that Belgian territory would be respected. Britain was therefore able to watch from the wings.*

But in the peace treaty which followed, the borders of France were altered without the consultation of the signatories of the Congress of Vienna. France ceded the *départements* of Alsace and Lorraine to Prussia – or rather, to the German Empire, for in 1871 the sovereigns of all the German states except Austria met at Versailles to embrace *das Kaiserlich Deutsches Reich* ('Imperial German Empire'†) under Wilhelm I. The Prussia of 1815, with a population of ten million, and only a little over nineteen million when Bismarck became chancellor, had now become a Germany of forty-one million – greater than the population of France; greater, indeed, than of any country west of Russia (although Bismarck would never see a *Grossdeutsches Reich*, which would not be accomplished until 1938 with the *Anschluss*, the incorporation of Austria in the Third Reich). The Concert of Europe was dead, the balance of power alarmingly out of poise.

Yet in the minds of European princes France had for so long been the threat to peace that it would be some time before the full

* In the Anglo-Prussian treaty, signed on 9 August 1869, Wilhelm declared it 'his fixed determination to respect the neutrality of Belgium, so long as the same shall be respected by France'. Two days later, Napoleon III made the same declaration. Britain declared in each treaty that if one side violated Belgian neutrality, she was prepared to cooperate with the opposing side. The treaties were for the duration of the war, plus twelve months. Thereafter the provisions of the treaty of 1839 were to apply again. However, the feeling towards Belgian neutrality was perhaps not quite so cut and dried as this suggests. There appeared in the press some Foreign Office 'kites', flown to sound public opinion. In the event of a German march through Belgium into northern France, could not England accept the situation provided Bismarck gave his word only to use a 'right of way' through the country? Liberal England of that day still recoiled from being drawn into continental quarrels. Besides, Lord Salisbury for one regarded France, not Germany, as the country threatening European peace.
† The tautology derives from the inability to translate *Reich* directly.

significance of Germany's emergence as the pre-eminent military–industrial power sank home. Meanwhile all that a humiliated France, as well as a humbled Austria and a still-wounded Russia, could do was try to copy the Prussian institutions that had delivered such spectacular victories: universal conscription, railway building, relentless improvement in weapons technology – and general staffs honing plans for war. And in the German *Reich* – Prussia especially – the army's achievements would feed a growing militarism which would then begin to feed on itself. It was as if the hall of mirrors at Versailles, in which the French were brought to sign the surrender, and in which Bismarck grandiosely proclaimed the *Reich*, was reflecting, magnifying and multiplying the uniformed glory of Europe. It was indeed a sort of collective military psychosis from which only Britain, in her island fastness, looked immune.*

For the time being, however, Germany seemed content to consolidate her new unity, albeit shaped by Bismarck's increasingly irritable, almost paranoid, temperament, which the weak and ageing king was not the man to check. As the most recent biographer of 'the Iron Chancellor', Professor Jonathan Steinberg, observes:

> In the Reich Constitution of 1871 Bismarck reproduced the semi-absolute features of the Prussian Constitution of 1850. He made certain that in the national government, as in the government of the largest federal state, he alone had the power of decision over everything from war and peace to stamp duty on postal transfers. He brooked no contradiction, terrified his subordinates and had no advisers.

Just so. In 1878, in the wake of yet another Russo-Turkish war, Bismarck stepped centre stage once more when he chaired a posthumous session of the Concert of Europe – the Congress of Berlin, a meeting of the great powers and the Ottoman Empire to unravel the tangled web that was the post-imperial Balkans, the particular trick being to balance the interests of Britain in the Mediterranean with those of Russia and Austria-Hungary. As a result, the Turks were

---

* 'Militarism', *militarismus*, variously defined as a doctrine that values war and accords primacy in state and society to the armed forces, was an accusation made of Berlin in the 1860s by south German democrats, Catholics and anti-Prussianists, and in turn by Bismarck – and others – of Napoleon III, alleging that he used the spectre of war with Prussia to promote cohesion at home.

obliged to fall back even further from the Danube, and Romania achieved full independence, along with Bulgaria, Serbia and Montenegro. However, with the release of the latter three from Turkish check, allowing Russia greater influence in their internal affairs, the Congress had unwittingly placed a pan-Slavic can of worms on Austria-Hungary's flank – on Prussia's flank, indeed, for the following year Bismarck brokered the 'Dual Alliance', a defensive pact with Austria principally against Russia, which Italy would join three years later.

The old Prussian king died in 1888 (the year that Moltke retired as chief of the general staff), to be succeeded by Crown Prince Frederick, who would himself die of throat cancer within months. At this point the throne passed to his son, who would rule as Wilhelm II, 'the Kaiser' ('Emperor') – known to every British Tommy as 'Kaiser Bill'.

And Wilhelm was a Kaiser with a mission, as well as unbounded self-belief. Two years later he dismissed Bismarck, a move that *Punch* famously caricatured in a cartoon of March 1890 as 'Dropping the Pilot'. From now on the new young Kaiser, the grandson of Queen Victoria, the cousin of the future Tsar Nicholas II, would continue alone the glorification of Prussia – of Germany, indeed. He would increase her power, expand her horizons, build a true overseas empire, Germany's 'place in the sun'. He would, in short, pursue a *Weltpolitik* – and by personal rule, finding, in Professor Steinberg's words, 'a group of dedicated courtiers who encouraged his megalomania'. As his biographer, Professor John Röhl, writes: 'With the help of his favourite Count Philipp zu Eulenburg [Wilhelm proceeded] to hollow-out the remaining constitutional constraints to exercise his personal power. In the military and naval spheres and in the making of foreign policy in particular his decisions now went virtually unchallenged.'*

But the Kaiser was no Bismarck. Steinberg again: 'The Iron Chancellor embodied and manifested the greatness of Germany. His

---

* John Röhl, 'The Long and Twisted Road to Sarajevo: Kaiser Wilhelm II and the Approach of War in 1914', paper given at the German Historical Institute, London, 2 Nov. 2010. It should be stressed, however, that not every manifestation of *Weltpolitik* would mean automatic conflict with Britain. Construction of the Berlin–Baghdad railway, for example, sometimes cited as a threat to the oilfields of the Persian Gulf on which the Royal Navy, converting to oil from coal, depended, was to London something of a paper tiger. The announcement on 3 July that the railway would be extended to Basra caused no appreciable concern, for the Foreign Office was close to concluding an agreement with Berlin on its operation.

image hung in every schoolroom and over many a hearth. Yet this image became a burden to his successors. Germany had to have a genius-statesman as its ruler. Kaiser Wilhelm II outdid the Iron Chancellor in military display, but failed the test. He could not control himself, still less the ramshackle structure that Bismarck had left him.'

Or, as Asquith himself would put it in his post-war memoir: 'From the seclusion of Friedrichsruh [the Chancellor's home in retirement] the formidable and menacing figure of Bismarck still dominated German opinion, and paralysed the Kaiser.'*

And then, in January 1901, Queen Victoria died. The Kaiser's pathetic lament in later years that if their grandmother had still been alive she would never have allowed the three first cousins – himself, the Tsar and King George V – to go to war with each other may have been absurdly fanciful, but Berlin's relationship with London was now no longer checked by any sense of grand-filial obligation; and Wilhelm had no great affection for his Uncle Bertie, the new King Edward VII.

* H. H. Asquith, *The Genesis of the War* (London, 1923).

Chapter Three

LESSONS

Mock not the African kopje.*

Rudyard Kipling, 'Two Kopjes' (1903)

'We had seven days' fighting right off at a stroke, and our regiment lost very heavily. The first day we lost 121 men and we had hardly been twenty minutes in action, and the worst of it is that we cannot see where the Boers are firing from . . .'

Private Thomas Heyliss, a soldier in 1st Battalion the Border Regiment, writing to a friend at home in Cumberland in January 1900, summed up the shock of first contact with a 'European' enemy, the Dutch settlers of the Transvaal and the Orange Free State – the Boers (literally, 'farmers'). His was one of two dozen infantry battalions, in a force of nearly 20,000 in all, ranged against a Boer *kommando* of some 6,000 militiamen – hunter-farmers, natural mounted infantry – under Louis Botha at the Tugela River in the early months of the Second (or Great) Boer War. Private Heyliss wore khaki and carried the new Lee–Enfield magazine-fed rifle, but still at heart a great many in the British army carried the musket and wore red, just as Heyliss's regimental forebears had when they sailed for the Crimea

---

* *Kopje* – a small hill rising up from the African veld; from Afrikaans *koppie*, from Dutch *kopje*, literally 'a little head' (from *kop*, head). *Kop* – a prominent, isolated hill or mountain.

47

half a century before – and just as the Gordons and Northamptons had when they too felt the fire of the Boers for the first time, in 1881 in the much smaller affair known as the First Boer War. Heyliss and his fellow infantrymen used the rifle as if it were a longer-range musket – firing volleys, usually from a standing position, shoulder-to-shoulder – rather than for individual marksmanship. And they preferred to manoeuvre in almost equally close order. In essence, the principles of fire and movement had hardly changed since 1815 – or, for that matter, since 1704 and Blenheim. On the other hand, as President Paul Kruger of the Transvaal put it, 'The Boers can shoot, and that is everything.'

It was not as if there hadn't been lessons to learn from more recent conflicts – the American Civil War, the Austro-Prussian War, the Franco-Prussian war – but on the whole these had been dismissed as wars special to their armies and locations. The Civil War had been an affair of militias, the other two the business of huge, conscript armies. The British army was a relatively small but experienced force of long-service regulars; there was no comparison with the rag-bag regiments of the hastily raised Union or Confederate armies, nor with continental troops drilled on the principles of Napoleon or Frederick the Great. There had, however, been lessons closer to home, metaphorically speaking – on the North-West Frontier:

> A scrimmage in a Border Station—
> A canter down some dark defile
> Two thousand pounds of education
> Drops to a ten-rupee jezail.

Kipling called the poem 'Arithmetic on the Frontier'; a hundred years later the idea it encapsulated so succinctly would be intellectualized as the concept of 'asymmetric warfare'. And it was not as if the Afghan *jezails* that brought down many a British infantryman were the equal of the Boers' German-made Mauser rifles; they were primitive muskets by comparison. The point was more about individual marksmanship. Kipling again:

> I fired a shot at a Afghan,
> The beggar 'e fired again,

48

An' I lay on my bed with a 'ole in my 'ed,
An' missed the next campaign!*

In truth the drill manuals of the 1890s had tried to deal with this challenge; but theory was one thing, its practical application by those who had not yet been convinced of the need for innovation quite another. For it was not just the Boers' accurate shooting that surprised Private Heyliss and his companions in the Border Regiment, it was their fieldcraft: 'we cannot see where the Boers are firing from'. They were in fact firing from a range beyond which the British soldier was accustomed to shoot – up to a thousand yards – and as hunters of the veld, concealment was second nature to them. In the opening month of the war they had severely mauled the army in Natal, laid siege to Mafeking and Ladysmith, and then in what quickly became known as 'Black Week', 10–17 December 1899, meted out serious punishment at Stormberg, Magersfontein and Colenso – names soon etched deep in the mind of the British public, as well as Private Heyliss's. Nor was the lesson lost on senior officers. Major-General Neville Lyttelton, commanding the 4th (Light) Brigade at Colenso (in 1904 he would become the first chief of the general staff), was struck by the contrast with his experience of commanding a brigade at Omdurman in the Sudan a year before: 'In the first, 50,000 fanatics streamed across the open regardless of cover to certain death, while at Colenso I never saw a Boer all day till the battle was over, and it was our men who were the victims.'

Having been given a humiliating bloody nose in Black Week trying to cross the Tugela, the commander-in-chief in South Africa, General Sir Redvers Buller, brave as the proverbial lion (he had won the Victoria Cross in the Zulu War), was therefore even more determined to drive on to relieve Ladysmith; and now, in the third week of January, he mounted an attack 20 miles to the west of his first attempt at Colenso, opposite the Rangeworthy Hills, of which one of the most prominent was called Spion Kop.

It was not a well-conceived operation, nor was it well executed. Reconnaissance was perfunctory, use of ground unimaginative; there was little coordination of fire and movement, and communications

* 'Private Ortheris's Song' (in *Life's Handicap*, 1915).

were not up to the demands of a complex battle. Wireless telegraphy (using Morse code) was in its infancy, no telegraph/telephone line was available, heliograph and semaphore flags had their limitations and were no use at night, when signal lamps were used instead, with the added risk of compromise. When things began to go wrong, therefore, commanders had only a tenuous grip on the action, made worse by a curious failure of junior leadership – the traditional boast of the British army – as the situation became confused.

It all culminated in a disastrous attack on Spion Kop by a brigade of infantry which, having climbed the slopes in the dark, found themselves on a false crest as daylight came, without cover and overlooked by Boer marksmen, who began pouring devastating fire into what became known as the 'murderous acre'. The Mauser, and the German-made (Krupp) guns of the Staatsartillerie – the only regular Boer troops – killed two hundred and fifty and wounded another twelve hundred in the space of forty-eight hours. One of Buller's 'gallopers' that day was Winston Churchill, back in uniform with the hastily raised South Africa Light Horse after his early adventures as a war correspondent. He scrambled up and down Spion Kop several times carrying messages, writing afterwards that 'Corpses lay here and there. Many of the wounds were of a horrible nature. The splinters and fragments of the shells had torn and mutilated them. The shallow trenches were choked with dead and wounded.'*

It was a spectacular demonstration that, for all the experience gained in many a colonial campaign, and thirty years after the battles of the Franco-Prussian War had pointed to the future, the British army lacked the moral and physical power to deal with a modern enemy, having neither the technical means nor the tactics to cope with long-range artillery and magazine-rifle fire, though these had been in service for a decade and more. Spion Kop was the Victorian army's nadir. Fortunately, the battle had not taken place in some unobserved corner on the far side of the world: the telegraph may not have been used to communicate orders in the field, but it certainly spread the news abroad. The man in the street – in London, Swansea, Manchester, Dublin, Aberdeen; anywhere, indeed, that the

---

* Winston S. Churchill, *London to Ladysmith via Pretoria* (London, 1900); see also his *My Early Life* (London, 1930).

booming popular press reached – learned the shocking details soon enough.* Before long, 'Spion Kop' (and then just 'the Kop') had become the name for the towering stands in many a football stadium.

The army itself was all too painfully aware of its failings, but it was not just the nation that was being told of them: so was the rest of the world. 'The vast majority of German military experts believe that the South African war will end with a complete defeat of the English,' wrote Count von Bülow, the German foreign minister, gleefully after Black Week: 'Nobody here believes that the English will ever reach Pretoria.'

In London the government nearly fell.

But although the army's prestige with foreign observers, especially German, suffered a severe blow (Bismarck may have dismissed the British army earlier as too small to be of any concern to him, but after Kitchener's Sudan campaign he had had no cause to doubt its acumen), the 'English' did indeed reach Pretoria – and Bloemfontein, the other Boer capital. Under the new leadership of Lord Roberts, the victor of Kandahar, and then of Lord Kitchener, the victor of Khartoum, the army recovered itself, beat the Boer field armies and then waged a determined, if costly, counter-guerrilla war against the 'bitter-enders' (the Boers who vowed to fight 'to the bitter end' when their governments signed the peace) until their final surrender in 1902.

But the cost, besides the humiliation, of having to put into the field nearly half a million British and imperial troops, including 250,000 British regulars, to subdue a vastly inferior number of armed Dutch settlers was staggering. While the Boers probably lost fewer than 4,000 killed in the field, British and imperial casualties were nearly 6,000 killed and 23,000 wounded, plus 16,000 deaths from disease and wounds. The money cost exceeded £220 million; income tax went up during the war (from 2d to 1s 3d in the pound: 0.83p to 6.25p), and so did the taxes on beer, tobacco and tea. No wonder Kipling would write of those early, bruising encounters:

---

* The lessons were certainly etched in the mind of many an officer: for one example of its impact in August 1914, see chapter 19, p. 391 below.

Then mock not the African kopje,
But take off your hat to the same,
The patient, impartial old kopje,
The kopje that taught us the game!
For all that we knew in the Columns,
And all they've forgot on the Staff,
We learned at the Fight o' Two Kopjes,
Which lasted two years an' a half.*

But learned it was. The men who had fought in South Africa and who went to France in August 1914 knew there was a direct line linking the African *kopje* to the BEF, beneficiaries of an altogether different training. And in August 1914 the Germans quickly realized it too. An officer of the Brandenburg Grenadiers, whose regiment had a rude shock in the first encounter with the BEF, at Mons in Belgium, would write: 'Wonderful, as we marched on, how they had converted every house, every wall into a little fortress: the experience no doubt of old soldiers gained in a dozen colonial wars; possibly even some of the butchers of the Boers were among them.'†

'The kopje that taught us the game!' Never in the army's history was there such wholesale upheaval – reform – as now followed the South African war. Never in so short a time, perhaps half a dozen years, ten at most, after the Treaty of Vereeniging had brought an intelligent and magnanimous‡ end to the war, had the army been so imbued with the impulse for change – from the very top to the very bottom. As early as 1904 a foreign military observer was noting the alteration in tactical movement: 'In their manoeuvres the British infantry showed great skill in the use of ground. Their thin lines of khaki-clad skirmishers were scarcely visible. No detachment was ever seen in close order within three thousand yards. Frontal attacks were entirely avoided.'§

* 'Two Kopjes', one of the suite of sixteen 'Service Songs' which close *The Five Nations* (1903).
† Walter Bloem, *The Advance from Mons* (London, 1930), originally published as *Vormarsch* (Leipzig, 1916).
‡ So magnanimous, in fact, that many of the Boers would fight for the King against the Germans in South-west and East Africa in the First World War – including Louis Botha. Jan Smuts, another Transvaal *kommando* leader, would actually command a British force in East Africa, and be appointed field marshal in the British army.
§ The irony, that in the apparent absence of any alternative, frontal attacks would become the staple of war on the Western Front between 1915 and 1918, could scarcely

For just as Private Heyliss of the Border Regiment had been given his crude lesson in fieldcraft, all the generals sitting at the cabinet table on 5 August 1914 had heard the Mauser and the Krupp artillery, had seen their effects and been thoroughly chastened by the experience. To quote Kipling one last time ('The Lesson', published in *The Times* a full year – remarkably – before the Boer War was over):

> Let us admit it fairly, as a business people should,
> We have had no end of a lesson: it will do us no end of good.
> Not on a single issue, or in one direction or twain,
> But conclusively, comprehensively, and several times again . . .

And this was the conclusion of the various committees of inquiry. The first, the Elgin Commission,* which began taking evidence in October 1902, and in the course of fifty-five days saw 114 witnesses and asked more than 2,000 questions, produced an excellent narrative by which the various branches of the army could act; but since it was less convincing on the question of reorganization of the War Office itself, a further commission was set up. The War Office (Reconstitution) Committee consisted of just three members – Lord Esher,† who had sat on the Elgin Commission, the future first sea lord Admiral Sir John (Jacky) Fisher and Colonel Sir George Clarke, who had been secretary of the Colonial Defence Committee and would become the first secretary of the Committee of Imperial Defence (CID) when it was formed the following year.

Esher took evidence in private and came up with three main recommendations. First, an 'Army Council' modelled on the Board of Admiralty should be established to decide on policy issues, replacing the confusion of responsibilities associated with the old model of a War Office (the civil ministry of the secretary of state for war – i.e. of the army) separate from the headquarters of the

---

have been imagined – although the lessons of the Russo-Japanese War warned of the consequences clearly enough.

* Chaired by the 9th earl of Elgin, Liberal peer and member of Gladstone's third administration, lately viceroy of India, and in 1905 secretary of state for the colonies (with Churchill as his under-secretary).

† Reginald Balliol Brett, 2nd Viscount Esher, very much a man of his times: historian and Liberal politician who retired early from politics to take a 'back-room' role in public affairs, with access to almost everyone who counted, including the King.

commander-in-chief* – the former in a hotch-potch of buildings in Pall Mall, the latter in the Horse Guards in Whitehall. Secondly, the post of commander-in-chief was itself to be abolished and a general staff formed instead within the War Office, with a chief (CGS†) and three subordinate divisions – operations (and intelligence), staff duties (organization), and military training – each headed by a director in the rank of brigadier- or major-general. Finally, the other three functional departments – those of the adjutant-general (AG), quartermaster-general (QMG), and master-general of the ordnance (MGO) – were all to be brought into the War Office, their respective heads sitting on the Army Council, with the CIGS as *primus inter pares.*‡

It was a superb model – better, in fact, than that of the Admiralty, since the members of the Army Council would have proper staffs. It would prepare the army for the First World War, see it through that war, and, indeed, see it through the Second World War and beyond.§ But not all the lessons of the Boer War had been conclusive, for the nature of the military art (it is not all science) means that officers with the same experience could hold contrary opinions on operational matters. However, there was no dissent over the principal lesson of

* In full, 'Commander-in-Chief of His Majesty's Land Forces in Great Britain and Ireland'. The army's terminology could seem pedantic, confusing and inconsistent – and sometimes was. Senior command appointments were termed as follows. Officers in command of brigades and divisions (usually brigadier-generals and major-generals respectively) were designated 'general officer commanding' (GOC) – e.g. GOC 5th Cavalry Brigade, GOC 1st [Infantry] Division – although referred to commonly in brigades as 'the brigadier' (the rank 'brigadier-general' was phased out from 1922, and 'brigadier' substituted) or, in both divisions and brigades, as 'the commander'. Officers in command of 'Commands' (*sic*), such as Aldershot Command, or, on mobilization, army corps (or, simply, 'corps') – usually lieutenant-generals – were designated general officer commanding-in-chief (GOC-in-C), but commonly simply 'GOC'. Officers in command of major detached commands such as the BEF or geographical commands such as India – full generals or occasionally field marshals – were designated commander-in-chief (C-in-C).
† From 1909 (and henceforward in this volume for clarity) 'CIGS' – chief of the *imperial* general staff.
‡ The AG (the second military member of the Council) had overall responsibility for the welfare and maintenance of the soldier – in particular, recruiting, pay and medical provision. The QMG fed, clothed, housed and moved the army, his department having four principal subordinate branches, each headed by a director (a major-general or brigadier-general): transport and remounts (horses), movements and quartering, supplies and clothing, and equipment and ordnance stores. The MGO was responsible for procuring all warlike equipment.
§ To the 'Heseltine reforms' of the mid-1980s, when the tri-service staff became pre-eminent. The author worked in the Directorate of Military Operations – the branch that, under Major-General Henry Wilson, drew up the plans for 1914.

South Africa: that firepower was the most decisive factor in war, and manoeuvre was necessary to avoid its destructive effect. Paradoxically, however, manoeuvre was itself made possible only by the *offensive* power of modern weapons: without the means to suppress *defensive* fire, troops in the open (at least by day) would be cut down by both long-range small-arms fire and by artillery. The terrible years of the trenches, from 1915 to the middle of 1918 – Churchill's 'desperate and vain appeals against the decision of fate' – were a bitter exploration of just how much offensive firepower was required to permit manoeuvre in the face of the defensive power of modern weapons.

But what was the army *for*? The question may have been implicit every year that Parliament voted supply – approved the army estimates – but in 1906 it was made explicit by Haldane when, rather unexpectedly, he found himself secretary for war in the new Liberal administration formed at the end of the previous year. In his first ministerial speech to Parliament, on 8 March 1906, he declared that 'the first thing we want is absolutely clear thinking about the purposes for which the Army exists and the principles on which it is to be organized'. It was typical Haldane, the Hegelian philosopher. Charged with reducing the army estimates, instead of taking the traditional approach of 'the same as before, but better (and cheaper)', he posed the existential question which spoke not only to the unresolved spectre of invasion but also, and ultimately more importantly, to the implications of the Entente Cordiale signed two years before.

Hitherto, Britain and France, while cooperating in various military ventures – notably of late the suppression of the Boxer Rebellion* – had been increasingly dangerous colonial rivals; the Entente was a marked advance, signalling a major strategic shift for both nations. Despite Haldane's question, however, the shift was never followed through to its logical conclusion of an alliance, with stated objectives and agreed methods, though the need was mooted as early as 1905 by Louis Mallet, private secretary to the foreign secretary in Arthur Balfour's Tory administration (the marquess of Lansdowne):

---

* A nationalist movement bent on eradicating the foreign 'spheres of influence' in China. It sparked intervention by a remarkable eight-nation military alliance comprising, ironically, all the major belligerents of the First World War save the Ottomans – Austria-Hungary, France, Germany, Italy, Japan, Russia, Britain and the United States.

'Unfortunately we have no treaty, no written engagement. If we had, there would be no need for anxiety and I believe that we should never be troubled with German ambitions again. It is the uncertainty attaching to the course we should take if war broke out which is at the bottom of the ceaseless intrigues of Germany.' That uncertainty – the 'great question', as Lansdowne's successor, Grey, called it – would be at the root of the drift that characterized British strategic thinking right up to August 1914.

The Entente was indeed a strange *rapprochement*, a sort of dalliance in which the wooed, France, would come to expect that the wooer, Britain, while not actually tying the knot, would willingly consummate the relationship when the time came. A cartoon by *Punch*'s Bernard Partridge suggested that from Berlin's point of view the Entente was a *mésalliance*. It showed John Bull (Britain) walking off with the trollop Marianne (France) in her scandalously short tricolour skirt, while Germany, the Kaiser himself, affects not to care – though his sabre shows below the hem of his long greatcoat. Yet when the time did come for the consummation in August 1914, it looked for a while as if John Bull would stand Marianne up. Why had she let him – encouraged him to – pay court in the first place?

Bismarck may have subdued and humiliated France in 1871, but he had not broken her. Indeed, the humiliation was a powerful spur to recovery, and he had to devote much effort thereafter to contain French revanchism, notably to isolate her from the other continental powers – principally Austria, with whom she might have made common cause in the wake of the Austro-Prussian war. In this he was largely successful, but after the pilot was dropped and Germany let the 'Treaty of Reassurance' (or 'Reinsurance') with Russia lapse, France was able to begin talks with Russia.* It was a transformational

---

* The Treaty of Reassurance was a secret agreement brokered by Bismarck in 1887 after the German–Austrian–Russian *Dreikaiserbund* (Three Emperors' League) collapsed in that year because of competition between Austria-Hungary and Russia in the Balkans. The treaty provided that each party would remain neutral if the other became involved in a war with a third great power, but that this would not apply if Germany attacked France or if Russia attacked Austria. Germany paid for Russian friendship by agreeing to Russian influence in Bulgaria and Eastern Roumelia and by agreeing to support Russian action to keep the Black Sea as its own preserve. The Kaiser would not renew the treaty in 1890 since by that time Austria's interests in the Balkans were becoming too great; and in any case, he believed that his personal relationship with the Tsar – as cousins – gave him another lever.

Punch *cartoonist Bernard Partridge encapsulates the defiance in the Entente Cordiale – in which, as seen from Berlin, Britain spurns the Kaiser in favour of unworthy France.*

moment reminiscent of 1807, when Napoleon and Tsar Alexander I had embraced on a specially built raft in the middle of the River Nemen to sign the Treaty of Tilsit (dashed five years later with the French invasion of Russia). When the French fleet visited Kronstadt in 1891 it was received with full military honours, the first time the Marseillaise had been heard officially (and legally) in Russia. The talks dragged on somewhat, but at the end of 1893 the formalities were completed. Paris could breathe a little more deeply.

Yet within a decade the poor showing of Russian arms in war with Japan (1904–5) would demonstrate the liability of Russia as a military ally, and Paris began to look for others.* Coming late to the game was not easy, however, for the Germans had quietly been paying court: the Kaiser had made a not unsuccessful visit to London in 1895, and in 1901 had attended the funeral of Queen Victoria (who had made him an honorary admiral in the Royal Navy). France watched with dismay, for with the most powerful fleet in the world and vast reserves of empire manpower, Britain, notwithstanding her relatively small standing army, was potentially *the* superpower; any understanding with Germany could prove disastrous.

The problem, from the perspective of both London and Paris (as well as from that of Berlin) was the former's policy of 'splendid isolation'. Apart from the half-hearted expeditions to Portugal to keep the peace in 1826, and a brief foray along the south bank of the Danube in 1854 prior to the invasion of the Crimea, Britain had not committed troops to the Continent proper since Waterloo, exerting pressure instead from time to time through shows of naval strength. By 1904, the year of the Entente, such a policy, unstated though it was, looked increasingly flawed. In part the Boers had seen to that: if it had taken nearly half a million troops to defeat 20,000 militiamen, what were the prospects of dealing in isolation with any of the continental powers – especially Russia threatening India, weak though the Japanese war had shown her to be?

The idea of a *rapprochement* with France was not new: as early as

---

* The Russo-Japanese War (February 1904 to September 1905) was a struggle for control of Korea and Manchuria, with Japanese pre-emptive attacks to secure victory before Russian reinforcements could arrive from the west. Decisive Japanese victories on land at Port Arthur and Mukden, and the spectacular naval victory at Tsushima, were followed by American mediation and the Treaty of Portsmouth (New Hampshire).

1881 the Prince of Wales had had exploratory talks with Léon Gambetta, soon to become the French prime minister, but the 'Scramble for Africa' continued to get in the way. Indeed, the scramble almost came to blows in the wake of the Sudan campaign – the so-called Fashoda Incident.* But the Russo-Japanese War was not just a distant demonstration of military and naval prowess, or the lack of it: as spectators, Britain and France found themselves on opposite sides, the unintended consequence of the Franco-Russian ('Dual') Alliance, and the Anglo-Japanese Treaty of 1902. Unintended, but hardly unforeseen, for Britain had signed the treaty as a means of mitigating Russian threats to her interests in the Far East; indeed, in retrospect the treaty can be seen as the first formal repudiation of 'splendid isolation'.†

The proverbial wise counsel averted any collision of spectators, however – though Scarborough lost a trawler and several men to the fire of Russian warships as the Baltic fleet made its way through the North Sea en route to Japan, the Russians somehow, scarcely credibly, mistaking the fishing fleet in the fog for torpedo boats. Both Britain and France thought it time to settle their underlying rivalry for the sake of a greater security, and indeed to allow both countries a freer hand colonially. A beginning had been made the year before the war by the expedient of a royal gesture: in the spring of 1903 the new king (Edward VII) had gone to Paris as a statesman, 'the uncle of Europe'. His charm offensive opened the way for the diplomats. The old suspicions were suspended and the following year the Entente was

---

* France, discomposed by Britain's continuing hold on Egypt, decided to stake a claim at Fashoda, an abandoned fort on the White Nile south of Khartoum. A hundred or so French–Senegalese *tirailleurs* under Major Jean-Baptiste Marchand made an epic, fourteen-month march by river steamer and foot across central Africa, arriving in July 1898. In September, Kitchener, flushed with his recent success in crushing the Mahdi's revolt, met him there. In the old cliché, Europe braced itself for war; but all that happened was that the two men sat down, opened a bottle of champagne, exchanged comradely soldierly stories and waited for their respective foreign offices to sort things out. In November, Paris abandoned the claim.

† The treaty, which was to run for five years before renewal, was primarily directed against the potential shared menace posed, it was believed, by France and, perhaps more probably, Russia in the Far East. The alliance obligated either power to remain neutral if the other found herself at war with a third power. However, should either power be obliged to fight a war against two or more powers, the other signatory was obliged to provide military aid. It was renewed and expanded in scope twice, in 1905 and 1911, and was the basis for Japan's declaration of war on Germany on 23 August 1914.

signed. As the French ambassador in London declared, 'we give you Egypt in exchange for Morocco'.*

If France harboured hopes that the Entente would give her a stronger hand in dealing with Germany, Britain did not see it that way; in fact, Lansdowne had been at pains to try to improve relations with Berlin – to capitalize on the Kaiser's albeit inconsistent and heavy-handed overtures – since 1900. However, Berlin begged to differ: manifestly the Entente was directed at Germany. Even so, given the centuries of enmity between Britain and France, and perhaps even the late alliance of Britain and Prussia against the 'Great Disturber' – Bonaparte – Berlin believed that with a little pressure the *mésalliance* could be put asunder. In March 1905, therefore, the Kaiser sailed to Tangiers and declared his support for Moroccan independence. To Berlin's surprise – possibly because Lansdowne's earlier approaches had been taken as a sign of weakness – Britain did not stand aloof; rather, she voiced strong support for France. With American mediation a conference was convened at Algeciras, in the shadow of the Rock of Gibraltar, and the Germans climbed down. From then on, in a perfect demonstration of the law of unintended consequences, Germany became, in the mind of the British general staff, the potential enemy; and the British army's attention began turning towards the Continent for the first time in ninety years.†

Haldane's challenge as secretary of state for war amounted to more than determining where to point the army, useful as that was: the nation's land forces as a whole – regular, volunteer and militia – needed the same measure of structural reform as that just carried through in the War Office. His two predecessors had tried, though each with a different purpose and method. William St John Brodrick

---

* Britain would control the eastern end of North Africa, and thus the route to India, while France would have the western end, from Tunisia through Algeria to Morocco. The Entente dealt also with hitherto intractable issues in Indo-China, and the rights of Breton fishermen off the coast of Newfoundland.

† There is some debate, however, as to how focused on a continental commitment Haldane himself was. He argued, for example, that the nation needed to be ready to reinforce India or the colonial frontiers, for which the Expeditionary Force was equally well tailored. Some historians also maintain that the pro-French option that he espoused in his memoirs was largely a *post facto* case of recovering his reputation after being forced to leave the cabinet in 1915 for perceived German sympathies. But the point is largely academic, since the rest of the War Office machine and the army looked increasingly across the Channel, not across the oceans.

had begun even while the war in South Africa was being fought, but his ideas vastly over-estimated the potential of post-war recruiting: Britain had never had to resort to conscription, not even during the Napoleonic Wars, and his proposals for six army corps could not have been realized without some measure of compulsory service. There were plenty of advocates of this, notably the recently retired commander-in-chief, Lord Roberts, fortified by the findings of yet another inquiry: the Royal Commission on the Militia and Volunteers, set up in 1902 and chaired by the duke of Norfolk, had found both bodies unfit for service.* Hugh Arnold-Forster, who succeeded Brodrick in October 1903, was more absorbed with the question of home defence, but as a 'navalist' he was less convinced of the need for any large force to deter or repel a landing. He made no progress – the debates on the recommendations of the Norfolk Commission were interminable – but he did set in hand the Esher proposals on War Office reconstitution. Elgin's principal criticism in the light of the Boer War experience, the lack of a mechanism for expanding the number of troops available in both the short and medium terms, remained unaddressed.

Haldane's success was twofold, if ultimately incomplete. First, he accepted the findings of the Norfolk Commission respecting the absolute need for the auxiliary forces (militia and volunteers) – and also the need radically to restructure them. In this he was helped by recent events, not least the Morocco crisis, which gave him considerable cross-party support for a root and branch reform. For example, the Conservative peer Lord (Thomas) Newton, whom Asquith would make a deputy war minister in 1915, urged desperate measures: speaking on the Commission's report in the House of Lords, he invited their lordships to 'suppose, for instance, that your house is in bad repair, and you call in an architect, and the architect says, "By an

---

* The Commission's report was issued in May 1904. Of the militia, it stated (paragraph 29): 'The evidence which we have received satisfies us that the drill and training at present undergone by this force is insufficient to fit its units at short notice to oppose trained troops in the field.' And in paragraph 33: 'We are forced to the conclusion that the Militia, in its existing condition, is unfit to take the field for the defence of this country. We think, however, that its defects arise from causes beyond the control of its officers and men.' Of the volunteers, paragraph 49 stated: 'We are agreed in the conclusion that the Volunteer Force, in view of the unequal military education of the officers, the limited training of the men, and the defects of equipment and organization, is not qualified to take the field against a Regular army.'

expenditure of a considerable sum of money I can put your house in order, but if you will take my advice you will pull it down and build a new one in its place." '

So pull down the house Haldane did – starting with the militia, the medieval relic. Since the days of Henry VIII it had been the responsibility of the lord lieutenant in each county of England, Wales and Ireland (and from 1794 of Scotland also) to muster and drill a force of a given size for home defence or internal security. In later years a form of conscription – the militia ballot – had been used to fill its ranks, but the ballot had not been used since 1820; so the militia had become a voluntary force, and not a very efficient one at that. In theory it should have been otherwise, for militia volunteers were meant to undertake initial training for several months before returning to civilian life, reporting thereafter for regular periods of training and an annual two-week camp. In return for this they received nominal military pay, meant to be a useful addition to the civilian wage; thus militia service was supposed to appeal to both agricultural and industrial labourers, as well as men in casual occupations, who could leave their civilian jobs for a well-paid 'holiday' and pick them up again afterwards. In reality, the militia was chronically under-recruited and poorly trained, except perhaps the artillery and engineer regiments, though these were few (until 1861 the militia had been an all-infantry force). And, critically, enlistment was for home service only. It was, however, a conduit of sorts into the regular army, for officers especially, and while many regarded it as something of a 'back door' way in, some famous names of the First World War took this route.

First to go was the name 'militia' itself, with its negative connotations of compulsion and inefficiency. Then the purpose was redefined: instead of a home guard, Haldane wanted a ready source of trained manpower to serve as reinforcements and battle-casualty replacements for the regular army at home and abroad in whatever contingency might arise. He therefore devised a structure that was both a holding organization for former regulars with a reserve liability and a training organization for civilians who were prepared to make a greater commitment in exchange for higher pay than the former militia rates. 'The Reserve' became the generic name for both these categories, the former regulars designated 'Army

62

Without conscription, the British army depended on volunteers and was therefore weaker than the armies of the continental powers. The creation of the Special Reserve in the decade before the war as an immediate source of battle-casualty replacements was one of the achievements of Richard Burdon (Lord) Haldane, the war minister.

Reserve'* and the part-timers 'Special Reserve' (SR).

Special Reservists, for all arms and services (except cavalry, for which there was no SR, save in Ireland), were given four months' basic training alongside regular recruits at regular rates of pay before being released to their former civilian occupations, whence they were called up each year for three weeks' continuation training at regular rates of pay, with an annual retainer, or 'bounty'. Crucially, the terms of service obliged all reservists to serve overseas if called up, which service in the militia had not.

It was a particularly effective way of building up the reserve of officers, trained initially in the junior division of the new Officers' Training Corps (OTC: later the public school cadet corps), which Haldane also instituted, and then in the senior division at university. Robert Graves, the poet and novelist, was commissioned via this route when the First World War broke out, as he describes in *Goodbye to All That*: although he was barely nineteen and on his way from school to Oxford, his OTC experience at Charterhouse was deemed sufficient to equip him to be a second lieutenant in the SR.†

But Haldane recognized that while he could do much to professionalize the Reserve, to tap into the old militia source of recruits would still need an occasional pinch of 'feudalism', to which Lord Newton in the debate on the Norfolk Commission had alluded wryly: 'I should have thought the fact of the voluntary system having broken

---

* Although most ex-regulars had a liability as part of their terms of enlistment – typically five years, after seven 'with the colours' (i.e. on active duty) – they could now profit from it by opting for one of two categories. A soldier choosing 'Section A Reserve' undertook to rejoin in an emergency that did not require general mobilization, for which he received 'retainer' pay of seven shillings a week, and was required to train for twelve days per year. The pay, on top of civilian earnings, was good – exactly the same as the basic pay of a regular private soldier – reflecting the higher possibility of call-out than the second, more common, category, 'Section B Reserve'. Those taking this option were liable to call-out only in the case of general mobilization, and received retainer pay at half the Section A rate. A man could serve for only two years as a Section A reservist, but could then transfer to Section B and in practice serve at least another seven.

† The junior OTCs, which replaced the various school rifle corps, clearly varied in quality, depending in part, of course, on the willingness of the cadets: Graves is rather dismissive of his time in the Charterhouse OTC, though *Goodbye to All That* (London, 1929) needs to be read generally with a pinch of salt, but it was evidently not without effect. Major-General Allan Adair, who was commissioned into the Grenadiers (SR) in 1916, and who would command the Guards Armoured Division in the Second World War, is much more positive about Harrow's OTC in his memoirs: 'Our OTC seemed to us as professional as some Territorial battalions. In 1912 our field day was organised by General ['Wullie'] Robertson, Commandant of the Staff College, Camberley': *A Guards' General* (London, 1986).

down must have forced itself upon my noble friend, the Lord Privy Seal (the Marquess of Salisbury), who is a colonel of a Militia regiment, because I read in a newspaper the other day that he was offering half-a-crown a head to people who would bring him recruits, as if they were plovers' eggs or something to eat.'

It was Haldane's genius to work with the weave, however, and occasionally it brought results that not even the best minds in the new War Office could have conceived. Perhaps the most original of the various new SR units, and certainly the most endearing – not least in offering a snapshot of pre-war England – was the 'Wolds Wagoners'.* Sir Mark Sykes, 6th baronet of Sledmere, owned 30,000 acres of prime farming land in the Yorkshire Wolds. He had served in South Africa as a militia volunteer with the Green Howards, and was convinced that the logistic demands of a future European war would be too great for the Army Service Corps (ASC) unless it increased its number of waggon drivers. The type of waggon the ASC used was mainly the pole-hitch rather than that with shafts, and since by the early 1900s the pole hitch had fallen out of favour in civilian use except in the Wolds, Sykes proposed to the War Office that the agricultural workers of East Yorkshire be signed up as reservist drivers, but exempted from military training since it might discourage farmers from releasing them, or indeed the farmworkers from volunteering.

Initially the War Office was sceptical, preferring the all-round utility of the trained soldier to the single-skill specialist. Nor did it help that the ASC had been the only branch of the army that had *not* been criticized for its performance in the Boer War. Undaunted, Sykes went ahead anyway, unofficially mustering drivers at his own expense, giving them the grades of 'wagoner', 'foreman' and 'roadmaster' (equivalent to private, corporal and sergeant) and designing a brass-and-enamel lapel badge with a bridled horse's head encircled, and a coloured-ribbon button-hole for their waistcoats, in lieu of uniform. He then invited Brigadier-General Frederick Landon (soon to be promoted major-general and director of transport and movements) to Sledmere to observe the driving competitions at the annual agricultural show. Duly impressed by what he saw (the ASC reckoned

* The Wolds Wagoners' single 'g' (the army always spelled 'waggon' with two) was another sign of their singularity. The ASC's march was an American song of the 1850s: 'Wait for the Waggon'.

it took six months to train a pole-waggon driver), Landon recommended incorporating the Wagoners into the ASC Special Reserve. They were signed up formally in February 1913, when the War Office took over the annual bounty payments – a sovereign for a wagoner, two for a foreman and four for a roadmaster. The drivers had called it the 'silly quid' when Sykes had paid it, since it seemed so easy to earn – a timed run round a figure-of-eight obstacle course at the annual Sledmere show, dismantling and reassembling the wheels and axles, and loading and unloading fifty-pound sacks against the clock. Though the full implications of the *King's* quid were probably barely contemplated, by the summer of 1914 there were 1,127 Wagoners, including farriers and harness makers – almost 10 per cent of the ASC's regular strength, a significant reinforcement.

The largest section of the SR – just as in the regular army – was the infantry, and Haldane now made a further modification to the famous Cardwell–Childers reforms of the late Victorian period.* Since 1881 the militia infantry had been mustered as the third battalion of the county regiment, with sometimes a fourth, fifth and sixth depending on the number of regular battalions, the militia designation being shown in brackets – hence, for example, 3rd Battalion the Norfolk Regiment (1st Norfolk Militia); 4th Battalion the Suffolk Regiment (Cambridgeshire Militia) – and headquartered at the new regimental depots in the county towns. From 1908, when the Special Reserve was created, the battalions were redesignated as, for example, 3rd (Reserve) Battalion the Royal Welsh Fusiliers (the famous 'c' spelling, 'Welch', came only officially after the war). With the improvements in training and pay, and the liability for service overseas, these battalions came increasingly to be seen as the 'second line' reserve in the regimental recruiting area, a sort of warehouse for spares, with a small training staff of regulars who, with the other depot staff, maintained the mobilization stocks and generally kept track of the regular reservists on their books, of whom there might be several thousand. Special Reserve officers now wore the same uniform as those in the regular battalions, and increasingly saw themselves in the image of

---

* Edward Cardwell and Hugh Childers, secretaries for war respectively in Gladstone's first and second administrations, formally linked infantry regiments with specific parts of the country and built depots for them in the county towns. Cardwell is usually described as the father of the regimental system.

the regulars – as Graves and, later, Siegfried Sassoon, reveal in their memoirs (both were commissioned into the 3rd (Reserve) Battalion of the Royal Welsh Fusiliers, and posted thence to the regular battalions in 1915).* Indeed, SR officers were now 'King's commissioned', as opposed to the old system by which they received their commissions from the lord lieutenant, and full members of the Reserve of Officers, like the former regulars. On the appropriate Order in Council, the SR battalions would call-up the Special Reservists and muster at the depot, thereafter guarding vulnerable points (such as docks and railway bridges, as well as military sites) and despatching men as required to make up losses – or simply numbers – in the regular battalions. They were not, therefore, organized into brigades and divisions. If the strength of the Special Reserve would never be as great as Haldane hoped, it was at least markedly more efficient than the militia had ever been; and, critically, its officers and men were available for immediate service with the regulars overseas, without even the need for the King's signing the order for general mobilization.

The Volunteer Force – originally the 'Rifle Volunteers' – were a different kettle of fish. Fiercely independent and proud of their patriotic origins half a century earlier during the invasion scares – answering Tennyson's (and the Secretary for War's) call to 'Form, riflemen, form!' – they, like the militia, had come forward in some numbers for service in South Africa, although their terms of service did not require it. So had the Yeomanry who, pre-dating the Volunteer Force by seventy years (*their* invasion scare had been prompted by the original Napoleon, not his nephew), were even more independently minded than the riflemen, as well as considering themselves a great deal 'superior'. In the early days of the Rifle Volunteers there had been a distinct class aspect to independence, for while the image of the regular army and militia was that of gentry and peasantry (and the Yeomanry, as its name implied, that of gentry and tenantry), the Rifle Volunteers saw themselves as a citizen army, their complexion distinctly middle-class. They disdained red coats, for example, which they saw as synonymous with muskets and rigid lines, preferring instead the more egalitarian and practical 'rifle green', or even, after

---

* Siegfried Sassoon, *Memoirs of an Infantry Officer* (London, 1930) is only thinly disguised as fiction.

the fashion of American volunteers, grey (or 'gray'). In turn, the regulars were all too pleased that these 'citizen soldiers' did not wear red and risk being mistaken for 'proper' soldiers.

From the 1880s, indeed, the War Office had been trying to get the volunteers under better regulation, mustering them – on paper at least – as volunteer battalions of the regular regiments.* Haldane decided to drop the name 'Volunteers', calling them instead the Territorial Force (from 1920, the Territorial Army – TA), since they were for service only territorially, that is, on home ground, and tried to link the Territorial battalions more closely with the parent regular regiment.† But to preserve their new efficiency he ring-fenced their funding, putting it in the hands of what he called 'County Associations' (he chose the name, he said, 'because that is a good term invented by Oliver Cromwell'), with the lord lieutenant, who had hitherto been in titular command of all auxiliary forces within his county, as president.

Yet Haldane's ultimate purpose for the TF remains unclear. It was organized as a field force, with an establishment of fourteen infantry divisions, plus supporting arms (artillery, engineers) and services, and fourteen Yeomanry brigades. Mobilized – or, strictly, embodied – and at full strength, which it never in fact achieved, it would have been over twice the size of the regular Expeditionary Force (EF) at 312,300, a figure far greater than necessary merely for home defence.‡ There was strong political opposition among the radicals in his own party, and in the Labour party, to extending the liability for service overseas to the TF, but he undoubtedly saw the force as the basis for expansion in wartime, which after further training and the necessary legislation could be sent as reinforcements for the EF in formed units (as opposed to the SR, whose job was to provide individual reinforcements and

---

* Accordingly, for example, the 5th, 6th, 8th, 9th, 10th and 25th Lanarkshire Rifle Volunteers were arbitrarily attached to the Highland Light Infantry (HLI) and renamed as the 1st, 2nd, 3rd (etc.) Volunteer Battalions. This duplication of numbers – for example, 1HLI, the regular battalion, and 1HLI(V), the volunteers – still seemed to emphasize the separateness.
† So the five volunteer battalions of the Highland Light Infantry, for example, now became 5th (City of Glasgow) Battalion HLI, 6th (City of Glasgow), 7th (Blythswood), 8th (Lanark) and 9th (Glasgow Highlanders) Battalions, with the suffix 'TF' in brackets.
‡ In September 1913 the TF actually numbered 236,389 men. It was 'embodied' rather than 'mobilized' because its peace establishment (PE) was in effect its war establishment, whereas the PE of a regular army was much smaller, requiring the mobilization of its reservists to bring it up to war strength.

replacements), or to relieve regular units in overseas garrisons. Besides, a liability for overseas service would simply have been counter-productive, putting off many recruits. Haldane did put measures in place to allow a unit or an individual to volunteer to be liable for overseas service, but without providing any inducement; when he tested the water in 1910, fewer than 10 per cent of the TF chose to be liable. He certainly contemplated contingency legislation for a grave national emergency, but decided that was a bridge best crossed when necessary, and not before. When they did come to the bridge, in August 1914, the new secretary of state, Kitchener, decided to cross the water by an entirely different means.

Nevertheless, Haldane had put the reserves as a whole onto a more professional and, as it happened, more economical footing (which was, indeed, his first design: soon after introducing the Territorial and Reserve Forces Bill in 1907 he was able to tell Parliament that the army estimates would be reduced for the following year by between two and three million pounds). And he now threw himself into promoting the new TF and SR, he and his ministers touring the country, speaking at county gatherings and to individual units, and opening branches of the OTC at schools and universities. Recruiting to the TF surged initially, fuelled by yet another invasion scare, but after 1910 it began tailing off. To Kitchener, observing from his new post in Egypt, the recruiting shortfall only confirmed his doubts about what he saw as merely a rebranding of the volunteers, for whom he had little time. Others at the centre of business, such as Major-General Douglas Haig, who as director of military training (then, from 1907, director of staff duties) was closely involved in the development of Haldane's ideas, were more enthusiastic. Whatever the shortcomings in recruiting, the fact was that there was now a proper *force* for the defence of the home base, rather than a lucky dip of volunteer units, with a stiffening of regular officers and NCOs in the key command, staff and training appointments, and all under the supervision of the War Office; and in the Army Reserve there was a robust system for augmentation and battle-casualty replacements for the Expeditionary Force.* Haldane had been able to 'echelon' the forces of the Crown

---

* In Ireland, where there was no TF, the former militia, now the Special Reserve, was 'double-hatted' with a home defence role – which, of course, meant also (perhaps even principally) internal security. Nevertheless, its two SR cavalry regiments – the North

(organize each of the three elements – regulars, TF and Reserve – in relation to the others) in such a way as to get the best out of them as individual constituents and as a whole – at the very least on paper; and in reality to a greater degree than first appears in August 1914.

But if the auxiliary forces taxed his energies the most, it was the first echelon, the Expeditionary Force itself, that was Haldane's most complete success – the force which the Kaiser would in August 1914 dismiss (allegedly) as Britain's 'contemptible little army'.

Irish Horse and the South Irish Horse – the only true SR cavalry in the army – would play an active role in France in August 1914. (King Edward's Horse, a relic of the Imperial Yeomanry raised during the Boer War in London from colonial expatriates, was transferred to the SR in 1913, and was mobilized, but remained Yeomanry at heart. It was disbanded in 1924.)

Chapter Four

THE CONTEMPTIBLE LITTLE ARMY

In every respect the Expeditionary Force of 1914 was incomparably
the best trained, best organized and best equipped British Army that
ever went forth to war.

The Official History, vol. 1

There is no hard evidence that in August 1914 the Kaiser actually
called the BEF a 'contemptible little army', but somehow the jibe
stuck, and its members were soon wearing it as a badge of pride, calling themselves 'the Old Contemptibles' and proceeding to deal with
the myth of Prussian invincibility with reciprocal contempt. Certainly
the sentiment echoed Bismarck's quip that if a British army landed on
Prussia's Baltic coast he would send a policeman to arrest it. After the
war, the Kaiser conceded that if he had said anything of the sort, it
would not have been that the BEF was contemptible, but that it was
'contemptibly little'; either way, he fatally equated size with quality.

Yet despite the official historian's encomium, the BEF, the dis-
posable land force of the United Kingdom, was indeed a little army by
continental standards. Without universal conscription, the norm for
every continental power, it could hardly have been otherwise. In
August 1914, for the offensive against Belgium and France, Germany
mustered some twenty-eight army corps of varying strength and quality, each numbering no fewer than about 40,000 men; the BEF
comprised just two, with the option of a third. However, the Kaiser's

71

chief of staff, Colonel-General Helmuth Johann von Moltke (the 'Younger Moltke'), was more circumspect than his sovereign in ascribing weakness to its small size, describing the British army (if not wholly intending a compliment) as 'that perfect thing apart'. Certainly neither he nor his imperial commander-in-chief, from the evidence of the preceding century, could have doubted the army's courage – the *foremost* quality (in Churchill's words), for it guaranteed all the others.

The Expeditionary Force, originally referred to as the 'Striking Force', was formally constituted on 12 January 1907 by special War Office order.* In essence Haldane's work with the BEF was a grand tidying-up exercise, bringing the bulk of the regular units in Britain, whose job had largely been to keep those policing the empire up to strength, into a coherent force capable of being sent abroad in time of war. Its exact destination and operational function were unspecified – India, to counter a Russian invasion, was one possibility – but the working assumption was that in the event of war with Germany it would cooperate with the French army somewhere on the Continent relatively close to the Channel ports.

But although the BEF was an all-regular force, for reasons of economy it was kept, so to speak, on short rations: the number of men it was allowed to recruit in peacetime, the so-called 'peace establishment' (PE), was considerably smaller than the number needed for war, what was known as the 'war establishment' (WE). The WE of an infantry battalion, for example – 30 officers and 992 other ranks – was 25 per cent greater than its PE. And because the battalions at home fed trained soldiers to their linked battalions overseas, they were invariably under-strength even at PE, perennially playing a game of 'catch-up'. The BEF therefore relied on the call-up of reservists (*not* the Territorials) to bring its units up to strength for war. It also relied on the reassignment of staff officers in various peacetime headquarters and training establishments such as the staff college (and even the War Office itself) to activate the dormant headquarters of

---

* Initially, 'British' was an unnecessary qualification: there were no allies for whom it might otherwise have been confusing. The prefix came into use only after the EF had landed in France, being first recorded in Parliament by Hansard on 26 August, when Asquith was asked a question on casualties. For clarity, however, from now on in the text 'BEF' will be used.

the commander-in-chief – GHQ – as well as two of the three corps HQs, and to reinforce the headquarters of the divisions and brigades, particularly in areas such as intelligence and communications.

For the first time in the army's history, however, units in peacetime were organized into the groupings in which they could go to war. Hitherto the arrangements had been ad hoc, as one Tory MP, Sir James Fergusson, complained just before the Boer War. Having been wounded while serving with the Grenadiers in the Crimea, he had seen for himself the inefficiency:

> If you send a single brigade to any foreign part the battalion is brought under a General whom they have never seen, and they only come to know him by degrees. What sort of a military system is that? Why should there not be brigades under the officers who commanded them in times of peace, and so, at least, to this small extent, we should be ready for the least emergency?*

If this seems obvious now, as it did to Fergusson, it was not to the Victorian army, which was essentially a colonial peace preservation force, with the emphasis on the lower-level regimental virtues of endurance and flexibility rather than on higher organization. The Crimean War had been a wake-up call, but the country had largely pressed the 'snooze' button; 'muddling through' was elevated to military precept, in part justified by the duke of Wellington's sceptical view of continental sophistication: 'The French plans are like a splendid leather harness which is perfect when it works, but if it breaks it cannot be mended. I make my harness of ropes: it is never as good looking as the French, but if it breaks I can tie a knot and carry on.'

The lash-up harness had not worked in the Boer War, however, and the spectre of the German army was now making the need for change apparent to all. Churchill himself had been in no doubt for some time, and in 1909, after another visit to the annual German manoeuvres, wrote home to his wife Clementine: 'This army is a terrible engine. It marches sometimes 35 miles in a day. It is in number as the sands of the sea – and with them all the modern conveniences.'

* Hansard: Debate on the Army Estimates, 1898.

No longer could the British army rely principally on a public-school education for the officers and fortitude for the other ranks; modern war, and especially the all-arms battle, as it would become known, required organization and method. Key to the success of campaigns was – still is – the higher command arrangements. In the British army these had always been improvised when the occasion demanded, and were invariably faulty. It usually meant that a campaign began with a series of bloody setbacks, leading to the replacement of the commander and his staff, after which there would be a heroic recovery and the army would win the last battle. Now, for the first time, a general headquarters (GHQ) was designed specifically for the purpose of commanding an expeditionary campaign under a full ('four-star') general. It was not quite a permanent headquarters, however: once a year it assembled for the army manoeuvres, and would otherwise form on mobilization, staffed by officers in earmarked appointments in the War Office and from the staff college, with permanently earmarked 'enabling' units such as a GHQ signals company. Although it was all still a shade extemporary, it was certainly better than previous arrangements – and in fact the GHQ was really no more disembodied than comparable headquarters in the continental armies.*

The BEF's actual fighting (as opposed to logistic) formations† were six infantry divisions, each comprising twelve infantry battalions grouped in three brigades, with supporting arms and services and a divisional cavalry squadron.‡ There was in addition a cavalry division for 'strategical' duties.§ All the divisions had permanently appointed

* Only in the Cold War would the British army maintain a permanent HQ at this level in peacetime – that of the British Army of the Rhine, which doubled as HQ Northag, Nato's Northern Army Group.
† The term 'formation' applies to levels of command above those of infantry battalions or cavalry regiments, which are known as 'units' (and their constituents – companies and squadrons – 'sub-units'): brigades, divisions, (army) corps and armies.
‡ The terms 'arms' and 'services' were always a little loosely employed: 'arms' were the infantry, cavalry and artillery, while 'services' embraced the engineers, medical, supply and administrative corps. Today the terms used are combat arms (infantry, armour, army aviation), combat support (artillery, engineers, signals, intelligence) and combat service support (supply, maintenance, medical and administrative). In 1914 the 'supporting arms' were the Royal Artillery, the Royal Engineers and – to all intents and purposes – the Royal Flying Corps.
§ *Cavalry Training* (1909) divides the function of cavalry thus: '(a) Independent or Strategical for strategical exploration under the instructions of the commander-in-chief. (b) Protective cavalry for the provision of the first line of security, under the direct

commanders and staffs, although they could expect to be augmented on mobilization. Initially they were to have been directly subordinate to GHQ, but such a wide span of command was soon acknowledged to be impracticable, even with good communications – which the BEF did not have (one of its two major weaknesses, the other being heavy artillery). Two army corps headquarters, commanded by lieutenant-generals ('three-star'), were therefore earmarked.* First Army Corps (I Corps), which in 1914 was Haig's, was based on the headquarters of Aldershot Command and was more or less fully manned; Second Army Corps (II Corps) was based on the much smaller Eastern Command headquarters and would have to be considerably augmented; a third headquarters was earmarked in case the need should arise, but its manning was more ad hoc. The Cavalry Division, the BEF's 'eyes and ears', answered direct to GHQ. At its full strength the BEF would number about 150,000, of which four-fifths would be more or less directly engaged in fighting.

Yet these innovations would have been so much window-dressing had it not been for the application of one brilliant principle recommended by the Esher Committee – that the new functional divisions and branches of the reformed War Office should be replicated at each subordinate level in the BEF (except that of the MGO, for procurement needed no subordination: it was a central business). There was now a straight chain-of-staff responsibility for each function – operations, supply, personnel etc. – from War Office down to brigade; and, in principle at least, the same people who ran the army in peace would do so in war. Indeed, this staff system of permanent, 'cloned' headquarters was perhaps the Esher Committee's greatest contribution to the army's readiness for war (then and since, for the system endures in essence today). And Haldane's in implementing it.

Although the BEF was a true all-arms affair, with a particularly capable cavalry element, it was a preponderantly infantry force, as

---

orders of the commander of the force they are protecting. (c) Divisional cavalry, forming part of a division of all arms, for scouting in connection with the infantry advanced, rear, or flank guards or outposts; or for intercommunication purposes.'
* Strangely, the term 'army corps' was not actually adopted until August 1914, although it had been in use in Wellington's day: '1st Army' and '2nd Army' were used instead. The last-minute change was to avoid confusion when operating alongside the French.

was every continental army, for the infantry was the only arm that could take and hold ground. As Field Marshal Montgomery was to say half a century later, with the experience of two world wars behind him, 'Without infantry you can do nothing, absolutely nothing at all.' And the British infantry of 1914 were famously good at three things: marching, shooting and fieldcraft. The first they had always been good at.* The second they had always been good at in terms of volleying – firing as a body, the effect more by volume than marksmanship – but by 1914 they had become extraordinarily good individual marksmen too. The third they had learned rudely at the hands of the Boers, and then practised for a decade on every patch of training ground in the country, and annually on manoeuvres in the English countryside.

Indeed, there was something akin to religious fervour in the embracing of what might be called Boer belief, Kruger's simple formula that 'the Boers can shoot, and that is everything'. One of its greatest apostles was Colonel Charles Monro, the new commandant of the School of Musketry, at Hythe on the Romney marshes, scene of the experiments with light infantry under Sir John Moore a century before. 'Musketry' may have had the ring of the past, but the word 'rifle' was after all merely a diminutive of 'rifled musket'. Before the Crimean War the infantry had carried the smooth-bore 'Brown Bess', wildly inaccurate beyond 100 yards and barely lethal at 300, but nevertheless effective as a volleying weapon in the hands of plentiful and well-drilled infantrymen. Only a few specialist corps, such as the Rifle Brigade and the 60th Rifles, carried rifled muskets. The Crimean War changed that; indeed, at its outset the War Office put in hand what today would be called an Urgent Operation Requirement. In

---

* Kipling had caught the essence of the infantryman's art in a poem of 1903, entitled 'Boots (Infantry Columns of the Earlier War)':

> We're foot—slog—slog—slog—sloggin' over Africa
> Foot—foot—foot—foot—sloggin' over Africa
> (Boots—boots—boots—boots—movin' up and down again!)
> There's no discharge in the war!

> Seven—six—eleven—five—nine—an'—twenty mile to—day—
> Four—eleven—seventeen—thirty—two the day before
> (Boots—boots—boots—boots—movin' up and down again!)
> There's no discharge in the war!
> [And six more verses in the same metre.]

1851 the French Minié rifle had been chosen as a replacement for the Brown Bess, and two years later the School of Musketry established to train instructors, but the pace of replacement had been slow; when Britain went to war in 1854, therefore, Miniés were bought as fast as the factories in France and at Enfield in England could make them, and thrust into the hands of the red-coated infantry en route to the war – some soldiers not exchanging their old muskets for new until they actually arrived in the Crimea.

Target shooting – taking individual aim – now became the requirement, but aside from occasional and salutary lessons in marksmanship on the North-West frontier, volley fire was still pre-eminent, and the School of Musketry remained something of a backwater, teaching the mechanics of the rifle and its fire rather than the tactics of its use. After the Boer War, however, the War Office appointed high-fliers as commandants and chief instructors at Hythe, all of them convinced 'musketry maniacs'. Monro himself almost single-mindedly put fire and movement at the heart of the infantry's agenda. In August 1914 he would command the 2nd Division in the BEF, rising to full general two years later. His successor at Hythe, Colonel Walter Congreve, who had won the VC at Colenso in the fighting before Spion Kop, would command 18th Infantry Brigade in the BEF, and he too would rise to full general.*

Under Monro and Congreve at Hythe the chief instructor was Lieutenant-Colonel Norman McMahon, who had won the DSO with the Royal Fusiliers in South Africa. Convinced by the evidence from the Russo-Japanese War of the coming superiority of the machine gun – what the military historian Basil Liddell Hart would call with chilling elegance 'the concentrated essence of infantry' – he had argued very vocally for each battalion to be issued with six, but when this was rejected by the War Office on grounds of cost he turned instead to the technique of rapid fire, which he proceeded to advance fanatically with his NCO instructors. He checked the initial post-Boer War enthusiasm for training in long-range marksmanship, arguing that in European warfare fields of fire of even 800 yards (intermediate range) would be unusual, the country being 'trappier' than that of the veld.

---

* His son, Billy, also Rifle Brigade, would win the VC posthumously on the Somme. The Congreves are one of only three father-and-son VC pairings, the others being the Robertses and the Goughs.

Three to four hundred yards would be the norm, he believed, which was also the point (German tactics stressed) at which the final assault was launched. And since German tactics favoured a steady advance by men in closer order than the British – it was said that reservists gained confidence from *das Tuchfühl*, 'the touch of cloth' – so McMahon argued that it was necessary to speed up the rate of fire, even at the expense of pinpoint accuracy. Rather than careful shooting at the glimpse of a head behind a rock on a *kopje*, what was needed was, as he called it, the 'browning' of a mass of targets – fire that, one way or another, forced them to ground.*

McMahon's innovations – he was known as *the* musketry maniac – were pivotal in the retraining of the British army, and he would live just long enough to see his efforts bear fruit in the BEF, in which he was to command a battalion of the Fusiliers.† So stunned would the Germans be by the sheer weight and effect of the BEF's rifle fire in August 1914 that one of their field intelligence reports is supposed to have suggested that the number of machine guns in a British infantry battalion was not two, as advertised, or even six, as McMahon had recommended – but twenty-eight. Even taken with the proverbial pinch of salt, the many testimonies to the infantry's shooting prowess are compelling.

It helped, of course, that for ten years they had had in their hands a superb weapon, the 'Rifle, Short, Magazine, Lee–Enfield' – the SMLE, or simply the '303', as it was known – superior in every respect to its nearest rival, the German Mauser. The SMLE's stopping power was formidable: its .303-inch bullet could penetrate 18 inches of oak, 36 inches of earth-packed sandbags, or two house bricks at 200 yards. But not least of its superior points was that it was indeed short – a barrel length of 25.2 inches (640 mm) as opposed to the Mauser's 29, and an overall length of 44.5 inches (1132 mm) to the Mauser's 62, though

---

* McMahon's 1907 lecture to the Aldershot Military Society – an influential group – was considered so important that *Field Service Regulations* were amended to include his strictures on firepower, not least that with only two machine guns a battalion needed one rifle for every yard of front it was meant to hold. The price of this – besides presenting a large artillery target to the enemy instead of the smaller target that a machine gun would have offered – was a reduction in the frontage that a battalion was expected to hold.
† Having then been promoted to command 10th Infantry Brigade, he was killed at Ypres in November 1914.

the weights of the two were about the same. It meant that the SMLE was handier when it came to the trenches: 'The butt was as good as the bayonet at close quarters,' was one Old Contemptible's opinion.*

The shorter barrel length had at first worried the shooting clubs, which presumed there would be a loss of accuracy at longer ranges, and, with the greater recoil, a slower rate of fire (because it would take fractionally longer to re-aim). The concerns proved unfounded; marksmanship improved dramatically, as did the rate of fire, for the SMLE had a fast-operating bolt action and a ten-round magazine that could be quickly recharged by clips of five.† Treasury restrictions limited riflemen to 250 practice rounds a year, not counting extra ammunition fired in competitions, but many hours were spent with drill ('dummy') rounds practising loading, firing and reloading, which was half the trick. Fifteen aimed rounds per minute became the standard rate on the order 'rapid fire' – the so-called mad minute – though a practised rifleman could manage twenty to thirty. In 1914 Sergeant-Instructor Snoxall of the School of Musketry reputedly set a record that still stands for a bolt-action weapon – thirty-eight rounds in a 12-inch target at 300 yards in one minute.‡ On active service each rifleman carried 120 rounds of ammunition (weighing 5 lb 8 oz – 2.5 kg), with a further hundred held in the battalion transport in 50-round cloth bandoliers which could be slung on the shoulder over the web equipment if required.§ The machine-gun section carried 11,500 rounds in forty-six 250-round belts.

But all this individual expertise would have been to no avail without good fire discipline. Since the duke of Marlborough's great

---

* Quoted in David Ascoli, *The Mons Star: The British Expeditionary Force 1914* (London, 1981). The bayonet added 17 inches to the SMLE. But bayonet fighting – or rather, *training* for bayonet fighting – was never the thing in the BEF that it later became on the Western Front. The pre-war army was more imbued with the idea of 'never putting a man where you can put a bullet'.

† Two chargers (clips) could be loaded in succession, which could not be done with the Mauser, and rotation of the bolt was much less abrupt during the forward and backward motion, making the 'racking', the ejection/chambering action, more like two motions than the Mauser's four.

‡ Corporal Fred Dray, East Lancashires, admitted: 'The best I ever managed was 24, but I'll let you into a secret. I shut my eyes, worked away at my bolt and clips, and finished up with a sore shoulder and a record number of "outers" [the outer ring of the target].'

§ Web equipment – 'webbing' for short – a sort of harness of pouches made from thick cotton canvas, was for the soldier's personal stowage of ammunition, water bottle, mess tins and the other immediate necessities of life in the field.

victories of the first decade of the eighteenth century – Blenheim, Ramillies, Oudenarde, Malplaquet – the British infantry had made an art of fire control, preferring whether in defence or attack to deploy in longer lines of two or three ranks rather than shorter ones of five and more (the French and Prussian method). This gave an obvious advantage of overlap, the penalty of not being able to bring as many muskets to bear made up for by firing faster. They had gained superiority in devastating volleys by both speed of reloading and mastery of fire control by 'platoons' (subdivisions of the company, about fifty men, a company until 1913 being just over 100 men), each platoon volleying independently, so that a rolling fire could be kept up. The junior company officers of the BEF, therefore, the lieutenants and second lieutenants (collectively 'subalterns'), inherited a devolved system, whereas in the continental armies fire control was the business of the company commander.

Because the platoon system was so well established, a last-minute (October 1913) change in the organization of the infantry battalion could take place with nothing more than, for some, bruised pride. Hitherto there had been eight companies in a battalion, which had suited the close-order methods of the previous century. For reasons of economy in the widest sense, and tactical efficiency, these were now doubled in size and halved in number, to four. The 100-man companies had been commanded by a captain, with a senior non-commissioned officer (SNCO) seeing to discipline and minor administration. Under the new organization, each of the four companies, usually designated A to D, or in the case of the Guards, 1 to 4, was commanded by a major or senior captain (referred to as a 'riding captain', since company commanders still had horses), with a captain as second-in-command and four subalterns, each in charge of a platoon of some fifty men (on paper, at least).* Each platoon had a sergeant, and sometimes a second sergeant, and each of the four sections of twelve men (now likewise permanent) a corporal and lance-corporal. Each company now formally had a sergeant-major (CSM), who wore a crown on his lower sleeve as his badge of rank, and a company quartermaster-

* Platoons had not hitherto been permanent commands, rather groupings within the company, and the subalterns had been unspecified company officers rather than platoon commanders – a system which, in a similar form, continued in the Gurkhas until the 1960s.

sergeant (CQMS), with a crown above three chevrons on his upper sleeve. In action, the CSM was responsible primarily for ammunition resupply, and the CQMS for water and rations.

The battalion itself was commanded by a lieutenant-colonel, with a major as second-in-command, a captain as adjutant – the lieutenant-colonel's executive officer – a captain or lieutenant commissioned from the ranks as quartermaster, responsible in war for all supplies and transport, one subaltern in charge of the machine guns and another of the signallers. The senior NCO (or, strictly, warrant officer) in the battalion was the regimental sergeant-major (RSM), whose badge of rank was the royal coat of arms worn on the upper sleeve. His responsibilities in peace were legion, but in action he was additionally responsible for ammunition and prisoners of war. Collectively these officers and NCOs were known as the battalion staff, and were joined on mobilization, if he were not on the strength already, by a regimental medical officer (RMO), a captain of the Royal Army Medical Corps – the only other cap-badge, save perhaps a padre's, that an infantryman would have seen routinely.

This, then, was the basic fighting unit of the BEF – a self-contained organization held together by a combination of family feeling and fierce discipline. In turn the battalions were grouped in fours into brigades.* It was the brigade commander who allocated the artillery support, usually a battery of (six) field guns to each battalion, and gave the commanding officer his tasks, but the notion of brigade battle was restricted by rudimentary communications and the limited ability of the artillery to centralize their fire. Battle was essentially the business of the battalions themselves; and, since fire control was by voice and whistle, it was often the self-contained business of the companies – or, indeed, of the platoons. A subaltern's job in the end came down to a mnemonic – 'DRINK': *D*esignation, *R*ange, *I*ndication (of target), *N*umber (of rounds), *K*ind (of fire). 'Platoon; at five hundred; strip-wood, men advancing from; five rounds; rapid . . . *fire!*'

The BEF was a young army, in absolute terms and in comparison with the overseas garrisons, which tended to have more soldiers with

---

* In turn the brigades were grouped – usually in threes – in divisions, commanded by a major-general. The division would also include artillery and engineers.

longer service. Although a man could sign on for twenty-one years, typically in the infantry his engagement would be twelve – seven 'with the colours' (actually serving with his regiment) and five with the reserve. In August 1914 there were only 4,192 men with fifteen or more years' continuous service with the colours – 2.5 per cent of the BEF's projected strength of 165,000 – and 46,291 with less than two years' service; indeed, many of the latter would be left with the rear parties since they were considered only partially trained.

A significant exception was the age of commanding officers and brigade commanders. Today an infantry commanding officer could be as young as thirty-seven, though more usually is between thirty-nine and forty-one, and a brigade commander forty-three to forty-five. By 1917 the average age for battalion commanders would be twenty-eight, and the mandatory upper limit thirty-five.* In August 1914, however, most infantry commanding officers were in their late forties, some in their fifties, while of the commanders of the fifteen infantry brigades that would initially land in France, the youngest was fifty-two and the oldest fifty-five. It is only possible to speculate on their level of fitness. Most of them had been steeled in their prime in South Africa, and while it is unlikely that they regularly took part in the route marches that were the staple of infantry training (they and key battalion staff had horses), some would have been active in the hunting field or on the polo ground, the tennis court and the golf course, and a soldierly pride and decent diet would, on the whole, have kept a check on their weight (as contemporary photographs bear out); there is no reason to suppose they were unfit. Yet it is equally unlikely that they would have had the 'aerobic' fitness or stamina of a commanding officer or brigadier today. And in some cases in August 1914 it is evident that the want of fitness told.

Ironically – for it might be thought that the saddle was a place for the older physique – the ages of command were rather lower in the cavalry. Here, commanding officers were by and large in their early forties (and a few were in their thirties), and of the five brigadiers,†

---

* Churchill was lucky to be given command of a newly raised battalion in 1915 at the age of forty-one.

† The term used in the old sense of brigade commander; the actual rank at that time was brigadier-general, which was ultimately replaced in 1928 by the present rank of, simply, brigadier.

two were forty-four (Gough and Chetwode), one was forty-nine (Briggs, who had been commanding a brigade for four years), and the two others fifty (the wiry De Lisle, who had been commanding for three years and was still playing polo off a high handicap) and fifty-three (Bingham).

The cavalry of the BEF consisted of every one of the sixteen regiments serving at home (there were a further twelve in imperial garrisons) and a composite regiment of the Household Cavalry (The Life Guards and The Blues). They were organized in five brigades, four of them forming the Cavalry Division (under the redoubtable Edmund – 'the bull' – Allenby), which answered direct to GHQ, with the fifth (Chetwode) acting as an independent brigade, also answering direct to GHQ. Two further regiments provided a squadron to each of the six divisions for reconnaissance, protection and communications.*

The actual role of the cavalry had been hotly debated for a decade. Two camps had formed behind two opposing conceptions – the 'mounted infantry' and the *'arme blanche'* – and the paper war between the two was intense. There were articles in professional journals and in newspapers; pamphlets were published, even whole books; official manuals were written and then rewritten. In 1910 Erskine Childers, author of the invasion-scare novel *The Riddle of the Sands*, who had served in the Boer War with the Honourable Artillery Company, a militia unit, published *War and the Arme Blanche*, reflecting the practical experience of South Africa and his conviction that the *arme blanche* – literally the (knightly) 'white arm', the sword and lance – had no place in modern war. He argued that the cavalry needed only the rifle, for the horse was merely the means of movement from one position to another. In this, he and others of the 'mounted infantry' camp were arguing for a return in part to the original concept of dragoons – men who, in Dr Johnson's definition,

---

* The WE of other ranks in a cavalry regiment was almost half that of an infantry battalion – 526 compared with 992 – but the number of officers about the same, 25 compared with 30. Unlike the infantry, however, the cavalry's WE was less than its PE since the PE included a margin for men in training – the cavalry did not have separate training depots – including men destined as drafts for the 'linked regiment' overseas. On mobilization, the part-trained recruits were to be mustered in 'reserve regiments' (at home) where their training continued until they were ready to be sent forward as casualty replacements – in much the same way as the SR infantry battalions functioned.

'fought indifferently on horse or foot' – except that Childers saw no role for *any* combat from the saddle, which was merely the place from which to control the horse or observe the enemy. In fact, mounted infantry (MI) companies had been formed towards the end of the previous century and had been used with mixed success in South Africa; as late as 1913 there was a School of Mounted Infantry at Longmoor in Hampshire (cavalry wags said the place was chosen because the Longmoor heathland was the softest ground in England onto which the MI could fall).* In 1913, however, the whole concept of mounted infantry was dropped, the horses (mainly cobs,† much sniffed at by the cavalry) withdrawn and the school closed. Ironically, many of the cobs would be impressed back into service in August the following year and sent as remounts to the divisional cavalry regiments – which, to their surprise, found them remarkably handy. In May 1914, however, the idea of greater infantry mobility was revived with the formation of cyclist companies – one for each of the BEF's six divisions – drawn variously from battalions to work with the divisional cavalry squadrons.

Given that whole books were written on the 'Great Cavalry Debate' – Childers himself wrote a second, *The German Influence on British Cavalry* (1911), a response to the joint criticism of *War and the Arme Blanche* by Sir John French and the Prussian General Friedrich von Bernhardi – any summary of the debate is unlikely to do justice to the sincerity or intellectual rigour of either camp. For there was more to this than enthusiastic horsemen wishing to preserve their knightly arm of

---

* There were three MI battalions, composite units consisting of men drawn from different regiments. Up to 1913 the BEF's order of battle included two 'mounted brigades' (one of two MI battalions and one cavalry regiment, and the other of one battalion and two regiments). If their efficiency was questionable, in South Africa they had had a certain romance, which Kipling – as ever – captured:

'M.I. (Mounted Infantry of the Line)'

I wish my mother could see me now, with a fence-post under my arm,
And a knife and a spoon in my putties that I found on a Boer farm,
Atop of a sore-backed Argentine, with a thirst that you could n't buy.
I used to be in the Yorkshires once
(Sussex, Lincolns, and Rifles once),
Hampshires, Glosters, and Scottish once! (ad lib.)
But now I am M.I.

[And six more verses, and chorus.]
† A cob is a type, not in itself a breed – a small horse, usually stoutly built, with strong bones and steady disposition. A cavalry troop horse had altogether more 'breeding'.

the service pitted against a resentment of privilege and peacockery. In the end the argument was resolved not by dialectical process so much as by a compromise brought about by circumstance. Since the duke of Wellington's day, the cavalryman, in addition to the sword (and, after Waterloo, the lance), had carried a carbine – a weapon similar to but (by definition) shorter than the musket or rifle. Carbines were handier in the saddle or when hastily dismounting, but fired lower-velocity rounds, and this plus the shorter barrel length meant inferior accuracy and a shorter effective range (in other words, reduced killing power). The new SMLE, however, was only 4 inches longer than the Lee–Enfield carbine with which the cavalry had gone to South Africa, and it made sense therefore to standardize and give them the same weapon.

Shooting at once improved, especially as it was now linked to pay (the better the marksmanship, the higher the pay), and the weapon was worthy of the hours that had to be put in on the ranges. While the 'shock effect' of the charge, sword or lance in hand, was still much prized by almost every cavalryman, now at last he also had the means to inflict severe damage at a distance, even when the numerical odds were against him. Indeed, to a limited extent he could now hold ground, although, mercifully for the horse, which was already bearing a growing weight of equipment, the cavalryman was not issued with an entrenching tool. Whatever the official manuals said about the rifle versus the *arme blanche*, cavalry commanders could from now on make a tactical choice – especially with the support of the regiment's two machine guns. It was a far cry from the Light Brigade's choice at Balaklava.

In appearance, indeed, there was now little difference between the infantryman and the cavalryman. While both the horseman and the foot soldier of the continental armies still bore a resemblance to their nineteenth-century forebears (the *poilu** of the French infantry even wore red *pantalons*), all ranks of every branch of the British army wore khaki, though a greener shade than the more familiar brown khaki of the Second World War and after.† The rank and file wore the

---

* Literally 'hairy one', an affectionate reference to the rustic character of the French infantryman.
† 'Khaki' is Persian, via Hindustani/Urdu, meaning (the colour of) ash or dust. The infantry had given up their red coats on campaign service in the 1880s – in India, Africa and elsewhere – but there was no European-weight khaki uniform until after the Boer War.

1902 pattern service dress (thick woollen tunic with, for the infantry, trousers – kilts or trews for Scottish regiments – or breeches for the mounted arms), and ankle boots with iron toecaps, iron plates on the heel and studded soles.* In 1914 the official issue was one brown and one black pair, but black soon afterwards became the only issue. Puttees – from the Hindustani *patti*, bandage – were worn to just below the knee,† and headwear was a stiffened peak cap (steel helmets were not issued until 1915), although the stiffener was removed on active service in some units, when it acquired the sobriquet 'the Gorblimey' – though the Scots regiments wore glengarries, or Balmoral bonnets ('tam-o'-shanters'). Officers' service dress was personally tailored in a superior cloth and to a different pattern, but at a distance looked much the same (though the Sam Browne belt, sword and absence of web equipment would be a fatal giveaway to German marksmen).

The effect of the 1902 pattern khaki could be startling. The German novelist Walter Bloem, a 46-year-old reservist captain in the 12th Brandenburg Grenadiers, would record his astonishment on first seeing a soldier of the BEF, a dismounted patrol of the 19th Hussars caught off guard near Mons: 'I had scarcely spoken when a man appeared not five paces away from behind the horses – a man in a grey-brown uniform, no, in a grey-brown golfing suit with a flat-topped cloth cap. Could this be a soldier? Certainly not a French soldier, or a Belgian, then he must be an English one. So that's how they dress now!'

Had Bloem encountered a member of one of the supporting arms or services he would have been no less intrigued. Except perhaps that the gunners – the Royal Artillery – would have been notably more smartly turned out. The gunners were in fact divided into three semi-autonomous elements – the Royal Horse Artillery (RHA), who

---

* Officially, 'Boots, General Service', but known universally as 'ammunition boots' (or 'ammo boots') from the archaic use of 'ammunition', embracing all military stores. The term 'ammunition loaf' – meaning issue bread – was used widely up to the middle of the nineteenth century.

† They were made of wool serge, with a length of cotton at the top (tapered) end, which was wrapped around the leg and tied off to secure them. The puttee was wound from the ankle (overlapping with the boot) to the knee for infantry, and the opposite way for cavalry, giving protection and support to the ankle and lower leg. The continental armies wore longer boots instead. Why the British army preferred the shorter boot and the puttee is not definitely established.

supported the cavalry, the Royal Field Artillery (RFA), supporting the infantry, and the Royal Garrison Artillery (RGA), who manned the heavier-calibre guns (and, later, anti-aircraft guns) which in earlier days had been called siege artillery. The standard unit was the battery of six guns (subdivided into three sections of two, each under subaltern commands), with an establishment of around two hundred men – gun numbers (those actually working – 'serving' – the guns), ammunition bearers, drivers, artificers – commanded by a major or senior captain. After the First World War the batteries were more or less permanently 'regimented' – grouped in threes or fours in a regiment under a commanding officer who was a lieutenant-colonel – but in 1914 they were mustered as 'brigades' for logistical and administrative purposes (the artillery brigade commander was a lieutenant-colonel).*

The gunners were, indeed, a magnificent arm – the RHA and RFA especially, with their six-horse teams – and superbly practised in their art. At least, as far as that art went, for if there was one element in which the BEF was weak in 1914, it was artillery (both numbers and weight of fire) – though no one imagined it before the fighting began. First, it lacked guns. The RHA and RFA were equipped with the excellent Royal Ordnance Quick Firing (QF) 13-pounder and 18-pounder respectively, and some RFA batteries with the QF 4.5-inch howitzer (high-angle fire).† The 13- and 18-pounders had been brought into service in 1904, and the 4.5-inch howitzer in 1910, but because of the poor performance of high-explosive shells in the Boer War, the Royal Artillery favoured the shrapnel round instead, which delivered a large number of individual 'bullets' close to the target and then ejected them explosively by a timed fuze in what was known as 'airburst' – acting in effect like a giant shotgun. The shrapnel round (originally 'spherical case shot'), invented by Henry Shrapnel who rose to be colonel-commandant of the Royal Artillery, had first been used in the

---

* Dispersal of the batteries among the infantry battalions in action was the standard procedure, however (and, indeed, the batteries were often in different barracks from each other in peacetime). The brigade commander therefore had little to do with the direction and control of fire. This would change during the course of the war as observation and communications improved, and as the lines solidified.

† QF guns were field pieces that fired rounds comprising propellant packed in brass cartridges with a shell fitted to the mouth, loaded through the breech, with a buffer/recuperator mechanism controlling the recoil; they were therefore quicker to reload and re-lay (re-aim).

Napoleonic Wars, and the gunners had developed it with possessive ingenuity throughout the following century. By 1914 the 13- and 18-pounder shrapnel rounds were perfection itself, but they were perfect for only one thing – killing men in the open, as well as horses, and gunners whose guns did not have shields. Once these had gone to ground or taken cover the danger was minimal, for shrapnel had no blast effect. It was therefore best suited for direct fire, when the gun layer (an artillery piece is 'laid' not 'aimed') could see the target, as opposed to indirect fire, where the gun is concealed and its 'fall of shot' adjusted by an observer. There were range limitations, too, compared with common shell – just short of 6,000 yards for the 13-pounder and 6,500 for the 18-pounder.

That said, the fire-effect – if the targets obliged – was spectacular. The 18-pounder shrapnel round contained 374 half-inch lead–antimony balls, lethal up to 300 yards from the burst, with best effect if the trajectory were flat and not plunging – which again made direct fire preferable, and at shorter range. British practice favoured a low burst, whereas the Germans generally fuzed their rounds to burst at a height of about 30 feet, which in August 1914 proved less effective. Firing at four rounds per gun per minute, a battery could shower a target with 9,000 bullets to the Vickers machine-gun section's 900–1,000 per minute, and at a significantly greater range. Little wonder, therefore, that both the infantry and, often as not, the gunners too, preferred the 18-pounders to fire in the direct role. The problem was, of course, that if the guns could see the target, the target could see the guns – as the Royal Artillery had learned painfully in South Africa, for the Boers' marksmanship had not been directed exclusively at the infantry. Both the 13- and the 18-pounder were therefore fitted with steel gun shields. But these could not protect all the gun numbers in action, nor of course the horses as they came forward to bring the guns out of action. If the infantry were advancing, this was not so much of a problem, but if they were withdrawing it meant that the guns would have to move before the enemy's guns and small arms got within their range, leaving the infantry unsupported at a critical moment; either that or risk being shot down getting the guns out of action at the last minute.

In fact, the debate over the use of artillery was every bit as heated as the 'Great Cavalry Debate'; it just attracted less public interest.

What the Boer War had shown – the Battle of Colenso in particular – was that when facing rifles accurate at 1,000 yards, and lethal at 2,000, the artillery simply had to keep its distance (or fire from concealed positions). By 1904, therefore, ranges at practice camps had doubled to 4,000 yards. But once the QF 13- and 18-pounders were introduced it appeared that the lesson of the *kopje* could perhaps be ignored, for it now seemed possible for the gunners to beat down the Mausers by rapid fire. The batteries could therefore expect to continue to give intimate support to the infantry. In any case, since the guns fired only shrapnel, and because fire could not easily or even usefully be concentrated, it made sense to parcel out the batteries among the infantry in much the same way as they had been at Waterloo.

The exceptions were the howitzer batteries (three per division, each of six guns), which carried three high-explosive (HE) rounds for every seven of shrapnel, and the single heavy battery of the RGA with each division. But the QF howitzer batteries were also expected to fire shrapnel direct, so the 4.5-inch gun had a shield too, even with a range of 6,000-plus yards; and the four 60-pounder guns of the RGA's heavy batteries, with a range of 10,000-plus yards, carried HE and shrapnel in the same ratio as the howitzers.

It wasn't just that HE ('Lyddite' and, later, TNT-Amatol) had proved disappointing in South Africa;* the preference for shrapnel was based on the generally accepted vision of future war, namely that it would be highly mobile and fought for key ground instead of on a continuous front or in depth, so that the infantry itself became the main target of attack. The shrapnel conviction became known as 'the spirit of close support', mirroring the infantry's belief in the 'mad minute' of rapid rifle fire, and the cavalry's fierce adherence to the *arme blanche*. The War Office manual *Field Artillery Training* (1914) promoted 'the moral effect of batteries advancing boldly'. Indeed, it spelled out the contract very plainly: 'Concealment, both as regards position and manoeuvre, must invariably be forgone for adequate reasons. To support infantry and to enable it to effect its purpose the

---

* Lyddite: principally picric acid, a heavily nitrated compound, manufactured from the late 1880s at Lydd in Kent. It was highly corrosive and thereby not wholly stable or predictable as an explosive in shells. TNT (tri-nitro toluene) and Amatol (a compound of TNT and ammonium nitrate) was much more stable, but the blast effects were not fully understood until later.

artillery must willingly sacrifice itself.' The Royal Artillery would win many a VC in August 1914 – and lose hundreds of men and horses – giving this intimate support to the infantry.*

This misjudgement, the gunners' equivalent of Spion Kop, was especially sad since the lesson of the Boer War had actually pointed strongly in the other direction: the artillery should take full advantage of the improved range and rate of fire of the new guns by concentrating the batteries' fire and by concealing them so that fire could be kept up indefinitely. But this had presumed that improved HE rounds would be developed, which they were not to any appreciable extent. Besides, there was what would prove to be a misperception among field artillery officers that the effect of HE lay not so much in the explosion itself as in the fragmentation of the shell case; and since the shrapnel round was demonstrably more effective in the business of scattering small pieces of metal about, logic suggested that there was nothing to be lost in the dispersion of the guns.† Besides, French artillery doctrine was going through a transformation in the years after the Entente, in line with the wider reaffirmation of the power of the offensive, and French artillerists had been respected since the time of Napoleon (himself a convinced artilleryman: 'It is with artillery that war is made'). The dictum therefore changed from 'the decision [action that brings success] is obtained by fire' to 'fire superiority makes the decision possible'; in other words, the role of the artillery was to neutralize rather than destroy. Not for the last time would the French belief in the intrinsic power of the offensive trump British experience.

This suited the Treasury, too. The ammunition scales for the Royal Artillery, the allocation of rounds, in 1914 would be based on the recommendations of the Mowatt Committee of 1901‡ – 1,000 rounds

---

* In fairness, the addiction to direct fire was not confined to the Royal Artillery. Major-General Jonathan Bailey, the pre-eminent British historian of artillery, in his *Field Artillery and Firepower* (London, 1989) concludes that 'In the event, all European armies were broadly guilty in 1914 of ignoring the potential of indirect fire.' In all, in the first three weeks' fighting the Royal Artillery would win eight VCs.

† This misunderstanding of blast effect – overlooking the physical impact of blast waves on the internal body – would contribute to the tardiness in recognizing 'shell shock' as a true clinical condition during the First World War.

‡ The committee was chaired by Sir Francis Mowatt, permanent secretary to the Treasury. The scale of ammunition to be held at first and second line – i.e. forward of the advanced depot – would be 528 rounds per gun, which compared well enough with both French and German scales; but after the war with Japan, the Russians had

per field gun in-theatre, with a reserve of 300 to be held in Britain and another 500 to be available from the factories within six months. No adjustment was made for the later introduction of the QF gun, nor in the light of the lessons of the Russo-Japanese war, where expenditure was far greater than had been assumed. The principle that 'the decision is obtained by fire' would have meant significant spending on ammunition stocks. Instead, emphasis was laid on the conservation of ammunition by thorough training. The doctrine of dispersion of batteries also meant a smaller manpower bill, with fewer artillery commanders, staff officers and signallers required to exercise centralized control. And so the Royal Artillery motto *Ubique* – everywhere – would apply primarily to the siting of the guns rather than to their reach.

Ubique was (is) a motto shared also by the other main supporting arm, the Royal Engineers, the 'sappers'.* They had four main functions – fortifications and sieges, mobility (especially bridge building), counter-mobility (principally, before the age of landmines, demolitions) and signals – as well as numerous ancillary responsibilities such as railways, water purification, surveying and postal services. They were, indeed, jacks-of-all-trades, and in extremis could fight as infantrymen, each sapper carrying a rifle. The basic unit of organization was the company or squadron (the term differed only to reflect the type of formation they supported – infantry or cavalry) of some 200 men, commanded by a major, subdivided into subalterns' commands of sections or troops, designated 'field' or 'signal'. The field companies were able to carry out most improvised military engineering tasks, but there was a separate 'bridging train' for the BEF comprising some 300 men and over 400 horses, most of them draught animals to haul the pontoon waggons.

In August 1914, however, the sappers' biggest challenge would not

---

concluded that 1,000 rounds were needed. However, the question of weakness in heavy artillery was not, according to Haldane's memoirs, one of cost, but the widespread belief in a war of movement and rapid decision, which argued for field rather than heavy guns: *Before the War* (London, 1920).
* A 'sap' was a narrow trench dug towards a fortress to allow explosives to be placed – something of a medieval practice that would be revived in the trenches after 1915 with the RE tunnelling companies. The Royal Corps of Sappers and Miners (essentially a labour organization) was absorbed by the Royal Engineers (essentially a body of officer specialists) after the Crimean War.

be building bridges but blowing them up. 'The service explosives available for hasty demolitions in the field are guncotton [nitro-cellulose] and cordite,'* declared the *Field Service Pocketbook* (1914). 'Other explosives may sometimes be obtained, the most likely being gunpowder and dynamite. Where a lifting effect is desired, gunpowder should be used; but, when a cutting or shattering effect is necessary, one of the others (high explosives) is better.' In other words, the *Pocketbook* was anticipating the need for the field companies and squadrons to find additional high explosive – dynamite, say – from local sources, not least because dynamite was not the safest explosive for rough handling and transport, and could not be used after exposure to moisture, when the nitroglycerine can separate and become unstable ('sweating'). Without modern plastic explosives such as Semtex, laying charges was a slow, laborious business: a large 'chamber' had to be made and then carefully packed with a large quantity of relatively low explosive. Gelignite, the first 'plastic' (or 'putty') high explosive, had been invented by Alfred Nobel (who had also invented dynamite) in 1875, but had not found favour with the army, who considered it to be still too unstable. When it came to demolition of iron or steel girder bridges, therefore, successive charges might have to be laid. However, since the prevailing doctrine envisaged a war of movement – and forward, not back – demolitions were seen as secondary to river crossings. Sappers would perform prodigious acts of valour during the retreat to the Marne, but time and again their incapacity for hasty demolition of ferrous bridges would cost them and the rest of the BEF dearly.

No less a burden would be borne in the retreat by the Royal Engineers' signal troops. Of the many weaknesses revealed in South Africa, none was more intractable than that of communications. Heliographs (using Morse code), like 'semaphore' flags, had been used to good effect; an army that saw most of its service in the colonial sun could not but have become proficient. But these methods had limitations even in sunny climes – the vulnerability of the signallers,

---

* Cordite had been developed as the smokeless replacement for gunpowder, and was the main propellant in British small-arms and artillery ammunition. It consisted of, by weight, 58% nitroglycerine, 37% gun-cotton and 5% petroleum jelly. It was extruded as spaghetti-like rods initially called 'cord powder', or 'the Explosive Committee's modification of Ballistite' – soon abbreviated to 'Cordite'. Both gun-cotton and cordite are low-order explosives.

easy interception of messages; and at night they had to be replaced by lamps, which had less range. Telegraphy – again using Morse – was well developed, and in European warfare there would be the advantage of extensive civilian (railway and post office) landlines to transmit messages, and even for telephony. There was also a presumption that an expeditionary force would, despite its name, operate on 'interior lines' – that is, within an ally's territory – as opposed to 'exterior lines' beyond it. And indeed the BEF would have this advantage in August 1914, just as the Germans would have the disadvantage of operating on exterior lines. In addition, 'field cable', insulated wire, could be laid at up to 6 miles an hour by Royal Engineers waggon and limber (which looked much like a horse artillery team), connecting corps headquarters with the divisions, and divisions with brigades.

Within artillery batteries, field telephones connected by lighter field cable (the responsibility of the batteries to lay) were available, though the Gunners did not think much of them before the August battles, preferring the tried and tested techniques of the past century. The sheer weight of enemy fire forced a rethink. GHQ's *Notes from the Front* (December 1914) would conclude that 'the amount of work and time devoted to visual signalling have not borne fruit in this war'. Or, as one artillery officer had it (from Millbank hospital in London): 'When the German infantry got within about 1,500 yards and the English artillery were beginning to get effective fire, our guns were bombarded with terrific rate of fire. Voice control was then no good, and no signaller could stand up. The [field] telephone was the only thing that was of any use.'

But for the most part, communications between headquarters in mobile operations was by mounted orderlies and despatch riders – on horses, motorcycles and, very locally, bicycles. What would have revolutionized command and control – whether of the fighting units themselves or the artillery – was wireless telegraphy (Morse), or better still, wireless telephony (voice). The Royal Navy had taken up wireless telegraphy (WT) with Guglielmo Marconi's experimental sets as early as the fleet manoeuvres of 1899, as a result of which the Marconi Company was asked to send engineers and equipment to set up five coastal stations in South Africa. Instead, in late November after the outbreak of war, these were diverted inland for deployment along a line from Durban to the diamond-mining town of Kimberley. The exercise was not a success, for which each side – Marconi and the War Office – blamed the other.* Thereafter senior officers were sceptical about the merits of wireless, especially given the size of the equipment (the batteries in particular), and although the War Office by no means threw over the invention, the early disappointments did not have the same galvanizing effect as the tactical and technical setbacks elsewhere in the army. The problem in large part lay with money: the War Office's financial secretary would authorize only a minimal sum for WT since there was still no endorsed continental commitment for the BEF. Only in 1912 was the Army Signal Service formed – not as a separate organization but within the Royal Engineers – and WT given serious attention.†

Nevertheless, by 1914 there were 'waggon wireless stations' to connect the BEF headquarters with the Cavalry Division, and pack-saddle sets connecting the cavalry divisional headquarters with its brigades, with ranges of up to 80 and 30 miles respectively. However, there had been nothing like the investment of money and interest needed to produce robust and handy field communications for the infantry divisions, and rather as the artillery disdained the field telephone, so the cavalry preferred to use the more reliable landline instead of its wireless waggons and pack-saddles. In August 1914, by the law of unintended consequences, this preference would prove providential: because the wireless telegraphy sets were not being used much to send and receive, the operators turned their attention to

---

* It was established much later that the severe thunderstorms of the South African interior during that summer had been a source of serious interference for the primitive receivers. Nor was it properly understood at the time that as the conductivity of the soil was poor, thorough 'earthing' was necessary. In July three of the rejected wireless sets were installed in the Royal Navy cruisers *Forte*, *Magicienne* and *Thetis*, blockading Delagoa Bay. With one ship acting as shore station and the others signalling at ranges of up to 50 miles, the interception of smaller, faster blockade-runners proved so effective that the Admiralty began negotiating a contract for installing sets in all ships. In August 1914, Germany had 17 government wireless stations; Austria-Hungary, 4; France, 18; Russia, 28; and Britain, 47.
† There were real advances in audio radio broadcast at this time, too. The first public radio broadcast had taken place as early as Christmas Eve 1906, made by Westinghouse Engineers from a transmitter at Ocean Bluff, Brant Rock, Massachusetts. Ships at sea heard a broadcast that included 'O Holy Night' played on the violin and a passage from the Bible. Perhaps because the transmission of reports and orders was seen as a staff rather than a command function, and also because of the obvious problems of security, the advantages of voice were not apparent to the army.

intercepting German radio communications, and with good results.*
But the arrested development of WT would prove especially unfortunate in one area – with the one invention with which neither
side had previously been to war: the aeroplane.

If there was one thing that proved the pre-war British army was not
closed to innovation it was the fixed-wing aircraft. On 21 September
1910 a retired Royal Artillery captain, Bertram Dickson, who had
learned to fly earlier that year, took off in a Bristol Boxkite machine
from a grass strip on Salisbury Plain, the tract of rough sheep-grazing
country in Wiltshire of which the army had bought a large part a
decade earlier. It was the third day of the annual army manoeuvres,
which that year involved some 60,000 men and extended across three
counties. 'Blue Force' and 'Red Force' were advancing towards each
other, each trying to establish the opposing force's strength and axes
– the classic role of cavalry. Red Force had an airship, the 'Beta', but
the weather had grounded it. Strong winds had also grounded the
Boxkite, but on the twenty-first it finally managed to take off.

Few taking part in the manoeuvres had ever seen an aeroplane – it
was only the year before that Blériot had flown the English Channel
– but the British and Colonial (later the Bristol) Aircraft Company,
founded earlier in 1910, had persuaded the War Office to let them
demonstrate what the Boxkite could do. Dickson was given the mission to observe the movements of Blue Force and report these to Red
Force headquarters. Half an hour after taking off, flying over Salisbury
Plain at about 200 feet, he located the Blue Force cavalry and turned
back to report the sighting. Although the army had installed a WT
transmitter–receiver in its new airship, the sets were too big for the
Boxkite. Rather than fly all the way to Red HQ, Dickson decided to
put down in a field close to the village of Wylye and telephone the
information from the post office. He was at once captured by Blue
Force cavalry – a patrol of the 4th Dragoon Guards, who would be the
first regiment of the BEF to make contact with the Germans in 1914.

Dickson was taken to Blue HQ, where the umpires tried to decide
what to do in the unprecedented case of cavalry capturing an aeroplane. While there he met Winston Churchill, then the home

---

* German electronic communications were in much the same state, the war catching
the modernization and expansion programme in midstream. The army's carrier pigeon
service, a branch of the Engineers (*Pionere*), had 21,000 birds to offset the deficiencies.

secretary as well as an officer in the Yeomanry, come to observe the manoeuvres. Churchill was an instant convert. Indeed, he would soon start taking flying lessons, although he never did get a pilot's licence: the wings on his air commodore's uniform in later life were as honorary as the rank (his crash landings were legion and legendary). However, when he became first lord of the Admiralty the following year he immediately began pressing the cause of naval aviation, just as in early 1915 he would press the cause of the tank after simply reading an outline specification (the first were ready for service in 1916). In May 1912 the Royal Flying Corps was formed from the Royal Engineers Air Battalion (balloons) and Royal Navy balloon and airship detachments, initially comprising a naval as well as a military wing. Just twenty-seven months later, in August 1914, after the elevation of the naval wing into the Royal Naval Air Service in July that year, four RFC squadrons consisting of twelve aircraft each would fly to France with the BEF (the balloon squadron deployed in 1915 once the Western Front had become entrenched). They would not, however, be equipped with WT; communication with the ground would be by signalling lamp.*

The BEF, then, while being without question 'incomparably the best trained, best organized and best equipped British Army that ever went forth to war', had some significant weaknesses, both technical and tactical. Its infantry relied on reservists to bring it up to fighting strength, some of whom would inevitably have lost their general 'edge', in fitness especially, and massed its riflemen into firing lines to make up for the paltry allocation of machine guns. The cavalry were still wedded to the *arme blanche* as the weapon of decision. The artillery was short of heavy guns; its field batteries fired only shrapnel and were all too ready to fire from exposed positions in order to give the infantry moral support. By contrast, all German field batteries, equipped with 15-pounders and light howitzers, fired HE as well as shrapnel; the 15 cm (5.9-inch) heavy howitzer fired an 11 lb bursting charge of HE; heavy mortars and siege howitzers – some with as large

---

* The aircraft were a mixture of BE2s (Nos 2 and 4 Sqns), Blériot monoplanes and Farmans (3 Sqn), and Farmans and Avro 504s (5 Sqn). The most numerous, the BE2 (Blériot Experimental), was designed by Geoffrey de Havilland and built at the Royal Aircraft (formerly Balloon) Factory at Farnborough. Its maximum speed was 63 knots (116 km/h) at 6,500 feet, with an operational ceiling of 10,000 feet and endurance of 3 hr 15 min; it was armed with a swivel-mounted Lewis gun manned by the observer.

a calibre as 42 cm (16.5 inches) – would give short shrift to fixed defences. The Royal Engineers had inadequate means of demolition to deal with girder bridges, and communications were not up to the demands of free-moving battle or the concentration and speedy application of artillery fire. Although the Army Service Corps used mechanical transport increasingly between the railheads and the divisional distribution points, the motive power forward of the corps rear areas was principally the horse; and once the infantry had detrained they marched on foot (only in October 1914 would the London omnibuses, green-painted, make their appearance). Operations therefore developed at a relatively slow pace – no faster, indeed, than those of the previous century. Yet the advent of the aeroplane changed dramatically the nature of higher command. For now it was possible to observe what the enemy was doing at a depth of around 80 miles (a return sortie by a BE2), and for GHQ to receive the information within two hours – by which time the enemy would only have been able to advance a maximum of about 10 miles. Cavalry could in theory reconnoitre to the same depth and pass the information back even more quickly by WT, but the aeroplane had literally an overview, and in depth, whereas cavalry had to build up a picture from what they observed across their front (where the enemy might have deployed their own cavalry screen to deny that observation). Having said that, cavalry did have the advantage of being able to gather more detailed information, such as the identity of the advancing units, from prisoners or captured equipment – and occasionally battle maps and operation orders – and were not fettered by bad weather or the dark. But in practice logistical constraints placed a limit on the cavalry's scouting range, and in August 1914 it would be the information gained by the RFC that would have a profound effect on the course of operations.

What, then, of the individual soldier of the BEF? Confident in his ability with the rifle, or the field gun, or the sword and lance, and hardened by the daily routine of the regular soldier, he was not in the least overawed by the prospect of superiority in opposing numbers; and he knew there was no superiority in quality. Even the reservist who had not been with the colours for years, despite the slackened muscles and the extra pounds, was tough-minded: his former service had made him so. Regular or reservist, the soldiers of the BEF were hardy professionals, regimented in units with strong identities, within practised brigade and divisional chains of command – in all, an unusually cohesive force. Beyond that, generalizations are as usual perilous. The Germans had an opinion of the British soldier, though. The reports from their field intelligence on the conduct of Old Contemptibles after capture would speak with grudging admiration of their resentment at being taken prisoner, of their truculent un-willingness to cooperate, and of their mental resilience. This would be in marked contrast to reports, later, on the Territorials ('not very soldierly'), the Kitchener battalions ('the finest of men, but not sol-diers') and from 1916 the conscripts, many of whom, from 'the underclass', would shock their captors as specimens of debased manhood. The BEF of August 1914 was materially and morally a world away from those who followed them into the trenches of subsequent years.

The real deficiency in the summer of 1914, however, was not in specific capabilities such as heavy artillery or machine guns, but in numbers – mass. The BEF was simply too small to make a strategic contribution, too small to stand out in a clash of great continental armies, and therefore too small to give London a say in the plans of war on land. It would be, to all intents and purposes, an ancillary of the French army, and ancillaries are not in a position to dictate terms. Had the legal questions surrounding the Territorial Force been resolved, allowing them to be deployed overseas at once to release regular units, the BEF might have doubled in size by early September. Had conscription been introduced at any time after 1910, an expeditionary force of at least 400,000 might have been fielded. But there had never been conscription in Britain, and a Liberal govern-ment would have been the last to introduce such a measure – especially when, despite all the evidence of German militarism, war seemed so dim a prospect. After all, it had been averted so far: good-will and wise counsel would surely continue to prevail?

Chapter Five

PLANS

If ever a plan deserved victory it was the [German] Schlieffen Plan; if ever one deserved defeat it was [the French] Plan XVII.

Field Marshal Lord Wavell, *Allenby: A Study in Greatness*

Armies make plans. However, military plans do not necessarily correspond to political intentions, and in consequence the functions and outlook of military staff officers can stand in marked contrast, even sometimes in conflict, with those of diplomats. In the century after the Congress of Vienna, diplomats increasingly saw their primary aim as avoiding war, while the military staffs saw theirs as gaining advantage in war by preparing detailed mobilization and campaign plans. For the diplomat, war represented failure, while for the staff officer it was neither failure nor success, but rather the bloody testing of his preparations – though, as Moltke stressed, war plans could play but a part, if a critical one, in the ultimate outcome. To what extent on the road to the First World War military plans developed a momentum of their own has long been the subject of debate. Mobilization in the days of conscript armies, because of the large number of reservists that short-service conscription generated, gave an army the numerical advantage over an adversary who did not mobilize or did so late. Not to mobilize in the face of mobilization by an adversary was therefore in effect to surrender. Mobilization was not itself a declaration of war, but if two adversaries were to mobilize and then pull back from the brink, demobilization would have to be carried out with strict mutuality, otherwise one side could find itself in the same perilous position as it would have had it failed to mobilize promptly. Unsurprisingly, therefore, and also because of the sheer expense of calling up the nation's reservists, there was no real example of such a demobilization in the century before 1914. Mobilization as good as meant war.

Yet the decision to mobilize was one of policy, and policy was reserved to government – or, in the case of absolute monarchy, to the monarch. The existence of mobilization plans did not alter this fact. Once the army was mobilized, its deployment for its offensive or defensive campaign was the business of the military staff; but again, the plan of campaign was subject to political scrutiny beforehand, since war was not a matter of military strategy alone (this is as true today as it was at the time of the Peloponnesian Wars two millennia and more before both Moltkes). On the contrary: war, wrote the pre-eminent – and Prussian – military philosopher Carl von Clausewitz in *Vom Krieg* (*On War*), first published in 1832, is not merely a political act but also a political instrument, a continuation of political commerce, a carrying out of the same enterprise with other means: 'Der Krieg ist eine blosse Fortsetzung der Politik mit anderen Mitteln'. Unfortunately the notion gained purchase that once war begins it becomes solely the business of soldiers. In Britain this was perhaps because the first full translation of Clausewitz to be published (by Colonel James Graham in 1873) renders *mit anderen Mitteln* not as 'with' but as 'by' other means, allowing the inference that the primary, non-military, means are at an end. With characteristic pithiness, Georges Clemenceau, prime minister of France from 1917, both reclaimed the true meaning and took Clausewitz's logic the next required step in proclaiming: 'La guerre! C'est une chose trop grave pour la confier à des militaires' ('War is too serious a matter to entrust to military men').

A. J. P. Taylor, the controversialist and first TV historian, claimed in his 1963 work *The First World War* that 'on 1 August Germany declared war on Russia; two days later, with hardly an attempt at excuse, on France. The First World War had begun – imposed on the statesmen of Europe by railway timetables.' Indeed, six years later, riding the wave of the 'futility and callous incompetence' school of Great War history epitomized by *The Donkeys* and *Oh! What A Lovely War*,* he took a second bite of the publishing cherry with *War by Timetable* (1969). But Taylor's fondness for startling claims was already well known: in his 1955 biography of Bismarck he had argued that the 'Iron Chancellor' had unified Germany more by accident than design. The idea of 'war by timetable' is just too easy. Railways were of course central to mobilization plans, and the building of new lines, in Russia especially, was closely monitored by staff officers in the various capitals to assess the relative advantage that increased railway capacity gave potential adversaries. After all, Moltke had said: 'Don't build forts; build railways.' Timetables certainly constrained options, and they shaped the military plans that gave rise to the timetables in the first place. But to claim that railway timetables imposed war on European statesmen is no more logical than saying that *Bradshaw's Railway Companion* imposed seaside holidays on the industrial classes of Victorian England.

'The enemy of a good plan is the dream of a perfect plan,' wrote Clausewitz; but that did not stop the dreaming in Berlin. Indeed, with the departure of the Elder Moltke as head of the *Grosser Generalstab* in 1888, the dreaming became increasingly fantastic, at its most dangerous remove from practicality between 1891 and 1906 during the tenure of General der Kavallerie Alfred Graf (Count) von Schlieffen. In 1906 he would hand over to his predecessor-but-one's nephew, Helmuth Johann von Moltke (the 'Younger Moltke'), and from his deathbed supposedly urge his successor: 'Only make the right wing strong!' By this he meant the right wing of the great wheeling movement through Belgium that would envelop Paris and trap the French army, hammer and anvil, against the German border. This was the essence of the plan that bore his name – the Schlieffen Plan, the plan of plans; the apotheosis of planning.

His inspiration was a perfect battle fought before the invention of gunpowder – before, indeed, the invention of the stirrup: Cannae. In 216 BC, near the present-day town of Barletta in southern Italy, the

---

* Alan Clark's *The Donkeys* (London, 1961) (see chapter 15), inspired the Charles Chilton radio play of the same year entitled *The Long Long Trail*, which was then put on the stage by Joan Littlewood and her Theatre Workshop in 1963, and on celluloid by Richard Attenborough in 1969, as *Oh! What A Lovely War*.

THE SCHLIEFFEN CONCEPT

Five armies wheeling through neutral Belgium
and Luxembourg (and even perhaps the
Netherlands), with two more holding between
Metz and Mulhouse against an expected French
offensive (Plan XVII).

German troop
movements

Anticipated French
offensive

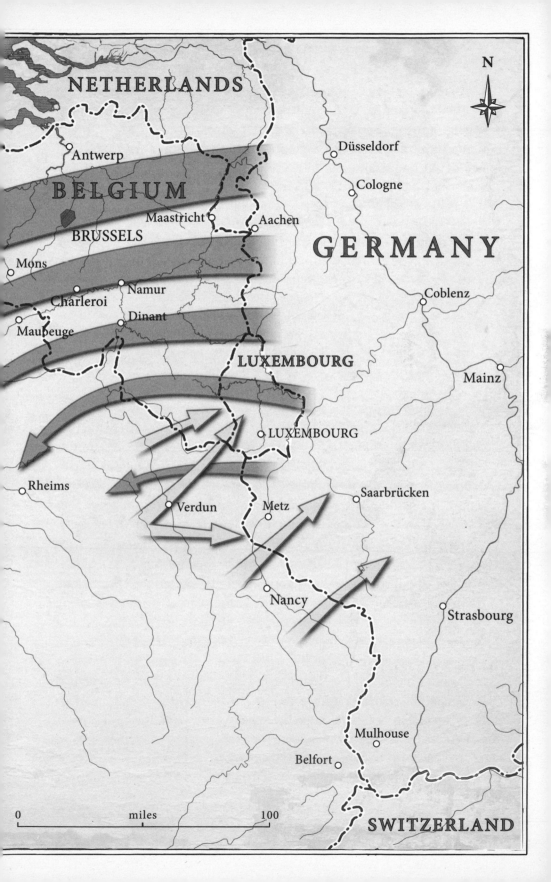

Carthaginian army of Hannibal defeated a Roman army twice its size by the bold gamble of presenting only a weak centre while sending cavalry and light infantry in a double envelopment deep into the Roman legions' rear. Sixty thousand legionary corpses attested to not just defeat but annihilation. Of Cannae, Schlieffen wrote:

> A battle of annihilation can be carried out today according to the same plan devised by Hannibal in long forgotten times. The enemy front is not the goal of the principal attack. The mass of the troops and the reserves should not be concentrated against the enemy front; the essential is that the flanks be crushed. The wings should not be sought at the advanced points of the front but rather along the entire depth and extension of the enemy formation. The annihilation is completed through an attack against the enemy's rear . . . To bring about a decisive and annihilating victory requires an attack against the front and against one or both flanks.*

Yet Rome ultimately won the Punic Wars, not least because Hannibal did not know what to do with his famous victory. Schlieffen did not intend making that mistake. The purpose of *his* Cannae was to defeat the French quickly before switching troops to the east to defeat the more slowly mobilizing Russians. For Schlieffen was presented with the classic Napoleonic challenge of having (potentially) to deal with two armies simultaneously, the terms of the Franco-Russian alliance stipulating that war with one party meant war with the other as well. And his plan was suitably Napoleonic: in essence, the 'strategy of the central position', whose design was to concentrate the greatest number of men into the principal battle while denying the enemy armies the opportunity to support each other. First a wedge had to be driven between the two, using part of the force to pin, or at least mask, one of the armies while the main body defeated the other quickly by a violent blow. A force would then be detached to pursue the defeated army and prevent its rallying, while the main body turned to deal with the other enemy army, which would now be wholly unsupported.

The strategy had worked for Bonaparte – but not always. The biggest risk lay in judging what proportion of the main force to

* *Alfred von Schlieffen's Military Writings*, trans. and ed. Robert T. Foley (New York, 2003).

detach to pursue the defeated army: too small and it might allow them to rally and return to the fight; too large and there might not be the strength remaining to deal with the other army. The latter is what happened in 1815, when the French dealt the Prussians a terrible blow at Ligny and almost knocked them out of the campaign. But because Bonaparte was unable to detach enough troops to maintain pressure on Blücher's men as they retreated, while he himself turned to deal with Wellington's army, the Prussians were able to recover and march to the eleventh-hour relief of their allies at Waterloo. In the Schlieffen Plan, the wedge was already driven between the armies by virtue of geography; the detail to be worked up lay therefore in the plans to mask the Russians mobilizing on the borders of East Prussia, while concentrating German strength for the paralysing blow against the French, then switching the victorious troops from west to east via the ultra-efficient German railway system. To that extent, the plan did indeed become a gigantic railway timetable, the elaboration of which was in the hands of the *Eisenbahnabteilung* (railway section), one of the strongest and most important branches of the general staff. Its chief was General Wilhelm Groener, who would become de facto head of the German army in late 1918. But the whistle and the green flag were in the Kaiser's hands – at least until he fumbled, and dropped them.

There is a question, however, as to what extent the Schlieffen *Plan* was reality or myth, a theoretical staff study rather than a sealed blueprint for a campaign. In a sense, for the BEF in France in August 1914 the answer did not matter: the Germans were marching through Belgium – to whose plan made little difference on the ground. It is more a matter for the *Kriegsschuldfrage*, the war-guilt question: to what extent were events in the month after Sarajevo determined by the existence of an aggressive and inflexible plan of campaign? From a British military perspective the more searching question is: what operational alternative was there to what the BEF actually did? Might the German plans have been more thoroughly overthrown in August and September 1914 than they actually were?*

The Schlieffen Plan, even as modified by the Younger Moltke, had elegance and daring, which is why Wavell wrote that it deserved to

---

* An answer is suggested in the final chapter.

succeed; but it had never been realistic.* Liddell Hart, the foremost British military thinker of the inter-war years, was particularly disparaging of the *Grosser Generalstab*: 'A swift victory over the main armies in the main theatre of war was the German general staff's solution for all outside difficulties, and absolved them from thinking of war in its wider aspects.'† These wider aspects were, not least, Belgian neutrality and Britain's reaction to its infringement. As the German-born Professor Holger Herwig writes in a much-admired recent work, '[Schlieffen] raised tactics to the level of operations, and subordinated statecraft to purely operational concepts.'‡ Hans von Seeckt, chief of staff of one of the corps on Schlieffen's right wing, and head of the army in the post-war *Reichswehr*, was even more categorical: 'Cannae: no slogan became so destructive for us as this one.'§ But Schlieffen also ignored a good few military, as well as political, realities, not least among them the number of troops available, 'time and space', and logistics; and it is this otherwise apparently inexplicable gap between theorizing and military logic – given the professionalism of the Prussian general staff – that has led some to the conclusion that the plan never existed beyond a sort of military doodle.**

For a decade after the Dual Alliance with Austria was contracted, even before the formalization of Franco-Russian military cooperation, Schlieffen's great predecessor at the head of the *Grosser Generalstab*, the architect of Bismarck's military victories, the Elder Moltke, had been

* Field Marshal Archibald Percival Wavell, 1st Earl Wavell, *Allenby: A Study in Greatness* (London, 1940). Wavell had been a captain in the directorate of military operations when Henry Wilson was its head.
† *The Real War (1914–1918)* (London, 1930), later republished as *A History of the World War (1914–1918)*. Basil Liddell Hart (1895–1970; knighted 1966) served on the Western Front briefly before being invalided to light duties from the effects of gas. His theories of 'the indirect approach' much influenced the German army in the 1930s, from which they developed the doctrine of *Blitzkrieg*.
‡ Holger Herwig, *The Marne, 1914* (New York, 2009).
§ See James S. Corum, *The Roots of Blitzkrieg: Hans von Seeckt and German Military Reform* (Lawrence, KS, 1992).
** One of Hitler's field marshals, Albert Kesselring, makes a telling remark about the *Grosser Generalstab*'s rarefied military intellectualism. Of the instruction at the pre-1914 staff college he writes that it was inadequate in too many practical fields, such as intelligence, logistics, air and naval warfare, applied science and 'anything to do with oil which soiled the fingers and hampered the tactician and strategist in the free flight of his ideas': 'Training and Development of German General Staff Officers', unpublished paper, US Army Historical Division European Command, quoted in Kenneth Macksey, *From Triumph to Disaster* (London, 1996).

pondering on Germany's two-front dilemma. Despite the complete-ness of his greatest victory, over the French in 1870, Moltke doubted that it could be repeated against a reorganized and reinforced French army and – notwithstanding his views on forts versus railways – France's strengthened border fortresses. He concluded that in a war on two fronts the only course was to stay on the defensive against France, check Russia by a sharp stroke at her advanced forces, and then turn westward to deal with the expected French offensive. It was still the Napoleonic strategy of the central position, but the mirror image of what Schlieffen would come to think. Since, however, in Moltke's esti-mation outright victory was not possible, the aim instead would be to cripple both opponents and thereby bring about a favourable peace. His immediate successor, Alfred Graf von Waldersee, endorsed the 'plan'; indeed, Bismarck actually curbed Waldersee's initial ideas on a more aggressive stance, in particular a pre-emptive war with Russia. But after the 'pilot', Bismarck, had been dropped in 1890, Waldersee fell out of favour with the thrusting new Kaiser. The tipping point came when he criticized the imperial tactics during the annual manoeuvres, which the young Wilhelm himself insisted on directing. The Kaiser promptly dismissed him and appointed Schlieffen in his place. From the outset, the new *Generalstabschef* found himself under royal pressure to take a more forceful stance towards France. Soon, to the Kaiser's delight, Schlieffen was able to oblige, questioning the feasibility of an offensive in the east alongside the Austrian army. By his calculation it would be impossible to gain any compelling victory over the Russian army or pre-vent it from retiring out of reach. Nor could he concede Moltke's assessment that the French fortifications ruled out an offensive in the west when there was the simple expedient of bypassing them by march-ing through Belgium. The Kaiser approved. The following year Schlieffen formally threw out Moltke's plan and began working on a scheme to ignore the 1839 treaty, the 'scrap of paper'. Liddell Hart remarks that 'his conception of war was dominated by the theoretical absolutes of Clausewitzian doctrine. So when he came to the conclusion that such absolute victory was unattainable in the East, he came back to the idea of seeking it in the West.'*

---

* Foreword to Gerhard Ritter, *The Schlieffen Plan: Critique of a Myth*, trans. A. and E. Wilson (New York, 1958).

Schlieffen developed his plan annually by degrees. At first he favoured an approach-march through the southern tip of Belgium to turn the French flank near Sedan, the very place where the campaign of 1870 had been decided. By 1905, however, to be sure of casting the net broadly enough to envelop the bulk of the French armies in the field, he was planning to go through the centre of Belgium in a great wheeling movement, with the tip of his right wing crossing the French border near Lille. But this in turn presented him with another problem: to avoid being delayed by the strong Belgian fortresses of Namur and Liège, he would have to outflank them by a march through the Maastricht corridor – violating Dutch territory. And in extending his right wing so, when it swung south he risked running into the strong defences of Paris, or, in turning south-east to avoid them, exposing his flank to a counter-stroke by its garrison. So he decided to extend his wheeling movement wider still – west of Paris.

Such a plan required huge numbers of troops, not least the detachments to mask the bypassed fortresses and to protect the long-stretched lines of communication. Thus Schlieffen calculated that he would have to shift the distribution of his forces significantly: nearly seven-eighths of the total available in the west would now be dedicated to the great wheeling movement, with the remaining eighth assigned to counter a possible French offensive across his own frontier – indeed, an increasingly probable one, for 'attack' was the new French doctrine (see discussion later in this chapter).

'It was a conception of Napoleonic boldness,' wrote Liddell Hart,

the decisive effect of arriving in the enemy's rear with the bulk of one's forces. If the manoeuvre went well it held much greater promise of quick and complete victory than any other course could offer, and the hazards of leaving only a small proportion to face a French frontal attack were not as big as they appeared. Moreover if the German defensive wing was pushed back, without breaking, that would tend to increase the effect of the offensive wing. It would operate like a revolving door—the harder the French pushed on one side [weakening their line elsewhere in order to do so] the more sharply would the other side swing round and strike their back.

Nevertheless, the concept required nerve not to water down the ratios. Hence Schlieffen's supposed dying words to Moltke: 'Only make the right wing strong!'

The vision of *corps d'armées* in Prussian field grey marching through Belgium *désunis*, cavalry to the fore, was certainly Napoleonic in its grandeur. It was also Cannae, but with a single rather than double envelopment. However, there was a crucial post-Punic, post-Napoleonic development to take account of – railways. And these favoured France, for while the German armies could deploy by train to the Belgian border, from there on, in the face of opposition from the Belgian army, including destruction of track and railway bridges, the *Landser* (the German 'Tommy') would have to advance by foot.* The French, meanwhile, would be able to use their extensive railway system, and its telegraph, both to assemble their armies and to switch them from east to west, and vice versa, as the situation developed. The German right wing, if indeed it was to swing west of Paris and then turn east at, say, Chartres on an axis Auxerre–Langres, would have to march over 600 miles before the culminating battle with the French armies meant to be waiting obligingly near the German border. Even without opposition this would be a two-month march, during which the French could redeploy by train at ten times the speed.

'The less he could count on an advantage in speed the more would depend on having a decisive superiority of strength, at any rate in the crucial area,' Liddell Hart goes on to observe. Schlieffen certainly knew this, and began creating additional army corps from reservists who were meant to be battle-casualty replacements (*ersatz Truppen*), instead incorporating them – and also the *Landwehr* (Territorials) – from the outset for subsidiary operational tasks in the main force. This was risky in the extreme, for besides the questionable quality of the *ersatz* units, it meant that their attrition began at once, even before they were called on to fill gaps in the regular divisions. It was a gamble, wishful thinking – but it was certainly bold. Indeed, it had something in common with Bonaparte's own throw of the dice in his 'Campaign of the Hundred Days', before meeting his Waterloo. Even

---

* *Landser* is a diminutive of *Landsknecht* (literally 'country servant'), a fifteenth-century term, disputed in origin but possibly used to distinguish troops recruited in lowland Germany from Swiss mercenaries. 'Tommy' is, of course, a diminutive of 'Thomas Atkins'. The exact origin of 'Thomas Atkins' is also disputed, despite definitive claims by some historians.

so, it gave only a slight numerical superiority over the French, a margin that would disappear with the addition of the Belgian and British armies; and by the time Schlieffen framed his final plan it is clear that he was very doubtful that Germany could actually attain the necessary superiority of force to execute it.

In a letter to *The Times* in 2011 on intervention in Libya, Lieutenant-General Sir John Kiszely, formerly director of the British tri-service Defence Academy, succinctly summed up the relationship between the political and the military in strategic decision-making:

> Strategy is the balancing of objectives (or ends), with the ways and means of achieving them. Politicians should, indeed, set the objectives they wish to achieve, but it is the duty of the Chief of the Defence Staff, and others responsible for strategic advice, to ensure that politicians understand the extent to which those objectives are achievable with the ways and means available. If the necessary ways and means cannot be found, the objectives must be modified. This is an iterative process, which requires continual discourse to ensure that objectives, ways and means remain in balance. If strategy is not formulated in this way, strategic failure beckons.*

And beckon it did in the years before the Great War, for Schlieffen's approach became increasingly fantastical, solving problems by double-counting and ignoring the political implications of more and more desperate expedients. At no stage does he appear to have warned the Kaiser and his cabinet that the chances of success were small compared with the risks, and that German policy ought to be adjusted to that grave reality, writing instead that 'it is necessary to violate the

---

* *The Times*, 1 Aug. 2011. Clausewitz was making the same point in *On War*, book VIII: 'It is an inadmissible and even harmful distinction to leave a great military enterprise or its planning to a "purely military" judgment; more, it is absurd to consult professional soldiers on a plan for a war in order that they may judge from a "purely military" stand-point what cabinets are to do.' After the war, the former German chancellor, Theobald von Bethmann Hollweg, would (in evident self-justification) write remarkably: 'In drawing up the plan of campaign, the political leadership had no share. Nor had it any in the changes to which Schlieffen's plan was subjected some time after the outbreak of war, or in the departures from the modified plan when it came to be executed in practice. During my whole term of office there was never any kind of council of war in which politicians intervened in the pros and cons of the military debate': *Reflections on the World War*, trans. George Young (London, 1920). He was, however, writing in reaction to the criticism by former general staff officers that politicians had interfered with planning and had therefore been responsible for the defeat of those plans.

neutrality not only of Belgium but also of the Netherlands [and Luxembourg]. But as long as no other expedient can be found, one has to make the best of these difficulties.' He could not have known how much he would be helped in these difficulties by the French themselves, whose purblindness when it came to the possibility of attack through Belgium would restore to the Germans a good deal of Liddell Hart's 'advantage in speed'.

In fairness to Schlieffen and his apparently cavalier attitude towards the neutrals, he did anyway perceive Belgian neutrality to be something of a sham – at least, later he did: in a memorandum of 1912 (he continued working on his grand ideas even in retirement) he would write: 'This country (Belgium) is regarded as neutral, but in fact it is not. More than thirty years ago it made Liège and Namur into strong fortresses to prevent Germany from invading its territory, but towards France it left its frontiers open.' The implication was that the French would have little difficulty in launching an attack through Belgium to envelop the flank of a German offensive. Indeed, earlier he had written: 'If, blindly trusting in the sanctity of neutrality, we were to attack along the whole front Belfort–Montmedy [along the Franco-German border], a practical and unscrupulous enemy would soon effectively envelop our right flank through Belgium and Luxembourg. Belgian counter-measures would be too weak or too late to be effective.' And then, in the tortuous logic and morality of the violation of neutral territory: 'In a war of aggression against France, the laws of self-defence would make it impossible for Germany to respect Luxembourg and Belgian neutrality. The French are now as convinced of this as we.'

The exquisite irony in the juxtaposition of 'war of aggression' and 'self-defence' goes unremarked.*

Now, it can be argued that Schlieffen regarded his plan as no more than a process of military appreciation to determine the optimum force structure for the army, perhaps even to argue for more resources, rather than as the basis for a campaign blueprint. The population of the German Empire was two-thirds as much again that of France, but

---

* Schlieffen had also persuaded himself that the Dutch were closet British allies. But from 1904 there was no real doubt in his mind of the nature of the projected war with France: his definitive draft plan of that year bore the title *Angriffskrieg gegen Frankreich* – a war of aggression against France.

only some 54 per cent of available imperial manpower was ever actually called up, compared with France's 80 per cent.* Budgetary constraints, an increasingly left-wing Reichstag and reluctance within the army itself (a deeply conservative institution) to recruit in the growing urban centres of population, which were perceived as politically unreliable, kept it at a peacetime strength in 1911 of 612,000, compared with France's 593,000. The law of unintended consequences also gave an advantage in reservists to the French: democratic mistrust of militarism, especially in the wake of the Dreyfus affair†, kept military service at two years, compared with the Germans' three. So although the French reservists were perhaps not as well trained as the German, the system produced a third more of them each year.

To what extent, by the time he came to relinquish his appointment in 1906, Schlieffen had abandoned the idea of marching west of Paris rather than east is still the subject of debate. Although his flights of fancy as the supreme staff theorist had been extraordinary, his experience of Prussia's nineteenth-century wars with Austria and France could not but have made him profoundly aware of Moltke's dictum that 'no plan of operations goes with any degree of certainty beyond the first contact with the hostile main force'. It is not unreasonable to believe that he considered his great wheeling movement to be merely preparatory to a series of unpredictable battles with the

---

* Germany in 1914 had a population of 68 million; France 40 million; Russia perhaps 160 million; Imperial Austria-Hungary 53 million; United Kingdom 46 million (of which Ireland 4.5 million); Italy 36 million; Belgium 7.8 million. See *Bulletin of the American Geographical Society*, Volume 46, 1914.

† In 1894 Captain Alfred Dreyfus, a young French artillery officer of Alsatian Jewish descent, was sentenced to life imprisonment for allegedly passing military secrets to the German embassy in Paris. He was sent to the penal colony at Devil's Island in French Guiana. Two years later, evidence came to light identifying a French army major named Ferdinand Esterhazy as the real culprit. Senior officers suppressed the new evidence, and a military court unanimously acquitted Esterhazy after the second day of his trial. The army accused Dreyfus of additional charges based on documents forged by a French counter-intelligence officer and accepted without full examination. Word of the framing of Alfred Dreyfus and of the cover-up began to spread, chiefly owing to a letter headlined 'J'accuse!' in a Paris newspaper by the novelist Émile Zola. The government was forced to reopen the case. In 1899 Dreyfus was brought back to Paris from Guiana, after almost five years in solitary confinement, for a second trial. The political and judicial scandal that ensued divided French society. Eventually, all the accusations against Dreyfus were proved baseless. In 1906 he was formally exonerated and reinstated as a major in the French army. He would serve with distinction in the war.

French army, rather than one great culminating clash; in other words, that he would fight where opportunity presented. Whole books have indeed been written on 'the Plan', one of the most recent, by the retired US infantry officer Terence Zuber, going so far as to claim: 'There never was a Schlieffen Plan.'*

Whether the plan was a mere *Denkschrift* (memorandum) or a detailed concept of operations, when Schlieffen's deputy, the Younger Moltke, succeeded him in 1906, the new Chief of Staff immediately began modifying the operational precepts, notably to avoid violation of Dutch territory (the Maastricht corridor). But Moltke would not revert to his uncle's strategy of 'Russia first'. Indeed, the overall strategy remained Schlieffen's: strike at once, in greatest strength, at France through Belgium (and Luxembourg), then transport the victorious armies by train to the east to defeat the plodding Russians, whose constitutional incompetence – demonstrated recently in the Russo-Japanese war – would only exacerbate the tardiness of their mobilization and deployment.

But during the Younger Moltke's time at the Königsplatz, the head-quarters of the *Grosser Generalstab*, hard by the new Reichstag building, neither France nor Russia was standing still. The latter's humiliation by the Japanese in 1905 was reassuring for Berlin, but alarming for Paris, and from 1908 the French began pouring money into Russia, both to modernize her infrastructure, the railways in particular, and to rebuild her army. These efforts culminated in a 'Great Programme' brought formally before the Duma, the Russian parliament, in 1913 and designed to bear its full fruits by 1918 – an unassailable peacetime strength of 800,000 men, with comparable numbers of artillery and machine guns. And then in August 1913, in direct response to recent German increases in recruitment, the French National Assembly extended compulsory military service by a year, increasing the army's standing strength by 100,000 troops, and authorized more spending on armaments.

The revitalizing of Russian arms was a real preoccupation with Berlin, the French increase less so. For with this increase came a

---

* Terence Zuber, *Inventing the Schlieffen Plan: German War Planning 1871–1914* (Oxford, 2002). This remarkable assertion prompted numerous rejoinders and conferences, a summary of which is contained in Hans Ehlert, Michael Epkenhans and Peter Gross, eds, *Der Schlieffenplan* (Paderborn, 2006).

change of operational doctrine, which actually played rather well to the Schlieffen–Moltke game. In 1911, against a worsening political situation in the Balkans and North Africa, the vice-president of the *Conseil supérieur de la guerre*, General Victor Michel (the commander-in-chief designate in wartime), submitted proposals for a modification of the existing defensive strategy – Plan XVI (French plans were unofficially numbered sequentially), adopted in 1909 – for what he feared would be a German enveloping attack west of the Meuse. Plan XVI anticipated a shallow hook through the Ardennes, and so concentrated the field army in Lorraine; but Michel proposed placing the bulk of his forces on the Franco-Belgian border to enable them to mount a counter-offensive. To boost the numbers required for such an extension of the fighting front he proposed incorporating reservists into the first-line order of battle (as he was inclined to believe the Germans intended doing), reviving the Napoleonic concept of the *demi-brigade*, a sort of cloning – half regular, half reservist. The *Conseil* rejected the plan out of hand. The French army – the French nation – had been suffering a sort of collective neurosis since the defeat of 1870, only exacerbated by the Dreyfus scandal: Michel's apparent defeatism was the antithesis of *La Gloire*, the animating martial spirit of the country since Louis XIV's day. The new war minister, the former soldier Adolphe Messimy (who would return to the army in August 1914), began looking for a new chief. He first asked the veteran 'colonial' General Joseph Gallieni, who turned down the appointment on the grounds that he was nearing retirement. Gallieni suggested Paul Pau, who had lost an arm in the war of 1870, but Pau was a convinced Catholic, and therefore was identified with the reaction against the prevailing post-Dreyfus anti-clericalism. Messimy would not have him. Pau resigned his commission, and General Joseph Joffre was appointed instead.

Joffre, though by training a sapper, with a reputation for plodding staffwork, had nevertheless embraced with a will the doctrine of *offensive à outrance* – offensive with the utmost hostility, to the limit, even to excess. He tore up Plan XVI and began work on a scheme more suited to resurgent *esprit militaire*. Eighteen months later he proclaimed grandiloquently in the new field regulations: 'The French army, returning to its traditions, henceforth admits no law but the offensive.'

Why? In part, *La Gloire*: digging trenches was not glorious. And there was the economic imperative: France (like Britain) could not realistically contemplate fighting a long war, so she had to prepare for a short one – and to keep it short she would have to seize the initiative soonest, and that could only be done by taking the offensive. But there was, too, a nagging anxiety that the temperament of the French infantryman was such that he could not – even if he wanted to – stand on the defensive against the more strictly disciplined Germans. After all, most of the reservists, being pre-1913 men, had only spent two years with the colours. And so the talk became all of *élan vital* and the superiority of the bayonet. Indeed, French tactics now required the *poilu* to unload his rifle before a bayonet charge so that he would not be tempted to pull the trigger, and would be intent only on giving point – *À la baïonnette! En avant!* In fact, so taken with the spirit of the bayonet was the French high command that it was even issued to the cavalry.*

And *élan vital* required all the trappings of the traditions to which the army was returning. In 1911 the Chamber of Deputies debated replacing the *poilu*'s red trousers with something more suitable for the modern battlefield, a grey-green uniform known as *la tenue reseda*. There was furious opposition, on the grounds that it was both ugly and too similar to German *feldgrau* (field grey). Alexandre Millerand, who would replace Messimy as war minister the following year, declared: 'Le pantalon rouge, c'est la France!' So in August 1914 the French army would march to war with *le pantalon rouge* – as well as the red *képi* (hat). As one British observer, Edward Spears, wrote, many officers 'thought it chic to die in white gloves'.

---

* New artillery regulations also appeared. Previously they had stressed the need for preliminary bombardment; now they decreed that the guns would fire only *during* the infantry's advance. Joffre's support for the development of heavy artillery continued to be very half-hearted: at the meeting at which Michel had presented his proposed revisions to Plan XVI to the *Conseil supérieur de la guerre* (in 1911), Joffre led the counter-argument, urging development of a light howitzer. In a meeting of the *Conseil* in October 1913, he even argued against giving heavy artillery to army corps: he did not want to 'burden' them and divisions with relatively immobile heavy artillery, preferring to group it at army level (despite the arrangements for target acquisition and command and control being not much better in the French army than in the British). He believed (by January 1914) that French artillery compared well with that of the Germans and could negate the latter's range advantage by skilful use of its own mobility. He had an almost theological belief in the famous *Soixante-quinze*, the 75 mm QF gun, which had a rate of fire of 20–30 rounds per minute.

They would march, however, to a compromise plan. Joffre's first preference – as Schlieffen suspected – was an offensive through Belgium and into Germany as soon as war was declared. The Belgian plain was, after all, the best going – much better than hilly Lorraine or the heavily wooded Ardennes. And it would mean easier lines of communication for the BEF, which the French general staff were convinced would come to their aid. Joffre presented his preference to the Conseil in January 1912. The prime minister, Joseph Caillaux (a Radical, who would lead the peace party in the war), rejected it outright: 'Not one French soldier will put a foot on the soil of Belgium if the Germans respect the treaties [of neutrality].' When Caillaux's government fell shortly afterwards, Joffre put his views to the new premier, Raymond Poincaré. However, Poincaré too refused to permit French forces to enter Belgium unless Germany had violated her neutrality. This might – perhaps ought to – have been the point at which Joffre resigned, but whereas Michel's plans had been based on the conviction that the Germans would attack deep through Belgium, Joffre in fact believed the weight of the attack would be in the east; it was not difficult for him therefore to give his characteristic shrug and turn his attention back towards Lorraine.

His new design (or rather, that of General Ferdinand Foch, lately commandant of the staff college), Plan XVII, called for the army's main strength to be concentrated on the German border. From there an offensive would be launched east and north-east either side of the Metz–Thionville fortresses by four armies comprising at least eight corps (with a fifth army held in reserve). One axis of advance was to be through the Ardennes and thence into Germany proper (the Saarland), the other into Elsass-Lothringen, as Alsace-Lorraine had been known since 1871. A variation, later known as Plan XVII(b), in case the Germans did violate Belgian–Luxembourg neutrality, would instead send the two northerly armies, plus the reserve, north-east into Luxembourg and Belgium to meet the offensive.*

---

* French plans were not perhaps as worked-up as is sometimes presumed. Joffre simply called Plan XVII a *plan de renseignements* – a term not easy to translate literally, but suggesting a preliminary design for battle based on the best estimate of the enemy's intentions. Or so Joffre would have us believe in his memoirs (*The Personal Memoirs of Joffre, Field Marshal of the French Army*, trans. T. Bentley Mott, London, 1932), in which he says he kept Plan XVII(b) secret, not telling either politicians or his corps commanders. Spears, in *Liaison 1914*, shows a map of 'Plan XVII(b) – Variation of

The plan relied on two assumptions. First, although in its detail the Schlieffen concept remained a secret, the broad implications of a war on two fronts were plain enough, and the question for the French general staff was therefore about numbers: how many troops would the Germans have to commit to East Prussia – and therefore how many would be available for an offensive against France? They calculated that the Germans would have to send at least twenty divisions to the east; in fact in 1914 they would send only nine.* Secondly, they believed that the *Grosser Generalstab* would not be willing to use reserve divisions as other than casualty replacements; Schlieffen, however, had been working on this very requirement – and Moltke would continue to do so. From these two assumptions Joffre and the *État-Major de l'Armée* – the general staff – deduced that the Germans would not have enough troops to defend their border with France *and*

---

original plan (a) ordered on August 2 when it became known that the Germans were violating neutral territory'. It is quite possible that the map is no more than a representation of what actually happened.

* Barbara Tuchman, in *The Guns of August*, claims that in 1904 an officer of the *Grosser Generalstab* betrayed the Schlieffen concept for money (variously reported as 60,000 francs – roughly £200,000 at today's value) 'in a series of three rendezvous with a French intelligence officer'. Other writers have made the same claim – concerning the so-called Vengeur ('Avenger': the Prussian's codename) documents – but the evidence is far from conclusive. Intelligence-gathering is a notoriously difficult area in which to establish anything with certainty; discovering German war plans would have been the principal object of the *Deuxième Bureau*, the intelligence branch of the French general staff, and the *Bureau* no doubt had routine contacts with German officers, but there is no absolute evidence of anything concrete gained, only a renewed effort to study railway-building near the Belgian border. In April 1914 the *Bureau* obtained the German mobilization (but not the actual campaign) plans, which might have suggested that reserve formations would be used for combat from the outset, though again it was inconclusive. In terms of deployment and lines of advance, a good idea of German thinking might have been gained by studying the railway-building plans – the elongation of platforms and sidings near the Belgian border, for example. But even this could be misleading (see chapter 12); indeed, it was the French staff's belief that these were probably German deception measures. Likewise, the rate of mechanization in the German army suggested to some in the *Deuxième Bureau* (and Michel) that a major advance through the flat country of Belgium, along its well-paved roads, was intended, rather than through the Ardennes. Capability is not the same as intention, but some answer to capability must be found nevertheless. However, the principal result of the 1904 intelligence windfall (if such it was) – the strategy of the two-front war, France first – was the *État-Major*'s calculation that the Germans would not have enough troops to mount a deep thrust through Belgium, an unshakeable appreciation that the British general staff accepted: in August 1911 Henry Wilson would tell Haldane that twenty-eight days after mobilization the Germans would oppose the Russians' thirty-six divisions ('only' thirty-six) with twenty-seven divisions, and Austria with thirty-six; for this had been Michel's appreciation too – and Foch's.

launch an invasion in strength through Belgium. He concluded therefore that a major attack by French troops in Lorraine would thwart the German main effort and therefore the entire campaign.

Despite the difficulties inherent in an attack in Lorraine against what he supposed would be the bulk of the German army, Joffre remained convinced of both its viability and its worth, for the strategy was not 'France alone', but the Franco-Russian Entente: if from the outset the Russians also attacked, the simultaneous two-front offensive would be more than Germany could withstand. He therefore pressed the strategy remorselessly in the annual Russo-French staff talks. It was, indeed, the inescapable import of article 3 of the original (1892) military convention: 'The available forces to be employed against Germany shall be, on the part of France, 1,300,000 men, on the part of Russia, 700,000 or 800,000 men. These forces shall engage to the full with such speed that Germany will have to fight simultaneously on the East and on the West.'

The military appreciation that led to the development of Plan XVII was brilliant in its technical gathering of data on the enemy's order of battle and railway capacity – up to a point, for ultimately it underestimated both; but the appreciation failed to follow through ruthlessly the logic of the fortified Franco-German frontier, the very logic that had led Schlieffen to his conclusion that the main effort must be in Belgium, the only place in which the fortified defences could be turned. In essence, the French were looking for somewhere to attack, because that was what *offensive à outrance* required. Attacking where the Germans were strongest would have potentially the most disruptive effect, so it suited the French general staff when they concluded that the Germans would mass for the assault on the border. Yet a plan that required the Germans to win quickly in the west so that they could then switch to the east would, logically, require the Germans to attack where the French were weakest. This would oblige them to hook through Belgium, even if only the south-eastern corner. Plan XVII, even XVII(b), could not deal with the obvious outcome of this logic – the Schlieffen Plan. For if Belgian neutrality was to be violated, it scarcely mattered that it was being violated only a bit, through the Ardennes: rape was rape. What was there anyway to stop a greater violation, in greater strength to envelop the French left – the Belgian army? Paris did not place much faith in them; so why should the Germans fear them? No: what was to stop the greater use of Belgium for the envelopment of the French army was that the Germans did not have enough divisions – or so the *Deuxième Bureau* calculated. The assumptions were elegantly self-serving; and entirely wrong.*

And so the great flaw of the doctrine of *offensive à outrance* became the Schlieffen Plan's opportunity, for Plan XVII drew the great weight of troops away from the 'place of decision', the left wing, for the main offensive into Lorraine. Conventional wisdom would have been to order those troops not in the main offensive to stand on the defensive, but the French army, 'returning to its traditions', admitted 'no law but the offensive'. So the four front-line French armies would each be concentrated for offensive action, and the fifth concentrated as the reserve. As a result the overall length of the French line would have to be reduced: it would simply not be possible to cover even half the length of the Franco-Belgian-Luxembourgeois border. It was all the more important therefore that the French continued to convince themselves that no attack could be mounted in strength through Belgium – that the Germans would not develop operations west of the Meuse.

The Schlieffen Plan and Plan XVII positively dovetailed with each other.

After the war, Joffre would strive to put a gloss on the French plan, suggesting that it was principally one of mobilization and concentration, with no fixed scheme of operations. But although any commander would try to build into a plan as much flexibility as possible to deal with the unexpected, Joffre's protestations were disingenuous. General de Castelnau, his deputy on the general staff (and in 1914 the commander of the French 2nd Army), explaining to a post-war parliamentary commission the difference between a concentration plan and an operational plan, would emphasize that Joffre always kept his cards close to his chest. Joffre, giving evidence himself, said that a commander could decide on an operational plan only after he received intelligence about what the enemy was doing. Yet even as the Germans began marching into Belgium, he would order

---

* There were some at the time – notably Churchill – who could not accept this analysis, but the combined authority of the French and British general staffs invariably carried the day in what passed for debate on the matter. See chapter 7.

the attack in Alsace-Lorraine as required by Plan XVII – and even an offensive into the Belgian Ardennes.

For the BEF, on the far left of the French line, it would be a fatal miscalculation.

Chapter Six

CALCULATIONS

It is an obvious truth that the times must be suited to extraordinary characters.

Edward Gibbon, *Decline and Fall of the Roman Empire*

In the unfolding military drama of the decade of preparation, the remarkable personality and endeavour of Henry Hughes Wilson loom large. Rarely in the nation's history has one soldier – and so relatively junior a one, in rank at least (first as brigadier- and then major-general) – so shaped the nation's policy, grand strategy and detailed war plans.

Wilson was not, as he is sometimes described, an Ulsterman. He was born in 1864 in Leinster, of the Anglo-Irish 'ascendancy', his father a JP and deputy lieutenant of County Longford, his mother from an old County Dublin family. He did however marry an Ulsterwoman, from Donegal.* He was an implacable Unionist, and from February 1922 would sit briefly as the Ulster Unionist MP for North Down until assassinated by the IRA the following month (thereby gaining the melancholy distinction, as a field marshal, of being the most senior officer to be killed by direct enemy action – if

---

* To be precise, his family traced their ancestry to a follower of William III ('King Billy') who landed with the army at Carrickfergus north of Belfast in 1690. One of his descendants, Wilson's grandfather, made a substantial sum of money in Belfast shipping, and bought his family estates in Leinster.

the IRA's doorstep murder could be dignified thus).*

Wilson had all the characteristics, good and ill, associated with Ireland's greatest export, general officers. He was dedicated, determined, hardworking, ambitious, meticulous, forthright, affable and witty, while at the same time sycophantic, opinionated, vitriolic, emotional and scheming. According to the editor of his diaries and first biographer, Major-General Sir Charles Callwell (another Anglo-Irishman, who would take over from Wilson as DMO in 1914), he had 'a bland ingenuousness of manner which he had cultivated successfully'. Above all, he was certain of his own judgement; but he also had the outsider-complex of the man from the marches, and, as his diaries reveal, an acute desire for recognition. Even as a brigadier-general he took an almost childlike pleasure in the praise of politicians, including those he despised, and of his seniors. He positively courted approval, and when he received it, it reinforced his self-assurance. His diaries stand in marked contrast to those of another future CIGS and fellow Irishman (himself an Ulsterman), General Sir Alan Brooke (later Field Marshal Lord Alanbrooke), Churchill's 'master of strategy' in the Second World War, in revealing an inability to recognize that the power of debate is not the same as the trick of being able to dazzle.

Ironically, Wilson had almost failed to gain a commission at all. Marlborough College in his time was neither the designer-label school of today nor the intellectual nurturer of later boys such as Sassoon, MacNeice and Betjeman.† His time there was inauspicious. After only three years, in 1880, when his father heard of an increase in officer cadetships at the Royal Military Academy Woolwich (for those bound for the gunners and sappers), he was withdrawn from the school to prepare for the entry exams. Despite the help of crammers, however, Wilson could not pass them, or even those for Sandhurst (which trained infantry and cavalry officers, and posed easier technical papers), failing five times. He was forced therefore to take a back-door commission via the Longford Militia, which wore the cap-badge of the Rifle Brigade (RB), and in 1885 managed to transfer to one of its

* Lord Roberts was to die within sound of the guns, while visiting GHQ in November 1914, and Lord Kitchener would drown when the cruiser *Hampshire* struck a mine off Scapa Flow in June 1916 en route to Russia.
† Marlborough was founded for the education of clergy sons in 1843, and so ill did it serve them that in 1851 there had been a famous 'rebellion' – quelled only after four days of mayhem, and ultimately overcome by masters sent from Dr Arnold's Rugby.

regular battalions – 1RB in India. Thereby he acquired not only a regular commission but also the status of 'black buttons' (which rifle regiments, something of an elite, wore rather than shiny ones), which, with his height, gave him useful cachet and presence.* The following year he saw action in the third Burmese War, in which he was wounded several times – notably in the eye, which gave him an unnerving stare, and the leg, which occasionally gave him need of a walking stick – itself another augmentation of his presence. During his convalescence at home in Ireland, and with 2RB in England and Belfast, he studied hard for the staff college entrance exam, went to Camberley in 1892 and passed out the following year. From November 1894 he worked in the intelligence department of the War Office, where his fluent French was something of an asset. Indeed, this fluency, acquired from a succession of French governesses, would be pivotal to his later career, and to the development of the military *entente*. After three years he was appointed brigade major (the principal staff officer) of the 3rd Brigade in Aldershot, and went with them to war in South Africa, but was soon appointed deputy assistant adjutant-general and assistant military secretary to the commander-in-chief, Lord Roberts. He had a 'good war', coming out of it with a DSO and a recommendation for brevet promotion to lieutenant-colonel. But he had seen no regimental duty for over ten years.†

Perhaps because of this, in 1902 he was appointed to command the 9th 'Provisional' Battalion at Colchester, in effect a holding unit for (in soldier's parlance) 'odds and sods', rather than a first-line one, and only a year later returned to the War Office. Here he fell out with the first CGS, Sir Neville Lyttelton, a former supporter as well as a fellow black-button man, who mistrusted his scheming. By now, however, Wilson had gained wider notice and other patrons, and in 1907 he was promoted temporary brigadier-general and appointed commandant of the staff college in succession to Colonel Sir Henry Rawlinson, yet another black button (King's Royal Rifle Corps). The

---

* The influence of the 'black-button mafia', as the rifle regiments were known, is sometimes overstated, but there is no doubt that the buttons conferred a certain prestige; and it is doubtful whether Wilson's lack of academic acumen would have put him high in the passing-out list at Sandhurst, whence the 'mafia' liked to recruit. That said, he was a fine linguist.

† A 'brevet' (rank) was a means of accelerated promotion, conferring unpaid supernumerary rank on those showing exceptional promise.

upgrading of the staff college post to one-star general (in part by Wilson's own hand while at the War Office) would give him an entrée to the *État-Major*, the French general staff, that as a colonel he might have found, if not impossible, then certainly not as easy, to acquire.

Wilson's proved a popular appointment, as his farewells three and a half years later testify. His affability and waggishness endeared him to the students, who were for the most part experienced officers in their thirties, while the staff – and students – appreciated his teaching innovations, such as the staff ride and war games.* His style was also markedly less didactic than it would later become, and he had a genius for lecturing; he was, after all, an Irishman.

At Camberley, however, his Francophilia soon took hold. He had first become interested in the campaigns of 1870–1 while a student at the college, and these now became a – perhaps *the* – focus of the syllabus, with battlefield tours and staff rides throughout northern France. It was all very much at one with Britain's new interest – at least the army's new interest – in continental operations following the Moroccan 'crisis' of 1905, with the sudden possibility of another Franco-German war. But the interest went deeper than mere battlefield visits. In 1906 the new foreign secretary, Grey, had authorized the War Office to begin secret staff talks with the French on the options for deployment of a BEF in the event of war with Germany. This green light (though to Grey's mind it was only ever amber), the unintended consequence of the Kaiser's misadventure in Morocco, was a classic of diplomacy. Paul Cambon, the long-serving French ambassador in London (he had been appointed in 1898, and would continue in post until 1920), wanting to probe Grey on the extent and depth of the British commitment to the Entente, had at his first call on the new foreign secretary suggested secret and deniable staff talks. The suggestion was couched in terms of 'if my government were to ask for assistance, and if your government were to agree to assist, it would be helpful to know what might be the possibilities . . .' It would hardly have come as a surprise to Grey, for another arch-schemer, *The*

---

* A staff ride is a systematic analysis of the site of a battle or campaign to understand the influences of physical factors such as geography. A war game is a simulation of an operation, not usually of an actual past battle or campaign, involving two or more sides but in which no units are actually deployed. Its purpose is to test the validity of a proposed plan of action or strategy, and/or to train commanders.

Times's assiduous and influential military correspondent, Colonel Charles Repington, had been advocating staff talks both publicly and privately since the Entente had been signed two years before.* A few days after Cambon's call, as if by chance, the DMO, James Grierson, met the French military attaché, the dapper artilleryman Colonel Victor Huguet, riding in Hyde Park (the improbability of Grierson's taking any form of exercise rules out true chance). So began the secret and deniable staff talks.

By May 1906, detailed railway movement plans were being drawn up, and at the same time exploratory talks were taking place with the Belgians through the British military attaché in Brussels, Lieutenant-Colonel (later Major-General) Nathaniel Barnardiston. These revealed that in the event of German invasion the Belgians intended concentrating the field army around Brussels to protect Antwerp. This would leave the great frontier fortresses of Namur and Liège unsupported, but the Belgian general staff considered them strong enough to withstand siege, nor did they think them susceptible to *coup de main* (a surprise operation). There was, however, concern that a German thrust from across the French border, through Sedan, could outflank them, although it was not clear how such a move would serve in a campaign to defeat France. Nevertheless it was a threat to the neutrality of Belgium, which was ostensibly Britain's primary interest, and the DMO, Grierson, concluded that he would have to get troops to the Upper Meuse by the tenth day of war if they were to be of any help. It was this, rather than any requirement to support the French, that galvanized the War Office's thinking about mobilization. But later in the year Grierson visited the Belgian army's annual manoeuvres, and was shocked by what he saw: 'The men were unintelligent looking, slack and I should say not well instructed. The infantry were of decidedly inferior physique, the artillery were badly horsed, and the cavalry and engineers only made a good impression.'

* Charles à Court Repington, 1858–1925: Eton, Sandhurst – and black buttons (Rifle Brigade). At Camberley he was a brilliant student, and laurels beckoned, but during a posting in Egypt in 1902 an affair with Lady Garstin, the wife of a British official, became public, in part through the testimony of Henry Wilson, and Repington was forced to resign his commission. Because of his sharp mind and acquaintance with many of the movers and shakers at the War Office and in the BEF, once the war began he became influential in the making and breaking of careers, and to some extent strategy. Detractors dubbed him 'the Playboy of the Western Front'.

Going on then to watch those of the French army, Grierson was by contrast impressed with everything he saw, judging the staffwork to be the best he had seen in any army in peace or in war. From here on, despite a lingering attachment to Antwerp, the British general staff would work increasingly on the assumption that the best way to protect Belgium was in concert with the French rather than the Belgian army.

The poor impression gained of the Belgians was unfortunate, to say the least, and it may also have been a false one. In 1815 there had been similar concerns, yet Belgian troops surprised Wellington by their steadiness at Quatre Bras, and took a terrible pounding at Waterloo itself without too much wavering. And they proved doughty fighters in 1830–1 when wresting the country from the Dutch. In fact, in August 1914 they would fight with uncommon – and of course unexpected – pluck. It is interesting to speculate on what the Belgians' impression was of Jimmy Grierson, a grossly overweight major-general from an army that had only recently had the devil of a job subduing 12,000 farming kin of their neighbours the Dutch. But then, the British army has always (thank goodness) had a higher opinion of itself than others have sometimes had of it.

Even if Grierson's assessment had been accurate in 1906, the Belgian army underwent considerable modernization in the years that followed, especially after 1910, spurred by their admirable new young king, Albert, who four years later would prove a steady and capable commander-in-chief. In any case, was Grierson's conclusion – to give up on the Belgians and throw in entirely with the French – while practical, entirely logical? Might he not instead have addressed some scheme of reinforcement, both physical and moral? The door might have been open – if not in King Leopold's fading years, then after Albert's accession. Even if the question of the Scheldt's navigability in international law could not be resolved, and the BEF's supply through Antwerp were therefore not feasible (see footnote on page 12 above), it would have been perfectly possible to run the lines of communication through Zeebrugge and the Channel ports – as long as the Admiralty obliged.

Henry Wilson was not a party to these staff discussions, but he was well aware of them, and indeed animated by them, not least through his personal contacts with Colonel Huguet. As Huguet relates in his

1923 memoir *Britain and the War*, when he had been appointed in 1903 no one in the *Ministère de la guerre* thought the British army could be of the slightest use from a military point of view; but his reports had argued – with increasing force and success – that 'an army which could so well profit by its lessons was worthy of respect no matter what its size may be'. In 1909, therefore, while still commandant at Camberley, Wilson decided to initiate an exchange with his opposite number at the *École supérieure de la guerre* (the French staff college), at that time Brigadier-General Ferdinand Foch. The idea of this was not only to study French instructional methods but, according to Wilson's friend and biographer Callwell, to get to know 'a French soldier who, already in those days, enjoyed a certain European reputation as a military writer and thinker on the art of war'.*

The resulting visit in December 1909 went very well, Foch being evidently surprised by Wilson's seriousness of purpose. Another visit was arranged for the middle of January, during which Wilson would put a very direct question to his opposite number: 'What would you say was the smallest British military force that would be of practical assistance to you in the event of a contest such as we have been considering?'

'One single private soldier,' Foch replied in an instant, 'and we would take good care that he was killed.' In other words, the moral effect of knowing that Britain was standing by France – that they were indeed allies – would be considerable, and the French general staff would do all it could to bind in the BEF; for if even one British soldier were to arrive, it would surely mean that more would be committed to follow, especially once blood had been shed. Foch's response might also have indicated that he expected a long war in which Britain's latent military strength would be decisive; if so, however, he did not, on the evidence of Wilson's papers, vouchsafe this judgement to his 'allied' opposite number. Then, according to Wilson's diary, '[Foch] also told me much of the Russian unpreparedness, and we talked at great length of our combined action in Belgium.'

This mention of Belgium is intriguing. It was a full year before

---

* Foch's two published works on strategy, *Les Principes de la guerre* (*On the Principles of War*), 1903, and *La Conduite de la guerre* (*On the Conduct of War*), 1905, were widely read.

General Michel, vice-president of the *Conseil supérieur de la guerre*, submitted his modifications to Plan XVI, which supposed that the main thrust of any German effort would be through Belgium; in January 1910, the focus was still on operations in Lorraine. But Foch would certainly have been in the know about developing thinking in the *État-Major*; indeed, Michel consulted him. And Michel, as related in the previous chapter, was only too keen to develop counter-offensive operations in Belgium, but from a strong defensive position along the border. By the end of these discussions, Wilson would seem to have got a pretty good grasp of the operational concept of Plan XVI, whether he had learned anything of it before from the War Office or not. Foch concluded by inviting him to come over for a staff tour in the summer – which indicates the 'access' Foch had with the *État-Major* – and accepted an invitation to visit the British staff college in May.

Wilson was clearly impressed. Had he not been a Francophile before, Foch would have made him one now.* On return to Camberley, having watched the way instructors at the French staff college insisted on tactical exercises being conducted at a fast pace – stimulating the students by exclamations of 'Vite, vite!' and 'Allez, allez!' – he introduced the same emphasis on pace to his own. They were soon known by staff and students alike as 'Allez, allez operations'.†

In the middle of the year, just after Foch's reciprocal visit, Wilson was recalled to the War Office, some six months ahead of the end of his tour at Camberley. He had hoped for a brigade – and, indeed, one was in the offing – but the CIGS, now Sir William Nicholson, a sapper who had been senior military attaché in Japan at the time of the Russo-Japanese War and had seen the fighting in Manchuria (though it does not seem to have made any profound impression on him), wanted him back as DMO to replace Spencer Ewart, who was to be adjutant-general, the second military member of the Army Council.

Ewart, who for a short time had been Wilson's contemporary (senior by three years) at Marlborough, had risen effortlessly. Tall and good-looking, he was devoted to his regiment, the Cameron

---

* And they had certainly made friends: Wilson would be invited to the wedding of Foch's daughter in Paris in October.

† The staff college – especially before its move to Shrivenham in 2000 to combine with those of the navy and RAF – frequently tended to conscious imitation of armies it believed superior in size or acumen. Perhaps understandably, during the Cold War the Germans were the model (and sometimes the Israelis). Now it is the Americans.

Highlanders, with whom he had distinguished himself in Egypt and the Sudan before becoming a brigade major in South Africa, after which he served entirely on the staff in Whitehall, never commanding. His promotion to lieutenant-general at forty-nine – the same age and year as that other rising star, Haig – bore witness to the esteem in which he was held at the War Office by both Nicholson and Haldane. And yet Wilson was not happy with what he found in the directorate of military operations – what Ewart had left behind. Two months into the job, he wrote in his diary: 'I am very dissatisfied with the state of affairs *in every respect* [emphasis added]. No rail arrangements for concentration and movements of either Expeditionary Force or Territorials. No proper arrangement for horse supply, no arrangements for safeguarding our arsenals at Woolwich. A lot of time spent in writing but useless minutes. I'll break all this somehow.'

If Wilson was correct (and the work he commissioned suggests he was), then assuming that Ewart and his staff were competent and industrious, two things can be concluded. First, the mobilization of the BEF and its despatch to the Continent was not the War Office's priority. Indeed, in spite of clouds on the Balkan horizon,* the directorate of military operations' perennial preoccupation remained India (both its internal security and the threat from and to Afghanistan, in particular Russian intentions†) and, increasingly, a possible Turkish threat to Egypt. Secondly, British politicians had not addressed, let alone answered, Grey's 'great question' (the extent to which the Entente Cordiale implied military support to the French) with anything like the precision required for the CIGS to derive a proper military strategy from which detailed planning could follow. That said, there was no reason why mobilization plans should not have been properly in hand. Where, when and how the BEF would be employed did not affect, say, the number of extra horses it needed to bring it up to its war establishment. It was this lack of planning that so

* War would break out between Italy and Turkey the following year, and between almost everyone else in the Balkans the year after that. See chapter 8.
† The concerns were alleviated somewhat by the Anglo-Russian Convention of August 1907, which firmed up boundaries (and therefore respective control) in Afghanistan as well as in Persia and Tibet; if not bringing the 'Great Game' to an end, this at least moved it into a lower league. This opened the way to the 'Triple Entente', an informal understanding among Great Britain, France and Russia based on the Franco-Russian military alliance of 1894, the Entente Cordiale of 1904 and the 1907 Anglo-Russian Convention.

exasperated Wilson initially, and he quite properly threw himself into the task of sorting it out. But he would never in his own mind be able to draw a distinction between mobilization and deployment (and, indeed, *employment*), so that the one increasingly drove the other. Alternatives were anathema: there was a best possible strategy and concept of operations, and Wilson saw it as his job to plan for it in every detail, and to convince all and sundry – the CIGS, the Admiralty, the secretary for war, the foreign secretary, anyone who would listen (and sometimes those who would not) – that it was the right and only plan.

Why was the 'great question', and the consequent questions of strategic policy, never settled? There was, after all, a body to deal with just these matters – the Committee of Imperial Defence (CID), set up formally in 1904. It had no executive powers, but it was the forum for considering the strategic implications of policy, and advising the cabinet and government departments accordingly. Its secretariat – a permanent secretary and two assistant secretaries (one naval, one army) – had five specific duties: consideration of all questions of imperial defence; obtaining and collating data from government departments; preparing papers in anticipation of the needs of the prime minister and the CID; advising on defence questions involving more than one government department; and 'corporate memory' – keeping records for use of the cabinet of the day and its successors. The CID was, however, a rather enigmatic body. The prime minister was its chairman and only permanent member; he invited others to attend on a more or less ad hoc basis, though ministers could apply to attend if a matter touching on their department was being considered. Also invited, as appropriate, were the chief ministers of the dominions.* But the 'great question' was high policy, a matter for the cabinet: unless Asquith, who had become prime minister in April

---

* The CID's permanent secretariat would become the war cabinet secretariat in 1916, introducing to cabinet meetings for the first time the practice of writing minutes. There were four standing sub-committees: Colonial (later Oversea) Defence; Home Ports (later Home) Defence; Co-ordination of Departmental Action; and Air. Its first secretary, in 1912, was Colonel Maurice Hankey – later Lord Hankey – a Royal Marines officer who had been assistant naval secretary. He would in turn become secretary of the war cabinet and then, in 1919, first permanent cabinet secretary, serving in this series of positions for a total of twenty-six years. Hankey, although a convinced navalist and never quite able to remain impartial in the matters considered by the CID, is nevertheless credited with bringing order and method – and not least proper minuting – to what otherwise tended to be a talking shop.

1908, wanted an answer, the 'great question' would not be put, and certainly not to the full cabinet, for the radicals (as opposed to the 'Liberal imperialists' – the likes of Grey, Churchill and Haldane*) would not have stood for a continental commitment, and the government's majority always looked shaky. In any case, as Asquith often said – even during the July crisis of 1914 – there were some matters of policy that could only be decided 'at the appropriate time', by which he meant when all the circumstances were finally known and all other possibilities comprehensively exhausted – what his opponents called the policy of 'wait and see'.

The Foreign Office's view of the great question was in the main that of Eyre Crowe, an official who after the war would become its head. In 1911, commenting on an article in the French press, he minuted:

> The fundamental fact of course is that the *Entente* is not an alliance. For purposes of ultimate emergencies it may be found to have no substance at all. For the *Entente* is nothing more than a frame of mind, a view of general policy which is shared by the governments of two countries, but which may be, or become, so vague as to lose all content—

—a passage containing so many expressions of uncertainty, in fact, as to be almost the perfect expression of Asquithian 'wait and see'.†
When, therefore, Wilson went back to the War Office in the summer

---

* The 'Liberal imperialists' took the pragmatic line that imperialism was the spirit of the age and should therefore be embraced, while the classical, radical Liberals argued instead for social and constitutional reform as the priority. Asquith always had a difficult balancing act in cabinet.
† It seems quite extraordinary, especially at a century's remove, that even after seven years in which to discern the substance of the Entente, and its consequences, such a conclusion could be reached. Sir Eyre Crowe (he was knighted later in the year) had strongly urged an anti-German policy in the decade before the First World War, despite or because of a German mother, a German education (he was seventeen before he first came to England, to sit the FO examination) and a German wife. In 1907 he had written a 'Memorandum on the present state of British relations with France and Germany', which much impressed Grey. Germany, he argued, aimed at the domination of Europe; concessions would only increase the German appetite for power, and the Entente must not be abandoned. He also asserted that favourable Anglo-German relations would best be strengthened by a forceful defence by Britain of her foreign interests. Stanley Baldwin, prime minister during Crowe's time as head of the FO (1920–5), would call him 'our ablest public servant'. Robert (Lord) Vansittart, Crowe's successor-but-one, thought him 'a dowdy, meticulous, conscientious agnostic with small faith in anything but his brain and his Britain'. Crowe and Grey made an interesting pair, but between them could not resolve the Entente's vagueness so 'as [*not*] to lose all content'.

of 1910, he found that the CID had not even begun to arbitrate between the two radically opposing views – the Admiralty's and the War Office's – of how war with Germany (if it ever came to war) should be made. But if he could not, for the time being, get an answer to the great strategic question – and certainly not the answer he wanted – he could at least invigorate mobilization planning, for at present this stood quite apart from decisions about deployment: no BEF, no strategic choice.

And with no area of planning was Wilson more dissatisfied than that of the supply of horses. Except for a few staff cars at the principal headquarters, and motor-bicycles in the Signals Service, the motive power of the BEF forward of the corps rear areas (to where supplies from the railheads were brought increasingly by motor-lorry) was provided by the horse. Horses hauled the Army Service Corps' waggons, which brought the combat supplies (ammunition, rations, fodder) forward from the corps distribution points. They hauled the artillery's guns and the waggons of the 'ammunition train'; they hauled the engineer stores and bridging, the signal-cable limbers, the infantry's transport – the waggons and Maltese carts for its machine guns, first-line ammunition, water, field kitchens, tents – and the field ambulances. They carried the cavalry, the general officers, the staff, the infantry's battalion and company commanders, and key officers such as the adjutant and medical officer. Even the Royal Flying Corps had the odd horse-drawn water-cart. The BEF simply could not go into action, let alone sustain itself, without that noblest of creatures.

But they were not all needed in peacetime, nor were there the men to look after them. The PE was the minimum number of horses deemed adequate for training purposes. Just as, on mobilization, individual reservists needed to bring their units up to WE would be recalled to the colours, so would the additional horses – except that there were no reservist horses. The intention was that they would be bought in from the civilian market. The same was the case (to an even greater extent) for the Territorial Force. The problem was that no one in the War Office had been able to say if the civilian market could meet the demand in terms of numbers, type and – critically – readiness. As a result of increasing mechanization there had been, for example, an observable reduction in the number of 'light trotting vanners' in the streets – horses which, singly or in pairs, pulled the lighter sort of closed waggon (or van): exactly the type of animal needed by the artillery. And while the mobilization of reservists was relatively straightforward – the depots kept track of them, sending them travel warrants and reporting instructions as mobilization approached, and then the executive telegram requiring them to report to their mobilization centre – bringing in horses required an altogether more active plan.

A start had been made. Speaking to the army estimates in the Commons in March the previous year, 1909, the secretary of state for war, Haldane, had reminded the house that in trying to establish the availability of horses in Britain, there was legislation long on the statute books, and good will and commonsense in the country. The legal provisions rested in

> the power under Section 114 of the Army Act – a power which the police have of taking a census of the horses that exist in the country. That has never been scientifically or systematically put in practice; but when I came to look into the matter I found that this had been done to a much larger extent than I knew, and that they rather liked the practice, because it enabled them to get to know people about the farms and various places in the most friendly fashion. In several of the counties, more than I had anticipated, a pretty thorough census has been taken. I have been in consultation with the Board of Agriculture with regard to the number of horses in the country. The exact figures it is not possible to obtain. Various estimates have been made, and I think the House may take it as certain that there are upwards of 2,000,000 horses in the country. Of course, all these horses are not fit for our purposes, and I should write off half, to be safe, in respect of horses under five years and not otherwise fit for the sort of work we should put them to. Of the remaining million it would be safe to again write off half, in respect of horses of type that you could not suitably use even for transport or artillery. That leaves us with 500,000 horses in the country able and fit for Army purposes—a number sufficient to mobilize the Army between three and four times over. There is that satisfactory feature in the situation. The only question is not whether the horses are there or not, but whether we can mobilize them ... The question was, therefore, how to organize these horses, and we naturally turned to the County Associations and to the police, who have power under Section 114 of the Army Act. I have myself had conferences with some chief-constables, and very interesting they have been. The result was that we came to the conclusion that we would try an experiment in one or

two counties to see how it worked, because we felt that if it worked well it would be adopted by other counties.

The experiments had not worked quite as well as Haldane had hoped, however, for the following year, 1910, he was thinking about a more systematic scheme of registration. On 23 June Lord Alexander Thynne asked in the Commons 'whether he has under consideration a scheme for the enumeration or registration, for military purposes, of all horses in civilian ownership,' to which Haldane replied that the answer 'is in the affirmative'. When asked by another member: 'When is this scheme likely to get beyond the stage of consideration?', he revealed the huge amount of work yet to be done (that Wilson found so frustrating):

A great deal of progress has been made with it. The hon. Member must remember that this has to go through the Quartermaster-General's department in order to make the necessary arrangements with the Commander-in-Chief [he meant the GoCs-in-C] ... This is the scheme which was discussed on the Estimates. We have not yet got to the stage of appointing registration officers. It is taking its course, and we shall at the proper time consult the associations on the point of the work to be done.

Seemingly, however, the Quartermaster-General's department was not giving the matter the highest priority. In late October Wilson's diary records that he 'got off my detailed queries to the QMG in regard to horses for mobilization'. The answer was prompt, and unwelcome: the next day he received the statement that the QMG's department was 'quite unable to give me the information I want . . . no one can tell me where the horses are coming from nor when they will come.' In other words, the situation was much the same as it had been before the Boer War, when by some intuitive process it was presumed where – very roughly – the necessary horses were, and that arrangements for their acquisition and mobilization could be improvised. Yet Wilson knew that this had not worked at all well for South Africa, and that it would work even less well when time was of the essence – as it clearly must be for any war on the Continent. 'What a scandalous state of affairs,' he exclaimed in his diary: 'I'll push this to the end.'

A month later he was writing of 'a long talk with Charles Heath [director of transport and remounts] about horse mobilization. He is taking my papers and will find out from the C-in-Cs when they expect to be mobilized; but the fact is clear and is this – that at the end of 1910 no one knows how long it will take to mobilize. A disgraceful state of affairs.'* But by January Wilson had had enough of dealing with the QMG. After a series of conversations with the CIGS he prepared a minute on the deficiencies of the mobilization procedures in general, and this the CIGS sent to Haldane.

It did the trick. On 20 January Haldane asked Wilson to lunch – alone – at his house in Queen Anne's Gate. Wilson spoke plainly, and left with the sense that Haldane had not been briefed as candidly as he ought to have been by the members of the Army Council, but that now he might galvanize matters. Which is what indeed seems to have happened, for two months later the War Office had at last settled on the requirement that the whole of the infantry of the six divisions would embark on the fourth day of mobilization, cavalry on the seventh, and artillery on the ninth. 'We will work this out in detail and see what will have to be done,' wrote Wilson in his diary, with evident satisfaction.

In the case of horse supply this meant that the War Office took on responsibility for the census from the Home Office, developing it into a registration scheme on which a robust mechanism for rapid mobilization could then be built. Committees of inquiry – 'horsing committees' – were now set up, notably under Sir Francis Acland, formerly financial secretary to the War Office, to establish the detailed requirement. A horse mobilization section was established in the War Office, and legislation enacted (by amendment to the Army Act of 1911) to allow nominated officers to enter any stable in the hours of daylight to record by type and number the horses suitable for army service – with the exception of royal stables and those of foreign embassies and fire brigades, and exempting the chargers of officers on

* This passage in Wilson's diaries (though in unusually clear handwriting) has caused much confusion. In the published version, Callwell, doubtless trying to be helpful, instead of 'Charles Heath' gives the abbreviation 'DST' – a straight error, perhaps of transcription (for DTR). The DST – director sea transport – was an Admiralty officer, hardly the most appropriate official with whom to be discussing the actual mobilization of horses, although it was his business to carry them across the sea (the War Office's DST – director supplies and transport – was not established until late 1914). Some authors have apparently taken to invention to solve the puzzle, 'director staff training' being perhaps the least appropriate rendering (Robin Neillands, *The Old Contemptibles*, London, 2004).

the active list and the horses of the Yeomanry. Failure to admit an authorized officer – usually the (regular) adjutant of the local Yeomanry regiment or TF battalion – would result in a search warrant and then prosecution. In the autumn of 1913, some considerable time after the registration scheme had been put in hand, a Wiltshire farmer called Knox, of Edington at the foot of the scarp on the western edge of Salisbury Plain – a man who had no doubt seen the army at its training more than most men – refused admittance to the registration officer, Captain A. V. Martin. The local deputy assistant director of remounts (DADR), Captain F. S. Kennedy Shaw of the Border Regiment, wrote to him asking if he might call and explain the situation. Knox refused. A series of patient and impeccably polite letters from Kennedy Shaw failed to move Farmer Knox, who objected to the way the registration was conducted, wanting a 'more businesslike' approach (presumably involving money). By this time Haldane had been elevated to lord chancellor, and Jack Seely appointed secretary for war. Knox's 'case' went progressively up the chain of command, eventually landing on the desk of the secretary of state himself. Seely directed to 'proceed with law' so as not to set a precedent for allowing refusal. Not surprisingly, Knox soon backed down.

His protest, however, was fortunately not repeated in the horse-owning population as a whole. Though some owners were distraught at even the thought of their beloved animals being taken, others for whom the horse was but a part of their business were happy to cooperate, especially in schemes of subsidies which provided for partial mobilization without need of the impressment laws. By such means the Army Horse Reserve (AHR) was created, with an establishment of 10,000 (mainly vanner types) for the Royal Artillery, and 15,000 saddle and draught horses for the rest of the army. These were to be at the QMG's call with forty-eight hours' notice, delivered to a collecting point up to 10 miles from their stable (on penalty of £50) for a payment of £4 per horse per year on contract for three years, plus its full market value if called up for service. By August 1914 the AHR was fully subscribed.*

But for general mobilization, the balance had to be made up by recourse to the law – impressment. Throughout 1912, therefore, over

---

* An indication of the comparative value of the £4 'retainer' – to both owner and the War Office – is that a government horse cost close on £30 a year in forage. The sum had been carefully arrived at by the horsing committees, having taken evidence widely.

500 officers – almost all regulars – in nineteen 'remount circles' within the army district commands in Britain, subdivided into purchase (census) areas, worked on the register (Ireland had a similar but separate system). DADRs were then responsible for setting up and maintaining the system of collecting the impressed horses and sending them to where the horse mobilization section of the War Office had identified the requirement. Some 900 'War Office purchasers' were designated, who were 'private gentlemen in prominent positions in the counties and, to a certain extent, retired officers'; these individuals would act as honest brokers when the time came (the arrangements for the TF and Yeomanry were essentially the same), while the actual 'takers' of the horses on the day would be the magistrates and the police.* Each command had a railway collection and distribution programme, helped in no small measure by the number of rail-horseboxes kept in sidings throughout the hunting counties.

By the end of 1913, three years after Wilson had vowed to 'push this to the end', the registration programme had identified in precise detail some 462,000 horses fit for military purposes in Britain (not far short of the earlier estimate, based on partial police census figures, of half a million out of a total equine population of two million), and a requirement of 140,000 (54,000 for the BEF, with a higher fitness requirement than for the TF, and 86,000 for the 'Terriers' and Yeomanry) of which 20,000 would be taken from Ireland. The census revealed a larger percentage than expected of heavy draught horses – some 189,000 – and so the establishment tables were rewritten to reduce the reliance on 'vanners' by some 6,000 and instead to take up 3,000 of the heavier types for the Royal Artillery ammunition trains and ASC supply columns. They were not as fast or handy, perhaps, and certainly not as handsome, but this 'two-for-four' substitution had the advantage of reducing the requirements for forage, shipping space and drivers.

Besides worrying the remount branch, however, increasing civilian mechanization also presented the ASC with possibilities. In the course of three years from 1908, the London General Omnibus Company

---

* Lieutenant-Colonel (later Lieutenant-General Sir George) G. F. MacMunn, DSO, RA, deputy director remounts, War Office, lecture delivered at RA Institution, Woolwich, October 1913.

had put 2,000 B-Type motor-buses on the streets to replace its horse-drawn buses (the horse-bus continued nevertheless, in part because it was subsidized by the Army Horse Reserve), and by 1913 had 4,000 drivers whom they had trained themselves. The War Office carried out several exercises with the motor-buses – some of them high-profile affairs promoted by the Automobile Association – but had no plans for their impressment on mobilization. Half of all the London buses would have been needed to transport one division's worth of infantry: what was the use of mechanizing only one of the BEF's six divisions when the others marched on foot? The logistic burden alone – the fitters, the spares, the fuel – would have been too much. In the event, motor-buses would cross the Channel not long after the BEF, but to see service elsewhere – bringing troops out of Antwerp after the hasty decision to reinforce the beleaguered Belgians.

Nevertheless, the War Office was alert to the potential of the petrol engine to ease its reliance on the horse (the Mechanical Transport Committee had been set up as early as 1903): in 1911 Haldane was reassuring Parliament that 'we are getting further and further in the direction of using different kinds of traction for Army purposes – even across rough ground and hard places, and there is a motor at Aldershot which will climb almost anything short of a precipice'; at which point an honourable member, possibly from the shires and doubtless 'from a sedentary position' (Hansard is not specific), asked, 'Will it jump?' Haldane was not to be dismayed (and probably ready to be sophistic when it came to the definition of 'jump'): 'Yes, I have seen it jump,' he declared. 'We are in the beginning of these things, and there is no doubt that traction will be assisted by motors in the Army just in the same way as it is being developed in civil occupations.'*

They were indeed 'in the beginning', not simply of mechanization but of a continental-mindedness about mobilization planning, and Wilson was ever dismayed that they had not made that beginning earlier. But by August 1914 the plans would be laid in such detail as might have impressed the *Grosser Generalstab* had they ever learned of

---

* The 'motor' concerned was almost certainly the 'Caterpillar No. 1' tractor built by Hornsby & Sons, agricultural machinery and traction engine manufacturers, of Grantham, Lincolnshire, from which, it can be argued, the tank was eventually – and belatedly – developed.

them, and it was above all Wilson's achievement – as, indeed, it should have been, for he was the director of military operations. But mobilization was one thing; where and how the BEF should be used was quite another – though, of course, the plans for one had considerable impact on those of the other. When Wilson had gone back to the War Office in 1910, not only were the mobilization plans, to his mind, in 'a disgraceful state of affairs', there was not even political or military common ground on strategy, and consequently no notion where the BEF was to embark and disembark. Another crisis in Morocco the following year would provide him with the opportunity to, as he saw it, bang heads together. Out of it, while heads were still dazed, would emerge an apparent strategic policy on which the War Office – meaning he, Wilson – could get down to *real* work.

Chapter Seven

THE SEA AND THE DRY LAND

or, the Battle of the Two Wilsons

Although the new War Office building towered over the Admiralty opposite (a modest Georgian house, with its later Adam screen and newly built Queen-Anne-style extension alongside the Horse Guards), the navy was pre-eminent in the mind of government. The War Office represented a perennially unwelcome demand on the exchequer, for sea power was both Britain's safeguard and the guarantor of her imperial wealth; an island nation, it was felt, should have no need of a standing army. It was not until 1660, with the restoration of the monarchy under Charles II, that the country had accepted that relying on a militia rather than regulars was a gamble that would bring catastrophic results; and that a nation with a growing empire needed more than locally raised troops to win and then secure its riches. Even then, continental entanglements were viewed askance as bringing little or no profit, and more usually great loss. British involvement in war on the mainland of Europe in recent times had come about through miscalculation, accident, misadventure – had been avoidable and therefore should have been avoided. Yet the pattern would continue after 1688, when the nation replaced its king – James II – with a Dutchman (William of Orange – King William III) with whom Louis XIV of France had an existential problem. And for the next century

Shakespeare's 'sceptred isle' – the 'fortress, built by nature for herself, / Against infection, and the hand of war' – became a true seat of Mars. But after each war, usually with the French, often with the Spanish and sometimes with Germans, the 'militia instinct' reasserted itself, and retrenchment would be the order of the day, with disbandment of the land forces hastily expanded to meet the contingency. Indeed, the cuts would usually be to a level below that at the outset of the war, almost as an act of penitence. When Britain lost the North American colonies in the 1780s, George III's ministers resolved to run down the army and build up the navy, for they concluded (rightly) that it had been the loss of sea control to the colonists' allies, the French, that had sealed the fate of the land campaign (though it was doomed in any case through bad generalship). The fact that sea control without an army could bring no decision was by the by. And as for the perpetual threat to these shores from France, the prevailing sentiment could be summed up in lines from Thomas Campbell's poem of 1800, 'Ye Mariners of England':

> Britannia needs no bulwarks,
> No towers along the steep;
> Her march is o'er the mountain-waves,
> Her home is on the deep.

So much, indeed, would the army be neglected in the decade after the loss of the North American colonies that when war did come with Revolutionary and then Napoleonic France, British troops could do next to nothing. It took fifteen years for the army to reconstitute itself into something capable of taking to the continental field – in Portugal and Spain – and getting to grips with the Napoleonic centre of gravity, the Grande Armée.

In the meantime, it was the Royal Navy that had had to carry on the fight, which amounted to capturing French and Spanish sugar islands in the Caribbean and thereby the treasure with which to subsidize Britain's continental allies, and strangling French trade through blockades and commerce-raiding. But sea power was principally about preventing defeat – if aggressively. British warships remained, as ever, the nation's 'wooden walls', and gained their most memorable victory in October 1805 when Nelson and his 'band of brothers' destroyed the better part of Admiral Villeneuve's Franco-Spanish fleet, which at Bonaparte's urging had broken out of the Mediterranean to seize control of the 22 miles of water that stood between the sceptred isle and the army of 150,000 imperial troops camped on the cliffs above Boulogne. 'Give me six hours' control of the Strait of Dover,' Bonaparte had told Villeneuve, 'and I will gain mastery of the world.'*

That day at Trafalgar, when Bonaparte's hopes for even a moment's control of the Dover strait were dashed for good, is hallowed in the annals of the senior service, but what had preceded it was an even greater feat of seamanship, and a demonstration of true sea power. For two years before Trafalgar, from June 1803 until July 1805, Nelson did not set foot on land – nor indeed on anything much but the deck of his flagship, HMS *Victory*; neither did the great majority of his sailors, nor those of the Royal Navy's northern squadrons, disembark. For almost as long, his second-in-command, Vice Admiral Cuthbert (Lord) Collingwood, never heard the splash of his flagship's anchor. For two whole years His Majesty's fleet remained continuously at sea off the coasts of Europe, watching for the French squadrons scattered in harbours from Brest in the north of the Bay of Biscay to Toulon in the Mediterranean, lest they try to break out and combine to sweep the Channel clear for the passage of – as it was optimistically called – *l'armée de l'Angleterre*. In 1801, Admiral John Jervis, Earl St Vincent, in a letter to the Board of Admiralty, made the celebrated remark: 'I do not say, my Lords, that the French will not come. I say only they will not come by sea.' Such heroic confidence was not without its price: perhaps half of Britain's gross domestic product had been poured into the navy since the 1780s. But the great US naval theorist Captain Alfred Thayer Mahan, in his super-influential work of 1890 *The Influence of Seapower upon History, 1660–1783*, grasped perfectly the significance of the two-year blockade and demonstrated the elegant power of his pen in asserting: 'Those far distant, storm-beaten ships, upon which the Grand Army never looked, stood between it and the dominion of the world.'

And nowhere was Mahan's work more influential than with the

---

* The fleets had combined at Cadiz, after Villeneuve had crossed and recrossed the Atlantic with Nelson in pursuit.

Kaiser and his naval minister, Admiral Alfred (later von) Tirpitz. 'I am just now not reading but devouring Captain Mahan's book and am trying to learn it by heart,' wrote the Kaiser to a friend: 'It is on board all my ships and [is] constantly quoted by my captains and officers.' And he grasped well enough the implications: Germany had acquired an overseas empire five times the size of the *Kaiserreich* (largely in Africa, but with increasing interest in the Pacific), and its merchant navy, second only to Britain's, used British ports around the world and relied on the protection of the Royal Navy; both the empire and its trade depended therefore on British sufferance. At any time the Royal Navy could mount a Nelsonian blockade of Germany's coast and seize her colonies. Tirpitz had even seen for himself what this dependence meant: in 1896 he had been given command of the East Asia Squadron, operating from Hong Kong; when it came to berthing and all the usual port functions, his ships constantly took second place to those of the Royal Navy. Either Germany must live with this – perhaps even using naval cooperation as a means of forging a wider *entente* – or she must build a fleet powerful enough to shed her dependence. The trouble was that such a fleet was incompatible with Britain's security strategy – essentially that of the 'wooden walls', which now had to protect a good many distant places too. This was no matter to the Kaiser, however: a large German fleet would positively frighten Britain into active friendship. It was a very Teutonic view of affairs, and it was also a fundamental misreading of the foundations of British security as well as of the psychology of the nation. Command of the sea, from the days of Raleigh's great statement of sea power, had been more important to Britain than any continental alliance: 'Whosoever commands the sea, commands the trade of the world, commands the riches of the world, commands the world itself.'*

Within weeks of Tirpitz's appointment in June 1897 (his predecessor, Admiral von Hollmann, not sharing the Kaiser's enthusiasm for capital ships, had been manoeuvred out) the new naval minister submitted a memorandum on the future German fleet. He identified the principal enemy as Britain, and the principal area of conflict as

* Sir Walter Raleigh, 'A Discourse of the Invention of Ships, Anchors, Compass, &c.', in *The History of the World* (1614), collected and published in 1829 as *The Works of Sir Walter Ralegh* [sic], *Kt.* (London, 1829; repr. 1965), vol. 8.

the North Sea between Heligoland, 30 miles off the mouth of the Elbe (which Britain had exchanged with Germany for Zanzibar in 1890*), and the Thames. He ruled out cruiser warfare – 'tip and run' attacks and commerce-raiding by heavily armed but lightly armoured ships – since Germany had so few overseas bases; the over-riding need was for battleships (heavily armed, heavily armoured) to take on the British fleet – specifically, two squadrons of eight, plus a flagship and two reserves, by 1905. This was not a purely military appreciation; indeed, it was akin to President Ronald Reagan's strategy of the late 1980s to outspend the Soviets on defence (through 'Star Wars' especially) in order to bring about seismic political change. On the assumption that Britain would have to stay ahead by a ratio of at least 3:2 to survive, Tirpitz calculated that the British economy would simply be unable to bear the strain at some point around 1920, and would then be forced into an 'alliance' (on Germany's terms) with the Reich. The Kaiser also believed – just as fancifully – that Britain would run out of manpower as well. Not without some opposition, the German parliament approved the estimates, and building began.[†]

On 2 December 1906 the Tirpitz programme was made obsolescent, however, with the launching of HMS *Dreadnought*, for one man at least had taken note of the lessons of the Russo-Japanese war. The decisive battle of Tsushima had convinced the new first sea lord, Admiral Sir Jacky Fisher, that above all what counted was long-range gunnery *as well as* heavy armour. *Dreadnought* – which became the generic name for the new class of capital ships built on this principle – was designed, laid down and built in record time. Every existing battleship was decisively outclassed by her all-big-gun battery and the speed she could develop with her revolutionary steam turbines – 21 knots (24 mph; 39 kph).[‡] The problem with the 'pre-Dreadnoughts',

* Without possession of Heligoland, the Kiel Canal could hardly have offered safe transit to German warships.
† The naval appropriations of 1898 provided for a fleet of nineteen battleships, twelve armoured cruisers (for fleet action) and thirty smaller cruisers. Two years later, the estimates authorized a further expansion: the fleet would comprise two flagships and four squadrons of eight battleships.
‡ The German Wittelsbach class could manage a top speed of 18 knots, but *Dreadnought*'s three-knot advantage – small as it seems – would not have been insignificant in a running fight, or indeed in transit from the home fleet's anchorage at Scapa Flow to the expected battle area off Heligoland. And at a cruising speed of 10 knots, *Dreadnought*'s range was 1,600 miles greater than *Wittelsbach*'s.

The Dreadnought Race, summed up in this Kladderadatsch *('Crash') cartoon of c.1909 – 'The Marine Painters of England and Germany: Uncle Edward [King Edward VII] to William [the Kaiser]: "Your little marine masterpiece is too ambitious; keep it as a study."'*

armed with four 8-inch guns and several of smaller calibres, was spotting and correcting the fall of shot: it was difficult to tell which shell splashes came from which guns. *Dreadnought's* ten 12-inch guns did away with that problem, as well as increasing both range and weight of fire (their secondary armament was now designed to repel attacks from torpedo boats). The following year the Germans responded with the Nassau class, which stretched their existing technology rather than innovating, introducing conventional triple-expansion piston engines to gain a few more knots, and a main armament of twelve 11-inch guns to equal *Dreadnought's* range of 20,435 yards (roughly 11½ miles or 18.5 km), though not in weight of shell.*

So began the 'dreadnought race', which was a contest not merely of numbers but of capability – a contest to produce faster and faster ships with thicker and thicker armour and bigger and bigger guns (as well as a programme to enlarge Fisher's Admiralty building to handle his side of the race). Together with two battle-cruisers,[†] Tirpitz's new programme would give Germany ten dreadnoughts in service or on the stocks in 1909, reducing the Royal Navy's numerical superiority to a ratio of 12:10 rather than the 2:1 it believed necessary (for the Admiralty had to take account too of the Austro-Hungarian and Italian navies). In 1909, therefore, Asquith announced an additional four 'super-dreadnoughts' with 13½-inch guns in a new configuration that allowed a full broadside (the weight of broadside now double that of 1906), hoping that this would induce Germany at last to negotiate a treaty of limitation. It did not, and so the appropriations were made for the four new ships, prompting something of a crisis for the Liberal government whose social welfare programme was already driving up taxes.

---

* It is sometimes suggested that the Germans rejected turbine propulsion on cost grounds: a royalty of one million gold marks would have been payable on every turbine to its British inventor, C. A. Parsons. However, since the Nassau class cost 33.5 million marks per ship, this would seem to have been an unlikely case of saving ha'p'orths of tar – although the Tirpitz programmes were tightly funded. A much more likely reason was the naval ministry's scepticism about using the turbine for propulsion in a ship of such size and displacement.

† These carried the same armament as dreadnoughts (hence dreadnought-class battle-cruiser) but had much thinner armour, relying instead on the consequential greater speed. It was a type for which the Germans had less admiration than did Fisher, but they could be built under the existing *Kaiserliche Marine* appropriations for armoured cruisers, rather than seeking further provisions for more capital ships.

The race was further stepped up with Tirpitz's 1912 estimates – a fleet of thirty-three battleships and battle-cruisers, which would have outnumbered the Royal Navy in home waters. With Austria-Hungary building four dreadnoughts and the Italians already with four and building two more, Britain was faced with a choice of either building more battleships, withdrawing altogether from the Mediterranean or seeking an alliance – or at least an understanding – with France. The only realistic option – and the one recommended by the new first lord of the Admiralty, Winston Churchill (appointed in October 1911) – was to have the French assume responsibility for checking Italy and Austria-Hungary in the Mediterranean, while Britain would in turn protect the north coast of France. And on this basis a formal agreement within the Entente (known generally as the Anglo-French Naval Convention) would be drawn up in July 1912.*

Underestimating Britain's ability to find 'allies' – notably Japan and France – and thereby to withdraw its own ships to home waters, was one of the several flaws in the Tirpitz plan. Another was under-estimating her resolve and capacity to build more ships. The naval estimates for 1912 and 1913 would lay down ten new super-dreadnoughts – ships of the Queen Elizabeth and Revenge classes, representing a further step-change in armament (15-inch guns), speed and armoured protection. In the same time Germany would manage to lay down only five, the Kaiser's priority returning to the army. Yet the race had changed the face of the oceans: in *Jane's Fighting Ships* of

---

* The French prime minister, Raymond Poincaré, was not impressed with the first draft, noting that there was still no formal commitment by Britain to come to France's aid in a war with Germany: 'To begin a military or naval convention by saying that it means nothing so far as the Governments are concerned is superfluous and quite out of place in such a convention. If the *Entente* does not mean that England will come to the aid of France in the event of Germany attacking the French ports its value is not great' (see Robert K. Massie, *Dreadnought: Britain, Germany and the Coming of the Great War*, London, 1991). Hardly surprisingly, several members of Asquith's cabinet were disconcerted by the implication that it *did* in practice commit Britain to just such a course. The final revision of the convention ran: 'If either Government had grave reason to expect an unprovoked attack by a third Power, or something that threatened the general peace, it should immediately discuss with the other whether both Governments should act together to prevent aggression and preserve peace, and if so what measures they would be prepared to take in common.' It may have sounded non-committal, but it allowed the admirals and their staffs on both sides to get on with their detailed plans (and why should they tell their political masters much, for they would only fuss?).

1906, Germany was ranked just fifth among naval powers (the United States was second, behind Britain, followed by France and Japan, and then, after Germany, Russia, Italy and Austria-Hungary). By 1914, *Jane's* would be placing Germany second. But despite this leap up the league table, by 1914 Germany would still have only twenty-four dreadnoughts and dreadnought-class battle-cruisers, while Britain would have thirty-eight (and would be able to impress at once three more battleships being built in British shipyards for Chile, Turkey and Brazil). It was a long way from the old two-power standard – that the Royal Navy should be able to outnumber any two other fleets combined – and a considerable way from the 2:1 superiority over the German fleet that Fisher had argued for (it was not much more than 3:2), but it was a definite superiority nonetheless.

For Britain, besides the cost to the exchequer, the dreadnought race had two major consequences. First, it fuelled, perhaps even created, the perception of hostility between the two countries. In an extraordinary article in the *Daily Telegraph* in October 1908, the Kaiser gave vent to his frustration, real or otherwise, in language reminiscent of a later German leader:

You English are mad, mad, mad as March hares. What has come over you that you are so completely given over to suspicions quite unworthy of a great nation? What more can I do than I have done . . . To be forever misjudged, to have my repeated offers of friendship weighed and scrutinized with jealous, mistrustful eyes, taxes my patience severely . . . I repeat that I am a friend of England, but you make things difficult for me. My task is not of the easiest. The prevailing sentiment among large sections of the middle and lower classes of my own people is not friendly to England. I am, therefore so to speak, in a minority in my own land . . . But, you will say, what of the German navy? Surely, that is a menace to England! Against whom but England are my squadrons being prepared? If England is not in the minds of those Germans who are bent on creating a powerful fleet, why is Germany asked to consent to such new and heavy burdens of taxation? My answer is clear. Germany is a young and growing empire. She has a worldwide commerce which is rapidly expanding, and to which the legitimate ambition of patriotic Germans refuses to assign any bounds. Germany must have a powerful fleet to protect that commerce and her manifold interests in even the most distant seas. She expects those interests to go on growing, and she must be able to champion them manfully in any quarter of the globe. Her horizons stretch far away.*

The second consequence was the renewed spectre of invasion: with a large fleet Germany might be able to land a significant force in these islands. This exacerbated the competition for resources between the Royal Navy and the army, for while the navy argued that building more ships was the proper safeguard against invasion, the army argued that prudence required a counter-invasion force in case of mishap – hence the TF and the earmarking of regular divisions for home defence (for, assuming that the purpose of an invasion across the North Sea was to keep any British striking force at home, all that would be necessary for German success when the time came was the mere threat – and timid politicians in London). But the more intractable – and ultimately more fateful – problem was the implication for continental strategy: in short, what, if anything, was to be done with the BEF? There would be a formidable German fleet to threaten – limit – its deployment; would the Royal Navy be strong enough to neutralize – keep in port – such a fleet, or if necessary destroy it?

When Henry Wilson went to the War Office in 1910 he had found no answer to the question: 'Whither the BEF?' This was hardly

* The article was concocted by Colonel (later Major-General) Edward Stuart-Wortley from the Kaiser's conversations with him (at Highcliffe Castle in Dorset where, on the advice of his uncle, Edward VII, the German Emperor had stayed in December 1907 to take seawater baths from Bournemouth Bay; and also from conversations at the annual army manoeuvres in Lorraine in September the following year). Stuart-Wortley submitted the article to the Kaiser for approval, who passed it to the chancellor, at that time Bernard von Bülow, asking him not to pass on the article to the Foreign Office. However, Bülow did pass it, probably unread, to the minister, Wilhelm von Schoen, requesting an official translation and any amendments that might be necessary. Schoen did not read it (some accounts say that he was away), and it was dealt with instead by the under-secretary, who read it but passed it without comment to a press official, who interpreted his instructions as meaning he should only correct any errors of fact. It was returned to Bülow who, still without reading it, returned the draft to the Kaiser saying he saw no reason not to publish. Unsurprisingly, publication caused a storm in Germany, as well as elsewhere. The Reichstag called for constitutional restraints to be placed on the Kaiser, which Bülow supported. The Kaiser promised to respect the constitutional formalities in the future, but gratefully sacked Bülow the following year when the Reichstag rejected the budget, replacing him with the arch-Prussian (though mildly Anglophile) Theobald von Bethmann Hollweg. The phrase 'lost in translation' springs to mind, but also deceit, incompetence and perfidy in Berlin. Stuart-Wortley would become the first general to be sacked after the débâcle of the Somme in 1916.

surprising, since there was no answer to Sir Edward Grey's fundamental 'great question', with which the foreign secretary had been toying ('struggling' seems too vigorous a word) since the signing of the Entente. So while Wilson threw himself into the neglected business of mobilization, he also embarked on what was little short of his own foreign policy towards France. He intensified his contacts with the influential Foch and began work on a concept of operations in which the BEF would fight on the left flank of the French, which hitherto had been but one of a number of options identified by the Directorate of Military Operations. The CIGS, Sir William Nicholson, appears to have been content for Wilson to work up the concept in more detail, if only because the identification of a concentration area – Maubeuge, close to the Belgian border and midway between the ports of entry and the French army's expected centre of gravity – would enable some sensible staffwork to proceed concerning movements and logistics. The trouble was that the Admiralty had very different ideas about strategy in the event of war, and refused to be a party to such plans.*

But then events played into Wilson's hands in the shape of a second Moroccan crisis.† In 1911 a rebellion had broken out against the Sultan, who by early April was besieged in his palace in Fez. Under the terms of the Algeciras Treaty which had concluded the first crisis, he appealed to Paris for help, and French troops, already landing at Rabat on the pretext of protecting European lives and property, despatched a flying column to Fez. In June the Spanish occupied Larache and Ksar-el-Kebir in the north-west of the country. On 1 July, SMS (*Seiner Majestät Schiff*) *Panther*, described sometimes as a light

---

* The essential work of a staff officer prior to the commander's decision is to identify all the factors influencing that decision and to suggest options. The staff of the Directorate of Military Operations would therefore have written many papers on the variable factors in a continental commitment, and identified several options for the BEF – including Antwerp and remaining initially in the United Kingdom. Detailed planning by the other departments to turn an option into a plan – notably that of the QMG for movement and supply – could to an extent begin as soon as an option was identified, but the effort involved in planning for several options was prodigious. Not surprisingly, the other departments looked to the DMO for a firm lead so that their staff could work up their own plans in the finest detail. The DMO's lead came from the CIGS.
† Britain's recognition by the terms of the Entente of France's 'sphere of influence' in Morocco had tempted the German reaction known as the 'First Moroccan Crisis' of 1905–6, which was resolved at the Algeciras Conference when France's 'special position' was formalized, and the policing of Morocco jointly entrusted to France and Spain (see chapter 3).

cruiser but in truth a gunboat – *Kanonenschiff* – arrived at Agadir in south-west Morocco. *Panther* had something of a reputation. In the previous decade she had thrown her weight around in the Caribbean and South America, testing the extent of the Monroe Doctrine.* Her arrival in Agadir was viewed in both Paris and London as more opportunism, the first step to establishing a German naval base on the Atlantic.

It is undeniable that the 'Agadir Crisis' contained elements of high farce – not least the appearance of *Panther* herself. A short, fat, light-grey steamer with twin smokestacks and two 4-inch guns, a crew of 120 and a brass band (John Masefield could have poetized her beautifully), she was hardly the ideal foreloper of Tirpitz's great battle fleet. But at the same time her arrival in the bay of Agadir threw Paris into some confusion, exacerbated by the circumstances arising from an accident in late May, when an aircraft had run out of control at the start of the Paris–Madrid air race, killing the French war minister, Henri Berteaux, and severely injuring the prime minister, Antoine Monis: just the opportunity for a *coup de main* by Berlin.

And so the *Panther* plot had been hatched – *Panther* purely because she happened to be the nearest ship, homeward bound after port visits in German East Africa, where doubtless her brass band had played the imperial national anthem, 'Heil dir im Siegerkranz' ('Hail to thee in victor's crown'), to the confusion of those who thought it sounded exactly like the British (for it was).

There had to be some reason for her entering sovereign waters, however, and the *Auswärtiges Amt* (German foreign ministry – colloquially 'Wilhelmstrasse', after the Berlin street on which it was situated) rose to the challenge with characteristic heavy-footedness. In a ploy not dissimilar to Bismarck's infamous Ems telegram, Berlin manufactured a petition from German firms appealing for help in warding off marauding natives. However, there were no German nationals in Agadir – or any European citizens for that matter: only Herr Wilburg, representative of the Hamburg business consortium, 70 miles away in Mogador. Since all telegrams in Morocco had to be sent in French, and therefore a code arranged, it was some time before

---

* Introduced in 1823 by US President James Monroe, who declared that further efforts by European nations to colonize land or interfere with states in North or South America would be viewed as acts of aggression requiring US intervention.

a message could be got to him to travel at once to Agadir – not, indeed, until the evening *Panther* had arrived to rescue him. But off he dutifully set next day on horseback in the scorching heat of the North African summer, along rough and precipitous tracks (though not in the least threatened by natives), managing to reach Agadir in the afternoon three days later. There, on the beach, exhausted, he fell asleep without making contact with the saviour-vessel. He awoke next morning to find a larger ship, the light cruiser *Berlin* (ten 4-inch guns), anchored in the bay, and at once began trying to attract her attention. *Berlin*'s crew at first took him for a Moroccan beachcomber; only when in frustration he placed his hands on his hips did their cultural awareness tell them that here was a European – the 'Endangered German', as he was wryly dubbed in Whitehall.

Der Panthersprung (the *Panther*'s leap), as it was soon known, aroused the predicted reaction in Germany. 'Hurra! Eine Tat [a deed]' thrilled *Die Rheinisch-Westfälische Zeitung* in prominent headlines: 'Action at last, a liberating deed ... the foreign policy of a great nation, a powerful state, cannot exhaust itself in patient inaction.' And yet another arch-schemer, Arthur Zimmermann, under-secretary of state at the Wilhelmstrasse, assured the Pan-German League that 'we are seizing this region once and for all. An outlet for our population is necessary.' It was clear that *der Panthersprung* was a fishing expedition. Even if a 'German West Morocco' was not to be on the cards, there could be compensations: Berlin now sought to manoeuvre Paris into colonial concessions elsewhere in exchange for a free French hand in Morocco.

London was not happy. Indeed, precautionary war measures were taken. At Grey's urging, the home fleet came to readiness at Portland, the Atlantic fleet cancelled its summer manoeuvres off Norway (which were to have been carried out with, of all people, the German high seas fleet), and large orders for additional naval ammunition were placed. Special guards were posted at government buildings, as well as on bridges and tunnels of the South Eastern Railway, which served the Channel ports. The days passed and Berlin seemed to be treating all enquiries by London with something akin to disdain. Even Lloyd George, by nature Germanophile and as chancellor of the exchequer not a regular member of the CID, became agitated. He decided quite independently to use his traditional Mansion House speech* to send a strong message to Berlin – which Asquith and Grey were more than content to let him do (his oratorical gifts could have been made for such an occasion).

It was ironic that it should be the least 'imperial' of the senior cabinet who would put the Kaiser and Bethmann Hollweg on their guard – but perhaps appropriate, since it would be he who would take Asquith's place as war leader at the end of 1916, bringing at last some energy to the task. Rising to his feet before the assembled financial power brokers of the City on the evening of Friday, 21 July, a hot evening in a particularly hot month, he began with the usual economic *tour d'horizon*, followed by a statement of Liberal values, and then, with suitable change of key and tempo, a declaration in the sing-song tones of the valleys that – *however* – peace 'is the first condition of prosperity'. And then, abandoning his extemporary style, he picked up the piece of paper whose words the prime minister and Grey had carefully approved: 'I would make great sacri-fices to preserve peace,' he assured the sea of bankers; 'I conceive that nothing would justify a disturbance of international good will except questions of the greatest national moment.' And then came the message to Berlin – nothing new or remarkable, but, delivered at that time, portentous and not to be ignored:

> But if a situation were to be forced upon us in which peace could only be preserved by the surrender of the great and beneficent position Britain has won by centuries of heroism and achievement, by allowing Britain to be treated where her interests were vitally affected as if she were of no account in the Cabinet of nations, then I say emphatically that peace at that price would be a humiliation intolerable for a great country like ours to endure.

Berlin would correctly interpret the speech as a warning that she could not impose an unreasonable settlement on France. Paris, likewise, would come to interpret it, though with rather less cause for certainty, as an affirmation of the muscular strength of the Entente. The French-born Princess Marie Radziwill, married to one of the

---

* The Mansion House is the official residence of the Lord Mayor of London and the venue for an annual speech by the chancellor of the exchequer on the state of the economy, addressed to the mayor and financial leaders of the City.

Kaiser's court, wrote from Berlin that the 'speech has poured oil on the fire'.*

Fortunately, meanwhile, the German stock market came to the rescue. On Friday, 1 September, scheduled talks in Berlin between the French ambassador and the German foreign minister, Alfred von Kiderlen-Wächter, were suddenly called off – for no more reason than that the ambassador, Jules Cambon (whose elder brother Paul was ambassador in London), was ill. Of this innocuous reason the foreign ministry, heavy-footed to the last, failed to inform the press. The following day there was panic at the Berliner Börse, with instructions to sell coming in from the provinces and continuing all week, and Monday – *der Schwarze Montag* – brought a run on the banks as nervous depositors withdrew their capital. The markets rallied towards the end of the week, but collapsed again on the Saturday. By the end of the month the Reichsbank had lost a fifth of its gold reserves trying to prop up the markets and the banks, and in order not to be driven off the gold standard altogether, the chancellor instructed Kiderlen-Wächter to back down over the Moroccan ambitions. *Panther* slipped her anchor and the crisis was past.†

One of the unintended consequences of *der Panthersprung* – perhaps ultimately the most significant – was the apparent endorsement of the 'Wilson–Foch' plan as the preferred strategy for the BEF. It would happen largely by haphazard, as so much in Asquith's government, and little would actually be made explicit, but Wilson and others

* Princess Radziwill's letters to General Count Mario di Robilant, whom she had met when he came to Berlin in 1885 as the Italian military attaché, covering the period from 1908 to her death in 1915, offer an invaluable insight to what might be called sceptical opinion in Germany – the views of those on the edge of the imperial–military circle. They were translated, edited and published as *This Was Germany: An Observer at the Court of Berlin* (London, 1937). As to the Kaiser's view of the crisis and the British response, he was perhaps more puzzled than troubled. In May he had come to London (with the Kaiserin) at the invitation of his cousin, the new king, George V, for the unveiling of a statue of their mutual grandmother, and the King had told him that the French occupation of Morocco should be accepted as a *fait accompli*. The Kaiser reported to the chancellor, Bethmann Hollweg, in terms that suggested he had hoped for support to head off what he saw as the latest French colonial move, and was disappointed only that Britain would not help.
† The face-saving Treaty of Fez was signed on 4 November. Germany accepted France's position in Morocco – in effect a French colony – in return for territory in the French Equatorial African colony of Middle Congo (now the Republic of the Congo), which became part of the German colony of Kamerun (and which, along with Togo, was captured by the allies early in 1916). The area was in the main a fever-ridden place, but it did give Germany a better outlet on the Congo River.

would believe that they had been given a clear signal. As the political temperature mounted in Berlin and Paris, not to say literally in Morocco itself, Asquith called a secret meeting of the CID on 23 August at which he asked for a presentation of the respective Admiralty and War Office plans. This was the moment Henry Wilson had been waiting for; indeed, he had pressed hard for the meeting. So had Winston Churchill, who as home secretary, though not a member of the committee, was responsible for certain aspects of security and therefore home defence. Besides, he was an indefatigable lobbyist on military matters, and had already sent Asquith a memorandum on the military situation in Europe.* The PM invited him to the meeting on the twenty-third, along with Lloyd George (by virtue of his sudden engagement with the crisis) and, naturally, the first lord of the Admiralty, McKenna, and the recently ennobled Haldane, together with Sir William Nicholson (CIGS), Sir John French (inspector-general of the forces, and presumptive commander-in-chief of the BEF), the first sea lord, Admiral of the Fleet Sir Arthur Wilson – and of course Grey.†

Only a month before, Henry Wilson had been in Paris, where he had had lunch with the French war minister. He had all his facts and figures at his fingertips – and on the huge maps of France and Belgium that hung on the walls of his office, and on which he had worked almost daily since becoming DMO. Now, on the morning of 23 August, he rolled these up and took them with him to No. 10. The committee met at eleven-thirty and would continue until six. The army – Wilson himself – would be given the floor first, and then in the afternoon would come the navy's turn, the first sea lord speaking for himself, for the Admiralty had no war staff. It would become known as the battle of the two Wilsons.

Physically imposing, even in frock coat – the soldiers wore plain clothes at the War Office – tall and spare, bright-eyed and eloquent even by the standards of his Irish descent, the DMO laid on a masterly performance. Standing in front of his maps, with their military

* CAB 38/19/50, 'Military Aspects of the Continental Problem'.
† Lloyd George's remarks after the war that only an inner circle, of which he was not one, was privy to strategic policy-making need to be considered in the light of his exposure at this meeting to the extent of what the Anglo-French staff discussions had produced.

symbols showing the various German, French and Belgian fortresses and the projected locations of the army corps, and arrows indicating the probable German lines of advance and of the French counter-offensive, for an hour and three-quarters he described the threat as the *État-Major* and the British general staff saw it. The German army, fully mobilized, he told his audience, would field 110 divisions (each division 15,000–20,000 strong). The figure was sobering – especially when the British contribution to the equation could be, at best, seven divisions. There would be, he said, a holding operation against the Russians by twenty-two or so divisions (with, it was supposed, Austrian support in the Carpathians), and Belgian neutrality would be disregarded in order to outflank the strong French frontier defences with the object of gaining a rapid, Sedan-like victory, after which the German army would rail its victorious divisions east to crush the slowly mobilizing Russian bear. Against the ninety or so divisions in the *Westaufmarsch*, the campaign against France, Wilson explained, the French would be able to field only eighty-five (keeping a further nine on the Italian border as an army of observation); and even if the Belgians put up serious resistance – adding their numbers to the calculation, which would even things up a little – the Germans could concentrate at their chosen point against the French line to achieve overwhelming local superiority.*

This gloomy assessment was sound enough, but would apply only if the French plans lacked the flexibility to switch troops to the 'area of decision'. However, Wilson's conclusion was that it all boiled down to 'relative strengths': France would probably be defeated unless the six infantry divisions and the cavalry division ('six plus') of the BEF were despatched at the outset of war.† And he went on to explain exactly how this was to be done – through the railway timetables, which the War Office were planning in such detail as even to allow

* The figures are generally thought to have been derived from the French intelligence coup of 1908. Yet sobering though they certainly were, they did not tell the whole story, for the *Grosser Generalstab* had by this time made plans to use reserve troops from the outset – both *Landwehr* and *ersatz Truppen* – in the *Westaufmarsch*.
† By October of the following year, Wilson had changed his mind: the BEF, even at six divisions plus the cavalry division, would *not* tip the scales (Wilson note, 12 Oct. 1912, in *A Guide to the Papers of British Cabinet Ministers*, London, 1974). This ought to have provoked a wholesale reassessment of the implicit strategy of a 'forward deployment' of the BEF, but it did not.

the troops ten-minute tea breaks every few hours, as well as the extensive arrangements at the ports of embarkation and disembarkation, the shipping schedules and details of the onward journey by rail to the concentration area at Maubeuge.* The plans were far advanced, Wilson declared confidently: the War Office had printed thousands of maps of Belgium and northern France.

The meeting was particularly well minuted, so that the tone and temper of the speakers are discernible. There was a surprising degree of confusion and then exasperation over what the navy could, or rather could not, do to get the BEF to France quickly – not least on the part of the first sea lord, Arthur Wilson, who was apparently unaware of the extent of the planning that had gone on between the general staff and his own director of sea transport. The discussion ranged wide and long, covering such matters as whether it would be possible to bring Russian troops to France – perhaps even through the Dardanelles, suggested Churchill, in ominous foremention of the name – until it was agreed that St Petersburg would not feel able to spare a single man from the defence of Russia's own borders. In any case, declared Sir Edward Grey, with equally ominous portent, the 'Turks were in close relations with the Germans, and we certainly could not force the Dardanelles in these circumstances'.

History, too, was certainly well to the fore in the minds of the statesmen as they considered the enormity of a continental commitment: Trafalgar was mentioned, not surprisingly when it came to control of the Channel; and Corunna – showing perhaps less confidence that a British expeditionary force could remain long in Europe. Even the duke of Marlborough was invoked: on the matter of the BEF's having to maintain contact with the French army if it withdrew from the Meuse south-east, Churchill said that he did 'not like the idea of the British Army having to retire into France away from its own country', to which the CIGS replied, no doubt with some relish,

---

* One can only admire the diligence of the respective staffs, for French railways had a rather different approach to timekeeping from the British. France had adopted Greenwich Mean Time in 1911, called 'Western European Time', but not the Greenwich meridian, which was only accepted in 1913 (after revelations of confusion in the rescue attempts after the sinking of the *Titanic*), when clocks were at last synchronized in London and Paris. And, although 'railway-time is always that of Paris', says Baedeker's *Northern France* (Leipzig and London, 1909), 'the clocks in the interior of the stations, by which the trains start, are purposely kept five minutes slow'.

that 'similar operations had often fallen to our lot before – for instance under Marlborough' – well knowing, of course, that Churchill was a descendant of the great captain-general.

The talk was certainly lofty, if occasionally airy. Time and again, however, Churchill brought the discussion back to questions of military detail: what would be the effect on the French, and therefore the BEF, of greater German strength (and therefore success) on the Meuse than was anticipated by the general staff? The memorandum he had submitted beforehand, 'Military Aspects of the Continental Problem',* assumed a significantly large attack developing *north* of the Meuse (which the general staff considered fanciful), and he cross-questioned Henry Wilson and the CIGS accordingly. The DMO was in no mood to give the Yeomanry major's ideas anything other than the politest brush-off: 'Winston had put in a ridiculous and fantastic paper on a war on the French and German frontier, which I was able to demolish,' he wrote in his diary. It was in fact a paper of extraordinary prescience which, had it been subjected to a thorough staff examination, would have pointed to the problems that actually arose in August 1914; and history might then have been very different. The problem was that the general staff believed – because it was the settled opinion of the *État-Major* – that the Germans would not have enough divisions to develop a strong offensive north (and therefore west) of the Meuse because of the number they would have to keep in East Prussia.

Professor Sir Michael Howard (OM, CH, CBE, MC), perhaps the pre-eminent British military historian of the past half-century, in his foreword to Professor John Gooch's *The Plans of War*,† writes: 'These men [the general staff] were not fools, and they certainly were not Blimps. The policies they advocated certainly led to unforeseen results; but their advocacy was based not on prejudice, but on hard and, within its limits, clear thinking, after careful examination of possible alternatives. Not, it must be admitted, of *all* possible alternatives.' And there's the rub: the ideal general staff identifies and examines *all* possible alternatives, so as to provide the policy-makers with genuine choices, and ought not to rule out anything as

---

* The paper is examined in the light of events below in chapter 21.
† John Gooch, *The Plans of War: The General Staff and British Military Strategy c.1900–1916* (London, 1974).

impossible where the material facts – in this case, the intention of the *Grosser Generalstab* – are unknowable. In the end decisions have to be made, but the job of the staff is to keep asking 'what if . . . ?'

As he finished answering the multitude of, to his mind, tedious questions, Henry Wilson turned to his namesake, the first sea lord, and, knowing that at last he would be able to expose the Admiralty's unwillingness to cooperate, asked if the Royal Navy could guarantee the safe passage of the BEF across the Channel – at which point (it was two o'clock) the meeting adjourned for lunch.

When it resumed an hour later, Haldane posed Wilson's question again; indeed, the secretary for war asked if the navy could not just convoy the BEF to France but transport it. Admiral Wilson, perhaps to the surprise of the meeting, replied that although he had not consulted on the matter, he did not believe there would be any insuperable difficulty (what he did not say was *when* – at what stage in the transition to war – they could be escorted). Asquith then invited him to present the navy's plans and elaborate on the short memorandum he had circulated before the meeting.

The presentation was as inept as the army's had been masterly. The first sea lord was twenty years the DMO's senior, brought out of retirement the year before to take over from Jacky Fisher. He was every inch a naval officer – bearded, taciturn, flinty, possessed of extreme self-confidence, and so demanding that his sailors had dubbed him 'old 'ard 'eart', and in some admiration, for he lived by his own severe precepts. But no warmth emanated from the professional head of the Admiralty as he spoke – and seemingly very little sense. In fact he spoke much against his will. He, like Fisher before him, believed that strategy was not to be divulged, that the effectiveness of naval plans in particular derived from their secrecy, and that this secrecy was best maintained by the first sea lord and his commanders-in-chief determining things *for* themselves and then keeping them *to* themselves. Accordingly, Wilson, like Fisher before him, had resisted the creation of a war staff. His exposition to the committee was, in Haldane's opinion (and certainly that of the soldiers present), rambling. It was certainly opaque, for he had no intention of vouchsafing naval secrets to a bunch of politicians. The concept he sketched was limply Nelsonian – a close blockade of the German coast by destroyers and light cruisers, while the battleships and battle-cruisers waited over the horizon for the German high seas fleet, which the blockade would provoke into sortie and which the Grand Fleet (the Atlantic and home fleets combined) would then annihilate. For this reason, he explained, there would initially be no ships to spare for escorts. Perhaps when the German high seas fleet had been sent to the bottom, troopships could then be escorted – not to France, he argued, where the tiny BEF would be wholly overwhelmed in the clash of the titan continental armies, but instead into the Baltic, where a landing in strength would threaten Berlin and draw off troops from the main fronts. The first sea lord was of the same mind as Fisher had famously been: 'The British army should be a projectile fired by the Royal Navy.'

But onto the Pomeranian coast? Haldane and the soldiers were astonished. This was a reversion to the old 'tip and run' strategy of the two Pitts. No doubt with memories of Bismarck's quip that if a British army attempted such a thing he would send a policeman to arrest it, they asked the first sea lord if he thought he could land a force big enough (and soon enough) to draw off any appreciable number of Germans from their drive west. Why, indeed, asked the CIGS, did the navy think itself better qualified than his staff to design a land campaign against the German army? Did the Admiralty, for example, possess maps of the German railway system? Poor Sir Arthur: instead of taking the enquiry as rhetorical, he tried to dismiss it with an imperious 'It is not the businesses of the Admiralty to have such maps', which invited the damaging (and deserved) retort: 'I beg your pardon, but if you meddle with military problems, you are bound not only to have these maps but to have studied them.'

And yet to characterize Sir Arthur Wilson as a bone-headed old sea-dog mired in the strategy of Nelson's day would not be to do him justice. Wilson was, like Nelson, a Norfolk man; his father was an admiral, his mother the daughter of the vicar of Swaffham. In the early 1850s he had been sent to Eton, and thence at thirteen to sea, where he saw action in the later stages of the Crimean War (in 1911 he had served longer than any man at active duty in either the army or the navy). He had served on the China station in the Second Opium War, accompanied the mission to Japan that had laid the foundations of the Imperial Japanese Navy, then returned home to various training appointments and to membership of the board established to enquire into the potential of the new Whitehead torpedo. He was thoroughly open to technological initiatives, and above all he was brave: in 1884 he had landed in the Sudan with the Naval Brigade during the campaign against the Mahdists, and won the Victoria Cross in hand-to-hand fighting at the battle of El Teb. But his preference for keeping things to himself was notorious, and the root of his undoing. In June 1904, as future appointments were being discussed, including the possibility of his becoming commander-in-chief in the Mediterranean, Rear-Admiral Prince Louis of Battenberg, the director of naval intelligence and himself a future first sea lord, wrote to the earl of Selborne, first lord of the Admiralty, about the

> curious trait of Wilson's to do everything himself [which] finds expression in other ways. He declines to have any more staff [as C-in-C home fleet] than the C.-in-C. at the Cape or the East Indies. He knows quite well what an enormous fleet he will have under him in war, as I supply him with the Order of Battle every month, and I know that he is making elaborate plans, but it is all done by himself alone and personally. If he were to go to the Mediterranean he would continue with exactly the same system. I don't say he could not do it, as he is a bachelor, and a pipe and a bit of biscuit does him for a meal any time, and he is probably able to work twenty hours a day and sleep in his clothes. I venture to think that he, in common with all Admirals I know (except Beresford and Fisher), does not know how to use a staff. The Mediterranean station must always remain our big training ground. What we want there is a C.-in-C. who will train and teach his Flag-Officers, his Captains, and train and teach his staff. That Wilson will not do, though he will have his fleet admirably prepared for war, and if the French [and this two months *after* the Entente Cordiale was signed!] come out he will beat them; of that there is no doubt. But if anything was to suddenly remove the C.-in-C. there would be chaos.*

Yet his reputation as a master of naval strategy – indeed, a genius, in Jacky Fisher's view – had been high enough for Asquith in 1909 to appoint him suddenly and without consulting anyone to membership of the CID. His 'clear and straight forward manner' had impressed ministers during the committee's inquiry into the Fisher

---

* He was not in fact appointed, being in any case close to retirement age. He remained with the home (Channel) fleet until 1907, when he retired from active duty and went to live in Norfolk with his sister.

naval reforms; Lord Morley, the secretary of state for India, noted that 'Sir A. Wilson strikes me, and I think the others of us, as much the best-balanced sort of man, to say nothing of his having proved himself as a first rate commander'. This was not something that would have been said of the DMO, for all his professionalism. Sir Arthur Wilson's mistake at the meeting on 23 August, besides his lamentable presentational skills in that particular company, was not his strategic vision but his venturing on to dry land in proposing the preposterous Pomeranian punt (though in 1905, when with Russia prostrate at the hands of the Japanese the Kaiser had been considering a lightning attack on France, the *Generalstab* had been all too wary of the effects on their plans of a British landing in Schleswig-Holstein – or the Scheldt estuary).

Sir Arthur's minister, the first lord of the Admiralty, McKenna, loyally backed him up, but spoke no more convincingly. Henry Wilson now counter-attacked by reminding the meeting where the principal danger lay, namely in the German army's superiority over the French: the *État-Major* placed little hope in sea power to avert the calamity awaiting them on the frontiers. Sailing what must have been perilously close to the wind even for him, the DMO alluded to a recent piece in *The Times* which reckoned that the Royal Navy was worth 500,000 bayonets to the French: 'Our navy is not worth five *hundred* bayonets to them. Indeed, Joffre [does not] value it at *one* bayonet.' Within the narrow confines of the land battle, this was obviously true enough – the Royal Navy had no wheels and would not be able to defend Paris, the Kaiser had told Prince Louis of Battenberg in 1905, and again during the Agadir crisis – but it was hardly a strategic view of the entire problem, and it showed just how deep was the lack of cooperation between the two services.

Asquith had begun the meeting by quoting what a sub-committee of the CID had concluded in examining the question two years before, 'that the expediency of sending a military force abroad or of relying on naval means alone is a matter of policy which can only be determined when the occasion arises by the Government of the day'. He ended the meeting by saying that he would deliberate on the matter further.

An hour later Henry Wilson received a note from Haldane: 'My dear General, You did admirably today. Lucid and real grip, your exposition made a real impression . . .' Indeed it did. Haldane had never regarded the BEF as solely a continental force (as the general staff increasingly had): he was a convinced supporter of Britain's traditional maritime strategy, and saw the BEF as the empire's central reserve for use in conjunction with – even in support of – her sea power. Yet the logic of the present position was – so far as it had been taken – indisputable. As the meeting broke up, he had told Asquith that he couldn't continue as war minister without a Board of Admiralty that could work with the War Office – in effect, saying that both first lord and first sea lord would have to go – and a naval war staff that could work on detailed plans alongside the general staff. Churchill had already impressed Asquith and Grey by his engagement with issues well beyond his departmental remit (and, indeed, by his remaining in London throughout August, when almost every other minister had decamped for the grouse moor, marina or fashionable resort and had had to be recalled; the first sea lord, for example, had been most reluctant to return from Scotland, where he was shooting). And yet Wilson's advocacy of sending the BEF at 'six plus' (six infantry divisions and the cavalry division – virtually every regular in the British Isles) looks more than a shade disingenuous when, only a month before, he had worked out that 'we can only just make the Cavalry Division, four Divisions, and the Army Troops mobile. The 4th and 6th Divisions will have no horses, no A.S.C. personnel, no mechanical transport or mechanical transport drivers, and no medical units. Then we are 2,500 officers short, and so on.' Indeed, the 'so on' was almost a show-stopper: the howitzer batteries could be fought with only four, not six, guns, and even then with only half the required scale of ammunition. The DMO's determination nevertheless to send 'six plus' is incomprehensible professionally; it only made the remotest sense as a token of solidarity with the French. The strength of the German army, on the other hand, was anything but token.*

Asquith took five weeks to make up his mind, and did so without benefit of any professional analysis. There was, of course, no defence staff (unlike today); the limited CID secretariat was not noticeably up to the job, and Asquith failed to create even an ad hoc staff to assess the issues. As Field Marshal Lord ('Dwin') Bramall writes in *The Chiefs*, a golden opportunity 'of developing a Defence Policy Staff to undertake the essential task of evaluating strategic options on an impartial national

---

* It is to Wilson's credit, of course, that by the time, three years later, that the BEF did sail for France, these deficiencies had been thoroughly rectified.

basis was lost'.* Instead, Asquith relied on his own instincts and a stream of advice from Churchill (though not, unfortunately, Churchill's assessment of the German threat). Just over a week after the battle of the Wilsons, in a letter to Haldane on 31 August, the prime minister was not much further forward in his deliberations than he had been at the end of the meeting: 'Sir A. Wilson's "plan" can only be described as puerile, and I have dismissed it at once as wholly impracticable . . . in principle, the General Staff scheme is the only alternative.'

It seems, therefore, that British strategy in the run-up to war was to be based on either a brilliant but partisan display by an Irish showman or an apparently superficial and unquestionably badly presented plan by a salty hero of a bygone age.

The general staff scheme was not the only alternative, of course, but it was the only one that Asquith could practicably expect the War Office to give him – especially as the whole business was being examined against a background of some urgency. He evidently pondered on matters for another month before reaching a decision. Not that at the end of his deliberations he issued any directive – rather, he made an appointment that seemed to signal which way the wind was blowing: on 27 September he offered Churchill the Admiralty. Haldane, though personally disappointed – for he too had wanted the Admiralty, feeling his work at the War Ministry was largely done – immediately offered every help with creating a naval war staff. And although there would be no resolution of Grey's 'great question', or even talks between British and French prime ministers, from then on the orientation of 'Upper Whitehall' – the Admiralty and War Office – was towards the rapid and safe despatch of the BEF to its concentration area at Maubeuge.†

By and large Asquith was content with this, though in November he attempted to clarify the position of His Majesty's government – or rather, to assert somewhat resentfully the primacy of ministers in the matter of policy – by stating that 'all questions of policy have been and must be reserved' for the decision of the cabinet, and that it was 'quite outside the function of military or naval officers to prejudge' them. This was

---

* Bill Jackson and Dwin Bramall, *The Chiefs: The Story of the United Kingdom Chiefs of Staff* (London, 1992).

† Churchill threw himself into the task with characteristic energy – and much else. Six months later, Jacky Fisher, the former first sea lord – whom Churchill would bring back out of retirement when war broke out – was writing to a friend: 'He [Churchill] is brave, which is everything! Napoleonic in audacity, Cromwellian in thoroughness.'

formally embodied in the cabinet resolutions for that month, and then for good measure communicated to the French foreign ministry.

And so, Britain having given no formal undertaking to France, Asquith reckoned there was no harm in the soldiers continuing to talk. In fairness to the War Office, although Henry Wilson would undoubtedly have been happy to dictate policy to the cabinet (indeed, his efforts had amounted to just that) he was not now fool enough to try; all he wanted was clarity of policy, which would enable him to bring total clarity to his war plans. Asquith's policy of 'wait and see' allowed him only generic planning; and generic planning was a difficult notion for a soldier. The trouble was, while the British government, because it did not wish any commitment, would see the talks as merely technical, the French government, because it did wish for a commitment, would regard the continuing talks as a token of earnest. Indeed, before the CID meeting on 23 August, Churchill himself had assumed the Entente to be a de facto treaty with France, his memorandum beginning 'It is assumed that an alliance exists between Great Britain, France, and Russia . . .' And the more talking there was, the more the Elysée believed there was an unspoken pledge.*

But Britain had not made plans in peacetime before, certainly not of this consequence, and the implications of ever closer cooperation

*Asquith had not entirely given up on alternatives. In October 1911 he asked the War Office to look again at the Belgian option – covering Antwerp and operating against the flanks of a German incursion. Churchill did likewise, pressing the point on the logic of reducing the number of divisions that the Germans would be able to pitch against France at the decisive point, for Wilson had conceded that up to a dozen divisions might be drawn off by cooperating with the Belgian army on the flank. However, Wilson's appreciation (which was that of the État-Major) that the Germans would not cross the Meuse in strength would then naturally draw the BEF deep into Belgium – to the Meuse, in fact. The difficulties that would arise from this were only too apparent given the low regard for the Belgian army and the Belgian government's refusal to cooperate in planning. The understandable desire to apply the BEF's strength at the point of decision, which Wilson was increasingly certain was south of the Ardennes, in the region Verdun–Maubeuge, relegated any Belgian option to a subordinate (and undesirable) position. The best that the general staff could do was to see such an option in terms of redeployment by land after entry to France; and so they continued with their detailed schemes for shipping and railing the BEF to a concentration area at Maubeuge. They kept a sort of watching brief on the 'With Belgium' option ('W.F.' was the shorthand for the 'With France' scheme being worked up by Wilson, though some historians have claimed that it stood for 'Wilson–Foch' – as, no doubt, did wags at the time). In April 1912 the military attaché in Brussels, Major Tom Bridges, was asked to probe the Belgian war ministry on the possibilities but managed to imply that the BEF would in the end enter Belgium with or without an invitation. This caused a diplomatic kerfuffle, and the FO had to deny any such intention, putting an end to all thoughts of contingency planning.

between the British and French general staffs – not merely about the mechanics of deployment but about how the BEF would be employed (as the very junior partner) – were largely lost on ministers for whom continental warfare was a wholly alien and abominable notion. Only Churchill, with his suggestion at the war council on 5 August 1914, the day after London declared war, that the BEF should be a strategic reserve for the Western Front, seems to have grasped the implications of allowing the BEF to be absorbed ever more closely into the French order of battle. Haldane might have done had he turned his powerful mind from organization to strategy – which was a distinct possibility now that naval cooperation was assured – but the following year, 1912, he was made lord chancellor, and his place taken by one of his junior ministers, Jack Seely, a Yeomanry officer whose DSO from South Africa was testimony to his dash and courage, but who was not, by general consent, the sharpest of minds (*The Times*'s Repington thought him complacent, and indeed within two years Seely would have to resign over his mishandling of the 'Curragh Mutiny'). And with the capable, if cautious – perhaps pedestrian – sapper, Nicholson, succeeded by Sir John French, another cavalry officer noted more for dash than intellect, the War Office lost a deal of its edge.* It is tempting to think that if Haldane had gone to the Admiralty and Churchill to the War Ministry – or, perhaps best of all, if Churchill had taken *both* portfolios – there would have been both cooperation between the two departments *and* rigorous scrutiny of the plans for the BEF. But in any case, as Lloyd George bemoaned in his memoirs, there were other issues demanding the cabinet's attention – 'Education, Temperance, Land Taxation – culminating in the most serious constitutional crisis since the Reform Bill – the Parliament Act, Home Rule, and the Disestablishment of the Church in Wales'. He recalled very decidedly that 'these subjects challenged an infinite variety of human interests, sentiment and emotion'.

With little interference from above, therefore, from now on the general staff (in truth, Henry Wilson) concentrated all their energy on the 'Foch plan' to the exclusion of any other options. Indeed, Wilson would spend more and more time either in France or with Colonel

---

* Repington believed the efficiency of the War Office to have declined by 50% with the departure of Haldane and Nicholson (and Murray as director military training).

Huguet, the French military attaché in London. The arrangements that on 23 August 1911 might have appeared to ministers as impressively thorough but broad began to get perilously restrictive and narrow. As early as 9 September, not three weeks after the CID meeting, Wilson had briefed Huguet on the green light to planning, and his friend the attaché had told him in turn 'where the French General Staff wanted us to go and what their plans are'. In effect, the BEF was becoming a two-corps reinforcement for the French fighting line.

Indeed, Wilson was already being recognized by the French for his work in this, Huguet telling him that if the DMO had been able to attend the recent French army manoeuvres the war minister 'was himself going to invest [him] with the Legion of Honour'. The evident esteem in which he was held in France might even have been going to his head, for something of his cocksure frame of mind at this time is revealed in two diary entries. When Churchill, still home secretary, had come to his office in the days before the CID meeting, 'He remained three hours with me . . . I was rather pleased with Winston.' And on receiving a despatch from the British military attaché in Paris describing an office call on the new chief of the *État-Major*, Joffre, he was pleased that 'In the main, Joffre seems to agree with me.'

A few months later he was cycling from the Belgian border to Verdun and the great battlefield of Mars-la-Tour, with its *Monument aux Morts 16 et 17 Août 1870*, a poignant sculpture representing *La France* who is supporting a dying soldier letting slip his rifle, with, at their feet, a child trying to take it up, while another grasps the anchor of hope. It evidently affected Wilson deeply, for 'I laid at her feet a small bit of map I had been carrying, showing the areas of concentration of the British forces on her territory'. Even though it cannot have been a serious security risk, as some writers suggest – Wilson is hardly likely to have marked a map in such detail; and in any case, who in the *Grosser Generalstab* could have believed such a find? – the action points at least to a certain loss of objectivity.

But to claim, as some historians have, as did Lloyd George, that in the three years before the shot was fired at Sarajevo the cabinet – certainly its key ministers – were wholly in the dark about the military staff talks, the planning and coordination for the despatch of the BEF to the Continent, is disingenuous. At the cabinet meeting on 1 November 1911, when the Agadir crisis was well past, the 'Liberal imperialists' – notably Asquith, Grey, Haldane and Churchill – were challenged about the military and naval conversations having taken place without the prior knowledge of the cabinet as a whole. There was a 'long and animated discussion', Asquith recorded, led by Lord Morley, lord president of the council, which was only brought to an end by the prime minister's postponing the subject for a fortnight so that tempers might cool (and, crucially, so that the imperialists could prepare a defence of their position). Churchill wrote to Grey a few days later urging him to take 'a very strong position about military consultations with the French' at the next meeting, and to Asquith that 'I think you and Grey will have to make the Cabinet face the realities next Wednesday.'

And Asquith appears to have done so, after his own fashion, for on the fifteenth Haldane wrote to his sister: 'We had a fight yesterday in the Cabinet over the General Staff preparations. McKenna attacked me rather viciously. But the P.M. steered things through.' While this is inconclusive evidence in respect of Lloyd George's claim that 'the cabinet devoted a ridiculously small percentage of its time to a consideration of foreign affairs . . . [while radical] subjects challenged an infinite variety of human interests, sentiment and emotion', it proves at least that Anglo-French military and naval cooperation was known to the cabinet as a whole.

So what? Perhaps only this: if Grey had been able to think through 'the great question', and the radicals had been prepared to discuss the nature of military and naval assistance to France in the event of an attack by Germany (whether violating Belgian neutrality or not), it is possible that the BEF might have been sent to France in 1914 at the right time, to the right place and in the right strength – and, as a strong strategic reserve, to decisive effect. Instead it would cross to France late, at barely two-thirds of its planned fighting strength, to fill a gap in the French line that could have been filled by the French themselves. And by the time the German advance was checked, and the opportunity created for a counter-offensive on the open flank in Flanders, all that the much-depleted BEF would be able to do was serve the mincing machine of Ypres.

That was the price of political evasion in cabinet, and tunnel vision in the War Office.

Above: Prussian militarism. *Left*: Otto von Bismarck (1815–98) in a cuirassier's uniform, although he had served but a year or so in his twenties. *Right*: Helmuth von Moltke (1800–91), architect of Bismarck's military victories and profound influence on subsequent military thinking.

Left: Kaiser Wilhelm II (left), with Helmuth Johann von Moltke (right) and Admiral von Tirpitz (centre).

Below: Kaiser Wilhelm and Moltke at the army manoeuvres in 1913. Although he had no military experience whatever, the Kaiser considered himself a military expert.

Left: The principal signatures on the 1839 Treaty of London – the 'scrap of paper' which guaranteed Belgian independence. Above: Entente Cordiale: K Edward VII initiates reconciliation with France by personal charm offensive in Paris, May 1903.

Left: Lord Haldane, lord chancellor, formerly war minister, and (right) Sir Edward Grey, foreign secretary, on their way to cabinet during the crisis of July 1914. Above: Major-General Henry Wilson, who as director of military operations at the War Office from 1910 to 1914 effectively dictated strategic policy.

Left: Brilliant, procrastinating, distracted: the prime minister, H. H. Asquith, in July 1914. **Above**: His chief distraction, the Honourable Venetia Stanley, Asquith's daily letters to whom are an invaluable guide to the cabinet's deliberations.

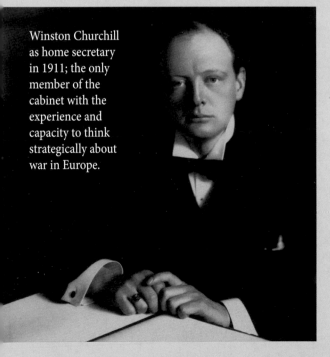

Winston Churchill as home secretary in 1911; the only member of the cabinet with the experience and capacity to think strategically about war in Europe.

Above: David Lloyd George, chancellor of the exchequer, presumed (wrongly, in the end) to be the leader of the anti-war faction of the cabinet.

Above left: The starting pistol. Gavrilo Princip seized after firing the fatal shots in Sarajevo, 28 June 1914. **Above right**: General Alexander von Kluck, commander of the German 1st Army on the great hook west through Belgium that crashed into the BEF at Mons on 23 August. British troops made full use of the rhyming possibilities of his name. **Right**: Prince Lichnowsky, the German ambassador, just before leaving London on 5 August, bitter at what the 'gangsters' and 'swine' in Berlin had done. **Below**: *Westaufmarsch*. German troops cross the Belgian border on 4 August in the first phase of the 'Schlieffen Plan'.

Two photographs, both posed, but both illustrating Belgium's real and spirited resistance to German encroachment. **Above**: troops (on the left 'firing' from the wrong side of cover) at an outpost in typical Flanders country; **below**: the extensive bridge and railway demolitions which significantly slowed the German advance.

German troops finally overrun one of the outer forts at Liège, 15 August.

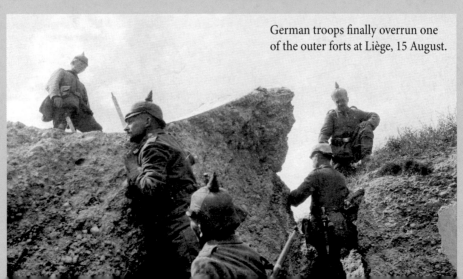

Above: Reservists of the Grenadier Guards, recalled by telegram to their regimental depot at Wellington Barracks, London, 5 August. Some BEF units were two-thirds reservists.
Left: Calling-up of registered horses, South Cave, East Yorkshire, also on 5 August. The BEF relied largely on horsepower still, and the equine mobilization procedures were as comprehensive as the human.

Below: Irish (and Grenadier) Guardsmen readying to march out of barracks for France.

Above: The 2nd Grenadiers leaving Wellington Barracks, Colonel Noel Corry at their head. Key officers in infantry battalions were still mounted at this time. **Below**: 1st Duke of Cornwall's Light Infantry entraining at the Curragh Camp outside Dublin, 13 August.

Lieutenant Hubert Harvey-Kelly of the Royal Flying Corps studying a map next to his BE2 aircraft near Whitby, Yorkshire, during his squadron's flight south from Montrose before the crossing to France.

Above: Cavalry of the BEF on the passage to France – without need of naval escort, Churchill having sent the fleet to battle stations before the outbreak of war.

Below: Troops leaving Boulogne for the BEF's concentration area at Maubeuge near the Belgian border. The detailed railway movement plans – on both sides – went largely without hitch.

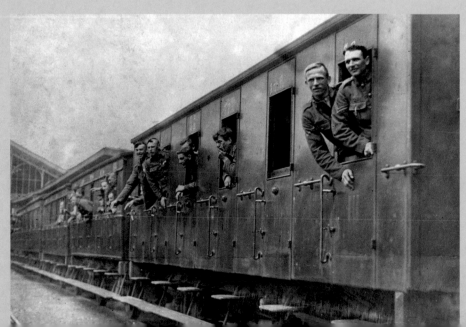

Chapter Eight

THE BONES OF GRENADIERS

The Balkans produce more history than they can consume.

Attributed to Winston Churchill

On 23 October the following year, 1912, Lieutenant-General Sir Douglas Haig, who in January had returned to England from his post as chief of staff in India to take command at Aldershot (earmarked as the headquarters of the BEF's I Corps on mobilization), wrote in his diary: 'Major P. Howell, Staff College, gives a most interesting lecture on the Balkans situation in the Prince Consort's Library.'*

Bismarck had famously told the Reichstag in 1876, when the region was again in ferment, that the Balkans were not worth 'the healthy bones of one of our Pomeranian musketeers' – which he later changed to Pomeranian *grenadiers* – but since that time the interests of Austria had, in the Kaiser's mind, become those of Germany too.† And now in

* The PCL still stands, much as it was in 1912, with an unrivalled collection of books, documents and maps on the history of the army. It was opened in 1860 to plans by Captain Francis Fowke RE, who designed the Royal Albert Hall and parts of the Victoria and Albert Museum. Howell's lectures were published the following year as *The Campaign in Thrace 1912: Six Lectures*. Because Aldershot was the army's principal garrison – 'the home of the British army' – and both Sandhurst and the staff college were nearby, the PCL became something of a military debating chamber.
† 'Der ganze Balkan ist nicht die gesunden Knochen eines einzigen pommerschen Grenadiers wert.' Balkan revolts against the Ottoman Empire threatened to extend to war between Austria and Russia, and Bismarck, mindful above all of the need to avoid war with Russia (he supposedly quipped: 'The secret of politics? Make a good treaty

1912 Austria was being drawn ever closer into those unhealthy places that had of late been the dominion of 'the sick man of Europe'. She had formally annexed Bosnia and Herzegovina four years earlier, in 1908 – in the first of four Balkan crises in six years, the last of which was to lead directly to the world war – after which an expansionist Serbia had (temporarily) given up her aspirations towards those provinces and turned her attentions south instead.* With Constantinople distracted by continuing internal tension, by Russian pressure to open the Dardanelles to the passage of her warships, and by war with Italy over the possession of Tripoli in North Africa, it seemed a propitious moment for the newly formed Balkan League (Serbia, Bulgaria, Greece and Montenegro) to seize more of the southern Balkans from the ailing Ottoman Empire. Mustering three-quarters of a million men, the League had begun to move on 8 October.

Henry Wilson, cutting short a long-planned tour of European capitals, returned to London. From here the situation looked even more precarious, for it became clear that Serbia was intent on acquiring a port on the Mediterranean, that Russia backed her, that Austria was strenuously opposed, and that France was expected to side with Russia, just as Germany was expected to throw in with Austria. On 12 November the Army Council, preparing for the worst, met to agree senior appointments in the BEF (Wilson was to have been deputy chief of staff).

Military events overtook political deliberations, however: the Balkan League was quickly victorious in the First Balkan War, Constantinople suing for peace in early December, and although fighting erupted briefly again in April 1913, for the time being the crisis was past. The speed with which victory had been gained – inside two months – nevertheless gave ammunition to the proponents of conscription. On this, however, Asquith remained utterly unmoved (and would remain so well into the war).

---

with Russia'), insisted: 'I am opposed to the notion of any sort of active participation of Germany in these matters, so long as I can see no reason to suppose that German interests are involved, no interests on behalf of which it is worth our risking – excuse my plain speaking – the healthy bones of one of our Pomeranian musketeers.'
* Germany had been more than ready to go to war at Austria's side in 1908, the Kaiser assuring Franz Ferdinand that 'Austria can depend on me. I will stand by you through thick and thin.' But Russia was enfeebled morally and materially by defeat at the hands of Japan, and without her Serbia was in no position to oppose Austria-Hungary.

Yet a common enemy was never going to be enough to hold together so disparate, so unlikely an alliance as the Balkan League, and in late June fighting broke out again, although this time the Turks stood principally as observers. Serbia, Greece and Romania quarrelled with Bulgaria over the division of their joint conquests in Macedonia. Serbia and Greece formed an alliance and attacked Bulgarian forces in Macedonia, while Romania in turn advanced into southern Dobrudja, Bulgarian territory. Within a fortnight there was an armistice, and a month later a peace treaty. By the middle of 1913 the Turks had been driven almost clean out of the Balkans, holding a mere bridgehead in southern Thrace, with Adrianople (modern Edirne) its furthest out-post not 150 miles from Constantinople – and Serbia had doubled the size of her territory and population.

Not everyone sighed with relief, however. The Kaiser's most recent biographer, Professor John Röhl, contends that to all intents and purposes the First World War was conceived – decided on – in November 1912, and then merely postponed. He reasons that to the Kaiser the First Balkan War promised a massive shift in the balance of power in favour of the Central Powers: 'He thrilled at the military advances of Bulgaria, Roumania, Serbia and Montenegro against Turkey and reviled the statesmen and diplomats working for peace as "eunuchs".'* In October 1912 he had tried to out-Bismarck Bismarck: 'The Eastern Question must be solved by Blood and Iron! But at a time that suits us! That is now!' He dreamed that the four Balkan Christian states would coalesce to form the 'Seventh Great Power' in the Concert of Europe, assuring Germany's domination. The crumbling of the Ottoman Empire – which Germany's ally Italy was doing so much to hasten in Libya – held out the prospect of extending German influence to Odessa, Suez and even to the Hindu Kush: 'The Central Powers will then be preponderant in the Mediterranean [and] hold sway over . . . the entire Mohammedan world!'

Unsurprisingly this view was not shared by Austria, growing increasingly alarmed at the expansion of Serbia on her southern bor-der. Nor was the creation of a 'Seventh Great Power' (which would be principally Orthodox, and therefore pro-Russian) attractive to the

---

* Röhl, 'The Long and Twisted Road to Sarajevo'. The German historian Fritz Fischer (1908–99) advanced the notion in the 1960s that German war aims had been established as early as 1912, and that the Kaiser chose to escalate the crisis of July 1914.

Grosser Generalstab and the Wilhelmstrasse. On the contrary, Austria's conflict with Serbia was a welcome opportunity to settle accounts with Russia and her western ally France before, in Professor Röhl's words, 'the multinational Danube Monarchy became too moribund and before the democratic tide in Germany itself rose even higher'.

Something of the Kaiser's capriciousness can now be seen. First came an adamant refusal to help Vienna – 'Under no circumstances [would he] march on Paris and Moscow' to stop Serbia reaching the Adriatic, he told his advisers on 9 November 1912 – while just days later he was enthusiastically embracing the policy urged on him by Moltke and his ministers: 'Germany's sword is already loose in its scabbard,' he was assuring the Austrian military attaché on the twenty-first; 'you can count on us.' Meanwhile – and tellingly, believes Professor Röhl – the Kaiser told his ambassadors in Paris and London to determine whether France planned to stand by Russia and with whom 'England' would side in the event of war. It was the answers he received from London to questions put by the ambassador Prince Lichnowsky to Haldane, and by the Kaiser's brother Prince Heinrich to King George V, that left the Kaiser in no doubt that Britain would take France's side in the event of attack. When Lichnowksy's report reached Berlin he summoned a 'war council' at which it was decided to pull back from the brink until the new Army Bill had raised the extra troops required for the modified Schlieffen Plan, until the submarine base being built at Heligoland was finished and the Kiel Canal linking the North Sea and the Baltic had been widened to take his dreadnought-class battleships (scheduled for completion in July 1914) – and until the German people had been won over to the idea of war against Russia.

Now the Austrians, who only days before had been given the green light to deal with Serbia, had to be reined back in. The Kaiser assured them, however, that it was but a temporary check, and, indeed, from the summer of 1913 onwards Vienna would again be receiving encouraging signals from Berlin – except that Germany would first have to deploy most of her forces to attack France before turning east, Moltke explained to his Austrian opposite number, Franz (Freiherr) Conrad von Hötzendorf: Germany had no fewer than 113 divisions at her disposal, 'but we have to consider the English who are sure to be on the side of France'.

In October 1912 the advance of the Serbian army into Albania brought an ultimatum from Vienna to Belgrade, to which this time the Kaiser did not object (nor did Moltke, nor the ministers), writing on a despatch from Vienna: 'Now or never! It's high time law and order was established down there!' At the unveiling that month of the vast monument commemorating the centenary of the defeat of Napoleon at Leipzig – the 'Battle of the Nations' – he assured Conrad: 'I shall go with you. The other Powers are not ready, they won't do anything to oppose you . . . I have always favoured peace, but there are limits . . . There comes a point when a Great Power can no longer stand aside but *must* draw the sword.' And then, going straight to Vienna, he told the Austrian foreign minister, Count Berchtold, that Russia would not be ready to fight for at least six years, and that 'in the forthcoming *racial* [italics added] struggle' Austria-Hungary and Germany would fight side by side: 'Whatever steps the Vienna Foreign Office now decided to take would be treated by him as an order . . .'

Professor Röhl concludes – aptly, given the centrality of railways to the story: 'Sarajevo now lay straight ahead and the road was clear.'*

---

* 'Clear road ahead' was, famously, the lookout's call on the footplate. There are, of course, other interpretations, and Röhl's is probably the minority view. But it is worth considering this report on the German war council of 8 December 1912 by Admiral Georg von Müller, chief of the imperial naval cabinet, and a 'hawk': '[Moltke said] "I consider a war inevitable – the sooner, the better. But we should do a better job of gaining popular support for a war against Russia, in line with the Kaiser's remarks." H.M. [the Kaiser] confirmed this and asked the secretary of state to use the press to work toward this end. T[irpitz] called attention to the fact that the navy would gladly see a major war delayed by one and a half years. Moltke said that even then the navy would not be ready, and the army's situation would continue to worsen, since due to our limited financial resources our opponents are able to arm themselves more rapidly. That was the end of the conference. There were almost no results. The Chief of the Great General Staff says: "War the sooner the better," but he does not draw the logical conclusion from this, which is: to present Russia or France or both with an ultimatum which would unleash the war with right on our side' (*War Premeditated: The War Council of 8 December 1912 Revisited*, quoted by Röhl, 'The Long and Twisted Road to Sarajevo'). Holger Herwig, for one, in *The Marne, 1914*, is adamant that the decision was not taken until later: 'The decision for war was made in late July 1914, and not at a much-publicized "war council" at Potsdam on 8 December 1912 . . . no one planned for a European War before 1914; the absence of financial or economic blueprints for such an eventuality speaks for itself.' Laying aside the caution that absence of evidence is not evidence of absence (see also contrary evidence in chapter 9), Herwig's view is not inconsistent with Röhl's: the *intention* to decide on war, when the circumstances were the most opportune (in about 'one and a half years'), is clearly evident in Müller's report; Herwig, however, fails to quote the report in full – omitting Müller's own damning assessment at the end.

*

The immediate consequence of these short Balkan wars was territorial and strategic. Greece gained southern Macedonia and Crete, Serbia the Kosovo region and tracts of northern and central Macedonia, and Albania became an independent state under a German prince (whose reign would last a fraction short of six months before he was forced to flee the country in September 1914). Bulgaria, having been frustrated in her desire to take the lion's share of Macedonia (indeed, perhaps even to move her capital from Sofia to Constantinople), would now look increasingly to Austria for support, while Serbia, forced by Austria to give up her Albanian conquests, would regard Vienna with greater hostility than ever – and, as a result, St Petersburg would regard Vienna likewise.

But there was a psychological consequence too. To London, the containment of the ferment *within* the Balkans, with the great powers staying above the actual fray, suggested (to the politicians at least) that this would somehow be the norm – that 'goodwill and wise counsel' would prevail. And it was this assumption, together with the inability to fathom the 'great question' – the extent of the guarantee to France implicit in the Entente Cordiale – that would ultimately prove Britain's undoing. So when on 28 June 1914 Gavrilo Princip, a Bosnian Serb, assassinated the heir presumptive to the Austrian throne, Archduke Franz Ferdinand, and his duchess (thereby flicking the switch that turned Professor Röhl's amber light to green), it did not register with any great moment in London. Asquith's letters to Venetia Stanley contain a passing, even arch, reference to being 'here [the War Office, whose portfolio he had taken after Seely's resignation] for an "obituary" on the Austrian royalties', and then nothing at all until 24 July, when he wrote that, even if it came to war, 'Happily there seems to be no reason why we should be anything more than spectators.' The many letters in between – sometimes several in a day – are full of remarkably sensitive detail on the continuing Irish home rule crisis, but not a word on the situation in Europe. Absence of evidence of disquiet is not, of course, evidence of absence of disquiet: in his 24 July letter he qualified his spectator-only view of events by conceding that 'we are within measurable ... distance of a real Armageddon' (an opinion he almost certainly gave also to the King); yet the whole tenor of Asquith's correspondence with Venetia Stanley, which he began in earnest in 1912, is such that had he truly been anxious he would have said so. Indeed, as events gained momentum the letters reveal a deep need for her reassurance.

Nor were Asquith's diary and letters the only contemporary records free of entries on the European situation. The diary of Captain (RN) Mansfield Cumming, head of the foreign section of the Secret Service Bureau, gives no sense of the imminence of war, the assassination passing wholly unremarked. Yet for six months and more Cumming had been working assiduously on establishing a network of agents along Germany's western frontier – including the 'Maastricht appendix' – to give early warning of attack and to continue reporting after war had started, and on cultivating his shipping-reporting agents in Denmark, but none of these was picking up signs of unusual activity. Nor did his increasingly close links with the French and the Russian secret services turn up hard intelligence, only a conviction that war would come at some time in the future. Two years earlier, after his first contacts with Colonel Charles-Édouard Dupont, head of the French *Deuxième Bureau*, he had written: '[Dupont] very strong indeed as to the vital necessity of our meeting each other and deciding now at once upon a plan of concerted action to be taken *when the crisis came*' (italics added). Earlier in 1914 Cumming had at last got approval and funding for his scheme to base an aeroplane in northern France to keep watch along the border with Germany (and presumably also the Belgian border with Germany), and as the echo of the shots in Sarajevo began seemingly to fade he actually bought the machine, though ironically the July crisis would overtake its deployment.*

And there was another, impartial, testifier to the general air of

---

* The foreign section of the new Secret Service Bureau (later the Secret Intelligence Service, SIS) had been established in 1909 on the recommendation of the CID, but inevitably it took time to establish its organization, procedures and focus, especially as funding was tight. It was only when the war settled into the more familiar landscape of the Western Front that the section really began to count. The major part of the intelligence establishing the German order of battle and dispositions in 1917 and 1918 – of key importance to GHQ in coping with the massive German offensive of spring 1918, and then the counter-offensive preceding the Armistice ('The Hundred Days') – was the work of SIS, whose agents were supplying a stream of information especially through neutral Holland (train-watching was a major activity) (Keith Jeffery, *MI6: The History of the Secret Intelligence Service 1909–1949*, London, 2010; correspondence with Sir John Scarlett, former DG SIS). Cumming used to initial papers he had read with 'C' in green ink; hence the custom of calling the head of service 'C'.

unconcern, and to the reaction to the assassination in particular. 'Colonel' Edward House, President Woodrow Wilson's special envoy, had arrived in London via Paris on 9 June after meetings with the Kaiser.* In his memoirs Sir Edward Grey recalls how House

> had just come from Berlin, and he had spoken with grave feeling of the impression he had received there; how the air seemed full of the clash of arms, of readiness to strike. This might have been discounted as the impression that would naturally have been produced on an American seeing at close quarters a continental military system for the first time. It was as alien to our temperament as to his, but it was familiar to us. We had lived beside it for years; we had known and watched its growth ever since 1870.†

House's impression might have been discounted, says Grey: 'But House was a man of exceptional knowledge and cool judgment. What if this militarism had now taken control of policy?'

If indeed. The fastidious Grey – like Lord Halifax, a generation later, who could not quite believe that men could be as evil as the Nazis appeared – could not grasp the essential coarseness and lethal absurdity of the Kaiser's nature, and the atmosphere he had created. What would he have made of His Imperial and Royal Majesty's complaint that his diplomats 'had so filled their pants that the entire Wilhelmstrasse stinks of shit'? The Kaiser would not have found bird-watching with Grey on the banks of the Itchen convivial, as former President Theodore Roosevelt had in 1910. Wilhelm II was another Charles I, but without the aestheticism. Believing in the divine right of kings and the moral superiority of his race, he would still be insisting, just days before the war, that only he, as a 'military expert', could understand the international situation which the 'civilian Chancellor [Bethmann Hollweg] still failed to grasp'.

* 'Colonel' was an honorific, customary in the southern United States (House was a Texan), given to a man of seniority and standing irrespective of military service, which House had not seen. House would be instrumental in advancing Wilson's 'Fourteen Points', the basis for the German surrender and the Armistice, and in drafting the covenant of the League of Nations.
† Viscount Grey of Fallodon, *Twenty-Five Years 1892–1916* (London, 1925).

But House himself, while not believing that Grey, with whom he had several long meetings, discounted his view entirely, was nevertheless struck by London's habituation to the armed camp across the Channel and the North Sea, and how the Irish home rule bill and women's suffrage were occupying His Majesty's ministers, even after the fateful shots in Sarajevo. 'The news of the Archduke's assassination reached London at the height of the Irish crisis and feminist agitation,' he records; 'and it created no more audible effect than a tenor solo in a boiler-shop.'*

Henry Wilson's diary, too, confirms that the boiler-shop noise was coming from Ireland, for the threat of armed resistance to home rule by the Ulster Unionists, led by the former Solicitor-General, Sir Edward Carson, and the uncertain response of the army, was monopolizing everyone's attention. With the war secretary Seely, Sir John French and the rest of the Army Council all having resigned not three months before in the wake of the 'Curragh Mutiny', it is hardly surprising.† Even so, for there to be no mention of the situation in Europe in the diary of the DMO until 25 July, the day after Asquith's letter to Venetia Stanley, is quite remarkable: a month 'lost' – a month of preparation; a month at least of thinking through the 'great question' again. For Asquith's 'Happily there seems to be no reason why we should be anything more than spectators' betrays his persistent, habitual complacency. It was no good basing judgements on what *seemed* to be; in matters of the defence of the realm the duty of

---

* Charles Seymour, *The Intimate Papers of Colonel House* (New York, 1926).
† Seely, acting for the cabinet, had somehow managed to give the GOC-in-C Ireland, Sir Arthur Paget (not the subtlest of officers), the impression that he was to seek the views of his command. This Paget did by putting a hypothetical question to his commanding officers along the lines: 'Would they obey an order to take coercive measures against the Unionists?' The great majority of officers of the 3rd Cavalry Brigade at the Curragh camp outside Dublin, several of whom were of the 'Anglo-Irish Ascendancy', including their brigadier, Hubert Gough, wrote to Paget that they would resign rather than obey such an order. Confusion ensued over a vague promise to let officers with a personal interest take leave during such operations, which to London's eyes amounted to connivance at mutiny, and Gough was summoned to the War Office. There followed much petulance on the part of Gough and Seely, and an uncharacteristic lack of 'grip' by French. The King was drawn in and matters became very unedifying, ending in what appeared to be a climb-down by Seely, who ascribed the affair to a misunderstanding. It was not a true mutiny – no one had disobeyed a direct order – but the press said it was, and the name stuck. The affair, although eclipsed by the outbreak of war within months, would nevertheless have deep repercussions for Anglo-Irish relations – far more so than is usually recognized.

the statesman was to see clearly what *might* be – every possibility, indeed.

Colonel House had.*

* In fact, House had already persuaded Grey to let him make overtures to the Kaiser on his behalf for what would be called, sixty years later, *détente*, writing to President Wilson on 3 July: 'Sir Edward Grey would like me to convey to the Kaiser the impressions I have obtained from my several discussions with this Government, in regard to a better understanding between the nations of Europe, and to try and get a reply before I leave. Sir Edward said he did not wish to send anything official or in writing, for fear of offending French and Russian sensibilities in the event it should become known. He thought it was one of those things that had best be done informally and unofficially.' And indeed House did write to the Kaiser in these terms; but by the time the letter arrived in Berlin, Wilhelm had left for his annual North Sea cruise. Yet what good it might have done is a very moot point. In January 1912 Asquith had sent the Germanophone Haldane to Berlin to try to negotiate an end to the naval 'arms race'. The initiative failed. Indeed, it worse than failed, for the Kaiser thereby managed to convince himself that his goal of forcing Britain to abandon 'the balance of power' had been achieved: 'England is drawing closer to us not in spite of but because of My Imperial Navy.'

Chapter Nine

A DEADLY QUADRILLE

When Austria is in trouble, every cripple must be at his post.

Jaroslav Hašek, *The Good Soldier Svejk and his Fortunes in
the World War* (1923)

The Imperial Austrian authorities had quickly established the facts.
While the assassins in Sarajevo – a team of six – were all Austrian subjects, they had been armed by Serbia and smuggled back into Austrian
territory by the Serb nationalist organization Narodna Odbrana
(People's Defence), set up in the aftermath of the Austrian annexation
of Bosnia and Herzegovina in 1908. The real string-pullers, however,
were the even more shadowy organization Crna Ruka, the 'Black
Hand', formed in 1901 by officers of the Serbian army and controlled
by Colonel Dragutin Dimitrijević, codenamed 'Apis' (supposedly after
the Ancient Egyptian bull-deity), himself one of the assassins of the
Serbian king and queen in 1903.*

* Strictly, the society was called Ujedinjenje Ili Smrt – 'Unification [or Union] or Death'.
Its aim was the uniting of all territories with significant Serb populations not ruled by
Serbia – 'Where there be Serbs there be Serbia'. It took its colloquial name from La Mano
Nera, an extortion racket originating in the Kingdom of Naples in the eighteenth
century and taken to the US by Italian immigrants in the 1880s, an early form of the
Mafia. Threats were accompanied by the black imprint of a hand, which clearly
appealed to the Serb extremists. The murder of the Serbian royal family had been
brutal even by Balkan standards, though the strange 26-year-old King Alexander
Obrenović (and Queen Draga, twelve years his senior) passed largely unmourned,
succeeded by the much admired and militarily able King Peter Karadordević.

Vienna now had its proof, if proof it needed, of Serb malevolence, and Vienna determined on condign punishment – war. And had the Austro-Hungarian army marched at once on Belgrade in a sort of hot pursuit, the rest of Europe might have stood aside. For even Russia's pan-Slavism had its limits: she could not underwrite every folly drafted in Cyrillic (she had not lifted a finger to help the Bulgarians the year before). But instead Vienna felt obliged to consult (from St Petersburg's perspective, conspire) with Berlin.* And it suited Berlin very well indeed to elevate the event from yet another piece of Balkan barbarism to an issue of international substance. For as Professor Röhl argues, the German decision for war would not be driven merely by hectic events in the Balkans: long-standing military and naval planning calculations were also determining policy, 'and the Kaiser and the General Staff believed themselves to be ready, albeit in the expectation that France would be crushed in five weeks and that the campaign against the hopelessly backward Russian army would be a walk in the park'.†

After all, the *Eisenbahnabteilung* had done its work: the new mobilization timetable for the increased provisions of the Army Bill of 1913 had been completed, and new railway lines and depots constructed. The *Finanzministerium* had bought large quantities of gold at a premium on the London exchange, and the *Reichsbank* stood ready to suspend the convertibility of its notes to prevent a run on its gold reserves. Tinned meat had been stockpiled in depots around the country, Dutch middlemen had been contracted to import vital supplies through Rotterdam, and agents had been found to coal His Imperial Majesty's ships in distant neutral ports. And – stuff of myth though it sounds – fast German passenger liners had been covertly crewed by German marines in readiness for war, while, as Professor Röhl wryly notes, 'Moltke took not one but two cures at Karlsbad in the vain hope of getting himself fit for the great racial showdown about to begin'. Britain – Germany's ultimate enemy in her quest for

* Sir John Keegan ascribes this to 'the precautionary mood of thought which decades of contingent war planning had implanted in the mind of European governments' (*The First World War*, London, 1998). To be fair to Austria, though arguably to go beyond fairness, her consultation might be construed as taking cognizance of the international repercussions of any action of hers. But no treaty – certainly not the Triple Alliance – obliged her to do so.
† Röhl, 'The Long and Twisted Road to Sarajevo'.

her proper imperial place in the world – remained an unknown quantity, and although the high seas fleet was not yet at anything like the strength needed to assure the defeat of the Royal Navy, Admiral Tirpitz could at least be satisfied that the Kaiser Wilhelm (Kiel) Canal had now been widened to take dreadnought-sized warships, and the *U-Boot* harbour on Heligoland fortified.

The Kaiser himself had been active, too. Once again, just as he had in November 1912 during the First Balkan War, on 16 June 1914 (twelve days *before* Sarajevo) he ordered Prince Lichnowsky to ascertain what would be Britain's stance in the event of a European war; and, just as he had in December 1912, he would later despatch his brother Prince Heinrich, an honorary admiral in the Royal Navy and a Knight of the Garter, who was yachting at the Cowes Regatta, on the same mission to King George V. His cousin assured the prince that 'England would maintain neutrality in case war should break out between the Continental Powers', but on learning of this, Asquith demanded a retraction: His Majesty's Government had no settled position, he insisted, but it did have obligations towards Belgian neutrality.* On that same day, 16 June, Moltke's deputy, Georg von Waldersee, summoned the military representatives of the three non-Prussian German kingdoms – Saxony, Württemberg and Bavaria – to the *Generalstab Hauptquartier* and ordered them to cease all written reporting until further notice. Professor Röhl asks the intriguing question: 'Did he have foreknowledge of the attempt on the life of Franz Ferdinand, at Sarajevo less than two weeks later?'†

Whatever was happening, by design or by chance, the Kaiser was

---

* Lichnowsky, suspected by Berlin of being too pro-British (the eternal ambassadorial disease of 'going native'), was largely kept in the dark. He would genuinely reassure Sir Edward Grey that Berlin wanted to act as mediator and restrainer with Austria-Hungary. But the use of family channels of communication was not helping: George V denied expressing himself so firmly to Prince Heinrich, and the 'retraction' – or rather 'clarification', since by the King's account there was nothing to retract – did not carry any weight at all with the Kaiser, who, at a crucial moment in the crisis (29 July 1914), would declare: 'I have the word of a King and that is enough for me!'

† This strange instruction to the military representatives was never likely to be effective, since (in peace at least) the officers' first loyalty was to their sovereign, not to the general staff. A fortnight later the Saxon ambassador in Berlin was writing to his king that the general staff wanted Austria to attack Serbia as quickly as possible because the time was right for a general war since Germany was more prepared for war than either Russia or France, while the Saxon military attaché, Lieutenant-General Freiherr von Leuckhart, reported that the general staff 'would be pleased if war were to come about now'.

playing his part to perfection – at least by the standard of bombast that had obtained at Potsdam since Bismarck's dismissal. On 5 and 6 July at the Neues Palais, the old Schloss Friedrichskron, he received his generals and Captain Hans Zenker, Tirpitz's representative (but not Moltke, who was still on his *Kur*), and his ministers, in separate audiences, and having assured himself that the army was ready for mobilization, he issued orders for the surreptitious mobilization of the fleet. Then, at the behest of the chancellor, Bethmann Hollweg (in Professor Röhl's words), 'he sailed off on his annual cruise to the Arctic Circle, ostensibly unaware of the crisis that he and his advisers had set in train'.

That 'ostensibly' is important. Historians sometimes cite the cruise as evidence of Berlin's unawareness of the gravity of unfolding events: how could the Kaiser, whose signature would be needed on the order for mobilization, set off for far northern waters if war was any sort of possibility, let alone imminent? In fact the royal yacht *Hohenzollern* anchored in the Sognefjord north of Bergen, from where she could return to Germany within twenty-four hours for the Kaiser to sign the mobilization order if needed (and he could sign it in even less time if there were a rendezvous at sea – or at Heligoland).

But events in Berlin – let alone the rest of Europe – were in any case no longer under the Kaiser's direct control. Moltke and the general staff, with the connivance, enthusiastic or otherwise, of the chancellor and the Wilhelmstrasse, now sought to engineer war with Russia and France in such a way as to make Germany appear the victim of Russian aggression, the single best way of uniting the country for the struggle to come – and even, perhaps, of securing Britain's neutrality. As the crisis mounted and the Kaiser returned, Tirpitz would ignore his orders to bombard the Russian Baltic ports, Bethmann Hollweg would keep him away from Berlin, and the Wilhelmstrasse would withhold or doctor his telegrams. All this might suggest, prima facie, that the Kaiser himself did not now want war; but given all the earlier evidence of his bellicosity, it more likely suggests that the key military and civil players – Bethmann Hollweg, Moltke, Tirpitz and the war minister General von Falkenhayn – were determined to handle the transition to war on their terms, not those of His Imperial Majesty, a meddling amateur with a belief in the divine right of kings. Whatever the truth, Haldane at the War Office hit the nail squarely on the head when on 20 July he forwarded to Grey a letter from Count Alexander Hoyos, the Austrian foreign minister's *chef de cabinet*, justifying the action that Vienna was about to take against Serbia, with his own comment: 'This is very serious. Berchtold [the Austrian foreign minister] is apparently ready to plunge Europe into war to settle the Serbian question. He would not take this attitude unless he was assured of German support.'

Indeed. In fact, German support was exactly what Vienna had been promised the day before the Kaiser left for his cruise. In what was in effect a blank cheque, Bethmann Hollweg telegraphed Vienna that, regarding Serbia, Austria-Hungary 'must judge what is to be done to clear the course', but that whatever was decided, Germany would be a faithful ally and friend. Lieutenant-General Hermann von Bertrab, chief of the survey department, who had had an interview with the Kaiser early on 6 July just before he had gone aboard *Hohenzollern* – the last officer to see him before he sailed – wrote to Moltke that His Majesty had told him that he had approved the decision by Vienna to march into Serbia, and that Germany would 'cover Austria in the event of Russia's intervening'.

Vienna took a fortnight and more to cash this blank cheque. Finally, on 23 July, Austria delivered an ultimatum to the Serbs. It was harsh and hostile, couched in terms which no practised foreign ministry could have supposed another sovereign nation might accept – certainly not in every detail.* And if there were lingering thoughts that Russia might sit out the crisis, that same evening, just as France's president (and former prime minister) Raymond Poincaré was setting sail for St Petersburg for talks, Vienna received a telegram thence counselling – warning – Austria-Hungary not to place undue demands on Belgrade. Even so, a shaken Serbian council of ministers met the following day and decided to comply with most of the Austrian demands, and to play for time – telegraphing St Petersburg for support. The Russian council of ministers agreed at once to back

---

* When Sir Edward Grey told his friend Prince Lichnowsky that 'any nation that accepted conditions like that would really cease to count as an independent nation', the Kaiser wrote in the margin of Lichnowsky's report: 'That would be very desirable. It [Serbia] is not a nation in the European sense, but a band of robbers!' Strictly, the Austrian démarche was not an ultimatum since it did not expressly threaten war as the consequence of non-compliance; it was a 'series of demands'. But the Entente powers – and others – referred to it as such from the outset.

Serbia to the extent of war if necessary. Meanwhile Bethmann Hollweg sent the Entente powers a note supporting the Austrian ultimatum and warning that their intervention would 'bring about inestimable consequences'.

The French government now formally warned Joffre that war was likely, while Belgium – 'brave little Belgium', as she would soon become to the British press – declared that she would uphold her neutrality 'whatever the consequences'.

The following day, 25 July, a Saturday, Russia initiated her 'period preparatory to war' measures, although the Tsar still recoiled from ordering even partial mobilization, while officially expressing 'the greatest anxiety' and warning that the country 'cannot remain indifferent' to Austrian threats against Serbia.

German observers in St Petersburg reported 'obvious war preparations', while in Berlin the foreign minister, Jagow, made a ploy to throw the Entente powers off the scent by publicly urging Austria to extend her deadline to the Serbs, while privately urging that she quickly attack them. Vienna, however, had already rejected an urgent Russian request to extend the deadline. At Sognefjord, the Kaiser – supposedly having read of the ultimatum in the Norwegian papers – curtailed his cruise and ordered the high seas fleet to return to home waters. In the middle of the afternoon, Belgrade, emboldened by the promise of Russian support, ordered general mobilization (having begun calling up selected reservists as early as 18 July). Two minutes short of the deadline the Serbian prime minister, Nikola Pašić, summoned the Austrian ambassador, Wladimir (Freiherr) Giesl von Gieslingen, and delivered Serbia's generally conciliatory but clever and evasive reply, adding: 'We accept your demands . . . for the rest, we place our hopes on your loyalty and chivalry as an Austrian general. We have always been very satisfied with you.'

Giesl replied in similar diplomatic terms, took his leave and rushed back to the embassy, where his staff were already burning papers and packing their belongings. As soon as he had studied the Serbs' note he sent the prepared reply to what Vienna had presumed would be the unsatisfactory response (he had in fact been instructed – and much earlier – to reject the Serbian reply whatever its contents). The Serb foreign ministry arranged for troops to escort the Austrian embassy staff to the railway station, which they reached without incident,

'Brave little Belgium': Punch *cartoon of 12 August 1914 – only a week after German violation of Belgian neutrality, already the doughty (and unexpected) resistance of the much inferior Belgian army was a cause for admiration and the call to arms. As yet, however, the stories of German atrocities had evidently not gained much purchase, for the 'Hun at the gate' looks more a bullying old fool than the heir of Attila.*

boarding the last train for Semlin, just across the Sava river, in Hungary.* There, Giesl made his way to the local garrison office, where the Hungarian prime minister, István Tisza, was the first to speak to him by telephone: 'Did it have to be?' asked Tisza forlornly, to which Giesl replied simply: 'Yes.' That evening Vienna issued orders for partial mobilization, to begin on 28 July.

With the formal departure of the Austrian ambassador from Belgrade, and in consequent expectation of an immediate offensive, the Serbian government now left the capital, which lay just across the river from Austria-Hungary, and the following day Serbian sappers blew the bridge over the Sava. Elsewhere too the wheels of mobilization were turning. St Petersburg reacted that evening, recalling troops to their quarters and giving immediate commissions to cadets at the military academies. Paris quietly recalled all generals from leave. In Rome, capital of the uncertain member of the Triple Alliance (but, with thirty divisions and a modern navy, potentially a decisive one), the foreign minister, the Marchese di San Giuliano, who had recommended to the Serbian ambassador that Belgrade nominally accept all Austrian demands and then entangle Vienna in prolonged negotiations, was still determined on neutrality – at least, perhaps, until the outcome of war became clearer. Under the terms of the Triple Alliance – a defensive treaty – Italy was not required to mobilize unless either Austria or Germany were attacked. The attempts by Moltke and Bethmann Hollweg to provoke Russia into the act of aggression were therefore of real significance to the balance of forces.

The following day, 26 July, St Petersburg ordered the partial call-up of reserves and put its military bases on alert. Ironically, Russia, the most backward of the great powers, had the flexibility in its staff procedures to take selective call-up measures – as did Serbia and Austria. On the other hand, Germany, the most militarily sophisticated, had an all-or-nothing system – thanks to the *Eisenbahnabteilung*'s rigid movement plans, which were predicated on the two-front war and in which mobilization and concentration were inextricably linked. However, the next day the *Stavka*, the Russian general staff, concluded that mobilization against Austria alone would be suicidal, and urged the council of ministers to think again.

* Now Zemun, a municipality of Belgrade.

Meanwhile Sir Edward Grey, alarmed but still believing in the civilized diplomacy that had appeared to accomplish so much in earlier crises, proposed a four-power conference with himself taking the chair, and the French, German and Italian ambassadors negotiating on their governments' behalf, during which Austria would suspend military operations. Prince Lichnowsky eagerly supported the idea in his telegram to the Wilhelmstrasse, which, anxious not to appear warmongering, passed it on to the Austrians telling them to look as if they were giving it serious consideration. The proposal would, of course, come to nothing.

On the afternoon of the twenty-sixth Churchill, less sanguine than Grey about a peaceful diplomatic outcome, secretly ordered the fleet to remain at Portland, where it had concentrated after the recent manoeuvres, and the naval reservists called up for the practice alert to remain with their ships. Some historians have suggested that this de facto mobilization of the fleet robbed London of a powerful signal in the days to come – the great gesture of mobilizing the Royal Navy, the one military machine in Europe that Berlin feared. Be that as it may, the fleet's fortuitous early readiness would be of incalculable value in the opening weeks of the war. The following day, 27 July, Churchill ordered the Mediterranean fleet to prepare to shadow potentially hostile warships, while the War Office quietly ordered certain key reserve officers to report to BEF headquarters units, and the GOC-in-C Southern Command (Sir Horace Smith-Dorrien) was ordered to place guards on vulnerable points in Hampshire, Dorset and Devon. Only now did *The Times* make the crisis its lead story, with a headline proclaiming 'PEACE IN THE BALANCE'. The cabinet met for an hour in the early evening to deal with the worsening situation in Ireland: troops of the King's Own Scottish Borderers had opened fire on gun-runners in Dublin and killed and wounded a good many bystanders. At the end of the meeting Grey briefly outlined his proposals for the four-power conference; but there was no discussion of Britain's obligations in the event of war.

At eleven in the morning of the next day, Tuesday, 28 July, Austria-Hungary declared war on Serbia. Pašić heard the news as he lunched in the aptly named Hotel Europa in Nish, southern Serbia, whither his government had sped. That evening, after long consultation with the Tsar, and despite the misgivings of the *Stavka*, the Russian foreign minister Sergei Sazonov announced partial mobilization against Austria, with placatory words towards Berlin. The Austrians' reaction was outright alarm: Conrad, the commander-in-chief, insisted that the foreign minister, Count Berchtold, press Germany to threaten to mobilize in order to force Russia to abandon its isolating mobilization against Austria alone. Meanwhile the German war minister, Falkenhayn, had ordered all troops on summer manoeuvres to return to their garrisons. In London, the Admiralty was stealing a march on the *Kaiserliche Marine*: Churchill gave the order for the fleet to sail – darkened – to Scapa Flow.

But across the Atlantic the *New York Times*, spectacularly wide of the mark in its editorial opinion, insisted that 'A general European war is unthinkable . . . Europe can't afford such a war, and the world can't afford it, and happily the conviction is growing that such an appalling conflict is altogether beyond the realm of possibility.'

Chapter Ten

THE GREAT QUESTION ANSWERED

On London fell a clearer light;
Caressing pencils of the sun
Defined the distances, the white
Houses transfigured one by one,
The 'long, unlovely street' impearled.
O what a sky has walked the world!

Alice Meynell, 'Summer in England, 1914'

On Wednesday morning, 29 July, the weather unusually cool (barely 17 degrees in London at midday), the cabinet met. The first item on the agenda was not the situation in Europe but – again – Ireland. It was dealt with speedily, however: changes were to be made in the Royal Irish Constabulary. Ministers then began their first substantive discussion of the continental crisis since the shots at Sarajevo (unbelievable as it seems), in particular the question of Belgian neutrality. Grey had prepared papers on the obligations under the London treaty of 1839 – at least, as the treaty was understood in 1870, when Gladstone had examined it on the eve of the Franco-Prussian War. Then the government's law officers had concluded that the guarantee of neutrality was never meant to have been conditional on unanimity among the signatories since any violation of that neutrality was likely to be perpetrated by one or more of them in the first instance. But Asquith's cabinet would not agree: several

189

ministers, possibly even a majority, took the view that the treaty of 1839 required collective action, even if – quite evidently – it could not be on the part of *all* the signatories. Nor was it clear whether Britain (and France) could take military action on Belgian soil uninvited by Belgium without putting themselves in breach of the treaty. There never was a treaty that more resembled a Swiss cheese.

Asquith told the cabinet, only a few of whom had been at the meeting of the CID on 23 August 1911, of the general staff's assessment: that if it came to war the Germans would indeed attack France through Belgium, but that the movement would be confined to the south-east corner, between the Sambre and Meuse rivers, in which case the Belgians might offer only token resistance and not call for help; and that there was also the possibility that the French would move into Belgium pre-emptively, thereby breaching its neutrality. In the discussion that followed, there was a view that if the violation were limited it might be possible for Britain to keep her sword sheathed, but that if the Germans looked like reaching the coast and occupying Belgium, then British interests would be threatened and the game would be a different one altogether. The cabinet would come to no decision, however, because Asquith would not press them to one (and they certainly would not consent to Churchill's request to mobilize the fleet fully).* They would not declare support for the other two members of the 'Triple Entente', although neither would they declare neutrality in all circumstances. Indeed, the cabinet's own state of collective uncertainty now became policy: Grey was instructed to be deliberately ambiguous, to tell the French ambassador not to count on British support and the German ambassador not to count on our not supporting France. Such a ploy was the very worst of a bad hand of options, for although, as Herbert Samuel, president of the Local Government Board, put it in a letter to his wife that afternoon, 'if both sides do not know what we shall do, both sides will be less willing to run risks', it allowed both the French and the Germans to take an 'optimistic' as well as a 'pessimistic' view of British intentions, encouraging them in their calculations of risk – in Berlin that Britain would stay above the fray, in Paris that she would stand

---

* Not that Churchill was straining for a fight: while wanting to take precautionary measures, he proposed that the crowned heads of Europe 'be brought together for the sake of peace'.

by her. It was a weak way to exercise the deterrent effect of hard power. But the fact was that the cabinet at this stage was clearly divided on the question of whether the Treaty of London was binding – certainly to military action. Asquith, doubtless in his metaphorical QC's gown, tried to sum up the cabinet's mind when he called on the King: 'It is doubtful how far a single guaranteeing State is bound under the Treaty of 1839 to maintain Belgian neutrality if the remainder abstain or refuse. The Cabinet consider that the matter if it arises will be one of policy rather than of legal obligation.'

The cabinet had 'decided not to decide', wrote John Burns, president of the Board of Trade. A decade's naval and military spending and planning had evidently been directed towards an indefinite policy. In his memoirs, Grey summed up the denouement of the decade's evasion of the 'great question':

> [I knew] That, if war came, the interest of Britain required that we should not stand aside, while France fought alone in the West, but must support her. I knew it to be very doubtful whether the Cabinet, Parliament, and the country would take this view on the outbreak of war, and through the whole of this week I had in view the probable contingency that we should not decide at the critical moment to support France. In that event I should have to resign; but the decision of the country could not be forced, and the contingency might not arise, and meanwhile I must go on.

Barbara Tuchman, whose *The Guns of August* (in Britain, *August 1914*) has long been the received narrative, writes gratingly: 'No more distressing moment can ever face a British government than that which requires it to come to a hard and fast and specific decision.' Perhaps she was getting in a return swipe for Churchill's (much) later remark that 'the Americans will always do the right thing . . . after they've exhausted all the alternatives,' but on this particular she was on to something: with diplomatic telegraph traffic becoming ever more clamorous, it was not at all obvious that Asquith's 'wait and see' was the right policy.*

The trouble was that the false lesson of the previous decade was

---

* Asquith himself appears to have been in no doubt that war was imminent, writing to Venetia Stanley that afternoon that 'it seems now as if nothing but a miracle cd avert it' – which made it doubly curious that there should have been anything else on the cabinet agenda that day.

confidence in, not just the desirability of, the diplomatic solution – the conviction that all it needed was for the right means to be found. Nevertheless, prudence required the priming of the machinery for going to war, otherwise the cabinet would have its choices curtailed when the time came to make a definitive decision. 'Precautionary period' was therefore declared, though not without some confusion. The 'War Book' had only recently been revised,* but Asquith's private secretary had to ring Maurice Hankey, secretary of the CID, to say that 'no one had the slightest idea how to start the ball rolling'. Hankey, who received the call while at lunch in the United Service Club in Pall Mall – not a bread roll's throwing distance from the German embassy – replied that each minister should tell his department to put its section of the book into effect. This was simple enough, and Hankey could have been forgiven for resuming his lunch without further ado, but one minister managed to tell his department that the precautionary period was to start 'next Monday' and then promptly leave London, while another was so engrossed in preparing a parliamentary speech that he omitted to tell his department until the evening. A cabinet secretariat, still two years from the making, would have saved a good deal of trouble.†

Meanwhile Belgium was bracing herself, ordering partial mobilization and reinforcing the great fortress at Liège, while in the Balkans

* From 1911 onwards, under the direction of the CID (principally Hankey), a 'War Book' was prepared summing up the measures that each government department would have to take at various stages of the transition to war – most critically at the declaration of 'precautionary period'.

† It would at least have been able to provide a more definitive chronicle of events: Wilson's diary says the War Office received the order on 28, not 29, July. There is, indeed, a real problem with dates and timings throughout the 'countdown'. Every message between capitals, for example, involved a time-span: the time the decision was actually taken, the time it was communicated to the official(s) responsible for communicating the decision to the other capital, the time it was sent (after the delay of encryption), the time it was received in the intended capital (sometimes via circuitous routes: the British Foreign Office used the telegraph via Aden to reach St Petersburg), the time it was decrypted, the time it was delivered to the ambassador, the time the ambassador delivered the message to the foreign ministry. The timing of messages, therefore, even with due allowance for different time zones, can be misleading, especially where a decision was taken in the evening. Dates can sometimes seem to be 'out' by twenty-four hours. Diaries, clearly on occasions written up some days afterwards, can be even more misleading. Perhaps one of the most reliable detailed chronologies is Clive Ponting's *Thirteen Days* (London, 2003). Though Ponting's conclusions are as controversial as any, his forensic handling of the complex international diplomatic record is impressive – as ought to be expected of a former senior civil servant in the Ministry of Defence.

the first guns of August actually began to fire, if half-heartedly – desultory shelling of Serbian positions by Austrian artillery the other side of the Sava, and of Belgrade itself by monitors on the river. In the Wilhelmstrasse, on learning of the Russian mobilization and movement to frontier assembly points, Jagow could now drop all pretence. He called in the Russian ambassador and told him that 'Germany will be obliged to mobilize as well. There is therefore nothing more to do: from now on diplomats will have to let the cannons talk.'*

Accordingly the Tsar authorized general mobilization; but then he received the most intriguing of what became known as the Willy–Nicky telegrams, the supposed cousinly attempts by the Kaiser to settle things 'within the family'. Russian mobilization would cause a European war, he argued; stopping mobilization would thereby stop the war. Accordingly, Nicholas ordered its halt, but later that evening, at the urging of the *Stavka*, reauthorized partial mobilization against Austria.

Churchill may not have been allowed to complete the mobilization of the fleet, but he was taking steps to enlarge it. Five hundred Turkish sailors had recently arrived on Tyneside to take possession of a dreadnought built by Armstrongs, but the first lord pre-empted them with a requisitioning order: at the stroke of the Churchillian pen the *Sultan Osman I* became the *Agincourt*, and the sailors re-embarked for the Bosphorus. The move is sometimes cited as one of the causes of Anglo-Turkish enmity, but in truth Constantinople had already signed a secret pact with Berlin.†

The following day, 30 July, saw the toppling of dominoes in slow motion. The Austrian foreign minister, Count Berchtold, had wired Jagow in the early hours to say that unless Russia immediately suspended its partial mobilization, Austria would order general mobilization. In Paris, the mood was of growing fatalism, with Joffre pushing for mobilization – or at least precautionary measures – arguing that each day's delay in mobilizing and concentrating would

---

* In 1914, of course, Russia's western continental borders were those of Germany and Austria-Hungary; there was no buffer in the form of Poland and the Baltic states as in 1939.

† The ship had been built in 1913 for the Brazilian navy and named the *Rio de Janeiro*, but after a collapse in the price of rubber, the mainstay of the Brazilian economy, the order was cancelled. The story of the Turks on Tyneside is told in Richard Hough, *The Big Battleship* (London, 1966).

cost 15–20 kilometres of French territory, since the mobilizing troops would have to assemble further and further back. Yet the president and prime minister, just returned from Russia, were determined not to let Germany manoeuvre them into any position that might look as if France were the belligerent. The French cabinet, sitting for the first time during the crisis with all its members present, approved certain precautionary measures, but not the call-up of reserves or requisitioning of transport and horses, and repeated the order for the cordon sanitaire – that French troops were not to approach within 10 kilometres of the border. 'France, like Russia, will not fire the first shot,' explained the telegram for London from the French foreign ministry at the Quai d'Orsay. The explanation given to the army, dismayed at being ordered, in effect, to surrender French soil without a shot, was that it was a necessary sacrifice to ensure British co-operation. It harked back to the battle of Fontenoy, in Louis XV's day, when, having been rebuked before for firing prematurely, the French commander reportedly invited les anglais: 'Messieurs, tirez les premiers.'

But during the morning the Kaiser received another Willy–Nicky telegram, telling him that his cousin had had to reorder partial mobilization. He angrily retorted: 'Then I must mobilize too!'

Moltke then heard disquieting news: Austria-Hungary was taking only defensive measures on the Russian border rather than preparing to mount offensive operations. This would free Russian troops to attack East Prussia – the very move that the Schlieffen Plan calculated on not happening. He frantically wired Conrad, his Austrian opposite number, urging full mobilization and preparations to take the offensive.

At about the same time in St Petersburg, Sazonov, the foreign minister, finally persuaded the Tsar to order general mobilization, which he then used as a bargaining counter with Berlin: Russia would halt its mobilization if Austria respected Serbian sovereignty.* Meanwhile the German chancellor, Bethmann Hollweg, determined that events should be controlled by himself rather than by the Kaiser or the general staff, turned down Moltke's demands for mobilization and

---

* The Russian view of mobilization – the Stavka having rather more flexible plans than the Grosser Generalstab – was that it should act as a deterrent; the Germans saw it as but the prelude to war.

wired London calling for British neutrality if war came. Grey, in accordance with the cabinet's line the day before, at once rejected the call for neutrality, but suggested that a settlement might be reached if Austria called a halt after taking Belgrade. On receiving Sazonov's proposal that Russia would halt her mobilization if Serbian sovereignty were respected – a proposal Jagow opposed outright – Bethmann Hollweg sounded out Vienna. Vienna must now have been in some confusion. Nevertheless, the imperial war council decided to order general mobilization – but directed against Serbia. Late in the afternoon St Petersburg went full steam on general mobilization, putting up proclamation posters, though without informing other capitals.

Moltke was beside himself with anxiety that the military advantage was being lost, and the following morning, aided by the war minister, Falkenhayn, would press Bethmann Hollweg to take a decision within twenty-four hours. Meanwhile the chancellor, just as anxious that any apparent Austrian intransigence over the details of the various mediation and mitigation proposals should not hand Russia and France (and Britain) a cause célèbre on a plate, was wiring Vienna urging that Grey's earlier proposal for a four-power conference be taken up. However, just before midnight brought that slow-toppling-domino day to an end, on receiving reports of Russian mobilization he reversed course.

As all this was playing out, the stress-creaks in the Entente were becoming unignorably audible. The French ambassador in London, Paul Cambon, having been told the day before what the cabinet had 'decided', pressed Grey to specify what precisely the British response would be if Germany attacked France. Grey, naturally, could give him no answer. Besides the indecision of the cabinet, he explained, there was public opinion to take account of (a consideration which contributed greatly to the indecision); and public opinion was not at all easy to gauge. *The Times* that morning of 30 July was insisting that Britain support the Entente, but the majority of the press urged neutrality, most notably the *Manchester Guardian* (today's *Guardian*) with its ultimate Little-Englander leader stating that 'we care as little for Belgrade as Belgrade for Manchester'. The only development in favour of intervention was that all parties in parliament – crucially, including the Ulster Unionists – agreed to adjourn debate on the Irish Amending (Home Rule) Bill indefinitely so as to present a united front. Grey, believing he must resign if Britain did not go to France's aid, could have been forgiven for quoting Psalm 6: 'My soul is also sore vexed . . . O Lord, how long?' Instead he assured Cambon that the cabinet would discuss the situation the following morning, 31 July (a Friday), and that he would inform the ambassador at once of any decision. In the event, however, no decisions would be taken, for news of the Russian mobilization would not reach London until late in the afternoon.*

Finally came word that the Italian fleet had begun mobilizing, and that the Dutch had declared neutrality.

But by now Henry Wilson too was getting thoroughly alarmed. On hearing of Grey's reply to the ambassador he had told Huguet's successor as French military attaché, Colonel le Vicomte de la Panouse, to 'get Cambon to go to Grey tonight and say that, if we did not join, he would break off relations and go to Paris'. He was also fretting that the CID had not met, and that the cabinet was deciding policy without asking for military opinion. He pressed the CIGS (since Sir John French's resignation in April, Sir Charles Douglas) to get Asquith, who still held the War Office portfolio, to agree the recall of the Territorials from their summer camps, and to cancel training of those about to go, for it would not be possible otherwise to put the railway movement plans for mobilization and deployment into action; but Asquith promised only to raise the matter in cabinet the following day.

With Friday came serious financial jitters. The City of London, whose business was business, a good deal of it international, was just as alarmed as Wilson, but for quite the opposite reason. Wanting to avoid war at all costs, since much of the money costs would fall to them, Lord (Nathan) Rothschild and a group of financiers went to see Lloyd George to urge neutrality. By the time they arrived at the Treasury, the Stock Exchange had had to close after severe losses, and the bank rate had risen from 4 per cent to 8 per cent. Later that day, when Berlin declared *Kriegsgefahrzustand* ('state of imminent war') there was a run on the German banks.†

---

* 'Nothing untoward happened at the Cabinet today' (Herbert Samuel, to his wife).
† Short of ordering general mobilization, *Kriegsgefahrzustand* put Germany onto a war footing: martial law, the borders sealed, covering troops sent to the frontiers, leave cancelled and troops recalled to barracks, the North Sea islands put on full alert, military guarding of the railways, press censorship of military news, interception of overseas mail etc.

In the afternoon there was another exchange of Willy–Nicky telegrams, wholly unproductive: the Tsar told his cousin that Russian mobilization could not be halted but was not intended as an act of war, to which the Kaiser replied that peace depended on Russia halting her mobilization. Meanwhile Jagow, in a move that even Bismarck might have thought unreasonable, instructed the German ambassador in Paris to demand that France declare neutrality within eighteen hours and turn over the fortresses of Verdun and Toul to Germany as pledges; and, in the same mood of ultra-Bismarckian diplomacy, Bethmann Hollweg sent an ultimatum to St Petersburg requiring a halt to mobilization within twelve hours.* Moltke, by now very worried indeed by all the prevarication, telephoned (not telegraphed) Vienna and over an open line warned that Germany was about to order mobilization and demanded that Austria concentrate her forces against Russia instead of Serbia, asking: 'Is Austria going to leave us in the lurch?'

Which is what it would have amounted to: for Moltke had prepared an ultimatum demanding free entry into Belgium to counter a pre-emptive French invasion – an entirely trumped-up threat – which was to be delivered to the Belgian government on the Sunday, 2 August.

That same Friday afternoon, the French socialist leader and militant pacifist (or at least anti-militarist) Jean Jaurès had an angry confront-ation with the under-secretary for foreign affairs, Abel Ferry, at the Quai d'Orsay. Having accused the government of being dupes of Russia, he warned: 'To the very end, we will continue to struggle against war,' to which Ferry replied dismissively: 'You wouldn't dare. You'd be assassinated on the nearest street corner!'

A few hours later he was – in the Café du Croissant, 146 rue Montmartre.†

At about the same time, in the Palazzo della Consulta in Rome,

---

* The ambassador in Paris, Freiherr Wilhelm von Schoen, did not issue the demand for the fortress-hostages, knowing that it would be rejected. The French learned of it only later, having intercepted the message and broken the code.

† Both Jaurès' assassin, the ultra-nationalist Raoul Villain, who was apprehended on the spot, and Gavrilo Princip, who fired the fatal shots in Sarajevo, would escape the noose. Princip had been a few days short of twenty at the time, the minimum age for the death penalty. Villain was not tried until 1919, when a jury somehow acquitted him. There was outrage in the socialist press in particular, not least because Jaurès' wife, as plain-tiff, had costs awarded against her. France, even after four years of war, was still evidently the country of Dreyfus. Villain would die in Spain fighting for Franco.

opposite the royal palace on the Quirinale, the Italian foreign minister San Giuliano told the French ambassador of the government's decision: the Triple Alliance was a defensive one, Austria's belligerence relieved them of any obligation to take military action, and in the event of war Italy would therefore remain neutral. For the French this was some comfort, promising distinct military advantage – which, in the event, Paris was slow to take. For although Count Cadorna, the Italian commander-in-chief, believed his army was in no condition for war (even after relatively easy victory in Libya), Joffre had had to assign at least two French army corps to cover the Alpine–Ligurian border, and there was now the potential to redeploy them.* On learning of Rome's decision, the Kaiser would write in his diary: 'Our allies drop away from us like rotten pears.'

Late that evening, after Joffre (arguing, correctly, that Germany was mobilizing by stealth) threatened to resign if mobilization were not ordered, and news of Russian mobilization had reached Paris, the French government resolved to order mobilization beginning on 2 August and to promulgate the decision at four o'clock the following morning, meanwhile issuing the *télégramme de couverture* (initiating protective measures) and warning the railways to get ready. When ministers heard of Jaurès' death there was an attack of nerves: would the 'forces of disorder' exert themselves within the borders of *La France* at the very moment the enemy was threatening from without? Joffre cancelled the order to move the 2nd Cuirassiers, stationed in Paris, towards the frontier.

But Berlin was still forcing the pace. Germany could now portray Russian mobilization as the act of aggression, and her own as one of defence. The Bavarian military attaché, Lieutenant-General Karl Ritter von Wenninger, who would be killed on the Eastern Front in 1917, described the scene in the Königsplatz that afternoon: 'Everywhere beaming faces, people shaking hands in the corridors, congratulating one another on having cleared the ditch.' Moltke had finally convinced Bethmann Hollweg that Germany must declare war on

---

* The Italians' decision was not quite as principled as first seems. Initially they had sought territorial compensations from Austria for taking her part in a war, which Austria was unwilling to concede. Indifference to principle, however, would eventually work to the allies' advantage: by May 1915 Italy had been persuaded to enter the war on their side.

Russia, but only later did the chancellor learn that German mobilization and deployment – the working out of the Schlieffen Plan – dictated an immediate attack on Liège in neutral Belgium. Brussels, still hopeful, but knowing what was to come, if not precisely when or in what strength, ordered mobilization to begin the following day. So did the Dutch and the Swiss. And in Constantinople the Porte called up all men between the ages of twenty and forty-five.

Asquith met Kitchener at lunch with Churchill. Kitchener's opinion, which could not have been unique, evidently impressed him, since he repeated it in his letter to Venetia Stanley that evening: 'If we don't back up France when she is in real danger, we shall never be regarded or exercise real power again.'*

In the early hours of Saturday, 1 August, the telegraph lines were abuzz with diplomatic traffic – so much so that London, fearing intercepts in Germany, began routing its telegrams for St Petersburg via Aden. One of them was a personal message to the Tsar ('My dear Nicky . . .') from the King urging a peaceful solution. It had been dictated by Asquith as the monarch sat sleepily in his dressing gown, roused from his bed at 2 a.m. by a prime minister 'still not quite hopeless about peace' (as he wrote to Venetia Stanley in the afternoon).

Not all the telegraphic traffic was accurate, let alone helpful, and the requests for repetition and clarification were increasing. London had asked Berlin if Germany would respect the neutrality of Belgium, to which the reply was ambiguous, even evasive. London had asked Paris likewise, and had received an unambiguous 'yes'. Grey now made one last confused and confusing approach to Lichnowsky. Before that day's cabinet meeting he telephoned the German embassy, according to Lichnowsky, and asked whether, if France remained neutral in a coming war between Germany and Russia, Germany would pledge not to attack her – implying (or rather,

---

* The opinion was, of course, as much political as military, if not more so, and Grey would use the same argument in the Commons on 3 August. There are echoes in the run-up to the Falklands War some eighty years later. On 31 March 1982, in the absence in New Zealand of the chief of the defence staff, the first sea lord, Admiral Sir Henry Leach, marched to the House of Commons to seek out the prime minister, Margaret Thatcher. 'Yes, first sea lord – what can I do for you?' asked a rather startled Mrs Thatcher on seeing Leach in uniform gatecrashing the emergency cabinet meeting. 'No, Prime Minister, it's what I can do for you,' replied Leach: 'if the Argentinians invade and we do nothing, our word would likewise count for nothing in the world' (Jackson and Bramall, *The Chiefs*).

wksy inferring) that Britain would be the guarantor of French ality. The ambassador at once assured him that Germany would pledge – and little wonder, for Germany's strategic situation would thereby have been transformed out of all recognition – and wired the joyous news to Berlin at 11.14 a.m. And then at lunchtime, while the cabinet was still in session (it began at eleven o'clock and sat for two and a half hours), Grey sent one of his private secretaries, William Tyrell, who spoke fluent German, to tell Lichnowsky that (in the words of the ambassador's subsequent telegram to Berlin), 'Sir E. Grey will this afternoon make proposals to me regarding English neutrality, even for the eventuality of our being at war with both Russia and France.' This was extraordinary in light of Grey's categoric reply to Bethmann Hollweg's telegram of the thirtieth asking for just such an undertaking, for nothing that had been said in cabinet could have suggested it.*

But the last grains of sand were already in the neck of the glass. The German ultimatums to Russia and France of the day before had now expired, and in the afternoon the Kaiser, with great ceremony and no little pomp, accompanied by his six sons and his brother Heinrich, drove to the Neues Palais to authorize general mobilization. Seated at a desk made from the timber of Nelson's flagship *Victory*, surrounded by his generals, and with tears of emotion in his eyes, at five o'clock in the afternoon of Saturday, 1 August he signed the order.

And then began six hours of what would, if the matter were not so grave, have been high farce as a result of the 'misunderstandings' between Grey and Lichnowsky. The Kaiser had not long put down his pen when Jagow rushed in with the news that a telegram had been received from London that seemed propitious. Ten minutes later the decryption was brought in – Britain's apparent offer to guarantee French neutrality. The Kaiser was jubilant: at a stroke, Germany had been handed success on a plate – the chance to destroy Russia without the intervention of France or Britain. His naval policy, his grasp of strategy, his personal diplomacy – all were vindicated in this

* The cabinet was heated, but again no overall position was reached, and Churchill was again refused permission to mobilize the fleet fully. It was also agreed that in the event of Britain's joining a European war the BEF would not be sent to the Continent, though this seems to have been a mere sop to cabinet unity at a moment when the actual decision was not necessary. Besides, two days earlier Asquith had told Sir John French that he would command any force the country sent across the Channel.

last-minute communication from the greatest imperial power on earth! He called Moltke and Falkenhayn back into the room and told them to deploy all their forces east.

Moltke was aghast: His Majesty must know that the *Grosser Generalstab* had no plans for war with Russia alone; it was not possible to improvise such a mobilization at short notice. Besides, he mistrusted both Britain and France. The Kaiser is said to have replied: 'Your uncle [the Elder Moltke] would have brought me a different answer.'

Bethmann Hollweg spoke in the Kaiser's support, as did Tirpitz, doubtless fearful of the Royal Navy's lead in the dreadnought race, but also arguing that it would be impossible to reject the British offer without then being seen as the provokers of war. Falkenhayn asked leave to consult Moltke separately, and when he returned not long afterwards announced that Moltke had agreed to study the re-deployment of forces east, though because of the existing plans it would have to be from their concentration positions near the French border (a clever ploy). The Kaiser was satisfied and instructed Jagow to telegram London accepting the 'offer' but explaining the little local difficulty of the railway timetables, and agreed to Tirpitz's suggestion that he send a personal telegram to his cousin King George.

While these telegrams were being drafted, Bethmann Hollweg suddenly remembered an important detail of the mobilization–deployment plans: as a preliminary, *16. Infanterie-Division* was to seize key points of the Luxembourg railways (which were run by the *Reichs-Eisenbahnen*), for although Luxembourg was a neutral under the terms of the Second (1867) Treaty of London, Schlieffen had feared that the French might seize them pre-emptively. The Kaiser told an ADC to get an order to the 16th Division not to move, but Moltke refused to sign it, whereupon he was ordered to leave the room, and the order was telephoned to the divisional headquarters at Trier *en clair*. However, the delay in transmission meant that at seven o'clock, with a precision that would have made Schlieffen proud, a company of the *Rheinisches Infanterie-Regiment Nr. 69*, under one Lieutenant Feldmann, crossed into the grand duchy and headed for Troisvierges – 'three virgins', an unfortunate choice of place for such violation – occupied the station and began tearing up the tracks. No sooner had they begun work than others of the regiment arrived in motor-cars to recall them. They were back inside Germany within half an hour, and before the inevitable telegram of protest arrived in Berlin.

The Kaiser's own telegram to London beat Jagow's by some minutes, and was delivered to Buckingham Palace in the early evening. Sir Edward Grey had gone to his club for a consolatory game of billiards with Arthur Murray MP, his parliamentary private secretary, when he received a call summoning him up The Mall. The King was bemused, not to say aghast, at learning from Berlin of an offer he had no knowledge of – that Britain and France were to be neutral in a war between Russia and Germany – and one that was so sharply at odds with what he understood the French position to be. Grey flatly denied any such undertaking to Lichnowsky, and at once drafted a reply along these lines for the King. He then went to No. 10, where Asquith agreed that the cabinet should meet the following morning for a thorough discussion of policy.

It was now the Kaiser's turn to be roused from his bed. On reading the King's reply, he summoned Moltke immediately to the Neues Palais and, greatcoat over his nightclothes, handed over the telegram and said to the chief of the *Grosser Generalstab* that he could now do as he wanted: all hope of peace (with France) was gone. Moltke, hugely relieved, returned to his office in the Königsplatz – and immediately sent a telegram to the 16th Division in Trier to resume the invasion of Luxembourg.

The dismay of the stationmaster of Troisvierges can only be imagined.

There had certainly been room for misunderstanding in the Grey–Lichnowsky exchanges. They were based on the proposition, discussed in cabinet, that if France went to war in order to support Russia, who was herself going to war to support Serbia, in a cause in which Britain had no vital interest, Britain could – should – stand aloof. And so, if a proposal were put to Russia and France along these lines, or even just to France, then if it were rejected Britain could wash her hands of the consequences. There was, however, a clear distinction to be made between this and the question of Belgian neutrality.*

---

* There were three distinct phases of conversation between Grey and Lichnowsky, some of it taking place by telephone, which together held out the possibility of French neutrality through the good offices of London. It is difficult not to conclude that the high stakes (which appeared to involve the untying of a Gordian knot), the tiredness of the principals involved, and even the subtleties of language – no doubt replete with conditionals and subjunctives – conspired to produce genuine over-optimism.

In St Petersburg the German ambassador, Count Friedrich Pourtalès, an immensely civilized man of Huguenot descent who had been in the post for seven years, having also been first secretary in the 1890s, was eventually admitted to the foreign ministry in the early evening. Sazonov had been at a council of ministers all afternoon in the old summer palace on Yelagin Island in the mouth of the Neva, a place chosen so as to be at arm's length from diplomats and telegrams. This turned out to be pure escapism, however. For six hours Pourtalès had held in his hands the declaration of war drafted in Berlin.

He now asked the minister if he was able to give a favourable reply to the 'request' of the night before to the suspension of mobilization. Sazonov refused to do so. Pourtalès asked him twice more, with the greatest civility, emphasizing the grave consequences of there not being such a reply. Still Sazonov refused, and so Pourtalès, now in tears, handed him the dread document – at which Sazonov merely glanced. Indeed, so high were emotions running that Sazonov did not notice that Pourtalès had by mistake handed him both versions of the diplomatic reply – one to be delivered if the response were negative, the other if positive. The two men embraced, Pourtalès asked formally for his passport, and it was settled that he would leave the capital the following day.

Communications did not improve. Pourtalès went back to his embassy and wired Berlin that Germany was now at war with Russia. Perhaps unsurprisingly, his message never reached the Wilhelmstrasse. Sazonov telephoned the French ambassador, Maurice Paléologue, who – remarkably for the son of a Romanian revolutionary who had fled Bucharest in 1848 after attempting to assassinate a Wallachian prince – was habitually slow in reacting. He did not get his telegram off to Paris until after one o'clock, by which time President Poincaré had learned the news from a shaken Russian ambassador. Meanwhile the British ambassador in St Petersburg, Sir George Buchanan, whom Sazonov had next telephoned, sent off his telegram to London via Aden. The irony was that Russia, while now at war with Germany, was not at war with Austria-Hungary; indeed, the two countries had not even broken off diplomatic relations, and now the *Stavka* hurriedly sent out orders for troops to withdraw 10 kilometres from the Austro-Hungarian border. At No. 10, Asquith at last sat down to pen his daily letter to Venetia Stanley – a long and indulgent one:

he had 'never had a more bitter disappointment', he began, for he could not now come to Anglesey to see 'your darling face, & be with you'.

On Sunday morning, the weather now sultry, Henry Wilson was becoming frantic. All his plans were based on the assumption that Britain would mobilize simultaneously with France, yet the cabinet was still undecided on anything. Italy, Denmark and Norway had declared neutrality, the Danes announcing a limited call-up for defensive purposes; Sweden, Switzerland and the Netherlands were mobilizing, but also 'defensively';* France, Germany, Russia and Austria-Hungary were variously at war, de jure or de facto. On Saturday night Churchill, more or less unilaterally, had ordered the fleet to mobilize, but Asquith would still not cancel the Territorials' summer camps to free the railways for the call-up of reservists, despite a memorandum from the Quartermaster-General saying that if the order were given by two o'clock that afternoon they would be able then to begin mobilization on Tuesday, 4 August, whereas a delay of twenty-four hours would mean they could not begin until the Thursday. Moreover, the QMG stressed that mobilization and the deployment of the TF to their home defence stations must be simultaneous, otherwise the move of the BEF to France would be delayed several more days.

As the cabinet met, as usual at eleven, it did so in two minds – one for intervention, on the grounds of Kitchener's 'we shall never be regarded or exercise real power again'; the other against, on the grounds that this was not Britain's fight and that there was no legal or moral obligation in the Entente to do so. But Asquith believed that there was in fact a third mind. In a note he had dashed off to his sister just beforehand he wrote:

> The ideas that on the one hand we can wholly disinterest ourselves and on the other that we ought to rush in are both wrong. And the real course, that of being ready to intervene if at a decisive moment we are called on, is difficult to formulate in clear terms. Yet I think this is what we must attempt.

---

* Though Sweden was giving cause for concern to the Foreign Office, suggesting that her neutrality might be conditional on Britain's not siding with Russia. It is possible that Berlin had offered the Swedes their pre-Napoleonic realm of Finland in return for active support.

What a pity – what a calamity for the nation, and, soon, for the BEF – that intervening at a decisive moment (and therefore place) had not been his guiding strategic principle since the CID meeting of August 1911. If it had, the War Office and the Admiralty, perhaps through the CID, would now have been able to tender alternative strategic options, all of them properly thought out and with detailed implementation plans. Instead, as far as the War Office was concerned, Asquith had just the one military option – that the BEF place itself on the left of the French line along the Belgian border; and on that particular option the clock was ticking fast.

In fact, Haldane too held Asquith's view, but for all his reading of Hegel and practice at the Bar, the caretaker at the War Office was also unable to 'formulate in clear terms' the middle course.

Grey began the meeting with an appeal for 'plain speaking' – this, too, a rather belated notion – because, he explained, he had to meet the French ambassador at half-past two and must be able to tell him what Britain proposed to do to help France, adding that Paris was 'relying on the entente'. And then he spoke plainly for himself: 'I believe war will come and it is due to France they shall have our support.'

The foreign secretary had finally answered the 'great question': the *quid* for the *quo* of the earlier Anglo-French colonial and naval agreements, the honour of the Entente, the necessities of empire – these required that Britain give France her military support at the hour of need. But where and how exactly was this support to be rendered? Grey was not specific. Nor did Henry Wilson's revised estimate, long known to the inner cabinet, that the BEF, even at six divisions plus the Cavalry Division, would not actually tip the balance of forces in France's favour, encourage him to any swift decision.*

Grey's opinion did not go down universally well, especially the suggestion that France was 'due' support. Lewis Harcourt, secretary of state for the colonies, passed a note across the table to Lloyd George asking him to 'speak for us [because] Grey wishes to go to war without violation of Belgium'. The non-interventionists, in the main the more junior cabinet ministers, had met beforehand at No. 11, the chancellor of the exchequer's residence, and decided that

* See footnote page 156.

unconditional neutrality was not an option, but that intervention should be contingent on 'certain events', such as 'the wholesale invasion of Belgium'.*

That qualifying 'wholesale' implied the possible acceptance of a limited violation of territory (calling to mind the general staff's assessment that a German incursion would not penetrate north and west of the Meuse), and in the ensuing cabinet discussion some brought up again the question of what the 1839 treaty actually required of Britain in guaranteeing Belgian neutrality, arguing that the passage of eighty years had created wholly different circumstances. It must now have occurred ruefully to many at the table that a late flowering of the Concert of Europe in the decade before might have debated, clarified and amended the treaty to advantage. In any case, it was all now too late, for even as the cabinet sat in council, German troops were tearing up the railways in Luxembourg, and in Brussels the German ambassador was taking from his safe the secret document he had just been ordered to deliver to the Belgian government – an ultimatum to allow the free passage of German troops, or suffer the consequences.†

Grey, having nailed his colours to the mast, now made it clear that he would resign if Britain stood aside in a Franco-German war. It appeared probable that Asquith, Churchill and Haldane (and others) would go too. Lloyd George evidently believed that the Germans

---

* From the diary of Jack Pease, President of the Board of Education. Pease was not a pacifist, but he had been educated at a Quaker school, Grove House in Tottenham (later Leighton Park, Reading), and was president of the Peace Society, as his grandfather and father had been. Indeed, the family emblem was the dove of peace with peapod in its beak. When volunteers were called for, however, 33% of Quakers of military age would enlist (Alan Wilkinson, *The Church of England and the First World War*, London, 1978). The note across the table had echoes – if to the opposite purpose – in Leo Amery's legendary interjection 'from a sedentary position' when in September 1939 Arthur Greenwood, standing in for the leader of the opposition, rose in the House of Commons to condemn Chamberlain's absurdly inadequate response to Hitler's invasion of Poland: 'Speak for England, Arthur!'

† Technically the ambassador was styled 'minister', since the (lesser) status of the German representation was legation not embassy. The document he was to deliver was in German, not diplomatic French, and because of its complex phrasing it would take the Belgian foreign ministry over an hour to translate. The ambassador/minister, Claus von Below-Selaske, was astonished – shocked, even – when he read the document, for although he was only lately come from Berlin he had no idea of the requirements of the Schlieffen Plan. He had only just told the Belgian press that 'your neighbour's roof may catch fire, but your own house will be safe'. Evidently the preamble in the document that Germany had learned that France was about to march into Belgium, and was thereby taking precautionary measures, did not convince him any more than it would convince the Belgian government.

would invade Belgium in large numbers anyway, in which case there was no point in forcing a decision until they did, when the cabinet response would be (more or less) united. And so the discussion turned towards the protection of the Atlantic, Channel and North Sea coasts of France from German attack, which was implicit, if not a formally binding obligation, in the naval agreements. This pleased the non-interventionists for two reasons: it was anyway undesirable – unacceptable – to have the German navy operating in waters so close to Britain; and it seemed to entail little prospect of actual fighting, since the Royal Navy considerably overmatched the German high seas fleet. Some members – including, of all people, McKenna, the former first lord – wanted to exclude French warships from the Channel too. Grey objected with the counter-intuitive argument that in fact this would favour France, for it would release her warships for action else-where, although his real reason was almost certainly the impossibility of excluding France from the sovereign right of self-defence. But to even the scales of neutrality, the cabinet agreed that in such circum-stances German cruisers and destroyers (but not dreadnoughts) would be allowed into the North Sea to protect their merchant shipping. Such complicated arrangements had been known since Nelson's day, but in Nelson's day there had not been the complication of long-range gunnery, submarines and torpedoes. This was an arrangement – even if it proved acceptable to Germany and France – that was bound to end in watery British graves, and more.

Asquith had been taking minutes of the meeting, in the form of another letter to Venetia Stanley, from which he now read to summarize the cabinet's view:

> 1. We have no obligations of any kind either to France or Russia to give them naval or military help. [Despite the naval agreement.]
> 2. The despatch of the Expeditionary Force to help France at this moment is out of the question & wd serve no object. [Even though the French believed its role on their west flank to be important.]
> 3. We mustn't forget the ties created by our long-standing & intimate friendship with France.
> 4. It is against British interests that France shd. be wiped out as a great power. [Asquith does not specify *vital* interests, but this is a categorical statement nevertheless.]
> 5. We cannot allow Germany to use the Channel as a hostile base.

6. We have obligations to Belgium to prevent her being utilized and absorbed by Germany. [Asquith writes utilized *and* absorbed, not *or*, leaving open the possibility that limited utilization might be acceptable.]

And, having summarized the cabinet's views but made no firm decision other than not to order the despatch of the BEF, and that the Channel would, so to speak, remain English, at about two o'clock he adjourned the meeting until six-thirty.

From her estate at Kleinitz, 100 miles or so south-west of Berlin (now Klenice, Poland), Princess Radziwill was also writing – to her long-time correspondent General di Robilant:

> Yesterday at six o'clock the telephone brought news of the order to mobilize. This morning three of my woodmen went off, this afternoon my cook and my little reader also departed, and from tomorrow there won't be a single able-bodied man left in Kleinitz. They are calling up all the men up to forty-five who have done military service and all the young men of seventeen will be enrolled this year.

Meanwhile, in the dingy office he shared with two French officers in the *Ministère de la Guerre,* the 27-year-old cavalryman Lieutenant Edward (Louis) Spears was beginning to feel uncomfortable; and it was not just the stifling heat, melting the asphalt pavements outside. Fluent in French, tall, debonair (his nickname in the regimental mess was 'Monsieur Beaucaire', from the popular novel about an urbane Frenchman in England), he had been sent by Wilson the week before to help coordinate plans for the reception of the BEF (he was almost certainly working too for Mansfield Cumming, head of the foreign section of the Secret Service Bureau, with instructions to make contact with agents in Belgium); but now 'France was mobilizing for war, and I, who belonged to the Army of a country that had not declared itself, had ceased to be a comrade and had suddenly become an object of suspicion.'* Indeed, a senior French officer told him 'in icy tones' that he would be required from now on to hand him letters for London unsealed. Elsewhere, however, the French general staff were finding

---

* Spears, *Liaison 1914*. At this time he spelled his name 'Spiers', but changed the spelling in 1918 because of the confusion its French pronunciation caused. He would have another liaison role in Paris, in 1940, as Churchill's emissary to Paul Reynaud, the French prime minister, in the rank of major-general.

real enemies to attend to. That morning there had been several incursions around Belfort in the right-angle of the borders with Germany and Switzerland, the old strategic route between the Rhine and the Rhône known as the 'Burgundian gate', scene of prolonged siege and bitter fighting in 1870–1. A *poilu* of the *44ème Régiment d'Infanterie de Ligne* had been killed by a German cavalry patrol near the village of Joncherey, a full 25 miles inside the border – Caporal Jules Peugeot, in peacetime a teacher (that he was at his post in command of a section of infantrymen on the morning of 2 August is testament to the efficiency of the French mobilization plan). But although mortally wounded, Peugeot had killed the man who shot him – Leutnant Albert Mayer of the *Jäger Regiment-zu-Pferd Nr 5* (mounted rifles). It was proof at last that the Germans were ranging freely across the border, and Joffre was now able to have the cordon sanitaire order lifted.*

As cipher telegrams arrived at the Foreign Office from every capital, with intermittent telephone calls, visits by ambassadors and attachés, and a trickle of 'human intelligence' from returning officers and officials, Asquith drove to the London Zoological Gardens to spend an hour in the bird sanctuary. It was almost certainly the best preparation he could have had for the resumption of the cabinet meeting, for its members had split into several groups which spent the afternoon trying to find their various ways out of the same maze. Besides, there was an anti-war rally of international socialists in Trafalgar Square which, though Asquith evidently did not think it would descend into sufficient disorder to prevent his getting back into Downing Street, was nevertheless an uncongenial backdrop to an effort at relaxation.† Grey, on the other hand, who as a keen and knowledgeable ornithologist would have liked nothing better than to

---

* Peugeot and Mayer were the first of their countrymen to be killed in the Great War, the Frenchman just twenty-one, the German a few months short of that birthday. Their bodies were taken to a nearby barn and laid out next to each other. After being claimed by his family on 3 August, Peugeot was returned home to Étupes, half a dozen miles to the west, and buried with full military honours in the cemetery. Mayer was also buried with full military honours – and at the expense of the officers of Peugeot's regiment – in Joncherey; his body was later moved to the German military cemetery at Illfurth near Mulhouse.

† In the event it was poorly attended, and described by the editor of the influential Liberal newspaper the *Westminster Gazette* as 'a feeble effort'.

pass a peaceful hour in the bird sanctuary,* went back to his office, where he met the French ambassador, Cambon, and gave him the assurance that 'if the German fleet comes into the Channel or through the North Sea to undertake hostile operations against the French coasts or shipping, the British fleet would give all the protection in its power'. He then went on to explain – in the words used in the confirmatory telegram to the British ambassador in Paris – that in the event of war Britain would not be sending the BEF to France, 'as it would entail the maximum of risk . . . and produce the minimum of effect'.

This latter assertion was rather more categorical than Asquith's second point in his letter to Venetia; but it was a late flowering of strategic common sense – were it not that at this stage no other option for the BEF had been studied. The 'maximum of risk' was a reference in part to the threat of invasion to a Britain denuded of regular troops, a return to earlier preoccupations (yet another invasion inquiry, in 1913, the third in eleven years, had concluded that it was desirable to hold back two of the BEF's six infantry divisions until the Territorials had been brought up to standard). And it was also perhaps, even intuitively, a reversion to that old default setting of British strategy: no continental engagement until it could no longer be resisted, but instead a recourse to economic warfare waged with the Royal Navy.†

Cambon asked Grey if the Germans knew of the naval guarantee, for Churchill, he said, had told his naval attaché that they had indeed been told. Grey replied that his information was 'quite wrong', that 'nothing has been said to any foreign representative except yourself', and would not be said until a public announcement were made. Some historians have branded this a straight lie, but this is less than fair to

* Grey's loneliness at this time – his wife had died childless in 1906, and he did not remarry until 1922 – was relieved in real measure by ornithology. He was known once to have missed a cabinet meeting for the prospect of a rare sighting. His 1927 book *The Charm of Birds* would become a bestseller.

† This had, after all, been the successful strategy on which Britain had based her defiance of Napoleon: the Royal Navy blockaded the Continent and ranged the world taking French colonies and gold, with which she then subsidized her coalition allies – notably Russia, Prussia and Austria. It was only after 1808 that Britain began seriously to commit troops to the continental fight – in Spain and Portugal. Admiral Sir Arthur Wilson had understood this all too well, even if at the CID meeting in August 1911 he had made such a hash of bringing the strategy up to date.

a foreign secretary who, whatever his faults, was having to deal with capitals and ambassadors as best he could before actual policy had been settled.* In fact Grey had spoken to Lichnowsky, but *before* the cabinet meeting at which the definite guarantee was decided; knowing the import of the 1912 naval agreement that allowed the fleet to concentrate in the North Sea, he had prudently told the ambassador that the German high seas fleet should refrain from any activity that might challenge the Royal Navy, specifying attacks on the French coast. Whether this 'warning' was to protect Britain's neutrality or the French coast (through whose ports, after all, the BEF would have to pass if it was decided to send it) is by the by: what Cambon needed to know was whether the Germans had been warned of *inevitable* consequences of attacking the French coast, which they had not been because when Grey spoke to Lichnowsky the guarantee had not yet been endorsed by the cabinet. This may seem like casuistry, but it could hardly be so in the prelude to war. Besides, Asquith had said the same when in an emotional state Lichnowsky had called on him at breakfast, 'very agitated poor man & wept', as he wrote to Venetia Stanley: 'I told him we had no desire to intervene, and that it rested largely with Germany to make intervention impossible, if she would (1) not invade Belgium, and (2) not send her fleet into the Channel to attack the unprotected North Coast of France.'

When the cabinet reassembled at six-thirty, Asquith could have had no certain idea which way he could take them collectively, save perhaps for a 'naval war' only, which Churchill, during the morning meeting, had commended in a note he passed across the table saying that 'the naval war will be cheap'. But during that meeting another note had been set before Asquith – in effect a blank cheque, though one with invisible strings attached. An hour into their discussions a letter from the Conservative leader, Andrew Bonar Law, had been brought into the room, which Asquith read aloud: 'It would be fatal to the honour and security of the United Kingdom to hesitate in supporting France and Russia at the present juncture; and we offer our unhesitating support to the Government in any measures they may consider necessary for that object.' Though it made no immediate impact on the course of the morning's discussions, it told every

* For an example of the accusation of unequivocal lying, see Ponting, *Thirteen Days*.

member of the cabinet what his personal future might be: if it came to an open split in the government, the Tories would support a pro-war coalition. As he went into the Cabinet Room, therefore, the prime minister's composure rested on more than an hour's avian sanctuary.*

In the event the resumed meeting proved 'peaceful', as one minister described it, focusing on the extent to which German violation of Belgium would require a British response. The general view was that if, like Luxembourg, as seemed the case from the early reports of the invasion of the grand duchy, Belgium made merely a token protest, and the incursion were limited to the south-east of the country, Britain could scarcely intervene as to do so would be, in the words of Grey's biographer, 'more Belgian than the Belgians'.† That her territory would be invaded was increasingly apparent, not-withstanding the Belgian foreign minister's opinion, given that morning to the British ambassador in Brussels, that despite the posturing threats from the Kaiser to King Albert there was 'no reason whatever to suspect Germany of an intention to violate neutrality' (it was, after all, a surprise to the German ambassador when he opened his safe). For it was plain from the study of the simplest road atlas that German troops now marching into Luxembourg had no practicable way into France except through Belgium. But the cabinet noted that if it came to war because of the violation of Belgian neutrality, Britain would not thereby be obliged to comply with any of the arrangements made previously with France. To Henry Wilson, the DMO, this would have been so much hot air: if the 'E' in BEF meant anything at all, it meant the one and only plan he had been working up with the French these past four years.

Although the cabinet had been, as it were, seeing through a glass darkly, Asquith realized that the War Office must have some clarity if the prompt despatch of the BEF were in the event to become policy.

---

* Asquith reckoned that three-quarters of the Liberal benches would be opposed to intervention 'at any price' (letter to Venetia Stanley).
† G. M. Trevelyan, *Grey of Fallodon* (London, 1937). Trevelyan's elder brother, Charles, a junior minister (not in the cabinet), was opposed to intervention even if the Germans invaded on a grand scale unless it were established that their object was to take Antwerp and the Belgian coast, thereby directly threatening British interests. He would resign on the declaration of war. As for Luxembourg, the *Corps des Gendarmes et Volontaires*, numbering at most some 300 men, concentrated mainly in the capital, could have done little, of course, but earn posthumous glory and impose a fearful moral penalty on Germany.

As soon as his ministers had left No. 10, at about eight o'clock, he called into the Cabinet Room the waiting CIGS, who had brought with him the staff captain railway transport to explain the technicalities of the movement plans. Asquith listened, and at length decided to halt all movement of the Territorials and make 5 August the first day of mobilization; but he told the CIGS that the decision to mobilize must remain secret for the time being. This, of course, was no help, and by midnight Asquith realized he could hold back no longer. He wrote out the authorization to mobilize the army – which did not of itself authorize the embarkation of the BEF, just the call-up of reservists and preparatory movement – and gave it to Haldane.

Next morning, Monday, 3 August, the Foreign Office learned of the German ultimatum to Brussels, and also that the Belgian government would not yet be appealing to the protecting powers for other than diplomatic support. But Brussels also made clear that Belgium would resist invasion vigorously; and, indeed, with that curious, hopeful fastidiousness that was to be repeated in 1940 – again to disastrous effect – Belgian troops on the border with France were ordered to fire on French troops if they tried to cross.

Grey now changed gear. Earlier he had summoned the Japanese ambassador and told him that if there were an attack on Hong Kong or Wehai (Port Edward), Britain would look to Japan for support under the 1902 treaty, and he now received Cambon to restate the promise of naval assistance, adding that this would mean that Britain and Germany 'would be in a state of war'. It hardly needed saying, for as soon as Sunday's cabinet meeting had finished, Churchill had told the Admiralty to exchange naval codes with the French navy and to put all bases at their disposal. Finally, just before Monday's cabinet at eleven o'clock, Grey saw Lichnowsky, who assured him that there would be no threat to the French coast 'as long as England remains neutral' – a strategic limitation that could not have been approved indefinitely by Moltke or Tirpitz. Indeed, when the Kaiser learned of Britain's guarantee he wanted to declare war immediately, and was only dissuaded by Tirpitz, who pointed out that the Royal Navy was already at her battle stations (Churchill's unilateralism had evidently gained London a little breathing space). Lichnowsky then made what he must have known was a hopeless bid to mollify concerns over Belgian neutrality by stating that Belgian 'integrity' would be maintained after the war. This might have been a legal mooting point, but since the original purpose of the 1839 Treaty had been to deny the great powers the use of the country to make war, a promise to hand it back after doing just that was plainly absurd.

When Grey briefed Asquith before they went into the Cabinet Room, both men knew that the game was up. Indeed, the prime minister had been kept company in his reverie of the small hours by the 'distant roaring' of the crowds that had gathered in The Mall to cheer the King: 'You remember Sir R. Walpole's remark,' he wrote later to Venetia Stanley: 'Now they are ringing their bells; in a few weeks they'll be wringing their hands.'* And as he entered the Cabinet Room, Asquith knew he would almost certainly leave it with fewer members than he began with, for he had received resignation letters from three ministers – Sir John Simon (attorney-general), John Morley (lord president of the council) and John Burns (president of the Board of Trade) – and there were others threatening. But he was confident that he could also count on the news from Brussels being more uniting than divisive, well aware that without the fig leaf of Belgian neutrality he could scarcely have carried some of the bigger names, notably Lloyd George.

As it turned out, the mood at the table proved far from acrimonious. Lloyd George, the 'conscience' of the non-interventionists, said that for him indeed the certain attack on Belgium made all the difference. This seems to have persuaded the three resigning ministers to say nothing publicly, and even to be in their places when Grey made his speech to the House in the afternoon (four, in fact, since the first commissioner of works and public buildings, Earl Beauchamp – 'Sweetheart' – also said he must go).† Herbert Samuel wrote to his wife that 'the Cabinet was very moving. Most of us could hardly speak at all for emotion.'

---

* Walpole's famous quip had been made against the background of growing hostility between Britain and Spain during the early eighteenth century over trade with Spanish colonies in the Americas. Several sea battles and minor skirmishes had taken place but Walpole as prime minister had defied the general clamour for war. In 1739 a British sea captain, Robert Jenkins, produced before the House of Commons his own ear, preserved in a jar of spirit, which he claimed had been cut off by a Spaniard attempting to take his vessel. The House was enraged and Walpole was obliged to declare war on Spain – to public rejoicing (hence his lament).
† In the event, only Morley and Burns resigned.

But what was there to speak of now? The ship of state was being taken by the current, engines turning but without steerageway.

Meanwhile, the government had to carry Parliament with it – the House of Commons at least – and so at three o'clock Grey rose to his feet at the despatch box and spoke for an hour. His style was more than usually conversational, wrote Asquith to Venetia Stanley, but it was 'a most remarkable speech . . . extraordinarily well reasoned & tactful & really *cogent*'.

It was in fact the first major statement on the crisis, and so Grey began with the background, but soon cut to the quick: 'Last week I stated that we were working for peace not only for this country, but to preserve the peace of Europe. To-day events move so rapidly that it is exceedingly difficult to state with technical accuracy the actual state of affairs, but it is clear that the peace of Europe cannot be preserved.' He did not want to finger culprits – 'to say where the blame seems to us to lie' – because he wished 'the House to approach this crisis in which we are now, from the point of view of British interests, British honour, and British obligations, free from all passion as to why peace has not been preserved'.

He then recalled members' minds to the first and second Moroccan crises, and spoke of the naval and military conversations that had followed from these. The French government, he reminded them, had understood during the first crisis of 1906 why Britain stood aloof, but had said subsequently:

> If you think it possible that the public opinion of Great Britain might, should a sudden crisis arise, justify you in giving to France the armed support which you cannot promise in advance, you will not be able to give that support, even if you wish to give it, when the time comes, unless some 'conversations have already taken place between naval and military experts.' There was force in that. I agreed to it, and authorized those conversations to take place, but on the distinct understanding that nothing which passed between military or naval experts should bind either Government or restrict in any way their freedom to make a decision as to whether or not they would give that support when the time arose.

He then gave a *tour d'horizon* respecting British interests, honour and obligations, concluding:

It may be said, I suppose, that we might stand aside, husband our strength, and that whatever happened in the course of this war at the end of it intervene with effect to put things right, and to adjust them to our own point of view. If, in a crisis like this, we run away from those obligations of honour and interest as regards the Belgian Treaty, I doubt whether, whatever material force we might have at the end, it would be of very much value in face of the respect that we should have lost. And do not believe, whether a great Power stands outside this war or not, it is going to be in a position at the end of it to exert its superior strength. For us, with a powerful Fleet, which we believe able to protect our commerce, to protect our shores, and to protect our interests, if we are engaged in war, we shall suffer but little more than we shall suffer even if we stand aside.

Perhaps, even while the BEF was mobilizing, Grey still had in mind Churchill's reckoning that a naval war 'will be cheap', but in human terms there never was a worse miscalculation than the claim that 'we shall suffer but little more than we shall suffer even if we stand aside'. He was, however, able to find some cause for cheer: 'The one bright spot in the whole of this terrible situation is Ireland. The general feeling throughout Ireland – and I would like this to be clearly understood abroad – does not make the Irish question a consideration which we feel we have now to take into account.' There would, in other words, be no stab in the back.

Andrew Bonar Law, leader of the opposition, rose in reply and said he would be brief, pledging publicly what he had offered privately in the note to Asquith: his party's unhesitating support of the government. And he managed to find another bright spot of consolation too: 'We have already had indications ... that every one of His Majesty's Dominions beyond the Seas will be behind us in whatever action it is necessary to take.'

John Redmond, leader of the Irish Nationalists, whose party held the balance in Westminster, rose and pledged the loyalty of Catholic Ireland (Sir Edward Carson, for the Unionists, had already visited Asquith and proposed a peace formula over home rule).

This left Ramsay MacDonald, leader of the two-score Labour MPs. His opposition was expected, and was both principled and pragmatic. He did not quite say that appeal to honour was the invariable refuge of the scoundrel, but he came close (Grey had used the word 'honour' seven times in his speech); and he was not persuaded that France was in peril of extinction: 'If France is really in danger, if, as the result of this, we are going to have the power, civilization, and genius of France removed from European history, then let him so say.' But MacDonald's most powerful argument – at least with the judgement of history – was pragmatism (or prudence): 'What is the use of talking about coming to the aid of Belgium, when, as a matter of fact, you are engaging in a whole European War which is not going to leave the map of Europe in the position it is in now?'

But there was no motion before the house, and so despite protests the speaker suspended the sitting until seven, when it was due to reassemble to receive the royal assent to a finance bill, when the matter could be debated on a motion to adjourn the house. In the event that evening, there was scarcely a debate. Lord Hugh Cecil, a Tory who had opposed intervention, would declare Grey's speech had been 'very wonderful . . . the greatest . . . delivered in our time or for a very long period . . . the greatest example of the art of persuasion I have ever listened to'; but a dozen or so Liberals did not agree, and the few that did were scarcely more than ambivalent. It took the protests of Arthur Balfour, the former Conservative prime minister, to move that the house adjourn and so halt the slide into acrimony.

It was not long afterwards that Grey was famously standing at a window of his room at the Foreign Office: 'It was getting dusk, and the lamps were being lit in the space below on which we were looking,' he recalled; and he remarked: 'The lamps are going out all over Europe; we shall not see them lit again in our lifetime.'

The following day, 4 August, the one lamp still lit, if dimly – Britain's – began to die with the news from Brussels that the Germans were across the frontier. A telegram from the German foreign minister to Lichnowsky cut no ice in Whitehall: 'Germany will not, under any pretence whatever, annex Belgian territory. Please impress upon Sir Edward Grey that the German Army could not be exposed to a French attack across Belgium, which was planned according to absolutely unimpeachable information.'

Just before two o'clock in the afternoon Asquith and Grey drafted a telegram to the British ambassador in Berlin – the ultimatum, the favourable reply to which must be received in London by midnight, or 'His Majesty's Government [would] feel bound to take all steps in their power to uphold the neutrality of Belgium'.

When the ultimatum expired and Britain declared war, the *Daily Mirror*, with a circulation at that time of nearly half a million, making it the second largest morning newspaper (and not in those days Labour-supporting), would declare in an echo of Grey's words in the House of Commons that 'Germany tried to bribe us with peace to desert our friends and duty. But Great Britain has preferred the path of honour.'

In a little-known secret memorandum written by the historical section of the CID, 'Report on the Opening of the War',* there is a breathtaking claim that the delay in mobilizing was all to the good:

> The refusal to mobilize on the same day as France would no doubt cause embarrassment to the army at the outset by hampering the staff plans, but on the other hand they [the government] could now assure the army that it would have the whole support of the country at its back, with incalculable possibilities in the future development of its strength.

A fat lot of comfort this could have been for the BEF, whose welcome by the French would in truth be far more heartening and important than the send-off by their compatriots – and whose principal concern anyway would be their reception by the Germans. Besides once again misleadingly conflating mobilization with deployment, in its frequent dissembling this report (written, of course, in the knowledge of the successful counter-attack on the Marne) shows the degree of disconnect between the military staffs and the policy-makers. Little wonder it was not declassified until 1965.

* CAB 17/102B, 1 Nov. 1914.

Chapter Eleven

THE CALL TO ARMS

For all we have and are,
For all our children's fate,
Stand up and take the war,
The Hun is at the gate!

Rudyard Kipling, 'For All We Have And Are' (1914)

Lieutenant Maurice Dease, the machine-gun officer of the 4th Battalion Royal Fusiliers (the Fusiliers were one of the few regiments that had four regular battalions), was at firing practice in Dorset when he received a telegram at eight-thirty in the evening on 29 July recalling his section to barracks on the Isle of Wight. The telegram was one of thousands despatched the length and breadth of the kingdom that afternoon after the War Office had declared 'precautionary period'.

Dease and his men packed up the machine guns and limbers at once, then lay down for a couple of hours' sleep before marching to Wool station at 3 a.m. to take the train to Portsmouth and the ferry back to Parkhurst. They arrived at 10.30, drew five thousand rounds of ammunition, filled twenty belts and re-packed the limbers ready to move. The order was for precautionary measures, not mobilization, but Dease's commanding officer was Lieutenant-Colonel Norman McMahon – 'the musketry maniac' – and he had orders to post sentries in the old invasion forts around the island in case of enemy landings. McMahon was wasting no time, and taking no chances.

But then, having hurried, Dease and his men, and 150 others of the battalion not on outpost, waited – the perennial military complaint. They waited, indeed, all that day and the next. Then on Saturday (1 August) the 4th Warwicks, a Special Reserve battalion, arrived straight from their annual camp and went under canvas in the adjacent fields, their orders, in the event of general mobilization, to take over the barracks and outposts when the Fusiliers quit them. The next day they must have wished the Fusiliers had indeed quit them, for there was torrential rain and still no orders for them to move. And then, just after midnight on the Sunday, Maurice Dease was called out to parade with fifty men, as his diary records, to be 'ready to move at a moment's notice'. The order to move never came, however, nor any indication why they might have been needed, so at eleven o'clock the next morning they stood down and went for another route march – the perennial military antidote to boredom, as well as one of the fundamentals of infantry prowess: 'The power of undertaking long and rapid marches without loss in numbers and energy is one of the chief factors of success in war.'*

Meanwhile, elsewhere, another Fusilier battalion was looking out to sea – the 7th, one of the regiment's two Special Reserve battalions. They too were at annual training, at Felixstowe in Suffolk, when the order arrived to be ready to repel invasion: 'My company had to go on outpost duty on the seashore only 300 yards from the camp,' recorded Captain Edmund Malone, a former regular. 'This seemed a silly proceeding. I had to guard a front of 200 yards along the esplanade. There were no troops on either flank, or in fact anywhere else on the east coast as far as we knew. Beery sentries fully armed, marched up and down the esplanade and terrified the inhabitants and trippers, who bolted indoors and barred their windows.' It might have been Walmington on Sea, thirty years later, and *Dad's Army*. And in varying degrees it was the same up and down the country, at railway bridges and docksides, and on beaches beginning to fill up for the bank holiday weekend, for the Special Reserve could be called up without the King's proclamation of general mobilization. For all the jitteriness, there would be only one casualty, however – a grey seal,

---

* *Infantry Training* (1914). A new version of the manual, reflecting the change to the four-company organization in October of the previous year, was hurriedly issued on 10 August.

shot by one of the Fusiliers when it failed to respond to a sentry's challenge. In Germany, in Stuttgart, a Serbian spy was shot as he tried to cut telephone wires – except that he turned out to be a *Reichspost* workman trying to repair them.

A few days later, to the relief of all, Malone and his battalion would be ordered back to London, for if general mobilization came there would be a real job for them – real vulnerable points to guard, and drafts to be found to fill up the ranks in the regular battalions.* Meanwhile in the 4th Battalion, especially with a man like McMahon in command, there was no sense of futility whatever. Although mobilization had not yet been ordered, the officers were told to settle their affairs – which meant, in the main, financial ('officers are particularly requested to pay their July mess bills with promptness', wrote the paymaster). And for Maurice Dease there was the additional responsibility of the precious machine guns, on which the battalion's safety and honour might well depend. Fortunately in the infantry there was no doubt about the weapon's importance. In the cavalry there were still mixed feelings, as C. S. Forester expresses in his novel *The General* (1936) – if perhaps a shade unfairly:

> Young Borthwick – Lieutenant the Honourable George Borthwick – was in an angle of a tributary ditch to the front with his machine-gun section, the men digging frantically with anything that came to hand, so as to burrow into the bank for shelter. Borthwick had been given the machine-guns, not as the most promising machine-gun officer in the regiment (a distinction the whole mess scorned), but because he had the most slovenly seat on a horse that had ever disgraced the ranks of the [fictitious] Twenty-second Lancers. Curzon [the commanding officer] realized with a twinge of anxiety that the reputation of the regiment suddenly had come to depend to a remarkable extent on how much efficiency young Borthwick had acquired at his job.

Dease, if not exactly typical, typified nevertheless the ideal of the infantry officer. He was a son of the Catholic gentry of Leinster, in Ireland, brought up to hounds and sent to school in England – first in London, and then Stonyhurst, the Jesuits' school in Lancashire. The

* Malone would be badly wounded in March 1918 while commanding the battalion, which, unusually for a Reserve battalion, had been sent to France in 1916.

Deases had lived at Turbotston in County Westmeath for 750 years, and one of them had been bishop of Meath during the rebellion of 1641, when he had dismayed many of his fellow clergy by preaching loyalty to the Crown. Maurice Dease had joined the OTC at Stonyhurst, and from there at eighteen he went via an 'army crammer' to the Royal Military College Sandhurst, from which in May 1910, not yet twenty-one, he was commissioned into his uncle's old regiment. The Fusiliers considered themselves a cut above most of the infantry of the line, and Dease's small private income would have been something of a necessity. He soon acquired a dog, 'Dandy', and a hunter, 'Palm', on which he followed the Isle of Wight foxhounds. Not surprisingly, especially with a reputation for efficiency, Dease was put in charge of the battalion's horse procurement in the event of mobilization. When therefore the order to mobilize reached the Fusiliers – at six o'clock in the evening of the fourth, the Tuesday after the bank holiday – he went at once to nearby Blackwater to make arrangements with the civilian purchasing officer as per instructions in the battalion's war book. But here the carefully laid plans of the War Office – which would have warmed the hearts of the *Grosser Generalstab* – met the reality of an English August and an unmilitarized society. The purchasing officer was 'an awful old dodderer', he wrote to his mother that evening: 'he has everything in an awful muddle & has lost his cheque book and everything'. But Dease, ever diligent and resourceful, managed to borrow some cheques from the paymaster, and arrange for a car to be at his disposal the following day.

Next morning, the first day of war, Dease, the purchasing officer and a civilian veterinary surgeon began their rounds of the stables listed in the Army Horse Register, and by evening had bought thirty animals – riding, draught and pack – at an average price of £45 5s. Much to Dease's relief, the owners brought them to barracks themselves, saving the need for collecting parties of Fusiliers. There the horses were branded by the vet with the allotted regimental number on a fore-hoof and shod where necessary.* The following day the trio

---

* The demands on farriers throughout the country would have been particularly heavy, for many of the horses had been turned away – put out to grass – for August, and consequently had had their shoes removed. Some of the hunt horses had been put out at the end of the season in the spring and had lost 'condition' – fitness – and some of the cavalry regiments had to do a deal of swapping and changing.

set out again, needing to buy a further fifteen to bring the battalion up to its establishment of fifty-six; this they managed to do by one o'clock at an average of £46 4s a horse, though the bulk of the riding horses (for the four company commanders and the battalion staff) were bought by 'regimental board' from the officers. One of them was Dease's own mount: 'I sold the "Palm" for £60 to the Government and the medical officer with the battalion will have him as a charger,' he wrote home, adding, 'I think he will do well. I have a better horse myself so have done fairly well over the deal,' and asking his father to use the £60 to settle his accounts.*

Better horses were indeed the common impression of the first days of mobilization. The 15th Hussars, in Aldershot, were particularly pleased that 'splendid horses joined – many from famous hunt stables', for they were smarting rather at having been given former mounted-infantry cobs on returning from India eighteen months earlier. What the owners felt about this equine call-up was mixed, to say the least. There were real concerns in the agricultural districts over the requisitioning of draught horses, for it was the middle of the harvest. Private owners were of course parting with cherished friends. Sir Edward Elgar, for all the patriotism of his music, raged to a colleague: 'Concerning the war I say nothing – the only thing that wrings my heart and soul is the thought of the horses – oh! my beloved animals.' Nevertheless, 165,000 horses of every sort and description were collected in just twelve days – eighty of them from as far away as the Isle of Arran, taken to the mainland by Clyde steamer. Maurice Dease was lucky in more than one respect with his, for although he had his work cut out getting harness to fit, at least he did not have any greys to camouflage with permanganate of potash dye.

However, the mobilization of this prodigious number of horses was if anything outdone by the complexity of mobilizing the reservists. Unlike their French and German counterparts, battalions were not localized – stationed in their respective recruiting areas; so, on receipt of his War Office telegram the reservist went first to his regimental depot, in the county town, to draw his uniform and equipment,

---

* 'Charger' was the term for an officer's horse of any arm or service; those ridden by other ranks, or draught horses, were variously called, most notably 'trooper' for a cav-alryman's mount (the rank 'trooper' did not replace 'private' in the cavalry until after the war).

before being despatched thence with a railway warrant to one of the regiment's battalions. He would probably have seen already the warning notices posted in public places, and made his tentative farewells. The process was simple enough, and it mattered not even if he were penniless: the War Office mobilization branch had thought of that. All he had to do was present his identity document (which carried his reporting instructions) at the counter of his village post office, and the postmaster or mistress would hand over five shillings subsistence money; he then presented his reporting instructions at the booking office of any railway station, and he would be given a ticket to the destination – his depot – stated in the document. And if his call-up meant leaving his family destitute, there was the Soldiers' Families Emergency Fund to call on, administered by the local town hall, until his first allotment of pay reached them. On the whole the reservist left to rejoin the colours in good heart; and most of them, the regular reservists especially, knew the world they were returning to.

Not all did, however. On 6 August, the second day of mobilization, Bill Maltby, a nineteen-year-old carter who had signed on as a 'Wolds Wagoner' the year before, was working in the fields 'in the middle of corn harvest when the postman turned up with the letter. I went home, got something to eat and got changed, and rode straight over to Sledmere.' But Sledmere – the seat of the Wagoners' founder, Sir Mark Sykes – was no longer the centre of operations: Maltby's orders, and those of all the other Wagoners, were to report to the Army Service Corps' northern depot in Bradford. So from Sledmere he cycled to nearby Fimber, where he caught a local train to Malton, changing there for York, and at York for Bradford. The railway network in Britain was then at its greatest extent, immeasurably speeding mobilization. The Driffield–Malton line of the former North Eastern Railway closed in 1958; had it not been open in 1914, Maltby and his fellow wagoners would have had to cycle 12 miles and more to Malton. As it was, by eight o'clock that evening more than 800 of them had arrived at Bradford, placing some strain on the depot: their first army meal was thick bread and cups of tea, and bed was the floor of a schoolroom. Two days later Wagoner Maltby was sent to Aldershot with a party of other Woldsmen to join Number 20 (Horse Transport) Company. Here he drew service dress and rifle, never having worn khaki before, nor having held a rifle, and was assigned a

Mark 10 General Service (GS) wagon and two-horse team. A fortnight later they would all sail for France.*

At least Sledmere to Bradford was just three short railway trips, and Aldershot a reasonable enough journey after that. Some of the ex-regulars had a very long and winding road. The 1st Battalion Gordon Highlanders were stationed in Plymouth, where several recently dis-charged Gordons had found work and wives. But as regular reservists their mobilization instructions required them to report first to the depot at Aberdeen to draw uniform and equipment, before taking the train back to Plymouth and reporting for duty at Crownhill Barracks. These, however, were the inevitable anomalies in a system designed to get 200,000 reservists (of whom 145,000 were ex-regulars), most of them infantrymen living within their old regimental recruiting areas, to where they were needed, passed medically fit for service and properly accoutred.

And it most certainly worked. The 1st Battalion Duke of Cornwall's Light Infantry, based at the Curragh outside Dublin – for whom mobilization came as a relief, for they had been guarding vulnerable points in Newry and Dundalk in case of attack by Unionist opponents of the home rule bill – had received 650 reservists, fully equipped, by 7 August, the third day of mobilization. These had first travelled to the Cornwalls' depot at Bodmin – although most were Cornishmen, living locally, many had moved to London or the Midlands in search of work – and thence by ferry across the Irish Sea. Now fully up to 'WE' (war establishment), the battalion would have a mere six days to get the reservists fit (and some were straining the buttons on their tunics), and their shooting eye back, for in the battalion mobilization instructions they would march out of barracks early on the thirteenth to entrain for the docks.

It was like clockwork: in every unit safe was a set of movement instructions, classified 'Secret', typically: 'Train No 463Y will arrive at siding B at 12.35 am August 10th. You will complete loading by 3.40 am. This train will leave siding C at 9.45 am, August 10th. You

---

* Bill Maltby might not have made the minimum height qualification (5 feet 3 inches) for enlistment directly into the Special Reserve, but no one was taking too much note of that when the Wagoners were formed – and certainly not on mobilization. He would survive the war; indeed, he would flourish in uniform, deciding to stay on as a regular in the ASC until 1923. Several of his fellow Wagoners would transfer to the infantry, and five would win the Military Medal.

will march onto the platform at 9.30 am and complete your entraining by 9.40 am.' The *Eisenbahnamt* of the *Grosser Generalstab* could not have arranged things better, or with a greater economy of words. Indeed, many officers thought the clipped organization decidedly un-British – 'the astonishing efficiency of it all', wrote Captain Arthur Corbett-Smith, conducting a party of Royal Field Artillery drafts, was entirely novel.

Not all the Cornish Light Infantrymen would board the trains, however, for those under nineteen were not allowed to serve overseas. One who was bitterly disappointed to be kept instead with the battalion's rear party was George Nathan, who had enlisted in May the year before, for he would not reach nineteen until November. In fact, Nathan – not a Cornishman but an East Ender, his father Jewish, his mother (as he said in his attestation papers) 'C of E' – was still only seventeen, having lied about his age at the recruiting office, the only honourable lie in the army's book. He must have been a remarkable recruit, however, for – tall, confident and capable – he was promoted lance corporal only six months after enlisting, and then corporal a fortnight after the rest of the battalion left for France. Once he was officially nineteen, he would go to France (in March 1915) with a divisional cyclist company, an acting sergeant, and two years after that would be commissioned into the Warwicks.* It was a time of greater imagination and mobility than is sometimes supposed: the Quartermaster-General of the BEF, and soon to be its chief of staff, Major-General William Robertson – known universally as 'Wully' – had enlisted (joined as a private) in the 16th Lancers and risen through every rank in the army; from December 1915 he would be its head – CIGS – and in 1920 field marshal.

But the BEF was not to be as strong as Henry Wilson had hoped and planned, the strength for which the great purchase of horses and call-

---

* George Nathan would have a remarkable life altogether. He was taken prisoner not long after commissioning, and in 1920 left the army to join the Royal Irish Constabulary's auxiliaries. Implicated in the questionable shooting of suspected IRA men, he left the following year and enlisted in the West Yorkshire Regiment, only to buy his discharge a year later. After a few years' drifting he enlisted again, in the Royal Fusiliers, but was dismissed with disgrace the following year. He tried his hand in Canada for a while, and then joined the International Brigade in the Spanish Civil War, where he was killed while in command of a battalion.

up of reservists had been designed. When the war council had broken up in the early evening of 5 August, the tacit assumption was that the force would comprise all six infantry divisions; but as rumours and fears of German landings on the east coast multiplied, Kitchener, now installed as secretary of state for war, and with his well-known (and justified) scepticism of the TF's capabilities, decided to send four only – 1st, 2nd, 3rd and 5th – plus the Cavalry Division, transferring the 6th from Ireland to England, and preparing to send the 4th later once the TF had got themselves organized.* And as far as he was concerned the BEF would be going not to Maubeuge but Amiens, for Maubeuge would be too close to the German thrust into Belgium to be a safe concentration area. In the event, however, Wilson simply carried on as planned, and the four divisions would indeed go to Maubeuge – which Kitchener conceded at a final war council on 12 August, two days after handing Sir John French written instructions for the BEF specifying Amiens, and three days after the lines-of-communication troops – the specialists and guards who would keep the deployment routes open and the troops supplied – had begun embarkation.†

Kitchener's part in the first month of the war is an interesting study in the art of strategy, specifically in where policy – the prerogative of the political leadership – ends, and where that of direction, even command, of operations begins. For the secretary of state now wore field marshal's uniform: whatever the protocol, his military rank (and experience) could not be ignored. And in the absence of clear decisions on policy, notably from Asquith, and strong military grip from the CIGS, Douglas, Kitchener simply apportioned to himself a strong measure of both so as to avoid the potential disaster that he all too clearly foresaw. For he was mistrustful of the French doctrine of *attaque à outrance* (all-out, no matter what) as well as fearful that if the BEF tried to detrain at Maubeuge they would simply be too close to the German advance to deploy properly. To his mind there was every possibility that the army's first taste of continental warfare for a

---

* The TF was unquestionably more efficient than the old volunteers, having been more closely aligned with the regulars and supervised by the general staff, but it had always been expected that they would have a proper period of training after embodiment before taking to the field. Wilson himself thought that the Territorials had 'no discipline' – the fundamental of any military force.

† For the BEF's complete order of battle, and notes on the organization and equipment, see the appendix.

hundred years would end in ignominious retreat. And in retreats lay the collapse of morale: the experience of Sir John Moore and Corunna cast a long shadow.*

Indeed, Kitchener's 'Instructions for the General Officer Commanding the Expeditionary Force proceeding to France' bear a remarkable similarity to those given to Moore in 1808, with their emphasis on cooperation to expel the invader: 'The special motive of the force under your command is to support, and cooperate with, the French Army against our common enemies. The peculiar task laid upon you is to assist the French Government in preventing, or repelling, the invasion by Germany of French and Belgian territory, and eventually to restore the neutrality of Belgium.'

This much was clear enough, but Kitchener then made the recurrent British caveat (echoing Canning's warning to Moore in 1808): 'It must be recognised from the outset that the numerical strength of the force – and its contingent reinforcements [the 4th Division, if circumstances permitted, and perhaps the 6th] – is strictly limited.' And he spelled out what operational limitations this implied:

> While every effort must be made to coincide most sympathetically with the plans and wishes of our Ally, the gravest consideration will devolve upon you as to participation in forward movements where large bodies of French troops are not engaged and where your force may be unduly exposed to attack ... In this connection I wish you distinctly to understand that your command is an entirely independent one, and that you will in no case come in any sense under the orders of any allied General.

---

* In September 1808, following the removal of General Sir Harry Burrard for his signing of the Convention of Cintra, Moore, the most admired soldier in Britain, was given command of the British army in Portugal. He advanced deep into Spain, ordered to cooperate with Spanish forces against the French, but the surrender of Madrid and the arrival of Napoleon with an army of 200,000 soldiers forced him to retreat to the coast in the depths of winter – January 1809. Although the army was eventually able to fight a successful battle at Corunna before being evacuated by the Royal Navy, with food, warm clothing and ammunition in short supply, and the French pressing hard, the discipline of some regiments during the retreat all but collapsed. The condition of the troops when they arrived in England caused a public scandal. Moore himself had been killed in the fighting at Corunna; it was widely believed that he would have faced a court martial had he lived for exceeding his orders, though in truth he had followed them faithfully. Sir Arthur Wellesley, later the duke of Wellington, then took command of the army which was sent back to Portugal.

Kitchener had already strayed into operational territory by specifying in the instructions that Amiens was to be the concentration area – an instruction later rescinded, conceding the reality of the railway movement plan based on Maubeuge – but he now went further, revealing his own perceptions of the relative fighting power of the BEF, the French and the Germans: 'Officers may well be reminded that in this – their first – experience of European warfare a greater measure of caution must be employed than under former conditions of hostilities against an untrained adversary.' And although the BEF, principally through its shooting – and no little courage – would show that it had gained by that experience of 'hostilities with an untrained adversary' (the Boers), Kitchener's circumspection would prove fully justified, for as the official historian put it, 'no steps had been taken to instruct the army in a knowledge of the probable theatre of war or of the German army'.

Did Kitchener believe that Sir John French needed riding on a tight rein? French had commanded the Cavalry Division in South Africa when Kitchener had been the army's chief of staff there, and then its commander-in-chief, and Kitchener wrote in his despatches that his 'willingness to accept responsibility, and his bold and sanguine disposition have relieved me from many anxieties'. Since then their paths had scarcely crossed; but on top of his habitual circumspection, and perhaps suspicious of the view of war from the cavalry saddle, Kitchener knew of the BEF commander's reputation. French was a supremely visceral cavalryman: money was for spending, whether one had it or not (he had to borrow £2,000 from Douglas Haig, when the latter had been his brigade major in Aldershot, to avoid scandal), and women were, in Nietzsche's words, 'for the entertainment of the warrior'. A wedding ring was no impediment.

The man who knew him best, perhaps, Haig himself, had no doubt about the matter, confiding to his diary that neither French nor his chief of staff, Lieutenant-General Sir Archibald Murray, 'are at all fitted for the appointments which they now hold at this moment of crisis in our country's history'. Murray had been commanding the 2nd Division since the beginning of the year, and Haig had been unimpressed with his handling of the division on exercise, and his ideas on fighting generally. French did not rate him either, and the two did not get on. Indeed, Murray was only appointed at the last minute: Wilson had been earmarked as chief of staff, but had then been judged too risky (his part in the Curragh 'mutiny' had in many respects been infamous), so he was made Murray's deputy. It is no exaggeration to say that from the outset Wilson worked to gain Murray's place, just as Haig worked to gain French's. This hardly made for cooperation, one of the fundamental, intuitive principles of war.*

Haig's concerns were whether French's 'temper was sufficiently even or his military knowledge sufficiently thorough'. This might seem to encompass the entire range of a general's necessary attributes, but there was another, and one that Haig possibly knew in his heart that he himself did not possess in such measure as his chief – the ability to inspire those under him. For French was warm and gener-ous, approachable and humane. He had the well-being of his men at heart, and they knew it; those with whom he came into contact – and he made it his business to be in contact (sometimes at the expense of more essential requirements of command) – loved rather than simply admired him. Was he, as some historians have suggested, dis-ingenuous? Whatever the answer, and notwithstanding the terrible miscalculations of 1915, with their badly conceived attacks, ten years on the no-nonsense Wully Robertson would write that he doubted 'if any other general in the army could have sustained in them to the same extent the courage and resolution which they displayed during the trying circumstances of the first six months of the war'.

This is a powerful endorsement, but it does not claim that another general could not have done *enough*, while bringing to bear the attrib-utes that French lacked. There was a saying in the army (then and now): 'Sweat saves blood; but brains save sweat *and* blood.'

Who were the 'other generals'?

Haig himself was a cavalryman, but rather more intellectually than instinctively (if obstinately) convinced of the role of cavalry. He was a careful Lowland Scot; probity was everything. He was never described as convivial, although he had been a member of the

---

* 'Cooperation' was not actually listed as one of the principles of war in *Field Service Regulations* – hence 'intuitive' – but in an article for the *RUSI Journal* in 1916 ('The Principles of War with Reference to the Campaigns of 1914–15'), the then Captain J. F. C. 'Boney' Fuller, who would become one of the great military thinkers of the inter-war years, reflecting on operations since August 1914, stressed the need for the additional principle of cooperation as well as 'economy of force'.

Bullingdon Club while at Oxford, but the early death of his father, a whisky magnate, had made him financially independent, and he had made a very good, if late, but entirely genuine match in Lady (Doreen, 'Doris') Haig, daughter of the third Baron Vivian, a lady-in-waiting to Queen Alexandra, which gave him an unusually strong voice with the King. He was a diligent and highly regarded staff officer who had done much to shape and implement Haldane's reforms. Yet he had not commanded a brigade (except for a few weeks in South Africa), let alone a division, and his command of the greater part of I Corps in the 1912 army manoeuvres had not been promising. In fact, some historians claim that he was 'decisively beaten', despite having the odds strongly in his favour, by the 'Blue' Force commander, Lieutenant-General Sir James Grierson, the former DMO and a Gunner. But this is a facile view; exercises are a notoriously difficult measure of senior command. They are good for practising procedures, movement, communications and the like, but since there are always artificial constraints on manoeuvre – and since, of course, they lack the ingredient of fire, particularly artillery fire – the outcome is always bound to be questionable. The world's press as well as its military attachés had been in East Anglia to watch the mock invasion of 1912, and the *New York Herald* had summed it all up with a nod to Marshal Bosquet's opinion on the Charge of the Light Brigade: 'magnificent, but it was not war'. The local press, in the form of the *Cambridge Evening News*, had been less literary but more brutal, with the headline: 'Futility of Manoeuvres. Bullet the Only Real Umpire'.

But *entirely* futile they were not. There is no doubt that during the manoeuvres Haig underestimated the value of aircraft in observation, whereas Grierson was clever in hiding his troops from the air and using the combined reconnaissance of aircraft and cavalry. While Haig, mounted, played the thrusting commander of the advancing ('Red') forces, Grierson, according to his diary, 'stayed in camp all day receiving reports and very soon located all the lines of march and halting places of the Red forces'. Haig may perhaps be forgiven a little: he had sailed for India, to be the Indian Army's chief of staff, only six months after Blériot had flown the Channel, and returned at the beginning of 1912 before the RFC had even been formed. Whatever the case, he certainly learned a lesson in the manoeuvres:

231

his diary entries for the first encounters of the war are full of remarks on air reconnaissance.*

Undoubtedly, however, Grierson was a step ahead of Haig in most respects except the literally vital one – fitness. Overweight – indeed obese – a bon viveur with cigar permanently lit, he was Edward VII to Haig's George V. And on the train to Maubeuge, at seven in the morning of 17 August, he would suffer an aortic aneurysm and die. Haig, who was on the same train, was asked what should be done, to which he replied that the train should proceed but that Grierson's death should be reported at once to Major-General Frederick Robb, commanding the lines of communication, as well as to Sir John French at Joffre's headquarters. Robb received the news quickly, and immediately telephoned the War Office; and then began a squabble of the familiar type over appointments. The selection of a corps commander was properly the business of the CIGS, but Kitchener, in his field marshal's uniform, was not to be trifled with. He insisted that Sir Horace Smith-Dorrien be sent out, though 'Smith-*Doreen*', as his detractors (including Haig) were wont to call him, had just been promoted (full) general and commander of the home army. Kitchener evidently believed that Smith-Dorrien would stand up to French; and it is instructive that the secretary for war believed this to be the first consideration. Might he also have been entertaining the possibility of needing to replace French, who would be sixty-two the following month, at an early stage, and considering that Smith-Dorrien (six years younger; four older than Haig – and having earned Kitchener's regard in South Africa and India) would be the man to appoint in his place?†

---

* The legend of the 1912 manoeuvres was embellished by the memoirs of Haig's former intelligence chief later in the war, Brigadier-General John Charteris, who, though he was not there, claimed that at the final conference of the manoeuvres in Cambridge on 19 September, in the presence of the King, the opponents were asked to explain their tactics and moves, and whereas Grierson was masterly – like Henry Wilson at the August 1911 CID – Haig set aside his written statement, which gave a clear and convincing account of his views, and to the dismay of his staff attempted to extemporize, and in the process 'became totally unintelligible and unbearably dull. The university dignitaries soon fell asleep, Haig's friends became more and more uncomfortable, only he seemed totally unconscious of his failure': Brigadier-General John Charteris (with John Buchan), *Field Marshal Earl Haig* (London, 1929). The evidence of the *Times* correspondent, Repington, who was there, disputes this.

† *Field Service Regulations*, 'issued by command of the Army Council' (of which the minister was chairman), is unequivocal on the respective responsibilities: 'The C.-in-C.

When French himself learned of Grierson's death he called London and asked for Sir Herbert Plumer as his replacement. 'Plum', a year older than Smith-Dorrien, was an apparently amenable, even buffer-ish, former mounted infantryman (who would in fact emerge as something of a star in 1917, with the accolade 'the soldier's general'). French may well have argued that as a four-star Smith-Dorrien was unnecessarily senior to fill the appointment of corps commander, but in truth the two were chalk and cheese, and had clashed several times over the role of cavalry in future war (Smith-Dorrien was firmly in the Lord Roberts camp in the *arme blanche* debate – the sword and lance versus the rifle). And some of the changes that Smith-Dorrien had introduced at Aldershot on taking over command from French in 1907 had seemed to him implied criticism. But Smith-Dorrien had impeccable infantry credentials, having first seen action in the Anglo-Zulu War (he had been present at Isandhlwana, and had been cited for the VC), and serving twice in the Sudan before going on to command his battalion in the Tirah Campaign (on the Afghan border) and then a brigade in South Africa. Against French's wishes he would take command of II Corps of the BEF.

But all three men – French, Smith-Dorrien, Haig – had one thing in common: none of them had absolute confidence in the mission. In this they shared Kitchener's misgivings too. French had wanted to go to Antwerp instead – and had said so at the war council of 5 August. Haig had wanted to go to France later, in greater numbers and decisive strength, and had said so to Haldane and the CIGS. But Smith-Dorrien had been even more decided. In the last week of July he had reviewed two thousand OTC cadets at their annual camp on Salisbury Plain and, according to one who heard him, told them 'that war should be avoided at almost any cost, that war would solve nothing, that the whole of Europe and more besides would be reduced

---

of the forces in the field is appointed by or subject to the approval of His Majesty's Government. Commanders, staff officers and heads of administrative services and departments will be nominated by the responsible military authority.' Kitchener may simply have been 'interfering' (as it was feared he would), but it is reasonable to infer that he was thinking in terms of the next C-in-C, and therefore that the appointment of the commander of II Corps was 'subject to the approval of HMG'. It did not help that on learning of Grierson's death Sir John French would write to Kitchener (as well as telephoning the CIGS) asking for Sir Herbert Plumer, thereby suggesting that the appointment was in his gift.

to ruin, and that the loss of life would be so large that whole populations would be decimated'.*

Did this matter? To the two corps commanders, perhaps not so much: they received their orders direct from GHQ. But the commander-in-chief had to decide what to do in the context of what the French were doing – rather as Sir John Moore had with the Spanish. With caveats amounting to ambivalence in Kitchener's directive, when the depth and strength of the German hook through Belgium took Joffre and his generals by surprise, Sir John French would have to discern the best course for the BEF. His own belief in the mission was therefore of the essence.

Meanwhile, as the BEF was getting itself to France – smoothly and as correct in every detail as could reasonably have been wished of any force, thanks to Henry Wilson's drive and meticulous forethought – French did not have to worry about the qualities that Wully Robertson said only he could have sustained when the going got really tough. Exceptions there most certainly were, but the general attitude of those who would soon be calling themselves the 'Old Contemptibles' might be summed up in the words of one of its regular NCOs, the backbone of the BEF – Sergeant David Brunton of the 19th Hussars: 'All was excitement and everybody very keen to get at the Germans, and for some of us, eager to be on active service again.'

For Brunton wore the South Africa medals, with five clasps, while it was almost certain that no sergeant in the 19th *Saxon* Hussars would be wearing any campaign ribbons at all. Before the autumn was out, however, the Saxons would have earned a good number of gallantry medals, many of them posthumous, and Sergeant Brunton would be wearing the ribbon of the Distinguished Conduct Medal.

---

* It must be admitted that the author can find only one account of this, by a Rhodes scholar then at Rossall School, Donald Smith, who was commissioned in the RFA the following year, and who after the war practised at the Bermuda bar and was a member of the Bermudan parliament (*Merely for the Record: The Memoirs of Donald Christopher Smith 1894–1980*, ed. John William Cox Jr, Bermuda, privately printed, 1982). On the other hand, Allan Adair, who was at the camp with the Harrow OTC, recalls Smith-Dorrien's urging the cadets to join the Reserves as quickly as possible (*A Guards' General*).

Chapter Twelve

AN ARMY WITH A COUNTRY ATTACHED TO IT

The authority of the C-in-C is supreme in all matters within the theatre of operations on land. He is responsible for the efficiency of the forces in the field, for the control and direction of their operations as a whole, and for the control of all territory under martial law.

Field Service Regulations, Part II: *Organization and Administration* (1909)

In the afternoon of Friday, 14 August 1914, Sir John French, with a small group of staff officers including Henry Wilson (but not, curiously, the BEF's head of intelligence, Colonel George Macdonogh) and Colonel Victor Huguet, the former French military attaché in London who was to be Joffre's head of mission to the BEF, crossed the Channel in the fast cruiser *Sentinel* and landed at Boulogne to an enthusiastic reception.* Before taking the special train for Dover, French had gone to the Admiralty to thank the first lord for his professional and

---

* Huguet had been sent from Paris a few days earlier with the French general staff's assessment of the situation, and was to be Joffre's official means of communicating with Sir John French. The head of the British military mission to the *Grand Quartier Général* – Joffre's own headquarters – was Major Sidney Clive, who would hold the post throughout the war. His diaries are a source of much detail on Joffre's decision-making. Huguet's purpose in London had been twofold: to get the deployment date brought forward, which he failed to do (the bank holiday throwing the movement plans), and to get Kitchener to agree to the BEF's concentration area being Maubeuge – as Joffre wanted – not Amiens; in this he was successful, since Sir John, once he had given up thoughts of Antwerp, had come to the same conclusion.

personal support, in Churchill's words 'solemn, radiant and with glistening eyes'.*

The first troops had arrived on 7 August, only two days after general mobilization began: these were the advance parties of the lines-of-communication units who would prepare the camping grounds. The main body of the BEF began crossing on the twelfth, not by warship but on 'shipping taken up from trade' (cross-Channel steamers and coasters of every description), with most of the troops making the voyage between the fifteenth and the seventeenth. Many were surprised by the absence of Royal Navy ships in the Channel – no escorts, no distant line of grey shapes keeping watch, not even smoke from funnels over the horizon; just here and there a destroyer cutting fast through the swell, bent on some business apparently unconnected with their passage to France. The BEF's safe conduct was in fact guaranteed by the Grand Fleet 600 miles to the north in Scapa Flow, and by the cruiser and destroyer patrols in the North Sea operating from bases the length of the east coast.† The first British casualties of the war had been 150 of the crew of HMS *Amphion*, leader of the 3rd Destroyer Flotilla at Harwich, when early in the morning of 6 August she had struck a mine laid by the *Königen Luise*, which the flotilla had sunk the day before off the Thames estuary. Ironically, before sinking the *Königen Luise* she had had to manoeuvre between her own destroyers and the ship taking the German ambassador to Holland, the Great Eastern Railway's steamer *St Petersburg*, to halt their fire (*St Petersburg* having hoisted the German flag). But if the Germans were quick off the mark with their minelaying – the *Königen Luise* had slipped out of Emden the night the ultimatum expired – the Royal Navy was sharper still. Or rather, the General Post Office's CS (Cable Ship) *Alert* was. Under the navy's orders, that same night she began dredging up the German communication cables in the Dover Straits, finding the first just after 3 a.m. and the last, fifth, cable just after 7 a.m., cutting the cables to Britain and patching the others running

---

* *Great Contemporaries*, London, 1937.
† Early on 4 August the Grand Fleet, commanded by Admiral Sir John Jellicoe, had left Scapa Flow on the first of its many 'sweeps' in the North Sea, its object to intercept German commerce-raiders 'jumping the gun'. At eleven o'clock that evening Jellicoe received the wireless message: 'Commence hostilities against Germany.' For three days the fleet cruised without seeing a single enemy ship, and on the seventh returned to Orkney.

to neutral countries into the British network. At a stroke, much of Germany's telephone and telegraph connection to the world beyond the Central Powers was destroyed – and British capacity increased. Elsewhere His Majesty's ships were severing and repatching the transatlantic cables.

In Boulogne Sir John French went immediately on a tour of inspection of the transit camps, some of them on the cliff tops where Napoleon Bonaparte's optimistically named *Armée d'Angleterre* had camped before Trafalgar, and then spent the night at Amiens. Next morning he went to see something of a novelty, the only military force ever to have left Britain other than by sea – Nos 2, 3, 4 and 5 Squadrons (sixty or so aircraft) of the Royal Flying Corps at their advance base.* Three days earlier they had taken off from Dover and crossed the Straits to Boulogne, from where they followed the coast to the mouth of the Somme, and then the river upstream to Amiens – 100 miles.† Not every aircraft had made it, however: on the twelfth, as the squadrons were leaving their stations for the staging field at Dover, a Blériot flown by Lieutenant Robert Skene, with Air Mechanic Raymond Barlow aboard, crashed on take-off from Netheravon airfield in Wiltshire, killing both men – the first BEF casualties of the war. There was, perhaps, no more prophetic an airfield than Netheravon: it had been selected in part because of the flat, rolled gallops on Salisbury Plain used by the nearby Cavalry School, which it displaced. After the war the cavalry would return only briefly to Netheravon, which would become instead the Machine Gun School (the airfield remains today).

French then boarded the train for Paris, reaching the Gare du Nord at 12.45 p.m. Here, his diary records, 'I was met by the British Ambassador . . . and the Military Governor of Paris. Large crowds had assembled in the streets on the way to the Embassy, and we were received with tremendous greetings by the people. Their welcome was cordial in the extreme.' After lunch at the embassy they went to the Elysée Palace, where French found President Poincaré in surprisingly

---

* Each RFC squadron had twelve operational aircraft, but the force had with it spare machines, as well as relief pilots.
† No. 5 Squadron crossed later, on 15 August. No. 2 Squadron, at Montrose, had the hardest task, its pilots actually starting on their southward flight to Farnborough on the third – the day before the ultimatum; after several accidents, none fatal, they did all reach Dover.

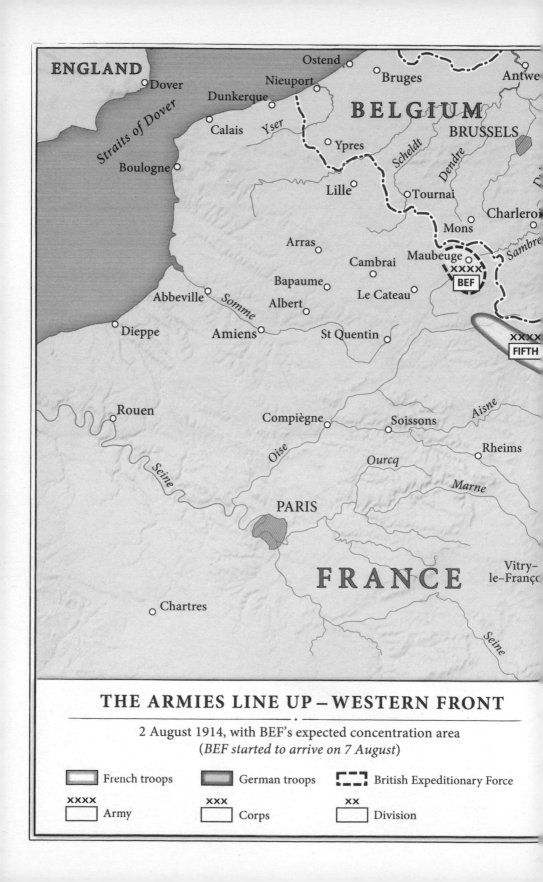

ENGLAND

Dover

Straits of Dover

BELGIUM

Ostend

Nieuport

Bruges

Antwe

Dunkerque

Yser

BRUSSELS

Calais

Ypres

Scheldt

Dendre

Boulogne

Lille

Tournai

Charlero

Mons

Sambre

Arras

Cambrai

Maubeuge

Bapaume

Le Cateau

XXXX
BEF

Abbeville

Somme

Albert

XXXX
FIFTH

Dieppe

Amiens

St Quentin

Rouen

Compiègne

Soissons

Aisne

Oise

Rheims

Seine

Ourcq

Marne

PARIS

FRANCE

Vitry–
le–Franço

Chartres

Seine

THE ARMIES LINE UP – WESTERN FRONT

2 August 1914, with BEF's expected concentration area
(*BEF started to arrive on 7 August*)

French troops	German troops	British Expeditionary Force
✗✗✗✗ Army	✗✗✗ Corps	✗✗ Division

buoyant mood, as well as René Viviani, the prime minister (since 13 July), and the war minister, Messimy, all full of optimism and notions of 'a victorious advance by the Allies . . . [the president speaking] playfully with me on the possibility of another battle being fought by the British on the old field of Waterloo'. Waterloo again – and Poincaré was not far off in his prediction of another battle there, for Mons was only 20 miles away.

Yet the president of France was not initially much impressed by the British commander-in-chief. And had Sir John French known why, his pride – which was his prime animating spirit – would have been severely bruised: 'Far from looking like a dashing soldier', wrote Poincaré in his memoirs, 'one would rather take him for a plodding engineer.'* What was worse, he now learned that the BEF would not be ready for action for another nine days.

But as French and Messimy pored over the maps that afternoon at the war ministry, the situation did not look at all bad: the French 1st and 2nd Armies were making progress in their offensive in Alsace-Lorraine, and the Belgians – perhaps surprisingly, and certainly heroically – were still holding the fortress of Liège in the face of the great German battering ram. However, the inconvenient intelligence reports about the strength of the German build-up on the Belgian frontier were not vouchsafed to French, for they did not suit the model of Plan XVII. So it did not seem to the commander-in-chief that there was any great need to hurry. The BEF had begun mobilizing three days after the French; its reservists, unlike those of many of the localized French units, had had to be recalled hundreds of miles, its units gathered up from all over the British Isles, transported by sea and then railed to a concentration area where all the elements could be properly married up. Sir John French was in no doubt that, to be effective and safe, the BEF must enter the line cohesively and properly found, not hasten into it short of men and the materiel of war.

The auguries for allied understanding were hardly good, therefore, despite French's upbeat reading of the Elysée meeting. And here Barbara Tuchman gets it wrong, attributing to Sir John French confusion rather than merely lack of percipience: 'The immediate purpose for which the BEF had come to France – to prevent her being

* *The Memoirs of Raymond Poincaré*, trans. Sir George Arthur (London, 1929).

Too little, too late? Sir John French, 'the little field marshal', arriving at the Ministère de la guerre in Paris on 15 August 1914, in advance of the BEF, which the Kaiser would supposedly call a 'contemptible little army'. Although the newspapers sent photographers to France as soon as war was declared, the Graphic's sketches, and those of its arch-rival the Sphere, remained popular – not least with the authorities, for the artists could use considerable licence: here Sir John French – and by extension the BEF – looks no smaller than the French officers greeting him.

crushed by Germany – appeared to escape him.' This was *not*, in fact, the purpose for which the BEF had crossed the Channel. Though it may have been the unspoken desire of some of the cabinet, it was not what had carried the cabinet as a whole, and Parliament and the country, into war; nor was it implied in Kitchener's instructions. Germany was 'the common enemy', but 'the peculiar task' of the BEF was 'to assist the French Government in preventing, or repelling, the invasion by Germany of French *and* Belgian territory, *and* eventually to restore the neutrality of Belgium' (italics added). Clearly the restoration of Belgian neutrality was now contingent on French assistance, which could only follow from preventing or repelling invasion, but this was not the same as Tuchman's vision of John Bull saving the fragile Marianne. Sir John French had his faults – lethal faults – but he had grasped the strategic object well enough; and two days later he would prove he understood full well the implications of the real situation once it was revealed to him – and grasped it, indeed, a good deal more quickly and more surely than did France's most senior generals. It is important not to write off Sir John French as *wholly* unsuited to high command. With the right chief of staff, he might have been good *enough*. But that night his diary betrayed no sense of incipient discord: he 'dined quietly' with his private secretary, Lieutenant-Colonel Brinsley FitzGerald, at the Ritz.

In any case, things began looking up the next day, Sunday, when he motored to Joffre's headquarters at Vitry-le-François, a sleepy little town 100 miles east of Paris in the valley of the Marne. Arriving just in time for lunch, at the *Grand Quartier Général* (*GQG*) he found an impressive air of 'calm, deliberate confidence' and indeed some jubilation since a captured German 'flag' had just been brought in.* Joffre and his equally bulky chief of staff, Henri Berthelot, proceeded to brief him on the situation and their intention: while maintaining the primary offensive in Alsace-Lorraine, they intended to attack in the north-east, beginning in five days' time (on 21 August), and wished the BEF to advance on the left of the French 5th Army,

---

* French's memoirs say 'flag', but judging by the reaction it must have been a regimental colour. It might, of course, have simply been taken from the regimental baggage, but at this stage of the fighting both the Germans and French were carrying their colours in the field, unfurled. The British infantry, on the other hand, had cased theirs on leaving barracks, and for the most part consigned them to the regimental depots.

north-east from the concentration area at Maubeuge towards Nivelles, as part of a great outflanking movement. One, possibly two, German army corps and a division of cavalry – no more – would be facing the BEF, though it was difficult to be precise, he explained.

It seems extraordinary, but French and Joffre had never met before, this in itself an indictment of the system of staff talks, which had become in effect a dialogue between Wilson and Foch. However, the two men formed favourable impressions of each other, so that, having first told Joffre that the BEF would not be ready before the twenty-fourth, as he had insisted to the president and Messimy, French now said he would do all he could to be ready for an offensive on the twenty-first. The best that can be said of this hasty re-calculation is that he may have felt that, facing lighter opposition than earlier supposed, he could take a gamble. Yet one, possibly two, army corps was a not inconsiderable force against which to pit one division of cavalry and four of infantry. It has been suggested that Joffre tricked French into going early, but this seems unlikely: on 16 August the outlook at *GQG* was sanguine in the extreme. All their calculations were based still on the conviction that the Germans would have to leave such a force on the eastern front to ward off a Russian *attaque brusquée* that they would not have enough troops to develop an offensive west of the Meuse (north of Namur) in any appreciable strength.*

If only they had known. If only Sir John French had known. Facing him would be not 'one, possibly two, army corps' but the whole of General Alexander von Kluck's 1st Army – four active corps, three from the reserve and three cavalry divisions; in all, some 220,000 men.† The Royal Flying Corps were still at Amiens; the French *armée de l'air* had evidently seen nothing untoward; agents on the ground likewise. On the sixteenth, all seemed to be going to plan – Plan XVII. French said he would go to 5th Army headquarters the following day,

---

* Despite the mutual favourable impressions, however, Joffre felt unable to accept a sensible operational request from French: 'As the British Army was posted on the left, or exposed flank, I asked Joffre to place the French Cavalry Division, and two Reserve Divisions which were echeloned in reserve behind, directly under my orders. This the Commander-in-Chief found himself unable to concede' (French, *1914*).

† On paper the strength of the 1st Army could be given as 320,000, and indeed some histories quote that number, but not all elements were mustered for the *Westaufmarsch*: some remained on counter-invasion duty in Schleswig-Holstein, for example.

and Joffre warmly commended to him its GOC – General Charles Lanrezac.

So the little fleet of Rolls-Royces set off once again, this time north-west, partway along the valley of the Marne, through an empty landscape – 'the crops were half cut, and stooks of corn were lying about everywhere' – to Rheims, where French and his entourage rendezvoused with the rest of the advance party at the Hôtel du Lion d'Or (Henry Wilson was pleased to be able to pun with *lit on dort*); here they found the chief of staff, Archie Murray, on his hands and knees, stripped to his underpants in the stifling heat, trying to make sense of the situation from the maps spread on the floor, oblivious to the constant procession of chambermaids. There was a 'flap', too, since the War Office codes had been mislaid, perhaps even left on the luggage rack of the train from Boulogne, and several telegrams had arrived, indecipherable without them. It was not as the staff college envisaged an advance headquarters. Sir John French did the sensible thing: he dined and then went to bed.

Next morning he set off for Rethel, 25 miles to the north-east along a good, straight road, taking with him once more Henry Wilson, the indispensable linguist and incorrigible Francophile (some would say *Francomane*), leaving behind the codeless staff and the heat of the plain as they climbed gently into the boskier country of the tributaries of the River Aisne – to the headquarters of the French army's 'star turn'. At ten o'clock the commander-in-chief of the BEF arrived in the town square and got out from his Silver Ghost looking 'very spick and span' according to Lieutenant Edward Spears, now the liaison officer at 5th Army – 'ruddy faced, his white moustache drooping over the corners of his mouth . . . clear blue eyes . . . upright bearing'.

Lanrezac came out to greet him, an altogether less military and appealing figure, thought Spears, 'a big flabby man with an emphatic corporation . . . weather-beaten and . . . swarthy, revealing his creole origin' (he had been born in Guadeloupe). But Lanrezac's appearance belied a shrewd brain: he alone of the French high command had begun to suspect that not all was as *GQG* believed. Indeed, he was becoming worried. His 5th Army had crossed the Belgian border and taken up positions along the Meuse, principally south of Dinant but also as far north as Namur, in preparation for its offensive into the Ardennes, but the Cavalry Corps, under *GQG* command, which had been covering his left flank, had been ordered to scout on towards the Belgian–Luxembourg border astride what was presumed would be the German axis of advance towards Sedan (of haunting memory – the rout of the French army in 1870): all that was now occupying some 15 miles' frontage between Dinant and the fortress of Namur was a single regiment – about 3,000 men. *GQG*'s assessment on 14 August that there were six German army corps and four (perhaps six) cavalry divisions in front of Liège did not disturb Joffre, but it did trouble Lanrezac: if he advanced into the Ardennes and the Germans crossed the Meuse and turned south, they could cut his lines of communication; likewise, if he held on the Meuse and the Germans crossed north of Namur, his flank would be turned. He had therefore asked *GQG* to allow him to leave a covering force on the lower Meuse and withdraw the bulk of his army to the area of the fortress of Maubeuge and to Givet on the upper Meuse – and (ironically) to change the BEF's concentration area from Maubeuge to Amiens.*

Joffre had been sympathetic, seeing 'nothing but advantage in studying a movement such as that suggested'; although, as French noted in his diary, he 'consider[ed] that the danger [was] far removed and by no means certain to materialize', the following morning (15 August) he had told Lanrezac he could move two corps north and adjust the 5th Army's line to face north as well as east, while remaining in a position still to mount an offensive into the Ardennes as soon as the situation was favourable. He told him also that he had asked Messimy to release three territorial divisions committed to coastal defence to take up a line between Dunkirk and Maubeuge to prevent the passage of cavalry, even though he was sure that any Germans west of the Meuse could be no more than a few ranging uhlans (cavalry).† Indeed, to Joffre the puzzling thing was the slowness of the German advance everywhere: there had yet been no debouch from the great fortress of Metz (the *attaque brusquée* he had been expecting

---

* Maubeuge was a Vauban fortress, built in the seventeenth century, but greatly extended after the Franco-Prussian war. It was not, however, in the same league as Namur or Liège.
† The following day at Haelen, on the Gette, 30 miles north-west of Liège, Lieutenant-General Leon de Witte's Belgian cavalry division, fighting dismounted with the (Belgian model) Mauser carbine, stopped in their tracks six regiments of the German II Cavalry Corps trying to cross the river. German losses were heavy. Still no alarm bells rang at *GQG*.

from the outset to disrupt French mobilization and deployment), no great activity further south before Nancy, although intelligence had suggested that an attack would come on the 12th, and – most baffling of all – no great advance south-west through Luxembourg and the south-east corner of Belgium towards Sedan. What, therefore, was the German game? Why had they bothered to march into Belgium and Luxembourg at all? The answer – to cross the Meuse in strength before wheeling south into France – would have been obvious except for one thing: all the calculations showed they did not have enough troops.

Yet during the afternoon of the fifteenth, while Sir John French was meeting the president, there had been quite an affair at Dinant, when jaegers (in German, *Jäger*: light infantry attached to the cavalry divisions) managed to force a crossing of the Meuse, provoking a very Gallic and successful counter-attack – with bugles and bayonets – in which a young lieutenant, Charles de Gaulle, distinguished himself and was wounded, but drawing in General Jean-François Sordet's Cavalry Corps (under direct command of *GQG*), which then crossed to the west bank and thereafter lost contact with the enemy. And when *GQG* learned that some 10,000 German cavalry had crossed the Meuse north-east of Huy roughly halfway between Namur and Liège, despite the Belgians' blowing the bridges, Joffre told Lanrezac to move the two corps north at once. He followed up the order at 8 p.m. with *Instruction Particulière* No. 10. This was based on an assessment that the enemy's main effort on the right wing (that is, in Belgium) would be with six army corps and four (perhaps six) cavalry divisions on an axis north of Givet. Lanrezac was instructed to leave one corps on the Meuse, bring up the rest of the 5th Army towards the Sambre and, in concert with the Belgians and the BEF, deal with these German formations. *GQG*'s assessment would prove an underestimate by a factor of almost three: the German *masse de manoeuvre* was not six but some seventeen corps.*

---

* Again, the question may be asked how such a miscalculation could be made. The French cavalry were undoubtedly having difficulty penetrating the German cavalry screens to discover what was following up. At this stage German radio discipline seems to have been good, revealing little about the order of battle. The *armée de l'air*, which could have rumbled the entire German scheme, was for any number of reasons (not least the extreme range of operating) simply not detecting the huge numbers of troops moving into Belgium north of the Ardennes. But it was all a symptom of a sort of 'cognitive dissonance' in *GQG* – the difficulty of coping with information that conflicts with a decided state of mind. Military intelligence works by gathering information from

When Sir John French now met Lanrezac, therefore, he found not the warm, composed atmosphere of the *GQG* the day before, but rather an air of frustration surrounding a man irked by Joffre's tardiness in recognizing the threat to his left wing. Nor were his host's manners those of the Cavalry Club, especially towards one who came late to the business and in underwhelming strength (the French 5th Army was almost three times the size of the BEF). In fact the headquarters as a whole was rattled, for even the urbane cavalryman Hély d'Oissel, Lanrezac's chief of staff, berated Huguet (whom he equated with the BEF) when he saw him: 'At last you're here. It's not a moment too soon. If we are beaten we will owe it to you.'*

Having exchanged salutes and civilities, the two army commanders went into conclave, neither of them speaking the other's language, nor able to understand it much better. Between generals with a map in front of them there is perhaps a sufficient common language for such a meeting to be useful, though why Wilson and d'Oissel were excluded, and Spears, who could have made the meeting more than simply useful, is puzzling to say the least. After half an hour the 'creole general' and the little field marshal emerged to rejoin their senior staff, gathered in the *Troisième Bureau*, the operations branch, studying the wall-map on which the progress of the Germans was plotted by flag pins. Whatever the accord that the conclave had been meant to create, their mutual (mis)understanding was now to be fatally sealed. Putting on his glasses, Sir John French approached the map, found the place that Lanrezac had obviously referred to in his sanctum, pointed with his finger, and began: 'Mon Général, est-ce-que—' whereupon his French failed him and he turned to Henry Wilson: 'How do you say "to cross the river"?'

Wilson obliged, and the field marshal proceeded boldly: 'Est-ce-que les Allemands vont traverser la Meuse à ... à ...?', but then he fumbled the pronunciation of the name. Huy was the place at which his finger pointed on the map – a perversely difficult name to

---

the widest possible range of sources and then trying to make sense of what it says about the enemy's intentions. It fails to work when the information-gathering means are only targeted to confirm pre-conceived assessments, and independent sources reporting contradictory information are discounted as 'rogue' because they do not fit the expected pattern. It still happens.

* Spears, *Liaison 1914*, quoting Huguet's *L'Intervention militaire britannique en 1914* (Paris, 1928).

pronounce, 'the "u" practically having to be whistled', wrote Spears, who witnessed the effort. Whistling was quite beyond the field marshal, however: 'Hoy,' he said at last, triumphantly.

'Que dit-il? Que dit-il?' demanded Lanrezac, with all the legendary contempt of his compatriots for foreigners unable to meet the exacting standards of the Académie Française. Henry Wilson explained that the field marshal wanted to know whether in his opinion the Germans were going to cross the river at Huy. Lanrezac shrugged his shoulders impatiently. 'Tell *le Maréchal*,' he said curtly, 'that in my opinion the Germans have merely gone to the Meuse to fish,' which Wilson translated as 'He says they're going to cross the river, sir.'

French's language skills may have been limited, but not his instinct for knowing when he was being patronized. The lack of rapport between the two men would cost many lives, and perhaps opportunities. Nevertheless the meeting managed to end with just enough military courtesies to imply willing cooperation, and Sir John French climbed back into his Silver Ghost to head for Le Cateau where his own headquarters were being set up, close to the BEF's concentration area at Maubeuge – now perilously close to the fighting.*

---

* The account of this exchange is Spears' in *Liaison 1914*, published in 1930 after the deaths of the principals and of Wilson. Spears did not witness it himself, but writes: 'A British officer has told me . . . ' – that is, hearsay; and the construction 'has told me' suggests rather recent hearsay at that. The editor of Wilson's diaries (published in 1927) refers to the account as being that of 'an officer who was present' (and who clearly understood the French), which makes Spears again the possible source, for he was present at Rethel, if not at the actual exchange between the generals. Indeed, it would have been natural for the editor, Major-General Sir Charles Callwell, to consult the man who was the liaison officer at Lanrezac's headquarters. The exchange is related uncritically in every book about the BEF, yet it has been disputed by French sources, which claim that the remarks were not made to Sir John French's face – a claim attested to by several French officers who were present – but at dinner that evening by Lanrezac to his staff, along the lines of 'I felt like saying to the *Maréchal* . . .', the inference being that the 'officer who was present' – perhaps Spears himself (for he would have been the only British officer at Rethel that evening) – later conflated, deliberately or otherwise, the two. Lanrezac became an object of opprobrium in the BEF after the retreat from Mons. Sir John French in his memoirs writes only that: 'He [Lanrezac] was a big man with a loud voice, and his manner did not strike me as being very courteous' (and *pêcher* is not difficult to grasp). Wilson makes no mention of the episode in his diaries, which would have been odd even for such an extreme Francophile as he. Nor, intuitively, and even allowing for the circumstances (Lanrezac was clearly rattled by developments on his left), does it quite seem right – a French general to a British field marshal, commander of a force that could be of assistance, even if later in the day than he would have wished. Whatever the exact truth of the exchange, however, the meeting clearly did not augur well for hearty allied cooperation, and, indeed, Sir John French in his memoirs would be excoriating about Lanrezac's conduct during the fighting.

*

En route *le Maréchal* called on the French territorial divisions that would be on his flank. Reaching Le Cateau in the late afternoon, he learned of Grierson's death, and also of a telegram from Kitchener asking for information on the situation of French troops in the BEF's area of interest. Murray got off a quick telegram in reply, and then French sat down to write at greater length:

My Dear Lord K,

With reference to your wire asking for information as to the position of French troops west of the line Givet–Dinant–Namur–Brussels, I have already replied by wire in general terms. I now send full details.

A Corps of Cavalry (three divisions less one brigade), supported by some Infantry, is north of the River Sambre between Charleroi and Namur. This is the nearest French force to the Belgian Army, and I do not know if and where they have established communication with them, nor do the French.

One French Corps, with an added Infantry Brigade and a Cavalry Brigade, is guarding the River Meuse from Givet to Namur. The bridges are mined and ready to be blown up.

In rear of this corps, two more corps are moving – one on Philippeville, the other on Beaumont. Each of these two corps is composed of three divisions. In rear of them a fourth corps assembles to-morrow west of Beaumont. Three Reserve divisions are already in waiting between Vervins and Hirson. Another Reserve division is guarding the almost impassable country between Givet and Mézières.

Finally, other Reserve formations are guarding the frontier between Maubeuge and Lille.

I left Paris on Sunday morning (16th) by motor, and reached the Headquarters of General Joffre (French Commander-in-Chief) at 12. They are at Vitry-le-François. He quite realises the importance and value of adopting a waiting attitude. In the event of a forward movement by the German Corps in the Ardennes and Luxemburg, he is anxious that I should act in echelon on the left of the 5th French Army, whose present disposition I have stated above. The French Cavalry Corps now north of the Sambre will operate on my left front and keep touch with the Belgians.

I spent the night at Rheims and motored this morning to Rethel, the Headquarters of General Lanrezac, Commander 5th French Army. I had a long talk with him and arranged for co-operation in all alternative circumstances.

I then came on to my Headquarters at this place where I found everything proceeding satisfactorily and up to time. I was much shocked to hear of Grierson's sudden death near Amiens when I arrived here. I had already wired asking you to appoint Plumer in his place, when your wire reached me and also that of Ian Hamilton [later to command at Gallipoli], forwarded – as I understand – by you. I very much hope you will send me Plumer; Hamilton is too senior to command an Army Corps and is already engaged in an important command at home.

Please do as I ask you in this matter? I needn't assure you there was no 'promise' of any kind.

Yours sincerely,
(Signed) J. D. P. French

The letter's uncertainty about the position and situation of the Belgians, expressed in an almost resigned way, suggests that French was already thinking that a retrograde movement was more likely than an offensive one. And Wilson made a telling, not to say curious, entry in his diary that evening: 'We hear of Castelnau [2nd Army] and Pau's [Army of Alsace] successes in Alsace which I don't so much like, as I think it means that the Germans are transferring corps from Alsace to Belgium.' He was assuming that the French success was due to the Germans' thinning out their defences in Alsace. They were not, of course; the troops in Belgium were, in effect, those that the French general staff had always calculated would have to be in the east to meet a Russian offensive. But how had he ever thought that Plan XVII had any chance of success if Alsace was indeed to be the German main effort, as the plan always supposed it would be? History has few examples of success in attacking the enemy's point of greatest strength.

By the next day (18 August) he was 'inclined to think now that we shall have 15 German corps in Belgium, of which 4 to 6 will be north of the river Meuse'. Sir John French in his fumbling attempts to pronounce 'Huy' had nevertheless put his finger not only on the map but on the essence of the only question that should now have mattered to *GQG*: *was* the German main effort to be in Belgium, with major forces north and west of the Meuse?

*

Germany was once more, in the words attributed to Voltaire, an army with a country attached to it – and the *Eisenbahnamt* was sovereign.* The Germans 'take to war as a duck takes to water', wrote the English-born Princess (Evelyn) Blücher in her Berlin diary, apprehensively and with mixed feelings, as mobilization continued apace: 'The marvellous military organization is, I must confess, overwhelming; everything goes off without a hitch . . . The German as a rule has no style . . . but put him in uniform and he looks smart at once.'†

Generalizations, of course, but apt nevertheless. The least 'Prussian' of Germans was not only smartened by uniform, he was transformed by it, especially given a little authority, as anyone who has stood on a platform of the *Deutsches Bundesbahn* today might imagine. The *Westaufmarsch* of August 1914 was the most prodigious movement of troops in history, and since. The *Grosser Generalstab* was driven by Moltke's maxim that 'a mistake in the original assembly of the army can scarcely be rectified in the entire course of the campaign', and aided by the dedicated efficiency of thousands of telegraphists and railway officials – 'our wonderfully ordered country, running like clockwork', in the words of the Princess. The *Eisenbahnamt* and its two dozen regional detachments had requisitioned 30,000 locomotives and nearly a million *Güterwagen* and *Personenwagen* (goods wagons and passenger carriages) to carry the eight armies and four cavalry corps – some 2.1 million men and 600,000 horses – to their assembly areas, four-fifths of them west across the Rhine. Between 2 and 8 August, 2,150 trains up to fifty-four *Wagen* long rumbled across the great Hohenzollern Bridge at Cologne, one every ten minutes. On the eighth, Captain Walter Bloem, a reservist officer of the 12th Brandenburg Grenadiers, paraded at dawn with his company in Frankfurt an der Oder, east of Berlin:

---

* Voltaire's words are variously rendered, including 'Whereas some states possess an army, the Prussian army possesses a state', and sometimes attributed to Count (Honoré) Mirabeau. Whatever the attribution, the phrase captures the essence of Fredrician Prussia, which the Kaiser had been only too happy to imitate – without realizing the danger of the ultimate outcome, that he himself would lose control of state affairs to his generals.

† Evelyn Blücher, *An English Wife in Berlin* (London, 1921). Her husband was Gebhard Blücher von Wahlstatt, the fourth Prince Blücher (1865–1931), an Anglophile descended from the great Prussian field marshal who had come to Wellington's aid at Waterloo. A devout Catholic (as was his wife – from the Lancashire recusancy), he would command an ambulance train formed by the Silesian association of the Order of Malta.

The hour of departure had been kept secret and Frankfurt did not expect its Grenadiers to leave so early. The streets were empty, only here and there frightened women's faces peeped through the curtained windows. The companies marched through the booking hall on to the platform alongside a train of tremendous length. Where were we going, east or west? The engine was facing west, but that meant nothing, perhaps just to mislead spies. The order was given, and in a moment the train was filled to bursting point with its living cargo . . . The public were not allowed on the platform except for one young and frail little lady, the wife of the battalion adjutant, married the previous day. She restrained her emotions most admirably, typical of her Prussian upbringing. The carriage doors were banged. The station master brought his hand to his red cap in salute, the whistle blew, one solitary white handkerchief waved, and the train moved off.

Not perhaps so different from the scene at Aldershot or Tidworth, Colchester or York, where it would have been 'English reserve' on the part of an officer's wife, but at least the BEF knew they were going to France; it was only when the Grenadiers' train reached the suburbs of Berlin and was switched to the main line running west that they were certain. 'As soon as this new direction was quite definite there was a general rejoicing,' wrote Bloem; 'for some undefinable reason the very thought of Russia gave one a shudder.'

The reason was probably 1812.

After an hour or so Bloem's train stopped at a country station, where the battalion were able to buy the morning papers, from which they learned of the atrocities in Belgium – though not those that were being read about in England: the Hunnic murder of women and children, the torching of buildings grand and humble. Instead, 'priests, armed, and at the head of marauding bands of Belgian civilians, committing every kind of atrocity, and putting the deeds of 1870 in the shade; of treacherous ambushes on patrols, and sentries found later with eyes pierced and tongues cut off, of poisoned wells and other horrors'.

The 'deeds of 1870' were those of the *francs tireurs*, literally 'free shooters': the unofficial French militias who, wearing no uniform, had wrought such havoc in the rear areas during the Franco-Prussian War. It was in part, perhaps even in large part, the determination to deter Belgian *francs tireurs* that the man appointed military governor,

THE TRIUMPH OF "CULTURE."

Brave, violated *little Belgium*: Punch *cartoon of 26 August, by which time reports of German atrocities had become widespread. Though used extensively for propaganda purposes, the reports were well grounded in fact, as men of the BEF attested after the counter-offensive in September. The 'culture' of the cartoon is a reference to the* Kulturkampf *('culture struggle'), the assertion of Prussian secularism under Bismarck, which in turn became a culture of militarism.*

Generaloberst Colmar von der Goltz, would issue the infamous reprisal orders in early September: 'It is the stern necessity of war that the punishment for hostile acts falls not only on the guilty, but on the innocent as well.' But even before that the field commanders were imposing rough justice (and injustice). And it would play very badly indeed with public opinion in Britain (and indeed in America), strengthening the sense of commitment to the cause: 'The only place for a gentleman now is France', wrote Robert Graves to his father that week, citing the violations among his reasons for seeking an immediate commission.*

But what Bloem and his Grenadiers did not read about were the severe delays being inflicted on Generaloberst Karl von Bülow's 2nd Army, wholly unexpectedly, by the Belgian army. The fortresses on the Meuse were holding out. And under the direct personal command of the King of the Belgians, some 117,000 regulars – a body of troops about the size of the BEF – reinforced by reservists, were taking post between the Gette and Dyle rivers to protect Brussels and Antwerp. This would further disrupt the German plan, but it also left the forts without intimate support. Another year and the king's concept for a more forward defence might have had time to take

---

* On 5 October, Goltz was even more explicit: 'In the future, villages in the vicinity of places where railway and telegraph lines are destroyed will be punished without pity (whether they are guilty or not of the acts in question). With this in view hostages have been taken in all villages near the railway lines which are threatened by such attacks. Upon the first attempt to destroy lines of railway, telegraph or telephone, they will immediately be shot.' Asquith set up a committee of investigation in December under Viscount Bryce, a former ambassador in Washington. It reported the following spring, and though its evidence handling has been strongly criticized, to the point that in the 1930s it seemed discredited, more recent scholarship has shown its four principal conclusions to have been broadly correct:

(i) That there were in many parts of Belgium deliberate and systematically organised massacres of the civil population, accompanied by many isolated murders and other outrages.
(ii) That in the conduct of the war generally innocent civilians, both men and women, were murdered in large numbers, women violated, and children murdered.
(iii) That looting, house burning, and the wanton destruction of property were ordered and countenanced by the officers of the German Army, that elaborate provisions had been made for systematic incendiarism at the very outbreak of the war, and that the burnings and destruction were frequent where no military necessity could be alleged, being indeed part of a system of general terrorisation.
(iv) That the rules and usages of war were frequently broken, particularly by the using of civilians, including women and children, as a shield for advancing forces exposed to fire, to a less degree by killing the wounded and prisoners, and in the frequent abuse of the Red Cross and the White Flag.

shape; as it was, unsupported, the fortresses' days were now numbered.

For the time being, however, Liège, with its ring of a dozen self-contained forts at a radius of 5 miles from the city centre, six on each bank of the Meuse, was a formidable obstacle to the unfolding Schlieffen Plan. The forts had all been built within the previous thirty years and were linked by tunnels, although they had not been fully modernized and incorporated some fatal design flaws; ironically, they had recently been re-equipped with Krupp heavy guns and mortars. An infantry division had joined the garrison on mobilization, so that there were around 47,000 troops in and about Liège, of whom over half were regulars. King Albert, in a handwritten order, charged them to 'hold to the end the position which you have been entrusted to defend' – the country's foremost citadel.

If this desperate order were fulfilled, it would not just be a long nail in Schlieffen's coffin; it would be revealing – indicative of the Germans' strategic intentions. For had they merely intended to neutralize Liège as a threat to the right flank and subsequently the lines of communication of a shallow hook through Belgium, as the French and British general staffs expected, they need only have masked the fortress-city with a single corps (Schlieffen believed a single division) and continued the march south and south-west. But since neither the French nor the British believed that the Belgian field army was in any condition to go on the offensive (an assessment the Germans could reasonably be thought to share), the violence of the attacks on Liège ought to have indicated another purpose – the need to clear the major axis west of the Meuse, and to secure the key railway junction which would be crucial to troop movement and logistics. King Albert appears to have believed that this was always the plan: if the Germans only intended taking the city to secure their flank, why sacrifice so much of the Belgian army merely to fulfil the obligation of resistance? Indeed, once the Germans did reveal their hand by the strength of the assault, he took the garrison commander's suggestion to release the infantry division (25,000 men) to rejoin the field army, ready to fight another day – and on the supposed main axis of advance west of the Meuse. Why Joffre did not share this analysis is unclear, especially when by 8 August General Otto von Emmich's X Corps had taken over 5,000 casualties battering against the ring of forts. It is difficult to avoid the conclusion that because the Belgians played no part in Plan XVII, Joffre's 'hymn sheet', *GQG* simply wrote them off, for there was no very convincing attempt to gain coherence on the Belgian flank even when the Germans' main effort was finally revealed.

The greater initiative would in fact come from London; and then in connection with the defence of Antwerp.

By 16 August, the day of Sir John French's first meeting with Joffre, there could have been no doubt about German intentions not just to mask but to take Liège. Having been thwarted in the attempt to 'bounce' the Belgians out, Bülow had been dealing with them as he would have done in the days of Blücher or Frederick the Great, or even the Teutonic Knights: he had brought up siege artillery – 305 mm Austrian howitzers made at the Skoda works in Pilsen, and 420 mm Krupp howitzers (nicknamed 'Fat – *Dicke* – Berthas' after the Krupp proprietress*). Both types fired armour-piercing, delayed-fuse rounds, which the fort-builder's art could not match. Within forty-eight hours they were literally pulverized into surrender, with the loss of 20,000 dead, wounded or captured. Fort de Loncin, built of unreinforced concrete 4 miles west of Liège, was destroyed by a single hit on the magazine, killing 350 out of the garrison of 500 instantly. On 15 August Liège's gallant commander, the 63-year-old General Gérard Leman, was found unconscious in the debris, almost asphyxiated by the fumes. The remnants of the last fort surrendered the following afternoon.[†]

But Liège's defiance had certainly imposed a delay on the Schlieffen–Moltke plan – a delay of at least forty-eight hours, invaluable to the BEF. Indeed, Sir John French's men might otherwise have been overwhelmed in the process of alighting from their trains

---

* Some writers have described Bertha Krupp – the 'Queen of Essen' – as corpulent, hence the name of the guns, and have said that this did not amuse her. In fact, Bertha Krupp von Bohlen und Halbach was rather svelte and attractive; the adjective described not her but the guns' appearance. British troops, perhaps with a better appreciation for alliteration, would adopt the name, but slightly changed – 'Big Bertha' – to apply to any of the large calibre Krupp artillery.

† Leman was at once brought before Otto von Emmich (who had known him before the war), to whom the gallant fortress commander offered his sword, asking that Emmich be sure to write in his despatches that he, Leman, had been found unconscious, thereby having carried out the King's instructions to the letter. Emmich refused the sword – a gesture of gallantry whose days were numbered.

at Maubeuge, just as Kitchener had feared. The defiance had cost 20,000 casualties or prisoners of war, but it had won the admiration of Europe for 'gallant little Belgium'.* It would do more than that, however; it would assure a remnant of sovereignty in two months' time. For the delay – perhaps as much four days – would mean that Belgian troops would just be able to hang on to a small corner of their country when by November Schlieffen had posthumously over-run the rest – a sovereign force still in the field rather than an army in exile (sustained by the wealth of the Belgian Congo). And it would, too, buy back for the BEF some of the time lost by tardy mobilization, though not all its compounded problems. Not least, the Belgians' defiance had undermined the absolute assurance of the German high command. For days after the bloody repulse of X Corps at Liège the Kaiser had been in a state of hysterical fury, berating Moltke for having brought Britain into the war because of a military imperative – the violation of Belgian neutrality – that within hours of the off had become a liability. And Moltke, for his part, came near to a nervous breakdown. With the news that his big guns had overcome all resistance, His Imperial Majesty would overcome his petulance and Moltke would appear to recover his equilibrium; but in truth the Kaiser had somehow lost his self-appointed image of Bismarckian infallibility, and Schlieffen's heir his credibility as a Frederician

---

* As early as 14 August, lines by – rather delphically – 'HM' (in fact, Hugh Macnaghten: a master at, and later vice provost of, Eton) addressed 'To the King of the Belgians' had been published in *The Times* summing up the sentiment (it is difficult to overstress the effect on British – and American – public opinion of both the Germans' conduct towards Belgium and the Belgians' defiance):

Multitudes upon multitudes they throng
And thicken: who shall number their array?
They bid the peoples tremble and obey:
Their faces are set forward, all for wrong.
They trample on the covenant and are strong
And terrible. Who shall dare to say them nay?
How shall a little nation bar the way
Where that resistless host is borne along?

You never thought, O! gallant King, to bow
To overmastering force and stand aside.
Safe and secure you might have reigned. But now
Your Belgium is transfigured, glorified,
The friend of France and England, who avow
An Equal here, and thank the men who died.

general. Moltke would soon be sacked. The Kaiser would be increasingly marginalized.

But for the moment he could savour a little victory. Even as the dust of the last fort was settling, the commander-in-chief of the *Kaiserreichsheer*, the Imperial German Army, was leaving Berlin to set up court, or rather *Grosses Hauptquartier* (Great Headquarters), at Coblenz, alongside Moltke's *Oberste Heeresleitung* (Supreme Army Command – *OHL*), which at last was leaving the capital too. That evening the Kaiser would dine off Frederick the Great's silver field service. War, to him, was history and theatre; for what else had he seen of it?

As for King Albert and his doughty Belgians, for now they were turning west. But the King, in personal command in the field still, had another decision to make: having bought himself time at Liège, could he force the Germans into another costly attack on Namur? With guns the size of the Skodas and Krupps the outcome would be only a matter of time, and the butcher's bill another heavy one unless the French 5th Army could come up from the Sambre to support them. Besides, if Namur were invested the only way out might be south into France, and every Belgian bayonet would be needed to continue the defence of national soil. Yet if Namur were to fall a gap would open ever wider between the Belgian right and the Anglo-French left. He therefore ordered the garrison to hold; but this time he would not press them to 'hold to the end'.

Meanwhile General von Kluck's 1st Army was marching through Liège. Though where it was headed was still not clear to *GQG*.

Chapter Thirteen

FEAR GOD. HONOUR THE KING.

An average march under normal conditions for a large column of all arms is 15 miles a day, with a rest at least once a week; small commands of seasoned troops can cover 25 miles a day under favourable conditions.

Field Service Pocketbook (1914)

> Kaiser Bill is feeling ill,
> The Crown Prince, he's gone barmy.
> We don't give a —
> For old von Kluck
> And all his bleedin' army.

BEF marching song (unofficial)

Four days after the fall of Liège, on 20 August, as Kluck's 1st Army got into its stride across the rolling country of French-speaking southern Brabant, Moltke informed its commander that 'a landing of British troops is reported at Boulogne: their advance from about Lille must be reckoned with. It is believed that a disembarkation of British troops on a large scale has not yet taken place.' The exact source of this intelligence is unclear, but a report in a Belgian newspaper the day before that the BEF had landed somewhere in France on the 18th had been picked up by Kluck and sent to Moltke's *OHL*.*

---

* Two days later, on the twenty-second, the German 1st Army would halt for two crucial hours to realign west in order to guard its flank against what Kluck believed was

259

Again, it seems extraordinary that a force of the BEF's size and distinctive appearance, even from the air, could have eluded the Germans. And it was not because they weren't looking for them. The *OHL* faced the same problems as the French *GQG* in gathering strategic intelligence, but they had a potential trump card – the Zeppelin. Moltke had five available on the Western Front, equipped with wireless, and each had a pre-allocated strategic reconnaissance mission, the two stationed at Düsseldorf and Coblenz to overfly Belgium and northern France respectively. But they were encountering the same problem as had the British dirigible in the army manoeuvres of 1910 on Salisbury Plain, the very problem that had accelerated the War Office's development of the aeroplane and the formation of the RFC – the weather. Four times in August 1914 Zeppelin Z9 took off from Düsseldorf to scout over Belgium for the BEF, but each time it was forced back by heat turbulence, or the wind, or even thunderstorms, its aluminium frame too vulnerable to damage.*

In fact, by the time of the *OHL*'s assessment that 'a disembarkation of British troops on a large scale has not yet taken place' the BEF's four leading divisions and the Cavalry Division had already completed their concentration at Maubeuge, and a fifth (the 4th Division) was

---

the BEF detraining at Tournai, but was in fact a French Territorial division. Moltke's message of 20 August – 'It is believed that a disembarkation of British troops on a large scale has not yet taken place' – would show how improbable was the Kaiser's supposed 'contemptible' order of 19 August, the only solid reference to which is *Source Records of the Great War,* Volume II, edited by Charles Horne (London, 1923): 'It is my Royal and Imperial command that you concentrate your energies, for the immediate present, upon one single purpose, and that is that you address all your skill and all the valour of my soldiers to exterminate first the treacherous English and walk over General French's contemptible little army.' Nor indeed was 'Headquarters, Aix-la-Chapelle' below the Kaiser's signature authentic: on 19 August his headquarters were still at Coblenz. The 'contemptible' remark is hardly out of character for the Kaiser, but the evidence is just not solid enough. It seems probable that a rumour, doubtless containing a grain of truth, became a magnificent propaganda opportunity.

* On the night of 25 August Z9 dropped nine bombs on Antwerp, killing or wounding twenty-six people and damaging the palace at which the Belgian royal family had taken residence. It was presumed that the Zeppelin had been guided to its target by a 'spy' with a powerful lamp (the man was summarily shot). With a sort of poetic justice Z9 would be destroyed in its hangar at Düsseldorf on 8 October by two 20 lb bombs dropped from 600 feet by Lieutenant (later Air Vice Marshal) Reginald Marix of the Royal Naval Air Service flying a single-seater Sopwith Tabloid (one of the fastest aircraft of the time) from Antwerp, a straight-line distance of just over 100 miles – a magnificent early strategic use of air power.

on its way to Southampton to join them. Sergeant Brunton of the 19th Hussars was mightily relieved, for the regiment that Sir John French had commanded were in the role of divisional cavalry, sending a squadron to each of the 4th, 5th and 6th divisions, and for several days it had looked as if only A Squadron, with 5th Division, would actually 'get at the Germans'.

On the whole the men of the BEF had had rather a good trip over, the sea calm, the August sunshine pleasant – although below decks the horses suffered a good deal in the heat – and the train journey through Picardy an agreeable excursion. Corporal Snelling of the 12th Lancers, who had never been abroad before, thought it 'just like Wiltshire' – and all apparently going wonderfully to plan. In his active service pay book, Army Book (AB) No. 64 – 'AB64' (which, unlike in peacetime, the soldier kept on his person rather than lodged with the paymaster), was pasted, as ordered, a special message from Lord Kitchener who, mindful of the many Corporal Snellings who had never been abroad before, and of the entirely novel experience for British soldiers of arriving in France as allies, wished to warn them of the dangers to their virtue and to the honour of both countries:

> You are ordered abroad as a soldier of the King to help our French comrades against the invasion of a common Enemy. You have to perform a task which will need your courage, your energy, your patience. Remember that the honour of the British Army depends on your individual conduct. It will be your duty not only to set an example of discipline and perfect steadiness under fire but also to maintain the most friendly relations with those whom you are helping in this struggle. The operations in which you are engaged will, for the most part, take place in a friendly country, and you can do your own country no better service than in showing yourself in France and Belgium in the true character of a British soldier.
>
> Be invariably courteous, considerate and kind. Never do anything likely to injure or destroy property, and always look upon looting as a disgraceful act. You are sure to meet with a welcome and to be trusted; your conduct must justify that welcome and that trust. Your duty cannot be done unless your health is sound. So keep constantly on your guard against any excesses. In this new experience you may find temptations both in wine and women. You must entirely resist both temptations, and, while treating all women with perfect courtesy, you should avoid any intimacy.

Do your duty bravely,
Fear God.
Honour the King.

KITCHENER,
Field-Marshal.

The instructions, as might be imagined, enjoyed a mixed reception. For the men of the BEF were no more 'plaster saints' than those of the earlier generation described by Kipling.* Private Frank Richards of the 2nd Royal Welsh Fusiliers, author of *Old Soldiers Never Die*, still considered to be the finest Great War memoir written from the ranks, gave his opinion:

> I believe we were the first battalion to enter Rouen . . . On arrival at a new station we pre-War soldiers always made enquiries as to what sort of a place it was for booze and fillies. If both were in abundance it was a glorious place from our point of view. We soon found out we had nothing to complain about as regards Rouen. Each man had been issued with a pamphlet signed by Lord Kitchener warning him about the dangers of French wine and women; they may as well not have been issued for all the notice we took of them.†

But whatever the details of compliance, no lasting damage was done, which, as many observers have pointed out, says much for the fundamental decency of British soldiers and the good sense of Frenchwomen – and, too, for the 'grip' of the British NCO. When the 19th Hussars arrived in Rouen, several days after the Fusiliers, Sergeant Brunton and a fellow NCO 'had a walk into the town. We visited the "Notre Dame" where "Joan of Arc" was burnt at the stake. Also had a light dinner and several wines at a Café à la France' – and yet they both remained in good enough order to entrain at midnight.

The special message did afford some inter-allied amusement, how-

---

* From 'Tommy' (1892): 'An' if sometimes our conduck isn't all your fancy paints, / Why, single men in barricks don't grow into plaster saints'.
† Frank Richards, *Old Soldiers Never Die* (London, 1933). Richards, a reservist recalled to the colours, may have been typical of the pre-war regular in his approach to the forbidden fruits, but he typified the Old Contemptibles' tough, raw courage too, winning both the Distinguished Conduct Medal (DCM) and the Military Medal (MM) during his four years' re-engagement.

ever, if of a rather painful kind. 'Is it an army your Lord Kitchener is sending us, or is it a girls' school?' the officers of the French general staff had asked Edward Spears, with tears of laughter in their eyes. But they would have their answer soon enough. On the twenty-first, Spears drove with one of Lanrezac's officers towards Maubeuge and got his first glimpse of the BEF:

> The first I saw were a small detachment of Irish Guards, enormous, stolid, in perfect step. Next came a column of artillery: I thought I should burst with inward gratification at the smartness of those gunners. They were really splendid, perfectly turned out, shining leather, flashing metal, beautiful horses, and the men absolutely unconcerned, disdaining to show the least surprise at or even interest in their strange surroundings ... I said nothing, but stole a glance at the French officer who accompanied me and was satisfied, for he was rendered almost speechless by the sight of these fighting men. He had not believed such troops existed. He asked me if they were the Guard Artillery! [There was, of course, no such thing in the British army.] Soon after this we received a shock, and my French companion was further impressed, but in a way he did not much like, for we drove headlong into a most effective infantry trap. At a turn in the road we were suddenly faced by a barrier we had nearly run into, and found that without knowing it we had been covered for the last two hundred yards by cleverly concealed riflemen belonging to the picquet. Had we been Germans nothing in the world could have saved us.*

There were less immaculate bodies of men on the march, however, for some of the reservists were finding the heat and the *pavé* hard going, and many a man had had his cap-badge, shoulder titles or buttons begged by a village Marianne (one way or another). The 1st Oxfordshire and Buckinghamshire Light Infantry, whose antecedents had been with Sir John Moore at Shorncliffe during the pioneering light infantry training in the decade before Waterloo, and who considered themselves a good cut above most of the infantry of the line, had been astonished by their welcome at Boulogne – still rapturous on

---

* The Irish Guards, 'the Micks', as a battalion were marching to their first battle. They had been formed in 1900, to honour the bravery of Irish troops fighting in South Africa, but had not reached full strength in time to deploy as a unit to the war. With them was Lieutenant the Hon. Harold Alexander – the future Field Marshal Earl Alexander of Tunis. The last of the five Foot Guards regiments, the Welsh, would not be formed until 1915.

the fourth day of disembarkation. As they marched to their bivouacs 4 miles up the steep cobbles, accompanied all the way by importunate girls and children, they were slowly divested of their regimentalia, one young officer only being able to keep his platoon in good order by handing out playing cards from the well-thumbed pack he carried, each bearing the Ox & Bucks distinctive bugle-horn badge.

Comments on the reservists' struggle to keep up were widespread, though hardly to be unexpected. The Cornwalls, who had left the Curragh on the thirteenth, reached Le Cateau early in the evening of the eighteenth, having entrained at Le Havre a full forty-eight hours earlier (the train did not leave until three in the morning and, like all the rest, had then trundled at no more than 20 miles an hour); and 'from there we were told we had a six-mile march to a place called Landrecies', records the adjutant, Lieutenant Arthur Acland. 'It turned out to be a good ten miles, and our weary reservists found it hard to manage. Many fell out, and all were beat when we got to our billets at 1 a.m. 19th.'* Captain Alexander Johnston was at the staff college when the BEF mobilized, and had at once been posted as signal officer to the 7th Brigade, in II Corps. On the eighteenth he 'went for a route march with the 3rd Worcesters – my own battalion – to get the men of my signal section fit and accustomed to their heavy marching order. We did not go more than 8 miles and my fellows went well though the reservists were somewhat distressed and obviously want hardening up.' Some men died on these marches; some had died marching even before embarkation.

The question of reservists' fitness has sometimes been represented as a major systemic problem, a serious flaw in the design of the BEF, though the Germans (and French) had the same problem but on an even greater scale, for the great bulk of the German army was reservist. As anyone who has ever been on a route march knows, there are always casualties even among fully conditioned men – the un-accustomed heat, a sudden drenching, a chafing boot, lack of sleep, change of diet, as well as the 'bugs' that at any one time (and especially in the days before antibiotics) play havoc in any formed body of troops. The antidote is, in large measure, 'march discipline',

---

* Lieutenant Arthur Acland, later Lieutenant-General Arthur Floyer-Acland, CB DSO MC (mentioned seven times in despatches during the war), Military Secretary 1940–2.

which, says *Notes from the Front* (collated by the general staff in October 1914), 'men who have not been with the colours during the last 4 or 5 years do not understand the necessity for'. The *Notes* were emphatic that

> It [march discipline] should be impressed upon all ranks and should be resolutely insisted upon at all training previous to the arrival in the theatre of war. There has been straggling, no doubt in great measure due to exhaustion during the first phase, but it is most necessary to tighten up march discipline again to prevent undue opening out and straggling . . . Each unit should detail an officer with a small party of selected non-commissioned officers and men to march in rear of the unit in order to enforce orders against straggling, leaving the ranks for water, and so forth.

The *Notes* included the eminently sensible advice that 'when a halt is necessary it should be made before reaching or after passing a village', the first rule of military discipline being the avoidance of temptation.

On 19 August one of the single most cost-effective branches of the army (in terms of morale), the postal service, surged into action. An Army Post Office Corps had existed on an ad hoc basis since the 1880s, but in 1913 it became a Special Reserve unit of the Royal Engineers, with a strength of ten officers and 290 other ranks, scaled for a BEF of six divisions. The RE Postal Section was one of the first units to mobilize, with an advance party sailing to France on 12 August to set up the Army Base PO in the Havre Club, whence it dispatched its first mail on the seventeenth, and received its first from home the following day. Field service postcards were issued to all ranks, who could cross out which of the several (generally) cheery messages did not apply and add a couple of words at the end; or if paper and envelopes were to hand something more discursive could be penned. On the nineteenth, Lieutenant Frederick Longman of the 4th Fusiliers wrote home somewhat idiosyncratically from Noyelles-sur-Selle, where they had been billeted in a cottage 'with feather beds':

> My dear Mother,
>   The censor is very strict so I fear I can give you no news except that I am exceedingly flourishing. I enclose particulars of a strange bat I caught, I hope to be able to recognise it from Millais when I return . . . Your first letter (Aug: 13th) arrived today . . .

He would never be able to identify the bat in J. G. Millais' *The Mammals of Great Britain and Ireland*, however, for he would be killed near Ypres on 18 October.

While the infantry were toughening themselves up with route marches about the concentration area of Maubeuge, and the cavalry attending to farriery and fodder, the RFC were at last taking to the air to look for Germans. They had had more accidents during the fly-up from Amiens, but having got to Maubeuge forty-eight hours ahead of the leading brigades, they had been able to recuperate in relative peace: 'We were rather sorry they had come,' wrote one of 3 Squadron's flight commanders, Captain Philip Joubert de la Ferté, two days later when the first of the infantry arrived,

> because up till that moment we had only been fired on by the French whenever we flew. Now we were fired on by French *and* English . . . To this day I can remember the roar of musketry that greeted two of our machines as they left the aerodrome and crossed the main Maubeuge–Mons road, along which a British column was proceeding.*

Overnight all four squadrons painted hopeful Union Jacks on the underside of their lower wings (the red, white and blue roundel would not be standardized until the following year).

Undaunted, however, by the hazards of what later generations would call 'friendly fire' (a contraction of 'fire from friendly [i.e. not enemy] forces'), on 19 August Joubert, together with Lieutenant Gilbert Mapplebeck of 4 Squadron, in a Blériot monoplane and a BE2 (Blériot Experimental) respectively, flew the RFC's first reconnaissance mission: Joubert to reconnoitre Nivelles–Genappe to report on Belgian forces there, Mapplebeck to find out whether there was enemy cavalry in the neighbourhood of Gembloux. Without observers, to save weight, they intended to fly together as far as Nivelles so that if one were forced down the other could report his whereabouts, but the weather was overcast and after taking off at 9.30 a.m. they soon lost their way and each other. Mapplebeck eventually found himself over a large town, which he failed to recognize as Brussels, though he later picked up his position and found Gembloux,

---

* Quoted in Sir Walter Raleigh, *The War in the Air* (London, 1922)

where he could see only a small body of cavalry moving (curiously) south-east. Low cloud forced him down to 300 feet over Namur, whence he followed the Sambre but missed Maubeuge and landed near Le Cateau; taking off again, he made it back to Maubeuge at about midday. Joubert, whose Blériot was slower than the BE, tried flying by compass through the banks of cloud, and after two hours' wandering landed near a barracks at Tournai, where the commandant gave him 'a most excellent lunch', but could give him little information. He took off again just after midday, lost his way once more, and two hours later landed at Courtrai, 20 miles further north and west. Here the gendarmerie, after first trying to detain him, gave him petrol and told him that the headquarters of the Belgian flying corps was at Louvain, HQ of the Belgian army, a dozen or so miles east of Brussels. This was too far for him to attempt to make contact, so he limped back to Maubeuge via Le Cateau, arriving at 5.30 p.m., having seen trains in the main stations and pickets on the roads to Brussels, but nothing else.* They had both been lucky in landing and being allowed to take off again: it would be three days yet before another pilot, Lieutenant R. M. Vaughan, rejoined them. He had made a forced landing near Boulogne after crossing the Channel, had been arrested by the French, and remained locked up for nearly a week.

The lack of information was significant, although its significance was not immediately recognized: where was the Belgian army? The day before, the eighteenth, Sir John French had held a conference with his corps commanders and their staff – or, rather, with Haig and Major-General Sir Charles Fergusson, GOC 5th Division, the acting commander of II Corps, for Smith-Dorrien back on Salisbury Plain was only just being told of his new appointment. French had had to rely entirely on *GQG*'s intelligence summaries, for there was precious little coming from London, nor direct from Brussels – except for a curious message from the British minister (ambassador), Sir Francis Villiers, that the King of the Belgians wished to see him, to which the field marshal had replied asking, not unreasonably, for the Belgians to

---

* As Air Chief Marshal Sir Philip Joubert he would be C-in-C RAF Coastal Command for the major part of the Second World War. The experience of these observer-less flights bore out the RFC wisdom of the time that reconnaissances without a trained observer (both to observe and to navigate, so that observations were accurately map-referenced) were essentially useless. The RFC reckoned that it took as long to train an observer as it did a pilot; the Germans considered that it actually took longer.

send a special train. In fact, as the conference was taking place King Albert was already beginning to pull back the army into the Antwerp perimeter, moving his headquarters from Louvain to Malines, midway between Antwerp and the capital, which the Germans would enter the following day. Had Joubert been able to fly on to Louvain on that first reconnaissance mission he would have been taken prisoner; as, indeed, would Sir John French if the Belgians had ever sent the special train – the first time in history that a commander-in-chief would have been taken prisoner before a single one of his soldiers had fired a shot.

But *GQG*'s assessments were ineffably upbeat. If large numbers of German troops were moving north and west of the Meuse, so much the better: it meant they were not elsewhere; and if they were not elsewhere, that elsewhere was now the 'zone of weakness' – the opportunity for counter-offensive envisaged by Plan XVII. And the zone of weakness was, it appeared, in the Ardennes, where General Fernand de Langle de Cary, a particularly dashing cavalryman (of the *Chasseurs d'Afrique**), stood watching with the 4th Army as large numbers of German troops crossed his front. Imbued with the proper spirit of *offensive à outrance*, he told Joffre that he was ready to attack their flank as they marched west, which Joffre was only too gratified to hear, for the offensive in Alsace-Lorraine was making progress and Lanrezac's 5th Army and the BEF had things well in hand on the extreme left flank – so Cary's blow looked as if it would unhinge the entire German plan (whatever that plan was).

Joffre decided to order General Pierre Ruffey's 3rd Army, on Cary's right, to attack as well; but what he had not grasped was that the troops marching across their front (Bülow's 2nd Army and part of Max von Hausen's 3rd (Saxon) Army) would soon be followed by troops that *GQG* had simply not taken account of – the duke of Württemberg's 4th Army. The French general staff still believed the German main effort to be on the Franco-German border; with a size-able number of troops left in East Prussia to hold against an *attaque brusquée* by the Russians, how could there be *three* armies moving on

---

* First raised in the 1830s from regular French cavalry posted to Algeria, they had famously cleared the (British) Light Brigade's line of withdrawal after the ill-starred charge at Balaklava, and still to this day retain cordial relations with the descendant regiments of the brigade.

the left? The French 4th and 3rd Armies would not simply be attacking into the flank of a marching army – a glorious opportunity to inflict a major defeat; they would in turn be presenting their own right flanks to the duke of Württemberg's 4th Army. It was doubly fortunate, therefore, that Joffre decided to detach two corps from General Noel de Castelnau's 2nd Army, which was about to renew its attack in Lorraine, to take part in the counter-stroke in the Ardennes, for when the tables were turned Cary and Ruffey would need all the men they could muster.*

Joffre's *Instruction Particulière* of 8 a.m. on the eighteenth conceded that the German right wing might comprise as many as fifteen army corps, but was confident that its mass would be brought successfully to battle in the Ardennes by Cary's 4th and Ruffey's 3rd Armies, and that if the Germans south of the Meuse then attacked the *left* flank of the 4th Army, they could in turn be countered by Lanrezac's 5th Army. And he managed to square the circle of the thinking behind Plan XVII (in particular, the relative locations of the German right and his own left flanks) by the expedient of wishfulness: 'The enemy may engage only a fraction of his right wing group north of the Meuse' – which could thus be dealt with by the Belgians and the BEF. To be on the safe side, however, and as they were not producing much intelligence, he decided to send Sordet's Cavalry Corps to the BEF's left flank.

In the absence of any intelligence of his own, Sir John French could hardly dispute any of this, and from the evidence of the diaries, Henry Wilson continued to preach the gospel of Joffre. French therefore told the conference on the eighteenth that as soon as their concentration was complete the BEF would take up a position north of the Sambre on a line running south-east from Mons to Givry, and that, 'should the German attack develop in the manner expected, we shall advance on the line Mons–Dinant [east, south-east] to meet it.'[†]

* It may be, as has been suggested, that Joffre had some early intimation that Lanrezac might need help if the build-up of German troops became too great, but there was no convincing sign of it at the time. The two corps would, however, prove a Godsend when the penny finally dropped and Joffre turned his attention wholly to the Marne.
† 'When our concentration is complete, it is intended that we should operate on the left of the French 5th Army, the 18th [French] Corps being on our right. The French Cavalry Corps of three divisions will be on our left and in touch with the Belgians. As a preliminary to this, we shall take up an area north of the Sambre, and on Monday the heads of the Allied columns should be on the line Mons–Givet, with the cavalry on the outer flank' (from C-in-C's instruction to corps and cavalry division commanders).

NETHERLANDS

Antwerp

Ghent

Scheldt

Demer

Louvain

xxxx
BELGIAN
ALBERT

Tirlemont

BRUSSELS

Senne

Dendre

Grammont

xxxx

Dyle

Ath

BELGIUM

Soignies

Gembloux

Namur

Canal

Mons

Binche

Charleroi

Sambre

xxx

Sorde

Meuse

Maubeuge

xxxx
FIFTH
LANREZAC

Dinant

xxxx
BEF
(Assembling)

FRANCE

Givet

0   miles   25

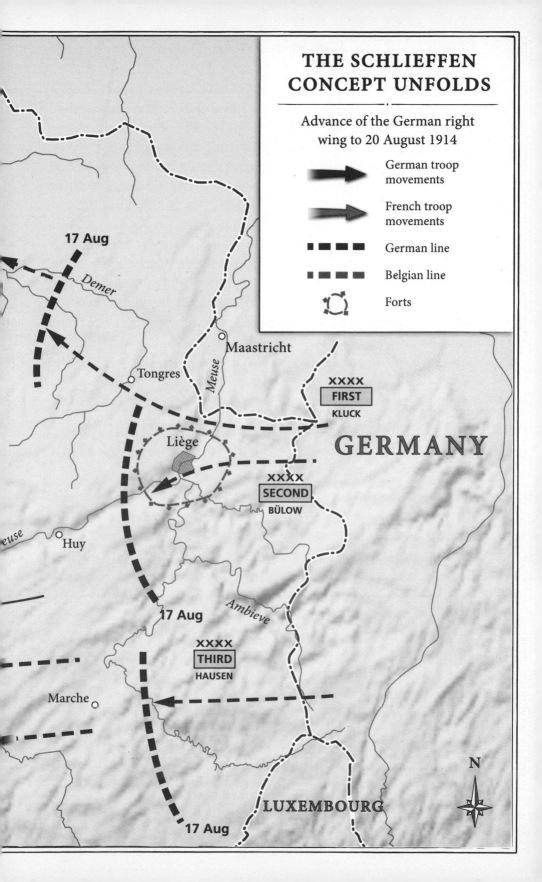

THE SCHLIEFFEN CONCEPT UNFOLDS

Advance of the German right
wing to 20 August 1914

German troop
movements

French troop
movements

German line

Belgian line

Forts

17 Aug

Demer

Maastricht

Meuse

Tongres

FIRST

KLUCK

xxxx

Liège

GERMANY

xxxx

SECOND

BÜLOW

euse

Huy

Ambieve

17 Aug

xxxx

THIRD

HAUSEN

Marche

17 Aug

LUXEMBOURG

N

One man seems instinctively to have understood the peril looming – that the German right wing was far stronger than anyone had calculated and threatened to overwhelm the BEF: Kitchener. *Seems* to have understood, because he wrote nothing down and kept his own counsel. After receiving French's telegrams of the seventeenth he had decided to send the 4th Division to France, the danger of German landings in Britain having receded. Given that at the same time he was issuing instructions for the creation of a vast new army to fight a long war, which would be recruited with the aid of the famous 'Your Country Needs YOU!' posters, it is inconceivable that he believed the BEF needed a fifth division for a grand advance over the Meuse and into Germany. Nor had Sir John French asked for it, though Wilson ranted in a letter home (with total disregard for the security being imposed on the most junior ranks) at the '*criminal* and *sinful*' decision to keep the 4th and 6th Divisions in England 'when they are so badly wanted here'. French himself had decided to form four of the lines-of-communication protection battalions into an independent brigade, the 19th, and order it forward to supplement his four infantry divisions. The plain fact was that Kitchener had never wanted the BEF to concentrate so close to the Belgian border, preferring instead Amiens: his sending the 4th Division looked very much like the despatch of a rescue force.*

On the nineteenth, therefore, as Joubert and Mapplebeck were flying over an apparently empty Belgium, GHQ was busy writing its operational instructions for the advance beyond the Sambre, where they expected to catch the Germans in the flank as the hordes of Prussian blue marched south and east towards the French border. The field marshal decided it was time to issue an Order of the Day – 'to be read out to all troops'. Commanders feel impelled to issue such orders before a big action, not least because, perhaps perversely, soldiers expect them to, but rarely do the orders come off to universal approval – as witness Kitchener's 'special message' to the BEF on its arrival in France. Sir John French had a certain touch, which was likely to make his messages rather plainer and to the point, but on

---

* It is difficult to avoid the conclusion that the only two men who understood that there was a huge qualitative difference between the army's recent experience of war (and its thinking) and the reality of war on the scale they were now facing – where the enemy was counted in numbers of army corps – were Kitchener and Haig.

this occasion it is interesting, perhaps even instructive, that he chose as his theme the idea of 'just cause' – a principle that 21st-century warriors might feel the need to acknowledge but one that was probably not uppermost in the minds of the BEF, buoyed up with a general mood of 'having a go at the Germans':

> Our cause is just. We are called upon to fight beside our gallant allies in France and Belgium in no war of arrogance, but to uphold our national honour, independence and freedom. We have violated no neutrality, nor have we been false to any treaties. We enter upon this conflict with the clearest consciousness that we are fighting for right and honour.
>
> Having then this trust in the righteousness of our cause, pride in the glory of our military traditions, and belief in the efficiency of our army, we go forward together to do or die for
>
> GOD – KING – AND COUNTRY.

Whether a private soldier of the Connaughts, say, thought his God, King and Country the same as those of a man in the Norfolks is a moot point, but even professional soldiers like a cause, otherwise they are merely mercenaries; and doubtless the commanding officers, in their own postscripts, placed the appropriate regimental interpretation on the words. The 4th Fusiliers' commanding officer, Norman McMahon, 'the musketry maniac', had addressed the battalion before they left the Isle of Wight, ending with a most economical and easily remembered statement of the regimental creed: 'A Royal Fusilier does not fear death; he is not afraid of wounds; he only fears disgrace . . .'

And who is to say that those words were without their effect when, on 23 August, the Fusiliers were to find themselves, with the rest of the BEF, not 'going forward together' but standing desperately on the defensive against a massive underestimation of the German right wing?

Chapter Fourteen

THE FIRST DUSTING

The first requisite is information. The air service and the cavalry must discover the direction of march and strength of the hostile columns, and until the former is known, the force should not be deployed, even when the enemy's line of advance may be foreseen.

Field Service Regulations, Part I: *Operations* (1909)

Early in the afternoon of Thursday, 20 August, GHQ issued Operation Order No. 5, launching the BEF's great forward movement north of the Sambre. Signed by Lieutenant-General Sir Archibald Murray, the chief of staff, it contained in detailed appendices the 'march tables' for the next three days – the Cavalry Division leading, followed by II Corps under the temporary command of Major-General Sir Charles Fergusson (GOC 5th Division), then Haig's I Corps – in all some 80,000 men.* But whereas operation orders usually begin with the 'situation' – a summary of all that is known of the enemy and friendly forces – because the mission and its execution follow logically from those factors (and generations of officers have been taught to mistrust any orders that do not begin thus), Operation Order No. 5 began with the worrying notice that 'Information regarding the enemy and allied troops will be communicated separately.'

* They would be reinforced the following day by the 19th Infantry Brigade (another 4,000 men), hastily formed from the lines-of-communication battalions which, their work now largely done, were being railed north.

274

Even worse, it never was, for events would overtake GHQ.

And so the primary stipulation of *Field Service Regulations*, the British army's painstakingly written new handbook of war, that 'The first requisite is information', was to be set aside in its first real outing in the field. Such is the gulf, sometimes, between theory and application; but so profound was this departure from what was after all a fundamental precept of war, and at the very outset of operations, that success was now more likely to be a matter of chance than calculation. Indeed, this stark failure by the general staffs of both *GQG* and GHQ set the BEF on a calamitous course from which it never truly recovered. Not only was the collection of intelligence dilatory, its interpretation was wishful. The logical process of the 'intelligence cycle' – a modern term, but the process was understood well enough at the time – provides information on which the commander decides his course of action. *GQG*, and in their wake GHQ, turned this on its head: having decided their course of action – Plan XVII – they interpreted the intelligence to confirm the correctness of the decision. That which tended to suggest the decision was wrong was effectively ignored, dismissed as inaccurate – 'it could not be true' – or distorted to fit the original assumption. The refusal in peacetime to admit the possibility that the German main effort would be on the right was bad enough; that it continued for so long once battle commenced is one of the great military failures of August 1914. The battle that was to follow Operation Order No. 5 – Mons – should never have taken place. It was at best a 'hasty defence' – never a satisfactory thing – and to all intents and purposes a 'meeting engagement', and such battles are the results of a failure one way or another to gain or correctly interpret intelligence.* Ironically, the battle of Waterloo, which had been fought a day's march to the north-east, had been preceded by a desperate meeting engagement – at Quatre Bras. And before that occasion, famously at the duchess of Richmond's ball, the duke of Wellington had at least had the good grace to say that 'Napoleon has hoodwinked me, by God!' By contrast, on the evening of 21 August,

---

* *Hasty defence*: 'A defence normally organized while in contact with the enemy or when contact is imminent and time available for the organization is limited. It is characterized by improvement of the natural defensive strength of the terrain by utilization of foxholes, emplacements, and obstacles.' *Meeting engagement*: 'A combat action occurring when a moving force, incompletely deployed for battle, engages an enemy at an unexpected time and place.' *NATO Glossary of Terms and Definitions*, AAP-6 (2010).

on receiving a report by the Cavalry Division of a much more extensive threat to the BEF than had been thought, Henry Wilson would blithely send this reply: 'The information which you have acquired and conveyed to the C-in-C appears to be somewhat exaggerated.'*

Sadly, the reaction of the divisional commander, Major-General Edmund Allenby – 'the Bull' – is not recorded.

Fortunately, however, the army's newest instrument of war, the aeroplane, would soon begin to penetrate this cloud of self-delusion – once it had been able to penetrate the actual clouds that shrouded the approach of 'Old von Kluck and all his b— army'. As GHQ were putting the finishing touches to the somewhat sketchy Operation Order No. 5, on 20 August, the RFC was beginning its second day of operations, this time with observers – but only two aircraft. Quite why only two is unclear even today: if the weather was good enough for two to fly, it was good enough for many more, and there were now nearly sixty machines sitting at Maubeuge. This was a moment when intelligence was of the absolute essence, when there was an acknowledged lack of it – as witness the operation order – and when there was no other direct way of gaining it. But GHQ were not expecting the Germans to be doing anything other than 'ranging with uhlans' west of the Meuse and turning, perhaps, east of it to meet the threatened attack by the French 4th and 3rd Armies – which the French themselves would surely be observing. Why, therefore, ask the RFC to do much more than take a look to see how far the 'ranging uhlans' had got?[†] The first aircraft on 20 August reconnoitred as far as Louvain and the outskirts of Brussels, seeing a force of all arms moving south-west of the capital, and another south-east into Wavre. A second patrol, south-west of Brussels (in a triangle Nivelles–Hal–Enghien), saw no sign of troops, and all the bridges intact. All this was useful negative information; but what would have been really helpful was to know just where were the 'as many as fifteen army corps' that Joffre's *Instruction Particulière* of 18 August had conceded might constitute the German right wing. To commit to

---

* In his diary Wilson wrote: 'During the afternoon many reports of Germans advancing in masses from north and east, also that Namur was going to fall [its evacuation was begun next day]. I can't believe this.'
† It is even more surprising as the RFC's commander, Brigadier-General Sir David Henderson, had written two highly regarded pamphlets: *Field Intelligence: Its Principles and Practice* (1904) and *The Art of Reconnaissance* (1907).

any large-scale movement without knowing was courting trouble.

It was foggy next morning, Friday the twenty-first, as the men of the BEF left their billets and bivouacs in the pleasant farms and orchards and the industrious villages of Hainault to strike out north for the Belgian border. In the afternoon it rained, the mist persisting, and the three reconnaissance flights that eventually managed to take off reported that the country immediately in front of the BEF was quiet, though just south of Nivelles there was a large body of cavalry with guns and infantry (later identified as the German 9th Cavalry Division), and another body of infantry moving south on Charleroi, leaving several villages ablaze. It is tempting to think that the RFC's *Beta* airship, left behind at Farnborough, would have been invaluable, and perhaps even more use than aeroplanes, at this stage – or for that matter, a regiment of armoured (or even unarmoured) cars. *Field Service Regulations (FSR)*, although originally issued in 1909, a year before the first aeroplane flew on army manoeuvres, and when the army's airships were still experimental, was remarkably prescient in recognizing the importance of air reconnaissance: 'The air service and the cavalry must discover the direction of march and strength of the hostile columns.' And the amendments to *FSR* issued in October 1914 were still strong on the role of airships, even without seeing them in France: 'Airships can, by their power of remaining motionless in the air, keep a large tract of country under observation.' The weather was poor (the Zeppelins had been kept in their hangars, after all), but the problem locally was visibility, not wind – not impossible conditions for the *Beta*.*

But while bad weather had grounded the RFC in the morning, it had not slowed the advance of Allenby's Cavalry Division, which entered Mons towards midday to a warm welcome. At once the division's intelligence officer, George de Symons Barrow, a somewhat 'passed over' Indian cavalry lieutenant-colonel whom Allenby had scooped up in London (where Barrow was home on leave) to fill the unofficial post in his headquarters, went to the telephone exchange at Mons station and

---

* *Beta* had been built in May 1910 and consisted of a long frame with a centre compartment for the crew and engines. A 35 hp engine drove two wooden propellers. At the army manoeuvres that year she remained in the air for nearly eight hours on one patrol. In 1912, re-equipped with a 45 hp engine, she had a maximum speed of 35 mph and could carry fuel for about eight hours with a crew of three.

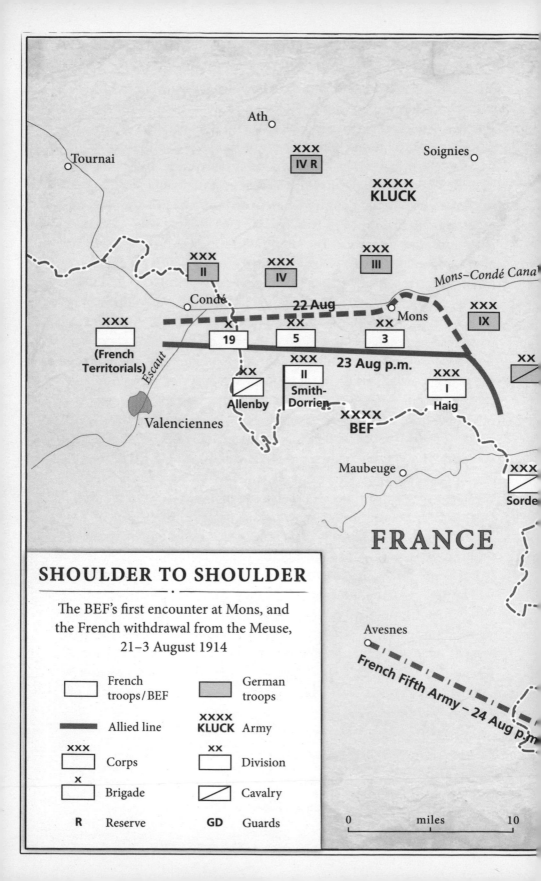

Ath

Tournai

Soignies

XXX
IV R

XXXX
KLUCK

XXX
II

XXX
IV

XXX
III

Mons–Condé Canal

Condé

22 Aug

XXX
(French Territorials)

Escaut

X
19

XX
5

XX
3

Mons

XXX
IX

XX

XX
Allenby

XXX
II
Smith-
Dorrien

23 Aug p.m.

XXX
I
Haig

Valenciennes

XXXX
BEF

Maubeuge

XXX

Sorde

FRANCE

SHOULDER TO SHOULDER

The BEF's first encounter at Mons, and
the French withdrawal from the Meuse,
21–3 August 1914

Avesnes

French Fifth Army – 24 Aug p.m.

	French troops/BEF		German troops
	Allied line	**XXXX** **KLUCK**	Army
XXX	Corps	**XX**	Division
X	Brigade		Cavalry
R	Reserve	**GD**	Guards

0   miles   10

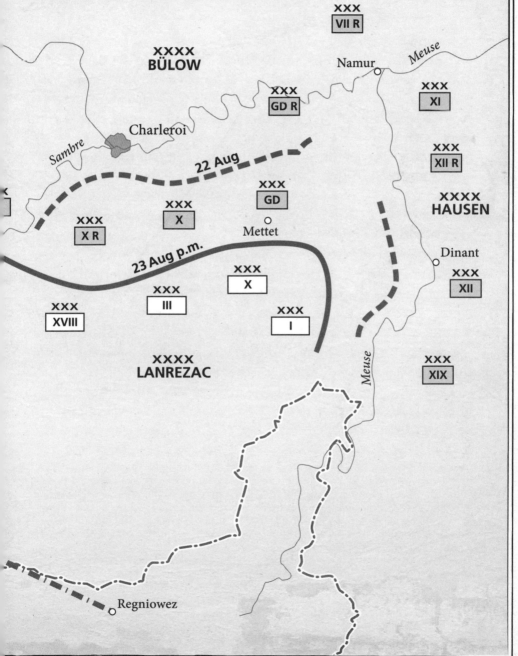

N

Nivelles

BELGIUM

xxx
VII R

Meuse

xxx
BÜLOW

Namur

xxx
XI

xxx
GD R

Charleroi

Sambre

22 Aug

xxx
XII R

xxx
GD

xxxx
HAUSEN

Mettet

xxx
X R

xxx
X

Dinant

23 Aug p.m.

xxx
X

xxx
XII

xxx
XVIII

xxx
III

xxx
I

xxx
XIX

xxxx
LANREZAC

Meuse

Regniowez

sat all day and far into the night ringing up all possible and impossible places in Belgium not known yet to be in German hands . . . Replies took the following forms: 'No sign of enemy here, but rumours they are in A—.' 'Germans are five miles distant on road to B—.' 'Have just received message from C— that enemy close to town; we are closing down.' A German voice or failure to get contact told that the enemy had already arrived. *

The intelligence was admittedly hearsay or presumption, but it was on such a scale that it could not be ignored – or should not have been; and yet Henry Wilson dismissed it as 'somewhat exaggerated'. In truth, it hardly needed the Cavalry Division to ride to Mons to telephone round Belgium: GHQ's intelligence section could have done the same from Le Cateau, and the RFC could then at least have been tasked with verifying the information gleaned. But at this stage there was still innate trust in *GQG*'s intelligence, sparse though that was.†

However, the Cavalry Division was at least able to make contact with the French Cavalry Corps. The GSO2 (general staff officer 2nd grade – in effect the division's deputy chief of staff), Lieutenant-Colonel Archibald 'Sally' Home, was sent to Fontaine l'Évêque, just to the west of Charleroi, where he found General Sordet 'very polite and punctilious [but the] horses very tired, they had been having a good doing'. Unlike British cavalry, who dismounted to lead their horses when they came to the walk, the French practically never did so, and their horses frequently stank, so bad were the saddle sores. In truth the corps had been run ragged for the past fortnight and had lost a sixth of their strength before firing a single shot. In any case, they were going to be no good to the BEF at Charleroi: they were meant to be covering the left, open, flank, not the right (the right flank was,

* General Sir George de S. Barrow, *The Fire of Life* (London, 1942). At fifty, Barrow was only three years younger than Allenby himself, but he had a spectacularly good war – hardly surprising, given the Mons initiative – becoming chief staff officer of the Cavalry Division, then of the Cavalry Corps when it was formed, then X Corps, and 1st Army, then commanding successively 1st Indian Cavalry Division, 7th Division, the Yeomanry Division, 4th Cavalry Division, XXIV Corps, and finally the Desert Mounted Corps in Palestine under Allenby.

† Joffre was also buoyed up by the news of the Russians' success in East Prussia, into which they had advanced almost a fortnight earlier. On 20 August the Germans were thrown back at Gumbinnen, and by the twenty-second the Russians had twenty-eight army corps in contact with the Germans. It could not be long, he reckoned, before this would have a drawing-off effect on the Western Front.

GQG assured them, covered by the solid mass of Lanrezac's 1st Army). So Sordet would somehow have to cross the BEF's entire front – not the most secure of manoeuvres.

Fortunately, late that Friday afternoon General Sir Horace Smith-Dorrien had at last arrived at II Corps headquarters at Bavai.* He had only received the telegram appointing him to command on the Tuesday morning, with an immediate summons to London to see Kitchener. There is no record of the interview that day, but in Smith-Dorrien's memoirs are the somewhat Delphic remarks:

> Lord Kitchener's first words to me, when I entered his room at the War Office that afternoon, expressed grave doubt as to whether he was wise in selecting me to succeed Grierson, since the C.-in-C. in France had asked that General Sir Herbert Plumer should be selected to fill the appointment. However, after thinking the matter over, he adhered to his decision to send me.[†]

In his rebuttal of Sir John French's memoir *1914* (published in 1919), which he wrote in 1919–20 but was allowed only to circulate privately because he was still in uniform, Smith-Dorrien states that Kitchener had said that the CIGS (Douglas) had 'just told him' that the appointment would be putting him in 'an impossible position' owing to the 'great jealousy and personal animus' shown to him by Sir John French over many years, and which was 'well known to the Army Council'. Whether that meant Kitchener had made the appointment *before* receiving Sir John French's request for Plumer is unclear, but he had nevertheless decided not to alter his choice, and this was a statement of a lack of confidence in *someone*. But the secretary of state – who was in any case acting outside his political authority (and it would have been better had French not asked for Plumer in his letter, thereby suggesting that it was indeed a matter within his authority) – would hardly have delayed Smith-Dorrien's departure unless he had something substantial to say. He certainly mistrusted

---

* A number of histories (including Richard Holmes's biography, *The Little Field Marshal: A Life of Sir John French*, London, 1981) date his arrival on the twentieth, but Smith-Dorrien's diary says firmly the twenty-first; and, indeed, the general chronology makes more sense thus. Either way, II Corps was preparing to move north on Mons, or was already on the move, when he arrived.
† Horace Smith-Dorrien, *Memories of Forty Years' Service* (London, 1925).

Henry Wilson, or at least Wilson's view of the situation. On 7 August – according to Wilson's diary – there had even been strong words between the two. Since the twelfth, when the *Times* military correspondent, Repington, had published a remarkable map showing the disposition of German corps in France and Belgium, Kitchener had grown ever more certain that Wilson's appreciation (which meant *GQG's*, essentially) was flawed; at the very least, therefore, he would have warned Smith-Dorrien of Wilson's dangerous over-optimism, as well as his undue influence over Sir John French. To speculate further would be vain; in any case, if Kitchener did indeed speak in these terms to Smith-Dorrien, he was, by inference, signalling his lack of confidence in the commander-in-chief.*

On 21 August, his staff having briefed him on the move forward, the new corps commander motored back to see Sir John French at Le Cateau: 'He received me pleasantly, and explained the general situation as far as he could, for the fog of war was peculiarly dense at that time,' he wrote in *Memories of Forty Years' Service*. In truth, 'pleasantly' was almost certainly a case of decorum, French being still alive at the time of writing. In the (earlier) rebuttal he says: 'I was not very cordially received.'

After receiving the new commander of II Corps with indeterminate pleasantness, French told him that they were to move next day to the general line of the Mons–Condé canal, I Corps on the right, II Corps on the left, 'but that it was only to be a preliminary step to a further move forward which would take the form of a slight right-wheel into Belgium, the British Army forming the outer flank, pivoting on the French 5th Army.'†

Smith-Dorrien almost failed to make it across the start line,

---

* Nevertheless, Kitchener was unable or unwilling to save Smith-Dorrien when French removed him from command of 2nd Army the following May. At the time of French's publishing *1914* both Kitchener and Douglas were dead. Sir John Fortescue, the great historian of the army, writing of French's account in the *Quarterly Review* in October 1919, described it as 'one of the most unfortunate books ever written'. Much of the correspondence with Smith-Dorrien, especially that of Edmonds, the official historian, is in the National Archives; its excoriation of French does not make pretty reading.

† Quotations in this and the following paragraphs are from *Memories of Forty Years' Service*. At this meeting, Smith-Dorrien asked French for formal permission to keep a diary, since, he explained, the King had told him to ask the C-in-C for such permission in order that he could write periodically to 'keep His Majesty posted in all pertaining to my command'. Sir John French could hardly refuse the King, but it could not have pleased him, knowing also that Haig too had a direct line to the Palace.

however, for soon after leaving Le Cateau, as daylight was beginning to fade, his car ran into a skirmish, 'the road blocked, bullets flying, and the sound of firing,' he relates, with an artillery battery 'in considerable confusion held up by sharpshooters across the road'. It turned out to be, in the modern vernacular, 'blue on blue' – mistaken identity.* The battery had been challenged by French Territorials; not understanding what they were meant to do, the gunners had tried to push on, so the French had opened fire, killing one and wounding two more – a miserable job for the battery commander to have to explain in the letter to the next-of-kin.

'This was a bad beginning,' reckoned a tired Smith-Dorrien, who seems to have taken matters in hand himself (which must have been an interesting experience for the French as well as the gunners – a four-star general reverting to subaltern): 'a brief parley arranged matters and I got to my head-quarters at 11 p.m., approved of the orders for the move next morning [the 22nd], and turned in.'

That night a worried Spears came to GHQ after a hazardous drive on roads full of horse transport, many of the drivers fast asleep. He told Henry Wilson that he feared General Lanrezac was about to abandon the idea of offensive action, in which case the BEF would be left in a perilous position if they continued to advance. Wilson could not believe it (another case of cavalry nerves, no doubt – Spears, 'Monsieur Beaucaire', was an 8th Hussar), but agreed that it would be a good thing for Sir John French and Lanrezac to meet the following morning. When Spears got back to 5th Army headquarters he learned that the French II and X Corps had been attacked that afternoon on the Sambre, to the east of Charleroi.†

Next day, the twenty-second, the clouds began to lift – literally and metaphorically. The RFC quickly got away twelve patrols and were soon reporting large numbers of troops approaching on the BEF's line of advance. The first plane to return, soon after eleven, had landed at

---

* Blue because in military map marking, the enemy is shown in red, and friendly forces in blue.
† Spears makes an interesting observation about the BEF's staff cars: they were prone to breaking down, unlike those of the French, because they had been bought 'straight out of the shop windows', and not run in and tuned up. The French, on the other hand, had requisitioned all theirs in good running condition. Some of the best of the BEF's cars were those given – loaned – by prominent figures such as the duke of Westminster and the earl of Derby, sometimes complete with chauffeur.

Beaumont, about 12 miles east of Maubeuge, for petrol, to be told that French cavalry had encountered German infantry north of the Sambre canal the previous afternoon, and had had to fall back – extraordinary news indeed, for there had been no word of it from the 5th Army. The next to return, just before midday, carried the first casualty to enemy fire, an observer, Sergeant-Major David Jillings. His plane had come under heavy rifle fire south-east of Lessines, not 20 miles north of Mons, and then, passing over a cavalry regiment just south-west of Ghislenghien, had met rifle and machine-gun fire. Indeed, the plane had drawn rifle fire all the way back to Ath, where Jillings had been wounded in the leg. By the end of the month a leg wound, even to an aviator, would not have rated a mention; but on 22 August it was a sort of signal that the BEF – the Royal Flying Corps, at least – had definitively passed from a peace to a war footing. And passed with some style: Jillings had almost certainly brought down a German Albatross by rifle fire (possibly with a single shot) near Lessines. He was awarded the MC in 1915 and later commissioned.

It would have been some consolation to GHQ had they known that the Germans had been as much in the dark as they were, at least about who was in front of them. Kluck actually learned of the presence of British troops not from a German plane but from an RFC one: 'It was only on the 22nd of August that an English cavalry squadron was heard of at Casteau, six miles north-east of Mons, and an aeroplane of the English fifth flying squadron was shot down that had gone up from Maubeuge. The presence of the English in front was thus established, although nothing as regards their strength.'*

The cavalry at Casteau was C Squadron of the 4th (Royal Irish) Dragoon Guards commanded by Major Tom Bridges who, by one of those strange coincidences of war, had recently been the military attaché in Brussels. Before the 2nd Cavalry Brigade had left Tidworth, its commander, Brigadier-General Henry De Beauvoir De Lisle, had gathered his officers together for a pep talk during which he asked Bridges his views on the strength of the Belgian fortresses. The former attaché gave a very accurate estimate of the holding power of Liège

* General Johan von Zehl, commanding VII Corps (Bülow's 2nd Army), *Das VII. Reserve-Korps im Weltkriege von s. Beginn bis Ende 1916* (1921), quoted in Herwig, *The Marne, 1914.*

but wholly over-estimated that of Namur.* And then De Lisle asked how long he believed the war would last, to which Bridges replied 'six months'. De Lisle thought otherwise: 'Make no mistake, gentlemen; we are in for a long and bitter war.' But he then rallied them with the promise that the first officer to kill a German with the new-pattern (1912) cavalry sword would be recommended for the DSO.†

And by another coincidence, it was Bridges' second-in-command, Captain Charles Hornby, who would gain that DSO. C Squadron had been pushed forward on the afternoon of the twenty-first to try to gain contact, but they met no Germans, learning only from refugees that 'uhlans' had bivouacked about 15 miles north.‡ It was yet another blisteringly hot day, the cobbled roads 'a proper bugger', recalled Farrier Arthur Newton of the 5th Lancers: 'I seemed to spend my whole time shoeing horses . . . It would have been better if we had ridden across country, but the orders were that we weren't to damage standing crops.' So Bridges decided to bivouac too.§

They were away again at dawn, and at six-thirty saw half a dozen 'uhlans',** as Bridges, along with everyone else, called all German cavalry with lances. They were in fact the 4th Cuirassiers of 9th

* Like everyone else, for no one had predicted the tactical circumstances in which Namur would find itself – effectively abandoned. Generaloberst Karl von Bülow's army laid siege on the twentieth, bringing up the big guns from Liège. It was all over by the twenty-fifth, at which point, by Schlieffen's plan, the road to Paris (or, at least, to the rear of the French army) lay open.

† De Lisle, who would succeed Allenby in command of the Cavalry Division, was never popular with his officers. It perhaps went back to his time as adjutant of the Durham Light Infantry in India, where he had trained and led the DLI's polo team to victory in the inter-regimental cup – a victory (the infantry over the cavalry) that should simply never have happened. He had later transferred to the 1st Dragoons (The Royals). Opinions of his character and ability are as mixed as those of Haig.

‡ Uhlan regiments were modelled on the Polish lancers of the Napoleonic era, though because all German cavalry – hussars, dragoons, cuirassiers – carried the lance, 'uhlan' became a generic term for men on horseback carrying lances. The lance consisted of a tube made of rolled steel-plate 3.2 metres long (10 feet 6 inches) weighing 1.6 kg (3 lb 9 oz), and a four-edged tempered steel spearpoint. By contrast, the lance carried by the British cavalry (lancer regiments) consisted of a steel head mounted on an ash stave, with an overall length of 9 feet 1 inch.

§ No such orders to avoid damage to crops had been given the Germans. To Kluck's regiments, damage to crops, and much else, was not just unavoidable; it was war. A few days later they would pour petrol over the medieval manuscripts in the library of Louvain's Catholic University and burn the place to the ground.

** All timings were Greenwich Mean Time (in modern military terminology, 'Zulu Time'), or Western European Time as the French called it. On 23 August 1914 at Mons sunrise was at 4.44 a.m., and sunset at 6.49 p.m. The time of first and last light – the sun's light from below the horizon (or, as the Highway Code has it, 'lighting-up time')

Cavalry Division, and they were ambling down the road, lances slung, unaware of Bridges' squadron, which he had moved into cover. He quickly ordered two troops to dismount for 'fire action', keeping the other two, under Hornby, mounted ready to charge.

At about 300 yards something spooked the Germans and they turned about, whereupon Bridges ordered the two troops to give chase, remounting the others and following at the trot. After a mile of galloping, Hornby came up against a half squadron of the Cuirassiers in a village street – and charged. As they clashed he drove his sabre into the chest of one of them, becoming the first man of the BEF to kill a German (barring, possibly, the slayer of the pilot of the Albatross the day before). His orderly, Private Tilney, had a hard time trying to follow suit, finding himself 'kept busy by a big blond German trying to poke his lance into me. I could easily parry his lance but could not reach him.'

The lance was not intended for close-quarter fighting, even less so in a confined space, and several 'uhlans' threw theirs down and tried to surrender. In the heat of the fighting, however, 'we weren't in no mood to take prisoners' wrote another trooper; 'and we downed a lot of them before they managed to break it off and gallop away'.

Again the Dragoon Guards gave chase.

Having put a few hundred yards behind them, the Germans dismounted and opened fire on their pursuers. Hornby and his men followed suit, bullets flying about their ears as they got the horses into cover behind a chateau wall. Corporal Ernest Thomas was one of the first into a firing position: 'I could see a German cavalry officer some four hundred yards away standing mounted in full view of me,' he recalled. 'I took aim, pulled the trigger and automatically, almost instantaneously, he fell to the ground'.

Kneeling, unsupported, at 400 yards – it was a fine shot, testament to the hours that the cavalry had put in at the butts before the war.

– varies depending on the cloud, but is generally about thirty minutes before and after sunset respectively. It is sometimes defined as the time at which colours can be discerned, but for soldiers it is the point at which night-time routine – strengthening the position, sentries, patrolling or sleeping – changes to that of day (and vice versa), with movement becoming respectively easier or more restricted. It is the point also at which an enemy attack is likeliest (particularly first light) and therefore when a body of troops stands to arms. The term 'stand to arms' (or simply 'stand to') means to adopt a position from which to fight in case of attack.

Thomas was the first man of the BEF to fire his rifle at the enemy (at least from the ground at other than aircraft).

The Germans now broke off the action and withdrew. Bridges concluded that he had run into the divisional advance guard, and expecting a follow-up in strength decided to withdraw before the squadron could be outflanked. The action had demonstrated, in miniature, the futility of the either/or absolutism of the *arme blanche* debate.

Elsewhere the cavalry were having similar dustings. Brigadier-General Sir Philip Chetwode's 5th (Independent) Cavalry Brigade, who were covering the advance of Haig's I Corps, ran into artillery and heavy rifle fire near La Louvière, which was answered with accurate rifle fire by the Scots Greys (the *arme blanche* debate already looking sterile) and the 13-pounders of E Battery. A patrol of the 20th Hussars, another of Chetwode's regiments, got to within 25 miles of Brussels before finding they had ridden into 'vast masses of Germans of all arms' and had to gallop for it in a hail of bullets, one or more of which brought down the horse of Private Thomas O'Shaughnessy. Remarkably, O'Shaughnessy was able to evade capture and managed to rejoin his regiment four days later in plain clothes (risking summary execution as a spy), having got through the German lines by playing deaf and dumb – 'not an easy subterfuge', says the regimental historian, 'for an Irishman'.*

But while the Cavalry Division was reporting enemy in large numbers approaching from the north and north-east, an RFC reconnaissance patrol spotted something even more ominous – a huge column (Kluck's II Corps), moving *westward* on the Brussels–Ninove road, and from Ninove *south*-west towards Grammont (Geraardsbergen). Brigadier-General Sir David Henderson realized at once what it threatened – a massive envelopment of the BEF's left wing. He took the report in person to GHQ. In fact, Belgian GQG had wired Joffre's headquarters the evening before to say that a German corps approaching Brussels appeared to be wheeling south. The information failed to reach GHQ, however – or, at least, to do so in the unequivocal language in which it had been sent from

* Lieutenant-Colonel L. B. Oatts, *The Emperor's Chambermaids: The Story of the 14th/20th King's Hussars* (London, 1973).

Brussels. Nor did the RFC report seem to make much impact.*

Wilson, though, clearly having thought a little more about Spears' report the night before, had persuaded Sir John French to take a drive to see Lanrezac (whatever else may be said of Wilson, his powers of persuasion were prodigious: after the 'pour pêcher' quip, Lanrezac was the last man that French wanted to see). They set out 'in the very early hours of a beautiful August morning', and then, quite by chance – the greatest of *good* chances (for the encounter would save the BEF a terrible mauling) – not far into the French sector a dozen or so miles south of Maubeuge they met Spears' car coming from the opposite direction, which they managed to flag down.† Spears records: 'I well remember the place' (as a subaltern meeting a field marshal undoubtedly would): 'quite a number of French soldiers, a couple of companies perhaps, were halted on either side of the road, and stared suspiciously at these strange, khaki-clad, red-tabbed officers.' He recounts how at dawn he had gone to the little hotel where the headquarters of Lanrezac's 5th Army were messing in the hope of some coffee and something to eat, and been surprised to find it full of dishevelled, disorientated civilians, mainly women and children. They turned out to be refugees from the fighting near Charleroi; but Spears makes no mention of any untoward appearance of the *poilus* at this impromptu rendezvous, which is significant in the light of Sir John French's account. Indeed, those Spears had seen earlier, not yet in action but all eagerness for it, were 'fine young fellows . . . Their lightheartedness and exuberance were contagious'.

There was an *estaminet* close by the chance rendezvous, which Wilson now commandeered as a conference room. Spears recalled a table 'piled high with dirty plates and cups . . . [that were] cleared aside and a map spread out'. There can have been few occasions in

---

* French records that 'At 5.30 a.m. on the 21st I received a visit from General de Morionville, Chief of the Staff to His Majesty the King of the Belgians, who, with a small staff, was proceeding to Joffre's Headquarters . . . He confirmed all the reports we had received concerning the situation generally, and added that the unsupported condition of the Belgian Army rendered their position very precarious, and that the King had, therefore, determined to effect a retirement on Antwerp, where they would be prepared to attack the flank of the enemy's columns as they advanced. He told me he hoped to arrive at a complete understanding with the French Commander-in-Chief.'

† They had possibly set out later than French recalled, since Spears had already visited several advanced units that morning to gain for himself an impression of the views of the operations staff.

history when a subaltern – even a lieutenant of hussars – has briefed a field marshal at so critical a moment; and certainly not in such comical surroundings, for the *propriétaire* now began defiantly, and noisily, washing the dishes in a tub in the corner of the room, stopped only with some difficulty by Spears' accompanying French officer to allow him to resume his briefing.

Spears began by giving the field marshal the situation as 5th Army headquarters understood it that morning. X Corps had been 'knocked about a good deal' but were still intact, and then he repeated what he had told Wilson the night before – that Lanrezac's appetite for the offensive was gone, and that the intelligence staff believed that the strength and extent of the German advance beyond the Meuse could mean but one thing: an enveloping movement on a huge scale. French asked about Sordet's cavalry corps, and when it might move to cover his left, to which Spears was only able to say that he understood it to have withdrawn to somewhere about Merbes-le-Château, between Charleroi and Maubeuge (to the rear and right of the BEF's I Corps).

French then asked where Lanrezac himself was, and on hearing he was at Mettet, south-east of Charleroi, some 30–40 miles' drive, decided not to continue. Spears tried to persuade him otherwise – testament to his unusual strength of character – but failed: a C-in-C's time was too valuable, said French, though in his own account he registers only his concern that there appeared to be 'some difficulty in finding General Lanrezac'.

It is perfectly understandable that the commander of the BEF would not want to waste time driving round the French countryside in search of Lanrezac, but it is difficult to imagine what could have been more valuable at that point than to speak face-to-face with the commander of the army on which the security of his own command largely rested. That he risked being received with the same off-handedness as the week before, and having to speak through interpreters, could be of no account: he needed to know, in detail and with absolute assurance, what the intentions were of the troops to his right, and what troops, if any, would be on his left. Sending Wilson, at least, would have been a better option than turning back for Le Cateau. Joffre would have thought nothing of 40 miles on French roads; but, then, his driver was the winner of the French Grand Prix, Georges Boillot, not a sergeant of the Army Service Corps.

What pressing concern reversed the commander-in-chief's intention? It seems, in fact, that he had already concluded that Lanrezac's 5th Army was not merely abandoning the idea of the offensive, it was abandoning the field: 'There is an atmosphere engendered by troops retiring, when they expect to be advancing, which is unmistakable to anyone who has had much experience of war,' he would write.

> It matters not whether such a movement is the result of a lost battle, an unsuccessful engagement, or is in the nature of a 'strategic manœuvre to the rear.' The fact that, whatever the reason may be, it means giving up ground to the enemy, affects the spirits of the troops and manifests itself in the discontented, apprehensive expression which is seen on the faces of the men, and the tired, slovenly, unwilling gait which invariably characterizes troops subjected to this ordeal. This atmosphere surrounded me for some time before I met Spiers [sic] and before he had spoken a word. My optimistic visions of the night before had vanished, and what he told me did not tend to bring them back . . . and therefore I decided to return at once to my Headquarters at Le Cateau.

Yet on return to Le Cateau, where he was greeted by the skirl of pipes of the Cameron Highlanders, the GHQ guard, the commander-in-chief made no change of plan and issued no new orders. There was no talk whatever – as Wilson's diaries confirm – of even halting the forward movement, let alone going on the defensive; and certainly not of any retrograde movement. French's memoirs say one thing, his actions another. It is fruitless to speculate why.

One man was taking no chances, however. The commander of the BEF might delay his decision to change course and then rely on his artillery to get him out of trouble; his chief of logistics could not. In a withdrawal, stores unloaded had to be reloaded (or else abandoned), waggons plying forward from the distribution points had to be turned round, roads cleared for the marching troops, new replenishment points found . . . And the hard-headed Quartermaster-General, Wully Robertson, was already discussing contingency plans with Major-General Robb, commanding the lines of communication, in case the BEF were indeed forced to retreat.* And soon the BEF would have

---

* In fact he was following *Field Service Regulations*: 'Orders for a possible retreat should always be thought out beforehand in case of need, but they should not be communicated to the troops before it becomes necessary to do so.'

cause to be grateful for his foresight, as well as for his robust decisions when the retreat actually began.

But for all the brilliance of his logistical staff work in the weeks ahead, it is difficult not to think that, seniority notwithstanding, Robertson should instead have been in the post for which his experience and temperament so perfectly suited him – the BEF's head of intelligence. That job was filled by Colonel (from November, Brigadier-General) George Macdonogh, lately head of Section 5 of the War Office intelligence division, concerned with internal security (what would become in part today's MI5). Macdonogh was brilliant; of that there was no doubt. He and a fellow sapper – James Edmonds, who would become in part the official historian of the Great War – had achieved such high marks in the staff college entrance exam in 1896 that the results, it was said, were adjusted to conceal the margin between them and their classmates (who included Robertson and Allenby). But Robertson had an impact that the intellectual, Jesuit-educated Macdonogh did not. Had he been in the other man's place in the BEF's 'deuxième bureau', there is every likelihood that on 22 August the infantry would have been digging defensive positions in front of the fortress of Maubeuge, not marching north in the expectation of going to it with the bayonet.*

For despite the growing evidence French, on seeing the reconnaissance reports brought by Henderson on the twenty-second, had reckoned that 'there still appears to be very little to our front except cavalry supported by small bodies of infantry'. And it was on this basis that he had sent a not discouraging, though a shade ambiguous, message to Lanrezac:

> I am waiting for the dispositions arranged for to be carried out, especially the posting of French Cavalry Corps on my left. I am prepared to fulfil the *rôle* allotted to me when the 5th Army advances to the attack. In the

---

* Macdonogh's effectiveness was undoubtedly reduced by suspicion of his Catholicism. He had been one of the few senior officers to advocate the use of force in Ulster during the home rule crisis (as had Churchill); the Curragh 'Mutiny' had opened fissures within the army, albeit tiny cracks compared with the gulf between the brass hats and the frocks. In 1916 he would return to the War Office as director of military intelligence and do brilliant work; but he suffered from poor relations with Haig and his chief of intelligence, Charteris, who in November 1917 would write to his wife: 'My chief opponents are the Roman Catholic people, who are really very half-hearted about the whole war and have never forgiven DH unjustly for being Presbyterian.'

meantime, I hold an advanced defensive position extending from Condé on the left, through Mons to Erquelinnes, where I connect with two [French] Reserve Divisions south of the Sambre. I am now much in advance of the line held by the 5th Army and feel my position to be as forward as circumstances will allow, particularly in view of the fact that I am not properly prepared for offensive action till to-morrow morning, as I have previously informed you . . .

Only late that evening did the penny at last drop. The remarkable Spears had been active all day, learning that Lanrezac's III Corps was falling back to a new ('unfortified') defensive line having been 'roughly handled' in the morning – one of its divisional commanders seriously wounded by rifle fire – and that 5th Army would in consequence be bowed back with its centre some 5–10 miles south of the Sambre. This would place the BEF at Mons about 9 miles ahead of the main French line, though Spears did not consider this calamitous. The 5th Army was certainly *not* beaten: its two 'wing' corps were intact, and there was every reason to suppose that the two centre corps would be able to recover, for 'the morale even of those units which had suffered most was good'. The problem lay not with the left-wing, XVIII Corps, but with the gap between it and the BEF, not least because two reserve divisions ordered forward by Lanrezac that afternoon to beef up the left would not reach the Sambre until late the next day. But Spears' worry was that Sir John French might still believe that Lanrezac intended attacking. At 7 p.m. therefore he set off again for Le Cateau, 'feeling anything but happy: the responsibility of having to report a situation so serious [with no information beyond what he had been able to glean himself] that it must necessarily profoundly influence British plans overwhelmed me with anxiety'.

He was also exhausted, but fortunately on arrival the eminently sensible Macdonogh gave him half a bottle of restorative champagne and – perhaps more importantly – reassured him in his estimate of the situation with more corroborating reports from the RFC.

Sir John French was dining late, but he came out at once to hear Spears' report. Having listened to it in silence – testimony to both its clarity and its authority – he told both Spears and Macdonogh to wait in the dining room while he and Sir Archibald Murray, the chief of staff, talked. Spears recalls his dismay on hearing, as he waited, the GHQ staff officers around the map-covered table and the liaison officers from I and II Corps discussing the general advance that was still planned for the following day.

After twenty minutes the door opened and a grim-faced Murray broke the spell. 'You are to come in now and see the Chief,' he said to the staff. 'He is going to tell you there will be no advance. But remember there are to be no questions. Don't ask why. There is no time and it would be useless. You are to take your orders, that's all.'

They did, and took them thence to their respective corps commanders, who received the orders rather differently. Smith-Dorrien, having only just taken over II Corps, remained 'in blissful ignorance of the situation', for he was allowed to sleep on. Haig, on the other hand, at I Corps, was dismayed at the order to take up a front from Mons to Peissant 'without delay', which seemed to him 'ill considered . . . in view of the condition of the reservists in the ranks, because it meant a forced march by night'.*

Doubtless he believed that all would be made clear at the conference Sir John French had ordered for five-thirty the following morning at II Corps headquarters.

And doubtless, too, before Spears' arrival, the commander-in-chief had himself been hoping for a decent night's sleep. Now he would have to cope with several hours fewer. But then another visitor arrived to disturb the chief's repose. Close to midnight, Colonel Huguet came to the chateau with one of Lanrezac's officers bearing an extraordinary request: *le général* wished the BEF to attack the flank of the German forces that were assailing 5th Army.

This was a sea change in the situation on Joffre's left flank – and had it not been for Spears' initiative, it would have been the first that French had heard of it. He pondered for a moment and then replied that he could not commit to an attack before discovering what lay to his front – 'until he got reports from his aeroplanes', Wilson says in his diary – but that he would at least stand on the Mons line for twenty-four hours. In the circumstances it was a good decision, which would only have been better had he made the decision to take up *proper* defensive positions on the Mons line – in other words, to dig

---

* Haig's diary is somewhat confused at this stage, the chronology not wholly reliable.

in. Clearly he felt impelled by straightforward loyalty to an allied general under pressure: if the RFC at daylight found no enemy to his front he could indeed incline his advance to the east to attack Lanrezac's Germans in the flank. But equally, too, he appears still to have been infected by Wilsonian optimism.*

However, the suddenness of the request and the part-withdrawal of 5th Army without telling him had their effect on French's trust in Lanrezac, which within days would precipitate an almost total breach between the two men. For it did not help that Lanrezac was evidently trying to conceal the state of affairs on the left flank, telling *GQG* that afternoon that the BEF was 'still in echelon to the rear of the Fifth Army', although at that very moment II Corps was arriving at Mons, as French had already told him – 'I hold an advanced defensive position extending from Condé on the left, through Mons to Erquelinnes' – and I Corps was well north of Maubeuge and level with the left wing of Fifth Army and Sordet's cavalry corps. In any case, if the BEF were in echelon to the rear, how could they attack the enemy in the flank? If Lanrezac did indeed know the true dispositions – as he must have, for Huguet had been given copies of the movement tables (and Lanrezac was asking for the attack to take place as soon as it was light) – even allowing for the fact that the BEF was still moving, and therefore a part of it would still be behind his left flank, what was the point of telling *GQG* a half-truth?

Could it have been that Lanrezac was preparing his alibi? Joffre had already removed several generals from command, notably in the 1st and 2nd Armies attacking in Alsace-Lorraine: they were sent to specially appointed quarters at Limoges in west-central France and isolated from all contact with either Paris or the army (coining the verb *limoger*). Lanrezac, having failed to make any forward movement as instructed by Joffre, would have been only too aware that a railway warrant for Limoges had probably been made out for him in pencil; any sign of retreat would see it inked in. How useful it would be therefore to blame the BEF's tardiness in

---

* French would never have described himself as innovative, but in many respects he was quick on the tactical uptake, realizing soon enough that the real intelligence he needed would come from the RFC – who had the necessary range and perspective – rather than from his beloved cavalry, who would be drawn inexorably into the actual fighting to help extricate the infantry during the prolonged withdrawal after Mons.

coming to his aid. This was certainly Spears' considered view.*

Meanwhile the last of the infantry were slogging up to Mons with rifle and pack, shepherded by the hussars of the divisional cavalry squadrons. Frank Richards could count himself lucky, though: he and the rest of the 2nd Royal Welsh Fusiliers were taking the train. As part of the hastily formed 19th Brigade they were being railed from various places along the lines of communication (in Richards' case, Amiens), where they had been guarding key points, to Valenciennes, not 10 miles from where they would first see – or rather, hear – action. But if they were welcome reinforcements on II Corps' left, they were certainly not an RSM's delight: 'The majority of men in my battalion had given their cap and collar badges to the French ladies they had been walking out with, as souvenirs, and I expect in some cases had also left other souvenirs which would either be a blessing or curse to the ladies concerned,' wrote Richards.

For single men in barracks don't grow into plaster saints.

---

* Lanrezac's memoirs are full of infelicitous references to the BEF compared with the French army at this time, of their 'not speaking the same language and having different mentalities' etc. As for the fear of being *limogé*, in less than a month fifty-eight senior officers would be sent to the rear. By December, 40% in all had been removed from post. But Sir John French is, it has to be said, unreliable in his recollection of, or explanation of, his decision to abandon the advance on the twenty-third. His diaries suggest it was the enemy situation that was the cause, although no new information reached him during the evening of the twenty-second (and *GQG* reports of increasing strength were still being considered a shade over-egged, though not by Macdonogh). His description in *1914* of the *poilus'* 'tired, slovenly, unwilling gait' on the morning of the twenty-second is reflected in his diaries, and conflicts with Spears' impressions. Spears had not, of course, 'much experience of war', but his description of the morale of 5th Army is *so* positive that it seems unlikely that he had merely failed to notice its absence. Nor, indeed, on the morning of the twenty-second had 5th Army's X Corps made much of a retrograde movement – certainly not enough to have the effect in the rear areas that French describes. Besides, as John Terraine puts it succinctly in *Mons: The Retreat to Victory* (London, 1960), the *poilus*, overloaded with equipment which made them lean forward on the march, as if bowed by fatigue, 'Straggling along in loose formation, all over the roads, out of step . . . were a startling sight to English observers; but they usually "got there", all the same.' It was surely Spears' report that changed the orders for the BEF from advance to defence; and perhaps the realization that if 5th Army had been so roughly handled, the Germans were indeed advancing in strength. Either way, it does not speak well of GHQ's coordination with 5th Army (relying on a single subaltern liaison officer), and its appreciation of intelligence. Sir Walter Raleigh's official history, *The War in the Air* (London, 1922, and therefore subject to correction by French) is unequivocal: 'Sir John French on the evening of the 22nd held a conference at Le Cateau, whereat the position of the Germans, so far as it was then known, was explained and discussed. At the close of the conference Sir John stated that *owing to the retreat of the French Fifth Army* [author's italics] the British offensive would not take place.'

Chapter Fifteen

MONS – THE STUBBORN RESISTANCE

Close country favours delaying action, but not necessarily a protracted defence, for it is often possible for the attackers to work up to the defenders unseen.

Infantry Training (1914)

'My F.O.O. [forward observation officer] looked at the slag heaps,' said Driver Walter Pursey of the Royal Field Artillery, 'and thought they were God's gift to an observation officer. We set off to climb one and within a couple of minutes our boots were sizzling, and down we came. No more slag heaps, and precious little observation.'*

The *Official History* describes the battlefield of Mons in all its novel challenge and awfulness:

The space occupied by the II Corps in particular, within the quadrangle Mons–Frameries–Dour–Boussu, is practically one huge unsightly village, traversed by a vast number of devious cobbled roads which lead from no particular starting-point to no particular destination, and broken by pit-heads and colossal slag-heaps, often over a hundred feet high. It is, in fact, a close and blind country, such as no army had yet been called upon to fight in against a civilised enemy in a great campaign.

---

* The forward observation officer was responsible for calling for artillery fire and sending corrections to the guns to adjust the fall of shot.

Private Jim Cannon of the 2nd Suffolks summed it up plainly: 'I took one look at it and thought what a bloody place to live. I took a second look and thought what a bloody place to fight.'

His brigade (14th), which had been stationed at the green and pleasant Curragh, consisted of 1st Duke of Cornwall's Light Infantry, 1st East Surreys and 2nd Manchesters as well as the Suffolks. They had marched from their billets at five o'clock the previous morning (22 August) and reached Mons at four in the afternoon, where, wrote the adjutant of the Cornwalls, 'We put out outposts and dug ourselves in.'* They did so because although GHQ's Operation Order No. 5 had said that gaining the line of the Mons–Condé canal was 'only to be a preliminary step to a further move forward', the BEF's field discipline required that they dig – if not deep – even at a temporary halt (the change in the situation heralded by Spears late the night before had not yet been relayed to the forward units). And it was as well that they lost no time in doing so, for the first Germans began arriving the next morning even as Sir John French was holding his dawn conference.

'It is more than usually difficult to piece together what went on at this conference,' says French's biographer Richard Holmes. This, if anything, is an understatement. Haig's diary, for example, times the meeting at 10.30 a.m. – some five hours out. But although few shots had yet been exchanged with the enemy, men were already tired. 'Sally' Home, Allenby's GSO2, records how, the evening before, the Cavalry Division had retired west on Quiévrain across the rear of Smith-Dorrien's II Corps to cover the BEF's left flank, leaving Chetwode's 5th (Independent) Cavalry Brigade to cover the approach of Haig's I Corps on the right – '15 miles over paved roads, the worst march I have ever done, on a tired horse and in the dusk. Arrived 11.30 pm – a long day.' Indeed it was, for they had been up at 3 a.m., and the day before at three-thirty. Not surprisingly, he writes on the twenty-third that '[I] had promised myself a long lie: result that I was woken at 3 am. Left at 4.30 with General Allenby for Conference . . .'†

---

* Journal of Captain Arthur Acland. They also set fire to the barges the length of the canal so that they could not be used as bridges.
† The regiments of the 2nd Cavalry Brigade, which formed the rearguard for the divisional move, did not reach their billets until two o'clock, although they would at least have the morning's respite. The Cavalry Division was undeniably tiring, however, which would be a major factor in Smith-Dorrien's decision to stand and fight at Le Cateau two days later.

Recollections, wilful or genuine, vary as to Sir John French's stated intention at Mons. The line of the Mons–Condé canal was being held by Smith-Dorrien's II Corps, with Haig's corps echeloned rear of them covering the right flank and facing east. It is probably at this conference that the tetchy exchange between the commander of the BEF and the commander of II Corps (neither of whom could have had much sleep), which Alan Clark quotes in *The Donkeys*, took place – or rather, might have taken place, for there is no reliable record of it. Indeed, it was almost certainly pure invention on Clark's part:

> Sir John French: The British Army will give battle on the line of the Condé Canal.
>
> Sir Horace Smith-Dorrien: Do you mean take the offensive or stand on the defensive?
>
> Sir John French: Don't ask questions, do as you're told.*

However, that the two men were at odds with each other early on there is no doubting. Haig writes little about the conference other than noting Wilson's airy confidence that the French offensives in the Ardennes and Alsace 'must succeed', and the difference between the estimate of the Germans' strength by, respectively, Sir John French and Wilson, and Macdonogh, 'who was not in the conference room' but who told Haig afterwards of the RFC's reports of all roads west from Brussels to Ath and Tournai being 'thickly covered with masses of German troops of all arms marching very rapidly westwards . . . Yet our C-in-C ordered my corps to press on!' The precise meaning of this last – pressing on – is unclear: it may have been simply to press on with the approach march (Haig's I Corps had not completed theirs), and to occupy the flank position south-east of Mons indicated at the conference; or there may have been a flicker of enthusiasm in Sir John

---

* *The Donkeys* (London, 1961), a much discredited book. Even the quote on the frontispiece ('Lions led by Donkeys'), from which the title is derived, Clark admitted to making up – as, indeed, he did his military credentials, claiming to have 'served in the Household Cavalry', whereas he had joined the training regiment at Windsor in February 1946 while in his final year at Eton, leaving at the end of the summer half (term). The author has not had the inclination to trawl through every last word of the Liddell Hart archive to see if this was something that he *didn't* make up (the task has defeated many previous researchers), but Clark's attribution of the exchange between French and Smith-Dorrien is to Sir James Edmonds, who was, anyway, nowhere near the conference. In fact, at the supposed time of the exchange Edmonds was on a train with the rest of the 4th Division, en route from Boulogne for Le Cateau.

French's mind still for the idea of a general advance after a day's skirmishing. Haig makes no mention of the possibility of retreat, though French's memoirs (confirmed by his diary) state plainly that he warned them to be ready for advance *or* retreat. Smith-Dorrien remembers the conference as follows (with no actual mention of retreat but with the acknowledgement that a local tactical withdrawal might be forced):

> At 6 a.m. the Chief appeared at my head-quarters, and, addressing his Corps and Cavalry Division Commanders assembled there, told us that little more than one, or at most two, enemy Corps, with perhaps a Cavalry Division, were facing the B.E.F. So it was evident that he too was in blissful ignorance of the real situation. Sir John was in excellent form, and told us to be prepared to move forward, or to fight where we were, but to get ready for the latter by strengthening our outposts and preparing the bridges over the Canal for demolition. I took the opportunity of emphasis-ing the weakness of my general line and the danger of holding on to the Mons salient, remarking that I was issuing orders for the preparation of a retired position south-west and clear of the town of Mons to cover, should a retirement become necessary, the advanced troops at Nimy and Obourg who would have to fall back behind Mons, as soon as things got so hot as to risk their being cut off. The Chief expressed himself in agreement, and approved my action.*

Sir John French's recollection of the conference in *1914*, written years later with the benefit of hindsight (corroborated in part by his diary, in its execrable handwriting), makes astonishing reading:

> Allenby's bold and searching reconnaissance had not led me to believe that we were threatened by forces against which we could not make an effec-tive stand. The 2nd Corps had not yet been seriously engaged, while the 1st was practically still in reserve . . . I entertained some anxiety as to the salient which the canal makes north of Mons, and enjoined on Smith-Dorrien particular watchfulness and care with regard to it . . . The air reconnaissance had started at daybreak, and I decided to await aircraft reports from Henderson before making any decided plan.

* All quotations from Smith-Dorrien from *Memories of Forty Years' Service*.

The weakness of the line to which Smith-Dorrien referred lay in its length – 7 miles – as well as its poor fields of fire and the bulge (the 'Mons salient'), which could be fired into from the flanks. The mere facts of the length of front and such a salient indicate that Sir John French could not have been expecting anything more than a light encounter. On the other hand, the strength of the position lay in the water obstacle, which meant that the Germans would have to concentrate their initial attacks on the crossing points – the bridges and lock gates – which in turn meant that the BEF's battalions could concentrate their defence on these points. It is unclear quite what French meant by 'particular watchfulness and care'. Smith-Dorrien's dispositions make it clear that he took the salient very seriously, with the 3rd Division almost wholly focused on it: the division covered but a third, at most, of II Corps' front, with the 5th Division covering the remainder.* II Corps had twenty-four hours, at best, to prepare its positions, but with the possibility of a subsequent advance, GHQ did not order the destruction of the bridges. Instead, the battalions placed outposts on the approach roads to force the Germans back if they tried to get up to the canal in small numbers – it was only some 60 feet wide at its narrowest – or to delay them by forcing them to deploy if they came on in greater strength, in which case the outposts would

---

* It was, naturally, a very linear defence, the canal for much of its length forming a perfectly straight line, but Smith-Dorrien had been mindful of his flanks, particularly the right. He had placed the 3rd Division (7th, 8th and 9th Brigades) right, and the 5th (13th, 14th and 15th Brigades) left. The 8th Brigade on the right was in touch with I Corps, the 2nd Royal Irish holding the hill of the Bois la Haut, just south-east of Mons, 1st Gordons and 2nd Royal Scots dug in about Harmignies, and 4th Middlesex in line from Bois la Haut to Obourg, north-east of Mons. The 9th Brigade, on the left of the 8th, comprised three fusilier battalions, the 4th (Royal), 1st Royal Scots (Fusiliers), and 1st (Northumberland) holding the outpost line on the canal from the left of the 4th Middlesex to the bridge of Mariette, some 6 miles, with the 1st Lincolns in reserve a mile south-west of Mons. The 7th Brigade were in reserve about Ciply, 2 miles south of Mons. The 5th Division continued the line along the canal westwards from Mariette, with the 13th Brigade holding the next 3 miles to Les Herbières, 1st Royal West Kents right, 2nd King's Own Scottish Borderers left, with the other two battalions, 2nd Duke of Wellington's and 2nd King's Own Yorkshire Light Infantry, in reserve in St Ghislain. To the left of 13th Brigade came the 14th, from Les Herbières, 2½ miles to the extreme left of the corps at Pommeroeul bridge, with the 1st East Surreys on the right, 1st Duke of Cornwall's Light Infantry on the left, the 2nd Suffolks and 2nd Manchesters in reserve. The 15th Brigade, a wonderfully English-counties formation commanded by Count Gleichen, 'Glick' to his friends in the Grenadiers, the son of Prince Victor of Hohenlohe-Langenburg (remarkably, an admiral in the Royal Navy) – 1st Norfolks, 1st Bedfords, 1st Cheshires, and 1st Dorsets – was preparing a position in rear about Dour.

withdraw across the canal and the sappers would blow the bridges behind them. Except that by the time it was clear that there would be no further advance there were not the sappers or demolition equipment to destroy all the bridges. Smith-Dorrien observes that II Corps' concentration at Maubeuge had not been completed, 'but the French were so insistent on our moving forward to cover their left flank that, although short of guns, field hospitals, and engineer units, the C.-in-C. decided to go without them'.

As ever, though, when at last the order was given to blow the bridges the sappers would work heroically to do the job.*

When the conference ended, at about nine o'clock, Sir John French did something that showed he had still not grasped the scale of the attack about to befall the BEF – nor, in truth, the need for personal command of what was to be a two-corps battle. For while Haig's I Corps might not expect much action initially on the right flank, their support would be critical in II Corps' withdrawal to the 'retired position' that Smith-Dorrien had identified – and vital if it came to any further withdrawal. Now, instead of waiting for the RFC reports, and with the sound of battle heard clearly to the north – which he dismissed as the Germans merely 'trying to "feel" our position all round' – Sir John French left his chief of staff, Archie Murray, at II Corps headquarters and drove to Valenciennes to see the 19th Brigade, who were just detraining, and to order them to prolong the line west from II Corps' left, west of St Ghislain, to Condé sur L'Escaut. Given his declared concern for the Mons salient, it is strange that he chose to reinforce the left flank, and to keep the brigade under GHQ's control rather than II Corps'; for it would have been of real value to Smith-Dorrien in the coming battle of the salient.[†]

French also wanted to speak to the commander of the French

---

*It was at the conference that French ordered the bridges to be prepared for demolition. However, Smith-Dorrien had already, at 2.30 a.m., sent an order to his two divisions to prepare them, and as soon as the conference ended he issued a further order directing them to be destroyed on authority of the divisional commanders in the event of a retirement being necessary. All the barges in the canal were sunk by small gun-cotton charges.

† If this criticism seems severe, or too reliant on hindsight or even modern practice, the C-in-C's absence from the battle should be compared with Smith-Dorrien's method of command on the twenty-third: his finger on the pulse and active direction of events stand comparison with the Iron Duke's that day ninety-nine years before on the ridge of Mont St Jean, two dozen miles to the north.

Territorial divisions flanking the BEF on the left, General d'Amade. By the book, going to see the Territorials was correct: commanders of flanking units and formations must liaise, though the rule is that they do so 'left to right'; strictly, therefore, it was for d'Amade to liaise with the BEF (he certainly didn't have anyone to liaise with on his left). But in the circumstances, this is too pedantic, and Sir John French had every right to want to see the flank for himself. It was also understandable that he would want to see the commander of the scratch 19th Infantry Brigade, and even its battalions, hitherto on lines-of-communication duty; but it was not absolutely necessary, and certainly not to deliver the orders in person, for he had already placed the brigade under Allenby's command (there is no record of why not under II Corps, for if the brigade were aligned with them on the canal, rather than held back and to the flank, it made more sense to do so – and Smith-Dorrien would hardly have been careless of his own flank. As it was, the Cavalry Division was now tethered somewhat by a force that could only move at the speed of a marching boot). Above all, it was extraordinary for the commander-in-chief to absent himself from his headquarters – with which he had no communications except by car and despatch rider – for so long: it would be early afternoon before he returned to his advance headquarters at Bavai, by which time six German divisions were in contact with II Corps, and the troops in the Mons salient were having to fall back.

The sound of battle as Sir John French left II Corps headquarters was the shelling of 8th Brigade in the Mons salient, and of the 4th Royal Fusiliers of 9th Brigade at Nimy on its western side.* The morning had broken in mist and drizzling rain – it had been torrential for a few

---

* Rifle fire from (probably) the German 31st (Thuringian) Infantry Regiment at about eight o'clock had killed possibly the first man of the BEF in a ground action – Private John Parr, a 16-year-old rifleman (the usual story of giving a false age on enlistment) of the 4th Middlesex to the right of the Fusiliers opposite the village of Obourg. Curiously, and impossibly, the date of death on his headstone in the Commonwealth War Graves Commission cemetery at St-Symphorien is 21 August. There are a number of fanciful stories about Parr being a bicycle scout, shot while on reconnaissance north of the canal, but the evidence is that he was killed with his platoon, possibly at an outpost in Obourg. There is correspondence in the files between the War Office and his mother when he was posted missing in which one of the company officers attests to seeing him on the twenty-third. That there is nothing more positive is indicative of the confusion of the fighting that morning (and the nature of the terrain), and the size of the infantry companies – some 200 men each.

hours either side of midnight – with German scouts soon almost literally stumbling on the outposts, and the Fusiliers had captured two 'uhlan' officers, whom they identified as 3rd Hussars, III Corps' cavalry. Similar skirmishes across the 7 miles of front would soon build up an accurate picture of what the BEF was really facing – the full weight of Kluck's 1st Army. Smith-Dorrien saw some of the fighting for himself: as soon as the conference was finished he 'motored to the left of [his] outpost line at Pommeroeul, and leaving the car crossed the bridge and saw an interesting scrap between the Cornwalls and German scouts'.* It must indeed have been an interesting experience for a man who had watched the Zulus attack at Isandhlwana.

One of the novel features of the BEF's first battle was that it took place not only in a built-up, industrialized area – for the first time in the army's history – but with civilians all about them, for they too had been caught unawares by the direction and strength of the German advance. As the morning mist cleared, promising another day of fine weather, the church bells rang and villagers began walking to mass in their Sunday best. Even the trains were still running in and out of Mons, crowded with holiday-makers.† Children brought coffee and rolls to the Fusiliers at Nimy. The day before, as they had rested in the *grand place*, the good citizens of Mons had brought them bread, eggs and fruit – and wine, too, though the officers were just able to stop them in time (a sweltering day and a tiring march . . .). And the battalion had not been short of help in the afternoon building barricades and digging scrapes.

Many of them also knew they were treading in the footsteps of history. To get here, the day before they had marched across the battlefield of Malplaquet, where in 1709 the duke of Marlborough had won a bloody victory before capturing the fortress of Mons, and in the evening had bivouacked but a couple of dozen miles from the field of Waterloo – though unusually, for most regiments bore one or the other, the Fusiliers bore neither battle honour on their colours.

---

* Of the day as a whole, the Cornwalls' adjutant Arthur Acland recorded in his journal the battalion's 'somewhat poor opinion of the Germans' rifle shooting'.
† The progress of the Germans was being monitored quite effectively by the Belgian state railways, however. When a patrol of the 1st East Surreys towards the east of II Corps' line crossed the canal soon after dawn, they found the railwaymen at Hautrage busily getting engines in steam to haul rolling stock to safety, south.

They knew that this bit of country was called the 'cockpit of Europe' – the place of battles for centuries – but not that within twenty-four hours they would be adding to that long list. Nevertheless, if there was optimism still flowing down the chain of command on the evening of the twenty-second, there was enough sixth sense and battlefield discipline within the brigades to take some serious precautions against attack. The Fusiliers worked until last light before resting – and even then they stood down only two in every three (a high state of alert), with strict orders to build no fires and show no lights. Conscious that the time was at hand, many wrote letters home.

The 4th Fusiliers designated their companies not in the usual line-infantry fashion – A to D – but W, X, Y and Z.* Colonel McMahon had sited Y and Z Companies forward on the canal, with X Company in support near battalion headquarters at Nimy station and W Company in reserve just north of Mons. Lieutenant Maurice Dease's machine-gun section was with Y Company at the northernmost fixed bridge, which carried the single-track railway line across the canal (the road bridge, 600 yards to the north, had been swung back). He had sited one Vickers machine gun on either side of the track on the home bank, in sandbag emplacements tucked into the buttresses, which could be covered by two rifle platoons dug in adjacent to the bridge (the section had worked late into the night strengthening the position, Dease himself filling sandbags with track ballast). Thus positioned, the machine guns would be able to enfilade any head-on attack (that is, fire down the file, the length of the column) but could be pinpointed more easily than if they had taken a position to a flank to rake the bridge end to end, especially if they were to remain in place to beat off a series of attacks. *Infantry Training* stressed that 'machine guns are essentially weapons of opportunity. The power of the gun is best used to develop unexpected bursts of fire against favourable targets'; nevertheless, it also stated plainly that 'when the situation calls for effective fire, fire effect must not be sacrificed to

---

* There is much speculation why (4RF were not the only battalion to do so). The four-company organization had only recently been introduced – hitherto the eight companies were numbered, not lettered – and it has been suggested that some regiments found that the regional accents of their soldiers sounded the letters A–D with insufficient distinction.

obtain concealment'. Dease must have sited his guns with the words ringing in his ears.

The artillery, too, were having a difficult time trying to find gun positions. *Field Artillery Training* (1914), in its section on 'Wood and Village Fighting', did not anticipate the sort of country in which the Royal Field Artillery (RFA) batteries now found themselves, dealing with villages as relatively small built-up areas with open ground between them rather than the conurbation that fringed the canal. Four 18-pounders of 107 Battery had managed to find a place on the eastern edge of Mons (near Hyon) from where they could, close to the limit of their range, support Y and Z Companies of the Fusiliers, but elsewhere guns had to be brought forward in pairs or even singly for action in the direct-fire role.*

The sappers, as usual, found themselves with more tasks than resources (their motto, like the gunners' – *Ubique*, 'Everywhere' – was never more apt), but only now was the critical shortage of demolition charges fully exposed. All night they had been helping the infantry to make strong points the length of the canal, and supervising Belgian volunteer labour preparing the fallback position. Early in the morning they received Smith-Dorrien's warning order to prepare the bridges for demolition, but all they had been able to do by first light was reconnoitre them – eighteen in all, and only four field troops for the job (each troop comprising three officers and seventy-four other ranks). But it was not only a question of a shortage of sappers and a lack of suitable HE – all the bridges were iron and steel;[†] there was a real problem with detonators. Not long before mobilization the Ordnance had withdrawn all the 'fuze instantaneous', which were out-of-date, and mobilization had run ahead of the replacement programme. The demolition parties would therefore have to use safety fuze and electrical firing, and there was only one exploder per section – twelve in all for the entire corps front.[‡] And since each bridge needed multiple (cutting) charges that had to be fired simultaneously for best effect, the work needed a good deal of ingenuity – which meant experienced

---

* Despite the obvious drawbacks of being at the limit of their range, there were advantages: the guns would probably be beyond the range of the German artillery, and they could keep firing for longer once the infantry began to pull back.
† See chapter 4.
‡ The exploder, the size of a large shoe box, generated the power to fire the detonator when the plunger was pushed down.

NCOs. The *Field Service Pocketbook* (1914) helpfully advised that 'other explosives [apart from gun-cotton and cordite] may sometimes be obtained, the most likely being gunpowder and dynamite', and one of the field company commanders sent men into Mons to try to get some, but without success. It remains one of the unexplained ironies of the battle that just about the only advantage in fighting in a built-up coal-mining area – the proximity of explosives and detonators – yielded nothing. Indeed, with only a little more notice the shot-firers (the men who fired the blasting charges underground) of the Borinage, as the region was known, might have been able to prepare all the bridges with gelatin-dynamite charges. But that said, if GHQ had been on top of the intelligence picture the crossings could all have been blown by first light without outside help.*

As it was, the work could not begin properly until eight o'clock, and since the bridges in the Mons salient were by then under fire it quickly proved hazardous in the extreme laying charges in the Fusiliers' area and in that of the 8th Brigade to their right. Lieutenant Wilfred Holt of the 56th Field Company RE was killed trying to get onto the 4th Middlesex's bridge at rue des Bragnons, and the rest of his section were captured.

Soon afterwards the German 18th Division began its attack on the salient, led by two brigades side by side, the 85th (Holstein) and 86th (Schleswig-Holstein) Regiments: many of them were ethnic Danes, the bounty of the Prusso-Danish War of 1864 (and many of whom – those who survived the war – would become Danish nationals once again after the plebiscite in 1920). It was to be a mutual baptism of fire: only the scouts of the Middlesex and the Fusiliers had traded shots with German cavalry so far, but the infantry of Lieutenant-General Ferdinand von Quast's IX Corps had yet to fire a single round (except at aircraft), the Belgians having fallen back on Antwerp before the right wing of Kluck's army could make contact. As ever, it was first

---

* Strictly, the Borinage was the mining region (from which the name derives) of south-western Belgium, in the province of Hainault, south-west of Mons, where coal had been dug since the Middle Ages. The American Charles White, in *The Belgic Revolution of 1830* (London, 1835) – about the revolution which, arguably, set Britain on its course for war – wrote: 'The Borains [the inhabitants of the Borinage], like the dark spirits of the melo-drame, rose from their mines, and helter-skelter pushed upon the capital.' It seems ironic that the Borains' emergence from the deep should have brought the BEF to these very same pit-heads eighty-four years later.

the noise that shook the defenders: 'I was frightened by [it],' admitted Private Robert Jack of the Middlesex; 'I'd never heard anything like it. Most of the shells were bursting well behind us, but there was also a strange whistling sound as the bullets came over . . . There were four of us in a rifle-pit and our officer walked over to us and I remember thinking: "Get *down*, you silly bugger." Later on I heard the poor man was killed.'*

In the main the attacks came in waves, the men shoulder-to-shoulder – *das Tuchfühl*, the 'touch of cloth' – eight battalions, some 7,000–8,000 men, against four companies (two each of the Fusiliers and Middlesex) numbering fewer than 1,000. Corporal Holbrook of the Fusiliers, the commanding officer's orderly and one of the best shots in the battalion, remembered the scene well, and his astonishment:

> Bloody Hell! You couldn't see the earth for them there were that many. Time after time they gave the order '*Rapid Fire*' . . . You'd see a lot of them coming in a mass on the other side of the canal and you just let them have it. They kept retreating, and then coming forward, and then retreating again. Of course, we were losing men, and a *lot* of the officers especially when the Germans started this shrapnel shelling and, of course, *they* had machine guns – masses of them! But we kept flinging them back . . . I don't know how many times we saw them off. They didn't get anywhere near us with this rapid fire.†

The Germans were raked, too, by flanking fire from the Middlesex's

---

* Quoted in Ascoli, *The Mons Star*.
† Quoted in Lyn Macdonald, *1914: The Days of Hope* (London, 1987). The officers, in order to observe the enemy and to control the fire, could not take the same cover as the riflemen. The stories of Germans mown down in masses have undoubtedly been exaggerated, however. Terence Zuber, a former US infantry officer and University of Wurzburg PhD (and author of *Inventing the Schlieffen Plan* – see chapter 5), writes in *The Mons Myth* (Charleston, SC, 2010), an analysis of the after-action reports of both sides, that the rushes from one tactical bound to the next, and the taking cover when under fire, were frequently mistaken for the effects of the BEF's musketry, whereas the tendency of the British infantry was to fire high (see, for example, the testimony of Lieutenant Roupell of the East Surreys on page 314 below). But British reports are simply too consistent to be wholly mistaken; and the fact is that much superior numbers were held off for a significant time by rifle fire alone. Zuber's is, nevertheless, an important corrective to the idea that the Germans only came on like cattle, and that for the BEF it was little more than a day on the rifle range; for such a reading does neither side justice.

machine guns and those of the Royal Irish ordered forward to support by the brigade commander, Beauchamp Doran (an Irishman and former commanding officer of the Royal Irish Regiment). Shrapnel from 107 Battery's 18-pounders near Hyon burst over them, as well as from guns firing direct, but it was first and foremost a battle of 'musketry' the whole length of the line – just as Waterloo had been. And it would be the last: from now on the BEF artillery would increasingly determine the ground on which a stand would be made.

On the receiving end of this musketry, principally at the hands of the East Surreys about Les Herbières, were Walter Bloem and his Brandenburgers. Beaten back in their first attack, they had re-formed and were advancing a second time, in short rushes:

> From now on the English fire gradually weakened, almost ceased. No hail of bullets greeted each rush forward, and we were able to get within 150 yards of the canal bank. I said to [Lieutenant] Gräser: 'Now we'll do one more 30-yard rush, all together, then fix bayonets and charge the houses and the canal banks.'
>
> The enemy must have been waiting for this moment to get us all together at close range, for immediately the line rose it was as if the hounds of hell had been loosed at us, yelling, barking, hammering as a mass of lead swept in among us . . . [Gräser is killed.]
>
> From now on matters went from bad to worse. Wherever I looked, right or left, were dead or wounded, quivering in convulsions, groaning terribly, blood oozing from fresh wounds. The worst was that the heaviest firing now began to come on us from the strip of wood that jutted out into the meadow in our right rear: It must be our own men, I thought, who could not imagine we had gone on so far and now evidently took us for the enemy. Luckily we had a way of stopping that: 'Who has the red flag?' Grenadier Just produced it, and lying on his back waved it wildly. No result; in fact the fire from the right rear became even heavier. The brave Just stood up and with complete unconcern continued to wave the red flag more frantically than ever. But still no effect.

And for the simple reason that the fire was from the East Surreys' machine-gun section and part of their C Company. 'My proud, beautiful battalion . . . shot to pieces by the English, the English we laughed at,' groaned Bloem. And when they advanced next day, the 'English' having withdrawn, he was astonished to find the sandbagged machine-gun emplacement in the wood, and how cunningly it was concealed: 'Wonderful, as we marched on, how they had converted every house, every wall into a little fortress: the experience no doubt of old soldiers gained in a dozen colonial wars; possibly even some of the butchers of the Boers were among them.'

No doubt; but it lay, too, in a tradition reaching much further back – to the loop-holed walls of Hougoumont and the little fortress of La Haye Sainte a couple of dozen miles away.*

Smith-Dorrien had ordered the troops in the salient to 'make a stubborn resistance' before withdrawing to the more defensible ground to the south of Mons. Stubborn it certainly was – and ironic, too, that the man who had done the most to transform the BEF's marksmanship into fifteen devastating rounds a minute (McMahon) was in command of the battalion (the 4th Fusiliers) that was now to bear the brunt of the Germans' renewed efforts to gain a crossing into the salient. By late morning his officers were becoming casualties in alarming numbers, and the machine-gunners too. Each time a machine gun stopped firing Maurice Dease would dash to it from his trench high on the canal bank 50 yards behind to get it into action again. Inevitably on one of these forays he was hit – in the knee. Y Company Commander, Captain Lionel Ashburner, urged him to go back to the battalion aid post in Nimy to have the wound dressed, but he refused. Having helped pull clear the wounded gunners from the left-hand gun and got replacements up, Dease ran as best he could across the railway track to the right-hand gun which had also stopped firing. Halfway across he was shot in the side, but still he managed to crawl to the cover of the sandbags, where one of Y Company's platoon commanders, Lieutenant Frederick Steele, made him lie down and get field dressings to the wounds. Dease became agitated each time one of the Vickers stopped firing, however, and not long afterwards crawled back to the centre of the track to control the fire of

* Bloem's account (in *The Advance from Mons, 1914*) should, however, be read with a degree of circumspection. Zuber believes that Bloem, a novelist (and therefore not to be trusted, one suspects Zuber implies), embellished his account of Mons (Zuber calls it 'lurid') and that it was published in English because it suited the purposes of the official historian (Brigadier-General James Edmonds), who also wrote the foreword. There may be truth in this, but the book was originally published in Leipzig in 1916; and with many of the named participants still alive, and in the prevailing mood of Germany at that stage of the war, it could hardly have been a work of very great distortion.

both guns. After a few more minutes the right-hand gunner was hit, so Dease crawled to the gun to take his place. A little later, with all but two of the machine-gun section dead or wounded, Dease himself was hit a third time (by some accounts, it may have been a fifth), and soon after he died.

Corporal Henry Parmenter, the surviving NCO, crawled to the gun in Maurice Dease's place, but was wounded in the head and fell down the embankment (which probably saved his life, for he was pulled into cover and taken to the regimental aid post). The lone fusilier manning the left-hand gun, the last of the section unscathed, was now wounded and his gun put out of action. Lieutenant Steele called to the riflemen along the bank for a volunteer who knew how the Vickers mechanism worked, and Private Sidney Godley, twenty-five, the son of a painter and decorator from East Grinstead, ran forward. He had been a fusilier for five years and evidently had picked up enough to chance his luck. Under heavy fire still, with Steele he hauled off three bodies from the gun and managed to get it working.

Soon afterwards, at about one-thirty, the battalion was ordered to withdraw, and Y Company began falling back. Godley continued to hold off the Germans even though he too had now been hit, and then a little later, with the water cooling-jacket riddled with bullets, the gun jammed and Godley was wounded again, this time a bullet in the head. Nevertheless, before collapsing he managed to heave the barrel into the canal.

'Machine guns skilfully handled may be of great assistance in movements of this nature,' says *Infantry Training* (1914); 'and the detachments must, if necessary, be prepared to sacrifice themselves to cover the retirement of their infantry.' If this seems incredible to read, it is what the Fusiliers' machine-gun section did. Maurice Dease and Sidney Godley were awarded the Victoria Cross, the first two of the Great War – and Godley would be informed of his not by his commanding officer but by the commandant of his prisoner-of-war camp, for although he had been left presumed dead, he was in fact found by the Germans and his wounds deftly treated.*

*By way of illustrating how difficult it is to be certain of the various accounts, it is worth mentioning that repeated attempts have apparently been made over the years to find the machine gun that Godley threw into the canal, but without success. Zuber, in *The Mons Myth*, says that the 84th Infantry Regiment war diary states that it captured two machine guns on taking the bridge. This does not mean that one or the other account

The Middlesex, to the right, had been having just as bad a time, not least because they held double the frontage of the Fusiliers and, with no continuation of the defensive line east, their right flank was vulnerable (the French had no troops north of the Sambre except for a few cavalry patrols, and the Royal Irish, holding the Bois la Haut, were a good 2 miles *behind* the canal, with the Royal Scots and the Gordons extending south-east from the Bois towards Harmignies to make touch with Haig's I Corps). Indeed, the Mons salient was rather more than the northerly kink in the line of the canal: it was also the eastward swelling into the no-man's-land that was bounded by the canal and the Sambre as far as their confluence at Charleroi – and which was already becoming free-ranging territory for Freiherr Manfred von Richthofen's Cavalry Corps, and would soon be manoeuvring space for Quast's IX Corps.

The Middlesex's commanding officer, Lieutenant-Colonel Charles Hull,* had sited two companies forward, each of about 200 men, B left, D right, with A and C Companies in support a thousand yards behind. C Company therefore was effectively the right-flank protection for the battalion – and on the right flank was the Bois d'Havre, offering a covered approach for the Germans. Having, with the 4th Fusiliers, sent the German 18th Division reeling mid-morning, the Middlesex were then faced with the 17th Division – Schleswig-Holsteiners and Mecklenburgers – supported by IX Corps' concentrated artillery, which many of the BEF's infantrymen thought

---

has been falsified: for example, Godley may well have heaved his gun over the side of the bridge and believed it had fallen into the canal; but the gun emplacement was sandbagged into the buttresses some yards back from the water's edge, so the gun might well have simply tumbled down the bank to the towpath. A severely wounded man – especially a defiantly brave one – can be forgiven for leaping to a conclusion. Zuber is a very considerable military historian, but he can be as uncritically accepting of German regimental accounts as he accuses British historians of being of their own (to take just one example, and a laughable one, he refers to a night patrol believing it heard the rustling of a British outpost, which turned out to be 'frost thawing on the sugar beets' – a curious meteorological phenomenon in August). Too often he uses 21st-century norms (and terms), and his remorselessly revisionist polemic frequently leads him to fight, as the Germans say, *von Gänseblümchen nach Gänseblümchen* – from daisy to daisy. Nevertheless, his analysis is frequently compelling. Godley received his VC from the King in 1919.

* Later Major-General Sir Charles Hull, commanding 16th (Irish) Division (and the father of Field Marshal Sir Richard Hull, who would command the 1st Armoured Division in Italy in the Second World War – a singular double for father and son – and be the last CIGS).

was being directed by the increasing number of German aircraft overhead.*

'Hold the front, feel for the flanks' had always been the Prussian army's maxim, and IX Corps' commander, Quast, a singularly aggressive-minded Prussian, was doing just this. Soon the forward platoons of the Middlesex were getting the uneasy feeling that there were Germans behind as well as in front of them. 'It was like sitting in a sack not knowing what was going on outside except that, whatever it was, it was noisy and dangerous,' recalled Private Tom Bradley of D Company: 'The place was swarming with Germans and by mid-morning they had even got round behind us . . . By noon we had lost all but one of our company officers.'

By noon the Germans had forced a number of crossings – the frontage was just too great for the Middlesex to cover every yard – and B and D Companies were being pushed back.† Both company commanders were soon either killed or wounded, together with the forty-year-old Major William Abell as he brought A Company forward to support B, and more sappers who were making a vain attempt to blow the bridges. In fact, only two of the eight bridges in the 3rd Division's sector would be blown, though not for want of courage on the part of the sappers, two of whom – Captain Theodore Wright and Lance-Corporal Charles Jarvis – would win the VC that day, coolly working under fire to lay the explosives.‡

Brigadier Doran now sent the 2nd Royal Irish forward to keep open the mouth of the sack so that the Middlesex and the Fusiliers could extricate themselves. They were met by artillery and rifle fire, and the

* *Die Fliegertruppen des deutschen Kaiserreiches* (usually simply *Fliegertruppen*), as the German army air service was known in 1914, had in fact no greater technological capability than the RFC, although their cooperation with artillery by signal lamp was perhaps more practised. Their influence on the direction of artillery at Mons was probably next to nothing.
† Musketier Oskar Niemeyer, from Hamburg, swam the canal and managed to swing the Nimy road bridge back across before being killed by fire from the Fusiliers. He is buried at St-Symphorien military cemetery, not far from Private Parr.
‡ Captain Wright and Lance-Corporal Jarvis were both wounded. Three weeks later Wright, thirty-one, was killed behaving just as heroically. Jarvis, thirty-three, a reservist (he had left the colours in 1907), worked for ninety minutes to lay twenty-two charges on the bridge at Jemappes, sending back his 'assistants' in the Scots Fusiliers when the fire became too hot. Wounded again two months later, he was invalided home and spent the rest of the war at Portsmouth dockyard. His father, Charles Alfred Jarvis, a coastguard at Fraserburgh, had himself been decorated for bravery by the Royal Humane Society.

Lieutenant-General Sir Douglas Haig, commander of I Corps – 53, fit and active, but doubting both the BEF's plan and the man at its head.

General Sir Horace Smith-Dorrien, summoned to take command of II Corps after Sir James Grierson's fatal heart attack, leaving the train at Folkestone for the crossing to France.

Left: The French commander-in-chief, General Joseph Joffre, with the commanders of the two armies he expected would see the bulk of the fighting under Plan XVII, Noel de Castelnau (2nd Army) in Lorraine and Paul Pau (Army of Alsace). **Below left**: General Charles Lanrezac, on whose left the BEF were to fight – a prickly man whose truculence at the outset made for poor relations with Sir John French. **Below right**: 'The most important subaltern in the British army': Louis Edward Spears, liaison officer with Lanrezac's 5th Army.

Lieutenant-General Louis Franchet d'Espèrey – 'Desperate Frankie' – who replaced Lanrezac in command of 5th Army before the counter-offensive on the Marne.

General Ferdinand Foch: as commandant of the French staff college before the war he had a profound influence on military planning, and on Henry Wilson.

Lord (Horatio Herbert) Kitchener, appointed secretary for war while a field marshal; his appearance in Paris in uniform greatly irritated Sir John French.

Field Marshal Sir John French (pictured here in 1915): according to Spears, 'the man who never lost his head'. But there were severe doubts as to his suitability for the highest command.

'The miracle on the Marne': General Joseph Gallieni, the diminutive but pugnacious commander of the Paris garrison, rushed troops forward in taxis and buses to hold the line of the river as the Germans closed on the city.

Above: 'Demain, en avant!' Cameronians crossing a pontoon bridge over the Marne in the great counter-offensive that began on 6 September. Henry Wilson wagered that they would be across the border into Germany in six weeks. **Right**: The high-water mark of the counter-offensive: the Cameronians by their shallow trenches on the Aisne ten days later. Despite the BEF's repeated attacks, and those of the French to their left and right, the Germans managed to hold firm. **Below**: Some of the RFA's 18-pounders during the BEF's redeployment after the Aisne battles – 'the race for the sea'.

Right: J Battery RHA in action near the Messines ridge in October, during what would become known as the First Battle of Ypres – a desperate attempt to outflank the extended German line, and in turn to prevent a breakthrough by fresh troops.

Above: 'From now on the spade will be as great a necessity as the rifle': 11th Hussars unhorsed and in rudimentary trenches towards the close of First Ypres, November. Deep trenches would soon stretch from the North Sea to the Swiss border.

Below: Movement restored: British cavalry passing the remains of Albert Cathedral, 22 August 1918. The 5th Lancers were the last cavalry regiment to leave Mons in 1914, and the first British troops to re-enter the city on 11 November 1918.

unnerving sight of fleeing patients from the mental hospital behind C Company's position.

Without the canal as both a barrier and a reference point, and under increasingly heavy shelling, the fighting on this flank now became intense and confused. D Company of the Irish were badly mauled and had to withdraw to the cover of Hyon. All the officers of A Company were soon dead or wounded, and C Company – numbering only thirty or so, the rest having gone forward to the canal with the machine guns earlier – had to drive back an attack with the bayonet, led by the company commander. Seeing D Company cut up badly, Quartermaster-Sergeant Thomas Fitzpatrick, a Cavan man, gathered up forty or so drivers, cooks and orderlies in the transport lines and took them forward to where he found the left-hand company of the Gordons (the battalion were strung out in scrapes the length of the Chaussée de Beaumont, which ran north-west from Harmignies) and joined them in defence of the crucial crossroads behind the Bois d'Havre. He did not abandon the position until eleven that night, having lost over half his party. It was distinguished conduct by any measure – not least by an NCO whose prime responsibility was D Company's water and rations – and he was subsequently awarded the Distinguished Conduct Medal, and commissioned the following year.

In the more open country of the right flank, with clearer sight-lines for the artillery forward observation officers, the gunners were at least able to fire as batteries rather than by sections or single guns. The three batteries of XL (40) Field Brigade were eventually disposed the length of the hill of the Bois la Haut and late in the afternoon were able to help stop in its tracks an attack by 75th Bremen Regiment. But they had their casualties too, including two battery commanders, one of them killed, and when it came to extricating the guns they would need the bayonets of the Gordons to clear the way.

By the mid-afternoon of that sweltering Sunday, the fighting had intensified in the 5th Division's area too as Kluck's weary III and then IV Corps wheeled into line and finally closed up to the canal. The East Surreys were only too eager to meet them with fifteen rounds a minute. 'The enemy came through the wood about 200 yards in front, they presented a magnificent target, and we opened rapid fire,' wrote one platoon commander, yet another Irish-born officer – the

22-year-old Lieutenant George Roupell, who would win the VC the following year:

> The men were very excited as this was their first 'shot in anger'. Despite the short range a number of them were firing high but I found it hard to control the fire as there was so much noise. Eventually I drew my sword and walked along the line beating the men on the backside and, as I got their attention, telling them to fire low. So much for all our beautiful fire orders taught in peace time!*

All along the canal from Mons to Condé now the infantry of the 5th Division were cutting down the flower of Brandenburg. Not a single German crossed the bridges or locks all afternoon, and many an outpost remained north of the canal until as late as six o'clock (about an hour before dusk). The GOC, Sir Charles Fergusson, would be removed from command in October when the division – a shadow of its Mons self – failed to press home the attack at Ypres; but on 23 August his judgement was as steady as it had been during the Curragh incident, when he had kept all but the 3rd Cavalry Brigade from heaping coals on the fire. His sappers were working hard on the bridges, and he was sure he could hold the line until the next morning.

When Sir John French returned to Bavai in the middle of the afternoon he found Murray jacketless, his shirt open to the waist, sitting over a map trying to make sense of the reports from II Corps about the situation on the right. In his memoirs French describes his reaction – that of a man who had spent the better part of the day at precisely the opposite end of the battlefield from that at which the decision was being made (or rather, being forced):

> After my conference with the Corps Commanders on the morning of the 23rd, I left General Smith-Dorrien full of confidence in regard to his

---

* Quality will out: George Roupell, born in Tipperary to a future commanding officer of the 1st East Surreys, would temporarily command that battalion in Germany on occupation duties in the winter of 1918–19, before being attached to the force sent to northern Russia in support of the Tsarist resistance to the Communist revolution, where he was taken prisoner and sent to Moscow; he was eventually repatriated in 1920. He was commanding 36th Infantry Brigade in May 1940 when German armour over-ran his headquarters. He and his staff captain evaded capture but were marooned by the Dunkirk evacuation. They worked as labourers on a farm near Rouen for two years until taken first into unoccupied France and then into Spain by the French Resistance, making their way to Gibraltar, and then home by ship.

position, but when I returned to my Headquarters in the afternoon, reports came to hand that he was giving up the salient at Mons because the outpost line at Obourg had been penetrated by the enemy, and that he was also preparing to give up the whole of the line of the canal before nightfall. He said that he anticipated a gap occurring in his line between the 3rd and 5th Divisions in the neighbourhood of Mariette, and he went so far as to make a request for help to the 1st Corps.*

It was, of course, rather more than just penetration of the outpost line: the Fusiliers and Middlesex had been driven back from the canal itself, and the right flank was being enveloped – and these battalions were commanded by two of the finest officers in the BEF, soon to be promoted to command brigades. Nor was Beauchamp Doran, the brigadier, inactive: he was exercising very direct control of his reserves, at times personally leading detachments into position. The problem was simply that II Corps was spread too thinly across a wide front – 21 miles – and the artillery was not able to play a full part in the battle (they should, after all, have comprised three, not two, divisions).

The other problem was Sir John French's own 'stubborn resistance' – to the idea that II Corps was facing any real danger. 'Up to this time,' he wrote in *1914*, even with all the evidence at last before him, 'there was no decided threat in any strength on Condé. Sir Horace, therefore, need not have feared an imminent turning movement, and, as regards his front, he was nowhere threatened by anything more than *cavalry supported by small bodies of infantry* [italics added].' For the source of this encouraging appreciation it is probably unnecessary to look further than Henry Wilson, who seems to have been occupying some parallel military universe, convinced by 'careful calculation' that the BEF was faced by one corps and a cavalry division, or possibly two corps. II Corps headquarters had positively identified two German corps and a cavalry division by late morning – *before* the attack extended to 5th Division's front. Nevertheless, 'I persuaded Murray and Sir John that this was so,' Wilson wrote in his diary, 'with the result that I was allowed to draft orders for an attack tomorrow.'

* French, *1914*. In his first despatch, written just two weeks later, he very clearly dissembles: 'About 3 p.m. on Sunday, the 23rd, reports began coming in to the effect that the enemy was *commencing* [italics added] an attack on the Mons line, apparently in some strength.'

Wilson's astonishing appreciation was not the view of the 8th Brigade, nor of 3rd Division as a whole, and certainly not of II Corps. Nor was it the view of the RFC, who had been in the air since dawn and who, not surprisingly, observed what they had observed the day before – but even further advanced. Needless to say, neither was it the view of Macdonogh (Sir John French's own chief of intelligence); but the orders for the attack survived until about eight o'clock, when a telegram from Joffre confirmed that there were at least three corps facing the BEF.

Yet Sir John French clearly resented Smith-Dorrien's withdrawal: 'Reports came to hand that he was giving up the salient at Mons because the outpost line at Obourg had been penetrated by the enemy, and that he was also preparing to give up the whole of the line of the canal before nightfall' – the tone is unmistakably disapproving, even disdainful. Yet it is difficult to imagine that James Grierson would have taken any other view than Smith-Dorrien's, had he still been the corps commander – nor indeed Herbert Plumer had he been appointed instead, for the 'Plume' was notably cautious. For any commander – let alone a commander-in-chief – to have so little confidence in the judgement of one of his key subordinates was a problem of disastrous potential. Nor did it make sense: II Corps commander was a peppery man, but he knew his business – and he was certainly getting about the battlefield. At about seven o'clock that evening Smith-Dorrien had learned that the Germans had penetrated his line near Frameries:

I had no troops left, and all I could do was to request the 5th Division to push out to their right, which they did by sending the 1st Bedfords to Paturages. Knowing the gap was appreciable owing to the left flank of the 3rd Division in retiring having failed to join up with the right flank of the 5th Division, and that if the Germans realised it there was nothing to prevent their pushing through in large numbers and rendering our position untenable—

—he sent a precautionary message to GHQ:

Third Division report at 6.47 p.m. the Germans are in front of his main position and are not attacking at present, they are, however, working round 3rd Division on left flank. If it should appear that there is a danger

316

of my centre being pierced I can see no course but to order a general retirement on Bavai position. Have I your permission to adopt this course if it
appears necessary?

Sir John French's account differs slightly, but tellingly (he had by
this time returned to his main headquarters at Le Cateau): 'Every
report I was now receiving at Headquarters pointed to the early
necessity of a retirement of the British Forces in view of the general
strategic situation, and I did not, therefore, deem it desirable to interfere with the 2nd Corps commander. Reports of German activity
on his front continued to be received from the G.O.C. 2nd Corps. At
7.15 p.m. he asked for permission to retire on Bavai.'

What French writes in his first despatch, however, is far more
emphatic: 'The right [he meant the *left*] of the 3rd Division, under
General Hamilton, was at Mons, which formed a dangerous salient;
and I directed the Commander of the Second Corps not to keep the
troops on this salient for too long, but, if threatened seriously, to draw
back the centre behind Mons.'

But the general officer commanding II Corps had not in fact 'asked
permission to retire on Bavai' (which implied that he wanted to do so
at once), only for the authority to do so 'if it appears necessary'. The
difference is neither pedantic nor insignificant. What is more, if every
report the commander-in-chief was receiving (not simply from
II Corps) 'pointed to the early necessity of a retirement of the British
Forces in view of the general strategic situation' (a remarkable change
of outlook since the three o'clock view that they faced only 'cavalry
supported by small bodies of infantry'), why was he not telling Smith-
Dorrien this and arranging with Haig how it was to be done? In short,
why was he not exercising command? The 'fog of war' is a concept
well known to all military commanders, but it should not be confused
with a smokescreen.

Fortunately, Smith-Dorrien was managing pretty well on his own:

I then jumped into a motor and went to General Haig's head-quarters at
Bonnet, some four miles away, and asked if he would allow Haking's 5th
Infantry Brigade, which was on the road about two and a half miles from
Frameries, to push on to cover the gap. I found Hubert Hamilton's [GOC
3rd Division] G.S.O.2, Lieutenant-Colonel F. B. Maurice, there on the same

quest. Haig readily gave his consent, and Maurice dashed off to tell Haking. The situation had, however, been almost restored by the 9th Brigade, and the Germans driven back before the 5th Brigade reached Frameries; but I would remark that although I had contracted my front to about twelve miles, it was still far too large for the troops I had and every man was practically in the front line, so that a break through, with no reserves to meet it, must have entailed retreat. Haking's borrowed Brigade remained to hold the gap.

The Germans, however, were in no better position to continue the advance than Smith-Dorrien was to stem it. They had taken many more casualties than II Corps. Curiously, the figures have never been reliably established, but they were probably in the region of 6,000–10,000 killed and wounded, the 12th Brandenburgers – Bloem's regiment – alone suffering over 500. Nor was there effective co-ordination between the commanders of IX and III Corps, for Kluck's headquarters seemed to have as poor a grip on the battle as Sir John French's. The great tide of field grey was content with its high-water mark that evening along a line about 3 miles south of the canal.

And now, at 8.40 p.m., Sir John French, even though convinced of the 'early necessity of a retirement of the British Forces in view of the general strategic situation' (he says 'British Forces' – the BEF – not merely II Corps), sent a peremptory order to Smith-Dorrien: 'I will stand the attack on the ground now occupied by the troops. You will therefore strengthen your position by every possible means during the night.'*

The first sentence was all that a corps commander needed to be told, especially one wearing four stars. The second reads distinctly tetchily. And it was the only formal order issued from GHQ the entire day.

Nevertheless Smith-Dorrien was confident enough that he could hold where he was, especially now that Haig's I Corps was in a position to give proper support. II Corps had lost nearly 1,700 killed and wounded, and as many unaccounted for, some of whom had been taken prisoner. I Corps had suffered very few losses, for they had

*It is worth remembering that 'the position now occupied by the troops' drawn on a map in a headquarters does not always tell the whole story: the 8th Brigade, for example, did not get into position, complete, until 3 a.m.

scarcely been engaged (an officer of the 1st Guards Brigade described it laconically as 'I Corps Rest Day'). Likewise the Cavalry Division and 19th Brigade on the left, whose battalions had not fired their first shots until about five o'clock, had lost relatively few men. The wounded were being evacuated with unprecedented efficiency by the Army Medical Services, or else tended by Belgian civilians, or even German field ambulances. The dead lay where they had fallen, in time to be buried by the Germans with due respect. Seventeen hundred casualties: the figure was trifling by the standards of the battles to come, but it represented some 5 per cent of the two divisions properly engaged, and probably 10 per cent of their fighting echelon – and concentrated in the 8th and 9th Brigades (half the casualties had been sustained by the Fusiliers, the Middlesex and the Irish, whose machine-gun sections had worked wonders, but at huge cost). It was not a loss to be alarmed by, but neither could it be ignored – and certainly not repeated daily for long.

Chapter Sixteen

SHRAPNEL MONDAY

> It must be a point of honour with troops never to retire, without
> orders, from a position they have been detailed to hold to the end.
>
> *Field Artillery Training* (1914)

Sir John French had only been able to snatch a very little sleep the night before Mons: the unexpected situation on the right had seen to that. And now, just as he might have been contemplating a few hours' repose before the BEF roused itself again to 'stand the attack on the ground now occupied by the troops', the most important subaltern in the British army arrived from General Lanrezac's headquarters with news that was truly hair-raising: the French 5th Army was about to retire some 15 miles, completely exposing the BEF's right flank.

The time of Spears' arrival at Le Cateau is disputed. French says 1 a.m.; Spears believes this is 'mistaken', and that it was 'much earlier . . . probably about 11', while some sources put it as early as ten. This is more significant than may at first appear. In his own account of the fighting, *1914*, French says that disquieting reports about the situation on his right had been arriving 'from late afternoon':

These were confirmed later in a telegram from French Headquarters, which arrived at half-past eleven at night. It clearly showed that our present position was strategically untenable; *but this conclusion had been forced upon me much earlier in the evening* [italics added] when I received a full

320

appreciation of the situation as it then appeared at French General Headquarters. General Joffre also told me that his information led him to expect that I might be attacked the next day by at least three German Corps and two Cavalry Divisions.

Sir John French was becoming tired. And the growing realization that he was faced by a stronger threat than he had supposed, and that all was not going well with Joffre's Plan XVII, would have wounded his pride – especially as it also vindicated Smith-Dorrien's earlier 'pessimism' and exposed his own misjudgement. And no doubt too he was wondering if he had been in the right place for most of the day. But it was not in Sir John French's nature, fortunately, either to flap or to despair: Spears would later write of him as 'the man who never lost his head, and on whom danger had the effect it has on a wild boar: he would become morose, furious for a time, harsh, but he would face up and never shirk'. But there was another element to his character, which he might have borrowed from Mr Darcy: 'My temper would perhaps be called resentful. My good opinion once lost, is lost forever.'* Such resentment was already dangerously prominent in his relations with Smith-Dorrien (the rancour going back years); it would now become a moving force in the case of Lanrezac. For Spears' news that the 5th Army was withdrawing without any 'by your leave' – or, indeed, notice (for Spears was acting on his own initiative in driving to GHQ, not the instructions of Lanrezac or his staff) – was to Sir John French nothing short of perfidy. If he, French, had stood his ground the following day, and had Kluck been agile (admittedly a big 'if'), the BEF would have been enveloped and destroyed. Why Lanrezac was prepared to precipitate a calamity on his left flank, which, after the destruction of the BEF, could have had no other outcome but the envelopment of his own army, is to this day inexplicable.†

---

* Jane Austen, *Pride and Prejudice* – which might, indeed, have been an appropriate subtitle for this book.
† The justification for Lanrezac's decision to withdraw – and there have been many attempts at justification, some of them frankly outlandish (such as learning from General Sordet that Sir John French had already decided to withdraw on Maubeuge) – is immaterial: to withdraw without consultation with the BEF was dishonourable, as well as *pas la guerre* (and it was certainly not for Spears alone to pass such information). When faced with calls to go his own way on the retreat from the bruising battle of Ligny, abandoning Wellington before Waterloo, Blücher had refused point blank, with the essence of allied cooperation: 'I have given my word to Wellington.'

Sir John French decided to withdraw only *after* hearing that Lanrezac was doing so, not on the basis of the earlier reports from Joffre and *GQG*. But if he did so bitterly, he was perfectly calm and resolute about it:

> I selected the new line from Jerlain (south-east of Valenciennes) eastwards to Maubeuge. This line had already been reconnoitred. The Corps and Divisional Staff Officers who were called into Headquarters to receive orders, especially those of the 2nd Corps, thought our position was much more seriously threatened than it really was and, in fact, one or two expressed doubts as to the possibility of effecting a retirement in the presence of the enemy in our immediate front. I did not share these views ... I determined to effect the retreat, and orders were issued accordingly. The 1st Army Corps was to move up towards Givry and to take up a good line to cover the retreat of the 2nd Corps towards Bavai, which was to commence at daybreak, about 4.30. Our front and left flank was to be screened and covered by the cavalry and the 19th Infantry Brigade.

But this was asking a good deal – and asking late, for it was one o'clock in the morning before GHQ summoned the principal staff officers of the three subordinate headquarters to Le Cateau for orders (Smith-Dorrien says eleven, but this is probably too early). Why written orders – even a 'warning order' (the barest outline of the intention, and key timings) – were not simply sent out at once is unclear, although Brigadier-General Johnnie Gough (Hubert Gough's younger brother), Haig's chief of staff, wired the outline of the orders as soon as the conference was finished – Haig's diary says he was wakened at 2 a.m. with a telegram from GHQ ordering a 'retreat' – and as a result I Corps was able to get the 1st Division moving by four o'clock.* But Smith-Dorrien's headquarters had no telegraph contact with GHQ, and precious time was lost for II Corps by doubling the journey – Bavai to Le Cateau and back (60 miles, at night, on roads

---

* This sounds easier than in fact it was. Even though I Corps had seen little fighting – certainly compared with II Corps – the 2nd Division's diaries, for example, speak of 'the infantry [being] done up after trying days without regular food and very little sleep', relating how in one position, 80,000 rounds of small arms ammunition had to be left in the trenches, as well as entrenching tools and other supplies, there being no transport and every man already carrying 300 rounds (about 11½ lb/5.2 kg) in addition to his rifle and personal equipment (Everard Wyrall, *The History of the Second Division*, London, 1921).

increasingly clogged by refugees), rather than simply Le Cateau to Bavai; and, writes Smith-Dorrien, 'it was past 3 a.m. ... when [Brigadier-General George Forestier-Walker, his chief of staff] returned to my head-quarters to say that the C.-in-C. had, in view of fresh information, decided that instead of standing to fight, the whole B.E.F. was to retire'. Almost as pressing as time was the question of coordination: 'I naturally asked him for the plan of retirement, and was told that G.H.Q. were issuing none, though he had gathered that the idea was for the I Corps to cover the retirement of the II, but that I was to see Haig and arrange a plan with him.'

If it had been merely a move while not in contact with the enemy, the procedure would have been reasonable enough: allow the commanders to rest, and let the chief of staff (Murray) give co-ordinating instructions to the chiefs of staff of the subordinate headquarters. But it was far from a routine move, and needed the personal stamp of the commander – French himself. A conference at either Haig's or Smith-Dorrien's headquarters would have been the ideal; or, failing that, an operation order detailing 'the plan of retire-ment' followed by a personal visit to the three headquarters (including Allenby's) in succession; but the staff procedure, principally in GHQ that morning, was lamentable.* For a start, it meant that Haig had to do his own staff work, for Gough was still at Le Cateau. In fact he lost no time, showing resource getting round the corps: 'Thanks to the motor I was able to give personal orders to all the chief commanders concerned in the space of an hour' (sending

---

* No doubt Wully Robertson, as he beavered away at the reversal of the logistic plans, was thinking 'I told you so', for earlier in the year, as director of military training at the War Office, he had overseen an exercise for GHQ in the gymnasium at Sandhurst in which Wilson had acted as chief of staff and displayed marked ignorance of some pro-cedures: 'If you go to war with that operations staff,' Robertson told French, 'you are as good as beaten' (quoted in Brian Bond, *The Victorian Army and the Staff College 1854–1914*, London, 1972). As for Forestier-Walker, II Corps' chief of staff, although Smith-Dorrien was always well pleased with him, it seems odd that he should have left GHQ knowing there were so many loose ends to be tied up. He probably took the prag-matic view, however, that since much time had already been lost, the priority was to get the battle procedure started for II Corps' withdrawal, and that face-to-face co-ordination with I Corps would simply have to follow. Why II Corps had set up headquarters where there was no telegraph link is another matter. Although it is the responsibility of the superior headquarters to provide communications to the lower, it is curious that the commanders of both the BEF and II Corps were content with this. At the very least there might have been a telegraph post established close by whence telegrams could be relayed – or even cable extended.

out written orders later). But in II Corps things were much slower, principally because the troops were strung out over 12 miles of defensive front, and by the time Smith-Dorrien could get out even a warning order they were under heavy shelling, followed soon after first light by attacks the length of the line.

But where, ultimately, were they retreating *to*? It was after dawn when Spears got back to 5th Army with Sir John French's message for Lanrezac. It positively dripped resentment: 'Should the left flank of the British Army be seriously threatened, the Commander-in-Chief intend[s] to retire on his lines of communication [south-west towards Amiens], in which case General Lanrezac must look after his own left flank, as the British would no longer hold themselves responsible for covering it.' Lanrezac had been sleeping, bootless and without his tunic but otherwise fully dressed, when a staff officer ushered Spears into his makeshift bedroom and threw open the curtains. Spears saluted and delivered the message, bracing himself for a furious retort, but the commander of the 5th Army received him in silence, gazing at the carpet. Having then dismissed the bearer of such disobliging news without remark, Lanrezac telegraphed Joffre at 6 a.m. and asked for instructions.

In truth, French's threat made little sense. Lanrezac's withdrawal would not place the BEF's *left* flank in any greater peril than it already was. And if the left flank were to be seriously threatened, how would withdrawing south-*west* make it more secure? Surely it would be turning the flank towards Kluck? Fortunately good sense prevailed with the arrival at Le Cateau of a telegram from Joffre asking that the BEF retire towards Cambrai instead, a proposal of which French was quick to acknowledge the wisdom: 'I am falling back slowly to position Maubeuge, Valenciennes . . . If driven from these positions I will act in accordance with your wishes.'

The warm accord of their meeting eight days earlier at Vitry-le-François was clearly paying dividends. Nevertheless, Joffre now realized how perilous it was to have his left flank not under command (for he could not rely on the Territorials), and began thinking how he might create a 6th Army on Sir John French's left, making the BEF the filling in the sandwich. It would be the culmination of the whole 'Wilson–Foch' project – in effect to make the BEF but one more army incorporated in the French order of battle.

And to Lanrezac, who had been faced with the prospect of both flanks *en l'air*, for the 4th Army had been emphatically thrown back in its offensive in the Ardennes, Joffre wired: 'The Fifth Army will manoeuvre in retreat, resting its left on the fortress of Maubeuge, and its right against the wooded hills of the Ardennes. Keep in touch with Fourth Army . . . continue to maintain liaison with the British Army.'

Maubeuge – its magnetic effect was working on the Germans as well as on *GQG*. That morning, Karl von Bülow, whom Moltke had now appointed Army Group Commander (of both 1st and 2nd Armies), ordered Kluck to direct II and IX Corps to pivot on the fortress so as to envelop Lanrezac's left (a move which, after Sir John French's change of heart, the BEF would in fact thwart). But to do that, Kluck would have to drive a wedge between the 5th Army and the BEF, and he was already intent on turning the BEF's other flank, the left. He simply ignored the order. Lanrezac, meanwhile, was not going near Maubeuge: he instinctively shied away from the decrepit old fortress as a fox that has seen a trap before, sending a message (by wireless, unusually) to its commander that the 5th Army could no longer cover the town.* Sir John French, on the other hand, was sorely tempted: although he had looked over the defences and concluded there was much work to be done, it seemed to offer haven, somewhere he could at least rest and reorganize. And yet the same instinct as Lanrezac's warned him otherwise, mindful (he would tell Spears after the war) of the fate of Marshal Bazaine in 1870, who in similar circumstances fell back on the fortress of Metz, only to be surrounded, pummelled and starved into surrender – three marshals, fifty generals, 135,000 men and 600 guns. It was, apparently, the ringing words of Lieutenant-General Sir Edward Hamley's great text *The Operations of War* (1867) that recalled him – 'the commander of a retiring army who throws himself into a fortress acts like one who, when the ship is foundering, lays hold of the anchor'.†

* The forts, though modernized after the Franco-Prussian war, were no match for what the Germans could evidently throw at them after the evidence of Liège, and were too near the town, which was in consequence a shell-trap. However, the French garrison at Maubeuge was to hold out until 8 September, for the Germans simply masked and bypassed it.

† Spears makes the rather lofty point that had Hamley used a less vivid image, French might not have remembered it. On the other hand, what would be the merit of dullness in a book of instruction? 'But when loud surges lash the sounding shore / The

John Terraine, in his admirably balanced *Mons* (1960), gives Sir John French praise for his decision to give Maubeuge a wide berth: 'He served the British Army well in that moment.' He did indeed, but only by – for the first time in the campaign – exercising judgement worthy of a commander-in-chief.

Meanwhile the men of Smith-Dorrien's corps were having a very mixed time in that hardest operation of war, withdrawal in contact, the first object of which is to break clean with the enemy, who will almost certainly be trying to fix the withdrawing force in place. A portion of the force has to hold him off by fire while the other moves back to a position from which it in turn holds off the enemy to allow the first portion to withdraw; and this continues until the enemy is no longer able to bring direct fire to bear (usually because the withdrawing force has moved behind cover), at which point the withdrawing force moves as a whole by the quickest means to its new position. Even then, indirect fire – artillery – will still be a threat. When troops are engaging the enemy they are deployed more or less in line; when they are withdrawing to another fire position – another 'tactical bound' – they are still essentially deployed in line, and movement is slow. Only when they have broken clean can they safely move in file, more quickly and under greater control. Switching from one to the other is time-consuming, and a commander – whether of a company, battalion or brigade – will not want to have to slow his withdrawal by being forced back into a firing line. 'When mounted troops are available, they will be used to cover the final withdrawal of the infantry from each successive fire position,' says *Infantry Training* (1914).

Cavalry *were* available, but not across the corps front as a whole, Sir John French's priority being the left flank. For the most part, the infantry would have to shift for themselves. The best way of covering their movement was by artillery (and here smoke rounds would have been of enormous advantage; but they were yet to be developed), and while the day before had been principally a small-arms battle, now

---

hoarse, rough verse should like the torrent roar.' And Sir John French was first a midshipman on HMS *Warrior*; the naval analogy would have resonated well with him. Actually, he recalled Hamley inexactly, if, nevertheless, appositely: in *1914* he writes: 'Hamley described it as "The anxiety of the temporising mind which prefers postponement of a crisis to vigorous enterprise." Of Bazaine he says, "In clinging to Metz he acted like one who, when the ship is foundering, should lay hold of the anchor."' Yet Hamley's book was published three years *before* the siege of Metz.

that the brigades were clear of the industrial sprawl astride the canal, the gunners could come to the fore – almost literally. And indeed they would fire so much that 24 August became known as 'Shrapnel Monday'.

But first, the order to withdraw: without radio, it had to be a relay of written and then spoken words, edited at each level to exclude those details required only by the receiving headquarters and add others appropriate to the subordinates – from II Corps headquarters to the two divisions; from divisional headquarters to the brigades; from brigade headquarters to the battalions; battalions to companies, companies to platoons, lieutenant to corporal and then (if he was lucky) to the rifleman himself. Nor could the withdrawal begin at once, for Smith-Dorrien had first to clear the roads of all his transport (carrying combat supplies and engineer stores), brought forward in the expectation of the advance continuing – a task not helped by the growing number of refugees flushed belatedly and bewildered from villages the length of the canal, shuffling along the *pavé*, with here and there a handcart filled hastily with children or an invalid, with pots and pans and bedding, accompanied by whatever domestic animals had been roped or driven into the flight. Smith-Dorrien could only hope they would clear the roads when he needed them. Meanwhile, to shorten his front and take the pressure off the 3rd Division, which had without doubt seen the worst of the fighting the day before, he ordered the 5th Division to hold its ground until the 3rd could get away (if only he had had his other, third, division . . .).

Get away they eventually would, but with a running fight to break clean, for at dawn Ewald von Lochow's III Corps renewed the attack, his orders to 'fix' the BEF's centre while Kluck prepared the attack on the open left flank. Heavy shelling across the 3rd Division's front was followed by an attack by the 6th Division – Brandenburgers – between Ciphy and Frameries. They were met by the same withering rifle fire of the day before, from the rearguards of the 7th and the 9th Brigades – the 1st Lincolns and 2nd South Lancashires – supported by the 18-pounders of the 109th Battery RFA. The German losses were again prodigious, not least in officers, but the rearguards paid a price too; as they withdrew, the South Lancashires lost nearly 300 men to enfilading fire from machine guns atop a slag heap.

In the 5th Division, the 1st Cornwalls did not get the 'surprising order', as the adjutant's diary put it, until eleven o'clock – 'surprising' because although they had had quite a fight along the canal the evening before, just before midnight they had 'got away well, without much loss, and with a somewhat poor opinion of the Germans' rifle shooting'. But they were certainly tired, having then marched 8 miles to the aptly named mining village of Dour, which they reached about two o'clock and where they slept in the street until first light (just after four o'clock), when they were sent to 'a prepared position which looked strong but which was really weak against their [German] Artillery, because the trenches were dug in mounds of slag which [reckoned the adjutant] I much doubted would have stood two shell bursts'. With Saturday night spent digging in along the canal, Sunday fighting, and no proper hot meal since leaving their billets on the Saturday morning, come Shrapnel Monday evening they were not at their best; yet they shared the common opinion of II Corps, voiced by Private Harry Pratt of the 1st Northumberland Fusiliers, that in withdrawing 'we'd simply wasted our time on the canal'. Perhaps that sense might have been modified had they been attacked that morning in their new positions, but despite 'a big fight going on just on our right' the Cornwalls managed to slip away through Dour 'in good order though the Germans plumped a series of shells into the town as we got going [but] lost only two or three men'.

If the infantry were beginning to feel the want of sleep, the Cavalry Division was feeing it even harder. 'Sally' Home had had only half an hour on Sunday night (on top of his two the night before), for the headquarters were on the march from Elouges on the extreme left of the line at four o'clock, ready for the covering action to extricate the 5th Division (whose move GHQ somehow thought 'was to commence at daybreak'). As they set off, Kluck's artillery began shelling II Corps' front, so Allenby took the division several miles south-west in the belief that the 5th Division had in fact quit its line. At eleven he got an urgent message from the divisional commander, Fergusson, recalling him to protect his left flank, which the Germans were now trying to turn. Doubtless spurred by the terrible thought that they had left the infantry in the lurch, De Lisle's 2nd Cavalry Brigade, with L Battery RHA, galloped back. Allenby had ordered them to put in a diversionary attack using any means 'including mounted action if necessary', while he himself followed with Brigadier-General Charles

Brigg's 1st and Hubert Gough's 3rd Brigades, with D and E Batteries, as fast as they could.

What happened next was at best confused and at worst a rerun of Balaklava. It began well: the magnificent L Battery, who a week later, at Néry, would win three VCs in the course of being destroyed, formed line on the north-east edge of Audregnies with a commanding view of the ground, and their six 13-pounders opened fire on the massed German infantry at 800 yards (in the three-hour action they would fire 450 rounds). Two squadrons of the 9th Lancers dismounted at once and opened fire: 'Directly in front of us,' recalled Corporal Harry Easton, 'was a field sloping downwards. The field had been cut and the sheaves of corn stooked and the first enemy line made a B-line for the stooks. We received the order "Rapid Fire Commence." They were such an easy target.' So easy, indeed, that at first Easton didn't hear the order to cease fire and retire to remount.

Why De Lisle was so intent on charging while his guns and small arms were having such effect is unclear, but charge they did – the Lancers right, the 4th Dragoon Guards left. They speared a few hapless scouts crouching behind the stooks, and then the German batteries ahead – nine of them along the Mons–Valenciennes road – opened up. And if this were not bad enough, the squadrons were then stopped in their tracks by barbed-wire fences and a railway embankment. 'We galloped about like rabbits in front of a line of guns,' wrote Captain Francis Grenfell of the Lancers, 'men and horses falling in all directions.'

The arrival of the 1st and 3rd Brigades on the left towards Angre took the heat off the 2nd Brigade, with D and E Batteries (following L Battery) coming into action fast and doing fearful execution among the massed infantry. 'Every shell burst low over them,' wrote 'Sally' Home with admiration. But the charge had cost the Lancers and Dragoon Guards over 150 killed, wounded and missing – and over 300 horses, which meant the better part of a regiment. It did nothing to endear De Lisle to the brigade, with both commanding officers openly critical of the order to charge, but, like Balaklava, it was somehow turned into a feat of arms: De Lisle said subsequently that Fergusson had told him: 'But for the Cavalry Brigade the Division would have been destroyed to the last man,' and he issued a Special Brigade Order commending 'the true cavalry spirit of the 9th Lancers in daring to charge unbroken infantry in order to save neighbouring troops, and that of the 4th Dragoon Guards in the effective support given, without hesitation or thought of danger'.

If there was any truth in Fergusson's remark it was down to L Battery – and, indeed, to the fire of the other two batteries, as well as the marksmanship of the dismounted cavalrymen – and certainly not 'the true cavalry spirit'. Nevertheless the story was quickly taken up by a press refreshingly (in those days) eager for good news, and stories were soon appearing of the 'cavalry charge to save the guns'. Ironically, however, 'the guns' (and the infantry) had been saved by the help of *dismounted* cavalry: Francis Grenfell, twice wounded in the charge, rallied a number of other lancers to haul away the 18-pounders of the 119th Battery, the horses and most of the gunners being dead or wounded. For this and his action in the charge he would be awarded the VC, as would the battery commander, Major (later Major-General) Ernest Wright Alexander.*

Some of the 5th Division's infantry did not get away so cleanly, however. In a gallant but confused rearguard action, fighting almost literally to the last round, the 1st Cheshires lost nearly 800 men killed, wounded or captured, including their commanding officer.†
Indeed, Brigadier-General Count Gleichen's very English-counties

---

* There is sometimes confusion about the 'first VC of the war'. The award of the first VCs was announced in the *London Gazette* of Friday, 13 November 1914 (though the War Office order is dated the 16th), and because it is a military list the recipients are listed in order of seniority, Captain Grenfell appearing before Lieutenant Dease. This does not imply precedence, however. Lieutenant-Colonel (as by then he was) Alexander's VC was not gazetted until 18 February 1915. Grenfell was killed in action that year, three months after learning of the award. While in hospital in England recovering from his 24 August wounds he was visited by the King, and also by Lord Roberts who, with a sharp recollection of the *arme blanche* debates, 'asked rather direct questions as to why we charged, and whom we charged, and who gave the order to charge'. Grenfell's cousin Julian, the poet, would also be killed in 1915.
† Lieutenant-Colonel Dudley Boger, though wounded, and one of his company sergeant-majors, Frank Meachin, managed to escape and in November were taken to Nurse Edith Cavell (a British nurse who had stayed behind when the Germans invaded) in Brussels by Belgian civilians, who arranged for Boger to have an operation. He and Meachin were given forged identity cards, and Meachin, disguised as a fish hawker, managed to get to Flushing, in Holland, and thence to Folkestone. Boger got as far as Villevorde before he was recaptured. Boger was not untypical of the older commanding officer of the BEF's infantry: at school with Henry Wilson, who was a year his senior, he had been promoted to lieutenant-colonel in June at the age of forty-eight. He was subsequently awarded the DSO for his command at Mons. Nurse Edith Cavell was executed by German firing squad on 12 October 1915.

brigade lost a third of its fighting strength in what turned out to be a vital flank guard action to save the division. And yet the day was another triumph, however imperfect, not only for the Gunners but for the School of Musketry at Hythe. Sixteen-year-old Trumpeter Jimmy Naylor, of the 80th Battery RFA, watched in awe an officer of the 2nd Battalion King's Own Yorkshire Light Infantry controlling the fire of his platoon:

> He was saying, *At four hundred . . . At three fifty . . . At three hundred.* The rifles blazed, but still the Germans came on. They were getting nearer and nearer and for the first time I began to feel rather anxious and frightened. They weren't an indeterminate mass any more – you could actually pick out details, see them as individual men, coming on, and coming on. And the officer, still as cool as anything, was saying, *At two-fifty . . . At two hundred . . .* And then he said, *ten rounds rapid!* And the chaps opened up – and the Germans fell down like logs. I've never seen anything like it, the discipline, the fire discipline of those troops.*

But where was Sir John French? Once again he was curiously detached from the battle. He had told Smith-Dorrien and Haig that they must coordinate the withdrawal for themselves, and there was merit in this, for Haig was the junior officer and his corps was de facto in a supporting role; or rather, there would have been had there been the time and method to do so, and had the enemy not disobligingly attacked II Corps within a few hours of the order to withdraw (it was only towards midday that the two corps commanders would be able to meet). But it required more from the commander-in-chief than simply giving his corps commanders *carte blanche* – especially as he had not seen or spoken to Smith-Dorrien since the early-morning conference of the day before, and the situation had changed very materially since then. In *1914* French writes: 'Personally, I have always been far more a regimental than a Staff Officer'; and yet he was in many ways treating the withdrawal as a staff exercise rather than as a practical problem – the sort a regimental officer would have dealt with routinely. It can only have demonstrated confidence in Smith-Dorrien, however grudging.

* Quoted in Macdonald, *1914.*

In fairness, there were other command matters that Sir John French felt obliged to attend to – some of which, in fact, he certainly was attending to. He spent a little time watching units of II Corps fighting to break clean, then motored over to the right of the line to watch those of I Corps retiring relatively unmolested; he visited Haig, and then drove to see General Sordet, whose cavalry corps on its odyssey to get across to the left flank of the BEF had got to Avesnes, well to the south of Maubeuge (it would be another twenty-four hours before they completed the move, pretty much worn out). And then he cheered himself a good deal by driving to Le Cateau, where the 4th Division was at last detraining, to see its commander, Major-General Thomas D'Oyly Snow, and lost no time ordering him to take up a position towards Cambrai to support II Corps as they fell back towards Le Cateau, though for some reason – perhaps thinking II Corps' head-quarters already had enough on its plate – he did not put the division under Smith-Dorrien's command but under the direct orders of GHQ. Indeed, GHQ was collecting an increasing number of independent formations – the Cavalry Division (and the 19th Brigade), the 5th Cavalry Brigade, and now the 4th Division – and yet exercising only the loosest control of the battle as a whole.

For whatever reason, he did not go to see the commander of II Corps. So Smith-Dorrien, on learning early in the evening that French had returned to his advance headquarters at Bavai, went to see him instead. It was another insufferably hot day, the fighting, although successful, had not been without loss, and the commander of II Corps was still irritated by the poor staffwork of the night before, which had contributed to his problems. And no doubt he found it difficult to conceal his frustration at having to seek out his commander-in-chief for orders. In his *Memories of Forty Years' Service* Smith-Dorrien says that he told French of 'the action of the II Corps and its positions'; and nothing could better illustrate – save perhaps the post-mortem on the battle to come at Le Cateau – the difference of opinion between the two men over what was tactical necessity. Smith-Dorrien describes how the order for the BEF to retire in the direction that Sir John French intended

necessitated a crab-like movement, the I Corps crowding in on the 3rd Division and that division on the 5th Division, and unless the last could edge off more to the west the time would come when some troops would be squeezed out . . . When therefore at about 3 p.m. pressure on the [left] flank and the fact that it was fighting a desperate action, put out of the question any edging of the 5th Division to the west, I directed the 3rd Division, then free of the enemy, to move across its rear . . . This move worked admirably, for it secured the west flank, gave the harried 5th Division an area to fall back into where both its flanks could be secure, and gave more shoulder-room to the I Corps, which was getting a bit compressed between Maubeuge and Bavai, chiefly owing to the fact that the direction of retirement rendered it necessary that some of the troops of the two Corps should use the same road for a time. Though this manoeuvre involved an interchange of positions of the two Divisions in subsequent movements no complications resulted.

This was not, however, Sir John French's opinion, at least not by the time he came to write *1914*:

[At Bavai] all reports and reconnaissances indicated a determined attempt to outflank us and cut across our line of retreat, but Allenby's cavalry was splendidly disposed and handled . . . There was some confusion in the retirement of the 2nd Corps. The 5th Division crossed the rear of the 3rd near Bavai, got to the east of them and somewhat on the line of the retreat of the 1st Corps, whose movement was thus hampered and delayed.

And as if this weren't damning enough, with the other hand he heaped praise on Haig and I Corps:

Our troops in this part of the line were very active and pushing . . . I went out from Haig's Headquarters to a high ridge, whence the ground slopes down towards the north and north-east, along a gentle declivity stretching almost to the canal which was some distance away. The situation of the 1st Corps was excellent, and the artillery positions were well chosen. From where we stood we could observe the effect of our fire. It was very accurate, and shrapnel could be seen bursting well over the enemy lines and holding his advance in complete check, whilst the German fire was by no means so effective. The infantry were defending their position a long way down the slope with great determination and tenacity. The steadfast attitude and skilful retreat of our right wing at Mons had much to do with the success of our withdrawal, and the short time I spent with the 1st Corps that morning inspired me with great confidence.*

'A big butcher's bill is not necessarily evidence of good tactics,' General Sir Archibald (later Field Marshal Lord) Wavell would reply to Winston Churchill in 1940 when the prime minister protested that the low casualty figures in Eritrea suggested the army had not put up much of a fight against the Italians. Certainly there had been mistakes in II Corps' battles – notably in the case of the Cheshires, who had ended up surrounded because the order to withdraw had not reached them – but casualty figures do give a rough indication of the degree to which troops have been engaged. On 24 August, I Corps' casualties were about 100; II Corps' were close to 2,000. Sir John French's relative praise should be judged accordingly.

Having made his report, Smith-Dorrien asked for 'instructions as to our further retirement'. According to *Memories of Forty Years' Service*, French replied that he could do as he liked, but that Haig intended to start at 5 a.m.: 'I [Smith-Dorrien] remonstrated, saying that unless we moved early we should have a repetition of that day (the 24th) when orders had been issued too late to avoid the enemy coming to close grips,' a remark that could not have endeared him to 'the Chief', who ' asked me what I proposed. I replied that I wished to start off my impedimenta [his 'logistic tail'], which had already been in bivouac several hours, soon after midnight, followed by the troops at such times as would ensure my rear-guards being south of the Valenciennes–Jenlain–Bavai [*sic*] road by 5 a.m.'

French apparently agreed, but remarking that Haig could still do as he intended, whereupon Smith-Dorrien turned his efforts instead towards Archie Murray, who was working in his shirtsleeves again on the other side of the room, asking him to induce the

---

* There is no doubt but that the 13- and 18-pounder batteries fought magnificently throughout the day – as did the howitzer batteries in the field brigades – and that shrapnel cut down the German infantry in swathes and slowed their advance; but the German batteries were not greatly troubled, it seems, by counter-battery fire, so continued to plague the infantry as they tried to break clean. And without sufficient heavy artillery firing HE, the BEF was not able to fire 'predictively' (from the map, i.e. selecting predicted targets) into likely concentration areas and choke points – harassing fire that denies the enemy free movement out of direct contact.

commander-in-chief to issue an order for the whole force to move early and simultaneously – which indeed Murray did.*

By first light the BEF was slipping away – back across the French border, to its new positions at Le Cateau.

---

* It might be taken as further evidence of hostility that Sir John French was prepared to concede this point to Murray, a three-star, having refused Smith-Dorrien, a four-star.

Chapter Seventeen

'VERY WELL, GENTLEMEN, WE WILL FIGHT'

And he is dead who will not fight;
And who dies fighting has increase.

Lieutenant Julian Grenfell, Royal Dragoons,
'Into Battle' (1915)

If the enemy presses hard, a sudden counter-attack, not followed up
too far, may give good results.

Infantry Training (1914)

Grumbling, which the old sweats had long held to be 'the soldier's right', was no longer confined to the ranks. 'I hope they know what they're doing,' wrote Lieutenant Roupell of the East Surreys – he of the sword-wielding fire-control along the canal. And 'Sally' Home, in Allenby's headquarters, was just as troubled, if more searching: 'The questions which must be asked are as follows: Why did we advance north only to retire? Why were we short of guns? Perhaps it is part of a general plan, I hope so! It is poor comfort to the rank and file who know little except that they are retiring.'*

---

* The reference to shortage of guns is difficult to fathom, for although in one sense there could never be enough, the RHA batteries with the Cavalry Division had not been inactive, nor those of the RFA with the infantry brigades. It is more likely that Home was remarking on counter-battery fire, requiring heavier guns firing HE.

But General Alexander von Kluck was not entirely in the picture either. From his headquarters at Soignies, 10 miles north-east of Mons, he issued an army order on the evening of the twenty-fourth which assumed the BEF would make a stand on the line Maubeuge–Bavai–Valenciennes. He directed his III and IX Corps to fix the BEF in place, III Corps attacking the BEF's left (Smith-Dorrien at Wargnies), and IX Corps the BEF's right (Haig, at Bavai), while IV Corps were to envelop the BEF's left wing, and Richthofen's Cavalry Corps, recalled from their fruitless search for the French Territorials further west, would drive into the British rear: 'The outflanking of the left of the British Army, on the assumption that it remained in position, appears to be guaranteed.'*

Not long after midnight, however, an air report reached him which seemed to indicate that the BEF (which he still assumed was six infantry divisions, not four) was withdrawing on Maubeuge, and he sent out hasty orders for the whole of the 1st Army to adjust its axis of advance more to the south. But the first-light air reports (which he received at 9 a.m.) came as a surprise: long columns of all arms were moving from Bavai along the road to Le Cateau, and numerous small groups – single companies, batteries, squadrons, and cars – were crossing the Selle, north and south of Solesmes: 'The enemy was marching in an almost opposite direction to what was supposed earlier in the morning.' He changed the orders once again: the First Army was to attack the BEF and halt the movement.

The Roman road from Bavai to Le Cateau was a Godsend to the marching troops – dead straight, the shortest distance between two points, although many of those who had slogged up it to Mons could only view their march back down again as a retrograde step, metaphorically as well as literally (all 20 miles of it). The road was also ideal for the staff officers of the BEF, for whom it served as a perfect boundary on their maps to separate I Corps and II Corps. It was, too, a navigational Godsend for the pilots of the RFC, who were taking off from one field not knowing where they would be landing on return. And now that the cavalry was in a running fight to help the infantry

---

* General Alexander von Kluck, *The March on Paris and the Battle of the Marne* (London, 1920).

337

withdraw – just as before Waterloo after the clash at Quatre Bras (and even more spectacularly in Sir John Moore's great retreat to Corunna) – the surest way of keeping track of the enemy was from the air. But on 'Shrapnel Monday' a more dreaded enemy had arrived – the west wind. It made it easy for the RFC to get at the Germans, but difficult to get away. As the authorized history of the corps relates, in August 1914 – and indeed for the rest of the war too – 'the road to safety always, while the west wind was blowing, lay uphill'.* Lieutenant George Pretyman, with Major Lionel Boyd-Moss as observer, trying to reconnoitre towards Valenciennes the following day, found (in the words of their flight report) that they could 'make very little progress against wind', becoming an easy target for ground fire just north of Cambrai: 'Engine put out of action by bullet. Glide two miles farther W. clear of enemy, and land. Burn machine and join French Cavalry retreating towards Arras. Commandeer two bicycles and go to Gouzeaucourt where we get car and report to H.Q. 12th Brigade near Le Catelet. Get back to St. Quentin about 11.30 p.m. and report to General Smith-Dorrien.' With exploits such as this recounted in the squadron messes, W. E. Johns, commissioned into the RFC in 1917, would have had no shortage of material for his *Biggles* adventures.

But before the BEF could take up its new positions at Le Cateau (and Smith-Dorrien his headquarters at St Quentin), it had to negotiate an awkward obstacle – the Forêt de Mormal, 10 miles long by 5 miles wide. It was – from the map, at least – devoid of practicable roads leading in the direction the BEF was moving. Consequently, although the Bavai to Le Cateau road was the inter-corps boundary – and therefore, in the mind of GHQ, the two corps would be moving in parallel and proximity – Haig's I Corps would in fact have to march *east* of the forest, which meant they would have to cross and re-cross the River Sambre, separating the two corps by up to 10 miles. There were, in fact, passable by-ways north–south through the forest had there been time for the cavalry to reconnoitre properly (a brigade at least could have found routes), but more ominously there were several good lateral roads running roughly north-west to south-east. If II Corps were to withdraw unhindered down the good roads west of the Mormal

---

* Raleigh, *The War in the Air.*

forest, the Germans following up would be able to probe these leafy routes at will, thereby threatening the flank of the slower-moving I Corps. Which is what indeed would happen that night – or, at least, would appear to happen.

But for now both corps were getting away fairly well, with Haig's, again, little troubled by the enemy. In fact it was the French who would hold up I Corps, for the tail of General Sordet's cavalry was still crossing the line of withdrawal in their ride to the BEF's left flank; and there was also a problem on the far right, where the 1st Division found themselves sharing a road with the French 53rd (Reserve) Division of Lanrezac's 5th Army, and the 2nd Division with both the 53rd and the 69th Divisions. In the heat of yet another stiflingly hot day these lapses of staffwork, or of discipline, caused friction and local delay, but little else. Certainly the German cavalry and jaegers, who should have been pressing the retreat hard, were not much of a hindrance: I Corps reached their billets that evening having suffered but thirty-two casualties.

Once again, however, Smith-Dorrien's II Corps had things rather harder, if nothing like as hard as the day before. The 5th Division was able to march down the Roman road in peace, though it was thronged with 'every kind of vehicle from six-horse farm wagons to perambulators, [which] everywhere delayed the marching troops, and made it impossible for motor cars carrying Staff officers to pass the columns'.* Carrying 50 lb of equipment, extra ammunition having been issued in many units, and sweating heavily in the unremitting heat, a good many men fell out – reservists mainly – though most of them straggled in after dark, drenched by a torrential downpour that began at five o'clock ('Good as a bath, and twice as refreshing,' thought one of them). The 3rd Division and the 19th Brigade and the Cavalry Division to their left, however, bore the brunt of Kluck's frontal and flank attacks, and the rearguards were in a running fight for much of the day, with 1st and 3rd Cavalry Brigades in a sharp action near Le Quesnoy to extricate the 2nd Royal Irish Rifles who were acting as 2nd Infantry Brigade's rearguard, the brigade itself forming the divisional rearguard. At about four o'clock a despatch rider from I Corps trying to find 3rd Division headquarters came across the Irish

* *Official History*, vol. 1.

on the road south-west of the village and showed the commanding officer, Lieutenant-Colonel (later Major-General) Wilkinson Dent Bird, a message for the divisional commander: 'two columns of the enemy close behind [the column] and one or two cavalry regiments, with artillery and infantry, moving on Le Quesnoy' (the intelligence must have come from the RFC). Bird was about to order the battalion back into firing lines when a galloper brought him a message from Lieutenant-Colonel Thomas Pitman, commanding the 11th Hussars in the 1st Cavalry Brigade: there were Germans approaching in large numbers, he would hold on as long as possible, but did not expect to be able to check them for long. They had dismounted and lined the railway embankment – good cover for men and horses – which ran north-west to south-east, crossing the Roman road almost at a right angle. Following Kluck's orders to adjust the axis of advance more to the south, the German infantry were therefore advancing diagonally across the cavalry's front 'in innumerable short lines', which the hussars' Lee–Enfields and machine guns were able to enfilade until they were 'shelled out' of the position.

The next time Pitman would see the railway line was almost exactly four years later during the great allied counter-offensive, the 'Hundred Days', when as Major-General Pitman he would gallop north with his 2nd Cavalry Division.

The action at Le Quesnoy was typical of many that day as II Corps marched for Le Cateau – an exhausting business, with steadily mounting casualties (100 in the cavalry, 350 in the infantry), and wearing on the nerves. But if the day before, 'Shrapnel Monday', had belonged to the artillery, on Tuesday the cavalry really earned their pay: 'Most of this day seemed to be spent in massing to form a target for enemy artillery, being scattered and then forming up again,' wrote Captain Henry Evans of the 4th Hussars. They began calling it wryly the 'Cavalry Division Field Day'.

But the Germans were tired, too; and the experience of fighting along the canal on the twenty-third and in the open next day had made them wary. Nor was Kluck concentrating his troops to decisive effect: his II Corps was pursuing d'Amade's Territorials south-west towards Cambrai, while IV Corps appeared almost to be marking time to let IV (Reserve) Corps, with its two divisions, catch up; and the formation that might really have imperilled the BEF – Georg von der

Marwitz's Cavalry Corps – still had a way to march.* If Kluck had not had to detach two corps to watch Antwerp, and had now been able to bring them to bear, the result might have been catastrophic for the allies; but the Belgians still had fight in them, and the day before had launched a sortie in strength to help the hard-pressed allied troops on the River Sambre and the Mons Canal. It came too late; but nevertheless the threat from Antwerp to the German right and rear could not be disregarded – which was the whole point of Sir John French's suggestion at the war council on 5 August that the BEF go to Antwerp instead of Maubeuge.

The pressure on the BEF was mounting, however, and signal intercepts were indicating that the left flank was indeed the German main effort.† The newly arrived 4th Division at Solesmes, 7 miles north-west of Le Cateau, now came into action in a prolonged fight to cover the withdrawal of the 3rd Division, which continued well into the night. They might have been served better if all their artillery had arrived, and if they had still had their cavalry squadron, for on the twenty-fourth GHQ had removed the divisional cavalry from both the 4th and 5th Divisions to reinforce and make up losses in Allenby's Cavalry Division. At a stroke the divisional commanders had lost their 'eyes and ears', as well as escorts and mounted orderlies for the headquarters and the signal companies. The fighting at Solesmes was so intense that the 4th Division's rearguard would not get away until after midnight, and none of the brigades would be able to get to their positions at Le Cateau until daylight.

But as night fell, Smith-Dorrien, who once again had not seen Sir John French all day ('This was unfortunate, as there were several matters I wished to ask him about'‡), began taking stock. In his dimly

* The German II Cavalry Corps comprised three divisions, each of three cavalry brigades (each brigade consisting of two regiments of four squadrons), an artillery regiment (three four-gun batteries) and a machine-gun company (six MGs); plus seven jaeger battalions (strictly, six, and one *Schützen*, or light infantry), each consisting of four light companies, a machine-gun company (six MGs), a cyclist company and a motor-vehicle column – altogether a formidable, and mobile, grouping of firepower.
† Many of these intercepts were made by the radio station atop the Eiffel Tower, the finest listening post that could have been devised.
‡ Smith-Dorrien, *Memories of Forty Years' Service*. It is the absolute responsibility of the superior commander to communicate with his subordinates – hence the basis on which signal troops are organized – and not vice versa (though, of course, the subordinate keeps the superior informed of the situation as it develops within his area of responsibility). Sir John French had many things on his plate at this time – not least

lit headquarters, the little *mairie* in Bertry, about 3 miles south of the Le Cateau–Cambrai road, it seemed to him that the position he had been given to hold was 'quite a good one – on rising ground with a fine field of fire and with several villages capable of defence along it. The right, or east flank was certainly turnable, but that did not matter as the I Corps were to go there.' But when it had become clear that I Corps was not going to appear before last light, 'I requested the Commander of the 5th Division to hold the ground on the north-east of Le Cateau until they arrived.'

However, to Sir John French's mind the Le Cateau position was not one actually to be held, rather to be occupied overnight prior to continuing the retreat (or 'retirement', as it was being called). Smith-Dorrien had received a warning order to this effect from Henry Wilson at about six o'clock, the orders themselves arriving at nine, and II Corps headquarters had issued orders to the divisions at 10.15 p.m. to continue the retirement at daybreak. This fact is important, for it shows that even at this late hour – before the 4th Division's tricky situation on the left was fully appreciated, and before learning that the I Corps was not going to arrive on the right flank for some time – Smith-Dorrien had every intention of quitting the position at first light.

Yet the fact that he issued orders – instigated the battle procedure* – was itself no assurance that the withdrawal could have been made at dawn, even if the situation on the left and right had been tidier. In an exercise at the staff college the battle procedure would have passed unremarked, but the reality on the night of the twenty-fifth was wholly different. Smith-Dorrien paints the scene, speaking of the 'fog of war' (which, of course, was interfering with Sir John French's vision too – and, indeed, Haig's):

Communication was most difficult, and although the Corps signallers,

---

trying to keep some sense of cohesion with Lanrezac on his right and d'Amade on his left – but his first function was the command of his subordinate corps and the Cavalry Division, to which he was giving less priority than was manifestly needed.

* 'Those procedures to be followed when preparing for tactical operations, the object being to ensure, by concurrent activity, that the time available to prepare for battle is used efficiently so that troops are properly prepared and briefed' (from the current *Army Field Manual*). The term was not specifically used in 1914, though the procedures were for the most part those of today.

under that most resourceful of men, Major A. B. R. Hildebrand, R.E. (now Brigadier-General, C.B., C.M.G., D.S.O.), performed miracles with their wires and cables, it was impossible to find out the positions of units until hours after they reached them. Then it was not as if I only had the II Corps to deal with, for mixed up with them, fighting and retiring together, were the Cavalry Division, the 19th Infantry Brigade, and the 4th Division, none of which were under me, but were reporting their movements to and getting their orders from General Head-quarters, twenty-six miles to the rear. It is true that General Head-quarters issued an order timed 1 p.m. 25th August, placing the 19th Brigade under the II Corps, but it was then with the Cavalry Division, miles away, and Heaven knows when it got the order.

In fact, the brigade only got the order at six the following morning – and from II Corps, not GHQ. Such is the nature of military operations; it is not a question of apportioning blame, but of recognizing the innately trying conditions under which battle procedure is carried out – Clausewitz's 'fog of war' (*im Nebel . . . Ungewißheit**) and what he called 'friction', the 'force' that in war makes simple things difficult.

At last, about 8 p.m. [as it was getting dark], I got news of the 3rd Division; the main bodies of the 8th and 9th Brigades had reached the vicinity of their allotted positions about Audencourt and Inchy respectively about 6.30 p.m.; but there was still no news of the 7th Brigade, nor did I get any until the small hours of the 26th, and then to the effect that it had reached its destination at Caudry about midnight, but with the loss of the 2nd Royal Irish Rifles, part of the South Lancashires, and the 41st Battery R.F.A. Next day I heard that these units had reached Reumont and bivouacked there at 2 a.m., and had only rejoined their Brigade at 9 a.m.

The 7th Brigade's condition, although worse than most, was not untypical of what all the troops had experienced at some stage during the day. The signal officer, Captain (later Brigadier-General) Alexander Johnston, was beside himself:

The heat was awful and the march seemed endless. A certain number of men began to tail off and straggled in an appalling manner. A retirement certainly seems to have a most demoralizing effect, discipline seems to

---

* 'War is an area of uncertainty; three-quarters of the things on which all action in war is based are lying in a fog of uncertainty to a greater or lesser extent.'

relax, little attempt seems to be made to keep to the ranks, and men fall out to get drinks or food or to lie down . . . [later] I then made my way back to the hill above Solesmes where there was a stiffish fight going on, the rearguard trying to hold the Germans back till the guns and transport could be got through the town . . . The General [brigade commander] told me to go with him into the Town to try to get the guns through . . . The confusion in the Town was appalling, the place being packed not only with our fellows but with civilians and the remnants of the French Territorial Regt, and the traffic was continually being blocked.*

Frank Richards, with 2nd Royal Welsh Fusiliers in the 19th Brigade on the left flank, but having crossed to the right in the course of the day, was carrying 200 rounds of ammunition and 'arrived in Le Cateau about midnight, dead-beat to the world. The Royal Welch [*sic*] camped on the square in the centre of the town. We were told to get as much rest as we could . . . I slept the sleep of the just that night, for about three hours. I could have done with forty-three.'

The exhaustion of the troops and congestion on the roads had not escaped Smith-Dorrien's notice, and as midnight approached he still had no news of Allenby's cavalry and the 4th Division, 'for they were not under me, though I had been given permission to call on the latter Division for help should I require it'. None of this is materially disputed in the war of words that broke out in 1919 with the publication of Sir John French's memoirs (long before the *Official History* more or less established the facts, although itself not entirely impartial). But now, as if the situation on the left of II Corps – the cavalry and the 4th Division's running fight to break clean – were not problem enough, Smith-Dorrien was beginning to hear worrying news from the right:

Rumours were afloat during the evening that the I Corps were heavily engaged, and reports came in that heavy firing was heard in the direction of Landrecies. This was serious as, if they [I Corps] were not nearer than that, it meant a gap of eight miles between the right of my Corps and the left of the I Corps. Thus it will be gathered that, with the exception of a

---

* *The Great War Diaries of Brigadier-General Alexander Johnston 1914–1917*, ed. Edwin Astill (London, 2007). Johnston was badly wounded in September 1917 at Ypres commanding the 126th Infantry Brigade, was evacuated to England and would not see active service again.

few units of the 5th Division, no fighting units were on the position before dark, that a great many of those of the II Corps were on the move until after midnight, and that the 4th Division only reached the position at daylight next day.*

Clausewitz is very definite on the demands of the 'fog of war': 'The first thing [needed] here is a fine, piercing mind, to feel out the truth with the measure of its judgement.' And in the early hours of 26 August the attempt to feel out the truth gave rise to one of the most controversial decisions in the history of the British army: should the commander of II Corps have stood and fought at Le Cateau the next day, or should he have continued the retreat?

Smith-Dorrien relates that 'some of the fog was cleared away by the arrival of General Allenby, accompanied by his G.S.O.I, Colonel J. Vaughan (now Major-General, C.B., C.M.G., D.S.O.) at my headquarters [the *mairie* in Bertry] at 2 a.m.' To say the least, however, this was a late hour after a long, hot day of rearguards, and famously the nadir of the spirit, from which Napoleon had coined the term 'two o'clock courage'. ('As to moral courage, I have very rarely met with two o'clock in the morning courage: I mean instantaneous courage.'†) But if some of the fog was now cleared away, it was only to reveal an alarming prospect. Allenby told him that his troops were much scattered, that his men and horses were 'pretty well played out' ('Sally' Home writes: 'No food for men or horses tonight'), and that he could not get in touch with GHQ, to whom he was still directly answerable. He asked what Smith-Dorrien was going to do, adding that unless he could get away in the dark, the Germans were so close that II Corps would be forced to fight at daylight.

This was not a state of affairs of which Allenby could have felt proud, for he had, to all intents and purposes, lost control of his division. 'Allenby's staff were useless,' thought Colonel James Edmonds, the 4th Division's chief of staff, and subsequently the

* In fact II Corps heard nothing from GHQ about I Corps throughout the day (Smith-Dorrien went in person to GHQ at about four o'clock, but by then the bulk of the staff and the commander-in-chief had already left for their new headquarters at St Quentin, some 20 miles to the south). It was perhaps as well that II Corps had heard nothing, for although it would have been useful to learn in good time that I Corps were unlikely to arrive at Le Cateau that evening, GHQ – based on Haig's reports – grossly over-estimated the threat on that flank.
† Comte de Las Cases, *Mémorial de Sainte Hélène* (London, 1823).

official historian: 'They never knew where his brigades were.' There was, by Allenby's own admission, some truth in this, for he did not know the whereabouts of all his brigades; but the nature of the retreat was making demands on the cavalry that its communications were not equipped to deal with. Wireless was unsatisfactory, if functioning at all; telephones were few and the connections haphazard. The only reliable means was galloper or despatch rider, and that depended on his knowing the location to which he was heading, and that to which he would be returning. With the enemy pressing forward, the BEF falling back, and night enveloping both, the difficulties were not insignificant.

However, Smith-Dorrien was not responsible for the Cavalry Division: their condition was bound to affect the security of his left wing, but his first concern was the troops under his direct command – and his orders were to continue the retreat. He therefore sent for the commander of the 3rd Division, Hubert Hamilton, whose head-quarters were close by, and asked if his troops could move off before daylight. 'Hammy', as he was affectionately known by his troops, was very definite: the division could not move before nine o'clock. This may seem surprising, given that the orders for the retreat to continue had been issued by II Corps headquarters at 10.15 p.m.; but even if the brigades had needed no further rest or replenishment, it is questionable whether, given the division's dispersal (the 7th Brigade still not fully accounted for), there was time enough to complete the necessary battle procedure. A disorderly withdrawal, with the Germans so close (uhlans supported by motorized jaegers) and the roads clogged with refugees and military transport, could have spelled disaster; the corps – the whole left flank, indeed – risked losing all cohesion, at which point Kluck's 1st Army might have overwhelmed them.*

---

* It has been suggested, by Zuber and others, that Hamilton's telling Smith-Dorrien only now that he could not move before nine o'clock – when the orders had been sent out at 10.15 p.m. – was culpable negligence. Yet there is no record of Smith-Dorrien's seeing this as extraordinary (even though he was notoriously quick-tempered), so it might be concluded that Hamilton was expressing a 'time clear of position' rather than the time when the first troops would begin to move rearwards. Hamilton was unusual in that most of his service had been on the staff – he had not commanded a battalion – but he was generally regarded as a level-headed infantryman, and one who was fre-quently to the fore. Indeed, six weeks later he would be killed during a personal reconnaissance during the fighting around Ypres. He was buried in a churchyard near

There was dead silence in the room as Smith-Dorrien pondered the options. As a major in the Sudan he had won a DSO in a bold action that went beyond his orders; but not to continue the retreat was another matter entirely. One way or the other, there was not a moment to lose: referring the dilemma to GHQ would cost him time, for although there was a telephone half a mile away at the railway station (for some reason it had not been extended to the *mairie* by II Corps or GHQ signallers) there was no knowing where Sir John French actually was. Smith-Dorrien, in his memoirs, makes the point that *Field Service Regulations* were clear enough, if ultimately making it a question of judgement: 'If a subordinate, in the absence of a superior, neglects to depart from the letter of his order, when such departure is clearly demanded by circumstances, and failure ensues, he will be held responsible for such failure.' Perhaps, too, he recalled the reprimand of Lord Lucan by the commander-in-chief, Lord Raglan, after the fiasco at Balaklava: 'Lord Lucan, you are a lieutenant-general and should therefore have exercised your discretion, and, not approving of the charge, should not have caused it to be made.'*

Smith-Dorrien was a 'full' general, with one more star than a lieutenant-general's three. He turned to Allenby and asked if he would accept orders from him. Allenby said he would. There was another portentous pause, and then the general officer commanding the II Corps made the decision – to depart from his orders: 'Very well, gentlemen, we will fight, and I will ask General Snow to act under me as well.'

Béthune, with Smith-Dorrien present and a representative of each regiment in the division as an honour guard. The only light was provided by car headlamps, and shellfire occasionally forced the chaplain to pause in the service. Smith-Dorrien concluded the service with the words: 'Indeed a true soldier's grave. God rest his soul.' His remains were later repatriated.

* Raglan's reprimand was in fact a fundamental statement of generalship. And there was a famously instructive reversal of Lucan's dereliction in this regard eighty-five years after Smith-Dorrien's dilemma in the altercation between the Supreme Allied Commander Europe, the US General Wesley Clark, and the then Lieutenant-General Sir Mike Jackson (later the CGS) commanding the NATO force preparing to evict the Serbs from Kosovo. The Russians had sent a flying column to seize Pristina airport, and Clark wanted Jackson to stop them. Jackson, who considered the order futile and likely to end in serious bloodshed, protested, but Clark repeated the order baldly, to which the lieutenant-general replied: 'Sir, I'm a three-star general, you can't give me orders like this. I have my own judgement of the situation' (General Sir Mike Jackson, *Soldier: The Autobiography*, London, 2007).

The problem was that the saving section in *FSR* was preceded by the instruction that 'a formal order should never be departed from, either in letter or spirit – (a) so long as the officer who issued it is present; (b) if the officer who issued the order is not present, provided there is time to report to him and await a reply without losing an opportunity or endangering the command.' It turned on the question of judgement. However, Smith-Dorrien did not intend a prolonged defence. He could hardly mount 'a sudden counter-attack, not followed up too far, [that] may give good results' as *Infantry Training* suggested, but he could give the enemy what he called a 'stopping blow' to allow II Corps to break clean and continue the retreat.

And for a time, at least, it seemed that Sir John French approved. Smith-Dorrien sent him a lengthy message by car at 3.30 a.m., which arrived at St Quentin about five o'clock (Wilson's diary says two o'clock, but this does not add up: all the accounts of those present put Allenby's arrival at II Corps headquarters at two o'clock). The hour or so that it took to motor from Berty to St Quentin was an indication of the congestion on the roads, for it was no more than 18 miles. Smith-Dorrien's message was immediately acknowledged by the commander-in-chief, with an update on the general situation, concluding:

> If you can hold your ground the situation appears likely to improve. Fourth Division must co-operate. French troops are taking offensive on right of I Corps. Although you are given a free hand as to method this telegram is not intended to convey the impression that I am not as anxious for you to carry out the retirement, and you must make every endeavour to do so.

But the message was more than usually ambiguous: the situation appeared 'likely to improve' if II Corps could hold its ground, yet Sir John French was 'anxious' for them to carry out the retirement. This was not the clarity expected of a commander-in-chief; but, then, he had just been roused from his sleep (by Wilson) after another exhausting day, and he would not allow Murray, the chief of staff, to be woken. An hour or so later, perhaps tutored by Wilson, he had quite changed his mind, and despatched his prize liaison officer, Colonel Jack Seely (the former secretary for war), to Bertry to say so. And just to make sure, he told Wilson to telephone Smith-Dorrien to say likewise.

The commander of II Corps was therefore called to the station at about 7 a.m. (after Seely's arrival, and two hours after the German attacks had begun) with the message that the commander-in-chief wished to speak to him. Instead he found the sub-chief of staff, Wilson, at the other end of the line, with French's instructions

> to the effect that I should break off the action as soon as possible. I replied that I would endeavour to do so, but that it would be difficult, and that I had hoped to be able to hold on until evening and slip away in the dark. Henry Wilson asked what I thought of our chances, and I replied that I was fully confident and hopeful of giving the enemy a smashing blow and slipping away before he could recover.

Despite GHQ's concern about the attacks on Haig's I Corps, which would inevitably delay their arrival on the Le Cateau position, Smith-Dorrien's confidence at the end of a long night was evidently infectious, for Wilson replied: 'Good luck to you. Yours is the first cheerful voice I have heard these three days.'

There is more than a suspicion of dissembling on Wilson's part here, for Smith-Dorrien records that these were unforgettably 'pleasing words'; it does not seem to have been the peremptory order to retire that Sir John French (in retrospect at least) believed he had told Wilson to issue.

Meanwhile, after the two o'clock decision to stand and fight, Forestier-Walker, Smith-Dorrien's chief of staff, and the rest of II Corps headquarters were being put to the test. Besides having to reverse the orders to the 3rd and 5th Divisions and the corps troops (artillery, engineers and logistics), there was the 19th Brigade to take in hand, and General Sordet's Cavalry Corps to inform, with a request that he continue to cover the left flank. Smith-Dorrien went in person to tell the 5th Division; Fergusson, the divisional commander, who was just about to issue orders for the continuing retirement, was relieved at the news. Crucially, however, there remained the 4th Division to inform: and its commander, Snow, received the message asking if he would fight under Smith-Dorrien's orders only at 5 a.m., just as he too was issuing orders for further withdrawal. He readily agreed: the division was very weary. Indeed, he wrote subsequently to Smith-Dorrien that it was impossible for him to have decided otherwise: 'When you sent to me the morning of the 26th to ask if I would stand and fight, I ought to have answered: "I have no other choice, as my troops are already engaged in a battle of encounter, and it must be some hours before I can extricate them." '*

In a rare lapse of circumspection, Sir John French's biographer, Richard Holmes, writes: 'Most historians would agree with Smith-Dorrien and his supporters that the stand at Le Cateau was justified.' For what is the opinion of historians when it comes to such a military judgement? The commander of the Cavalry Division believed that II Corps would be forced to fight at daylight, the commander of the 3rd that he could not get away before nine, and the commander of the 4th that he had no choice but to stand and fight. As Sir John French himself wrote in *1914*, 'As to this decision, a commander on the spot, and in close touch with his Divisions and Brigades, is in the best position to judge of what his men can do.' Except that, having said so, he then tried to claim that authority for himself: 'I had, late on the evening of the 25th, before leaving for my Headquarters at St. Quentin, visited several units of the 2nd Corps in their bivouacs and, though tired indeed, they had not struck me as being worn out troops.'†

* It was a desperate decision, for the 4th Division 'lacked the very essentials for a modern battle. It had none of the following: Divisional Cavalry, Divisional Cyclists, Signal Company, Field Ambulances, Field Companies R.E., Train and Divisional Ammunition Column, or Heavy Artillery. Let the reader think what that means – no troops to give warning, neither rapidly moving orderlies nor cables for communication, no means of getting away wounded, no engineers, who are the handy men of an army, no reserve ammunition, and no long-range heavy shell fire' (Smith-Dorrien, *Memories of Forty Years' Service*).

† 'Late on the evening' is tricky. GHQ issued orders for the retreat to continue at 7.30 p.m.; these could hardly have been finalized without the presence of the C-in-C. In any case, it is Smith-Dorrien's view that a mistaken impression might have been gained – even by someone as experienced as Sir John French – by seeing more of the rear echelons than the fighting ones: 'with the exception of a few units of the 5th Division, no fighting units were on the position before dark . . . I specify "fighting units," as all transport and impedimenta accompanied by baggage guards, cooks, clerks, sick, etc. had moved off from our line positions on the night of the 24th about midnight and had therefore mostly reached their new positions in the course of the next morning, so a large number of men were to be seen cooking, washing, and waiting for the arrival of their Corps. I mention this as a good deal has been written on the subject as evidence that troops were in camp early, for I feel sure these detachments I have mentioned were mistaken for the actual fighting troops.' In fairness to French, in the small hours of 'Shrapnel Monday' he had thought people unduly pessimistic, and been proved right:

But what was the trouble in which Haig's I Corps was embroiled that so alarmed GHQ? Sir John French was woken at two o'clock with the news that the Germans had followed up aggressively, that the corps was heavily engaged, the headquarters at Landrecies was itself under heavy attack, and that Haig was calling for help, as the situation was 'very critical'. Henry Wilson (Murray being asleep) told the commander-in-chief that there was a very real chance of the Germans' driving a wedge between I and II Corps.

What in fact had happened was that a single German regiment of three battalions (*Infanterie-Regiment 27*), with artillery support, had managed to close on the town by way of several of the tracks through the Forêt de Mormal and attack the outposts of the 4th (Guards) Brigade. A running street-fight had ensued in which Haig, uncharacteristically, lost his head, ordering all papers to be destroyed and the headquarters to move at once. He had been off colour for twenty-four hours, and dosed heavily by the headquarters medical officer (probably with kaolin and morphine, for earlier he had been prostrated with diarrhoea), but this could hardly account for his hasty conclusion that I Corps was in peril, especially as neither the 1st nor the 2nd Division's headquarters was in the least troubled. But the corps was certainly off balance, in large part due to the crossing and recrossing of the Sambre and the mingling with Lanrezac's units. Sir John French, now not unreasonably beginning to wonder if the real threat to the BEF was on the right rather than the left – or perhaps even both, a double envelopment – ordered Haig to direct his retirement on Guise, due south, rather than south-west towards Busigny and II Corps, and sent a message to Smith-Dorrien at 3.50 a.m. asking if he could help. This, of course, crossed with Smith-Dorrien's message telling GHQ he was going to make a stand at Le Cateau, and brought the predictable reply that he could not move. At five o'clock French even sent a request for help to Lanrezac, of all people – though, to his credit, on receiving the message (via Huguet) the commander of the 5th Army ordered

---

'The Corps and Divisional Staff Officers who were called into Headquarters to receive orders, especially those of the 2nd Corps, thought our position was much more seriously threatened than it really was and, in fact, one or two expressed doubts as to the possibility of effecting a retirement in the presence of the enemy in our immediate front. I did not share these views' (see page 322 above).

his left wing to do what it could to shield I Corps' withdrawal.*

But if the reaction to the street-fight at Landrecies shows Haig's judgement in poor light, it at least demonstrates his fighting spirit. 'If we are caught, by God, we'll sell our lives dearly!' he rasped as he rushed to find the brigade commander, Brigadier-General Robert Scott-Kerr, to tell him to put up barricades – and then in person to the billets of the Irish Guards to have them form a 'reduit' (a strongpoint on which to fall back).† It must have been a queer moment for the Micks' commanding officer – battle orders direct from the corps commander – as well as quite a task, for the battalion was so soundly asleep that even the sudden shellfire failed to wake some of them (two subalterns were actually left behind when the brigade quit the town). And there were the inevitable moments of high farce, which Kipling recounts in the regimental history: 'One of the regimental drums was seen and heard going down Landrecies main street in the darkness, strung on the fore-leg of a gun-horse who had stepped into it as a battery went south. A battalion cooker, the sparks flying from it, passed like a fire-engine hastening to a fire, and men found time to laugh and point at the strange thing.'‡

Doubtless as Haig was rushing to the barricades he was also ruing his choice of headquarters – so far forward and on the edge of an unsecured forest. Time and again in his history of the Irish Guards Kipling emphasizes that 'a battalion's field is bounded by its own vision', but that night the same was true of I and II Corps. Both Haig and Smith-Dorrien clearly had the impression of a dam about to burst before them, whereas Sir John French perceived there was a deal more water the dams could take. Just before midnight, however, Haig decided to break out from his supposed encirclement, telling Charteris, his chief of intelligence, to get into the front of the staff car and choose the best route. 'I asked for five minutes to study the map,' wrote Charteris in his memoir of Haig,

---

* He issued the order at 7 a.m.: 'The British I Corps is hard pressed by German forces debouching south and perhaps south-east from Landrecies. The Group of Reserve Divisions and the XVIII Corps are ordered to face this attack with such forces as they can dispose of, and to counter-attack so as to disengage the British I Corps which is retiring south from Landrecies.'
† Charteris, *Field Marshal Earl Haig.*
‡ Rudyard Kipling, *The Irish Guards in the Great War* (London, 1923).

Then off we started. It was rather eerie work, it was quite dark and of course no lights on the car. There was a little mist, which was helpful in one way, but it made it more difficult to find the road. There was still a good deal of firing, and it looked rather a forlorn hope to try to get through. But anyhow it was better than staying in Landrecies and having sooner or later to surrender, which seemed the alternative.*

They did get through, but Charteris reckoned it 'a close shave'. Certainly if Smith-Dorrien's experience of leaving GHQ on the first night of his new command was anything to go by, it would indeed have been a close shave – the risk not so much the Germans as the French, or even his own troops. Two days earlier B Squadron of the South Irish Horse had been attached to I Corps headquarters as protection troops; the consequences of such a 'blue on blue' – Haig being shot by Irishmen – do not bear thinking about.

As soon as Haig made it out of Landrecies he found the 1st Division's headquarters and told Major-General Sam Lomax to mount a rescue operation for the 4th Brigade. As dawn broke, however, the situation at last became clear: the 4th Brigade needed no assistance. The I Corps was able to resume the retreat unmolested – but due south rather than south-west.

The whole affair had been a triumph for Oberst Ernst von Below's *Infanterie-Regiment Prinz Louis Ferdinand von Preußen (2. Magdeburgisches) Nr. 27*. The regiment had fought at Ligny with Blücher, at Sadowa with the Elder Moltke, and again at Sedan, but never could they have achieved so much as at Landrecies, where they had stood to the 4th (Guards) Brigade all night, sent the 1st Division on a futile march, forced the commander of the I Corps to bolt, put GHQ in a spin, and turned the heads of the French XVIII Corps in Lanrezac's 5th Army. Above all, at dawn they had sent the I Corps marching east of the Sambre, putting ever more distance between them and Smith-Dorrien at Le Cateau.†

* Charteris, *Field Marshal Earl Haig*. Charteris, at least, appears to have been prepared to think prior to acting, along the lines of Abraham Lincoln's 'Give me six hours to chop down a tree and I will spend the first four sharpening the axe.'
† This whole extraordinary affair at Landrecies is given an equally extraordinary gloss in Sir John French's memoirs, *1914*: 'When darkness fell on the 25th, the enemy had sent forward advance troops in motors and lorries through the Forêt de Mormal in pursuit of the 1st Corps. This culminated in a violent attack on Landrecies, which, however, was splendidly driven off with heavy loss to the enemy . . . Sir Douglas Haig, although his troops were very tired and handicapped also by heavy rearguard fighting,

still proceeded to carry out the instructions he had received, and the retirement of the 1st Corps was continued in excellent order and with complete efficiency.' That said, however, for some Landrecies was no picnic, and it produced I Corps' first VC. Lance-Corporal George Wyatt of the 3rd Coldstream twice dashed from cover under very heavy fire at close range to extinguish burning straw so that the position could be held, and, although wounded in the head, he continued firing until he could no longer see because of the blood pouring down his face. The RMO bound up the wound and ordered him to the rear, but he returned instead to the firing line. In April 1915 Major-General Lomax would die of wounds sustained near Ypres at the end of October.

Chapter Eighteen

'A DAY WILL BE WRITTEN IN STORY'

The guiding principle in all delaying action must be that when an enemy has liberty to manoeuvre, the passive occupation of a position, however strong, can rarely be justified, and always involves the risk of crushing defeat.

Field Service Regulations, Part I: *Operations*

'The 26th August, the anniversary of [the battle of] Crécy, dawned hot and misty, with some prospect that the historic weather of A.D. 1346 would be repeated, and the certainty that in an almost similarly desperate situation, the stout hearts of our island race would again triumph over superiority of numbers, and rob the enemy of what he considered an easy prey.'

The remarkably purple prose of the *Official History* sets the tone for its subsequent description of Le Cateau, the British army's biggest battle since Waterloo. Crécy, one of the great combats of the Hundred Years War, had been a victory against the odds for the English longbowmen, who were now metamorphosed into English riflemen 75 miles east of that momentous medieval battlefield – which had inspired poetry no less extravagant than the *Official History*'s prose:

His is the battle! his wholly!
For to-day is a day will be written in story
To the great world's end, and for ever:—
So, let him have the spurs, and the glory!

355

*

The 'him' of the poem* was Edward, Prince of Wales, the 'Black Prince'; the spurs and the glory of Le Cateau were meant to be Smith-Dorrien's. And at first Sir John French was content for it to be so, writing in his first despatch to Kitchener:

> I cannot close the brief account of this glorious stand of the British troops without putting on record my deep appreciation of the valuable services rendered by General Sir Horace Smith-Dorrien. I say without hesitation that the saving of the left wing of the Army under my command on the morning of the 26th August could never have been accomplished unless a commander of rare and unusual coolness, intrepidity, and determination had been present to personally conduct the operation.

Yet the following year he would tell Haig that he regretted not court-martialling Smith-Dorrien.

Such a court martial was a preposterous notion, involving as it would have the calling of evidence which (at the very least) must have raised doubts as to the competence of GHQ in general and Sir John French in particular. Indeed, it would have cast doubt on the competence of a good many more senior figures, including Haig and Allenby. The court martial of General Sir Horace Smith-Dorrien is one of the great trials of alternative history. Whatever its findings, the general conclusion could only have been that the retreat from Mons was not the higher command's finest hour (it is of course difficult to find any retreat in the army's history that earned its leaders abundant laurels, for retreat is unquestionably the most difficult operation of war).

Smith-Dorrien's view that the defensive position at Le Cateau was 'quite a good one – on rising ground with a fine field of fire and with several villages capable of defence along it' needs tempering. It was chosen by GHQ but the details of how it was actually to be defended were, naturally, left to the two corps commanders (or rather to II Corps' commander, since I Corps would never make it to the field). It had been the same at Waterloo: the duke of Wellington had

---

* 'Crécy', from Francis Palgrave's *The Visions of England: Lyrics on Leading Men and Events in English History* (London, 1881).

identified the ridge at Mont St Jean as a good place to make a stand but left the detailed disposition of the army to his chief of staff, Colonel Sir William de Lancey (or DeLancey), as he himself was drawn forward to the battle at Quatre Bras. *Infantry Training* (1914) says of the choice of a defensive position:

> The object must be to obtain the maximum of fire effect on all ground over which the enemy can advance, with the minimum exposure to his fire. An extensive field of fire from the position offers many advantages, but if the enemy be very superior in artillery a restricted field of fire combined with comparative security from his guns may give better results.

The position at Le Cateau would have made a perfect staff college study in the difficulties of resolving these conflicting demands.

There is some evidence that Wellington, when he made his prospective reconnaissance of the ridge at Mont St Jean in the weeks before Napoleon crossed the border, sited the line further forward, and that it was de Lancey, in making the detailed dispositions, who pulled the bulk of the line back. No such adjustment took place on 26 August, as the *Official History* explains:

> Officers had been sent ahead [to the rear; the enemy is always 'to the front'] to reconnoitre the position, but most of the units did not come on to it until dark, and heavy rain had interfered with the observation of those which reached it earlier in the day. Moreover it was difficult to identify places by the map; for the only one then available was the French uncontoured hachured map of the 1:80,000 scale, to which British officers were not accustomed.* When the troops stood to arms about 4 A.M. [at first light] under orders to continue the retreat, there was a heavy ground mist, so that, though the troops were approximately in position, there was little opportunity, or apparent necessity, to rectify the line and choose the best ground to repel a determined attack by superior numbers.

---

* Hachures: strokes drawn in the direction of the slope, the thicker, shorter and closer ones representing the steeper slopes, the gentler slopes shown by thinner, longer and further-apart strokes. British officers were trained to use the Ordnance Survey maps, whose contour lines joined points of equal height. These were much more accurate in locating a specific point (vital in calling for – 'predicting' – artillery fire). But a hachured map can in fact give a better impression of topography at a glance, and for staff purposes may therefore sometimes be superior.

Reading between the lines and other accounts, it is clear that a number of units were in the wrong place (at Waterloo the regiments arriving after dark were shepherded into position by officers with lanterns; at Le Cateau the circumstances were not as favourable) – and not only the wrong place but in positions in which they were needlessly exposed once the mist cleared, and which, in the expectation of moving off at once, the battalions had not properly laid out. It was understandable, given the general exhaustion, but it was a lapse in field discipline nevertheless. Occupying a defensive position at night is almost as difficult as withdrawing from one in contact, especially without good maps – or even poor ones, for on crossing the Belgian border during the march up to Mons the maps of France had for the most part been 'back-loaded'; many would be the stories of commanding officers making their way through the whole retreat with a small road atlas. Amazingly it was the same for the French army too: their stores were full of maps of Germany – which would not be needed for four years.

'But if the enemy be very superior in artillery . . .' Here was the rub. The BEF had not been forced out of their positions at Mons by weight of artillery fire alone, and they had not stood so long in position in the following two days as to feel the effect of any prolonged bombardment; they had not yet developed therefore a proper respect for high explosive, especially that of the howitzers. The infantry, in defence, could take cover against shrapnel, but HE could blast them mercilessly in their trenches, even ones that had been dug well – which at Le Cateau by and large they had not been – and demolish the buildings in which they took cover. At Crécy the English longbowmen had been spared the artillery of the day – crossbow bolts – because the Genoese mercenaries had allowed their strings to get soaked in the downpour preceding the battle, thereby losing range; at Le Cateau, the British infantryman would discover for the first time in history what it was to be 'fixed' by artillery.

The II Corps position was in essence a line from Beauvois to Le Cateau (a distance of about eight miles) angled back at each end. The 3rd and 5th Divisions had changed places during the withdrawal (no mean feat of staffwork), so the 3rd was now on the left of the II Corps line, and the 5th was on the right with a brigade (Brigadier-General Stuart Rolt's 14th) east and south of the town of Le Cateau to guard the right flank and make contact with Haig's I Corps (who, of course, would never arrive). When Major-General Snow agreed to act under his orders, Smith-Dorrien posted the 4th Division on the extreme left, angling back almost forty-five degrees from the Cambrai–Le Cateau road, to secure the corps left flank – the one he believed was the most threatened (indeed, believing that Haig was coming on to his right he had had no real concern for his other flank).

Cambrai itself, 7 miles west and north of Beauvois, was still held by d'Amade's Territorials (whose resilience, as part-time troops, was questionable), with the space in between occupied, in the very loosest sense, by General Sordet's worn-out Cavalry Corps. Some of these were in the neighbourhood of Walincourt, 2½ miles south of Esnes, where the 12th Brigade (of the 3rd Division) had placed its outer flank.

On the right of the II Corps front, the Selle, not much more than a stream, ran south to north forming a right-angle with the road at Le Cateau in which the three brigades of the 5th Division were crowded, less two battalions of the 14th Brigade either side of the road east of the town. The Selle was the notional inter-corps boundary, and the divisional commander, Sir Charles Fergusson, expected to be able to pull the battalions back into the right-angle once Haig's I Corps arrived.

In the centre and left of the II Corps front the 8th and 9th Brigades of the 3rd Division held the high ground overlooking Inchy, midway between Le Cateau and Beauvois, and the 7th occupied Caudry, 2 miles further along the road to Beauvois.

Neither the 3rd nor the 5th Division's positions had much depth – the brigades were largely 'in the shop window' – nor any reserve to speak of. Allenby's Cavalry Division had to suffice: the 1st Cavalry Brigade and part of the badly scattered 2nd formed the depth flank guard on the right, while the 3rd Cavalry Brigade were still well to the east trying to make contact with I Corps (though they would come back in during the morning just to the south of Le Cateau). The 4th Cavalry Brigade were posted in Selvigny to watch the left flank.

It was not ideal ground for what Smith-Dorrien had called a 'smashing' or a 'stopping' blow. If his intention had been merely to *delay* the Germans, then the long fields of fire all along the corps front would have been useful: the advancing troops would be forced to make the

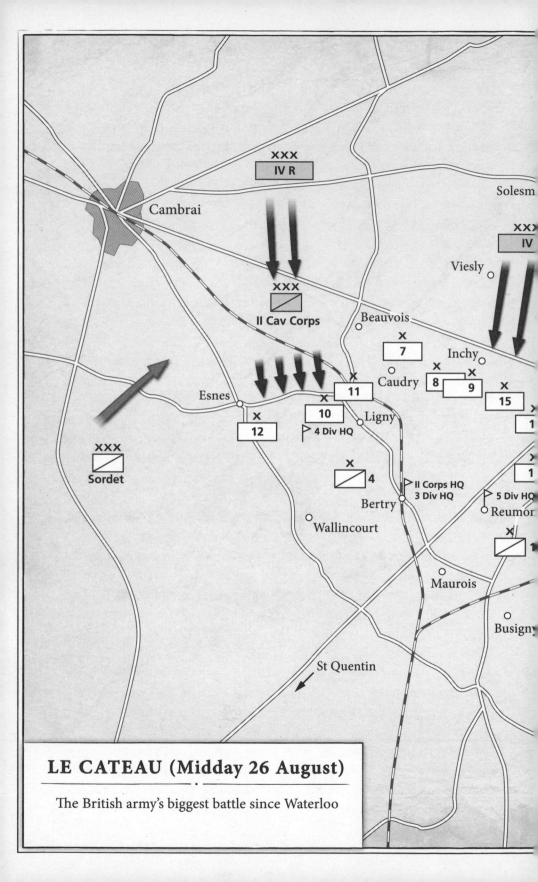

XXX
IV R

Cambrai

Solesm

XXX
IV

Viesly ○

XXX
II Cav Corps

Beauvois ○

x
7

Inchy ○

x
8

x
9

Caudry ○

x
15

x
11

Esnes ○

x
10

Ligny ○

x
12

▷ 4 Div HQ

XXX
Sordet

x
4

▷ II Corps HQ
3 Div HQ

▷ 5 Div HQ

Reumor ○

x
4

Bertry ○

○ Wallincourt

x

Maurois ○

○ Busigny

St Quentin
←

LE CATEAU (Midday 26 August)

The British army's biggest battle since Waterloo

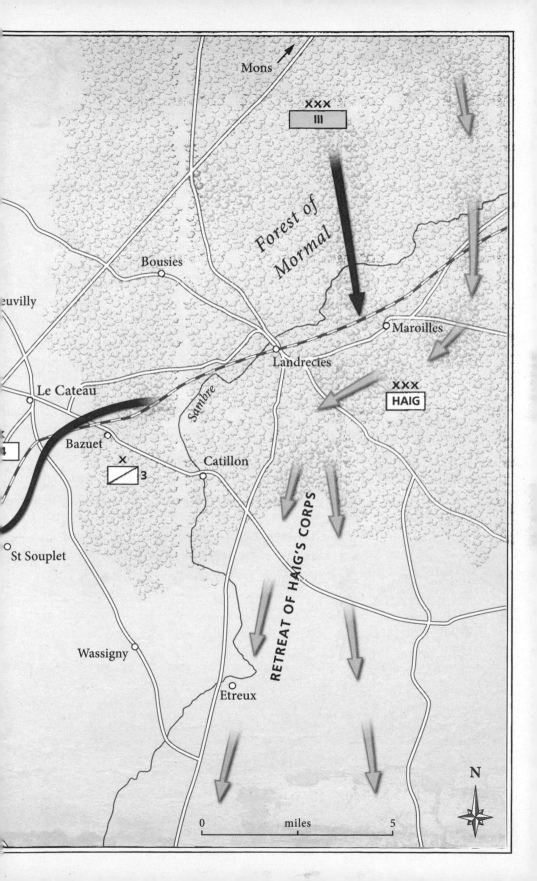

Mons

XXX
III

Forest of
Mormal

Bousies

euvilly

Maroilles

Landrecies

Le Cateau

Sambre

XXX
HAIG

Bazuet

X
3

Catillon

St Souplet

RETREAT OF HAIG'S CORPS

Wassigny

Etreux

0   miles   5

N

usual preparations and deploy for the assault, which would take time, and then the defenders could slip away before the attack developed fully, to repeat the tactic on the next suitable piece of ground. But the purpose of Smith-Dorrien's 'smashing' or 'stopping' blow – terms not in any official pamphlet – was to render the enemy incapable of following up the withdrawal with the vigour they had been showing the previous two days. The corps could then put some distance between itself and the leading German elements and regain cohesion – in short, break clean. Such a blow would not merely mean forcing the Germans to deploy but inflicting heavy casualties; and this in turn would mean receiving the attacks, beating them back and then doing the same again – until nightfall, when the defenders could quit the positions on the forward slopes without being observed (and, more importantly, without being shelled). It was a tall order, not least because it flew in the face of the warning in *Field Service Regulations* that 'the passive occupation of a position, however strong, can rarely be justified, and always involves the risk of crushing defeat'. For over such a frontage and with the troops available, there was little chance of other than a passive defence.*

It is not clear how far the battalions understood that the idea was to deliver a 'smashing blow' and then break clean: some units did not even receive the order *not* to retire at daybreak, and only held their ground to conform with what they saw about them. But to begin with it didn't matter: they just wanted to fight rather than keep running away. The II Corps reserve, the 19th Brigade, who had marched perhaps the furthest since Sunday (although they had had the good fortune of being railed up to Mons) and like the 5th Division had crossed the field from left to right, stumbling into Le Cateau itself at midnight with German cavalry still on their heels, were on the move again before daybreak. As Private Frank Richards relates,

* The warning appears in these specific words (as an amendment, in bold type) in the 1914 edition of *FSR*, issued on 10 November, though its import appeared in the original (1909) edition. It is tempting to think – though it cannot be established – that these ringing words were inspired by the experience of Le Cateau, which, by mid-October, Sir John French saw in a very different light from that of his initial despatch, and that they were meant thereby to be a standing rebuke to Smith-Dorrien. Le Cateau was certainly not being held up in the amended *FSR* as an example of what a 'stopping' or 'smashing' blow could achieve.

we were rousted at 4 a.m. and ordered to leave our packs and greatcoats on the square. Everyone was glad when that order was issued; the only things we had to carry now, besides rifle and ammunition, were an extra pair of socks and our iron rations . . . At dawn we marched out of Le Cateau with fixed bayonets. Duffy ['a time-serving soldier with six years service'] said: 'we'll have a bang at the bastards today.' We all hoped the same.

The infantry of the German 7th Division (IV Corps) were quick to begin infiltrating on the right flank, getting into the outskirts of Le Cateau itself and surprising the Cornwalls and East Surreys posted east of the Selle, while using the cover of the mist in the valley to get on to the high ground – from where their artillery would be able to enfilade the 5th Division. The 5th's own guns were for the most part deployed on forward slopes, mindful of *Field Artillery Training*'s desperate injunction: 'To support infantry and to enable it to effect its purpose the artillery must willingly sacrifice itself.' Indeed, more than one battery had been ordered forward from behind a crest so that the infantry brigade it supported could see the guns rather than simply their effect. The problem was, of course, that they then became targets for the German artillery – especially when the teams came forward to extricate them. The 5th Division would have to abandon nearly half its artillery by the end of the day's fighting, the horses lying dead in their harness all over the forward slopes. Things were a little better in the centre, where the 3rd Division used gun positions on the reverse slope, but because communications over the ridgeline were difficult, their supporting fire was less effective (although most of the guns would survive to fight another day).*

In any case, no real pressure built up in front of the 3rd Division before midday, by which time the 5th had been in serious action for six hours. So, too, had the 4th Division on the left flank. Indeed as Major-General Snow would tell Smith-Dorrien later, the division had been in continuous action since the afternoon before, which was why he believed he had no option but to stand and fight at dawn. But the division was not yet as tightly handled as the other two, which had been in action, or preparing for it, for the better part of a week now. Not long after 6 a.m., 1st Battalion the King's Own, in the 12th

---

* 'Saving the guns at Le Cateau' would become a favourite subject for cigarette cards, the Royal Artillery adding three VCs that day to its growing tally.

Brigade, was caught in one of the worst lapses of field discipline of the retreat when the commanding officer, Lieutenant-Colonel Alfred Dykes, believing his troops were screened by Sordet's cavalry, ordered the companies to pile arms, remove equipment and rest, despite being on a forward slope – though he could see the Lancashire Fusiliers digging in vigorously on the crest behind. When horsemen appeared from the trees 1,000 yards in front of the battalion, Dykes took no notice, assuming them to be French (if the divisional cavalry squadron had still been with the 4th Division there might have been no confusion). Moments later machine guns opened up in long, raking bursts, killing eighty-three men including Dykes himself, wounding 200, and horse artillery accounting for another hundred with shrapnel in the scrambling minutes that followed. Those King's Own who emerged unscathed were extricated only by the spirited support of the 1st Royal Warwicks from the 10th Brigade, one of whose platoon commanders was Lieutenant Bernard Law Montgomery. What is extraordinary about this regimental disaster is that Dykes had won the DSO while adjutant of the 2nd Battalion at Spion Kop in the Boer War, where the searing experience of small-arms fire from dominating ground had made such an impression on the army as a whole. Despite the débâcle, however, the King's Own reorganized and fought doggedly later in the day – exactly as the second battalion had done after the débâcle of Spion Kop. The BEF was a mentally toughened army.*

But if the long fields of fire had caught out the King's Own, they were doing the Germans no favours either. Across much of the II Corps front, lines of field grey topped by the spikes of the distinctive *Pickelhaube*† advanced down the forward slopes, giving the BEF's marksmen and gunners full opportunity. Private Frederick Spicer of the 1st Bedfords (who would be commissioned and rise to lieutenant-colonel) wrote in his diary:

---

* Zuber's treatment of the King's Own affair in *The Mons Myth* is characteristically over-stated: 'The battalion had been smashed in minutes . . . The 12th Brigade was now down to two battalions . . . Both battalions had effectively been destroyed.' This is simply not true: the King's Own remained a fighting entity, and so did the Lancashire Fusiliers, who took an almost equal number of casualties in the course of the fighting throughout that day. The 12th Brigade mounted a counter-attack in the early afternoon to recover the ground they had been forced off, though unsuccessfully.
† The leather (formerly metal) *Pickelhaube* helmet had a cloth cover (*Überzug*) for wear in the field. It was the standard headdress of the infantry and much of the cavalry. *Pickel* = 'pick(axe)'; *Haube* = 'bonnet'.

It must have been midday or later when the enemy infantry began to attack our immediate front. We had a real hour's hard work firing our rifles. Luckily we had brought plenty of ammunition with us, and we needed it. Line after line of German infantry advanced only to be mowed down by our rifle and machine gun fire. The battery of the 15th Artillery Brigade in the dip of ground [close behind] did great execution. The enemy suffered such enormous losses that they were unable to force us from our positions, and themselves had to withdraw from our front for a time until they were reinforced.

The 4th Division, after its disastrous start, spent much of the rest of the morning under heavy artillery fire, fending off probing attacks by dismounted cavalry and by jaegers in their distinguishing grey-green tunics and squat black shakos. It was much the same with the 3rd Division in the centre, Captain Alexander Johnston describing the impact, literal and metaphorical, of the German 5.9-inch (15 cm) shell with its 11 lb bursting charge of HE – 'they make a most awful report and in buildings do a fearful lot of damage . . . The German infantry showed no inclination to assault, there had been a considerable lull on their fire until they commenced their high explosive [i.e. not shrapnel] shell fire, which I believe was a last resort' – and remarking on 'the disaster' to the 8th Brigade to the right of his, the 7th, 'which had been caught by the German artillery when crowded in a village nearby'.

But the left flank and the centre were not the real points of weakness. As the RFC was soon able to confirm, the 5th Division were slowly but surely having their right flank turned: Captain (later Air Commodore) Lionel Charlton, landing near II Corps headquarters at Bertry,

found Smith-Dorrien in considerable anxiety as to his left about Haucourt and Selvigny. Having been on that flank at 9.30 a.m., I was able to reassure him as to its safety, and made another ascent to confirm my previous reconnaissance. During the reconnaissance I was able to report that the enemy had made no progress, though their shell-fire had increased. I was sent up again to examine the right about Le Cateau, and on reporting at 2.45 p.m. the General told me that the Fifth Division had been unable to withstand a most determined artillery attack, and had come back. He added that he had no doubt he would succeed in getting them back somehow, and requested me to inform Sir Archibald Murray. I left at 3.0 p.m. and reported to General Headquarters as ordered.

There is no doubt that during the retreat the RFC were a more valuable means of gaining intelligence than the cavalry, who were increasingly – and with increasing desperation – employed in the protective role.*

But there was yet no news of Haig's I Corps – they were, in fact, still marching south and east – and in the early afternoon the commander of the 5th Division, Fergusson, told Smith-Dorrien that his men were beginning 'to dribble away under their severe punishment', and that if he were to make any sort of orderly withdrawal it would have to be soon. The Germans had already penetrated between his 13th and 14th Brigades, practically wiping out the 2nd Suffolks, including their commanding officer, Lieutenant-Colonel Charles Brett; they had brought up artillery for direct fire at short range and were heavily shelling his own headquarters.†

With only the 19th Brigade as reserve, two battalions of which he had already had to deploy, Smith-Dorrien had no choice but to take Fergusson's advice. He therefore sent out the executive order to begin withdrawing along the routes his headquarters had already prescribed, beginning with the 5th Division, and sending what remained of the corps reserve – a field battery, the 1st Cameronians and the 2nd Royal Welsh Fusiliers – to take up a position astride the Roman road from Le Cateau to Maretz to cover their retirement. Frank Richards was not impressed: the 1st Argyll and Sutherland Highlanders, one of the other battalions in the brigade, had had what he considered a good fight in support of the 15th Brigade (and 'lost half their battalion'), but the Fusiliers were 'fed up' because 'we simply marched

---

* This should not have come as a surprise, except perhaps in respect of just how accurate and useful the RFC's reconnaissance was. In a report to *GQG* on the meeting between Sir John French and Lanrezac on 17 August, the 5th Army's chief of staff, Hély d'Oissel, stated: 'The British cavalry will never be available to participate in the operations undertaken by General Sordet's Corps. It will be employed as mounted infantry in the line, and cannot be counted on for any other purpose.' Doubtless French would have disputed this reading, but clearly Lanrezac and his staff had concluded that that was the import of the field marshal's concept of operations.
† The Suffolks had sailed from Dublin numbering 28 officers and 971 other ranks. When the battalion mustered at Bohain the day after Le Cateau they numbered two officers and 111 other ranks. The majority of the losses were men who were wounded and taken prisoner.

and countermarched during the whole time that this was going on'. They got a grim enough picture of what they were missing as they did so, however: 'In every village we marched through the church had been converted into a field hospital and was generally full of our wounded.'

Fergusson's division began withdrawing at about half-past three, and in the process possibly lost as many men – and certainly more guns – than in the fighting up to that time, for they were having to withdraw up the forward slopes of the spurs under cover of, in the main, nothing but the rifle fire of the rearguards. Captain Arthur Acland, adjutant of the Cornwalls, was especially grateful to Gough's 3rd Cavalry Brigade, 'which came up most opportunely. If it had not been for them, A. & D. Co'ys could never have got away, I'm sure. We had Germans on three sides of us and the rest of our people. We were jolly lucky to get out as we did.' He was in fact doubly lucky, for he had borrowed one of the commanding officer's horses to take the order for withdrawal to the companies: 'I don't quite know why I did it . . . The poor animal was hit in the head and just behind my leg, through the side. He died very soon after. I then remembered I was not on manoeuvres.'

It was quite evidently a desperate scrabble all across the front, as Smith-Dorrien recalled:

The troops were so hopelessly mixed up, and so many leaders had gone under that a regular retirement was almost impossible, especially too as the enemy was close up and pressing hard. Thanks, however, to the deter-mined action of Major Yate of the Yorkshire Light Infantry, who sacrificed himself and his men in holding the Germans off, the troops of the 5th Division got back on to the road.* Luckily the 15th Infantry Brigade was intact, and they about Troisvilles, the 19th Brigade about Maurois, and the R.H.A. guns of the cavalry farther to the east and south kept the enemy off and prevented the envelopment of our flank and enabled the troops to get away. When the 3rd Division saw the 5th retiring they took it up, and finally the 4th Division. Both these two last-named Divisions, less heavily assailed than the 5th, and with their flanks better guarded, could have remained where they were certainly until after dark and had little difficulty

---

* One of Le Cateau's four VCs was awarded to Private (later Captain) Frederick Holmes of the King's Own Yorkshire Light Infantry.

in retiring, in comparatively good order, the 9th Brigade in perfect order taking all their wounded with them. If the 4th Division were slightly more mixed up and irregular in their formations, it was due to the fact that they were immensely handicapped by their shortage of the necessities for fighting a battle (already described), largely in consequence of which their losses had been so heavy, amounting to about 25 per cent. of their war strength.*

But where was Haig's I Corps? GHQ didn't know, having only the most tenuous telephone contact with his headquarters after the Landrecies alarm; so the RFC had been told to find them. Lieutenant (later Air Vice-Marshal) Amyas Borton and Lieutenant Francis Small took off mid-morning in a Henri Farman, accompanied by Lieutenant Donald Lewis in a BE2 fitted with wireless. Borton and Small managed to make contact by landing close to a cavalry patrol, which was able to take a message to Haig, but Lewis lost contact with them, circled for an hour drawing fire, and eventually had to return to St Quentin with his damaged aircraft and a hand wound. However, Borton and Small now found they were unable to wait for a reply: two uhlans appeared in the distance and it became a race to start the engine and get away. GHQ would remain in the dark for many hours more about the I Corps' situation and movements.

So would many in the corps itself, for although they were under nothing like the pressure II Corps was facing, the route of the retreat – hemmed in by the Forêt de Mormal to the west and Lanrezac's 5th Army to the east – imposed its own 'friction', which the merest enemy pressure only seemed to exacerbate. Sergeant John McIlwain of the 2nd Connaught Rangers, in the 5th Brigade (2nd Division), records how, at about four o'clock that morning,

> our officers, who were wearied as ourselves, and apparently without orders, and in doubt what to do, led us back to the position of the night before. After some consultation we took up various positions in a shallow valley. Told to keep a sharp lookout for uhlans. We appeared to be in some covering movement. No rations this day; seemed to be cut off from supplies. Slept again for an hour or so on a sloping road until 11 am. We retired to a field, were told we could 'drum up' as we had tea. I went to a nearby

* *Memories of Forty Years' Service.*

village to get bread. None to be had, but got a fine drink of milk and some pears. Upon the sound of heavy gunfire near at hand we were hastily formed up on the road . . . By evening we mustered half-battalion strength. 'C' had about half a company. Over the whole Major Sarsfield took command, the Adjutant, Captain Yeldham, was also present. Colonel Abercrombie and 400 or so others were captured by the Germans.

Little wonder that the I Corps no longer believed it could join II Corps at Le Cateau. GHQ had come to that conclusion too – and perhaps with some discomfiture, for it was GHQ's function to maintain the cohesion of the BEF, and it does not take hindsight to see the threat that the Forêt de Mormal presented to that cohesion. Had Haig been able to – been ordered to – marry up with II Corps at Le Cateau, the threat to Smith-Dorrien's right wing would have been minimal. Indeed, there would have been a good chance of I Corps striking a smashing blow at the left flank of the German IV Corps. But once again, GHQ was playing more a loose coordinating role than one of command, not least because the chief of staff, Murray, was by now in a state of nervous collapse. Indeed, he got through the day only with the help of an injection given him by the headquarters medical officer.

For Sir John French, as his diary makes all too clear, the 568th anniversary of the battle of Crécy was a black day indeed. Not only was he losing grip on his command, he had the most disagreeable prospect of a meeting with Lanrezac. Joffre, whose *Instruction Générale* No. 2 GHQ had received during the night, had summoned the commander of the 5th Army, Lanrezac, and d'Amade, commanding the Territorials, to the BEF's headquarters at St Quentin with the intention of taking a firm grip on the rearward movement. The 5th Army's failure to make any progress with its counter-attacks had disturbed him, to say the least, but 'Papa' Joffre was not dismayed: plans were already in hand for his winning stratagem – a new *masse de manoeuvre*, the 6th Army, was being assembled around Amiens under the 66-year-old General Michel-Joseph Manoury, an artillery officer of coolness and resource.

The meeting of the four – Joffre, Lanrezac, d'Amade and Sir John French – took place in a house decorated in the 'neo-pompeian style', records Spears, although Lanrezac was late arriving: 'The windows and shutters were closed in the dimly lit chamber where the conference was held, and everyone spoke in an undertone as if there were a corpse in the next room.' Joffre asked French for a report on the situation of the BEF, which Henry Wilson proceeded to give on the field marshal's behalf, and then Lanrezac and his chief of staff arrived, and Joffre asked him to do likewise. The commander of the 5th Army did so, concluding his remarks 'with a touch of asperity' by referring to *Instruction Générale* No. 2, saying that he could not be expected to carry out the order to rest his left on St Quentin as the BEF barred the way. Joffre simply replied that he could retire instead on La Fère, and turned again to Sir John French for an acknowledgement. French, irritated not only by the presence of Lanrezac but with what he took to be a recurrence of his truculent manner, 'pointed out with acerbity' how precarious the BEF's position was: 'he had been cease-lessly attacked by overwhelming numbers, whereas the Fifth Army, attacked by an enemy inferior in strength, had continuously held back behind his own, and had finally retired headlong without warn-ing or explanation'.*

Wilson translated this – bowdlerized it, says Spears – and Lanrezac replied in (to Sir John French's mind) an off-hand, 'academic' way. Joffre looked hard at his subordinate, who was quite possibly working on the assumption that his railway warrant to Limoges was in the chief's pocket, but made no direct response. He embarked instead on an explanation of *Instruction Générale No. 2*, with its expectation of a grand counter-offensive in early September from positions to which the 5th Army and the BEF would in the meantime retreat. When Joffre had finished, Sir John French looked blank and said simply that he had no knowledge of the order, turning to Wilson for enlighten-ment – who replied that the order had been received, but had yet to be translated and studied.

Joffre appeared disconcerted (and his colleagues astonished), and with good reason. It beggars belief that the operations staff – of which Wilson was the deputy chief and, in Murray's prostration, the de facto head – had found anything more worthwhile to do than translate such a document, especially knowing that the French commander-in-

---

* He appears not to have known of Lanrezac's positive response to the request for help to the I Corps during the night.

chief was about to come to St Quentin to hold a conference. Wilson does not mention the event at all in his diaries, and neither does his editor, Callwell, who instead – after a passing reference to the fight at Le Cateau – writes: 'Since the retreat from Mons had begun, Wilson had been performing invaluable service at GHQ.' If he had, Sir John French could have been forgiven at that moment for thinking otherwise.

Joffre, however, in his imperturbable, elephantine way, went over the order again, but in a low, unemphatic voice that seemed to suggest he had already lost confidence in it. Silence followed the repetition, broken at length by the plucky if over-optimistic d'Amade, who suggested that his Territorials might launch a counter-attack into the German right flank – which Joffre dismissed impatiently (not surprisingly, since d'Amade had said earlier that his men gave way as soon as they saw German cavalry). And there the conference ended, with nothing absolutely decided, and very little discussed. It might in fact have been totally fruitless had traditional hospitality not come to the rescue: Sir John French invited both Joffre and Lanrezac to stay to lunch. Lanrezac made his excuses and left for his own headquarters, but Joffre accepted, and in the course of a meal whose menu is (sadly) unrecorded, he confided to the field marshal that he was far from satisfied with the way the 5th Army was being handled, and – with winning candour – admitted that his own plans had miscarried.*

When Joffre had left, GHQ turned its mind once more to the retreat, Sir John French, his personal staff, the dosed-up Murray and the ever-blithe Wilson leaving for Noyon, 15 miles south-west, in a little convoy of motor vehicles. 'To see the heads leaving, preceding the retreat, when no one knew anything but that things were going badly, had an immensely depressing influence on the rest of the staff and on all the troops in the town,' thought Spears – who recalled how in similar circumstances a French general had left his headquarters in

---

* In Paris the war minister, Messimy, was already paying the price for the failure of Plan XVII: on the day of Le Cateau he resigned, his place taken by the old socialist and future president, Alexandre Millerand. Like Seely – and, later, Churchill – Messimy would expiate his sins in uniform, rejoining the army as a reserve captain. By the end of the war he was commanding an infantry division; Seely, the Canadian Cavalry Brigade. It is diverting to speculate to what height Churchill would have risen if he had stayed in uniform after 1916 (assuming his reckless courage had not got him killed).

the direction of the enemy, 'for the sake of morale', before taking a side-road and driving south again. It would probably have been for the best if the field marshal had been able to sleep during the hour's drive, for his mind must otherwise have been turning over the events of the past four days, and perhaps recollecting the doubts he had entertained – and voiced – at the war council on 5 August. He had wondered if it were not better to go to Antwerp, to stiffen the Belgians when they – inevitably – fell back within its defences. Then Amiens had been mooted as a concentration area rather than Maubeuge, and now Joffre was telling him to fall back in the direction of that same city before they launched a counter-offensive. Was there not a terrible irony? For there at Amiens the BEF might have been at this very moment, with five divisions, not four, ready in every respect for battle – instead of this Corunna-like retreat and who-knew-how-many casualties. Sir John Moore's Spanish allies had let him down, forcing him to make that infamous march for the sea. Was it to be the same with allies again?

'It was after 4 p.m.,' records Smith-Dorrien, 'when my head-quarters were retiring from Bertry, that I rode with my Staff to watch the 5th Division pass along the road south of Maurois. I likened it at the time to a crowd coming away from a race meeting.' At twenty-one, Lieutenant Smith-Dorrien had seen troops streaming away from the battlefield of Isandhlwana, those few that had escaped the Zulu spears – a defeat that had stunned the nation. But if Isandhlwana were going through Smith-Dorrien's mind now, he did not say so, for the scene was altogether different: 'It was a wonderful sight – men smoking their pipes, apparently quite unconcerned, and walking steadily down the road – no formation of any sort, and men of all units mixed together. The curious thing was that the enemy were making no attempt to follow. They respectfully kept their distance behind the rear-guards, and later allowed the latter to retire without pressing them.'

It could only have been a 'wonderful sight' to a commander who had witnessed enough of war and men to see below the surface. Earlier Captain Alexander Johnston had been made 'sad and anxious for the future to see Englishmen behave like this', making their way back 'in a disgraceful manner' before the order to withdraw, although he adds: 'Of course these were only the bad men or men whose officers had been hit and were therefore out of control, and one always found plenty of splendid fellows holding on gamely even if their officers had gone.'

Indeed, some men did not get the order to retire, and went on fighting late into the night, confusing the Germans as to the BEF's intention and direction of withdrawal. And the French were giving stout support on the left, as Smith-Dorrien readily acknowledged:

> I had a momentary shock about 5 p.m. on getting clear of the village of Maretz, about three miles south of Maurois on the Roman road, for I suddenly heard very heavy artillery fire away to the north-west, which I reckoned was behind the 4th Division outer flank and feared the enemy had got behind Snow; but was much relieved, on galloping to a hill about a mile in that direction, to recognize the short sharp crack of the famous 'seventy-fives,' and then I knew they were French guns and probably Sordet's, and this they turned out to be.

Frank Richards recalled the 2nd Royal Welsh Fusiliers' withdrawal with characteristic soldier's phlegm: 'We retired all night with fixed bayonets, many sleeping as they were marching along . . . We were carrying our rifles all shapes and it was only by luck that many a man didn't receive a severe bayonet wound during the night.'

The last shots they had fired that day were at 'uhlans' galloping towards them in the dusk, Richards believed – at 600 yards. Except that they weren't uhlans but Sergeant Brunton's squadron of the 19th Hussars. And the shooting was deadly accurate.

That evening, Colonel Huguet wired Joffre from Noyon: 'Battle lost by British Army, which seems to have lost all cohesion. It will demand considerable protection to enable it to reconstitute.'

Chapter Nineteen

'C'EST LA FRANCE QUI VOUS SUPPLIE'

Half-hearted measures never attain success in war, and lack of
determination is the most fruitful source of defeat.

Field Service Regulations (1914)

It speaks volumes for Joffre that in spite of receiving Huguet's message
he did not falter. Indeed, he seems to have been invigorated by the
threat of collapse on his left flank, Spears having the distinct impression 'that the *GQG* was laying a firm hand on the direction of
affairs, and that drift and vacillation were at an end'. Joffre now sent
Lanrezac explicit instructions to counter-attack, craftily worded so as
to appear to be responding to the commander of the 5th Army's own
appreciation of the situation at the meeting the day before: 'You have
expressed to me your intention of throwing back by a counter-
offensive, well supported by artillery, the troops which are following
you, as soon as you have left the wooded region where the employment of your artillery is difficult. Not only do I authorize you to carry
this out, but I consider such an attack to be indispensable.' He added
that Lanrezac was to take no account of the condition of the BEF –
thereby thwarting the one, and obvious, cause for objecting to the
orders.

And then he sped to Noyon in his Peugeot, driven by Georges
Boillot, to boost Sir John French's spirits. The gesture would change

374

nothing as far as the field marshal's determination to retreat was concerned, however, and Joffre himself cannot have been encouraged by the experience. If Huguet thought Le Cateau was a battle lost, he could only have been reflecting the atmosphere in GHQ, which was in the end a thing of Sir John French's creation. The commander-in-chief would have been well aware of the duke of Wellington's dictum that a good general knows when to retreat and has the courage to do so, but Wellington's retreats had always been to advantage; the fate of Sir John Moore's army must have seemed the likelier model at this moment. Huguet evidently sensed all this: thinking that the news 'Battle lost by British Army' would go badly with the British public, he prompted Joffre the following day to send a warm message of appreciation for the BEF – '[which] by engaging itself without hesitation against greatly superior forces, has powerfully contributed towards assuring the security of the left flank of the French Army . . . [which] will not forget the service rendered'.

It was a great pity that Smith-Dorrien had not been at Noyon when Joffre called, for he would have been able to lighten the darkness. If Sir John French had allowed him to, that is. The commander of II Corps had arrived at GHQ in the early hours (not best pleased to have discovered it had moved from St Quentin without telling his own headquarters) and roused the field marshal and his staff: 'There was a convenient billiard-table in the room with a white cover,' he recorded; 'and spreading a map thereon I explained briefly the events of the day. Sir John appeared relieved, though he told me he considered I took much too cheerful a view of the situation' (which is confirmed by French's diary).

It is difficult, even after all these years, to fathom quite why GHQ, which had left St Quentin in the early afternoon, and none of whose principal staff officers had been forward even as far as the headquarters of the II Corps at Bertry, should have been so misleadingly gloomy when Smith-Dorrien himself was, at the very least, satisfied. It is the habit – the duty – of officers to maintain a cheerful face in the event of setbacks, but Smith-Dorrien had no hope of maintaining a fiction: if II Corps had suffered such a defeat as to render it incapable of fighting, the Germans would have followed up and destroyed the corps in detail. This simply did not happen. Indeed, II Corps was allowed to resume its retreat, and would continue for ten days in decent order and at very little cost in rearguards. For the truth was that they had indeed delivered a checking blow to Kluck's 1st Army. The stand at Le Cateau had for whatever reason dulled the ardour of his infantry and even his cavalry, and it thoroughly confused both Kluck and his staff, who became convinced that the BEF was trying to withdraw down its lines of communication – which they wrongly believed to be north-west through Cambrai and Lille to Calais (in fact, Kitchener was already considering changing the main port of entry from Le Havre to St Nazaire – further *south*).*

Kluck therefore now directed the 1st Army south and west in pursuit.

Meanwhile the II Corps marched almost due south. Not, however, in perfect order. The 'crowd coming away from a race meeting' had several faces, not all of them admirable, as Alexander Johnston had related at Caudry even while the race was still being run. One liaison officer, Christopher Baker-Carr, would describe how, while motoring about the lines of retreat next day, he kept coming across little groups of men who, when asked who they were, would reply: 'We're all that's left of the Blankshire Regiment, sir. All the rest got done in yesterday. Not a soul except us is left alive,' to which he would reply that if they kept heading south down the road for a couple of miles more they would come across 'three or four hundred sole survivors' of their regiment bivouacking in a field. 'This happened not once,' he writes, 'but twenty times . . . in the utmost good faith.'[†]

---

* Zuber, characteristically, marks down Le Cateau as a defeat. He correctly highlights the failings – largely the command arrangements – but criticizes Smith-Dorrien for failing to 'manoeuvre or counter-attack'. 'Manoeuvre' is easier to write than actually to do with exhausted soldiers on foot. The only force capable of manoeuvring was the Cavalry Division, but its brigades – rightly or wrongly – were spread about the battle-field on contact duty. They did little fighting during the day – witness the official figure of fifteen killed – but took up the classic role of cavalry in the retreat that evening. Zuber is right to point to the over-estimates in accounts such as Terraine's and Ascoli's of German strength actually brought to bear in the battle, but what is beyond question is that the German artillery greatly over-matched the British in both numbers and weight. Even this, though, is not quite the point: Le Cateau was a far from ideal defensive position, with too few troops to hold the ground adequately, yet the German 1st Army – which as the attacker held the initiative – failed to concentrate decisively. Neither could – or would – it follow up. Zuber says this was because it was dark; but if II Corps had suffered the demoralizing defeat he portrays – if it was 'not a cohesive, combat capable force for at least two days' – the pursuing troops should have been able to go through them like a knife through butter. You cannot have it both ways.
† C. D. Baker-Carr, *From Chauffeur to Brigadier* (London, 1930).

Disorientation is born of any number of things, but tiredness was universal, and it gave rise to some unedifying incidents. The remnants of the 1st Warwicks (who had put in the spirited counter-attack to extricate the King's Own the previous day) and the 2nd Dublin Fusiliers had stumbled into St Quentin on the morning of the 27th, some of the last men to do so. The commanding officers, Lieutenant-Colonels John Elkington and Arthur Mainwaring, sought out the mayor to ask for food and other help, but the mayor, believing that the Germans would arrive at any moment, agreed only on condition that they sign a document promising not to fight in the town, which they duly did. Whether they signed as an expedient or not, it was tantamount to a surrender document, and both officers would be court-martialled. Besides, their men were showing no signs of either quitting the town or making a stand: in the absence of determined leadership they had simply given up.* But the situation was saved by the arrival of a squadron of the cavalry rearguard under no other than Major Tom Bridges, whose men had fired the first shots at Mons on the twenty-second. Having failed to galvanize the commanding officers into action, he decided to take things in hand for himself:

> The men in the square were a different problem, and so jaded it was pathetic to see them. If one only had a band, I thought. Why not? There was a toy shop handy which provided my trumpeter and myself with a tin whistle and a drum, and [despite Bridges' shattered cheekbone and con-cussion] we marched round and round the fountain where the men were lying like the dead, playing 'The British Grenadiers' and 'Tipperary,' and beating the drum like mad. They sat up and began to laugh and even cheer. I stopped playing and made them a short exhortation and told them I was going to take them back to their regiments. They began to stand up and

---

* The affair bears a striking similarity with the retreat to Corunna, where some of the battalions disintegrated for lack of grip. Those that did not were kept together frequently (although not exclusively) by the lash. Many a soldier afterwards praised its use as the only thing that did the job, with particular admiration for one of its fiercest exponents, Major-General 'Black Bob' Craufurd, commanding the Light (Infantry) Brigade. The lash had long been abandoned in the British army; there was still 'field punishment', a sort of military stocks, but this was hardly suitable in a war of move-ment. It is not an over-simplification to say that discipline was best where the men feared their NCOs – in the sense of 'God-fearing' – and admired their officers. Allan Adair, on joining the Grenadiers, was told very firmly that his job was to 'show his guardsmen how to die'.

fall in, and eventually we moved slowly off into the night to the music of our improvised band, now reinforced with a couple of mouth-organs.*

During one of the periodic setbacks in the Peninsular War, an aide-de-camp of the duke of Wellington anxiously pointed to men running back from the fight, to which the duke replied simply: 'Oh, they all do that at some time. The question is, will they rally?' Certainly on the evening of 26 August the II Corps staff had made prodigious efforts to make sure the troops would, if called on, stand to and fight again. The knack was to disentangle the confusion of units, so officers were posted at road junctions directing the regiments to the routes allocated to their respective divisions. Smith-Dorrien himself rode as far as Estrées, one of the main rallying points, which he reached at last light (about 7.15 p.m.), transferring there from his horse to 'an excellent motor and A1 chauffeur placed at [my] disposal . . . by the generosity of Lord Derby' and setting off in the now pouring rain to St Quentin to report to Sir John French. At which point he discovered – to his fury – that GHQ had moved. So before driving the 35 more miles to Noyon he went to the station to find the director of railways, Colonel David MacInnes, to ask what trains he could give him for the weary and wounded. MacInnes told him he had orders to send all trains away, but agreed to keep them until Smith-Dorrien returned from Noyon – which he did, at dawn, with 'Wully' Robertson's permission ('blessing' would have been more like) to use any trains that MacInnes could spare. Still not done, Smith-Dorrien then took up quarters at the *mairie* with his personal staff – which, handily, included Prince Henri d'Orléans as liaison officer – and then watched his troops march through the town, diverting the most

---

* Tom Bridges, *Alarms and Excursions: Reminiscences of a Soldier* (London, 1938). Both colonels, in their late forties and bearing South Africa medal ribbons, were charged variously with cowardice and scandalous conduct, and 'shamefully delivering up a garrison to the enemy'; while they were acquitted of cowardice they were cashiered – dismissed with disgrace. Elkington at once enlisted in the ranks of the French Foreign Legion; fighting heroically throughout 1915, he was commissioned, badly wounded, and decorated with the *Medaille Militaire* and *Croix de Guerre* – and in 1916 pardoned, restored to his rank in the British army, and awarded the DSO personally by the King. Bridges himself would later command a division, before losing a leg at Ypres in 1917.

'Strange how potent cheap music is', says Amanda in Coward's *Private Lives*. But the Warwicks were further lifted some days later by better music: Field Marshal Montgomery, in his memoirs, describes the reviving effect of hearing the regimental band playing their jaunty regimental march 'The Warwickshire Lads'.

exhausted-looking to the railway station. Some of these were from Sergeant Brunton's squadron – horseless after the 'blue on blue' encounter with Frank Richards' Welsh Fusiliers. They had marched all night with the infantry, 'not knowing where we were going, and some caring less . . . The only way we got along was by linking arms and helping each other.'

Captain Acland of the Cornwalls had got along the same way: he and another officer 'walked arm in arm to keep us from rolling too much like drunken men . . . We had no notion where we were going, or what was behind us. We did know we were playing a big game. We knew the rules of the game, but we didn't know what the game was. If we hadn't known the rules, we wouldn't have got there' – a fair definition of professionalism.

It is difficult not to contrast Smith-Dorrien's energy in the aftermath of Le Cateau with the apparently torpid, despondent state of GHQ. Murray had again collapsed, and Henry Wilson sent Major-General Thomas Snow, commanding the 4th Division (which GHQ for some incomprehensible reason was still retaining under direct command), an instruction which, however jauntily worded, could only have had the most dismal effect: 'From Henry to Snowball. Throw overboard all ammunition and impedimenta not absolutely required, and load up your lame ducks on all transport, horse and mechanical, and hustle along.'

He even sent the same order to II Corps, which Smith-Dorrien countermanded as soon as he heard of it (earning a rebuke from Sir John French later).

Only 'Wully' seemed to be acting with both good sense and realism. He had ordered the ground dumping of ammunition and rations at various points along the line of retreat in accordance with *Field Service Regulations*: 'In order to restore the moral[e] and efficiency of the fighting troops supplies of ammunition and food should be deposited alongside these roads.' The French artist Paul Maze, working as an interpreter with the BEF, noted that in village after village 'a big pile of rations, topped by sides of beef, [was] erected like a monument in the middle of the square . . . a godsend to the troops'. It was a hugely wasteful, *in extremis*, method of resupply, but Frank Richards, with a group of stragglers trying to find his company, was grateful for the forethought: 'All along the road we took was broken down motor lorries, motor cycles, dead horses and broken wagons. In a field were dumped a lot of rations. We had a feed, crammed some biscuits into our haversacks and moved along again.' Fortunately, as the diary of the 4th Hussars recorded, fodder for the horses was in plentiful supply too, for 'the country was full of oats, cut but not harvested'.

Indeed, 'Wully' had done the BEF a great service before they had even set foot in France, for while commandant of the staff college, before Henry Wilson, he had stressed – unfashionably – the need to look at withdrawal as a phase of war:

> Our regulations justly lay stress on the value of the offensive; but if this teaching alone is given, think what may be the effect on the troops when they are ordered to retire instead of to go forward – that is, to abandon that method of making war by which alone, according to the training they have previously received, decisive victory can be achieved. Think, too, of the disintegration and demoralization which nearly always accompany retrograde movements, even when an army has not been previously defeated. It seems to me that there is particularly no chance of successfully carrying out this operation in war unless we thoroughly study and practise it beforehand during peace.*

Disintegration and demoralization: in fact the immediate but very real danger to the BEF was not Kluck's 1st Army overwhelming a disorganized II Corps, but the widening gap between it and I Corps. By 28 August Haig was some 15 miles to the east, and into the gap the German cavalry naturally tried to drive. Allenby's men were now having to cover the BEF's left (where, too, Sordet's Cavalry Corps was fortunately reinvigorated) and also to help screen II Corps, and they were well below (mounted) strength, the result as much of exhaustion as of enemy action. The commanding officer of the 18th Hussars believed that after Le Cateau 'No regiment had more than two squadrons, and some had only one.' All that could be found to fill the gap between Haig's and Smith-Dorrien's corps therefore was Gough's 3rd and Chetwode's 5th (Independent) cavalry brigades, Chetwode still trying to act as rearguard for the I Corps. It certainly suited Gough to be under command of Haig, for he was in a state of semi-mutiny as

* Quoted in Bond, *The Victorian Army and the Staff College.*

far as Allenby was concerned. He had quite arbitrarily taken his brigade over to the right flank before Le Cateau with the express purpose of, as he told Chetwode on meeting him unexpectedly, 'getting as far away from the Bull as possible' (little wonder that James Edmonds thought Allenby's staff were 'useless', that 'they never knew where his brigades were' – though it was evidently not entirely their fault).*

Both brigades would see some brisk action on 28 August against the Prussian Guards Cavalry Division, Gough's with their rifles and the support of E Battery RHA, while further east Chetwode's used both fire and manoeuvre – notably a charge by the 12th Lancers – to check the advance.

While all this was going on and GHQ was moving yet again, this time to Compiègne, Sir John French decided to take a look at II Corps for himself. The daily 'states' – the reports from the subordinate head-quarters giving the number of casualties and 'effectives' – would by now have been telling him of marked losses, but the great unknown was the category 'missing'. Unless a man were present at his corporal's roll call he had to be discounted from that unit's strength. That he might turn up with a dozen others an hour after the states were submitted was neither here nor there. So the evening states for the twenty-seventh, which Sir John French would have seen on the morning of the twenty-eighth, would have presented a very different – and more disastrous – picture of the losses in both men and materiel than that which would ultimately emerge.† In any case – and this is understandable, laudable even – the field marshal seems not yet to have

---

* Gough's remark is quoted by Edmonds (Liddell Hart Collection, Cambridge). According to Edmonds, Allenby maintained that it was merely Gough's 'little way', although Edmonds believed that in private 'the Bull' was more bitter, believing Sir John French to have been weak not to reprimand him. Why French should favour Gough – the Curragh 'mutineer' who had been the cause of his downfall – is unclear, however. That Gough was a capable, thrusting cavalry commander is perfectly evident; that he was also tiresome and self-regarding is equally plain.

† 'States will be furnished by subordinate commanders to their superiors daily or as often as may be ordered. States will show the general fighting condition of units, i.e. their strength in officers and men, horses, guns, and the amount of ammunition in possession . . . After an action, or during a prolonged operation, in order that commanders may immediately be made acquainted with the condition of their commands, states showing the losses, as far as they are known, in killed, wounded and missing, giving the names and units of officers, will be forwarded through the usual channels with the least possible delay': *Field Service Regulations*, Part II: *Organization and Administration* (1914).

bitten the bullet of continental warfare as far as losses were concerned. He was a man of the South African veld: at Paardeberg, one of the major and decisive battles of the Boer War, British casualties had been 350 killed and 1,250 wounded or captured; at Elandslaagte earlier, one of the first clear-cut British tactical victories, in which he himself had led the Cavalry Division with conspicuous success, the casualties had been 55 dead and 205 wounded. But these were high numbers for a country which had thought of its army in terms of an imperial police force. The French called British squeamishness over casualties 'Veldtitis'. To be hearing now of losses upwards of 20,000, and half the artillery, would have been almost bewildering.*

And yet when the field marshal finally saw II Corps he had 'a most agreeable surprise', for they were not, he wrote in his diary, cowed, like beaten troops: 'I met the men and talked to them as they were lying about resting. I told them how much I appreciated their work and what the country thought of them. I told them also of Joffre's telegram and its publication in England. The wonderful spirit and bearing they showed was beyond all praise.'

And then he concluded with an observation that summed up – without perhaps his being conscious of it even as he wrote – the fundamental flaw in British military strategy: '½ a million of them [soldiers of the BEF] would walk over Europe!'

For Britain had sent not a quarter of that number to France, and quality could only tell as far as it could stretch. Yet again he must have been wondering if at the war council on 5 August he should have held out for Antwerp. Yes, the sortie launched bravely from there on the twenty-third had been stopped in its tracks, and Belgian troops were once more falling back into Antwerp's ring of forts, the left (north) flank of which rested on the Dutch border, and the right (west) midway between the Scheldt and Dutch Flanders south of the estuary. And, true, there was the possibility therefore of being effectively surrounded by the Germans and by Dutch territory – although there was still freedom of movement all along the Belgian coast. Or perhaps he should have seconded Churchill's suggestion of concentrating well

---

* The total losses were eventually established as: Cavalry Division, 15 [sic]; 3rd Division, 1,796; 5th Division, 2,366; 4th Division, 3,158; 19th Infantry Brigade, 477. Of the total 7,812, 2,600 were taken prisoner, including many wounded (and thirty-eight guns). Three infantry commanding officers had been killed.

to the rear of the French army to form a strategic reserve (the very asset that Joffre did not have, and which he was now hurriedly creating in Manoury's 6th Army)? It is not surprising that Sir John French was entertaining – even beginning to implement – the idea of withdrawing altogether from the line; of resting, regrouping, re-equipping and then re-entering the fight at the right time and the right place.

And yet there were many in the BEF who had seen little action to date, and some none at all. The 2nd Infantry Brigade, in I Corps, for example, had scarcely fired a shot. One officer who had yet to draw his pistol, let alone fire it, was Lieutenant Evelyn Needham, a Special Reserve officer with the 1st Northamptons. On the twenty-eighth his sergeant asked why they were still retreating: 'I said it was a "strategic retirement". He looked blank. I felt a fool.'

The retreat went on.

Not that I Corps was without the will to fight; quite the contrary. The day before (27 August) the 1st Guards Brigade were acting as rearguard for the 1st Division: 'By some error of judgement,' wrote Haig in his diary, 'this rearguard remained too long in its position north of Etreux, and the greater part of the [2nd Royal] Munster Fusiliers was surrounded in a village and killed or captured. Only some 7 officers [and] 250 men returned.' So defiantly had the battalion fought that the Germans apparently sent for one of their chaplains (presumably Catholic – history does not relate) to bury the many dead.*

Haig himself, recovering from whatever it was that had laid him low on the twenty-fourth and disconcerted him on the night of the twenty-fifth, had been trying strenuously to narrow the gap between the two corps, and on the twenty-eighth, receiving an RFC report that the Germans were moving from east to west across his front, he sent word to Lanrezac that he was ready to cooperate in any attack on the enemy's exposed flank if Sir John French approved.

French, however, did *not* approve, and shortly after midnight, in a message every bit as petulant as his exchanges with Smith-Dorrien hitherto, demanded to know why the commander of I Corps had made a 'confidential promise of support' to Lanrezac – though Haig recorded that when French sent for him that afternoon ('about 35 miles distant and road difficult to find and very hilly') he apologized

---

* They would be replaced by the 1st Cameron Highlanders, hitherto the GHQ guard.

for its tone. Nevertheless, on 29 August Lanrezac's 5th Army would have to fight (at Guise) by themselves, for when a 'very worried' looking Joffre arrived at Compiègne that same afternoon, try as he might he could not persuade the field marshal, fortified in his resolve by a resurgent Murray (who kept tugging at French's tunic), to join in the offensive – or even to hold his current positions. Poor Spears would be berated by all and sundry when Lanrezac learned that no help would come from I Corps, not even from its under-used artillery. But there was even worse: for they learned that, in Haig's words, 'Sir J French decides that our Army must fall back . . . Retreat to begin at once'.

No wonder Joffre left GHQ, as he put it in his memoirs, 'de très mauvaise humeur'.*

In fact, that morning of the twenty-ninth, watched over by Joffre personally, Lanrezac would drive the 5th Army to some success. His attack towards St Quentin – which Kluck had occupied not long after Tom Bridges had led out the demoralized Warwicks and Dublin Fusiliers – soon ran into stiff opposition and exposed his right flank to Bülow's 2nd Army, but he judged the situation well and switched Lieutenant-General Louis Franchet d'Espèrey's I Corps to his right to meet the threat. Franchet d'Espèrey had already shown himself to be both a vigorous and a capable commander, and he now made his name with Joffre by hurling back Bülow's Guard and X Corps. Suddenly, and for the first time in over a week's fighting, the enemy was in full retreat. Nor was it just Joffre's approval that ensued: the BEF now had a French general to cheer, although inevitably they would drolly anglicize his name to 'Desperate Frankie'. But although Bülow was reeling, and Kluck was unwilling to go to his help, Lanrezac's 5th Army was too exposed to hold its new ground, and Joffre now ordered him to break off and withdraw south-east – which he began to do the next morning, 30 August, a Sunday. It was exactly a week since the BEF's battle at Mons.

In his diary that day, Sir John French confided that 'I have decided

---

* Curiously, in his diary Haig wrote that Lanrezac had been defeated and was falling back, and that Joffre wanted I Corps to hold its present position to cover the 5th Army's left flank. This reflects more on the pessimism of GHQ than on Haig, who could not have been looking for so rapid a French defeat given that he had urged supporting the attack.

to retire behind the Seine to the west of Paris, if possible in the neighbourhood of St. Germain. The march will occupy at least 10 days.' He did not, however, tell Joffre; only that – 'emphatically' – he could not fill the gap between Compiègne and La Fère, where Lanrezac's left now rested. It is perhaps as well, for such a shell-burst of an announcement would very likely have caused a rupture between the two men, who, despite events, still had a measure of affection for each other.

The news was received in London with dismay and mystification. Sir John French's letters and telegrams just did not add up. They had first been full of vim: even on the twenty-ninth he was describing the spirit of his troops as 'quite wonderful', while two days later the BEF, II Corps especially, were, he said, 'shattered'. On 1 September Asquith would write to Venetia Stanley that he was 'certain it will be found that French has greatly underestimated his total losses, which are much more likely to work out at 10,000 than 5,000. In fact if it were otherwise, it is impossible to account for his telegrams, in which (*Secret*) he speaks of his force as "shattered" & quite unable to take a place for the time being in the forefront.' Yet the casualty figures were not painting a picture of catastrophic defeat. Even 10,000 casualties (Asquith was near the mark) could not justify Sir John French's assertion that the BEF was shattered and unable to stay in the fight.*

Kitchener had sent a telegram asking for clarification; the reply was petulant and unclear. Asquith to Venetia Stanley again:

A telegram came in just before midnight [31 August], and I had a conference just after 12 p.m. downstairs with Kitchener, Winston, McKenna & Jack Pease (who had dined with us) being also there, & later Lloyd George. We came to the decided conclusion that the only thing to be done was for Kitchener to go there without delay, & unravel the situation, & if necessary put the fear of God into them all. He is a real sportsman when an emergency appears, & went straight home to change his clothes and collect his kit, & started by special train from Charing Cross about 1.30a.m. this morning. Winston provided him with a fast cruiser at Dover, whence he was to make his way to Havre & Paris.

---

* As noted above, the casualties at Le Cateau are generally reckoned to be 7,812 killed, wounded or captured (the greatest number of British casualties in any battle since Waterloo), and thirty-eight guns lost, with German casualties of around 5,000.

Unfortunately for the mood of the coming meeting with Sir John French, the clothes into which Kitchener changed were his field marshal's uniform.

As the fast cruiser carrying the uniformed secretary of state for war cut through the light swell in the Dover Straits, dawn broke mistily in the valley of the Oise. The 1st Cavalry Brigade, commanded by Brigadier-General Charles Briggs, had bivouacked for the night at Néry, a rather prettier village than those about Mons, the buildings mainly of stone rather than brick, but otherwise an undistinguished little farming place surrounded by beet fields. The ground was more wooded as it fell, slightly, to the north towards the L'Automne stream, which ran north-west into the Oise, and from which the mist was rising. About 600 yards to the east was a shallow ridge running north–south, parallel with the road. By some accounts it was supposed to have been occupied by French cavalry, although this degree of mutual support seems unlikely. In any case, if the ridge had been identified as a 'concern', the brigade might have been expected to take the pre-caution at least of making contact with its occupants. What is more likely is that because the village was occupied as darkness fell, after an exhausting day, and the brigade expected to resume its march at first light, no one took much notice of the ridge. Néry was, in any case, just the spot for a cavalry bivouac: the 5th Dragoon Guards had found billets at its northern end, the 2nd Dragoon Guards ('the Bays') and the 11th Hussars were in farm buildings in the middle, and L Battery RHA was in an orchard just to the south. At four-thirty, with the first signs of daylight, Brigadier-General Briggs gave the order to prepare to move. The regiments saddled up and the battery's six 13-pounders were hooked in (reveille had been at 3.30 – testament to the mounted soldier's longer day), but because the mist was still thick Briggs stayed the actual order to move off. The 5th Dragoon Guards and the Bays sent clearing patrols north and south, which returned at about five-thirty with nothing to report. Meanwhile L Battery let down the limber poles and began watering the horses by sub-sections at the nearby sugar-beet factory.*

---

* Letting down the poles took the weight off the horse's neck and back. The drill was adopted if expecting to move off soon, the order being 'without unhooking [the guns], poles down'. A picture of the scene can be gained by imagining the King's Troop RHA

Briggs had also ordered the 11th Hussars to reconnoitre the higher ground to the east and south-east, and so just after half-past four Second Lieutenant George Tailby, a grandson of the legendary Squire Tailby of the Leicestershire hunting field, led out his first patrol of the war, with six chosen troopers. They scoured the open ground between the village and the ridge for three-quarters of an hour, the visibility very poor. Then the mist began to shift a little. And there, 200 yards ahead, were horses, long cloaks and spiked helmets. Tailby's leading file opened fire from the saddle, the Germans spurred towards them, and he ordered: 'Files about, Gallop!'

They were not long galloping before Tailby's charger, Ronald (the name of Lord Cardigan's horse at Balaklava – Cardigan himself an 11th Hussar) crossed his legs in a hole and both fell heavily. The mist thickened obligingly, Ronald struggled up, Tailby managed to remount and they made it back to the road near Vaucelle, the next village north, where the patrol turned for Néry. Half a mile down the road they came on an *estaminet*, its doors open and a *feldgrau* cloak on a table, which Tailby took as a prize – or evidence – before leading the patrol back into Néry through the lines of the 5th Dragoon Guards, whom they warned but who seemed disinclined to believe them. His commanding officer, Lieutenant-Colonel (later Major-General) Thomas Pitman at first thought he might have mistaken French cavalry for German, but the cloak settled the question. Pitman just had time to report to the brigadier before the Germans opened fire.*

The mist lifted suddenly and a ranging shell burst over the battery. Seconds later small arms and machine guns the length of the ridge and three batteries over 'open sights' (very short range) poured fire on the southern edge of the village, where the Bays were standing to and L Battery was drawn up in full view.

With poles down, the teams stood little chance: as the horses tried to bolt, the poles drove into the ground. Chaos ensued. More shells

---

(the terms battery/troop were interchangeable) drawn up on Horse Guards for the annual 'Trooping the Colour', but in khaki and with twice as many horses, for the present-day ceremonial unit does not have the six ammunition waggons and all the others a battery took on active service – waggons for the forge and the horseshoes, for fodder, rations and the quartermaster's stores. All the King's Troop's guns were, however, fired in action during the Great War.

*From a talk given by Lieutenant-General the Lord Norrie, one of the 11th Hussars' subalterns at Néry, to the Royal Artillery Historical Society in 1967.

burst and men and horses began falling like proverbial ninepins. The battery commander, Major the Honourable Walter Sclater-Booth, his second-in-command Captain Edward Bradbury and his three subalterns were standing near some haystacks when the first shell burst. Sclater-Booth was at once felled by shrapnel. Bradbury, shouting for gunners, raced to the 13-pounders, followed by the subalterns and 28-year-old Sergeant David Nelson from County Monaghan. They managed to unlimber three guns and turn them towards the ridge, Bradbury taking command of one, Lieutenant Jack Giffard another, and Lieutenants John Campbell and Lionel Mundy the third. Before Campbell's gun could fire a round, however, it was knocked out by a direct hit, so he and Mundy ran over to Bradbury's, and the remaining two 13-pounders soon began to answer. After a very few rounds Giffard was cut down by shrapnel and the rest of the detachment either killed or wounded. Bradbury was now joined by the battery-sergeant-major, George Dorrell – at thirty-four a veteran of the Boer War (he had joined at fifteen) – back from watering the horses, but the ready ammunition in the limbers was now exhausted, and the fire was taking a steady toll of gunners crawling across to the ammunition waggons. For well over an hour the unequal duel continued, until at last, while trying to fetch up more ammunition, Bradbury was mortally wounded by a shell that severed both his legs. Dorrell and Nelson, both wounded, continued to fight the gun to its last round.

All three would be awarded the Victoria Cross, and after recovering from their wounds both NCOs would return to service and be commissioned. Dorrell would rise to lieutenant-colonel, and Nelson to major, although he would be killed in action in 1918. The battery had lost 150 horses (the Bays a similar number) and a quarter of its men had been killed or severely wounded, with many more *hors de combat*. It would take the villagers a week to dispose of the bloating carcasses. After Néry, lowering poles was forbidden.*

But the action, for all that it had started so badly – and in truth as a terrible failure of field discipline – ended in some triumph. The

---

* The VCs and No. 6 Gun – the last to cease action – are on display at the Imperial War Museum. L Battery was all but destroyed as an operational unit and was withdrawn to England to re-form, in April 1915 going from frying pan to fire – Gallipoli. The Battery was awarded the singular battle honour 'Néry', and L (Néry) Battery is today a sub-unit of 1st Regiment Royal Horse Artillery.

brigade commander, Briggs, had been quick off the mark, sending (motorcycle) despatch riders off to Allenby at St Vaast and to the 4th Division headquarters at Verberie, both about 3 miles to the north-west, ordering the 11th Hussars to prolong their hastily established defence line to the north edge of the village, and the 5th Dragoon Guards to counter-attack the ridge. This they did, largely with (dismounted) rifle fire, driving-in the German 3rd Cavalry Brigade, who believed they were under attack by greater numbers, but at the cost of the death of their commanding officer, Lieutenant-Colonel George Ansell.*

Meanwhile an attack by the 17th German Cavalry Brigade towards the sugar-beet factory was held off by fire from the Bays and the Hussars until the arrival of the 4th Cavalry Brigade and I Battery sent by Allenby, the RHA's 13-pounders opening up at 1,200 yards, quickly silencing the German guns and preventing the teams from hauling them away. The 1st Middlesex, sent up by the 4th Division, began arriving from the south and adding their fire, so that, having now pinned the Germans, Briggs could order the 11th Hussars to take the guns, which they did, swords drawn (and blooded) – the first guns (twelve *Feldkanone*) to be captured by the BEF. German casualties were 200, with half as many again made prisoner. A wireless message from the 4th Cavalry Division intercepted that afternoon read: 'Attacked by English at dawn, cannot fulfil mission.'†

There was no time to bury the dead, however. The sickening business of leaving behind fallen comrades was the price of continuing the withdrawal and recovering the guns, much damaged as they were. Once the wounded had been got away, the dead –

---

* His son, Colonel Sir Michael (Mike) Ansell, joined the 5th Dragoon Guards after the war, and in 1940 became the youngest commanding officer in the army when at the age of thirty-five he took over the 1st Lothian and Border Yeomanry in France. He was wounded (and blinded) and captured at St Valéry after the fighting withdrawal to the sea, during which he was awarded the DSO. His son, Major-General Nicholas Ansell, commanded the 5th Dragoon Guards in the 1970s, and was the author's principal instructor at the staff college. Asked by a German officer on the course, who did not know of the connections, why, having taken a law degree at Cambridge, the then Colonel Ansell had joined the army, he answered simply: 'It's in the blood.'
† On 5 September, Otto von Garnier's 4th Cavalry Division could muster only 1,200 sabres – some 3,000 fewer than at the beginning of the campaign. Surprising as it may seem, the action at Néry was a major contributor in this attrition – wounded, lamed and lost horses, their riders therefore *hors de combat*, and many others disorientated in the escape running into Lanrezac's men and being killed or captured.

twenty-three from L Battery alone – were buried in shallow graves or laid in cover as best they could be, the bodies labelled and the field pay books collected to send to the records office. There was no shortage of French hands to help with the grim work.*

And yet it was extraordinary how, in the middle of such a battle, a soldier might have little idea of what had really happened. Sergeant Brunton, now back with his squadron having recovered some of the horses scattered in the aftermath of Le Cateau, and a few replacements (on 29 August he noted: 'Had a check roll of my troop, and find I have only 24 men and 19 horses left out of 38 men and 35 horses') had been sent with his troop to reinforce the 11th Hussars. Of Néry, having been on 'mounted picquet' during the night, all he noted in his diary was: 'Get men out, grumbling and cursing but has to be done. All are tired and done up. We have hardly had any sleep for a week, and haven't washed or shaved ... In action today against enemy's cavalry. Slight losses. Heavy artillery duels going on. Feel done up but in good spirits. Queen's Bays suffered heavy.' It is a remarkably understated account of the action (in fact the Bays had few casualties, except horses). It was not untypical of the 1914 regular, however – 'grumbling and cursing but has to be done'.†

Néry was not the only sharp and bloody fighting that day. Further east, Haig's Corps, now rapidly closing up to Smith-Dorrien's, was having its first real battle. Covering the move of the corps through the forest at Villers-Cotterêts was the 4th (Guards) Brigade, who were attacked in strength in the early afternoon. The forest was intersected by broad paths – rides – down which the German machine-gunners

---

* The Commonwealth War Graves Commission Cemetery at Néry, the work of the great programme of recovery and reburial in the aftermath of the war, has only twenty identified graves; the remainder are identified communally. Some of those who fell that day, such as Colonel Ansell, are buried in the French national cemetery at Verberie, where the cavalry field ambulance's dressing station was located during the action.
† Brunton, a thoroughly decent and experienced regular, was also recording some of the wilder rumours that inevitably buzz round any bivouac. For example, on 28 August: 'Two Army Service Corps men shot today outside barracks for throwing rations off a convoy, while being pursued by Germans' – almost certainly a misreporting of Wully Robertson's orders to ground-dump (the first soldier to be executed by firing squad was a deserter, on 8 September). And inevitably, too, there were the rumours of spies: 'Also a German spy caught and shot. He had three (3) uniforms on. German, French, and over all an English cloak and puttees on.' And the weather was still baking hot. But in this, Brunton was in exalted company, for Horne, Haig's artillery commander, was writing to his wife of 'spies everywhere', and remarking that 'one knows little of what goes on elsewhere'.

could pour continuous fire, and a running fight developed as the brigade fell back steadily, supported by two batteries of the Royal Field Artillery. The battle soon became chaotic, the firing often at point-blank range. Two platoons of No. 4 Company made a counter-attack in which nearly everyone was killed, wounded or taken prisoner. Among them was the nineteen-year-old Lieutenant George Cecil, not long out of Sandhurst, who died sword in hand leading a bayonet charge – grandson (the first of five to be killed) of the Marquess of Salisbury, the prime minister who had been the advocate of 'splendid isolation'.

In all, the brigade lost over 300 men at Villers-Cotterêts; and the 6th Infantry Brigade, which in turn covered the withdrawal of the Guards, lost half as many again. The commanding officer of the Irish Guards, Lieutenant-Colonel the Honourable George Morris, was killed by machine-gun fire.* Brigadier-General Robert Scott-Kerr was severely wounded (he would not see active service again), and command of the brigade devolved on Colonel Noel Corry DSO (he had been promoted from lieutenant-colonel in July) of the 2nd Grenadiers, who led them for five critical days until relieved on 6 September. Four days after returning to command his battalion he was sent home, by Haig, for having withdrawn without orders from an exposed position, a shallow hill, at Mons. Both he and Morris had protested to Scott-Kerr and the divisional commander that it was 'another Spion Kop' – it could be overlooked – but had been ordered to hold it nevertheless. Just before midnight on the twenty-third – the day of the fighting along the canal – the commanding officer of the 2nd Royal Irish Rifles, Lieutenant-Colonel Wilkinson Bird, came to see him to say that

---

*Morris, the second son of the 1st Baron Killanin, of Galway, was a Catholic, educated at the Oratory School. He had originally been commissioned into the Rifle Brigade, transferring to the 'Micks' when the regiment was formed in 1900. He was several times mentioned in despatches in South Africa, and as an instructor at the staff college was highly regarded as a tactician. Later in September his elder brother, who had succeeded to the title, went to the site of the battle (the area having been retaken in the French counter-offensive), and excavated the graves in which the Guards' dead had been communally buried, unmarked and unrecorded, and managed to identify Morris's remains and those of three other officers, including George Cecil (whose mother had gone to Villers-Cotterêts earlier to enquire of her son, still officially posted as 'missing'). These he had reinterred in a plot he bought in Villers-Cotterêts cemetery, and the remains of the other Guardsmen reinterred – with Catholic ceremony (for many were Irishmen) – properly recorded and decently marked, until the Imperial War Graves Commission began their work of systematic reburial in 1919.

he had been ordered to withdraw from positions nearby, and that this would leave the Guards' left flank open. Since Bird's battalion was in not just another brigade but another corps – Smith-Dorrien's – this was a fine example of cooperation. And as Bird went on to be a major-general, his judgement could clearly have been reckoned sound. Corry went back to find Scott-Kerr, who had himself commanded the 1st Grenadiers, to ask permission to withdraw, but the brigadier was not at his headquarters, and it was uncertain whether he had gone to the 2nd Division's headquarters or elsewhere. Corry therefore ordered both his battalion and the Irish to quit the hill, telling his second-in-command that if there were any trouble over the decision he would cite *Field Service Regulations*, which gave a subordinate latitude in circumstances where a superior could not know the changed situation. As the Guards were pulling back, however, they were met by Scott-Kerr, who ordered them to reoccupy the position, which they were in the process of doing when the order arrived from I Corps to begin a general withdrawal. Morris, had he not been killed, would probably have been relieved of command too – although as a 'star' he would have been an awkward case to explain. There was clearly something amiss in the brigade. Between the divisional and brigade commanders, and the two commanding officers, the affair had evidently been badly handled from the outset, but in the BEF's circumstances at the time, justice was always going to be rough – and Haig himself was still finding his feet in command.*

*

* *Field Service Regulations* might well have borne out Corry's decision (especially as a full colonel) had it come to court martial, for chapter II, paragraph 13, of Part I does not simply permit a subordinate to disobey orders in certain circumstances, it requires him to: 'If a subordinate, in the absence of a superior, neglects to depart from the letter of his orders when such a departure is clearly demanded by circumstances, and failure ensues, he will be held responsible for such failure' (the passage Smith-Dorrien quoted in defence of his decision to stand at Le Cateau: see page 347). The whole question turns, of course, on the judgement that the departure is 'clearly demanded by circumstances'. Therein lies the basis for dispute, which courts martial – of necessity convened some time after the event, and removed from the immediate environment of battle – have notorious difficulty in settling. 'The system' must somehow have sensed the nuances in this case, however. On returning to England Corry was given command of the London Reserve Brigade, as a temporary brigadier-general, and then the following year was appointed to command the 3rd Grenadiers, with whom he fought with distinction at Loos, with occasional periods in acting command of the 2nd Guards Brigade. He retired in 1920 with the honorary rank of brigadier-general.

While the cavalry and RHA were doing battle at Néry, and the Guards at Villers-Cotterêts, Sir John French was locking horns with Kitchener 40 miles to the south-west, at the British embassy in Paris. He had been dismayed to see not the 'politician', the war minister, in a frock coat but, so it seemed, a minister who thought himself a soldier still: 'K. arrived dressed in khaki as a F.M.!' he wrote in his diary. But then, Kitchener *was* a field marshal: he wore uniform to the War Office – and in the short time between leaving Downing Street just after midnight and catching his train an hour or so later, he had quite possibly not given much thought to orders of dress. What he *had* given his mind to, though, was visiting Joffre and the troops. 'The Ambassador [Bertie] objected strongly to this and so did I,' wrote French; 'We had rather a disagreeable time.'

French's objection to a field marshal senior to him inspecting the troops was that it would undermine his own position as commander-in-chief ('[I told him] I would not tolerate any interference with my executive command and authority'). It certainly might have done if Kitchener had seen for himself the condition of the troops, especially those in I Corps who had yet to see any hard fighting, and if he had been able to speak to the corps commanders. Sir John French had a strong interest in keeping Kitchener's penetrating gaze distant. He might also have heard something of the rumours – he certainly did later – that Kitchener was thinking of making himself the supreme military commander at the War Office as well as minister (and seeing Joffre would be a preliminary to such a move). There was in fact a grain of truth in this. Kitchener was already in many respects acting as a commander-in-chief, relegating the CIGS to a subordinate role, often as not by simply keeping him in the dark about his ideas. And French may also have sensed – though he did not confide it to his diary – that there was a level of command missing. He was having the greatest difficulty exercising tactical control of the BEF's operations and at the same time coping with the political and military demands of an independent command within what amounted to an alliance. A Marlborough or a Wellington in such a position would have found the middle course. But the duke of Marlborough was fifty-four at the battle of Blenheim, and the duke of Wellington forty-six at Waterloo; Sir John French was sixty-two, and age may have told. Besides, French had neither the experience, the aptitude, nor the taste for the 'political'.*

The upshot of the meeting was that Kitchener did not visit Joffre or the troops (and nor would he become supreme military commander). Instead he returned to London that evening – surely the most momentous day trip to Paris until Churchill's in May 1940; and a more successful one, for unlike Churchill he managed to keep his interlocutor in the war. 'French's troops are now engaged in the fighting line,' he wired to Asquith before leaving, 'where he will remain conforming to the movements of the French army, though at the same time acting with caution to avoid being in any way unsupported on his flanks.'

It was just as well that Kitchener took the train for London straight afterwards, for had he gone with French to GHQ he would have witnessed the most remarkable scenes – 'a panic-stricken flight', wrote 'Chauffeur-to-Brigadier' Christopher Baker-Carr: 'Rumours of thousands of uhlans in the woods nearby . . . Typewriters and office equipment were flung into waiting lorries, which were drawn up in serried ranks in front of the château. It was a pitch-black night, lit up by a hundred dazzling headlights.' Wully Robertson had just sat down to a leg of roast mutton, which was hurriedly wrapped in newspaper and thrown into one of the lorries: 'It was none the worse next day, except for being cold,' he would recall. Lorries, cars, horses, staff officers, clerks, signallers, orderlies, guards – off they all sped into the safety of the night for the next staging post in the race for the Seine. All, that is, except the adjutant-general, Sir Neville Macready, who was sitting down with his staff to dinner in an outbuilding of the chateau. He was only discovered when a diligent GHQ medical officer returned to see if one of French's orderlies, confined to bed, was fit to move. It was fortunate indeed that the war minister in khaki was on his way back to England.

---

* Lord Gort VC, fifty-four, would have the same trouble with another BEF in France, in 1940. He could never master the Janus-like requirement of the commander-in-chief, looking simultaneously in two directions (several, indeed); at one time he was known, despairingly, as 'the best platoon commander in France'. However, Gort had a great redeeming feature, best described by the then Major-General Bernard Montgomery, whose judgement of commanders rarely conceded them capability, and who said of Gort's decision to break off the fight and go for Dunkirk: 'As a commander he did not see very far, but as far as he did see he saw very clearly' (*The Memoirs of Field-Marshal the Viscount Montgomery*, London, 1958). Sir John French perceived something – perhaps only that he was in the middle of a mess not of his own choosing – but could not resolve the blurred image enough to recognize what the problem truly was.

But in that caveat 'at the same time acting with caution to avoid being in any way unsupported on his flanks' Kitchener, the meticulous sapper, had from the point of view of allied cohesion given Sir John French a sort of *laissez-passer*. He hardly needed to have done so, for a commander of French's experience needed no reminding to secure his flanks, especially after all that had happened since 23 August; Kitchener had now, unintentionally, made it a discretionary condition of continuing the fight. 'Conforming to the movements of the French army', which was clearly Kitchener's priority, became in the mind of the commander-in-chief entirely secondary to staying a march ahead in the great strategic retirement so as not to expose his flanks. And a worrying gap – some 25 miles – would now open between the BEF and Lanrezac, which Joffre would try to fill by conjuring a new cavalry corps under General Louis Conneau (an Anglophile, fortunately; the son of Napoleon III's doctor in exile, who had once been a cadet at Woolwich), but which hardly made for the safety of either the BEF or the 5th Army.

Joffre's mind was becoming ever clearer, however – in almost inverse proportion to the confusion in the German high command. Indeed, he was beginning to take the first steps that would set up the great counter-stroke known as the Battle of the Marne – or, in the more alliterative terms of the newspaper headlines, the 'Miracle of the Marne'. Although he was still thinking in terms of an attack by the 3rd, 4th and 5th Armies against the inner flank of Schlieffen's great revolving door, he was also still reinforcing Manoury's new 6th Army on the extreme left, which he would place under the overall command of his old teacher, the veteran colonial fighter General Joseph Gallieni, brought out of retirement to be military governor of Paris, still a considerable garrison. Together with the 6th, the garrison would be a formidable *masse de manoeuvre* opposite the outer Schlieffen wing, which was now within 30 miles of the capital (on 30 August a German Taube plane had dropped bombs and scattered leaflets on the 10th *arrondissement*, just a mile from the Île de la Cité).* But fortune was at last favouring Joffre, for the RFC, and the *armée de l'air* flying

---

* Paris, not surprisingly, was beginning to tremble. Most newspapers had stopped publishing, the bigger hotels were being turned into hospitals, and the stations – except, for obvious reasons, the Gare du Nord – were full of Parisians trying to get away from what they imagined would be the fate suffered by the city in 1871.

from Paris, were reporting increasingly that the movement of Kluck's troops was shifting south-eastwards. And then a bloodstained map found on a dead German staff officer was rushed to *GQG*, where a jubilant *Deuxième Bureau* saw the numbered pencil lines that indicated the axes of advance for the 1st Army's corps *south-east* – the perfect gift of intelligence. Only much later would they be able to fathom why – that Kluck and Bülow were having to comply with the movement of the armies to their left: the old Schlieffen anxiety about not enough troops on the right – 'only make the right wing strong!' – was becoming reality.

German troops were certainly feeling the strain, and showing it too, with increased drunkenness reported by their chain of command (Scott-Kerr had observed in the attacks at Villers-Cotterêts that the enemy appeared to be 'doped up') and slower rates of advance. The BEF, on the other hand, though its own charge-sheets were mounting, was reviving, Smith-Dorrien recording in his diary that 'the troops have recovered their spirits, and are getting fitter every day, and all they want is the order to go forward and attack the enemy.' Soldiers do not like evading their business – fighting – and the memory of Sir John Moore and the slow leaching of discipline during the snow-bound retreat to Corunna a century before was etched deep. Yet Sir John French was not yet convinced that the BEF could make any sort of stand, let alone go forward and attack. Three days later he would write in his diary that 'a great deal of looting and irregularity is going on', and that Smith-Dorrien had told him that the loss in officers 'demoralizes the men'. Smith-Dorrien's diary does indeed confirm this, but his argument was for turning and fighting rather than for quitting the field (on 6 September a welcome draft of battle-casualty replacements would join from England, which strengthened his view). Both French and Smith-Dorrien knew that a century before, Moore's ragged army at Corunna had at the last minute risen from its frozen torpor at the call of the drum and the bugle and fought the French magnificently to a standstill – allowing them to be taken off by sea to fight another day. Could the field marshal convince himself that his own men might do the same?

On 3 September the BEF crossed the Marne, the last obstacle on their march to haven west of Paris. Sergeant Brunton and his troop 'had a swim . . . washed underclothes, and dried them in sun'.* They were more than ready to turn and face their hesitant pursuers. And by now the German 1st Army's change of direction was incontrovertible. At five o'clock that evening Macdonogh was able to report to *GQG* that there were no enemy advancing on the BEF's front. It seemed that, having failed to outflank the BEF, and presuming that the British were quitting the fight, Kluck was now determined to envelop Lanrezac's 5th Army instead. If he succeeded, the Schlieffen Plan had worked – and without the necessity of marching round Paris, or investing it. Moltke would have another Sedan – another Cannae indeed. But what if the BEF were not quitting the fight – and, even worse, if there were French troops as yet unaccounted for (or, at least, underestimated) on this wing? In turning south-east Kluck was presenting his right flank to the BEF and to Manoury's 6th Army. But what in fact Moltke had agreed to was that Bülow's 2nd Army should do the enveloping, while the 1st Army 'in echelon to the rear of the Second' would guard the open flank, for he was evidently not prepared to write off the BEF or the resolve of the Paris garrison. 'First reckon, then risk' had been the maxim of the Elder Moltke; his nephew was trying hard to follow that advice.

But Joffre, urged on by Gallieni, knew what to do, and that now was the time to do it. Conveniently, the government had left Paris for Bordeaux; it was almost as if the decks were being cleared for action – a sort of invitation to *GQG* to do what it willed. Joffre rose to the occasion with all the power of his pen: 'The time has come to profit by the adventurous position of the German First Army and concentrate against that Army all the efforts of the Allied Armies of the extreme left.'†

So would begin his *Instruction Générale* for the Battle of the Marne. But first there was a most disagreeable duty to perform. He must remove his old protégé Lanrezac from command, replacing him with Franchet d'Espèrey. This he needed to do for two reasons. Lanrezac, he was sure, simply did not have the instinct for the fight. But he also

---

* Though like many in the BEF he had no very great idea where he was. He thought, in fact, that they had spent the night in Chantilly, though this was in the middle of the French 6th Army's area. He had no map, and if a village or a town sign was missed, there was nothing to go on but what he was told by his squadron leader – doubtless without spelling. His diary is therefore in many places a fascinating record of an English NCO's phonetic transcription.
† See Spears, *Liaison 1914*.

knew that if he was to persuade Sir John French to turn about – to join in his great counter-stroke – he must make a gesture. 'Limogeing' Lanrezac (the second army commander in four days to suffer this fate, for on 30 August Joffre had sacked General Emmanuel Ruffey, the 63-year-old commander of the 3rd Army) would create some sense of obligation, as the commander of the BEF would be bound to feel that it had been done in part as a result of his own dissatisfaction. On 4 September therefore Joffre drove to Sézanne, 40 miles south-west of Rheims, to the 5th Army's headquarters. Lanrezac came out of the school in which he had placed his flag to greet his chief, and the two began walking up and down the playground. From time to time they stopped as one or other seemed to emphasize a point, but as Spears observed, Lanrezac was not looking directly at Joffre, and Joffre himself was talking more than he usually did. At length the two men simply walked out of the playground – '[and] I never saw General Lanrezac again'.*

Where did he go? First there was the sullen drive to Paris, and then the long, melancholy railway journey to Bordeaux, where protocol required that he present himself to the war minister – and thence the final, despairing train to Limoges. But for some time, wrote Spears, there was a rumour that he had been incarcerated 'in one of the grimmest of the Paris forts'. Certainly it was what Sir John French would believe (and probably even hope): 'Lanrezac has been put in arrest with 4 other generals and is to be tried, it is said, by Court-Martial,' he noted in his diary that evening, in the eastern suburbs of Paris; to the King, he wrote that 'the fat pompous political general' had been sacked. But he was still making plans to withdraw behind the Seine, which would just conform with the realignment of the 5th and 6th Armies and so be possible to square with Kitchener, though it would not have been Joffre's choice. For the field marshal was as yet in no mood to risk the BEF when the French themselves seemed to be falling apart. Two army commanders relieved in four days . . .

Joffre therefore had to make a special plea for the BEF's cooperation.

---

* Joffre then drove to meet Franchet d'Espèrey at the crossroads where he had told him to wait, and asked if he felt his shoulders were 'broad enough and strong enough for command of an army', to which the commander of I Corps simply gave a Gallic shrug of them, and said he would do his best. 'Good,' said Joffre; 'you are the commander of the Fifth Army from tonight' (Spears, *Liaison 1914*).

If Sir John French refused, Joffre would almost certainly have to protest to Paris – or rather, to Bordeaux – and thereafter, if London wished to remain in the fight, it would inevitably mean the 'Limogeing' of Sir John French himself. The unspoken stakes were therefore about as high as they could get when at three o'clock the following morning (5 September) Joffre sent GHQ, 'by hand of personal officer', a copy of his orders for the grand counter-attack. The officer, Captain de Galbert (who would be killed at the head of a battalion of *Chasseurs Alpins* in 1916), returned mid-morning with a not entirely encouraging, but nevertheless courteous, promise of 'further consideration' (there had been much to-ing and fro-ing the day before over two quite different plans suggested by Gallieni and Franchet d'Espèrey). Joffre wired to say that he was coming to see the field marshal, and set off on another white-knuckle drive with Georges Boillot for Melun on the banks of the Seine, in the south-eastern outskirts of Paris, where GHQ had found a billet. Spears, remarkably, managed to get there from the 5th Army just as Joffre was arriving, and went with him into GHQ's villa next to the French Red Cross hospital, where Sir John French was waiting with Murray, Wilson and Sidney Clive (the British liaison officer at *GQG*). A squadron of the North Irish Horse kept guard outside.

Joffre put his cap on the table, facing French (and behind him Murray, 'looking aloof and rather worried'), and with his back half turned towards the window, began talking 'in that low, toneless, albino voice of his'.* He said that he had come to thank the British commander-in-chief for having taken a decision on which the fate of Europe might well depend (to conform with the movements of the 5th and 6th Armies), to which Sir John French bowed. He then went on to explain the movements of the German 1st Army, paying especial tribute to the work of the RFC in its reporting, 'on which so much depended', and to whom he owed the certainty which enabled him to make his plans in good time.

Sir John French signalled that he understood, without need of translation.

So Joffre began to explain his plan, with evident conviction and

* The account that follows is based on Spears, *Liaison 1914*, and Callwell, *Field Marshal Sir Henry Wilson*.

very vividly. The next twenty-four hours would be decisive, he said; if not taken full advantage of, the great opportunity would never present itself again. He had already issued the orders to his troops: the time for retreating was over. And now he turned to the BEF. His plan depended entirely upon British cooperation, he said, and its success on their action. He was earnestly requesting all that the BEF could give, and seemed to have reserved his greatest eloquence for the final appeal. Turning squarely to face the little field marshal, he clasped his massive hands together 'so tight as to hurt them' and said, 'Monsieur le Maréchal, c'est la France qui vous supplie.'*

And then his hands fell to his side, as if the effort had exhausted him.

'We all looked at Sir John,' recalled Spears, intensely conscious of the high drama being played out in this little Paris suburb, where trams still clanked in the street outside, and children watched the soldiers swim: 'He had understood and was under the stress of strong emotion. Tears stood in his eyes, welled over and rolled down his cheeks.'

He tried to reply but language failed him. Turning to Clive, he said: 'Damn it, I can't explain. Tell him that all that men can do, our fellows will do.'

A massive, mustachioed *général d'armée* wringing his hands, begging on behalf of *La France*, and a British field marshal with tears rolling down his cheeks – 'Marianne' imploring 'John Bull': one day it 'would probably furnish the theme of a great historical picture', wrote Spears (though it never has). But soldiers, after allowing themselves a brief moment of high emotion, are invariably recalled to earth by some military detail – and by their staff. After the proverbial pregnant pause, Archie Murray, now apparently quite recovered from his own state of prostration, stepped forward and said, very coldly, that it was quite impossible for the BEF to move at six the following morning as Joffre had asked; they could not be ready before nine.

Three hours – would anyone have noticed the delay? Would it have made the slightest difference to the armies on the left and right of the BEF? Could not even just the Cavalry Division have begun its forward movement at six? Murray's prosaic intervention is curious, to say the

* 'It is France who begs you.'

least, and appears to represent the accumulated resentment of a fortnight's growing sense of betrayal – of misalliance indeed.

But for now, the time for retreating was over. Gallieni, reporting on the rest of the day's efforts at coordination between the 6th Army and the BEF, would end his telegram to *GQG* with three words that summed up the optimism of the hour: 'Demain, en avant!'*

---

* 'Tomorrow, forward!' There is – inevitably – another and significantly different account of the meeting: that of Joffre in a letter to the new war minister, Millerand, written shortly after the meeting, in which he writes that he told Sir John French that history would judge the absence of the British army severely, that he thumped the table, and that his final words were 'Monsieur le Maréchal, the honour of England is at stake.' It is possible that this was simply *l'esprit de l'escalier*, or that it was designed to show the new minister the firmness of the commander-in-chief. Whichever it was, it is as well that he did not use those words to Sir John French, who would have considered himself, and rightly, the arbiter of English (*sic*) honour at that moment, and who was far more likely to be sobbed into advance than bullied out of retreat. Spears, for one, would not have misheard or misunderstood the taunt.

Chapter Twenty

'EN AVANT!'

The advance . . . should be carried through with the utmost vigour and resolution, and all ranks should understand that they must press forward until the enemy is driven from the field.

'The Assumption of the Offensive', *Field Service Regulations*

It is well to consider a few statistics. First, the BEF. In thirteen days they had marched nearly 200 miles from Mons – the infantry on their feet, the cavalry half and half. Which of them was better off is hard to say: the reckoning afterwards was that an infantryman got an average of four hours' sleep in twenty-four during that fortnight, a mounted man – cavalry or gunner – an hour less, for he had his horse to attend to before he could lie down, and before he could march again. 'I would never have believed', wrote one officer, 'that men could be so tired and so hungry and yet live.' Another, in the 4th Division's artillery, asked two of his sergeants how long they thought they had been in France: 'Six weeks,' they said; 'perhaps seven.' It was only when he produced a calendar that they would believe it was only two. And whatever Sir John French or Sir Horace Smith-Dorrien thought of their morale as a whole, the men of the BEF were not in universally high spirits. Charteris, Haig's intelligence officer, noted that 'they were very glum, they marched silently, doggedly, never a whistle or a song, or even a ribald jest, to help weary feet along the road. Staff officers moving up and down the line with orders were

402

glowered at gloomily.' On 5 September, the day before the counter-attack on the Marne began, 20,000 men were posted missing – more than a fifth of the BEF's fighting element. A quarter of these would in time rejoin – there were men scattered about the whole line of the retreat, some still north of the canal at Mons, trying with varying degrees of determination to find their units – but a high proportion of those killed, wounded or captured were from II Corps, and many of them were officers. Although the battle-casualty replacements that arrived on the sixth would numerically fill up the ranks, the losses in experienced leaders would tell in the days to come, and indeed in the years to follow. But the claim still made that 'half the artillery' was lost is quite wrong: the losses were about 10 per cent. Losing half the artillery would have made it very difficult for the BEF to mount offensive operations.*

On 5 September, the BEF made up about 5 per cent of the allied bayonet (infantry) strength in France – on the face of it, scarcely a critical mass; but two factors made the BEF more important at that moment than its relative strength suggested. First, of course, was the geography of the battlefield: the BEF was centrally placed for the counter-stroke against the 'Schlieffen flank'. Second was its quality: despite the tactical mistakes, its five divisions (soon to be six: the 6th Division was being sent out too, but would not join until the middle of the month) had inflicted significant casualties on Kluck's 1st Army. They had forced the Germans to keep fighting, exhausting them, making heavy demands on their combat supplies and wearing down their materiel (and the RFC, an unproven auxiliary when the BEF had sailed for France, was now prized equally by GHQ and the French as a primary and most reliable source of battlefield intelligence). For Kluck did indeed have serious logistical problems. The allies might have preferred to have been operating on exterior lines – advancing through Belgium and into Germany rather than falling back on their

* For inflated losses, see e.g. Herwig, *The Marne, 1914*, p. 228. In fact, forty-two guns had been lost in the retreat from Mons, thirty-eight of them at Le Cateau (even those of L Battery were recovered after Néry, much damaged though they were). The five infantry divisions and the Cavalry Division (plus 5th Cavalry Brigade) together had sixty-five batteries, each of six guns; and each infantry division had a heavy battery of four guns – in all, just over 400. The distortions probably arose through calculating the thirty-eight lost at Le Cateau as a percentage of II Corps' two divisions; yet even this inaccurate method would still give a loss of only about 25%.

interior lines of communication – but the ever-extending external lines of the Germans were now groaning with the strain. By 5 September the 1st Army's railhead had managed to move to Chauny, just south of St Quentin, but it was still a full 40 miles behind the fighting troops and the distance was increasing by the day (60 miles was considered the maximum). Third-line transport, which took supplies from the railheads to the divisions, was being worked to death: 60 per cent of the mainly iron-wheel-rimmed trucks of the mechanical transport companies were broken down, and there were not nearly enough waggons for fodder, which led to some brusque requisitioning from French and Belgian civilians. Of the 220,000 men mustered at the start of the campaign, 11,000 had been killed or wounded or were missing, and almost as many were posted sick, largely from exhaustion and aggravated blisters (and some from want of food) – hardly surprising in a march of over 300 miles since detraining at the Belgian border. The detachment of II Corps to pin down the Belgians at Antwerp had left about 160,000 – a reduction of perhaps some 30 per cent in the 1st Army's fighting strength.*

'Unshaved, scarcely washed at all for days . . . faces covered with a scrubbly beard, they look like prehistoric savages,' wrote Walter Bloem: 'Their coats were covered with dust and spattered with blood from bandaging the wounded, blackened with powder smoke, and torn threadbare by thorns and barbed wire.' The 1st Army, although by no means a spent force, was no longer the great unstoppable machine that had wheeled through Belgium – or even that had borne down on the BEF at Mons. The Germans were now numerically weaker than the allies on the *Schwenkungsflügel*, the 'swinging' or 'pivoting' right wing – the wing that had mattered most in the Schlieffen Plan, the wing that was meant to execute the twentieth-century Cannae, replicating Hannibal's spectacular victory, but which had failed to envelop the allied left, becoming instead simply the high-water mark of the invasion of France. Kluck's 1st Army was outnumbered by half as many infantry battalions again and by 200 guns (850 in all – many of them French super-heavies of Manoury's 6th Army and the BEF, which together comprised 191 battalions). Bülow's

---

* While allied strength was building, therefore, Moltke's was steadily falling. It did not help that he had sent the Guard Reserve and XI Corps (from the 2nd and 3rd Armies respectively) to the Eastern Front on 25 August.

2nd Army, and the half of Max von Hausen's 3rd (Saxon) Army west of Sedan against which Ferdinand Foch's 9th Army (another of Joffre's conjuring tricks) was to hurl itself, were likewise outclassed, Franchet d'Espèrey and Foch between them mustering twice as many battalions and 250 more guns (nearly 1,100 in all).

It was now, on 5 September, the thirty-fifth day of mobilization; Schlieffen had calculated victory on the thirty-ninth or fortieth day.

But the French had bled too. Nine months before Captain John Macrae would write the poem forever linking the poppy to the sacrifices of the Western Front – 'In Flanders fields the poppies blow' – a German officer on the staff of the 6th Army, Major Rudolph (Ritter) von Xylander, used the image to describe the devastation in Lorraine: 'It looked extremely horrific everywhere: the farmsteads burned down; in many fields the French [in *le pantalon rouge*] lay as if in a field of poppies.'* Another wrote of his shock on coming into a small town, and behind a smouldering ruin finding the 'bloody shirts and pants, knapsacks and rifles' of 190 French soldiers buried the day before. It was hardly a huge number in the great scheme of things, the overall *Westaufmarsch* – and certainly not in terms of the grinding machine that the Western Front would become – but on the human scale that was the soldier's immediate view of the battlefield ('a battalion's field is bounded by its own vision'), it was numbing nevertheless. And yet another *Ritter*, on the staff of the *Oberste Heeresleitung* (OHL) – Karl von Wenninger, not a Prussian, perhaps significantly, but Bavarian – was shaken by the widespread sight of 'burned down villages, overturned wagons, dead horses, fresh graves . . . wounded horses with deadly sad eyes aimlessly wandering, the air filled with burning sweet smells' of flesh both animal and human.

It looked as if the vials of the wrath of God had been poured upon

---

* Xylander's diary, quoted in Herwig, *The Marne, 1914*. Macrae's three-stanza poem, published in *Punch* in December 1915 (having previously been rejected by the *Spectator*), was composed quickly for the burial of a friend killed in action. The 'blow' of the first line is sometimes rendered 'grow', since that was Macrae's first draft, subsequently altered for publication. The first stanza runs:

In Flanders fields the poppies blow
Between the crosses, row on row,
That mark our place; and in the sky
The larks, still bravely singing, fly
Scarce heard amid the guns below.

a great swathe of northern and eastern France. And no one was more aware of it, and of the fatigue of the troops he would ask to take back his nation's ravaged territory, than Joffre himself. Their *pantalons rouges* had faded to the colour of 'pale brick', wrote one of his staff officers, their long blue coats were 'ragged and torn', and their eyes were 'cavernous in faces dulled by exhaustion'.

Joffre told the war ministry to comb out every barrack and depot for replacements for the quarter of a million men who had been killed, wounded or captured, or had gone 'missing' or sick (more than twice as many as the BEF had come with to France) in the 400-mile-long 'Battle of the Frontiers', and then issued an Order of the Day which left no one in doubt as to the effort now expected and the price those taking part must prepare to pay:

> At the moment when the battle upon which hangs the fate of the country is about to begin, all must remember that the time for looking back is past; every effort must be concentrated on attacking and throwing the enemy back. Troops that can no longer advance must at any cost keep the ground that has been won, and must die where they stand rather than give way. Under present conditions no weakness can be tolerated.

It seems a curiously flat exhortation for a man who had reduced Sir John French to tears, with 'le pays' for 'country', rather than *La Patrie* or *La France*, and 'die where they stand' when the whole idea was *'en avant!'* But that was Joffre at his most 'imperturbable', the adjective most frequently assigned to him. Certainly Franchet d'Espèrey – 'Desperate Frankie' – would cast his own orders in a more ringing tone, resonant even of Nelson's signal before Trafalgar: 'It is important that every soldier should know before the battle that the honour of France and the salvation of the homeland depend upon the energy he displays in tomorrow's fighting. The country relies on every man to do his duty.' And then, after a blood-chilling warning of 'all the rigour of court martial' for any who showed weakness, the new commander of the 5th Army played a magnificent card, ending on the promise of laurels for the highest of soldierly virtues rather than the threat of retribution for the lowest: 'Acts of courage and energy will be reported without delay so that they may be rewarded on the spot.'

The BEF heard the news that they were to turn to face the enemy –

to run at him, indeed – with relief, and in places with actual rejoicing. Almost unbelievably, some had yet to see action: the 2nd Oxfordshire and Buckinghamshire Light Infantry, for example, in the 2nd Division (Haig's corps), had not had a man killed. 'The decision to advance gave everyone a wonderful uplift,' said one. 'During the retreat there was a joke I remember which went: "If they give us a medal for this it should have a pair of boots on it." '*

Sir John French's own Order of the Day called on them to 'push on vigorously to the attack'.

At first light the following morning, 6 September, close on a million French and 100,000 British troops began the counter-offensive – a great forward movement between Paris and Verdun, a front of some 150 miles, against the 750,000 Germans of the *Schwenkungsflügel*. The proverbial boot was now on the other foot, but it was a boot worn thin by a fortnight's fighting and marching – in the case of some of the French troops, three weeks' fighting and marching.† Weariness and wariness would, in many instances, combine to produce the same hesitancy that the Germans had displayed since (in the BEF's case) Mons, while the Germans, still superior in artillery across the whole front of the counter-offensive (some 3,300 guns to the allies' 3,000), would frequently display the same resource and stubbornness that the BEF had shown in their delaying actions. Indeed, as the scale of the offensive was unveiled – at first the Germans thought it must be a series of aggressive rearguard actions, until they discovered Joffre's Order of the Day that evening – the mood at *OHL* verged towards euphoric. Oberst Gerhard Tappen, chief of operations, burst into a staff meeting with the news: 'Well, we finally get hold of them. Now it will be a fierce fight. Our brave troops will know how to do their job.' In other words, there would be no more evasion by the enemy, the BEF and the French melting away before the fight: the 'Day of Decision' was at hand, and 'brute force' would decide it.‡

Brute force together with *Truppenpraxis*, a term that does not translate simply into military English – 'the practice of handling

---

* Quoted in Ascoli, *The Mons Star*.
† It was not just the footwear of the infantry that was wearing thin: the BEF's cavalry had already fitted their reserve horseshoes, and even these were now almost worn through. It was only a consignment arriving from England between 6 and 9 September that would keep them going during the march to the Aisne.
‡ Tappen's diary, quoted in Herwig, *The Marne, 1914*.

forces in battle', perhaps, a combination of tactics and procedure, but linked to 'operational art', which is the correlation of tactical detail with the over-arching goals of strategy. *Truppenpraxis* was the meat and drink of the *Grosser Generalstab*, the reason for its existence. In the 1st and 2nd Armies its test had come. For it could not be a matter of holding everywhere: the key lay in defeating the two armies on the wings of the offensive – Manoury's on the (allied) left, and Foch's on the right – before Franchet d'Espèrey's 5th Army and the BEF could make a decisive breakthrough in the centre. Hurl back those two wings, and any attack in the centre would lethally expose its own flanks. If the Germans could see this, so too could Joffre and Sir John French: what would defeat the stratagem of hurling back the flanks was dazzling progress by Franchet d'Espèrey and the BEF.

Yet while the vigour and resolution demanded by Orders of the Day and *Field Service Regulations* were communicable to the BEF's brigade commanders, and probably to those commanding battalions, it was another matter getting the message further down the chain. For two weeks the infantry had plodded in retreat – 'slogged', in army parlance – the enemy on their tail throughout; changing gear now to advance rapidly into a space empty of Germans (or so they were told), to close with them (wherever they were) and seize them by the throat, would take more than throwing a lever. It was the same with the cavalry. Sergeant Brunton's diary for 5 September makes no mention of the advance next day, merely that he had been on picquet with his troop all night, and was simply pleased that 'people at a farm bring my troop cooked eggs and coffee for breakfast'; later in the day on the sixth, he noted, they had 'rather a hot time of it' in action, though the casualties were small, and there were 'very heavy artillery duels'. He did take part in a charge, however, in which his horse came down, and he 'had to shoot her as she had an open joint at knee'. Towards evening, 'enemy aeroplanes [were] very active . . . which kept us on the move', and they 'had to bivouac on roadside' that night, with 'no fires to be lit; result no hot tea or cooked food'. It was solid enough, but not exactly 'push[ing] on vigorously to the attack', in the words of Sir John French's Order of the Day.

Brunton's squadron were in action soon after dawn on the seventh, escorting I Battery RHA – another 'hot time', in which they 'got enemy on the run'. They 'had to bury quite a lot of Germans', which was chivalrous enough, but there was nothing in *Field Service Regulations* about burying the dead, especially not the enemy, during the advance. It was as if a pace for doing things had been established in the retreat from Mons, perhaps an unspoken sense now of being in a longer game than had first been thought, and that conservation of effort was to be a guiding principle.

But it was not entirely the fault of the junior leaders. Brunton's squadron buried the dead because they were given the time to. Ironically, the quintessential cavalryman, Sir John French, rather than combining Allenby's division into a striking force or using them as strategic cavalry, had formed them into two brigade groupings to act as protective cavalry for the leading corps of the BEF.* Five cavalry brigades, even if under-strength, across a front of 15 miles – it was not an onerous covering task, and they were bound to make faster progress than the infantry, even having to deal with the occasional German rearguard. From time to time they simply had to wait for the infantry to catch up.

There were, however, some spirited actions, including a charge by the 9th Lancers against Prussian 'uhlans'. The Lancers had been reconnoitring the high ground above the village of Le Montcel ('Moncel' in English texts), forty of them, led by the commanding officer, Lieutenant-Colonel (later General Sir) David 'Soarer' Campbell, when a German squadron appeared, part of the 1st *Garde Dragoner* of Richthofen's Cavalry Corps.† Sergeant James Taylor describes how, as they closed up to the village,

> The Colonel put us behind some haystacks and went on ahead with his trumpeter. The next thing we knew he was galloping back, and we could see why. About 500 yards away there was a line of German cavalry advancing towards us, and I remember the adjutant saying: 'By God, Colonel, they're going to charge us!' And they were! Then Colonel Campbell gave the order, very quiet and matter of fact: 'Follow me, gentlemen.' And off

---

* There was now a third corps in the BEF: III Corps had been formed on 30 August under Lieutenant-General William Pulteney, comprising the 4th Division, the 19th Brigade and (when it arrived) the 6th Division. For the moment it was a useful if incomplete BEF supplement, on the left flank.
† Their full titles reveal the irony of the clash. The Prussians were 1. *Garde-Dragoner-Regiments, Königin Viktoria von Großbritannien und Irland*, while the 9th were the 9th Queen's Royal Lancers, though their Queen was not Victoria but her aunt by marriage, Adelaide, William IV's consort – formerly Adelaide von Saxe-Weiningen.

we went. I drew my sword [sergeants and above carried swords rather than lances] ... we hadn't had time to form a proper line – none of that knee-to-knee stuff – but we were going a much stronger gallop than the Germans and we met the left half of their line with a fair old clash.

Frederic Coleman, an American who had volunteered with two dozen other members of the Royal Automobile Club as additional drivers (with their cars), happened to see it:

Behind a friendly stone wall I stopped and took out. Diagonally, across the broad road that led north from the village, came a line of horsemen ... Then from the left shot other horsemen, one [Campbell] well ahead ... riding like mad, full tilt at the ranks of German pride ... [whose] pace was slow compared with the whirlwind rush of the smaller band. I was on the wall as the impact came ... I wondered that none of the chargers funked it ... Not one charger 'refused'.

The winner of the 1896 Grand National – Campbell (on 'The Soarer', hence the nickname) – was unlikely to have a refusal. He even managed at the gallop to shoot the German squadron leader. Sergeant Taylor too 'got [an uhlan] with my sword and fetched him out of the saddle' though he, Campbell and the adjutant were wounded in the mêlée. Moncel was possibly the last lance-to-lance charge of the war.

Meanwhile the RFC was reporting a general movement of German troops northwards, although the extent of the gap between Kluck's 1st and Bülow's 2nd Armies took longer to establish – as did the fact that it was occupied by little more than a cavalry screen. For the several rivers along the line of advance – the Grand Morin, the Petit Morin, the Marne itself and then the Ourcq – were well defended by machine guns and jaegers, and while the RFC might report that there were few troops compared with what the BEF had faced in the retreat, on the ground it felt at times much the same as before. On 8 September, Private Frank Richards, with the 2nd Royal Welsh Fusiliers in the new III Corps on the left, recalled

marching up some rising ground. Down in the valley in front of us ran the River Marne. On each side of the river was a village. A fine bridge had spanned the river but it was now in half, the enemy having blown it up. We advanced down the hill in extended order. The enemy were supposed to be holding the two villages, and we had to take them. We were met by a hail of bullets. The men on the right and left of me fell with bullet wounds in the legs, and a sergeant just behind me fell with one through the belly. We were having heavy casualties but couldn't see one of the enemy. We lined the edge of a little copse and opened fire on the villages, aiming at the windows of the houses. But the hidden enemy were still keeping up an intense rifle-fire, so we doubled back up the hill and under cover.

It may have been a reverse case of the Germans' mistaking the BEF's rapid fire for machine guns, for the German cavalry divisions and their jaegers were equipped on a far better scale than the BEF's two guns per regiment.

Whatever the source of the bullets that had sent the Fusiliers back up the hill into cover, it delayed the crossing. 'When it was dusk we carried on with the attack,' continued Richards:

We advanced and got into the grounds of a big château. Everything was now quiet, and from the château my platoon advanced quietly into the village. The first house we came to was locked. We heard some groans in the yard of the house and found an officer of the King's Own Lancaster Regiment who was badly wounded. He told the Second-in-Command of the Battalion, who was with us, that the enemy was strongly entrenched the other side of the river. He said it was quite possible there were still a lot of them left in the village we were now in. We also came across the dead bodies of three other officers of the same regiment; I expect they had been reconnoitring the village earlier in the day.*

They only managed to force a crossing the next morning. It had been the battalion's hardest fighting to date.

The Marne, with its steep wooded sides, was well suited to delaying actions, but even so, the advance was in places cautious to the point of hesitancy, as if in danger of springing some gigantic trap. An RFC patrol in the early afternoon of the ninth saw large bodies of German troops in the neighbourhood of Château-Thierry, and infantry moving on Domptin to the west of the 3rd Infantry Brigade – and the

---

* This was the same battalion that had been caught in the open at Le Cateau.

whole of the I Corps was halted for two hours until the situation could be cleared up. It must have been difficult at times for the cavalry to know what was wanted (screening the infantry or rapid advance): afterwards, Haig 'met the 5th Cavalry Brigade moving at a walk and delay[ing] the advance of our infantry. I motored on and saw Chetwode [brigade commander]. At my suggestion he at once trotted on. I explained to him that a little effort now might mean the conclusion of the war.'*

By the evening of the ninth, Haig's I Corps and Smith-Dorrien's II Corps were across the Marne, but the III Corps was still mostly south of the river. The advance had begun at first light on the sixth: in four days only 37 miles had been made – in contrast with the same distance, from Mons to Le Cateau, covered on 24 and 25 August. Private Joe Clarke of the 2nd Connaughts (I Corps) likened it to being on 'a train that stopped at every station. We would do half a mile, then halt for an hour, and then move on for a bit. There was some shelling and machine-gun fire but nothing to worry about. I think we could have done a lot better.'†

The trouble was the flanks, again. They had worried Sir John French throughout the retreat – on the left the shaky French Territorials, on the right the unreliable Lanrezac – and he was determined now to keep aligned with Franchet d'Espèrey's left wing. Meanwhile, un-fortunately for Joffre and any high hopes he may have had for keeping the Germans on the run, Kluck had been able to extricate his remaining two corps from the fight and slip them west across the Marne for a counter-attack on Manoury's 6th Army as they struggled across the Ourcq.‡

On 10 September the hot weather broke. Rain fell so heavily that under the abnormal weight of traffic the roads were soon churned up, slowing the advance even further. Bülow's 2nd Army was now in full retreat, however, thrown back with *élan* by Franchet d'Espèrey's 5th

---

* He later added to his diary: 'The enemy was running back. It was the duty of each one of us to strain every effort to keep him on the run.' Given Haig's scepticism about a short war before he left England, it is difficult to judge how serious a possibility he believed this to be.
† Quoted in Ascoli, *The Mons Star*.
‡ On 9 September the Belgians began another plucky sortie from Antwerp, which succeeded in tying down German troops who were otherwise beginning the move south to rejoin the 1st, 2nd and 3rd Armies.

Army, which with General Louis Conneau's cavalry corps could now at last make progress, hindered only by the elements. Manoury's 6th Army, on the BEF's left, was making accelerated progress too. But on the BEF's front Richthofen's rearguards were still giving trouble, although the signs of retreat – abandoned vehicles and equipment, stragglers – were having their heartening effect. Sergeant Brunton at last 'learned that the enemy are in retirement and that we have in conjunction with French troops saved Paris'. And he was in no doubt of the service they had done hereabouts too: 'One town we passed through today was a pitiful sight. The Huns had played hell with it and many young girls violated.'*

The BEF took 1,500 prisoners that day for fewer than 350 casualties, and bivouacked for the night just a few miles south of the valley of the upper Ourcq, crossing it the next morning before realigning the advance north and slightly east rather than north-west as before. Haig reckoned the delay and the realignment a mistake since it allowed the enemy close on his front to get away. He wrote that he had been able to press them hard the day before, recording with satisfaction 'an intercepted wireless message from the German General [Richthofen] commanding the Cavalry Corps in our front . . . He wished infantry to cover his retirement across the river!'

If only they could keep up that pressure and momentum . . .

By midnight on 12 September all three allied corps had got across the Vesle, the lower tributary of the Aisne, making the greatest progress to date, but against no opposition but the rain. This was at once both satisfying and ominous. Kluck had evidently disengaged, and it could be for but one purpose: to occupy the ground of his own

---

* Brunton makes a similar claim two days earlier: 'Rode through [indecipherable] today. Germans have destroyed and burnt the town and committed acts on the female population too awful to write about.' There are numerous other accounts in the same vein. Brigadier Horne, for example, wrote to his wife on 10 September: 'The Germans seem to delight in smashing and spoiling everything they can. They leave the villages & houses they occupy in a dreadful state, & ill treat the poor people awfully.' There is no doubt that the manifestation of the Vandal spirit of old, and the Kaiser's unfortunate exhortation to the Hunnic spirit during the Boxer Rebellion in 1900, which had earned the sobriquet 'Hun' for his own troops, shocked all ranks alike. 'Mercy will not be shown, prisoners will not be taken,' he had told them. 'Just as a thousand years ago the Huns under Attila won a reputation of might that lives on in legends, so may the name of Germany in China, such that no Chinese will ever again dare so much as to look askance at a German.' Little wonder that Kipling's 'The Hun is at the gate!' had such resonance in Britain.

choosing on which to bring to a halt the allied counter-offensive – the high ground to the north of, and overlooking, the Aisne. That night the RFC, whose flying – and, more critically, observation – was already seriously restricted by the bad weather, was hit as hard as in any artillery bombardment by a violent storm just as it was moving its operating base forward to Saponay, 10 miles south of the Vesle. Four aircraft of the 5th Squadron were completely wrecked, and others badly damaged. One pilot, having made a forced landing, saved his machine only by running it up against a haystack, laying a ladder over the front skids and piling paving-stones on the rungs before managing to tie it down. Half of the 3rd Squadron's machines were blown over, one of them lifting 30 feet before crashing on top of another. When dawn came, David Henderson, the GOC, had no more than ten aircraft operational.

Had the weather been favourable, the RFC, on the evidence of their form to date, would almost certainly have confirmed what was suspected, that the Germans were indeed digging in on the heights above the Aisne. Whether the BEF – or, for that matter, the French – could have found the extra energy to attack in force on the twelfth, before the Germans could dig deep enough, is another matter. What might have made a difference, however, was HE ammunition with the field artillery, and more heavy guns. As it was, there were some doughty efforts at getting across the Aisne during the night, Brigadier Aylmer Hunter-Weston (who would come in for much criticism as a divisional commander at Gallipoli, and then in command of a corps at the Somme) leading his 11th Brigade in person across a partially demolished bridge and up the slopes beyond, driving into the German outposts with the bayonet as first light approached.

They may have been slow off the mark on 6 September, but now that they could lock horns, the BEF wanted to fight. Throughout that day, the thirteenth, and the next, in driving rain and bitter wind, the battalions launched increasingly desperate attacks to dislodge the Germans, the fighting becoming very determined indeed, as the tally of VCs testifies. Lance-Corporal William Fuller of the 2nd Welsh was cited for bringing in wounded under sustained heavy fire; Bombardier Ernest Horlock for repeatedly returning to his gun after having his wounds dressed; Captain William Johnston, a sapper, for repeatedly ferrying the wounded across the Aisne and returning under heavy fire with ammunition; Private Ross Tollerton of the 1st Cameron Highlanders for bringing the wounded into cover and staying with them, and still fighting, after his company had retired; Private George Wilson, 2nd Highland Light Infantry, for attacking and capturing a machine gun single-handed, shooting the seven men of the detachment. On the fifteenth Sergeant Brunton wrote in his diary: 'A valley we rode through during the afternoon was aptly described as the "Valley of Death". Heaps of graves of our poor fellows and twisted remains of one of our convoys.'

But men could only stand so much. Some of the 3rd Division near Chavonne broke in a German counter-attack, falling back to the river in an unseemly rush. Haig was uncharacteristically phlegmatic: 'It was impossible to rely on some of the regiments in the 3rd Division which had been so severely handled at Mons and Le Cateau.'*

By now, though, it was clear that the Germans could not be driven off the heights in the way they had been driven back from the Marne, and from the Grand and the Petit Morel, and the Ourcq and the Vesle. Sir John French ordered the BEF to dig in. On his left and right the French were doing the same. It must have come as yet another

---

* Haig's diary, as any, must be read with care. Although he is by no means easy on those under his direct command – witness the affair of the Grenadiers' commanding officer at Mons – he can appear denigrating of others who are not 'his'. An entry for 20 September describes De Lisle's (2nd Cavalry Brigade) telling him that the 1st West Yorks, newly arrived with the 6th Division, and under Haig's temporary command, 'left their trenches and ran back to Paizey [sic] village headed apparently by the Colonel of the battalion. De Lisle and the 4th Dragoon Guards drove back a good many of the infantry at the point of their swords to the trenches.' Yet the divisional history paints a rather different picture: 'At dawn on the 20th September, the enemy delivered a heavy attack on the I Corps and on the French left, driving in the *Tirailleurs d'Afrique* and turning the flank of the West Yorks. The echeloned company formed front to the flank, and the supporting company followed suit. The Germans annihilated the right front company, and, using the white flag ruse, apparently captured some of the next company. Major Ingles, collecting a proportion of the front companies, withdrew a short distance and counter-attacked, but was unsuccessful and lost his life in this gallant endeavour. At about 1 p.m. a counter-attack was delivered by the Sherwood Foresters, who were in Brigade Reserve, the support company of the West Yorks, under Lt.-Col. Towsey, and a squadron of the 18th Hussars from Paissy. These, advancing over the perfectly open ground, recaptured the trenches and gallantly held them against further attacks. In this affair the West Yorks suffered casualties amounting approximately to 15 officers and 600 other ranks, the Sherwood Foresters also losing 12 officers and 180 other ranks.' Towsey was *not* removed from command, as might have been supposed had he run to the rear ahead of his battalion. Indeed, later that month he was wounded, and the following May, at Ypres, he was mentioned in despatches – the first of *five* mentions. By the end of the war he had the DSO, CMG and CBE, and command of a brigade. He seems an unlikely 'Duke of Plaza Toro'.

surprise to the ever-optimistic Henry Wilson, who two days earlier, on the thirteenth, had opined to Joffre's chief of staff that 'unless we make some serious blunder we ought to be at Elsenborn [across the German border] in four weeks'.*

German counter-attacks, more deliberate, now followed, and in turn more attempts to drive them off the heights. In the fortnight's fighting after crossing the Aisne the BEF would suffer 12,000 casualties; in the advance from the Marne they had taken fewer than 2,000.†

Barely a week later, however, writing to his old soldier-friend the duke of Connaught, Sir John French would put his finger on the sea change that was taking place on the Western Front: 'Nothing but the most powerful and efficient entrenchments will avail against the modern *heavy* artillery which is brought into the field.'

And at the end of September he would write to the King that from now on 'the spade will be as great a necessity as the rifle'.‡

At the *Oberste Heeresleitung*, Moltke, in a state of nervous collapse, reportedly told the Kaiser: 'Your Majesty, we have lost the war.'

On 14 September he was replaced by the Prussian war minister, General Erich von Falkenhayn.

It was the end of the Schlieffen Plan.

---

* In fairness to Wilson, Joffre's chief of staff, Henri Berthelot, thought *three* weeks.
† French losses in the advance were about 18,000 killed, 112,000 wounded and 80,000 missing. The Marne was, self-evidently, principally a French victory. German casualty figures for its seven armies in the west between 1 and 10 September were 99,000, including some 28,000 killed or missing.
‡ In his memoirs, he elaborates: 'I can remember sitting for hours at the mouth of a great cave which lay high up the southern bank of the river, within about 400 yards of the village of Missy and to the eastern flank of it, from which point I saw some of the first effects of the 6-in. siege howitzers which were sent to us at that time [by the Naval Division, as in South Africa]. Missy lay along the bed of the stream on both banks, and the Germans occupied a curiously shaped, high, conical hill which was called "Condé Fort." This was situated about 600 yards north of Missy, and reached by a steep ascent from the banks of the river. The hill completely dominated the village. On the day of which I am writing (September 24th), it was very interesting to witness the clearance of this hill by our high-explosive shells. We could see the Germans flying in all directions to the rear, and we subsequently got reliable information that their losses on this occasion were very heavy.'

Chapter Twenty-One

THE RACE TO THE SEA; AND
WHAT MIGHT HAVE BEEN

Time ... is less likely to bring favour to the victor than to the
vanquished ... An offensive war requires above all a quick,
irresistible decision ... Any kind of interruption, pause, or
suspension of activity is inconsistent with the nature of offensive
war.

Carl von Clausewitz, *On War*

The counter-attack on the Marne was indeed the end of the Schlieffen
Plan; but it was also the beginning of Churchill's 'desperate and vain
appeals against the decision of fate' – appeals that on the Western
Front would ultimately cost the lives of over half a million men of the
British army.*

On the Aisne, meanwhile, the armies began digging in. At first they
dug simple, shallow rifle-pits, but as more and heavier artillery was
brought up, the trenches were dug deeper and became more elaborate,
the Germans generally with the advantage of the better ground.
Both sides began 'feeling for the flank' again – trying to find the end

---

* The figures produced in the 1920s by the Central Statistical Office put the number of
British lives lost on the Western Front at 564,715. Nearly 200,000 (the great majority
from action in France and Flanders) were discharged as invalids, with what today would
be called 'life-changing' wounds.

417

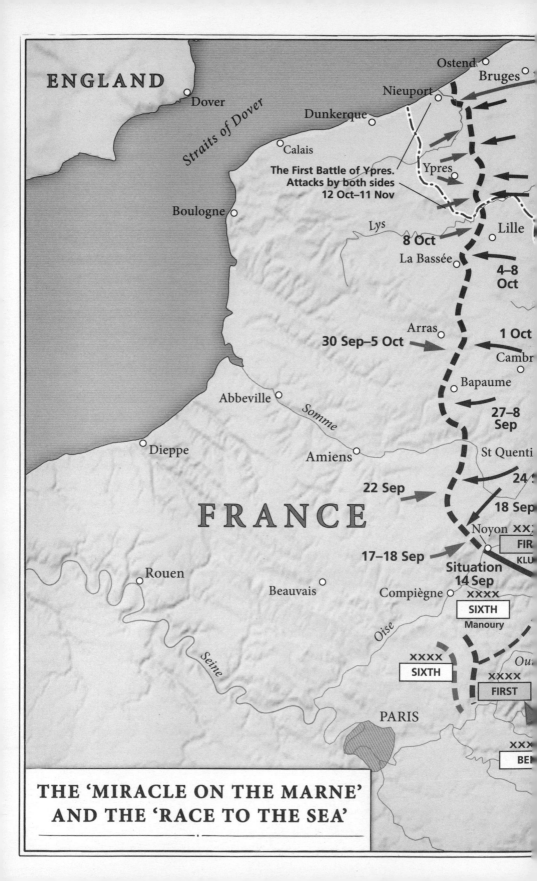

ENGLAND

Dover

Straits of Dover

Ostend

Bruges

Nieuport

Dunkerque

Calais

The First Battle of Ypres.
Attacks by both sides
12 Oct–11 Nov

Ypres

Boulogne

Lys

8 Oct

Lille

La Bassée

4–8
Oct

Arras

30 Sep–5 Oct

1 Oct

Cambr

Bapaume

Abbeville

Somme

27–8
Sep

Dieppe

Amiens

St Quenti

22 Sep

24

18 Sep

FRANCE

Noyon XX

FIR

KLU

Rouen

Beauvais

17–18 Sep

Situation
14 Sep

Compiègne

XXXX

SIXTH

Manoury

Oise

XXXX

SIXTH

Ou

Seine

XXXX

FIRST

PARIS

XXX

BE

THE 'MIRACLE ON THE MARNE'
AND THE 'RACE TO THE SEA'

N

6 Oct
XX
GIAN

Antwerp

City fell
10 Oct

Ghent

BRUSSELS

Louvain

Maastricht

Aachen

BELGIUM

Liège

Dendre

Meuse

Charleroi

Namur

Mons

Sambre

Maubeuge

Ardennes Forest

Cateau

LUXEMBOURG

XXXX
SEVENTH
HEERINGEN

LUXEMBOURG

XXXX

XXXX
XXXX
SECOND
BÜLOW

Rethel

Argonne

XXXX
FIFTH
CROWN PRINCE

Aisne

XXXX
THIRD
HAUSEN

XXXX
FOURTH
ALBRECHT

XXXX
FIFTH
Franchet
d'Espèrey

Rheims

Forest

Metz

XXXX

Marne

XXXX
FIFTH

XXXX
SECOND

XXXX
THIRD

XXXX
FOURTH

XXXX
NINTH
Foch

XXXX
FOURTH

0   miles   50

Nancy

XXXX
SECOND

TH

of the opponent's line, to force the defender to fall back so as not to be enveloped. At first it was local, the French on the left attacking with troops already in the line and the Germans likewise, before becoming more deliberate, with both Joffre and Falkenhayn trying to find 'fresh' troops for the task. For whatever the dashed hopes of the Schlieffen Plan, Moltke's successor had first to make sure the situation did not, at the very least, get any worse. Surmising that the British, having been thoroughly blooded, would now reinforce the BEF, he thought it well to capture the Channel ports and cut their supply lines – except that the lines of communication did not run through the northern Channel ports. Besides, the *Grosser Generalstab* was still hankering after its Cannae: opportunities might be created from unexpected tactical success. After all, a fortnight earlier, General Paul von Hindenburg's 8th Army had destroyed the better part of the Russian 2nd Army at Tannenberg, which for a while at least took the pressure off the *Oberste Heeresleitung*. For the time being, the flanks of both sides hung tantalizingly in the air, with 200 miles of open country to the west: perhaps there was still time to knock out France (and now the British) and then turn east with all the efficiency of the Prussian (and, they must hope, the French and Belgian) railway system to defeat the Russian bear?

During late September and early October there was a continuous series of battles in Picardy, Artois and Flanders, Joffre having matched the efficiency of the *Eisenbahnamt* by moving General Noel de Castelnau's 2nd Army from Lorraine to Amiens, while Falkenhayn moved Crown Prince Rupprecht's (Bavarian) 6th Army opposite him to St Quentin in a remarkable but little-known railway race (through Luxembourg). On 17 and 18 September the French attacked at Noyon; the Germans countered by attacking on the French flank towards Montdidier. On the twenty-second the French attacked north of Roye; and again the Germans countered by attacking on the flank. On 27 and 28 September Rupprecht struck near Albert, but Castelnau managed once more to halt them. With each attempt the line was prolonged west and north, in what would become known as 'the Race for the Sea', though the object was not so much reaching the coast as re-establishing a war of manoeuvre.

The search for the open flank now moved even further north, towards Arras. Two infantry corps and one of cavalry from Castelnau's 2nd Army, under General Louis de Maud'huy, advanced up the River Scarpe towards Vimy. Rupprecht tried to outflank him and on 3 October sent his reserve corps north of Arras and the IV Cavalry Corps further north towards Lille. By the evening of the 4th Maud'huy was in serious danger of being cut off, having lost contact with his cavalry to the north, and a gap having opened on his southern flank. He told Joffre he would have to withdraw, and asked in which direction. Joffre, desperate to protect the industrial areas of Artois, ordered Maud'huy to hold his ground, and at once set about reorganizing the northern armies. Maud'huy's detachment became yet another new army, the 10th (remarkable promotion for a man who in July had been commanding a brigade), and the 2nd and 10th, along with any other troops in the area, mainly Territorials, were grouped together under the command of Ferdinand Foch, as Joffre's deputy. The front held; for the moment the crisis was over.

Sir John French, and Kitchener, watching this slow-motion race for the sea, had been getting anxious, and had decided that the BEF must shorten its lines of communication as soon as possible, not least by resuming its place on the left flank of the French, rather than remaining sandwiched between armies. It were better, in any case, that Calais, Boulogne, Dunkirk or Dieppe (perhaps even Ostend and Zeebrugge) replace St Nazaire as the port of entry – or 'base', as it was called in *Field Service Regulations*. Besides, if the Channel ports fell into German hands, the Channel itself would soon be full of mines and U-Boats. Churchill, as first lord of the Admiralty, was only too well aware of the threat, and was already preparing to send a Royal Marines Brigade and two more of the Royal Naval Division – reservist sailors not required for ships' crews, half-retrained as infantry (among them, hastily commissioned, Rupert Brooke – 'Now, God be thanked Who has matched us with His hour, / And caught our youth, and wakened us from sleeping . . .'). With aircraft of the Royal Naval Air Service and an improvised force of armoured cars, as well as his own (personally chosen) Yeomanry regiment, the Oxfordshire Hussars, they were to screen the northern ports – and later, at the beginning of October, would sprint to Antwerp to stiffen the resolve of the Belgian garrison.*

On 29 September Sir John French sent a note to Joffre:

> Ever since our position in the French line was altered by the advance of General Manoury's 6th Army to the River Ourcq, I have been anxious to regain my original position on the left flank of the French Armies. On several occasions I have thought of suggesting this move, but the strategical and tactical situation from day to day has made the proposal inopportune. Now, however, that the position of affairs has become clearly defined, and that the immediate future can be forecasted with some confidence, I wish to press the proposal with all the power and insistence which are at my disposal. The moment for the execution of such a move appears to me to be singularly opportune.

The opportuneness lay in part with the imminent arrival of significant reinforcements, including the newly formed 7th and 8th

---

* In the early hours of 3 October, Grey and Kitchener, in Asquith's absence in Wales, asked Churchill to go to Antwerp to assess the Belgians' holding power. 'I don't know how fluent he [Churchill] is in French,' wrote Asquith to Venetia Stanley when he got back to London, 'but if he was able to do himself justice in a foreign tongue, the Belgians will be listening to a discourse the like of which they have never heard before. I cannot but think that he will stiffen them up to the sticking point.' He did indeed stiffen them up, the Belgian prime minister agreeing to continue the defence of Antwerp if allied troops could protect the withdrawal routes of Belgian forces still outside the perimeter. Churchill promised further British reinforcements and telegraphed London that the two naval brigades should be sent at once, and the Royal Marines Brigade from Dunkirk, all of which was agreed. A naval rating accompanying the party described Churchill's inspection of the forward positions thus: 'Mr Churchill was energetic and imperative. He discussed the situation with his own staff and some of the Belgian officers, emphasizing his points with his walking stick . . . he appeared on occasions to criticize the siting and construction of the trenches . . . To me it appeared that Mr Churchill dominated the proceedings and the impression formed was that he was by no means satisfied with the position generally. He put forward his ideas forcefully, waving his stick and thumping the ground with it. After obviously pungent remarks he would walk away a few steps and stare towards the enemy's direction.' On the morning of the 5th, Churchill sent a telegram to Asquith with the magnificent proposal that 'if it is thought by HM government that I can be of service here, I am willing to resign my office and undertake command of relieving and defensive forces assigned to Antwerp in conjunction with Belgian army, provided that I am given necessary military rank and authority and full powers of a commander of a detached force in the field.' It was received in cabinet with much laughter, but not by Kitchener, who said he was willing to give Churchill the rank of lieutenant-general – a remarkable reversal of his earlier disdain for the soldier-reporter. Common sense prevailed, however: there were others who could be sent to Antwerp, but few who could be sent to the Admiralty. General Rawlinson was despatched to take command, but he did not arrive for forty-eight hours, so during that time Churchill conducted himself as if he simply were indeed a lieutenant-general.

Divisions (both almost exclusively regular) and the leading elements of the Indian Corps and the Indian Cavalry Corps (via Marseilles, as Churchill's 1911 memorandum had suggested). 'In other words,' Sir John French explained, 'my present force of six Divisions and two Cavalry Divisions will, within three or four weeks from now, be increased by four Divisions and two Cavalry Divisions, making a total British force of ten Divisions (five Corps) and four Cavalry Divisions.'*

Joffre agreed at once, and the BEF began its move west.

At the same time, French began preparing to send an infantry and a cavalry division to Antwerp, but on 8 October King Albert was forced to abandon the city, leading the Belgian army west and south along the coast until they could take up a coherent line of defence on the River Yser.† A week later, in yet another attempt to outflank the German line, the BEF crossed into Belgium, to Ypres, to attack east along the Menin Road. As they did so, the Duke (Albrecht) of Württemberg's 4th Army, which had been railed from the Upper Aisne and reinforced by fresh troops from Germany, and from the siege of Antwerp after its surrender on 10 October, attacked the Belgians on the Yser. They were eventually halted when on the twenty-first the King ordered the sea-locks at Nieuport to be opened, flooding the surrounding country.

By now Sir John French had some 250,000 men at his command. Urged on by Foch, he went onto the offensive along the Menin Road on 21 October. His forces soon ran into trouble, however, the speed of the redeployment of Rupprecht's Bavarians and Albrecht's 6th Army taking both GQG and GHQ by surprise. A month's hard – at times, desperate – fighting would follow. Many of the newly formed Cavalry Corps went into action for the first time – dismounted, the horses being sent to the rear and the men taking up their rifles to hold Messines Ridge south of Ypres. The first regiments of the Territorial Force would be blooded too (those that had volunteered in sufficient numbers for

* On 6 September Chetwode's 5th (Independent) Cavalry Brigade had been placed under Gough's orders; a week later, together with Gough's own 3rd Cavalry Brigade, they were designated the 2nd Cavalry Division, with divisional units added as they arrived.
† Some of the marines and sailors of the Naval Division were only able to escape by crossing into Dutch territory south of the Scheldt, whereupon they were interned. The 'neutrality' of the Scheldt itself was never, in the end, put to the test, since the only British vessel to enter Antwerp was a hospital ship to evacuate the wounded, which was allowed passage specifically after Dutch permission was sought.

INDIA FOR THE KING!

The 'imperial concentration': although the British army was small by comparison with those of the continental powers, it had the resources of the empire to call on, not least India – as suggested by this Punch *cartoon of 9 September 1914, portraying Indian troops charging to war. By the middle of October two Indian corps (one of cavalry) would be in action in France and Belgium.*

service overseas) – the London Scottish, the first Territorials to go into action, losing half their strength in the process. And the Germans would have their first sight of the turbans, pugarees and Gurkha pill-boxes of the Indian Corps. At Hollebeke on 31 October Sepoy Khudadad Khan of the Duke of Connaught's Own Baluchi Regiment won the first ever Indian VC, when it looked as if the Germans might break the line: 'The British Officer in charge of the [machine-gun] detachment having been wounded,' ran the citation, 'and the other gun put out of action by a shell, Sepoy Khudadad, though himself wounded, remained working his gun until all the other five men of the gun detachment had been killed.' He would later receive a Viceroy's Commission as *subedar*.

That last day of October was indeed a desperate time, the moment when it looked as if the dyke would rupture, a day when individual soldiers in individual regiments made a difference. If there were to be an accolade of saver of that dyke it would almost certainly go to the 2nd Worcesters, the only troops left in front of Ypres that morning as the Germans managed to capture Gheluvelt, key to the Ypres–Menin gap and therefore to the open country beyond. The battalion had already been reduced to 400 (less than half its embarkation strength in August), and they would lose another 200 recapturing this vital ground. Major Edward Hankey, who had taken command a month before when the battalion's lieutenant-colonel was promoted to command the brigade, led what remained of the Worcesters across 1,000 yards of open fields, under artillery fire, to drive the Germans from the grounds of the Chateau Gheluvelt, managing then to hold on against the inevitable counter-attacks just long enough for reinforcements to be cobbled together from the rest of the brigade to plug the hole.

On 11 November there was another crisis astride the Menin road, when the 1st and 4th Brigades of the Prussian Guard attacked, breaking through the defence line and getting to within 2 miles of Ypres. Only the bayonets of the 2nd Oxford and Buckinghamshire Light Infantry and a scratch force of Grenadiers, Irish Guards and the Royal Munster Fusiliers were able to restore the situation – but at shattering cost, including the loss of the brigadier, Charles FitzClarence, who had won the VC at Mafeking.*

*He is the highest-ranking officer inscribed on the vast and moving Menin Gate Memorial commemorating those with no known grave.

The attack of the Prussian Guard, however, like that of the *Garde Impériale* at Waterloo, was the high-water mark of the German offensive at Ypres, and in the days that followed the fighting slackened. The BEF dug in – just as they had on the Aisne – but deep, and the Western Front began its consolidation into a continuous line of trenches that would eventually stretch from the North Sea coast to the Swiss frontier. But the fighting in October and November, on top of the August retreat and the counter-attack on the Marne, was the end of the old BEF – the four divisions that had marched up to Mons, and the fifth and sixth that had joined them thereafter. The casualties for the six weeks of the First Battle of Ypres, as it became known, were 58,155 (7,960 dead, 29,562 wounded, 17,873 missing, the remainder classified 'sick'); the BEF had arrived in France with around 80,000 infantry, which by the end of October had increased to 130,000, and which on paper stood at about 150,000 by the close of First Ypres. On 30 November the officially recorded figure for casualties of all kinds since the beginning of hostilities was 86,237.* Most of these were in the infantry, where the officers and NCOs led from the front. The conclusions hardly need spelling out. The 1915 edition of *Debrett's Peerage* was delayed for many months until the editors had been able to revise the entries for almost every blue-blooded family in the kingdom.

Regulars from all over the empire would now be recalled and fed piecemeal into Flanders, reinforced in equally piecemeal fashion by the Territorials once the necessary legislation had been enacted, and then from the summer of 1915 by the men of Kitchener's 'New Armies', the volunteers who were flocking in their many tens of thousands to answer the secretary for war's famous poster-call 'Your Country Needs YOU!', until in January 1916 conscription was introduced.

Need so many – the core of the professional army – have died in those first two months? In his memoir of the BEF's opening battles, *Forty Days in 1914*, Major-General Sir Frederick Maurice, Henry Wilson's successor-but-one as DMO (1916–18), writes plainly of the missed opportunities: 'We have in the end gained complete victory [his book

---

* The projected regular strength of the British army in 2020 is 82,000, including Gurkhas.

was published in 1919], but we could have gained it more quickly had our Governments been organized for war.'* This is the point at which, therefore, while recognizing that the BEF was standing (with the French) in the path of the greatest military juggernaut the world has ever seen, we must scotch any idea that what happened in the 'Battle of the Frontiers' was inevitable. Actions have consequences; and inaction has consequences too. Quoting the historian E. H. Carr is a perilous business, but in this he is worth the risk: 'Nothing in history is inevitable, except in the formal sense that, for it to have happened otherwise, the antecedent causes would have had to be different.'†

The futile encounter-battle on the Mons–Condé canal, the ensuing battle at Le Cateau and the subsequent retreat – these need not have happened if the BEF had concentrated at Amiens rather than Maubeuge, as both Sir John French and Kitchener had wanted at the 5 August war council (at which Churchill had suggested they should concentrate well to the rear of the French army to form a strategic reserve) – and as Lanrezac himself had suggested to Joffre as late as 15 August. On 21 September, Haig – whose handling of I Corps in the fighting at Ypres was to earn him considerable acclaim – wrote in unequivocal terms to the King's assistant private secretary, Major Clive Wigram, whom he had

---

* Maurice is a controversial figure. In December 1915, when Sir John French was recalled and Haig appointed in his place, Wully Robertson, by then the BEF's chief of staff, was appointed CIGS and took Maurice back to London with him. Robertson's relations with Lloyd George, who displaced Asquith in December 1916, were never good, and in February 1918 he was forced to step aside. Maurice, fearing that Haig would be next to go, took drastic action. Lloyd George had given misleading statistics to Parliament on the strength of the British army on the Western Front – a matter of significance, given the defeats in March and April during the Germans' great offensive – and Maurice wrote to Robertson's replacement, Wilson, pointing out the inaccuracies. Wilson ignored the letter and, though knowing it would be the end of him, Maurice wrote to *The Times* (the letter was published on 8 May) plainly accusing Lloyd George of misleading Parliament. Publication naturally caused a storm, though it was short-lived, for Maurice had not reckoned on Lloyd George's oratorical and dissembling abilities. Asquith, leader of the disaffected Liberal faction in the House of Commons, called an emergency debate on 9 May, but Lloyd George successfully implied that the origin of the misleading statistics was Maurice's own office, at one stroke discrediting both Maurice and (more usefully) Asquith himself. Maurice was suspended from his post and forcibly retired, but denied a court martial – in which he had expected to be able to prove his case. *Forty Days in 1914* cannot therefore be regarded as wholly impartial; nevertheless its analysis is compelling.
† *What is History?* (London, 1961). Edward Hallett Carr, 1892–1982, was assistant editor of *The Times* 1941–6, tutor in history at Balliol College, Oxford, 1953–5, and fellow of Trinity College, Cambridge, 1955. To describe Carr, a Marxist, as a controversial historian would be to weaken the word 'controversy' beyond recognition.

known in India: 'I am glad you already realize how wrong it was to have rushed the Army north to Mons by forced marches before our reservists had got their legs. GHQ had the wildest ideas at this time of the nature of the war and the rôle of the British Force.'

Had this alternative plan been adopted, though, would it have meant that the Germans would have been able to turn the flank of Lanrezac's 5th Army?

No. From 20 August, when Moltke told Kluck that 'a landing of British troops is reported at Boulogne: their advance from about Lille must be reckoned with', both the *OHL* and Bülow, commanding (ineffectively) the 1st and 2nd Armies as an army group, were acutely conscious of the danger to the 1st Army's (Kluck's) flank. Two days later, the 1st Army halted for two critical hours to realign west in order to meet what Kluck believed was the BEF detraining at Tournai but turned out to be French Territorials. By 24 August – the date Sir John French had originally given to President Poincaré and Joffre before agreeing to bring it forward to the twenty-first – the BEF would have been ready at Amiens to take the offensive. Its divisions could then have been transported via the excellent French railway system the 50 miles to St Quentin, whence it would have posed too great a threat to the 1st Army's right for Kluck to have risked trying to envelop Lanrezac's 5th Army south of Maubeuge.* In the meantime, Lanrezac would have had to shift for his own left flank; but this was, in essence, what he was doing anyway in the withdrawal on 22 August. Without the BEF on the Mons–Condé canal, Kluck would of course have had a free run south through Mons, but he could not have presented a flank to the fortress of Maubeuge without impunity, nor could he have made any real turning movement north of Le Cateau because of the Forêt de Mormal – and, anyway, Lanrezac was already taking precautions by withdrawing to the Sambre. Lanrezac's position would have been little different from the actual situation on 26 August since the BEF had by then been driven away to the south and

---

* *Field Service Regulations* Part I says that 'it is generally calculated that in the case of a division no time will be gained in moving it by rail, even on a double line, unless the distance is over 60 miles', which is why no attempt was made to move by rail to Mons, although *FSR* also acknowledges that fatigue of the troops was a factor to be taken into account. Since time would not have been of the absolute essence in such a move to St Quentin, and so many reservists were involved, railing would have been preferable in the August heat.

west, and the gap was opening up – except, of course, that Kluck's 1st Army would have been in greater strength and better shape without the encounters with British rifle fire. From 27 August the course of events would, at worst, have been no different from actual events, the BEF retreating from St Quentin on the same line – but without the losses incurred at Mons and Le Cateau, with greater cohesion between its two corps, and perhaps with much better cooperation and contact with the French. Its subsequent performance in the Marne counter-offensive might then have been more spirited, with a chance of 'bouncing' the Aisne heights and preventing the Germans from consolidating.

But Churchill had put his finger on the bigger issue in his memorandum to the Committee of Imperial Defence for the meeting on 23 August 1911: what was the *strategic* role of the BEF? In the discussion at that meeting on the BEF's status of command, Reginald McKenna, the then first lord of the Admiralty, had suggested that 'if a British force were to be sent at all, it should be placed under French command'. Perhaps McKenna knew that this would not be palatable to the general staff (which indeed it wasn't, as Henry Wilson at once protested), thereby advancing the cause of the naval option; but in any case, 'Mr Churchill dissented emphatically', say the minutes: 'The whole moral significance of our intervention would be lost if our Army was merely merged in that of France.'

This was a moot point – perhaps Churchill was thinking of his illustrious ancestor's difficulties with the Dutch field deputies in the war with France – but it needed mooting nevertheless: how was Britain to exert the greatest moral effect – and, implicitly, at the lowest cost? But there was more at stake than this. The question was really what was to happen *after* the Germans had invaded; for, having the initiative and therefore being able to concentrate, they would certainly force the frontiers at one point or another. Churchill had grasped the difference between merely winning battles and winning the war: 'France will not be able to end the war successfully by any action on the frontiers. She will not be strong enough to invade Germany. Her only chance is to conquer Germany *in* France' (italics added).

This, he said, would mean the French *accepting* invasion, including even the investment of Paris, but such a policy might depend on knowing that the British would be coming to France's aid on land – which, by return, would depend on our knowing what were the French intentions. This was, of course, a view entirely at odds with that of the French general staff, who did indeed envisage the invasion of Germany, or at least, certainly to begin with, that former French territory occupied by Germany (Alsace-Lorraine) – which for a few days in August 1914 was largely what happened. However, Churchill's bold assertion was based on the calculation that by the fortieth day of mobilization

> Germany should be extended at full strain both internally and on her war fronts, and this strain will become daily more severe and ultimately overwhelming, unless it is relieved by decisive victories in France. If the French army has not been squandered by precipitate or desperate action, the balance of forces should be favourable after the fortieth day [and improving] . . . Opportunities for the decisive trial of strength might then occur.

It could easily be supposed that this memorandum had been written in late 1914 rather than the summer of 1911: the fortieth day of German mobilization was 9 September, the day the BEF crossed the Marne on its way to the Aisne. Historians have sometimes commented on Churchill's prescience, but none has ever fully examined his conclusion that the French must accept penetration of the borders and organize to defeat the Germans thereafter, the part the BEF might play in such an operational plan, and the possible outcome.

So how did Churchill see the BEF's contributing to these 'opportunities for the decisive trial of strength'?

In short, by generating a BEF that could act decisively 'instead of being frittered into action piecemeal' – the argument, indeed, that Haig was making at the time of the 5 August war council, and in his preceding letter to Haldane: 'so that when we do take the field we can act decisively'. Churchill envisaged the immediate despatch of a BEF of four divisions plus the Cavalry Division, for its 'moral effect', to be joined by the two remaining divisions 'as soon as the naval blockade is effectively established' (and the threat of invasion thereby ended).* These would assemble not at Maubeuge for incorporation in the French line of battle, but well to the rear, at Tours, more or less

---

* It is indeed ironic that it would be Churchill's own daring that established the 'blockade' before even a shot was fired on the Western Front. As for the BEF's potential, in August 1914, in addition to the 247,500 currently serving troops of the regular army, the Army Reserve was 145,350 strong and the Special Reserve had another 64,000 men. Some of these, but only a very few, had joined the TF.

equidistant between St Nazaire and Paris. As soon as the colonial forces in South Africa could be mobilized, the 7th Division would be recalled from there and its stations in the Mediterranean. To these would be added 15,000 Yeomanry and TF cyclist volunteers. And – perhaps the greatest gamble (though in fact it would eventually happen) – six out of the nine divisions of the Indian Army could be brought to the BEF, 'as long as two native regiments were moved out of India for every British regiment' (Churchill was as aware as any – and more than most – of the peculiar mathematics and chemistry of the Indian Army): a further 100,000 troops, 'brought into France via Marseilles by the fortieth day'.*

In total, by 14 September this would have furnished a BEF of some 290,000 (Haig had written to Haldane of 300,000), which the actual arrival of the 7th and 8th Divisions and the Indian Corps before Ypres shows was perfectly possible. And, although Churchill does not mention it, there would also have been time to assemble additional heavy artillery.

But what, meanwhile, of the gap which a BEF at Tours would have left in the French line of battle? In his letter to Haldane, Haig had made the filling of this gap, so to speak, a fundamental assumption: 'I presume of course that the French can hold on (even though her forces have to pull back from the frontier) for the necessary time for us to create an army . . .'

The answer lay with the nine French divisions – two corps – earmarked for the army of observation on the Italian border. These could have been put at notice to move as soon as the Italians declared their neutrality on 3 August (a decision confirmed to the second war council by Grey on 6 August), and the move begun as soon as French intelligence could confirm that the Italian army, although recalling some reservists to the colours, was not moving to a war footing (Austria was, after all, the more recent enemy, and France the ally: there was every reason for Rome to fear an Austrian grab in Venezia). If such a redeployment sounds injudicious – perilous even – in the event this is what did indeed happen: the French Army of the Alps was stood

---

* Had this been done at once in August 1914, rather than, as it was, in the late autumn, the sepoys and sowars might also have had a rather less brutal time of the weather. Troops could be spared from India because, of course, as Churchill wrote in the memorandum, 'we should be allies of Russia' – with no fear therefore of invasion.

down on 17 August (at which time much of the BEF was still encamped near their ports of landing). Though it would have been a last-minute affair, its six in-place divisions (five of them regular), which were surplus to Plan XVII, would have been available to redeploy to the left of Lanrezac's 5th Army, where, indeed, the erstwhile commander of the Army of the Alps, d'Amade, had already been sent to take command of the Territorial divisions. The great advantage that the French enjoyed – though they failed to make full use of it – was that the Schlieffen Plan unfolded at walking pace, and on exterior lines, observable by air, while the strategic movement of French troops, on interior lines, could be conducted at the speed of the railway engine. Never, before or since, has a commander-in-chief had so much time in which to make his key decisions. That is the real import of A. J. P. Taylor's quip about 'war by railway timetable' – *not* that Europe's leaders were forced into war by movement schedules. The Elder Moltke had said it to Bismarck: 'Build railways, not forts.'

If these dispositions had been made, there is no reason to suppose that the situation at the end of September would have been any different from that which actually transpired – with French forces mounting a successful counter-attack on the Marne, and then the stalling on the Aisne.* There was an undoubted moral effect in having the BEF in the line, and it certainly 'punched above its weight', but it is unreasonable to suggest that the French would not have been able to manage things on their own if they had been able to replace the BEF with the same number of their own regulars. Joffre, seeing the enemy, as it were, off guard, had brilliantly improvised and delivered a blow on the Marne that had sent the flower of Brandenburg reeling; but it was not enough. In the terminology of modern doctrine, he had executed the first two of the four requirements of victory – 'find' and 'fix': he had found the weak point, Kluck's and Bülow's flank, and he had fixed them – temporarily (which is all that can be expected) – on the Aisne. What he then had to do was 'strike' and then 'exploit' (as suggested by Churchill's 'Her only chance is to conquer Germany in France').

---

* Indeed, with an army of two French corps (from the Italian border) under full command on Lanrezac's left, there should have been greater cohesion during the retreat. In fact, these divisions did take part in the Marne counter-offensive, and Manoury's 6th Army would therefore have had to be reinforced by two other corps to compensate for the absence of the BEF; but these were available in Lorraine given timely decision by Joffre.

However, at the time of launching the counter-offensive on the Marne Joffre had not been able to create a striking force to exploit success. What he needed was what the BEF could have offered had it been allowed to build its strength at Tours – a fresh, strong, virtually all-regular army numbering nearly 300,000. It should have been the winning move.

Not, however, simply to attack on the Aisne, to apply more brute force where brute force had already exhausted itself. What was needed was overwhelming force applied as a lever rather than as a sledge-hammer. The German flank was not just open in a localized way after the retreat to the Aisne; the entire *Schwenkungsflügel* – the 'pivot' or 'swing' wing – was extended in an east–west line through mid-Champagne and southern Picardy, and it was beginning to bow back on the right. Indeed, with each successive encounter on the extremity of the flank, even as the Germans brought up new troops, the line backed further north rather than projecting further west.* In the third week of September, with Antwerp still holding out, the BEF, some 300,000 strong, fully equipped, its reservists fighting fit, and with the RFC to direct its advance, could have launched a massive counter-stroke from Abbeville, a major rail junction, east between Arras and Albert (or even more boldly, further north between Arras and Lille), on a front of at least 30 miles – with strong reserves and artillery, screened by the Cavalry Corps, with the Indian Cavalry Corps ranging further north towards the high ground at Vimy.

With a simultaneous offensive by the French along the Aisne – indeed, across the whole front, to fix the Germans in place so that they could not further reinforce the right – all that Falkenhayn's 1st, 2nd and 4th Armies would have been able to do to avoid being enveloped would have been to turn through 90 degrees to face west. But their pivot point would have had to be somewhere that did not form too sharp an angle and therefore a dangerous salient, and with Belgian forces perhaps making another sortie from Antwerp, it is probable that this pivot point would have to have been Rheims, or even Verdun.† In any case, with the BEF pressing hard, and taking

---

* The shortest distance to the sea would have been along the Somme, but the Allies were too strong to allow it.
† It would have been no good the Germans' realigning north–south too far west, for in doing so they would have presented their right flank to Antwerp; and at this stage the Belgian field army was still to be reckoned with.

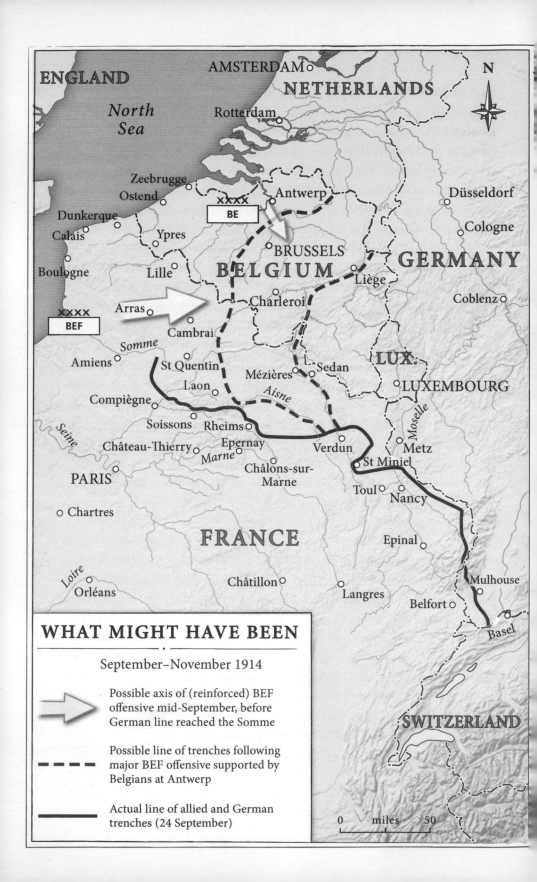

ENGLAND

*North
Sea*

NETHERLANDS

AMSTERDAM

Rotterdam

N

Zeebrugge
Ostend

Antwerp

Düsseldorf

Cologne

Dunkerque
Calais

Ypres

xxxx
BE

Boulogne

Lille

BRUSSELS

BELGIUM

Liège

GERMANY

Coblenz

Arras

xxxx
BEF

Charleroi

Cambrai

Somme

Mézières

Sedan

LUX.

LUXEMBOURG

Amiens

St Quentin

Laon

Aisne

Compiègne

Seine

Soissons

Rheims

Château-Thierry

Epernay

Marne

Verdun

St Miniel

Moselle

Metz

PARIS

Châlons-sur-
Marne

Toul

Nancy

Chartres

FRANCE

Epinal

Loire

Orléans

Châtillon

Langres

Belfort

Mulhouse

Basel

SWITZERLAND

WHAT MIGHT HAVE BEEN

September–November 1914

Possible axis of (reinforced) BEF
offensive mid-September, before
German line reached the Somme

Possible line of trenches following
major BEF offensive supported by
Belgians at Antwerp

Actual line of allied and German
trenches (24 September)

0   miles   50

account of its own extended lines of communication, in particular the railheads, there would not have been the manoeuvre space for Kluck's 1st Army to change direction through 90 degrees west of a line running north–south through Mons and Maubeuge. Had Falkenhayn got intelligence of the move of the BEF to Abbeville he might have made an orderly withdrawal from the Aisne to the Mons–Maubeuge line, dug in and brought up heavy artillery to halt the BEF's advance; but this in turn would have given the BEF the option of avoiding making a direct attack and again threatening to turn the German right flank – further north, between Mons and Brussels. In the best case for the allies, with the Germans unable to find a natural line on which to try to halt the BEF, and a renewed offensive by Franchet d'Espèrey's and Foch's armies to threaten the 1st, 2nd and 4th Armies' lines of communication, Falkenhayn would have had to pull back to the Meuse below Namur. He would then have had to garrison the river with all the troops he could find as allied strength built up on the Lower Meuse as far as Liège and within closing distance of the Dutch border in the Maastricht corridor.

Supposing, then, that at that point the Germans had been able to check further allied progress east – even perhaps, by a desperate reverse-Schlieffen transfer of troops from East Prussia – the situation in the west would have seen a strategic sea change. Joffre, to exploit, could now have used the growing Russian strength on the Eastern Front to his advantage: Falkenhayn would have been truly caught between two giant hammers. And with the Germans now on the defensive, Joffre would have had the choice of where to concentrate. With so catastrophic an end to the whole Schlieffen 'plan', it is not impossible to imagine the Kaiser's suing for terms.

However, on 4 September the Triple Entente powers had signed a pact: 'The British, French, and Russian Governments mutually engage not to conclude peace separately during the present war. The three Governments agree that when terms of peace come to be discussed, no one of the Allies will demand conditions of peace without the previous agreement of each of the other Allies.' All could not go quiet on the Western Front unless the Germans ceased fire on the Eastern.

It was ironic that, by this pact, the British were now in effect pledged to the defeat of the Germans not just in France but in Russia too – an object that would have been scarcely conceivable to the cabinet a week before the war began. Of course, in December 1917 a new (Bolshevik) Russian government would conclude a very separate peace, but that was not an option for a nation with 'honour', the noun that had propelled Britain to war. It is possible, therefore, to imagine the war entering 1915 with a return to the Elder Moltke's view of the two-front problem: stay on the defensive against France, check the Russians by a paralysing stroke (another Tannenberg, perhaps), and then turn westward to counter-attack when the inevitable allied offensive came – the aim being, since outright victory was no longer possible, to cripple both opponents and thereby bring about a favourable peace.

But the allies would have been in a vastly superior strategic position to that in which they actually found themselves in 1915. The possession of most of Belgium would have been significant in terms of the extra men and materiel available. And the failure of Germany to achieve victory would not have been lost on the neutrals. It was almost certainly impossible that Britain could have avoided war with Turkey, but if it were possible in May 1915 to persuade Italy, who in August 1914 had been in alliance with Germany and Austria, to enter the war on the allies' side – as she did, against Austria-Hungary on 23 May, and Germany on 28 August – it should also have been possible to persuade the Dutch and the Danes to consider their position too. The Dutch obligation to defend Belgian neutrality under the Treaty of London was sufficiently vague to permit the application of diplomatic pressure, especially once the Germans had been removed from the southern Dutch border. It seems likely at least that some way would have been found to open the Scheldt to allied shipping, and to close the 'breathing line' to Germany. The Danes were in just as ambiguous a position, if for different reasons. They had no connection with any treaty, only a pragmatic decision to make: which side would win? Or rather, how might the peace terms work to their advantage? Their neutrality was weighted towards Germany, but a Germany fighting defensively on the Meuse would not have been the same as a Germany in possession of almost all of Belgium and a large slice of northern France. There was Danish territory to recover in Jutland, and although in the event the Treaty of Versailles would restore a large part of Schleswig to Denmark (and, indeed, would have given her all of it, and Holstein, had the Danes not feared German irredentism),

Copenhagen could not have counted on it. There was, again, room for the diplomats to work.

At the very least the BEF counter-stroke, forcing the Germans back into Belgium, perhaps as far as the Meuse, would have given the allies far better ground on which to fight – and with a strong Belgian army, and a much shorter front (and therefore more reserves). At the very best, an offensive by British, French and Belgian armies on the Meuse in the spring of 1915, perhaps being allowed to use the Maastricht corridor, with Dutch–Danish action directed against the Kiel Canal and Heligoland, could have ended the war that summer.*

That said, the German army's (the German nation's) visceral ability to fight on, despite all logic, was formidable, as the rest of the war demonstrated. However, the ground on which the allies fought need not have been the same; and the war was not immutably programmed to run until November 1918. At best the Dardanelles campaign to circumvent the deadlock on the Western Front need not have been attempted. The 1916 Easter Rising in Ireland might not have taken place, or at least might not have taken the same embittering course, for Britain would not have appeared to be on the ropes (there was more than a little opportunism in the IRA's decision to 'declare war'); and with some sensible concession to home rule the Union might still today have been of Great Britain and Ireland (always assuming, of course, that Ulster could have been placated – a big 'if'). Perhaps the greatest bounties, however, would have been the failure of the Bolshevik Revolution in Russia before it even started, and a Germany in which fascism did not take hold.

Is this all too fanciful?

Three decades on, in the summer of 1943, after he had been exerting his indomitable will on the nation and its armed forces for three years of war, Churchill startled a group of his close associates by remarking that 'whoever had been in power – Chamberlain,

---

* In desperation, Moltke had pulled the IX Reserve Corps out of Schleswig-Holstein to reinforce the 1st Army. From September the Danish border and the Kiel (Kaiser Wilhelm) Canal were all but unguarded – a superb opportunity for attack by land and also from the sea, especially supported by a good plan of misinformation and deception: the rumours of impending Russo-British landings on the Belgian coast had already unnerved the OHL into creating a new army – the 7th – in Belgium, under the commander of the former 7th Army in Alsace-Lorraine, Falkenhayn's predecessor at the Prussian war ministry, Josias von Heeringen. It would have been an infinitely better prospect for success than the campaign in the Dardanelles.

Churchill, Eden, anyone you liked to mention – the military position would now be *exactly the same*. Wars had their own rules, politicians didn't alter them, the armies would be in the same position to a mile.'* This 'Tolstoyan summary', as one of Churchill's biographers, Ronald Lewin, puts it, was surely 'Winnie' at his most perverse, fuelled perhaps by a little brandy and post-Alamein relief, and masked by cigar smoke – Winnie the soldier still, defiantly growling from some long-remembered battlefield. He was forgetting, perhaps even conveniently, his own politician's part in the bloody fiasco of the Dardanelles and Gallipoli. For just as wars have consequences, so do battles – which is why they are fought – and likewise the operational plans which determine in large measure where and how those battles are fought. And the principal assumptions on which plans are made are primarily political, not military; hence Asquith's assertion at the CID meeting in August 1911 that 'the expediency of sending a military force abroad or of relying on naval means alone is a matter of policy which can only be determined when the occasion arises by the Government of the day.' The fact was, however, that the politicians had lost control of military strategy (and in this, of course, British politicians were not alone), their failure to show effective interest allowing a momentum to develop in the staff conversations whose outcome then became the strategy because once revealed, during the crisis, there seemed to be no alternative.†

By refusing to recognize what this implied – a decision deferred indefinitely – and instead basing all its plans on the assumption of simultaneous mobilization with the French and the incorporation of the BEF into the deployment plans of the French general staff, the War Office failed both the army and the country. Since the War Office was both a department of state and a military headquarters, this was

---

* Lord (Maurice) Hankey, related by Lord (C. P.) Snow, quoted in Ronald Lewin, *Churchill as Warlord* (London, 1973).

† Clausewitz identified the inherent tensions in 'policy and planning' thus: 'No major proposal required for war can be worked out in ignorance of political factors . . . [Likewise,] if war is to be fully consonant with political objectives, and policy suited to the means available for war, . . . the only sound expedient is to make the commander-in-chief a member of the cabinet' (*On War*). To an extent, this is what the CID did; but ultimately it only gave the illusion of integration, for the CID could not usurp the cabinet's decision-making or executive function – and key members of one were not members of the other. The nearest that Britain came to 'the sound expedient' was 'the hazardous experiment', as Asquith called it, of Kitchener's being made secretary for war.

both a political and a military failure – and, since the secretary of state for war was a member of the cabinet, ultimately a failure of cabinet government.

However the war began – by German design, by the negligence of statesmen, by the purblindness of generals – there was nothing inevitable about its course. Churchill said memorably, before the great clash of dreadnoughts at Jutland in 1916, that the Royal Navy – in particular the admiral commanding the Grand Fleet, Sir John Jellicoe – could lose the war in an afternoon. In August 1914, however, the decisive ground was not the North Sea but the Franco-Belgian border. And though government and the War Office may have failed them, the men of the BEF, the 'Old Contemptibles', paid the price of honour on that decisive ground, and paid it scarcely flinching – in honour, as they had been variously exhorted, of the King, the nation, the British army, or the regiment. They fought what they knew was *the* good fight because, as Sir John French had told them, 'Our cause is just.' And despite the shortcomings in planning and preparation over the years, the pride and prejudice in the senior echelons as the nation went to war, and the mistakes by commanders and staff in the first encounter battles, they fought *a* good fight – because, when all else is going wrong, that is what professionals did (and do).

> These, in the day when heaven was falling,
> The hour when earth's foundations fled,
> Followed their mercenary calling
> And took their wages and are dead.
>
> Their shoulders held the sky suspended;
> They stood, and earth's foundations stay;
> What God abandoned, these defended,
> And saved the sum of things for pay.

Postscript: Desperate Appeals Against the Decision of Fate

The British Army on the Western Front (and Gallipoli), 1915–1918*

In his memoirs, General Sir Horace Smith-Dorrien describes how, in the fortnight between the declaration of war (and the appointment of Lord Kitchener as secretary of state for war) and his being sent to France to command II Corps after the death of Sir James Grierson, he had several discussions with Kitchener on the expansion of the army:

> I was very insistent that, rather than use all available material for creating entirely new Divisions, it were preferable to build up on the existing Territorial Army, splitting each unit so as to provide many more cadres, and filling up the cadres thus created by recruits and the many trained ex-officers and men who offered themselves from civil life. I argued that this system of expansion would provide efficient units in the shortest time, and would leave available for training purposes a very large number of excellent instructors who would otherwise be merged into the fighting ranks. Lord Kitchener was sympathetic, as he always was, and asked me to draft a scheme. This I did, but it was not accepted.

Indeed it was not. Kitchener decided instead to use the Territorial Force (as it was then known) to reinforce the BEF as soon as legislation could be enacted. And after a slow start (although some

---

* Adapted from Allan Mallinson, *The Making of the British Army* (London, 2009).

units, almost to a man, had immediately volunteered for overseas service), individual TF units, then brigades, and finally divisions, were sent to France to fight alongside the regular army. Meanwhile, Kitchener appealed for volunteers to serve 'for the duration of the war'. They were to be trained by regulars and mustered in 'Service' (short for 'General Service', as opposed to 'Home Service') battalions, in the case of the infantry, or in corresponding units of the other arms and services. They were not to take the place of reservists, who were posted as individual replacements to existing battalions, but would serve in units consisting of other volunteers, led as far as possible by regulars. They were, indeed, to be an expansion of the regular army, not another type of reserve – the 'New Army'.

The response to the call for volunteers was remarkable, and the mass improvisation of their training no less astonishing. While some of the recruits were doubtless thankful of an excuse to exchange a life of hardship or tedium for one which promised excitement and a little local fame, the motive of the vast majority appears to have been simple patriotism – for 'King and Country' – or else a sense of local solidarity, of 'mateship'. For at the same time that individual recruits were flocking to the army's recruiting centres, Kitchener gave local grandees leave to raise battalions en bloc (often initially at their own expense) with the simple promise that those who enlisted together would be allowed to serve together.

The promise of serving together proved powerful. In Liverpool the earl of Derby, the great mover and shaker of the commercial north-west (and subsequently director-general of army recruiting), called on the office workers to form a battalion: 'This should be a battalion of pals, a battalion in which friends from the same office will fight shoulder to shoulder for the honour of Britain and the credit of Liverpool.' And so were born the 'Pals' battalions. But instead of one battalion, between 28 August (a Friday), as the BEF was in full retreat after Le Cateau, and 3 September Liverpool raised four, the clerks of the White Star shipping company forming up as one platoon, those of Cunard as another, and so on through the warehouses of the Mersey waterside, the cotton exchange, the banks and the insurance companies – men who knew each other better than their mothers knew them, and now doing what their mothers would never ordinarily have countenanced: going for a soldier – at least 'for the duration'.

Across the Pennines in Barnsley two battalions of Pals were raised, officially designated the 13th and 14th (Service) Battalions, York and Lancaster Regiment. Most of the recruits here were miners, many of whom had worked underground since they were 13 and so were not averse to the prospect of three square meals a day and work in the open air for a year or so. In the cities north of the border the response was the same. Glasgow raised three Pals battalions for the Highland Light Infantry, which were named after the institutions from which they had spontaneously sprung: Glasgow Tramways (15th Battalion, Highland Light Infantry), Glasgow Boys' Brigade (16HLI) and Glasgow Commercials (17HLI). Newcastle boosted the Northumberland Fusiliers by two such institutional battalions – the Newcastle Commercials (16NF) and the Newcastle Railway Pals (17NF) – and by no fewer than twelve 'tribal' battalions: six of Tyneside Scottish and six of Tyneside Irish, forming two whole brigades. Perhaps the most exclusive-sounding of the Pals was the Stockbrokers' Battalion (10th Battalion, Royal Fusiliers), and the most endearingly unmilitary (to modern ears, at least) the 21st Battalion, West Yorkshire Regiment – the 'Wool Textile Pioneers'. John Keegan writes:

> The Pals' story is of a spontaneous and genuinely popular mass movement which has no counterpart in the modern, English-speaking world and perhaps could have none outside its own time and place: a time of intense patriotism, and of the inarticulate elitism of an imperial power's working class; a place of vigorous and buoyant urban life, rich in differences and in a sense of belonging ... to any one of those hundreds of bodies from which the Edwardian Briton drew his security and sense of identity.*

But although the Pals battalions were of their own time and place, and although their experience was frequently tragic, the sense of unit identity which came from recruiting from a single locality gave them instantly both high morale and self-regulation (which the army has sought to emulate ever since). The alacrity with which recruits came forward was confirmation that the Cardwell–Childers regimental system, based on geographical identification, had been the right model for the infantry, even if in a way those two fine reformers had never imagined. But how were these Commercials, Railwaymen,

---

* John Keegan, *The Face of Battle* (1976).

Miners, Accrington Pals, Grimsby Chums and Wool Textile Pioneers to be made into soldiers capable of fighting the German or the Turk? The answer, in truth, was improvisation. It was one thing to form a command structure – there were retired officers and NCOs ready to step forward, and the Pals battalions found it easy enough to 'elect' their company officers and NCOs – but quite another to find the cadre of regular or even Territorial officers and NCOs to instruct them.* For while Kitchener might reasonably have expected the regular army to be a ready source of training staff when he issued his call for volunteers, the mounting losses in the BEF soon put paid to this idea. And so reservist NCOs with the most recent service were diverted to the new battalions, as were officers on home leave from India, usually with the 'sweetener' of promotion – anything, indeed, that the authorities could think of to attract them.

So successful was the call to arms that there was not only a shortage of trainers but also a chronic shortage of uniforms, rifles, ammunition and accommodation. Men drilled with broom handles in the clothes in which they had enlisted; they slept under canvas, or in seaside lodging houses. Only boundless good spirits and forbearance seemed in plentiful supply. There were New Army battalions that formed with only one regular officer – in the case of the 8th (Service) Battalion East Surrey Regiment a captain, who drew up his new command and asked those who felt they could control six to eight other men to step forward (a bold step which clearly worked well, since several of these self-selected NCOs went on to win commissions, and the battalion's war record proved second to none).

The battalions were conceived of not as reinforcements for existing brigades and divisions but as parts of entirely new Kitchener formations (brigades, divisions, corps), each successive 100,000 men forming a replica BEF, termed unofficially K1, K2 etc. Some Kitchener formations were already thoroughly militarized. In Northern Ireland the Ulster Volunteer Force, which earlier in the year had threatened armed resistance to the implementation of the home rule bill, in

---

* One of the best and most successful (perhaps against the odds) examples was the earl of Derby's brother, the Honourable Charles Stanley, at forty-three a decorated captain in the Reserve of Officers with service in the Sudan and South Africa. With Derby's intervention he was made temporary brigadier-general and took command of the four Liverpool Pals battalions comprising the 89th Brigade.

effect turned itself into the 36th (Ulster) Division, with an unsurpassed fighting record on the Western Front.* In the south of Ireland, too, the traditional source of manpower for virtually every regiment of the army at one time or another, the spirit of volunteering was no less strong, if somewhat more complicated. The 'Irish Volunteers' had been formed as a counter to the UVF, and their leaders – not so extreme as those who would take up arms in 1916 – now decided that the cause of home rule would be best advanced by a show of loyalty to the King, exactly as the UVF's leaders believed that volunteering safeguarded Unionism. Two divisions were formed – the 10th and 16th – predominantly but by no means wholly Catholic (as the 36th Division was by no means exclusively Protestant). The 5th (Service) Battalion of the Connaught Rangers was raised in Dublin in August – unusually, for Dublin is in Leinster, not Connaught – and a second Service battalion the following month in Cork (in Munster). The 5th were fortunate enough to have the excellent Sergeant McIlwain (see chapter 18) posted to them as a sergeant-major after Ypres, when his much depleted 2nd Battalion of the Connaughts was amalgamated with the 1st.

Before the war it was reckoned that it took about eleven months to make a soldier – and this with the full resources of the regular army. The first of Kitchener's divisions, the 18th, was judged ready to deploy to France in May 1915, even though it was a K2 formation (that is, raised as part of the second 100,000). Its early readiness was attributable in part to the imagination and energy of its commander, Major-General Ivor Maxse, who had made his name in the Sudan campaign and South Africa and had commanded the 1st (Guards) Brigade from Mons to the Aisne. Maxse's ideas about training were innovative – 'drilling for initiative', as he called it, insisting that all tactical movements must be planned and rehearsed with nothing foreseeable left to chance (what would later be known as 'battle drill'), so that the commander's mind was then free to apply the drill to the particular situation. He was impressed by the quality of the recruits, and his training concept had obvious resonance with men used to making decisions for themselves. Not all Kitchener divisions were so fortunate, and some, though in theory fully trained, would be

* Four out of the nine VCs awarded on the first day of the Somme were won by the 36th (Ulster) Division.

plunged into action before they were able to get used to conditions in the field.

On 2 January 1915 Sir John French received a letter from Kitchener that could have been penned by Pitt a century or so before: 'The feeling here is gaining ground that, although it is essential to defend the line we now hold, troops over and above what is necessary for that service could better be employed elsewhere. The question where anything effective could be accomplished opens a large field and requires a good deal of study. What are the views of your staff?'

The letter revealed the usual symptoms of the chronic British strategic disease: seeking easier victory somewhere other than where victory might achieve the strategic ends – through what would later be derided as 'stratagems of evasion'. Kitchener's question was reasonable enough in that it recognized that battering the army's head against the brick wall of the German defences on the Western Front was going to be both costly and unproductive; but the idea that the Germans could be defeated other than by defeating the German army did not recognize the reality of the German state. 'Finding the flank' was one thing at the tactical level, but quite another at the strategic.

But the opportunity seemed to present itself after Turkey entered the war on the side of Germany and Austria in November 1914. The war cabinet's thoughts – in particular those of the first lord of the Admiralty, Winston Churchill – turned to the eastern Mediterranean and the twin prospect of opening up warm-water lines of communication to Russia and defeating Germany by 'knocking away the props'. If Turkey were defeated, he argued, Italy, Greece and Bulgaria, who were still sitting on the fence, would come in on the allied side. This could be achieved at little cost, he further argued, believing that the Dardanelles could be forced by a handful of obsolescent warships. Kitchener had misgivings but the war cabinet gave way, and in February a naval bombardment of Turkish forts commanding the Dardanelles Straits began. By the middle of March the efforts to force the straits had come to grief, with both French and British warships destroyed by Turkish shore batteries and mines. At this point the stratagem's 'economy of effort' was abandoned and Kitchener agreed to commit ground troops. The Mediterranean Expeditionary Force (MEF) was formed under command of General Sir Ian Hamilton, consisting of the 29th Division – the country's only strategic reserve – and the Australian and New Zealand Corps (Anzac), which was assembling in the Suez Canal zone.

Hamilton's record is as controversial as French's. The campaign would be a costly failure, but the margin between failure and brilliant success at Gallipoli was narrower than is sometimes supposed. The peninsula was by no means impregnable, although the Turkish army was experienced and its discipline formidable. The problem lay in the quality of some of the MEF's subordinate commanders and the lack of training in many of its battalions, those of the New Armies especially. Indeed, Hamilton himself had only thirty-five days to prepare for what was to be the first machine-gun-opposed amphibious assault in the history of warfare.

His plan for multiple landings on 25 April, given that the months of naval bombardment had forfeited strategic surprise, was feasible enough. He intended the 29th Division to land at Helles on the tip of the peninsula and then advance on the forts at Kilitbahir; the Anzacs were to land some 15 miles up the coast on the Aegean side and advance across the peninsula to cut off any Turkish retreat and prevent reinforcement of Kilitbahir; the French (for this was an allied operation) would make a diversionary landing on the Asian shore; and the Royal Naval Division would make a demonstration in the Gulf of Xeros to confuse the Turkish high command as to where the main effort lay.

The execution of the plan was not up to its conception, however. The Anzacs, under the exceptional 49-year-old British officer Major-General William Birdwood, a Bengal Lancer, gained tactical surprise by landing before dawn without a preliminary bombardment. Thereafter, in crude terms, he simply ran out of luck. The 29th Division, under the far less exceptional Aylmer Hunter-Weston, simply impaled themselves on the cliffs and machine guns at the southern tip of the peninsula in broad daylight after a preliminary naval bombardment that would have left the dullest Turk in no doubt as to what was about to happen.

The Gallipoli peninsula thereby became a salient every bit as lethal as Ypres, and with the added complications of supply across open beaches, water shortage, intense heat and insanitary conditions. Despite suicidal gallantry on the part of both British and Anzac troops

446

(and French too), none could get any further than 3 miles from the beaches. As on the Western Front, barbed wire, machine guns and artillery put paid to any thoughts of tactical manoeuvre: the only alternatives were head-on attack or evacuation. Sergeant-Major McIlwain, whose battalion of Connaught Rangers was part of the 10th (Irish) Division in 'K1', recounts one such assault:

> Attack begins at 4 p.m. Small parties of 'A' 'B' and 'C' Coys attack after heavy bombardment. We [D Company] are in reserve. Our people have heavy casualties. Major Money commanding attack from sap [trench extending towards enemy lines] where I am with him. After dark when fighting has slackened, and the trenches chock full of Irish and Turkish dead and dying, seemed owned by no acting force. Capt Webber takes up us the reserve (about 50 strong) to occupy the position. At bifurcation of trenches the Captain goes north and sends me to command right and occupy where practicable. I did not see him again. The dead being piled up quite to the parapet I take my party over the top in rear and with about 20 men occupy portion of trench nominally Australian as many wounded Anzacs are there. Not long there when Turks bomb us [throw grenades] from front and left flank, also snipe us along the trench from left. My men with few exceptions panic stricken. By rapid musketry we keep down the bombing. My rifle red almost with firing. By using greatcoats we save ourselves from bombs. Turks but ten yards away drive us back foot by foot. Have extraordinary escapes. Two men killed beside me following me in the narrow trench and I am covered head to foot in blood. Casualties alarming and we should have fought to the very end but for the 18th Australian Battalion a party of whom jumped in amongst us and held the position until reinforced. When able to look about me I find but two Rangers left with me. The rest killed, wounded, or ran away before or after the Anzacs had come.

Hamilton was relieved of command in the middle of October and replaced by Sir Charles Monro. In this, at last, the troops were lucky: Monro was fresh from command of the 3rd Army on the Western Front, and as commandant of the Hythe School of Musketry after the Boer War he had been the architect of the infantry's education in marksmanship and the new tactics of fire and movement. He was independent-minded and his reputation stood high, and he lost no time in assessing the situation and reporting to the war council that there was no future in the campaign – which advice they accepted, if grudgingly, for it had also been Hamilton's opinion.

By 8 January 1916 the peninsula had been evacuated. And, just as at Corunna and later at Dunkirk, the evacuation was a sort of brilliant parting shot in an otherwise dismal campaign: remarkably, 134,000 men were taken off without a single loss, and with the Turks oblivious of what was happening almost literally under their noses – a masterpiece of deception, organization and command that would be studied at the staff college for years afterwards. If only the same degree of ingenuity had been there from the outset. If only the same guileful tactical methods could have been used six months later on the Somme, indeed: for if surprise could be achieved in the withdrawal, there was no reason in principle why it could not be achieved in the offensive.

The cost of the Gallipoli campaign had been massive. British casualties were at least 75,000, including 21,255 dead, a great many from dysentery and enteric fever.* The New Army battalions suffered particularly high losses, especially of officers – none more than the 6th (Service) Battalion, the Yorkshire Regiment (Green Howards), where only the quartermaster survived unscathed. And these losses were all the more calamitous for their cost to operations on the Western Front: the lack of reserves at the Battle of Loos in late September and early October 1915, for example, was a critical factor in the failure of the British autumn offensive in Picardy. Nor did the casualty lists do anything for recruiting, which took a dip towards the end of 1915 – rather as yellow fever in the West Indies had hampered recruiting during the Napoleonic Wars. Confidence in British generalship among the Anzac troops (and, just as important, their governments) fell dangerously, although regard for Birdwood remained high; and a general sense of failure hung upon the nation. On the positive side, the failure at Gallipoli put the Western Front back at centre stage as the decisive theatre of war, although it would take another year at least for the politicians to accept the full consequences of this.

Perhaps the most dispiriting aspect of the campaign was its predictability (for all that taking the peninsula was by no means an

---

* Australian casualties were 28,000 (7,600 dead); New Zealand's 7,250 (2,700 dead); French (estimated) 27,000 (10,000 dead); and Indian 5,000 (1,400 dead).

impossible concept). Its planning took place after a full six months of fighting on the Western Front, by which time there could have been few illusions about the nature of modern warfare. Aircraft would have been particularly useful in reconnaissance and artillery spotting, and Hamilton's chief of staff had asked for them early on during the planning; but the request was turned down flat by Kitchener. The navy had aircraft, some of them ship-based, but they were not well integrated with the action ashore. The greatest lesson, however, that amphibious operations were fraught with special dangers and required planning and resources of an exceptional kind, would eventually see a spectacular pay-off, though with another high-priced lesson in between, thirty years later in the Normandy landings.

If several military heads rolled after Gallipoli (though not enough: Hunter-Weston showed no more acumen when in command of a corps at the Somme later in the year), none rolled so famously as that of one politician – Winston Churchill. In November 1915, in characteristic form, he left the government, put on soldier's uniform and went to France – to command one of Kitchener's battalions of the Royal Scots Fusiliers.* But if Churchill's time at the Admiralty had brought about one of the most calamitous and futile campaigns in the army's history (an experience which did not, however, entirely cure him of strategic gambling), it also did a very great deal to place in its hands a weapon that would do much to help it overcome the stalemate of the trenches.

The tank was neither Churchill's invention nor his conception, as is sometimes over-enthusiastically claimed, but without him its potential might not have been recognized so early or its development pressed so effectively. And it came about from that same thrusting impatience which had placed him so often in the middle of the action as a young man. As war was declared the first lord of the Admiralty had sent Royal Marines and the ad hoc Royal Naval Division to help defend Antwerp, and in the weeks before the trenches reached the Belgian coast the 'jollies and bluejackets' were able to range along the flat roads of west Flanders in a veritable circus of improvised armoured cars and London buses. When Antwerp fell and the division

---

* Churchill commanded 6th Battalion Royal Scots Fusiliers until May the following year, when the battalion was amalgamated with the 7th. He saw service in the trenches and was recommended for brigade command.

was re-embarked, its buses went to the army as troop transports and many of the surviving armoured cars were sent to the Middle East. The instinct for mobility remained, though, and Churchill set up the Admiralty Landships Committee out of which emerged the machine whose image the new Tank Corps would wear, and still wears, as its cap-badge.

The English-speaking world calls them 'tanks' because that is what they were called in the deception measures during their despatch to France: they were shipped as 'water tanks'. The French, when they were told of the invention and developed machines of their own, called them with Gallic panache *chars* (*de combat*) – chariots. The Germans, when they learned of them the hard way and made some of their own, called them with Teutonic pedantry *Panzerkampfwagen* – armoured fighting vehicles (later simply *Panzer*). Much is revealed in military language. And largely for the same reasons of deception, the Tank Corps was originally known as the Heavy Section, Machine Gun Corps, and the first men in tanks wore crossed machine guns as their badge. But before the tank was ready for service the British army would receive its greatest ever shock, whose effects would change the course of the war and are still felt, consciously or otherwise, even today – the Somme.*

Through 1915, then, the Kitchener battalions had begun to enter the field. By the spring of 1916, K1–5 (Kitchener's first 500,000) had either seen action or were deployed and ready. But the BEF's commanders had understandable reservations about their capability, for the Western Front had become largely a business of siege warfare. To some extent its routine of constant labour – digging, repairing, wiring, carrying forward ammunition and stores – was easy enough for the New Army battalions to cope with. In its turn in the line, a battalion would typically spend four days in the fire and support trenches, four in close reserve half a mile or so to the rear, and four resting out of range of field artillery. Out of the line they would be at

---

* This is a contentious assertion, but ever since the Somme the army has been casualty conscious in a way that it never quite was before 1916. The losses in 1914 and 1915 were generally seen as the price to be paid for fighting in the big league, and largely unavoidable. The Gallipoli débâcle sounded a warning bell, but did not adversely affect the appetite for offensive operations on the Western Front. The casualties on the Somme changed everything, however. And they haunted politicians and soldiers alike in the inter-war years and during the Second World War.

training and recreation. But in 1916 the training of the New Army battalions was directed more towards individual trench skills and fitness than to battalion and company battle drills and tactics (and 'musketry' occupied nothing like its place in the pre-war army). In short, Kitchener's men could look after themselves, but they had scant practice in how to advance in the face of the enemy. The techniques of fire and movement seemed to be yesterday's story – the experience of the few months of 1914 before the trenches reached the coast. Now it was down to the bomb (grenade) and the machine gun, and occasionally the bayonet. The routine of trench warfare seemed to operate as a suppressant even to thinking about mobility. To an extent senior officers had willed this, or at least accepted it, but many of them were all too aware of the limitations it now imposed. The only part of the army still movement-minded (other than, of course, the Royal Flying Corps) was the cavalry, and they could only manoeuvre once the infantry had punched a hole in the defences. To the very end, Haig saw the winning of the war in terms of the collapse of a part of the German front line so that mobile troops – horse-borne – could exploit tactical success and restore the war of manoeuvre by which the decision would be gained. It was loosely, and often irreverently, referred to as 'galloping through the "G" in Gap'. Knowing the want of training in the New Army battalions, however, senior officers sought a simpler way of crossing no-man's-land to break open the German defences; and as the last of the K5 battalions were arriving in France in the spring of 1916, some thought they had found one in the experience of a battle in March the previous year – at Neuve Chapelle.

By 1915 the BEF had grown to such a strength that it had been reorganized into two armies – 1st Army, commanded by the newly promoted General Sir Douglas Haig, and 2nd Army, commanded by Horace Smith-Dorrien (until in May 'Wully' Robertson told him he was 'for 'ome'). Haig's stock stood particularly high after he had kept his head and held the line at First Ypres, and so Sir John French delegated to him the spring offensive in Artois (Pas de Calais). Although the offensive came to nothing other than a long casualty list, Haig had a measure of success at Neuve Chapelle. Here, after a huge but brief artillery bombardment, the attacking divisions (two regular British and two from the Indian Corps with a number of integrated British units) made progress, though not without cost: 11,200 casualties were taken during the three days' fighting, including six battalion commanding officers. But if the attack was in the end a disappointment – the Germans were able to recover more quickly than the British could exploit their own local success – it seemed to show what artillery could do when there was enough of it. In fact, Haig had been able to concentrate 340 guns – almost as many as the BEF had taken to France the previous August – against the German salient, a ratio of one gun to every six yards of front attacked. It followed, by his reasoning, that as great a concentration of guns firing for longer against the German line elsewhere would achieve even better results.

There were two flaws in this analysis, however, the first cruelly hidden. The bombardment at Neuve Chapelle had been brief – thirty minutes on the fire trenches and then a further thirty on the support lines – because of a shortage of shells (which would soon become the great 'Shell Scandal', forcing Asquith to form a coalition government and a separate ministry of munitions under Lloyd George). The brevity of the bombardment was regarded not just as the consequence of weakness but as *the* weakness, though in fact a degree of surprise was achieved by that very brevity, and it was this that made for success more than the actual damage inflicted by the guns. A prolonged bombardment naturally forfeited surprise; it served notice on the defenders that they would have to stand to and repel attack, and to senior commanders that they must move reserves ready to reinforce and counter-attack. The longer, too, that a battery fired, the more likely it was to be detected and put out of action by counter-battery fire. The success at Neuve Chapelle was more the result of surprise and the shock of the hurricane bombardment – what the Germans afterwards described as 'the first true drum-fire [*Trommelfeuer*] yet heard' – than of obliteration. If the artillery did not keep German heads down long enough, the assaulting troops would never make it across no-man's-land. Indeed, this much was obvious from one sector of the Neuve Chapelle attack, where a howitzer battery had been delayed getting into position and failed to fire on its designated target: the Germans in the untouched trench had been so quick to their machine guns when the noise stopped that 1,100 men fell to their fire. The lesson was clear either way, therefore: if the bombardment did not destroy the defenders, when it lifted the battle would be a straight race for the parapet.

The other flaw in the analysis lay in the assumption that the Germans – and their barbed wire – would be as vulnerable to artillery fire in the future as they had been at Neuve Chapelle. But in that part of Artois the water table is high (whence the 'artesian well'): the German trenches had had to be built up as much as dug down, and in consequence were more vulnerable to artillery. In the valley of the Somme, however, where Haig, who by 1916 had replaced Sir John French as commander-in-chief, had decided to mount that year's allied offensive, the Germans had burrowed deep (30 feet in places) into the chalk. And not only were the Germans dug in deep, in the second full year of static warfare the barbed wire defences in no-man's-land across the whole of the Front were thicker and deeper than ever. In other words, Neuve Chapelle was to the Somme as the English Channel is to the Atlantic.

Haig delegated the planning and execution of the Somme offensive to the man who had commanded IV Corps at Neuve Chapelle, Lieutenant-General Sir Henry Rawlinson (who had briefly been sent to Gallipoli to help plan the evacuation), and who now commanded 4th Army. Rawlinson's plan of attack would rely on a long obliterating bombardment which would destroy both the Germans in their dug-outs and the barbed wire which protected them, enabling Kitchener's under-trained infantry simply to march the several hundred yards across no-man's-land and occupy what remained of the enemy trenches. And because they would not advance across no-man's-land at more than walking pace (the rate at which the artillery barrage would 'creep' – a new technique – from the fire trenches to the support trenches) they would be able to carry the extra ammunition, defence stores and rations needed before resupplies could be brought forward – a load per man of some 60 pounds (27 kg).

Haig had also hoped that his attack would be able to use the new secret weapon – the tank. He was impressed by what had emerged from the Admiralty Landships Committee – an armoured rhomboid box on caterpillar tracks which did indeed look like the water tank of its cover name. It was armed with either machine guns or quick-firing 6-pounders mounted on sponsons either side, had a crew of eight and moved at walking pace. Haig had at first been sceptical, but began to think the tank might have potential after seeing a demonstration of its barbed-wire-crushing and trench-crossing capability, and therefore its potential to help his infantry cross no-man's-land and punch the hole through which the cavalry could gallop. Unfortunately, technical problems meant that none would be available before September 1916. He had been willing to wait, but the Germans had opened a surprise offensive against the border fortress of Verdun in Lorraine, and Joffre urged him to make the attack no later than the end of June, else 'the French army would cease to exist'.

The seven-day preparatory bombardment on the Somme looked and sounded impressive – 1,500 guns firing 200,000 rounds a day (in the end, the shell count was nearer 1.7 million, since the French added their weight on the right) – but because of the length of front to be attacked (12 miles), the inadequate number of guns for the task, their varying accuracy and the failure rate of the ammunition (perhaps as many as one in three shells proved either duds or misfires), the weight of fire was proportionately only half that at Neuve Chapelle. John Masefield, poet laureate from 1930 to 1967, had served on the Western Front as a medical orderly before going to the Dardanelles to write propaganda for the Foreign Office. The result, *Gallipoli*, a work of great lyrical beauty, apparently so raised the public spirits in lauding what there was to be proud of in an otherwise inglorious episode, that he was sent to France in October 1916 with a brief to do the same for the Somme.* He looked at what he could of the old battlefield, spoke to whom he could, including Haig, and read what he could. And of that first morning of the British army's most debilitating battle ever, 1 July 1916, Masefield would write:

> It was fine, cloudless, summer weather, not very clear, for there was a good deal of heat haze and of mist in the nights and early mornings. It was hot yet brisk during the days. The roads were thick in dust. Clouds and streamers of chalk dust floated and rolled over all the roads leading to the front, till men and beasts were grey with it.
>
> At half past six in the morning of 1st July all the guns on our front quickened their fire to a pitch of intensity never before attained. Intermittent darkness and flashing so played on the enemy line from Gommecourt to Maricourt that it looked like a reef on a loppy day. For one

---

* In *Gallipoli* Masefield wrote, for example: 'On the body of a dead Turk officer was a letter written the night before to his wife, a tender letter, filled mostly with personal matters. In it was the phrase, "These British are the finest fighters in the world. We have chosen the wrong friends."'

instant it could be seen as a white rim above the wire, then some comber of a big shell struck it fair and spouted it black aloft . . .

In our trenches after seven o'clock on that morning, our men waited under a heavy fire for the signal to attack. Just before half-past seven, the mines at half a dozen points went up with a roar that shook the earth and brought down the parapets in our lines. Before the blackness of their burst had thinned or fallen, the hand of Time rested on the half-hour mark, and along all that old front line of the English there came a whistling and a crying. The men of the first wave climbed up the parapets, in tumult, darkness, and the presence of death, and having done with all pleasant things, advanced across the No Man's Land to begin the battle of the Somme.

The 'race for the parapet' had begun. But a race it scarcely was, for on the one side lines of smart new khaki advanced at the march, while on the other, when the bombardment shifted on to the reserve trenches, files of fossorial field grey sprinted up the steps of the deep dug-outs to man the machine guns in the contest for the green fields beyond. It was – remains – the greatest set-piece attack, the greatest battle, in British history: eleven divisions in line (and two more in an adjacent diversionary attack) – $13 \times 18,000$ men.

The German Maxims opened up in long raking bursts, the arcs of fire interlocking so that every inch of ground was swept by bullets. The silent, waiting artillery batteries sprang into life, the guns laid on pre-adjusted lines just in front of the barbed wire, so that there was no need of corrections. And into this hail of lead, high explosive and shrapnel marched that glorious if part-trained infantry: pre-war regulars who had somehow made it this far, Territorials toughened by a year at the front – and, above all, the New Army battalions, Kitchener's men. One way or another, every man a volunteer.

Some to begin with seemed to be entering into the spirit of the expected walk-over. In the 8th East Surreys, the battalion formed by the single regular captain who had sensibly asked for those who felt they could control six to eight other men to step forward, one company went into the attack dribbling footballs across no-man's-land. The game did not last long: 147 officers and men were killed and 279 wounded before they reached the German fire trench. But as one of the few battalions to gain its objective that day, it reaped an impressive array of gallantry awards: two DSOs, two Military Crosses, two Distinguished Conduct Medals and nine Military Medals. The 'Football Attack' caught the imagination of the country, with graphic accounts in the press; the regimental museum in Guildford has one of the tragic leather balls.

The 1st and 2nd Barnsley Pals (13th and 14th Battalions, York and Lancaster Regiment), attacking side by side in 31st Division further north, got nowhere. The 1st Pals went over the top 720 strong; by the middle of the afternoon there were but 250 of them left. The 2nd Pals fared slightly better, losing 300 before the brigade commander called them off. Both battalions were lucky, however, for besides being in the support wave their brigadier was the 34-year-old Hubert Conway Rees, a regular infantryman robust enough to halt their attack. Elsewhere, the plan continued as if nothing untoward were happening. In front of the Barnsley Pals had been another Pals battalion – the 12th East Lancashires, the 'Accrington Pals', 730 men from the close-knit cotton mill towns of 'Blackburnshire'. After the first half an hour, 600 of them were killed, wounded or 'missing' (in other words, there were no remains of them after shelling). The brigadier wrote of them and the rest of his brigade:

> The result of the H.E. shells, shrapnel, machine-gun and rifle fire was such that hardly any of our men reached the German front trench. The lines which advanced in such admirable order, melted away under fire; yet not a man wavered, broke the ranks or attempted to go back. I have never seen, indeed could never have imagined such a magnificent display of gallantry, discipline and determination.

Robert Graves was lucky to have missed the first day (he had been sent back to England for an operation on his nose to allow him to breathe properly in the new gas mask): three out of five of his fellow officers in the 1st Battalion Royal Welsh Fusiliers were killed. His fellow subaltern-poet Siegfried Sassoon, who had just won the MC, would have been one of them too, except that his company was held in reserve. Sassoon had spent a good deal of the day and night before the battle crawling about in no-man's-land trying to make wider gaps in the barbed wire with his new wire-cutters, bought on leave at the Army and Navy Stores, so that the New Army battalion of the Manchester Regiment which was to attack from their trench might have a better chance: 'it seemed to me that our prestige as a regular battalion had been entrusted to my care on a front of several hundred yards,' he wrote later. Wilfred Owen, who had enlisted in the ranks in 1915 and would soon be commissioned into the Manchesters, was lucky, too, to be away from the front in an officer training battalion. (It was here that he wrote much of his poetry: 'My subject is war, and the pity of war. The poetry is in the pity.') He would be killed a week before the Armistice leading an attack with the Manchesters, for which like Sassoon he would win the MC.

Isaac Rosenberg, one of the few acknowledged greats of the war poets not to have been commissioned, was serving with the 11th Battalion, the King's Own, a 'Bantam battalion' (consisting of men under the 1914 minimum height of 5 feet 3 inches) and therefore not assigned an assault role on 1 July, being employed instead on fatigue duties and burials. In the days that followed he would write what the American literary critic and Second World War infantry officer Paul Fussell called the greatest poem of the war: 'Break of Day in the Trenches'.* It is a short, stark meditation on mud, rats and poppies, with none of the spirit that had motivated men to flock to the recruiting offices in their hundreds of thousands – including Rosenberg's own 'Bantams', pint-sized men determined to do their bit. Yet it was these very men who went over the top on 1 July, their ardour perhaps just a little diminished by recent experience, but not much:

> The darkness crumbles away.
> It is the same old druid Time as ever,
> Only a live thing leaps my hand,
> A queer sardonic rat . . .†

And Sassoon was no doubt thinking of the men of the Kitchener battalions of Rosenberg's regiment, the King's Own – the Royal Lancasters – when he wrote:

---

* Paul Fussell, *The Great War and Modern Memory* (Oxford, 1975).
† Isaac Rosenberg was killed while serving with the 11th King's Own on 1 April 1918.

But to the end, unjudging, he'll endure
Horror and pain, not uncontent to die
That Lancaster on Lune may stand secure.*

At the end of the first day of the battle of the Somme the casualties numbered 57,470 men, including that fearful category 'missing'. Of these, 19,240 were soon listed as 'killed in action'.

Soldiers and politicians have walked ever deeper in the shadow of the valley of the Somme. The casualty lists which for months filled the newspapers imprinted themselves equally indelibly on the mind of the nation. And the lists included only the names of the officers.

The casualties on the first day of the battle were almost as great as the duke of Wellington's in the entire Peninsular campaign. Yet at the end of that first day's fighting no single person had a complete grasp of the scale of the disaster. The day after the battle Haig recorded in his diary that the estimates were 'over 40,000 to date', adding that 'this cannot be considered severe in view of the numbers engaged, and the length of front attacked'. Rawlinson had expected 10,000 a day. But quite apart from the underestimating of its cost, the attack had not been successful, and as yet Haig did not grasp this either. On 8 July he wrote: 'In another fortnight, with Divine Help, I hope that some decisive results may be obtained.' He did not in fact finally abandon ('close down' is the rather euphemistic term) the Somme offensive until the middle of November.

Yet even as the true scale of the losses became widely known, morale did not crack, as it did in the French army the following year in the wake of the failures of their renewed offensives. There were, however, some 'indications of a loss of fighting spirit': Haig records his dismay, for example, at the 49th (West Riding) Division, made up primarily of Territorial units, who appeared to have made no gains for proportionately fewer casualties than other formations. On 9 July the 11th Battalion of the Border Regiment, a 'Pals' unit formed in 1914 by the earl of Lonsdale and known throughout the army as 'the Lonsdales', simply failed to carry out a night attack when ordered (or rather, what was left of the battalion failed, for out of 800 men they

* 'The Redeemer' (from *The Old Huntsman*, 1918).

had lost 500 killed, missing or wounded, including twenty-five of their twenty-eight officers on the first day). It was not mutiny: there was no outright refusal to obey orders, no desertions; the attack just didn't happen.

When the divisional commander learned of it he ordered exemplary punishment for the commanding officer (a captain who had been brought in from another battalion in the same brigade after the losses of the first day) and what few other officers were left, including even the regimental medical officer (RMO). The disciplinary papers wound their way up the chain of command, gathering more and more exclamations of outrage at the acting commanding officer's failure, and that of the RMO who had reported the men mentally unfit for duty, castigating also the Lonsdales' pathetically small remaining band of NCOs. Eventually the papers arrived at GHQ (Haig's headquarters) where the chief medical officer, the wonderfully named Surgeon-General Sir Arthur Sloggett, pointed out one or two facts that had been overlooked in the atmosphere of scapegoating after 1 July: the internal cohesion of the brigade had been severely shaken; the brigade commander himself appeared unfit for duty, as indeed did the Lonsdales' acting commanding officer; and the RMO had been asked his opinion of the state of the battalion's nerves, which was not within his capability to judge. Haig, sitting outside the 'bubble' of 5th (Reserve) Army, which was commanded by the ever-certain Gough of Curragh fame and which had taken over responsibility for that part of the front, was able to agree with Sloggett, and matters were quietly rearranged. The Lonsdales were rested and reinforced, and they fought well again later in the year; by the end of the war, the officers involved had all been decorated.

It was a demonstration that though its limits are indistinct, endurance is finite: the Lonsdales' experience was perhaps extreme, but there were other cases of battalions having lost not so much their nerve as their confidence. Still, most persevered as before, continuing to lose men in steady numbers, particularly young officers. After the Somme, however, they were increasingly reinforced – and, for the first time in the nation's history, by conscripts. A Military Service Act had been passed in January 1916 making virtually all men between the ages of nineteen and forty-one liable for call-up – except, controversially, men in Ireland.

459

This and the 'industrial scale' of the Somme offensive now changed the face of regimental soldiering. David Jones, a private soldier in a Kitchener battalion of the Royal Welsh Fusiliers, and one of the outstanding literary voices to emerge from the war, writes in the foreword to his *In Parenthesis* (1937):

> The latter [date – July 1916] marks a change in the character of our lives in the Infantry on the Western Front. From then onward things hardened into a more relentless, mechanical affair, took on a more sinister aspect. The wholesale slaughter of the later years, the conscripted levies filling the gaps in every file of four, knocked the bottom out of the intimate, continuing, domestic life of small contingents of men.

The losses of the Somme did not at first deter offensive action, however; certainly not the following year, although Lloyd George, who in December 1916 had replaced Asquith (whose son Raymond had been killed on the Somme) as prime minister, tried to apply the brakes: the huge attacks around Ypres, popularly known as Passchendaele, were both costly and just as futile as those of the year before. Only after the war did the impact of the Somme take full effect in the collective professional mind of the army – and, indeed, in the minds of individual officers.*

It was not that Haig and his senior officers were indifferent to the losses, that they had all somehow undergone compassion bypass surgery – the imputation of the *Oh! What A Lovely War* school of history. And in any case, the army commanders had no option but to recognize the reality of their finite resources of manpower. When, for example, tanks at last made their appearance on the Somme, at Flers on 15 September – a mere handful of them, because of production problems and breakdowns – Haig was finally convinced of their potential in helping the infantry across no-man's-land, and began pressing for as many as possible to be sent to France. And when a diversionary amphibious landing in Belgium was discussed the following year, he suggested flat-bottomed landing craft with ramp

---

* Not least because at regimental level these losses could be truly staggering: 'In early 1914 we [Grenadier Guards] had 84 [officers] serving in our three battalions, whereas during the next three years the Regiment, expanded to five battalions, had lost 199 officers killed and a further 127 had been wounded' (Adair, *A Guards' General*).

fronts from which tanks could be disgorged to overcome the enemy's defences. The British army on the Western Front was, indeed, technically innovative – more so than the German, if not always as tactically agile.

Just occasionally there were glimpses of what could be done with smart tactics. An assault on the German salient south-east of Ypres, the Messines Ridge, by Sir Herbert Plumer's 2nd Army in June 1917 was the first successful large-scale offensive operation of the war, a meticulously planned and cunning all-arms battle making use of extensive mining, precision artillery fire, tanks, gas and an assault before dawn. And in November that year 450 tanks attacked at Cambrai on firm, unbroken ground north of the Somme, penetrating the German line by sheer surprise and firepower, although as in previous attacks the success could not be exploited before the Germans were able to recover and seal the breach. Spring 1918 brought the massive German offensive known as the *Kaiserschlacht* ('Kaiser's battle'), for Wilhelm had personally ordered Ludendorff, effectively commander-in-chief, to add more men to the planned offensive to make them up to one million. It failed, and the allied counter-offensive began in August. This was a sustained three-month effort (the 'Hundred Days') which included American troops just arrived in France, and Italian pilots, and involved sophisticated all-arms co-operation and close air support. Mechanical, aeronautical and ballistic technology had all advanced apace: Blériot had spluttered across the English Channel not ten years before, yet by November 1918 over 1,000 aircraft were flying in close support of Haig's armies – on reconnaissance, artillery spotting, and in ground attack sweeps with bombs and machine guns. If only radio technology had advanced as quickly (Marconi had sent radio signals across the Channel in 1899), commanders would have had the means to exploit the full potential of tanks, aircraft and artillery. Nevertheless, the Hundred Days was undeniably Haig's victory, and one which until relatively recently had not been fully acknowledged. Some historians now maintain, in fact, that it was the British army's greatest victory.* Certainly in November

---

* The Battle of Amiens which began the offensive in earnest on 8 August with a surprise tank attack by Rawlinson's 4th Army broke through the German lines, destroyed six divisions and forced the line back 9 miles in one day. Ludendorff called 8 August the 'Black Day of the German Army'.

1918 the British army stood second to none. The French generalissimo Ferdinand Foch, who had been hastily appointed to overall allied command when the German offensive opened – the first time there had been a unified command in the whole course of the war – wrote to Haig after the Armistice:

> Never at any time in history has the British Army achieved greater results in attack than in this unbroken offensive . . . The victory was indeed complete, thanks to the Commanders of the Armies, Corps and Divisions and above all to the unselfishness, to the wise, loyal and energetic policy of their Commander-in-Chief, who made easy a great combination and sanctioned a prolonged gigantic effort.

In fact, in those final Hundred Days the BEF engaged and defeated 99 of the 197 German divisions on the Western Front, taking nearly 200,000 prisoners – almost 50 per cent of the total taken by all the allied armies in France in this period. And the soldiers were, for the most part, men who had joined since August 1914, led by a remnant of pre-war regular officers and NCOs who had not forgotten how war was meant to be made. Some of the August 1914 men may at times have doubted whether this mass, improvised and latterly conscripted army could ever come up to the mark. Robert Graves did, but by 1918, convalescing in England, he had changed his mind, which he brilliantly conveys by transposition to Caesar's day and the XXIII Legion (the Royal Welsh Fusiliers being the old 23rd Foot):

'Is that the Three-and-Twentieth, Strabo mine,
Marching below, and we still gulping wine?'
From the sad magic of his fragrant cup
The red-faced old centurion started up,
Cursed, battered on the table. 'No,' he said,
'Not that! The Three-and-Twentieth Legion's dead,
Dead in the first year of this damned campaign—
The Legion's dead, dead, and won't rise again.
Pity? Rome pities her brave lads that die,
But we need pity also, you and I,
Whom Gallic spear and Belgian arrow miss,
Who live to see the Legion come to this,

Unsoldierlike, slovenly, bent on loot,
Grumblers, diseased, unskilled to thrust or shoot.
O, brown cheek, muscled shoulder, sturdy thigh!
Where are they now? God! watch it struggle by,
The sullen pack of ragged ugly swine.
Is that the Legion, Gracchus? Quick, the wine!'
'Strabo,' said Gracchus, 'you are strange tonight.
The Legion is the Legion; it's all right.
If these new men are slovenly, in your thinking,
God damn it! you'll not better them by drinking.
They all try, Strabo; trust their hearts and hands.
The Legion is the Legion while Rome stands,
And these same men before the autumn's fall
Shall bang old Vercingetorix out of Gaul.'*

By November 1918 they did indeed 'bang old Vercingetorix [the Kaiser] out of Gaul [France]'.

At 11 a.m. on 11 November 1918 – the eleventh hour of the eleventh day of the eleventh month – the 15th Hussars, a regiment that like many had hung on to its cherished traditions throughout the war, mustered its remaining trumpeters and sounded 'Cease Fire'. It was an extraordinary moment, for the ceremonial call (all calls were ceremonial, for the trumpet had long ceased to be carried in the field) had not been heard for over four years. Moreover, the regiment was mustered in a field not a dozen miles from where they had heard the first shots fired on 22 August 1914. During that time, Britain had mobilized in all some 5,397,000 men. Over a million and a half of these – army, navy and latterly air force – had been wounded; and some 703,000 killed.†

In a beautiful wooded cemetery at the end of a suburban lane at St-Symphorien in the outskirts of Mons (all the cemeteries of the Commonwealth War Graves Commission, worldwide, are lovingly tended) the body of Private John Parr of the 4th Battalion Middlesex Regiment lies a few paces from that of Private George Ellison of the 5th Royal Irish Lancers. The Middlesex had been one of the battalions

---

*Robert Graves, 'An Old Twenty-Third Man', from *Fairies and Fusiliers* (1928).
† *The Longman Companion to the First World War* (Harlow, 2001).

that had put up so heroic a fight on the Mons canal on 23 August 1914; the 5th Lancers had been the last cavalry regiment to leave Mons in 1914, and the first British troops to re-enter the city on 11 November 1918. The date of Private Parr's death shown on his headstone is 21 August, which is uncertain (see footnote on page [302]). Private Ellison was killed on the morning of 11 November 1918, it is believed only 90 minutes before the ceasefire.

Private Parr and Private Ellison are sometimes referred to as, respectively, the first and the last British soldiers to die in action in the First World War. It is impossible to establish the accuracy of that claim, but there is poignancy in their lying so close, and at Mons: they had died hearing some of the first and the last shots of the war, and were buried within a few miles of where they fell. Their memorial stones face each other across a narrow strip of grass; and indeed in their experience of war – the war of movement of 1914, and the war of movement restored in the closing months of 1918 – they were not worlds apart.

Yet the public image of the war is too often only that which stood between those years – the trenches of the Western Front, the most extensive and bloodiest siege in history. From the soldier's point of view at least, there has to be balance in the way the Great War is assessed. It was, like Caesar's Gaul, divided into three parts; and no one part should be allowed to diminish the feats, or the terrible cost, of the other two.

APPENDIX

The British Expeditionary Force, August 1914 – Order of Battle

General Headquarters (GHQ)

Commander-in-Chief: Field-Marshal Sir J. D. P. French

Chief of the General Staff (CGS): Lieutenant-General Sir A. J. Murray

Sub-CGS: Major-General H. H. Wilson

General Staff Officer Grade 1 (GSO1) (Operations):
   Colonel G. M. Harper

GSO1 (Intelligence): Colonel G. M. W. Macdonogh

Adjutant-General: Major-General Sir C. F. N. Macready

Quartermaster-General: Major-General Sir W. R. Robertson

Major-General Royal Artillery: Major-General W. F. L. Lindsay

Chief Royal Engineer (CRE): Brigadier-General G. H. Fowke

Cavalry Division

General Officer Commanding (GOC):
   Major-General E. H. H. Allenby

GSO1 (chief of staff): Colonel J. Vaughan

Brigadier-General Royal Horse Artillery (RHA):
   Brigadier-General B. F. Drake

1st Cavalry Brigade (Brigadier-General C. J. Briggs)
      2nd Dragoon Guards (Queen's Bays)
      5th (Princess Charlotte of Wales's) Dragoon Guards

11th (Prince Albert's Own) Hussars
2nd Cavalry Brigade (Brigadier-General H. De Lisle)
    4th (Royal Irish) Dragoon Guards
    9th (Queen's Royal) Lancers
    18th (Queen Mary's Own) Hussars
3rd Cavalry Brigade (Brigadier-General H. de la P. Gough)
    4th (Queen's Own) Hussars
    5th (Royal Irish) Lancers
    16th (The Queen's) Lancers
4th Cavalry Brigade (Brigadier-General Hon. C. E. Bingham)
    Household Cavalry (Composite) Regiment
    6th Dragoon Guards (Carabiniers)
    3rd (King's Own) Hussars

Divisional troops

    III Brigade Royal Horse Artillery (RHA)
        D Battery
        E Battery
    VII Brigade RHA
        I Battery
        L Battery
    1st Field Squadron, Royal Engineers (RE)

I Corps

General Officer Commanding-in-Chief (GOC-in-C):
  Lieutenant-General Sir D. Haig
Brigadier-General General Staff (BGGS):
  Brigadier-General J. E. Gough
Brigadier-General Royal Artillery (BGRA):
  Brigadier-General H. S. Horne
CRE: Brigadier-General S. R. Rice

1st Division

GOC: Major-General S. H. Lomax
GSO1: Colonel R. Fanshawe
BGRA: Brigadier-General N. D. Findlay
CRE: Lieutenant-Colonel A. L. Schreiber

1st (Guards) Brigade (Brigadier-General F. I. Maxse)
    1st Coldstream Guards

1st Scots Guards
1st Black Watch (Royal Highlanders)
2nd Royal Munster Fusiliers

2nd Infantry Brigade (Brigadier-General E. S. Bulfin)
  2nd Royal Sussex Regiment
  1st Loyal North Lancashire Regiment
  1st Northamptonshire Regiment
  2nd King's Royal Rifle Corps

3rd Infantry Brigade (Brigadier-General H. J. S. Landon)
  1st Queen's (Royal West Surrey) Regiment
  1st South Wales Borderers
  1st Gloucestershire Regiment
  2nd Welsh Regiment

Divisional troops

  A Squadron, 15th (The King's) Hussars
  1st Cyclist Company
  Artillery
        XXV Brigade Royal Field Artillery (RFA)
                113th Battery
                114th Battery
                115th Battery
        XXVI Brigade RFA
                116th Battery
                117th Battery
                118th Battery
        XXXIX Brigade RFA
                46th Battery
                51st Battery
                54th Battery
        XLIII (Howitzer) Brigade RFA
                30th (Howitzer) Battery
                40th (Howitzer) Battery
                57th (Howitzer) Battery
        26th Heavy Battery,
                Royal Garrison Artillery (RGA)
  Engineers
        23rd Field Company
        26th Field Company

2nd Division

GOC: Major-General C. C. Monro
GSO1: Colonel the Hon. F. Gordon
BGRA: Brigadier-General E. M. Perceval
CRE: Lieutenant-Colonel R. H. H. Boys

4th (Guards) Brigade (Brigadier-General R. Scott-Kerr)
    2nd Grenadier Guards
    2nd Coldstream Guards
    3rd Coldstream Guards
    1st Irish Guards

5th Infantry Brigade (Brigadier-General R. C. B. Haking)
    2nd Worcestershire Regiment
    2nd Oxfordshire and Buckinghamshire Light Infantry
    2nd Highland Light Infantry
    2nd Connaught Rangers

6th Infantry Brigade (Brigadier-General R. H. Davies, NZ Staff Corps)
    1st King's (Liverpool Regiment)
    2nd South Staffordshire Regiment
    1st Princess Charlotte of Wales's (Royal Berkshire Regiment)
    1st King's Royal Rifle Corps

Divisional troops

    B Squadron, 15th (The King's) Hussars
    2nd Cyclist Company
    Artillery
        XXXIV Brigade RFA
            22nd Battery
            50th Battery
            70th Battery
        XXXVI Brigade RFA
            15th Battery
            48th Battery
            71st Battery
        XLI Brigade RFA
            9th Battery
            16th Battery
            17th Battery

XLIV (Howitzer) Brigade RFA
    47th (Howitzer) Battery
    56th (Howitzer) Battery
    60th (Howitzer) Battery
35th Heavy Battery, RGA
Engineers
    5th Field Company
    11th Field Company

II Corps

GOC-in-C: Lieutenant-General Sir James Grierson
    (from 21 August, General Sir Horace Smith-Dorrien)
BGGS: Brigadier-General G. T. Forestier-Walker
BGRA: Brigadier-General A. H. Short
CRE: Brigadier-General A. E. Sandbach

3rd Division

GOC: Major-General H. I. W. Hamilton
GSO1: Colonel F. R. F. Boileau
BGRA: Brigadier-General F. D. V. Wing
CRE: Lieutenant-Colonel C. S. Wilson

7th Infantry Brigade (Brigadier-General F. W. N. McCracken)
    3rd Worcestershire Regiment
    2nd Prince of Wales's Volunteers (South Lancashire Regiment)
    1st Duke of Edinburgh's (Wiltshire) Regiment
    2nd Royal Irish Rifles

8th Infantry Brigade (Brigadier-General B. J. C. Doran)
    2nd Royal Scots (Lothian Regiment)
    2nd Royal Irish Regiment
    4th Duke of Cambridge's Own (Middlesex) Regiment
    1st Gordon Highlanders

9th Infantry Brigade (Brigadier-General F. C. Shaw)
    1st Northumberland Fusiliers
    4th Royal Fusiliers (City of London Regiment)
    1st Lincolnshire Regiment
    1st Royal Scots Fusiliers

Divisional troops

C Squadron, 15th (The King's) Hussars
3rd Cyclist Company
Artillery
XXIII Brigade RFA
107th Battery
108th Battery
109th Battery
XL Brigade RFA
6th Battery
23rd Battery
49th Battery
XLII Brigade RFA
29th Battery
41st Battery
45th Battery
XXX (Howitzer) Brigade RFA
128th (Howitzer) Battery
129th (Howitzer) Battery
130th (Howitzer) Battery
48th Heavy Battery, RGA
Engineers
56th Field Company
57th Field Company

5th Division

GOC: Major-General Sir C. Fergusson
GSO1: Lieutenant-Colonel C. F. Romer
BGRA: Brigadier-General J. E. W. Headlam
CRE: Lieutenant-Colonel J. A. S. Tulloch

13th Infantry Brigade (Brigadier-General G. J. Cuthbert)
2nd King's Own Scottish Borderers
2nd Duke of Wellington's (West Riding) Regiment
1st Queen's Own (Royal West Kent) Regiment
2nd King's Own (Yorkshire Light Infantry)

14th Infantry Brigade (Brigadier-General S. P. Rolt)
2nd Suffolk Regiment
1st East Surrey Regiment

1st Duke of Cornwall's Light Infantry
2nd Manchester Regiment

15th Infantry Brigade (Brigadier-General Count Gleichen)
1st Norfolk Regiment
1st Bedfordshire Regiment
1st Cheshire Regiment
1st Dorsetshire Regiment

Divisional troops

A Squadron, 19th (Queen Alexandra's Own Royal) Hussars
5th Cyclist Company
Artillery
XV Brigade RFA
11th Battery
52nd Battery
80th Battery
XXVII Brigade RFA
119th Battery
120th Battery
121st Battery
XXVIII Brigade RFA
122nd Battery
123rd Battery
124th Battery
VIII (Howitzer) Brigade RFA
37th (Howitzer) Battery
61st (Howitzer) Battery
65th (Howitzer) Battery
108th Heavy Battery, RGA
Engineers
17th Field Company
59th Field Company

III Corps

(formed in France on 30 August 1914)
GOC-in-C: Lieutenant-General W. P. Pulteney
BGGS: Brigadier-General J. P. Du Cane
BGRA: Brigadier-General E. J. Phipps-Hornby
CRE: Brigadier-General F. M. Glubb

4th Division

GOC: Major-General T. d'O. Snow
GSO1: Colonel J. E. Edmonds
BGRA: Brigadier-General G. F. Milne
CRE: Lieutenant-Colonel H. B. Jones

10th Infantry Brigade (Brigadier-General J. A. L. Haldane)
    1st Royal Warwickshire Regiment
    2nd Seaforth Highlanders (Ross-shire Buffs,
       The Duke of Albany's)
    1st Princess Victoria's (Royal Irish) Fusiliers
    2nd Royal Dublin Fusiliers

11th Infantry Brigade (Brigadier-General A. G. Hunter-Weston)
    1st Prince Albert's (Somerset) Light Infantry
    1st East Lancashire Regiment
    1st Hampshire Regiment
    1st Rifle Brigade (Prince Consort's Own)

12th Infantry Brigade (Brigadier-General H. F. M. Wilson)
    1st King's Own (Royal Lancaster) Regiment
    2nd Lancashire Fusiliers
    2nd Royal Inniskilling Fusiliers
    2nd Essex Regiment

Divisional troops

    B Squadron, 19th (Queen Alexandra's Own Royal) Hussars
    4th Cyclist Company
    Artillery
        XIV Brigade RFA
            39th Battery
            68th Battery
            88th Battery
        XXIX Brigade RFA
            125th Battery
            126th Battery
            127th Battery
        XXXII Brigade RFA
            27th Battery
            134th Battery
            135th Battery

XXXVII (Howitzer) Brigade RFA
 31st (Howitzer) Battery
 35th (Howitzer) Battery
 55th (Howitzer) Battery
31st Heavy Battery, RGA
Engineers
 7th Field Company
 9th Field Company

6th Division

(embarked for France on 8 and 9 September)
GOC: Major-General J. L. Keir
GSO1: Colonel W. T. Furse
BGRA: Brigadier-General W. L. H. Paget
CRE: Lieutenant-Colonel G. C. Kemp

16th Infantry Brigade (Brigadier-General E. C. Ingouville-Williams)
 1st The Buffs (East Kent Regiment)
 1st Leicestershire Regiment
 1st The King's (Shropshire) Light Infantry
 2nd York and Lancaster Regiment

17th Infantry Brigade (Brigadier-General W. R. B. Doran)
 1st Royal Fusiliers (City of London Regiment)
 1st Prince of Wales's (North Staffordshire) Regiment
 2nd Prince of Wales's Leinster Regiment (Royal Canadians)
 3rd Rifle Brigade (The Prince Consort's Own)

18th Infantry Brigade (Brigadier-General W. N. Congreve)
 1st Prince of Wales's Own (West Yorkshire) Regiment
 1st East Yorkshire Regiment
 2nd Sherwood Foresters (Nottinghamshire and Derbyshire
  Regiment)
 2nd Durham Light Infantry

Divisional troops

 C Squadron, 19th (Queen Alexandra's Own Royal) Hussars
 6th Cyclist Company
 Artillery
  II Brigade RFA
   21st Battery

42nd Battery
53rd Battery
XXIV Brigade RFA
110th Battery
111th Battery
112th Battery
XXXVIII Brigade RFA
24th Battery
34th Battery
72nd Battery
XII (Howitzer) Brigade RFA
43rd (Howitzer) Battery
86th (Howitzer) Battery
87th (Howitzer) Battery
24th Heavy Battery, RGA
Engineers
12th Field Company
38th Field Company

Army troops (under GHQ)

5th Cavalry Brigade (Brigadier-General Sir P. W. Chetwode)
2nd Dragoons (Royal Scots Greys)
12th (Prince of Wales's Royal) Lancers
20th Hussars
J Battery, RHA

Composite Regiment
A and C Squadrons North Irish Horse (Special Reserve)
B Squadron South Irish Horse (Special Reserve)

Siege artillery (RGA)
No. 1 Siege Battery
No. 2 Siege Battery
No. 3 Siege Battery
No. 4 Siege Battery
No. 5 Siege Battery
No. 6 Siege Battery

Infantry
1st The Queen's Own Cameron Highlanders (GHQ guard)
(from 14 September with 8th Infantry Brigade)

Royal Flying Corps
GOC: Brigadier-General Sir D. Henderson
GSO1: Lieutenant-Colonel F. H. Sykes
2nd Aeroplane Squadron
3rd Aeroplane Squadron
4th Aeroplane Squadron
5th Aeroplane Squadron

Lines of communication defence troops
(from 22 August formed into 19th Infantry Brigade, commanded by Major-General L. G. Drummond)

2nd Royal Welsh Fusiliers
1st Cameronians (Scottish Rifles)
1st Duke of Cambridge's Own (Middlesex) Regiment
2nd Princess Louise's (Argyll and Sutherland) Highlanders
1st Devonshire Regiment (from 14 September with 8th Infantry
    Brigade)

Note: Every infantry regiment of the British army was represented by one or more of its battalions, except the Green Howards and the Border Regiment, whose home-service battalions were kept back in the Channel Islands and at Pembroke docks respectively until October, when they joined the BEF as part of the 7th Division.

Note on strengths

Cavalry division: four cavalry brigades (twelve regiments), and divisional troops
    Strength 9,269 all ranks
    9,815 horses
    24 × 13-pounders
    24 × Vickers machine guns

(Infantry) division: three infantry brigades (twelve battalions), and divisional troops
    Strength 18,073 all ranks
    5,592 horses
    76 guns (54 × 18-pounders, 18 × 4.5 inch howitzers,
        4 × 60-pounders)
    24 × Vickers machine guns

APPENDIX

The total 'ration strength' of the BEF in August 1914 (five divisions) was approximately 110,000.

Rifle strength: 66,000

Sabre strength: 7,600 (including 5th (Independent) Cavalry Brigade and
    divisional squadrons)

Guns: 430, including five RHA batteries, but excluding RGA.

PICTURE ACKNOWLEDGEMENTS

Every effort has been made to trace copyright holders, but any who have been overlooked are invited to get in touch with the publishers.

Endpapers (hardback edition only): *With the field guns on the Western Front* by Fortunino Matania, 1914, published in 'With the British Army on the Western Front' in 1916 for *Tatler* and *Sphere*: © David Cohen Fine Art/Mary Evans Picture Library.

Illustrations in the text

Mirrorpix: p. 14; Imperial War Museum/ PST 12140: p. 63; Getty Images: pp. 102 (Schlieffen portrait), 145; © Illustrated London News Ltd/Mary Evans: p. 241.

Picture sections

(Clockwise from top left on each page/spread.)

Section one

Prince Otto von Bismarck, 1894: Mary Evans/Süddeutsche Zeitung; Marshal Helmuth Karl Bernhard von Moltke, *c*.1870: Getty Images; Kaiser Wilhelm II, Vice-Admiral Alfred von Tirpitz and Lt-Gen. Helmut Johann Ludwig von Moltke, 1900: Getty Images; Kaiser Wilhelm II and Gen. Helmut Johann Ludwig von Moltke on manoeuvres, 1913: PA Archive/Press Association Images.

'Scrap of paper', 1839, detail of a First World War recruiting poster: © Philip Cartoy/Alamy; Edward VII greeting the French President M. Émile Loubet on his arrival in Paris, May 1903: Bodleian Library, MS. Photogr. c. 4, fol. 100; Herbert Asquith, July 1914: Mirrorpix; Venetia Stanley, *Tatler*, 28 July 1915:

Alamy; end of the retreat from Mons, September 1914: © The Art Archive/Alamy; staff conference, Le Cateau, 26 August 1914: Imperial War Museum/Q 51480; action at Nery, 1 September 1914: Imperial War Museum/Q51484.

Louis Félix Marie François Franchet d'Espèrey: © The Art Archive/Alamy; Gen. Ferdinand Foch, 1914: Getty Images; D Coy, 1st Battalion, the Cameronians, crossing a pontoon bridge over the Marne at La Ferté-sous-Jouarre, 10 September 1914: Imperial War Museum/Q51493; machine-gun position, Aisne, 17 September 1914: Imperial War Museum/Q 51497; J Battery, RHA, moving through a village near Amiens en route for Ypres, October 1914: Imperial War Museum/Q56310; J Battery, RHA in action near the Messines Ridge, October 1914: Imperial War Museum/Q56311; mobilization of troops, Battle of the Marne, September 1914: © UPPA/Photoshot; Lord Kitchener leaving a conference, September 1914: © Imperial War Museum/Robert Hunt Library/Mary Evans; Field Marshal Sir John French, 1915: The Print Collector/HIP/TopFoto.

Men of the machine-gun section of the 11th Hussars in the trenches at Zillebeke, winter 1914–15: Imperial War Museum/Q 51194; British cavalry passing Albert Cathedral, 22 August 1918: Getty Images.

INDEX

Note: Page numbers in **bold** indicate illustrations and maps

Abbeville 433, 435
Abell, Maj. William 312
Abercrombie, Col. 369
Acland, Lt (Capt.) Arthur 264, 303*n*, 367, 379
Acland, Sir Francis 135
Adair, Maj.-Gen. Allan 64*n*, 234*n*, 377*n*
Admiralty 2*n*
Admiralty Landships Committee 450
Agadir Crisis (1911) (Second Moroccan crisis) 150–2, 154*n*
aircraft 95–6 *and n*
  Beta airship 277 *and n*
  German 408
  increased use by end of war 461
  Lewis gun 96*n*
  for reconnaissance 97, 276–7
  refused for Gallipoli 449
  types 96*n*
  Zeppelins 260 *and n*
Aisne, river 413, 414
  trenches 417–18
  vulnerability of German flank at 432–3
Albania 173, 174
Albert, king of the Belgians 126
  abandonment of Antwerp 423
  command of army 254–5, 258
  withdrawal to Malines 267–8
Alexander II, Tsar 27*n*
Alexander, Lt the Hon. Harold (FM Lord Alexander of Tunis) 263*n*
Alexander, Maj. (Maj.-Gen) Ernest Wright, VC 330 *and n*
Alexander Obrenovíc, King of Serbia, assassination 179*n*
Alexandra of Denmark, marriage to Prince of Wales 33*n*

Algeciras, conference (1905) 60, 150
Allenby, Maj.-Gen. Edmund, Cavalry Division 276, 277
  and Gough 381 *and n*
  at Le Cateau 345–6, 359
  retreat from 380–1 *and n*
  and Néry 389
  withdrawal from Mons 328
Alsace-Lorraine
  ceded to Germany 43
  French 1st and 2nd Armies in **238–9**, 240, 250, 268–9
  and French Plan XVII 116, 120
American Civil War 48
American War of Independence 141
Amiens
  French 2nd Army at 420
  plan for deployment of BEF at 13, 227
  what if . . .? 427–9
Amiens, Battle of (1918) 461–2 *and n*
ammunition 79, 90–1
  ground dumping of 379
  shortages for volunteers 443
Amphion, HMS 236
Anglo-French Naval Convention (1912) 147 *and n*, 211
Anglo-Japanese Treaty (1902) 59
Anglo-Prussian Treaty (1869) 43*n*
Anglo-Russian Convention (1907) 129*n*
Ansell, Lt-Col. George 389 *and n*
Antwerp 12*n*, 13, 341
  abandonment of 423
  Belgian withdrawal to 382, 412*n*, 421 *and n*, 433
  bombing by Zeppelin 260*n*
  as supply route 126
Ardennes, German advance 268–9

Army Council 7n, 177
  establishment of 53–4 and n
  meeting (5 Aug.) 7–8
Army Horse Reserve, creation of 136
Army Medical Services, evacuation of
  wounded, Mons 319
Army Post Office Corps 265
Army Reserve 62, 64, 430n, 431
  mobilization 14
  see also Special Reserve
Army Service Corps 65, 97
Arnold-Foster, Hugh 61
Arras 421
artillery
  75 mm QF (French) 115n
  bombardment at Neuve Chapelle 452
  comparative strengths before Marne
    404–5
  counter-battery fire, Mons 334n, 336n
  debate over use 88–90
  direct and indirect fire 88
  German: HE 358, 414; siege 256
  superiority over BEF 376n, 414
  HE rounds 89 and n, 90
  Krupp breech-loading field guns 42
    and n
  losses 403n
  need for more heavy artillery 416 and n,
    431
  QF 4.5-inch howitzer 87
  QF 13-pounder 87–8
  QF 18-pounder 87–8
  range 88–9
  rate of fire 88
  shortage of shells 452
  shrapnel rounds 87–8, 89
Artois 420
  Pas de Calais spring offensive (1915)
    451
  trenches 453
Ashburner, Capt. Lionel 309
Asquith, H. H. (Herbert Henry), prime
    minister 2
  on assassination in Sarajevo 174–5
  on Bismarck 46
  cabinet meetings: 1 Aug., decision for
    war 200 and n; Nov. 1911 168; 29
    July, decision not to decide
    189–92; 2 Aug. 204–9, 214
    (continuing delay in despatch of
    BEF) 208; discussion of Belgian
    neutrality 206, 212; suggestion of
    'naval war' 211)
  and decision for mobilization 212–13
  and estimates of losses after Le Cateau
    385
  and General Staff Plan (1911) 164–5
    and n
  inquiry into Goltz's reprisals 254n
  and Kitchener 199
  as Liberal leader (from 1916) 427n, 460

  and new battleships 146
  and 'precautionary period' 192
  secret meeting of CID (Aug. 1911) 155,
    162, 438; assessment of strategic
    plans ('wait and see') 163–5
  and war council (5 Aug.) 8, 9, 11–12
Asquith, Mrs 20
Asquith, Raymond 460
Audregnies, near Mons 329
Australian and New Zealand Corps
    (Anzacs) 446–7
  casualties at Gallipoli 448n
Austria-Hungary, Dual Monarchy 12, 37
  and Balkans 37, 170
  Bismarck's ambitions in 34–6, 37
  Dual Alliance pact with Germany 45
  and expansion of Serbia 171–2, 173
  and France 56
  and Italy 35
  naval shipbuilding programme 147
  partial mobilization (28 July) 186
  reaction to assassination in Sarajevo
    179–80
  and Russian mobilization 193, 194–5
  shelling of Serbian positions 193
  ultimatum to Serbia (23 July) 183 and n
  war with Serbia 12, 187–8
  withdrawal of ambassador from
    Belgrade 186
Austro-Prussian War (1866) 48
Automobile Association 138

Bailey, Maj.-Gen. Jonathan 90n
Baker-Carr, Maj. Christopher, liaison
    officer 376, 394
Balaklava, Battle of (1854) 347
balance of power
  Britain's view of 24–5
  and unification of Germany 43
Baldwin, Stanley, prime minister 131n
Balfour, Arthur, MP 217
Balkan League 170–1
Balkan Wars
  consequences of 174–6
  First (1908) 170
  Second 171
Balkans 169–78
  Austria and 37, 170
band, improvised (at St Quentin) 377–8
    and n
barbed wire 453
Barlow, Air Mechanic Raymond 237
Barnardiston, Lt-Col. (Maj.-Gen.)
    Nathaniel 125
Barnsley, 'Pals' battalions 441
Barrow, George Symons, Cavalry
    Division intelligence officer 277, 280
    and n
battalion, defined 10–11n
Bavai
  GHQ at 314–15, 332–3

Roman road to Le Cateau 337
bayonet fighting 79 *and n*
Bazaine, Marshal, at Metz (1870) 325
Beauchamp, Earl, resignation 214
BEF (British Expeditionary Force) xix, 7*n*, 11
  age and experience xxi–xxii, 81–3, 97–8
  arrival and first days 235–7
  crossing into Belgium 423
  deployment 227–8
  efficiencies and deficiencies xx–xxi, 96–8
  fighting formations 74–5 *and n*
  first rifle shots 286–7
  formal constitution (1907) 72
  and French Army: disposition **238–9**; plans to integrate with 15, 166
  gap between BEF and Lanrezac 395
  GHQ: at Bavai 314–15, 332–3; independent formations 379; loses control over battle at Mons 332; loses coordinating role at Le Cateau 368, 369, 371–2; moves to Compiègne 381; moves to Noyon 378–9; pessimism before Marne 375–6, 379, 384*n*; retreats to Seine 394, 399; at St Quentin 369–70, 375
  Kitchener's message to 261–2
  at Marne 396, 402–3, 408–9, 423
  at Mons **278–9**, 292
  on Mons canal line 282
  'Old Contemptibles' 71
  Order of Battle 465–77
  'peace establishment' (PE) 72
  plans for deployment 12–13, 15–16; expected concentration area (Maubeuge) 12–13, 150, 156–7, 164, 227, **238–9**; possibility of counter-attack from Abbeville, *what if . . .?* 433, 435; Wilson's 155–9
  reorganization (1915) 451
  size (divisions) 10, 74, 135, 138, 156 *and n*, 163, 205, 227; limitations of 16, 98, 228
  strength at Ypres 423, 426
  threatened envelopment of left wing 287–8
  'war establishment' (WE) 72
  see also Army Reserve; British army; Special Reserve
Belfort, German incursions 209
Belgian army 125–6
  abandonment of Antwerp 423
  in Antwerp 412*n*, 421 *and n*, 433
  and German attack on Yser 423
  and Marne 412*n*
Belgium
  admiration for 257 *and n*

expectation of German invasion through 128, 165*n*, 190–1
  fortresses 108, 125
  German invasion 1
  and German ultimatum 206 *and n*
  independence (1830) 25
  mobilization 192–3, 199
  plans in event of invasion 125
  possibility of forcing German army back into, *what if . . .?* 437
  resistance to invasion 12, **185**, 213, 240, 254–8
  rumours of atrocities 252, **253**, 254 *and n*
  talks with 125
Belgium, neutrality of 1, 26 *and n*, 43 *and n*
  British obligations towards 181, 189–90, 206
  French support for (1914) 184
  Schlieffen Plan and 110–11
Below, Oberst Ernst von 353
Below-Selaske, Claus von, German ambassador to Belgium 206*n*
Benedetti, Count Vincent, French ambassador to Prussia 41
Berchtold, Count, Austrian foreign minister 173, 183, 188, 193
Bernhardi, General Friedrich von 84
Berteaux, Henri, French war minister 151
Berthelot, Henri, chief of staff to Joffre 242, 416*n*
Bertie, Sir Francis, ambassador in Paris 393
Bertrab, Lt-Gen. Hermann von 183
Bertry, Smith-Dorrien's headquarters 342, 372
Bethmann Hollweg, Theobald von, German chancellor 149*n*
  and Austria 183, 184
  call for British neutrality 194–5
  and Kaiser's cruise to Arctic 182
  and Russia 186, 197
  on Schlieffen Plan 110*n*
  'scrap of paper' remark 17, 19
Bingham, Brig.-Gen. the Hon. C. E. 83
Bird, Lt-Col. (Maj.-Gen.) Wilkinson Dent 340, 391
Birdwood, Maj.-Gen. William, Anzacs 446, 448
Bismarck, Otto von 40*n*, 44, 45
  ambitions for Prussia 29, 32*n*, 36
  and Austria 34–6, 37
  on Balkans 169–70
  and Disraeli 29
  and 'Ems Telegram' 40–1
  and France 37–8
  and Italy 35
  and Russia 107
  and Schleswig-Holstein 32–4
  view of British army 34, 71

Bloem, Capt. Walter, Brandenburger Regt
86, 404
mobilization 251–2
Mons 308–9 and n
Blücher, Gen., at Ligny (1815) 321n
Blücher, Princess (Evelyn) 251 and n
Boer War (1899–1902)
casualties 51
communication 49–50
financial cost 51
lessons learned xx, 52–5
Boer War, First (1881) 47–52
Boger, Lt-Col. Dudley 330n
Boillot, Georges, driver to Joffre 289,
374, 399
bombardment
preparatory, at Somme 454
risks of 452–3
Bonaparte, Napoleon
and Congress of Vienna 23–5
and war on two fronts 104–5
Bonar Law, Andrew, and Tory support for
pro-war coalition 211, 216
Bordeaux, French government move to
397
Borinage mining region, around Mons
306 and n
Borton, Lt (Air Vice Marshal) Amyas, RFC
368
Bosnia (and Herzegovina) 37, 170
Botha, Louis 47, 52n
Boxer Rebellion 55
Boyd-Moss, Maj. Lionel, RFC 338
Bradbury, Capt. Edward, RHA 388
Bradley, Pte Tom 312
Bramall, FM Edwin, Lord 163–4
Brett, Lt-Col. Charles 366
bridges
girder 92
Mons Canal 300–1, 305–6
Bridges, Maj. Tom 165n, 284
improvised band, St Quentin 377–8
and n
Briggs, Brig.-Gen. Charles, 1st Cavalry
Bde 83, 328–9
Néry 386–7, 389
Bright, John, MP, on Crimean War 24
Bristol Aircraft Company 95
British army
active strength (1 Aug. 1914) 11n, 48
battalion (defined) 10–11n
failings in Boer War 49–51
finite resources of manpower 460
march discipline 264–5
purpose of 55–6, 165–7
reforms xx; Cardwell–Childers 66 and n,
442
regiment (defined) 10–11n
senior command appointments 54
and nn, 74
staff college 128 and n

total mobilization 463
and unified command with French
(1918) 462
see also Army Reserve; BEF (British
Expeditionary Force); Special
Reserve; Territorial Force
British army, units:
Armies, 1st Army and 2nd Army (from
1915) 451
Corps
I Corps 75
action at Villers-Cotterêts 390–2
delayed before Le Cateau 349, 359,
366, 368–9
Marne 412
to Sambre 353
widening gap with II Corps 353,
380–1, 383
II Corps 75
at Le Cateau 358–9
at Mons 301, 302, 314, 318
move due south 375–7
no telegraph link with GHQ 322,
323n
tiredness, and disorientation 376–9
withdrawal 323–4, 339–40
III Corps 409n
Cavalry Corps, Messines Ridge 423
Divisions
3rd Division
Le Cateau 349, 350, 358, 359, 363,
365
Marne 415
Mons 327, 339–40, 341
4th Division 272
Le Cateau 349, 350 and n, 359, 363,
365
at Solesmes 341
5th Division
Le Cateau 349, 350, 358, 363, 365–6
Mons 314, 327
7th Division 422–3, 431
8th Division 422–3, 431
29th Division, Dardanelles 446
36th (Ulster) Division 444
49th (West Riding) Division 458
Cavalry Division 75, 277, 319
Le Cateau 349, 350, 376n
Mons 328–9, 339
Cavalry Division (2nd) 297n, 423n
Brigades
1st Cavalry, Néry 386–7
1st Guards 383
2nd Cavalry 284, 329–30, 415n
2nd Infantry 339, 383
3rd Cavalry 329, 367, 380–1, 380–1
and n, 423n
3rd Infantry 411
4th Cavalry 389
4th Guards 351–3, 390–1
5th Cavalry 287, 297, 380–1, 412, 423n

6th Infantry 391
7th Infantry 327, 359, 365
8th Infantry 302, 359, 365
9th Infantry 302, 327, 359
10th Infantry 364
11th Infantry 414
12th Infantry 359, 364*n*
13th Infantry 366
14th Infantry 297, 358–9, 366
19th Infantry 274*n*, 295, 319, 339
  Le Cateau 349, 362, 366
Regiments
2nd Dragoon Guards (Queen's Bays),
    Néry 386, 390
2nd Dragoons (Scots Greys) 287
4th Dragoon Guards 284, 329, 415*n*
4th Hussars 340
5th Dragoon Guards, Néry 389
9th Lancers
    at Marne, cavalry charge 409–10 *and n*
    Mons 329
11th Hussars 340
    Néry 386–7, 389
12th Lancers, charge 381
15th Hussars 223
    sounding of 'Cease Fire' (Nov. 1918)
    463
18th Hussars 22, 380
19th Hussars
    Néry 390
    and Royal Welsh Fusiliers 373
20th Hussars 287
60th Rifles 76
Argyll & Sutherland Highlanders, 1st
    Bn 366
Bedfords, 1st Bn 364–5
Border Regiment, 11th Bn (Lonsdales
    Pals) 458–9
Cameronians, 1st 366
Connaught Rangers 444
    2nd Bn 368–9
Dublin Fusiliers, 2nd Bn 377
Duke of Cornwall's Light Infantry, 1st
    Bn 225, 226, 264
    at Mons 297, 303*n*, 327–8
East Lancashires, 12th Bn ('Accrington
    Pals') 456
East Surrey, 1st Bn 297, 363
    Mons 303*n*, 308, 313–14
East Surrey, 8th Bn 455–6
Gordon Highlanders, 1st Bn 225
Irish Guards 263 *and n*
King's Own, 11th ('Bantam') Bn 457
King's Own Royal Lancaster 363–4,
    457
King's Own Scottish Borderers 187
Lancashire Fusiliers 364
Lincolns, 1st Bn, Mons 327
Manchester Regt, 2nd 297, 457
Middlesex Regiment, at Mons 307–8,
    311–13

Oxfordshire and Buckinghamshire
    Light Infantry, 1st Bn 263–4, 407
Oxfordshire and Buckinghamshire
    Light Infantry, 2nd Bn 425
Royal Fusiliers, 4th Bn 273
    mobilization 219–20
    Mons 302, 303–4 *and n*, 311, 312–13,
    315
Royal Fusiliers, 7th Bn 220
Royal Irish Rifles, 2nd Bn 308, 311
Royal Munster Fusiliers, 2nd 383
Royal Scots 311
Royal Warwickshires, 1st Bn 364, 377
Royal Welsh (Welch) Fusiliers 67, 373,
    462–3
Sherwood Foresters 415*n*
South Lancashires, 2nd Bn 327
Suffolk Regt, 2nd, Le Cateau 366 *and n*
Ulster Volunteer Force 443–4
Warwicks, 4th (Spec Res Bn) 220
West Yorkshires 415*n*
Worcesters, 2nd Bn 425
York and Lancaster Regiment, 1st and
    2nd Barnsley Pals 456
Yorkshire Light Infantry 367
Yorkshire Regiment (Green Howards),
    6th (Service) Bn 448
Other formations
Rifle Brigade 76, 122–3 *and n*
Royal Artillery 22, 86–91
    ammunition allocations 90–1
Royal Field Artillery 87, 305
    107 Battery, Mons 308
    109 Battery RFA, Mons 327
    XL (40) Field Brigade, Mons 313
Royal Garrison Artillery 87
Royal Horse Artillery 86–7
    E Battery 287, 381
    I Battery 389, 408
    L Battery 328–9
        Néry 386–8; 'letting down the
        poles' on limbers 386–8 *and n*
Royal Engineers 91–5, 97
    Army Signal Service 94
    and Mons canal bridges 300–1, 305,
    306
    organization 91
    signalling 92–5
    use of explosives 92 *and n*
Tank Corps 450
British Empire, support of 216
British Expeditionary Force *see* BEF
Brodrick, William St John 60–1
Brooke, Gen. Sir Alan 122
Brooke, Rupert 421
Brunton, Sgt David, 19th Hussars 234,
    261, 262, 373, 390 *and n*
    crossing of Marne 396–7 *and n*
    on German atrocities 413 *and n*
    at Marne 408–9, 415
Bryce, Viscount 254*n*

Buchanan, Sir George, ambassador to Russia 203
Bulgaria 45, 171, 174
Buller, Gen. Sir Redvers 49
Bülow, Bernard, Count von 51, 149*n*
Bülow, Generaloberst Karl von, 2nd Army 268, 397
  at Liège 254, 256
  Marne 412–13
  St Quentin 384
  and withdrawal of Lanrezac 325
Burns, John, president of Board of Trade 191, 214

cables, transatlantic 237
  undersea, German 236–7
Cadorna, Count, Italian commander-in-chief 198
Caillaux, Joseph, French prime minister 116
Callwell, Maj.-Gen. Sir Charles 122, 248*n*
Cambon, Jules, French ambassador to Berlin 154
Cambon, Paul, French ambassador in London 124, 195, 210, 211
Cambrai 359
  tanks (Nov. 1917) 461
Campbell, Lt-Col. (Gen. Sir) David 'Soarer', 9th Lancers 409–10
Campbell, Lt John 388
Campbell, Thomas, 'Ye Mariners of England' 141
Cannae, Battle of (216 BC) 101, 104
Cannon, Pte Jim, 2nd Suffolks 297
Cardwell, Edward, army reforms 66*n*, 442
Carr, E. H., *What is History?* (1961) 427 *and n*
Carson, Sir Edward 177, 216
Casteau, cavalry headquarters 284
Castelnau, General Noel de, French 2nd Army 269, 420
  and French war plans 119
Castlereagh, Lord, Congress of Vienna 25
casualties xx
  advance from the Marne 416 *and n*
  before Marne 403 *and n*
  Boer War 51
  British: total 463; Western Front 417*n*
  burials 389–90 *and n*, 409
  First Battle of Ypres 426
  first British (crew of HMS *Amphion*) 236
  first days 209, 220–1
  first RFC 237
  French, advance from the Marne 416*n*
  Gallipoli 448 *and n*
  German: before Marne 404; at Mons 319; Néry 389
  Le Cateau 376*n*, 381 *and n*, 382*n*, 385
  Mons 318, 319, 330, 334

Pas de Calais spring offensive (1915) 451–2
Somme 450 *and n*, 458
cavalry
  age and experience 82–3
  capture of aeroplane 95–6
  function of 74–5*n*
  mounted infantry/*arme blanche* debate 83–5
  protective role 366 *and n*, 409
  reconnaissance role 97
  and trench warfare 451
  war establishment 83*n*
Cavell, Nurse Edith 330*n*
Cecil, Lord Hugh 217
Cecil, Lt George 391 *and n*
Chamberlain, Neville 4*n*
Charleroi 288
Charlton, Capt. (Air Commodore) Lionel, RFC 365–6
Charteris, Brig.-Gen. John 232*n*, 291*n*, 352–3, 402
Château-Thierry, Marne 411–12
Chavonne 415
Cherbourg 28
Chetwode, Brig.-Gen. Sir Philip, 5th (Independent) Cavalry Brigade 83, 287, 297, 380–1, 412
Childers, Erskine
  army reforms 66*n*, 442
  on role of cavalry 83, 84
China
  Boxer Rebellion 55
  Second Opium War 27
Christian IX, king of Denmark 34
Churchill, Winston
  assumption about Entente Cordiale 165
  in Boer War 2*n*, 50
  command of Royal Scots Fusiliers 449 *and n*
  and Dardanelles 445–9
  enthusiasm for aircraft 95–6
  first lord of the admiralty xviii *and n*, 2–3, 164
  on French chance of victory in France 428–9
  on Jellicoe 439
  on Lloyd George's memoirs 18*n*
  and mobilization of fleet 4, 187, 188, 204, 213
  and naval blockade 207–8, 430 *and n*
  offer to assist Belgian army in Antwerp 422*n*
  on political influence on war 437–8
  and proposal for deployment of BEF 13, 15, 430–1
  and secret meeting of CID (Aug. 1911) 155, 157–8, 164
  and securing of Channel ports 421, 422*n*

and strategy xxi, 15, 147; role of BEF, *what if . . .?* 429–31; suggestion of 'naval war' 211
and tanks 449–50
and war council (5 Aug.) 8, 11, 13, 15, 166
City of London, stock market 196
civilians, at Mons 303
Clark, Alan, *The Donkeys* 101 *and n*, 298 *and n*
Clark, US Gen. Wesley 347*n*
Clarke, Col. Sir George, on War Office (Reconstruction) Committee 53
Clarke, Pte Joe 412
Clausewitz, Carl von 100
'fog of war' 343, 345
on plans 101, 110*n*
on policy and planning 438*n*
Clemenceau, Georges, prime minister of France 100
Clive, Maj. Sidney, BEF liaison officer 235*n*, 399
Coleman, Frederic, driver 410
Colenso, Battle of (1899) 49, 89
Collingwood, Vice Admiral Cuthbert, Lord 142
combat arms, defined 74*n*
combat service support, defined 74*n*
Committee of Imperial Defence (CID) establishment (1904) 130 *and n*
relations with Cabinet 438*n*
secret meeting (Aug. 1911) 155–63
secret memorandum ('Report on the Opening of the War') 218
Commonwealth War Graves Commission 390*n*, 391*n*, 463–4
communications 39
audio radio 94*n*
Boer War 49–50
carrier pigeons 95*n*
despatch riders, and gallopers 93, 346
field telephones 93
heliograph 50, 92
Royal Flying Corps 96
semaphore 50, 92
telephone landlines 94; interception of German radio 95
timings of messages about mobilization 192*n*, 199–203
waggon wireless stations 94
see also telegraph
Compiègne, BEF GHQ move to 381
'Concert of Europe' 24–5
and cooperation with France 29
Congo 154*n*
Congress of Berlin (1878) 44–5
'Congress System' (of Europe) 24 *and n*
Congreve, Col. Walter 77
Congreve, W. (Billy), VC 77*n*
Conneau, General Louis, new French cavalry corps 395, 413

Conrad von Hötzendorf, Franz, Freiherr, Austrian war minister 172, 188, 194
conscription
British introduction (Jan. 1916) 426, 459
French army 38 *and n*, 113
Prussian army 38 *and n*
Corbett-Smith, Capt. Arthur 226
cordite 92 *and n*
Corry, Col. Noel 391, 392*n*
Corunna, Battle of (1809) 228*n*
Corunna, retreat to (1809) 377*n*, 396
Craufurd, Maj.-Gen. 'Black Bob' 377*n*
Crécy, battle of (1346) 355–6
Crimean War 24, 27 *and n*, 347
Crna Ruka ('Black Hand'), Serb nationalists 179
crops, damage to 285 *and n*
Crowe, Eyre 131 *and n*
Cumming, Capt. Mansfield, RN, Secret Service Bureau 175, 208
Curragh Mutiny (1914) 8, 177 *and n*, 291*n*
cyclist companies 84

Daily Mirror, on declaration of war 218
Daily Telegraph, Kaiser's article in 148–9 *and n*
d'Amade, Gen., French Territorial divisions 340, 432
Cambrai 359
and meeting at GHQ 369, 371
Mons 302
Dardanelles campaign 437, 445–9
de Gaulle, Lt (Gen.) Charles 246
De Lisle, Brig.-Gen. Henry De Beauvoir, 2nd Cavalry Bde 83, 284–5 *and n*, 329–30, 415*n*
Dease, Lt Maurice, VC
background and career 221–2
death 310
and horse procurement 222–3
machine gun section at Mons 304–5, 309–10
and mobilization 219–23
declarations of war
Austrian 12, 187–8
British 217–18
German 1, 5*n*, 198–9, 201
problems of chronology 3–6, 192–204
DeLancey, Col. Sir William, Wellington's chief of staff 357
Denmark 35*n*
declaration of neutrality 204
possibility of war with Germany, *what if . . .?* 436–7
and Schleswig-Holstein question 32–4
Derby, earl of, and Liverpool 'Pals' battalions 441
deserters, execution of 390*n*
Dickson, Bertram 95

Dimitrijević, Col. Dragutin, Crna Ruka
179
Directorate of Military Operations 150n
Disraeli, Benjamin (earl of Beaconsfield),
'splendid isolation' 29
d'Oissel, Hély, Lanrezac's chief of staff
247, 366n
Domptin, near Marne 411–12
Donop, Maj.-Gen. Stanley von,
Master-General of the Ordnance, at
war council (5 Aug.) 9n
Doran, Brig. Beauchamp 308, 312–13,
315
d'Orléans, Prince Henri 378
Dorrell, Battery Sgt Maj. George 388
Douglas, Gen. Sir Charles, CIGS 15, 196
at war council (5 Aug.) 10, 15
Dour, village near Mons 328
Downing Street, No. 10, electricity in 1
Dray, Cpl Fred 79n
Dreadnought, HMS 144
Dreyfus, Capt. Alfred 112 and n
Dual Alliance (Austro-German) 45, 106
Dual Alliance (Franco-Russian) 59
Dublin 187
Dupont, Col. Charles-Édouard 175
Dykes, Lt-Col. Alfred 364
dynamite 92

Easton, Cpl Harry 329
Edmonds, Col. James, 4th Div chief of
staff 291, 309n, 345–6, 381 and n
Edward VII, King
accession 46
and Entente Cordiale 59–60
marriage 33n
Elgar, Sir Edward 223
Elgin, Victor Bruce, 9th Earl of 53n
Elgin Commission 53–4
Elkington, Lt-Col. John 377 and n
Ellison, Pte George, last British casualty
463–4
Elouges 328
Emmich, General Otto von, X Corps
255–6 and n
'Ems Telegram' 40–1
English Channel
plans for troop movement across 15n
ports 420, 421, 422n
'Entente Cordiale', early use of term 26
Entente Cordiale (1904)
discrepant assumptions about 165–7
and Grey's 'great question' 129–30
and n, 150
implications of 55–6, 57, 58, 59–60
equipment
cavalry 85
web (webbing) 79 and n
Esher, Reginald Brett, 2nd Viscount 53
and n
Esher Committee, and staff system 75

Esterhazy, Maj. Ferdinand 112n
Estrées, rallying point 378
Eugénie, Empress, exile 42
Eulenburg, Count Philipp zu 45
Europe
American view of war in 188
British view of xx, xxi, 58, 60, 140–2
'Congress System' 24 and n
Evans, Capt. Henry 340
Ewart, Gen. Spencer 128–9
Expeditionary Force (EF)
liability for service overseas 68
see also BEF (British Expeditionary
Force)
explosives 92 and n
detonators 305–6

Falkenhayn, Gen. Erich von, German
war minister 182, 188, 416
and Channel ports 420
dispositions after Marne 420, 433,
435
and mobilization 195
farriers, demands on, at mobilization
222n
Fashoda Incident (1898) 59 and n
fate xviii–xix, 417
Feldmann, Lieutenant 201
Fergusson, Maj.-Gen. Sir Charles, GOC
5th Div
as acting commander of II Corps 267,
274, 314
Le Cateau 349, 359, 366, 367
Fergusson, Sir James, MP 73
Ferry, Abel, French under-secretary for
foreign affairs 197
Fez, Treaty of (1911) 154n
Field Artillery Training, manual (1914)
89–90
on 'Wood and Village Fighting' 305
Field Service Pocketbook (1914)
on explosives 92, 306
on marching 259
Field Service Regulations
and air reconnaissance 277
on assumption of offensive 402
on daily 'states' 381n
on determination 374, 408
ground dumping of ammunition and
rations 379
on information 274, 275
on latitude for subordinates 347, 348,
392 and n
on machine guns 78n
on mobilization 4n
orders for retreat 290
on passive occupation of position 355,
362 and n
on role of C-in-C 232–3n, 235
on use of railways 428n
fieldcraft 49, 76

firepower (tactics), and manoeuvre 55
Fisher, Admiral of the Fleet Lord ('Jacky')
    9, 53, 144, 164*n*
FitzClarence, Brig. Charles, VC 425
FitzGerald, Lt-Col. Brinsley 242
Fitzpatrick, QM Sgt Thomas 313
Flanders 420
    devastation of countryside 285 *and n*,
        405
flanks 42, 312
    BEF on French left 207, 242–3 *and n*,
        244–5, 250, 280–1, 421–2
    BEF's threat to German 259–60*n*,
        268–9*n*, 369, 371, 428
    French threat to German 168, 268–9
        and n, 293, 428
    German threat to BEF's 297–8, 300*n*,
        301–2
    German threat to French 247, 293–4,
        321, 324–5, 428–9
    importance to Schlieffen Plan 104,
        108, 111, 255–6, 397, 408, 417,
        420–1
    Sir John French's concern for 395,
        412
    vulnerability of German (at Aisne)
        417, 420–1, 432–3
Foch, Gen. Ferdinand, French 9th Army
    405
    advance towards Vimy 421
    expectation of German strength 158
    at Marne (on allied right wing) 408
    and overall command for Hundred
        Days 462
    and Plan XVII 116
    and Wilson 127–8
'fog of war', and decision on Le Cateau
    342–3, 345
Forester, C. S., *The General* 221
Forestier-Walker, Brig.-Gen. George, chief
    of staff to Smith-Dorrien 323 *and n*,
    349
Forêt de Mormal 351
    I Corps and 338, 368
Fortescue, Sir John, on French 282*n*
four-power conference, proposed by Grey
    (July 1914) 187, 194
Fowke, Capt. Francis, Prince Consort's
    Library 169*n*
Frameries (Mons), German penetration of
    line at 316
France
    1830 revolution 25
    and Agadir Crisis 151–2
    and Alsace-Lorraine 43
    and Bismarck 37–8
    border fortresses 107
    and British cabinet decision (29 July)
        190–1, 195
    British military cooperation with 55–6,
        58, 164–5

British relations with (from 1830s) 13,
        26–9, 151–2
    expectation of invasion of Germany
        430
    German demand for neutrality 197
    knowledge of Schlieffen Plan 117 *and n*
    military reputation 37–8
    population 111–12 *and n*
    railways 13 *and n*, 109, 157 *and n*, 428
        and n, 432
    Royal Naval protection for 207–8, 210,
        213
    and Russia 56, 58, 113, 118
    Second Empire 38, 39–40
    see also Entente Cordiale; French army;
        French army, units
Franchet d'Espèrey, Lt-Gen. Louis
    and 5th Army at Marne 406, 408,
        412–13
    and French I Corps 384, 405
    to replace Lanrezac 397 *and n*
Franco-Prussian War (1870–1) 16, 40–3,
    48
    peace treaty (1871) 43
Franz Ferdinand, Archduke xvii
Franz Joseph, Emperor, and Dual
    Monarchy of Austria-Hungary 37
Frederick, king of Prussia 45
Frederick VII, king of Denmark 32
French army xx, 37–8, 431, 432
    artillery 90, 115*n*
    attacks after Marne 420–1
    campaign plan (flawed) 15
    conscription 38 *and n*, 113
    and Dardanelles campaign 446, 448*n*
    Garde Nationale Mobile (reserves) 38
    GQG optimism 242–3, 244–5, 268–9
    mobilization 13, 193–4
    need for replacements, before Marne
        406
    officers 38
    Plan XVI 114–15
    Plan XVII 115–20, 268
    Plan XVII(b) 116 *and n*, 118
    poor military intelligence 246 *and n*
    strength 112, 404–5
    superiority of German over 156, 162
    and unified command (1918) 461–2
    and withdrawal of British I Corps 339
French army, units:
Armies
    5th Army (Lanrezac) 244–5, 369,
        384–5, 397; withdrawal 290–5,
        320–1, 339
    6th Army (Manoury) 369, 383, 395,
        408, 412–13
    9th Army (Foch) 405, 408, 421
Corps
    Cavalry Corps (Sordet) 246, 269, 280,
        332, 380
    I Corps (Franchet d'Esperey) 384, 405

French army, units (*cont.*)
Divisions
2nd Division 339
53rd (Reserve) Division 339
69th Division 339
Territorial Division (d'Amade) 302, 340, 359, 432
French, FM Sir John 7, 10*n*, 166, 233
arrival in France 235–6, 237
character 229, 230, 321; lack of political aptitude 393–4; strategic ability 242, 294*n*
and French assessment of German strength 269
and Haig 229–30, 383–4
and II Corps 332, 381–2
intention to retire beyond Seine 383, 384–5
and Joffre 242–3 *and n*, 369–71; Joffre's plea for BEF cooperation 398–400
Kitchener and 229–30, 249–50, 393–5, 445
lack of military intelligence 267
and Landrecies 353–4*n*
and Lanrezac 244–8, 288–9; reaction to withdrawal 290, 291–4, 295*n*, 320–1, 324–5
later reputation 282 *and n*
Le Cateau 369–71, 381–2, 381 *and n*
and Marne: order to dig in 415–16; orders before 407; use of cavalry 409
and Mons 301, 331; and I Corps at Mons 332–3; intentions at Mons 297–302; message to all troops 272–3; return to Bavai 314–15
and need for heavy artillery 416 *and n*
offensive along Menin Road 423, 425
and Poincaré 237, 240, **241**
pre-war planning: misgivings about BEF mission 17, 233–4; plan for deployment of BEF 12–13, 15; and secret meeting of CID (Aug. 1911) 155; at war council (5 Aug.) 10, 12–13, 17 *and n*
and 'Race to the Sea' 421–3
recalled (Dec. 1915) 427*n*
and role of cavalry 84, 409
and Smith-Dorrien 281–2, 298 *and n*, 321, 331, 344–5, 356
and Smith-Dorrien's need to retreat 316, 317, 318
and Smith-Dorrien's request to fight at Le Cateau 342, 347–9, 350, 356
and withdrawal towards Maubeuge 322–4
French navy 147 *and n*
modernization 27 *and n*
Fuller, Capt. J. F. C. 'Boney' 230*n*
Fuller, LCpl William, VC 414
Fussell, Paul 457

Galbert, Capt. de 399
Gallieni, Gen. Joseph, military governor of Paris 114, 395
Gallipoli campaign 446–9, 454*n*
effect of failure of 448–9
Gambetta, Léon 59
Garnier, General Otto von, 4th Cavalry Division 389*n*
Gastein Convention (1866) 36
gelignite 92
general headquarters (GHQ)
establishment and responsibilities 74–5
see also BEF
George V, King
and British neutrality 202
and Kaiser 154*n*
and Prince Heinrich 172, 181
and Tsar 199
German air force (*Fliegertruppen*) 312 *and n*, 408
German army
at 2 Aug. (positions) **238–9**
apparent slowness of advance 245–6
artillery 88, 96–7
atrocities 413 *and n*
battle of the Marne: comparative strength before 404–5; digging in above Aisne 414, 415–16; logistical problems 403–4; reaction to counter-offensive 407–8, 420; retreat 413
and BEF withdrawal 340, 381; fatigue and drunkenness 340, 396; misinterpretation of 376
crossing of Meuse (15 Aug.) 246
invasion of Belgium 1
Kaiserschlacht spring offensive (1918) 461
mobilization 251–2
at Mons 313, 337; attack on BEF II Corps 302 *and n*; penetration of II Corps line at Mons–Condé canal 316–17
Mons salient 306, 307–8, 311–12
offensive at Ypres 425–6
possibility of turning Lanrezac's flank, *what if . . .?* 428–9
railway section (*Eisenbahnabteilung*) 105
reservists 109
strength 5, 112, 404–5, 404*n*
superiority over French 156, 162
view of soldiers of BEF 98
view of Territorials and conscripts 98
vulnerability of flank at Aisne 432–3
see also Schlieffen Plan
German army, units:
Armies
1st Army: checked by II Corps 375–6; move south and west 376, 396; strength 244*n*, 404–5; to halt BEF withdrawal 337

2nd Army (Bülow) 254, 384, 404,
412–13
3rd (Saxon) Army 268, 405
Corps
II Cavalry Corps 245n, 340–1 *and n*
III Corps 303, 327, 337
IV Corps, Le Cateau 363
IX Corps 306, 311–12, 313, 337
X Corps, St Quentin 384
Divisions
6th Division, Brandenburgers, Mons
327
7th Division 363
9th Cavalry Division 285–6
16th Infanterie-Division, Luxembourg
201
17th Division, Mons salient 311
18th Division, Mons salient 306, 311
Prussian Guards Cavalry Division 381
Brigades
3rd Cavalry Bde 389
17th Cavalry Bde, Néry 389
Prussian Guards, 1st and 4th Bdes
425–6
Regiments
1st Garde-Dragoner-Regiments 409n
3rd Hussars 303
12th Brandenburgers, Mons 318
31st (Thuringian) Infantry Regt 302n
75th Bremen Regiment, Mons 313
85th (Holstein) Regiment 306
86th (Schleswig-Holstein) Regiment
306
Infanterie-Regiment Nr. 27 351–3
Prussian Lancers 409–10 *and n*
Rheinisches Infanterie-Regiment
Nr. 69, Luxembourg 201
uhlan cavalry regiments 285 *and n*
German Confederation (from 1848) 32,
36
German navy
battleships 144 *and n*
building of 143–4, **145**, 146–8
'Dreadnought Race' **145**, 146
Nassau class battleships 146 *and n*
not ready for war 173n
Wittelsbach class 144n
German war council (Dec. 1912),
inevitability of war 173n
Germany
ability to fight 437
and Agadir Crisis 150–4
Army Bill (1913) 180
and Austria 170n, 183
Bismarck's plans for 29, **30–1**
declaration of *Kriegsgefahrzustand* 196
and n
declarations of war: on Britain 3–6; on
France 1; on Russia 5n
empire 143
intentions towards Belgium 15–16, 255

intentions for war with Russia 182
militarism 44 *and n*, 44n, **253**
as military state 250–4, 251n
mobilization timetable 180
perception of hostility of Britain 148–9
population 111–12 *and n*
Reich Constitution (1871) 44
restrictions on reporting by
non-Prussian kingdoms 181 *and n*
unification 37, 43
view of Boer War 51
view of Entente Cordiale 56, **57**, 58, 60
Gheluvelt, Ypres–Menin gap 425
Giesl von Gieslingen, Freiherr Wladimir,
Austrian ambassador to Belgrade
184
Giffard, Lt Jack 388
Gladstone, W. E. 29, 39, 43
Glasgow, 'Pals' battalions 441
Gleichen, Count 'Glick', 15th Brigade
300n, 330–1
Godley, Pte Sidney, VC 310
Goltz, Generaloberst Colmar von der,
reprisals against Belgian *francs tireurs*
254 *and n*
Gooch, Prof. John, *The Plans of War* 158
and n
Gort, Lord, VC 394n
Goschen, Sir Edward, ambassador to
Germany 3, 18–21
return from Berlin 21
Gough, Brig.-Gen. Hubert, 3rd Cavalry
Bde 83, 177n, 329, 367, 380–1 *and n*
on Allenby 381 *and n*
Gough, Brig.-Gen. Johnnie, Haig's chief
of staff 322, 323
Graham, Col. James 100
Graphic, The **241**
Graves, Robert 20, 254
'An Old Twenty-Third Man' 462–3
and Officers' Training Corps, *Goodbye
to All That* 64
at Somme 456–7
Great Britain
avoidance of war on mainland Europe
58, 60, 140–2
declaration of war on Germany 217–18
and global reputation 199 *and n*, 215
perception of hostility towards
Germany 148–9
possibility of neutrality 194–5, 200,
202
'splendid isolation' 29, 58
and support for France 195, 199–200
view of Balkan wars 174–6
Great War
'Cease Fire' 463
expectation of length 16–17, 272
first days 235–58
what might have been, *what if?* . . .
426–39, **434**

Greece 171, 174
Greenwich Mean Time 157n, 285n
Grenfell, Capt. Francis, 9th Lancers 330 and n
Grey, Sir Edward, foreign secretary xvii–xviii, 2, 124, 210n
  and Agadir Crisis 152, 153
  on Austrian ultimatum to Serbia 183n
  and Belgian neutrality 189–90, 206
  and cabinet meeting(s) 2 Aug. 209–10, 214; decision for war and support for France 204–5; speech on decision for war 215–16
  and Cambon 210–11
  on 'Colonel' House 176, 178n
  'great question' 129–30, 150, 191
  and intercepted German telegram 19
  'lamps' remark 217
  and Lichnowsky 200, 202 and n, 211, 213
  proposal of four-power conference (July 1914) 187, 194
  secret meeting of CID (Aug. 1911) 157
  and war council (5 Aug.) 8
Grierson, Lt-Gen. James 7n, 125, 316
  and 1912 manoeuvres 231–2
  on Belgian army 125–6
  death 232, 249
Groener, General Wilhelm, head of railway section 105
guncotton 92
gunpowder 92
The Guns of August (1962) xix and n

Haig, Lady (Doreen, 'Doris') 231
Haig, Lt-Gen. Sir Douglas, I Corps 169, 230–1, 274
  and 1st Army (from 1915) 451
  on 3 Div at Marne 415 and n
  appreciation of scale of war 272n
  before Le Cateau 349, 351
  on casualties on the Somme 458
  and declaration of war 5
  engagement at Villers-Cotterêts 390–2
  on error of march to Mons 427–8
  Landrecies 351–3, 353–4n
  and later strategy 451–2
  at Marne 412, 413
  at Mons 298, 301, 318–19
  and Mormal forest 338, 368
  order for withdrawal to Guise 351
  pre-war planning: and alternative strategies xxi, 16; misgivings about BEF mission 16, 233–4; proposal for deployment of BEF 13, 15–16
  and reserve forces 69
  and Sir John French 7, 229–30
  and Somme offensive 453–4
  and tanks 460
  and unified command with French (1918) 462

widening gap with II Corps 380–1, 383
and withdrawal of French 5th Army 293
Haking, Brig., 5th Infantry Brigade 317
Haldane, Richard Burdon, Viscount, lord chancellor 2, 166
  and decision for war 205
  on mechanization 138
  and Norfolk Commission reforms 61–2, 64–70
  and purpose of army 55 and n, 60–1 and n, 69–70
  and reserves 64–5, 69–70
  and secret meeting of CID (Aug. 1911) 155
  as secretary of war 55
  and supply of horses 133
  visit to Berlin (1912) 178n
  and war council (5 Aug.) 8
  and Wilson 135, 162–3
Hamilton, Gen. Sir Ian
  Dardanelles 445–7
  at war council (5 Aug.) 8
Hamilton, Maj.-Gen. Hubert, GOC 3rd Div 317
  and Le Cateau 345–7n, 346
Hamley, Lt-Gen. Sir Edward, The Operations of War (1867) 325
Hankey, Lt-Col. Maurice 11n, 131n
  and declaration of 'precautionary period' 192 and n
Hankey, Maj. Edward 425
Hannibal, and Cannae 104
Harcourt, Lewis, at cabinet meeting 2 Aug. 205
Harding-Newman, Capt. John 5
'hasty defence' 275 and n
Hausen, General Max von, 3rd (Saxon) Army 268, 405
Havilland, Geoffrey de 96n
Heath, Charles 134–5
Heeringen, Josias von, Prussian war minister 437n
Heinrich, Prince 200
  and George V 172, 181
Heligoland 144 and n
Henderson, Brig.-Gen. Sir David 276n, 287, 414
Henderson, Sir Neville, British ambassador in Berlin (1939) 4n
Herwig, Prof. Holger 106, 173n
Heyliss, Pte Thomas 47–8, 49
Hildebrand, Maj. A. B. R., RE 343
Hindenburg, Gen. Paul von, 8th Army 420
History of the Great War (Official History) xx, 71
  on Le Cateau 355–6
  on maps 357
  on Mons battlefield 296

Hohenzollern-Sigmaringen, Prince
Leopold of 40
Holbrook, Cpl, 4th Fusiliers 307
Hollebeke, Messines Ridge 425
Hollman, Admiral von 143
Holmes, Pte (Capt.) Frederick, VC 367*n*
Holmes, Richard 350
Holt, Lt Wilfred, RE 306
Home, Lt-Col. Archibald 'Sally', Cavalry
Division 280, 297, 345
Mons 328–9, 336
Hopkins, Gerard Manley, 'The Wreck of
the *Deutschland*' 40*n*
Horlock, Bombadier Ernest, VC 414
Hornby, Capt. Charles 285, 286
Horne, Brig 413*n*
horses 97
census of 133, 135
fodder 380
heavy draught 136, 223
horseshoes 222*n*, 407*n*
impressment 136–7
mounted infantry 84 *and n*
procurement at mobilization 222–4
Wilson and supply of 132–8
House, 'Col.' Edward, US special envoy
176–8 *and n*
overtures to Kaiser 178*n*
Housman, A. E., 'Epitaph on an Army of
Mercenaries' xxi–xxii
Howard, Prof. Sir Michael 158–9
Howell, Maj. Philip 16, 169
Hoyos, Count Alexander 183
Huguet, Col. Victor, Joffre's head of
mission to BEF 125, 235 *and n*, 293
report of loss of battle of Le Cateau
373
Wilson and 126–7, 167
Hull, Lt-Col. (Maj.-Gen. Sir) Charles, at
Mons 311 *and n*
'Hundred Days' counter-offensive (1918)
461–2
Hungary 37 *and n*
Hunter-Weston, Brig. Aylmer 414, 449
Dardanelles 446
Huy, crossing of Meuse at 247–8
Hyon, near Mons 313

Imperial War Graves Commission *see*
Commonwealth War Graves
Commission
Indian Army 431
casualties in Gallipoli 448*n*
Indian Cavalry Corps 423
Indian Corps 423, **424**, 425
infantry 75–6
marching on foot 97
marksmanship 77–8
platoon system 80–1 *and n*
reorganization of battalion structure
80–1

Infantry Training (manual) 220 *and n*
on counter-attack 336, 348
on defensive position 296, 357
on machine guns 304–5, 310
Ingles, Maj. 415*n*
intelligence, military
contribution of air reconnaissance
276–7
failings of 274–7, 280, 283–5, 287–8,
293–4
French problems 246 *and n*
German problems 260, 275–6, 284
on position of Belgian army 267–8
Ireland
Easter Rising (1916) 437
Kitchener formations from 444
resistance to home rule (1914) 177,
189, 216
Special Reserve 69–70*n*; North Irish
Horse 69–70*n*; South Irish Horse
70*n*, 353
Irish Amending (Home Rule) Bill,
adjourned 195–6
Isle of Wight, at mobilization 219
'Italia Irredenta' 35
Italian navy 147
Italian pilots, in 'Hundred Days'
offensive (1918) 461
Italy
and Austria–Serbia tension 186
declaration of neutrality 12*n*, 198
and n, 204, 431
at declaration of war 12
mobilization of fleet 196
war with Austria-Hungary (May 1915)
436

Jack, Pte Robert 307
Jackson, Lt-Gen. Sir Mike 347*n*
Jagow, Gottlieb von, German foreign
minister
and Austria 184
and demand for French neutrality 197
letter to British ambassador 3, 19–21
and Russian mobilization 193
Jane's Fighting Ships (1906 and 1914)
147–8
Japan
declaration of war on Germany (23
Aug.) 59*n*
Grey's request for support 213
Jarvis, LCpl Charles, VC 312 *and n*
Jaurès, Jean, French socialist leader,
assassination 197 *and n*
Jellicoe, Admiral Sir John 439
Jillings, Sgt-Maj. David, RFC 284
Joffre, Gen. Joseph 162, 406
assessment of German strategy (15
Aug.) 245–6
assessment of strength of German
forces 268–9 *and n*

Joffre, Gen. Joseph (*cont.*)
  and Belgian resistance 255–6
  and creation of 6th Army 324, 369,
    383
  demand for mobilization 198
  imminence of war 184, 198
  Instruction Générale No. 2 369, 370
  Instruction Particulière (18 Aug.) 269,
    276–7
  Instruction Particulière No. 10 (15 Aug.)
    246
  and Lanrezac 384; dismissal 397–8;
    and Lanrezac's withdrawal 293–4,
    321, 325; order to counter-attack
    at Le Cateau 374–5
  and Le Cateau, meeting with French
    369–71
  and Marne: after Marne 420–1;
    decision to counter-attack 395–6,
    397, 433; need for replacements
    before Marne 406; plea for BEF
    co-operation for counter-attack
    398–400
  and Maud'huy 421
  new cavalry corps 395
  and Plan XVII 114–20
  and report of loss of battle of Le
    Cateau 374
  and Somme offensive 454
  support for Belgian neutrality 184
  threat to left flank 247, 293, 324
  and visit of Kitchener to Paris 393,
    394
Johns, W. E., RFC 338
Johnston, Capt. (Brig.-Gen.) Alexander
    264, 343–4, 376
  Le Cateau 365, 372–3
Johnston, Capt. William, VC 414
Jones, Pte David, *In Parenthesis* (1937)
    460
Joubert de la Ferté, Capt. Philip, 3 Sqn
    RFC *and n* 266–7
July crisis xviii–xix

Kennedy, John F., US President xix *and n*
Kennedy Shaw, Capt. F. S. 136
Kesselring, FM Albert 106*n*
Khan, Sepoy Khudadad, VC 425
Kiderlen-Wächter, Alfred von, German
    foreign minister 154
Kiel Canal 33, 144*n*, 181, 437*n*
Kilitbahir, Dardanelles 446
Kipling, Rudyard
  'Arithmetic on the Frontier' 48
  'Boots' 76*n*
  history of Irish Guards 352
  'Mounted Infantry of the Line' 84*n*
  'Private Ortheris's Song' 48–9
  'The Lesson' 53
  'Two Kopjes' 47 *and n*, 52
Kiszely, Lt-Gen. Sir John 110

Kitchener, FM Lord
  appeal for volunteers (poster) 272, 441
  appreciation of German strength 269
    and n, 272 *and n*
  Boer War 51
  and flaws of Wilson's appreciation
    281–2
  to France for meeting with French
    385–6, 393
  'Instructions for General Officer
    Commanding the Expeditionary
    Force proceeding to France' 228
  on likelihood of long war 272
  meeting with Asquith 199
  message to BEF troops 261–2
  misgivings about BEF mission 228,
    233–4
  'New Armies' 426, 443–5, 450–1
  and 'Race to the Sea' 421
  relations with Sir John French 229–30,
    249–50, 393–5
  and Smith-Dorrien 232, 281–2 *and n*,
    440
  strategic thinking 16, 227–9, 445
  and use of reserves 69, 440–1
  and war council (5 Aug.) 8 *and n*
Kluck, General Alexander von, German
    1st Army 243
  advance across south Brabant 259 *and n*
  attacks at Mons 303, 327, 339
  and BEF withdrawal from Mons 337,
    339
  counter-attack against French 6th
    Army 412
  danger of BEF to flank, **what if . . .?**
    428
  disengagement at Marne 413–14
  envelopment move 287, 325, 397
  logistical problems before Marne 403–4
  move south and west 376, 396
Knox, Mr, farmer 136
Königen Luise, mine-layer 236
Kosovo 347*n*
Kronstadt, visit of French fleet (1891) 58
Kruger, Paul, president of Transvaal 48,
    76
Krupp von Bohlen und Halbach, Bertha
    256*n*

Ladysmith, siege of 49
Landon, Brig.-Gen. Frederick 65
Landrecies, engagement at 351–3, 353–4*n*
Langle de Cary, Gen. Fernand de, French
    4th Army 268–9
Lanrezac, General Charles, GOC French
    5th Army
  attack towards St Quentin (29 Aug.)
    384–5
  decision to withdraw 290–5, 321 *and n*;
    French's reaction 321–2
  dismissal 397–8

and French 244–8, 288–9, 369–71
German attempt to envelop 397
German threat to flank, *what if . . .?*
    428–9
and Haig's I Corps withdrawal 351–2,
    383–4
and Joffre 245
and Le Cateau 369–71, 374
Lansdowne, marquess of, former
    secretary for war 18*n*
Le Cateau
    BEF withdrawal to 335, 349–50 *and n*
    French's GHQ 282–3, 284, 290
    Roman road from Bavai 337
Le Cateau, Battle of (26 Aug.) 355–73
    choice of position 356–8
    controversy over decision to fight
        336–56, 350–1 *and n*
    dispositions 359, **360–1**, 362
    lapse in field discipline 358, 363–4
    units in wrong place 358
Le Montcel (Moncel), cavalry charge
    409–10
Le Quesnoy, action at 339, 340
Leman, Gen. Gérard, commander of
    Liège 256 *and n*
Leo XIII, Pope 40*n*
Leuckhart, Lt-Gen. Freiherr von 181*n*
Lewin, Ronald 438
Lewis, Lt Donald, RFC 368
'Liberal imperialists' 131 *and n*
    at Nov. 1911 cabinet meeting 167–8
Liberal Party, opposition to intervention
    in support of Belgium 212*n*
Libya, Italy and 171
Lichnowsky, Karl Max Fürst von, German
    ambassador in London 6 *and n*, 172,
    211
    Grey and 200 *and n*, 202 *and n*, 211,
        213
    and Kaiser 181, 181*n*, 183*n*
    return to Berlin 20
    telegram from German foreign
        minister 217
Liddell Hart, Basil 77, 106 *and n*, 107
    on Schlieffen Plan 108, 109
Liège, fortress 108, 111, 192, 284–5
    fall of 258
    resistance to German assault 240,
        254–5, 256
Ligny, battle of (1815) 105
Liverpool, 'Pals' battalions 441
Lloyd George, David, chancellor of the
    exchequer 2, 152–3
    at cabinet meeting (2 Aug.) 206–7, 214
    and ministry of munitions 452
    on political dereliction at war council
        17–18, 18*n*
    as prime minister xxii*n*, 460
    and secret meeting of CID (Aug. 1911)
        154 *and n*

Lochow, Ewald von, III Corps 327
Lomax, Maj.-Gen. Sam, 1st Div 353
London, Treaty of (1839) 12*n*, 26*n*, 37,
    189–90, 206
London, Treaty of (1851) 33
London, Treaty of (1867), and neutrality
    of Luxembourg 201
London General Omnibus Company
    137–8
Longman, Lt Frederick, 4th Fusiliers
    265–6
Lonsdale, earl of 458
Loos, Battle of (1915) 448
Louis of Battenberg, Prince, first sea lord
    9 *and n*, 161
Louis Philippe, king of France 25, 26–7
Louise, Princess 20
Louvain, Catholic University 285*n*
Lucan, Lord 347
Ludendorff, Gen., and *Kaiserschlacht*
    spring offensive (1918) 461
Luxembourg 201, 212
    German seizure of railways 201–2
Lyttelton, Maj.-Gen. Neville 49, 123

Maastricht corridor 12, 108, 113
MacDonald, Ramsay, on decision for war
    216–17
Macdonogh, Col. (Brig.-Gen.) George,
    BEF head of intelligence 235, 291
    and n, 292, 316, 397
Macedonia 171
machine guns
    allocation 85, 96
    cavalry view of 221
    superiority of 77
    Vickers, rate of fire 88
McIlwain, Sgt John 368–9, 444, 447
MacInnes, Col. David 378
McKenna, Reginald, home secretary 3,
    429
    and secret meeting of CID (Aug. 1911)
        154, 162
McMahon, Lt-Col. Norman 77–8, 273
    mobilization 219–20
    at Mons 304, 309
MacMunn, Lt-Col. G. F. (Lt-Gen. Sir
    George) 137 *and n*
Macnaghten, Hugh, poem to Belgium
    257*n*
Macrae, Capt. John 405 *and n*
Macready, Sir Neville, BEF
    adjutant-general 394
Mahan, Capt. Alfred Thayer, naval
    theorist 142–3
Mainwaring, Lt-Col. Arthur 377 *and n*
Mallet, Louis 55
Malone, Capt. Edmund 220–1
Malplaquet, battle of (1709), battlefield
    303
Maltby, Bill, Wolds Wagoner 224–5 *and n*

Manchester Guardian, support for
neutrality 195
manoeuvres 55, 76
1912 training 231–2 *and n*
Manoury, General Michel-Joseph, 6th
Army 369, 383, 395, 404
at Marne (on allied left wing) 408,
412–13
Mapplebeck, Lt Gilbert, 4 Sqn RFC 266
maps
of France 358
French uncontoured 357 *and n*
march discipline 259, 264–5
Marchand, Maj. Jean-Baptiste 59*n*
Marconi, Guglielmo 93, 461
Marix, Lt (Air Vice Marshal) Reginald,
RNAS 260*n*
marksmanship 76–80
Boers' 48–9
linked to pay 85
long-range 77
rapid fire 77
target shooting 77
volley fire 80
Marne, Battle of the (6 Sept)
battle 407–16
battlefield 403
BEF advance 412–13
German counter-attacks 415
German prisoners 413
Joffre's decision to counter-attack
395–6
preparations 402–16
situation at 14 Sept **418–19**
strategy for German army 407–8
Marne, river 410, 411–12
BEF crossing of (3 Sept.) 396–7
I & II Corps across (9 Sept.) 412
Martin, Capt. A. V. 136
Marwitz, Gen. Georg von der, Cavalry
Corps 340–1
Masefield, John
Gallipoli 454*n*
on Somme 454–5
Maubeuge 245*n*
fortress of 325
plan for deployment of BEF at 12–13,
150, 156–7, 164, 227
Maud'huy, Gen. Louis de, new 10th
Army 421
Maurice, Lt-Col. (Maj.-Gen. Sir) Frederick
317–18
Forty Days in 1914 (1919) 426–7 *and n*
Maxse, Maj.-Gen. Ivor, training of
Kitchener's units 444
Mayer, Lt Albert 209 *and n*
Maze, Paul 379
Meachin, CSM Frank 330*n*
mechanization
'Caterpillar No. 1' tractor 138*n*
London omnibuses 97, 137–8, 450

possibilities for 137–8
see also tanks
Mediterranean Expeditionary Force 445–6
'meeting engagement' 275 *and n*
Melun, near Paris, GHQ at 399
Menin Gate Memorial 425*n*
Menin Road, Ypres 423, 425–6
Messimy, Adolphe, French war minister
114, 240, 245, 371*n*
Messines Ridge, Ypres 423, 425
battle (1917) 461
Metz, fortress 245
Meuse, river, crossing of (15 Aug.) 246
Michel, General Victor, and Plan XVI
114, 116, 128
militarism 44*n*
military plans
at 29 July cabinet meeting 190–1
adoption of General Staff scheme
(1911) 164–5, 168
and political intentions 99–101, 110
and n, 437–9
Military Service Act (1916) 459
militia
county regiments 66–7
reforms (1902) 62, 64–7
Millerand, Alexandre, French war
minister 371*n*, 401*n*
Milne, Admiral Sir Berkeley, C-in-C 3
The Missiles of October (1974) xix
mobilization 4*n*, **14**, 219–34
Asquith's decision on 212–13
CID memorandum on delay 218
complex chronology of 192–204, 192*n*,
199–203
decision for 189–218
effect of improved communications on
39
efficiency of 225–6
'embodiment' of reserves **14**, 68 *and n*
as political decision 100–1
'precautionary measures' 5 *and n*
'precautionary period' 192 *and n*
Moltke, Col.-Gen. Helmuth Johann von
(the Younger)
and Austrian measures on Russian
border 194–5, 197
on BEF 72
and Belgian resistance 257–8
and declaration of war on Russia
198–9, 201
and 1st Army move to south and west
397
on inevitability of war 173*n*
on Marne 416
modifications to Schlieffen Plan
113–14
and report of landing of BEF (20 Aug.)
259–60 *and n*; **what if . . .?** 428
and Schlieffen 101, 105
use of reserves 437*n*

Moltke, Helmuth von (the Elder), chief
    of Prussian general staff 35 *and n*, 39,
    42, 101
and war on two fronts 106–7
Moncel (Le Montcel), cavalry charge
    409–10
Monis, Antoine, French prime minister
    151
Monro, Col. (Gen. Sir) Charles 76
    Gallipoli 447–8
Monroe doctrine 151 *and n*
Mons, Battle of (1914) 296–319
    battlefield **278–9**, 296–7, 303–4
    dispositions 300*n*
    and failure of intelligence 275–6
    German advance (shoulder to
        shoulder) 307–8
    German confusion in 318
    gun positions 304–5
    'Shrapnel Monday' (24 Aug.) 327–34
        and n
    superior German artillery 358
    withdrawal of II Corps 323–4, 326–8
Mons–Condé canal 282, 297, 300*n*
    and demolition of bridges 301 *and n*,
        305–6
    German crossings 312, 315
    and Mons salient 299–300, 309, 311
Montdidier, German counter-attack at
    420
Montenegro, independence 45
Montgomery, FM Viscount 76, 394*n*
    as Lt at Le Cateau 364
Moore, Sir John 228 *and n*, 396
morale 459
    after Mons 396, 402–3
    after Somme 458–9
Morionville, Gen. de, chief of staff to
    King Albert 288*n*
Morley, Viscount 162
    as lord president of the council 168,
        214
Morocco
    First Crisis (1905–6) 150*n*
    independence 60
    Second (Agadir) Crisis (1911) 150–2,
        154*n*
Morris, Lt-Col. the Hon. George 391
    and n
mounted infantry, cavalry as 83–4 *and n*
Mowatt Committee (1901) 90–1 *and n*
Mowatt, Sir Francis 90*n*
Müller, Admiral Georg von, on German
    war council (Dec 1912) 173*n*
Mundy, Lt Lionel 388
Murray, Sir Archibald, BEF chief of staff
    244, 249, 274, 292–3, 334–5 *and n*,
    399
    delay in BEF move to Marne 400
    and Haig 229–30
    and Le Cateau 369

Mons 301, 314
    unwell 369, 371, 379
Murray, Arthur, MP 202

Namur, fortress 108, 111, 258
    fall of 284 *and n*
Napoleon III, king of France 26, 28,
    40–1, 42
Napoleonic Wars 141
Narodna Odbrana (People's Defence),
    Serb nationalists 179 *and n*
Nathan, George, Cornish LI 226 *and n*
naval blockade 207–8, 210*n*, 430 *and n*
Naylor, Trumpeter Jimmy 331
Needham, Lt Evelyn 383
Nelson, Admiral Viscount 141–2
Nelson, Sgt David 388
Néry, battle of 386–92
Netheravon airfield 237
Netherlands
    declaration of neutrality 196
    defensive mobilization 199, 204
    Maastricht corridor 12, 108, 113
    possibility of war with Germany, *what
        if . . .?* 436
Neuve Chapelle 451, 452
Nevinson, Henry, journalist 18
New York Herald 231
New York Times, on unthinkability of war
    in Europe 188
Newcastle, 'Pals' battalions 441
Newton, Arthur, farrier, 5th Lancers 285
Newton, Thomas, Lord 61, 64
Nicholas I, Tsar 27*n*
Nicholas II, Tsar
    and George V 199
    and Willy–Nicky telegrams with Kaiser
        193, 194, 197
Nicholson, Sir William, CIGS 128, 150,
    166
    and secret meeting of CID (Aug. 1911)
        155, 157–8
Nicolson, Harold 5–6, 20
Niemeyer, Musketier Oskar 312*n*
Nieuport, opening of sea-locks 423
Nimy, near Mons 302, 303
Nobel, Alfred 92
Norddeutscher Bund 36, 41
Norfolk, duke of, on Commission on
    Militia and Volunteers 61–2 *and n*
North Africa, British interests in 60*n*
North Sea, access to 207–8
North-West Frontier 48
Norway, declaration of neutrality 204
Noyon
    French attack (17 and 18 Sept) 420
    Sir John French at 374–5

Officers' Training Corps 64*n*
Oliphant, Lancelot 6
Omdurman, Battle of (1898) 49

Opium War, Second 27
Orsini, Felice 28 *and n*
O'Shaughnessy, Pte Thomas 287
Ottoman Empire 23 *and n*, 171
    and Balkan unrest 170–1
    and Germany 193
    mobilization 199
    war with 436, 445
Ourcq, river 410, 412, 413
Owen, Wilfred 457

Page, Walter Hines, US ambassador in
    London 6–7n
Paget, Sir Arthur, GOC-in-C Ireland 177n
Paissy 415n
Paléologue, Maurice, French ambassador
    to Russia 203
Palmerston, Lord 22, 28
    on Belgian independence 25
    and Schleswig-Holstein question 32
'Pals' battalions 441–3
    in action 456, 458–9
    Stockbrokers' Battalion 442
    training 442–3
    'Wool Textile Pioneers' 442
Panouse, Col. le Vicomte de la 196
Panther, SMS, and Agadir Crisis 150–4
Paris
    Eiffel Tower, radio station 341n
    German bombing (30 Aug.) 395
    threat to 395n
Paris, siege of (1870–1) 42 *and n*
Paris, Treaty of (1814) 23
Parmenter, Cpl Henry 310
Parr, Pte John, first BEF casualty in
    ground action 302n, 463–4
Parsons, C. A., turbine engine inventor
    146n
Pas de Calais spring offensive (1915) 451
Passchendaele (1917) 460
passports, diplomatic 4n
Pašić, Nikola, Serbian prime minister
    184, 187
Pau, Paul 114
Pease, Jack, president of Board of
    Education 206n
Peninsular War 378
Peter Karadordevíc, king of Serbia 179n
Peugeot, Caporal Jules 209 *and n*
Picardy 420
    autumn offensive (1915) 448
Pitman, Lt-Col. Thomas, 11th Hussars
    340, 387
Plumer, Gen. Sir Herbert 233, 461
Poincaré, Raymond, French prime
    minister 116, 147n, 183
    meeting with Sir John French 237, 240
Poland 26
Ponsonby, Sir E. 20
Ponting, Clive 192n
poppies 405 *and n*

Portsmouth (New Hampshire), Treaty of
    (1905) 58n
Portugal 58
postal service, field service postcards 265
Pourtalès, Count Friedrich, German
    ambassador to Russia 203
Pratt, Pte Harry 328
'precautionary period', declaration of 192
    and n
Pretyman, Lt George, RFC 338
Princip, Gavrilo xvii
prisoners, German, taken by BEF at
    Marne 413
Prussia
    Bismarck's ambitions for 29, 32n, 36
    enlargement 24, 29, 36
    'Falk Laws' 40n
    Junker caste 37 *and n*
    nature of state 40 *and n*
    navy 33n
Prussian army
    conscription and reserves 38 *and n*
    officers 39
public opinion, British 195
Punch cartoons, dismissal of Bismarck 45
Pursey, Driver Walter, RFA 296

Quakers 206n
Quast, Lt-Gen. Ferdinand von, IX Corps
    306, 311–12

'Race for the Sea' **418–19**, 421–3
radio technology 461
Radziwill, Princess Marie, letters to
    Gen. Count Mario de Robilant 153–4
    and n
    on German mobilization 208
Raglan, Lord 27n, 347 *and n*
railways 173 *and n*
    advantages for troop movements 428
    and n
    Berlin–Baghdad 45n
    French 13 *and n*, 109, 157 *and n*, 428
    and n, 432
    German 251–2; timetables 42, 100–1,
    105
    German requisitioning of French and
    Belgian 404
    Luxembourg 201–2
    and mobilization 225–6
    Prussian 39
    and Schlieffen Plan 109, 432
Ranke, Robert von, consul-general 20
'rapid fire', at Mons 307 *and n*
Rawlinson, Col. (Lt-Gen.) Sir Henry 123,
    422n
    Battle of Amiens 461n
    and Somme offensive 453, 458
Reassurance, Treaty of (1887) 56 *and n*
recruitment 61
    Army Reserve 64n

effect of casualties on 448
Officers' Training Corps 64 *and n*
and reserve forces 69
Special Reserve 63, 64–5
Redmond, John, and loyalty of Catholic
    Ireland 216
refugees: from Charleroi 288; from
    villages on Mons canal 327
regiment, defined 10–11*n*
Reichsbank, suspension of convertibility
    of notes 180
Repington, Col. Charles, *Times*
    correspondent 125 *and n*, 166 *and n*,
    282
Richards, Pte Frank, Royal Welsh Fusiliers
    295, 344
    at Le Cateau 362–3, 366–7, 373,
        379–80
    at Marne 410–11
Old Soldiers Never Die (memoir) 262 *and n*
Richthofen, Freiherr von, Cavalry Corps
    311, 337, 409, 413
Rifle Volunteers *see* Volunteer Force
'rifle volunteers', Palmerston's 28
rifles
    ammunition 79
    'Brown Bess' 76
    for cavalry 85
    Chassepot (French) 38, 42
    Dreyse (Prussian breech-loading) 35, 38
    jezail (Afghan) 48
    Lee-Enfield magazine-fed: Boer War 47,
        77; SMLE ('303') 78–9 *and n*, 85
    Mauser 50
    Minié (French) 38, 77
    muskets 76
    shortages for volunteers 443
Ritter von Wenninger, Lt-Gen. Karl 198
Robb, Maj.-Gen. Frederick 232, 290
Roberts, FM Lord 8–9, 51
Robertson, Maj.-Gen. William ('Wully')
    226, 427*n*
    and BEF retreat 290–1, 324*n*, 378,
        379–80, 394
    order to dump ammunitions and
        rations 379–80
Robilant, Gen. Count Mario di, Princess
    Radziwill's letters to 154*n*
Röhl, Professor John 45 *and n*, 171, 173
Rolt, Brig.-Gen. Stuart, 14th Bde 358–9
Romania 45, 171
Rosenberg, Isaac, 'Break of Day in the
    Trenches' 457
Rothschild, Nathan, Lord 196
Rouen 262
Roupell, Lt George, VC, East Surreys
    307*n*, 314 *and n*, 336
Royal Automobile Club, volunteer
    drivers 410
Royal Commission on the Militia and
    Volunteers (1902) 61–2 *and n*

Royal Flying Corps 96
    base near Amiens 237, 243
    damaged by violent storm (12 Sept) 414
    effect of wind on 337–8
    reconnaissance: first sorties 266–8; of
        German positions 276–7, 283–4; at
        Le Cateau 365–6 *and n*; at Marne
        410
Royal Irish Constabulary 189
Royal Marines Brigade 421
Royal Naval Air Service 96, 421
Royal Naval Division 421, 446
Royal Navy 28, 58, 439
    Admiral Sir Arthur Wilson's plans
        (Aug. 1911) 159–62
    at declaration of war 2–3, 4
    numerical superiority 147–8
    plans for 140–68
    and protection of French coasts 207–8,
        210
    shipbuilding programme 144 *and n*,
        146, 148
    wireless telegraphy 93
Ruffey, Gen. Emmanuel, dismissed 398
Ruffey, Gen. Pierre, French 3rd Army
    268–9
Rupprecht, Crown Prince, 6th (Bavarian)
    Army 420, 421, 423
Russell, Lord John 29
Russell, William Howard 28*n*
Russia
    and Battle of Tannenberg 420
    Bolshevik Revolution (1917) 436, 437
    interest in Dardanelles 170
    mobilization 186, 193–5, 194*n*
    partial mobilization against Austria
        193–4, 203
    and Poland 26
    relations with Austria 174
    relations with France 56, 58, 113, 118
    and Serbia 171–2 *and n*, 183–4, 188
    and Triple Entente pact 435–6
    and *what if . . .?* 436, 437
Russian army 113, 280*n*
Russo-Japanese War (1904–5) 58
Russo-Turkish war (1877–8) 44–5

Sackville-West, Vita 6
Sadowa (Königgrätz), Battle of (1866) 36
St Nazaire 421
St Quentin
    BEF GHQ at 369–70, 375
    II Corps at 377
    Lanrezac's 5th Army attack 384–5
St-Symphorien cemetery 463–4
St Vincent, Admiral John Jervis, Earl 142
Sambre, river 274, 338, 351
    attack on French II and X Corps 283
Samuel, Herbert 190, 214
San Giuliano, Marchese di, Italian
    foreign minister 186, 198

Sarajevo 37
  assassination of Archduke Franz
      Ferdinand xvii; British indifference
      to 174–6
Sardinia, kingdom of 28n
Sarsfield, Maj. 369
Sassoon, Siegfried 67, 456, 457–8
Sava bridge (Serbia/Austro-Hungarian
      border) 186
Saxe-Lauenburg, duchy of 33
Sazonov, Sergei, Russian foreign minister
  and Austrian declaration of war on
      Serbia 188
  and Austrian mobilization 194–5
  and German declaration of war 203
Scapa Flow 4, 144n
Scarpe, river 421
Scheldt, River 26, 126
  status of 12 and n, 423n
Schleswig-Holstein 32–4
Schlieffen, Alfred, Graf von 101, 104–5
  on Belgian neutrality 111
  and political realities 106
Schlieffen Plan xix, 101, 102–3, 104–13
  and advance of German right wing
      270–1
  and alternative BEF strategy 105,
      428–9
  based on walking pace 109, 432
  development of 108–9
  ended at Marne 416
  French knowledge of 117 and n
  and Joffre's counter-attack at Marne
      395
  and Liège 199, 255, 256–7
  need for troop numbers 109–10
  and neutrality of Belgium 110–11
Schoen, Wilhelm von, German
      ambassador in Paris 149n, 197n
School of Mounted Infantry, Longmoor
      84
School of Musketry, Hythe 76–7
Sclater-Booth, Maj. the Hon. Walter 388
Scott-Kerr, Brig.-Gen. Robert 352, 391,
      396
'Scramble for Africa' 59
Secret Service Bureau 1, 175 and n
Sedan 108
  fall of (1870) 42
Seeckt, Hans von 106
Seely, Colonel Jack 8
  and Curragh mutiny 177 and n
  at Le Cateau 348–9
  as secretary for war 136, 166
Selle, river 359
Serbia 45, 170, 179–88
  Austrian ultimatum to 183 and n, 184
  gains in Balkan Wars 173, 174
  nationalist organizations 179 and n
  relations with Austria 174
shell shock 90n

ships
  Dreadnought class 144 and n, 145
  ironclads, French 27 and n
  long-range gunnery 144, 146
  requisitioning of Turkish dreadnought
      193
  steam turbine engines 144
Shrapnel, Henry 87
Simon, Sir John, attorney-general,
      resignation 214
Skene, Lt Robert, RFC 237
Sloggett, Surgeon-General Sir Arthur
      459
Small, Lt Francis, RFC 368
Smith, Donald 234n
Smith-Dorrien, Gen. Sir Horace, II Corps
      187, 232, 281–3, 282n
  and 2nd Army (from 1915) 451
  and decision to counter-attack at Le
      Cateau 336–56, 375; decision
      347–9; and French's order 350–1
      and n; intentions 359, 360; on
      position at Le Cateau 356–7;
      withdrawal after 378–9;
      withdrawal to Le Cateau 339–40
  and Kitchener 232, 281–2 and n, 440
  misgivings about BEF mission 233–4
  at Mons 301, 302, 315; and Mons
      salient 309, 316–18, 323–4; and
      Mons–Condé canal line 298,
      299–301 and n; withdrawal from
      Mons in contact 326–8
  and morale (before Marne) 396
  relations with French 232, 298 and n
  visit to French (after Mons) 332–3
Smuts, Jan 52n
Snelling, Cpl, 12th Lancers 261
Snow, Maj.-Gen. Thomas D'Oyly 332,
      347, 349, 379
  at Le Cateau 359, 363
Snoxall, Sergeant-Instructor, School of
      Musketry 79
Soignies, Kluck's HQ at 337
Solesmes, near Le Cateau 341
Somme, Battle of the 454–60
  casualties 450 and n, 458
  'Football Attack' 455–6
  'race for the parapet' 455–6
Sordet, Gen. Jean-François, French
      Cavalry Corps
  at Dinant 246
  FM Sir John French and 269, 289, 332
  and Le Cateau 349, 359
  to BEF left flank 269, 280, 332, 380
South Africa
  colonial forces 431
  wireless telegraph stations 93–4 and n
Spears, Lt (Maj.-Gen) Edward, liaison
      officer with French 5th Army xviii,
      115, 244
  on dismissal of Lanrezac 398

first view of BEF 263
and French 5th Army withdrawal 283,
321
and French mobilization 208–9 *and n*
and Joffre's request for BEF cooperation
399–400
and Lanrezac 288–9, 295 *and n*, 324–5
on meeting of French and Lanrezac
247–8 *and n*
on Sir John French 288–9, 325–6*n*,
370, 371
Special Reserve **63**, 64–7, 430*n*, 431
fitness 264–5
mobilization **14**, 67, 223–6
Wolds Wagoners 65–6, 224–5
see also Army Reserve
Spicer, Pte Frederick 364–5
Spion Kop 49–51
staff college 128 *and n*
'staff rides' 124 *and n*
Stanley, Hon. Charles 443*n*
Stanley, Venetia, Asquith's
correspondence with 2, 174–5,
203–4, 385
Steele, Lt Frederick 309–10
Steevens, G. W., journalist 5*n*
Steinberg, Prof. Jonathan 44, 45–6
stock markets
Berlin 154, 196
London 196
Strachan, Sir Hew, on relations with
France 27
strategy xxi, 39, 382
alternative 105, 428–31
failures of British thinking (1915) 445
thinking of war council (5 Aug.) 15–17
Stuart-Wortley, Col. (Maj.-Gen.) Edward
149*n*
Sweden, declaration of neutrality 204
and n
Switzerland, defensive mobilization 199,
204
Sykes, Sir Mark, and Wolds Wagoners 65

tactics
firepower 55
frontal attacks 52 *and n*
Messines Ridge (1917) 461
Tailby, 2nd Lt George 387
tanks 449–50
delay in use of 453–4
at Flers (Somme) 460
names for 450
Tannenberg, Battle of (1914) 420
Tappen, Oberst Gerhard 407
Taylor, A. J. P. 100
Taylor, Sgt James 409–10
Taylor, Joseph, gunsmith 28*n*
telegraph 93
in Boer War 50
French system 109

no link between Corps and GHQ 322,
323*n*
Prussian use of 39
wireless 93–4 *and n*
Tennyson, Alfred, Lord, 'The War' 28
Terraine, John, *Mons* (1960) 326
Territorial Force (Army) 11, 98, 204,
227*n*, 426
first action at Messines Ridge 423, 425
formation 68–70
size (1913) 68 *and n*
to reinforce BEF 440–1
Territorial and Reserve Forces Bill (1907)
69
Thomas, Cpl Ernest 286
Thynne, Lord Alexander, MP 134
Tilney, Pte 286
Tilsit, Treaty of (1807) 58
The Times
'Peace in the Balance' headline (July
1914) 187
and support for France 195
see also Repington, Charles
Tirpitz, Admiral Alfred (von) 143
and German shipbuilding programme
143, 144, 147
on readiness of fleet 181
underestimation of Royal Navy 147
Tisza, István, Hungarian prime minister
186
Tollerton, Pte Ross, VC 415
Tours, alternative position of BEF at,
what if . . .? 431, 433
Towsey, Lt-Col., West Yorks 415*n*
Trafalgar, Battle of (1805) 141–2
training
1912 manoeuvres 231–2 *and n*
changes after Boer War 52–5
improvisation for Pals battalions 442–4
of Kitchener's volunteers 441–5, 451
transport
BEF staff cars 283*n*
improvised armoured cars 450
London omnibuses 97, 137–8, 450
see also horses
trench warfare 450–8
and lack of mobility 451
trenches 450–1
consolidation 426
first 417
German 453
Trevelyan, Charles, resignation 212*n*
Triple Alliance, Italy and 186, 198
'Triple Entente' 129*n*
pact (3 Sept.) 435–6
Troisvierges, Luxembourg 201, 202
Truppenpraxis 407–8
Tsushima, battle of (1905) 144
Tuchman, Barbara 191
The Guns of August (1962) xix *and n*
on purpose of BEF 240, 242

Turkey *see* Ottoman Empire
Tyrell, William, private secretary to Grey
    200

Ulster Unionists 177, 195
uniforms
    boots 86 *and n*, 407 *and n*
    French 85, 115
    German, *Pickelhaube* helmets 364
    hats 86
    khaki 47, 85–6
    puttees 86 *and n*
    Sam Browne belt 86
    service dress 86
    shortages 443
United States of America
    American troops in 'Hundred Days'
        offensive (1918) 461
    not at Congress of Vienna 24*n*
    view of war in Europe 188
    see also House, 'Col.'; Wilson, Woodrow

Vansittart, Robert, Lord 131*n*
Vaughan, Col. J., at Le Cateau 345
Vaughan, Lt R. M., RFC 267
Verdun, German offensive 454
Vereeniging, Treaty of (1902) 52
Vesle, river 413
Victoria Crosses
    first Indian 425
    first two 310
    Le Cateau, RA 363*n*
    Marne 414–15
    Néry, RHA 388 *and n*
    Somme 444
Victoria, Queen 46, 58
Vienna, Congress of (1815) xvii, 23–5
    art. 65, on conjunction of Netherlands
        (Belgium) and Holland 24–5
    and Bismarck's 1866 Prussia–Germany
        36
    and Prussian borders 24, 29
Villain, Raoul, assassin of Jaurès 197*n*
Villeneuve, Admiral 142
Villers-Cotterêts, I Corps action at 390–2
Villiers, Sir Francis, ambassador to
    Belgium 267
Vimy, French advance to 421
Viviani, René, meeting with French 240
Voltaire, on Germany 250–1 *and n*
Volunteer Force (Rifle Volunteers) 67–8
    and n
    as home defence force 68
    see also Territorial Force
volunteers
    'Pals' battalions 441–3
    reforms 61*n*
    response to Kitchener's call 441–3

Waldersee, Alfred, Graf von 107
Waldersee, Georg von 181

Walincourt, near Le Cateau 359
Walpole, Sir Robert 214 *and n*
'War Book' 192 *and n*
war councils
    1st (5 Aug.) 8–17
    final (12 Aug.), on deployment of BEF
        227–8
    German (December 1912) 173*n*
    individual recollections of 17*n*
'war games' 124 *and n*
war guilt (*Kriegsschuldfrage*) xviii–xix, 105
War of Jenkins' Ear 214*n*
War Office 2*n*, 7
    failure to incorporate BEF into French
        deployment plans 438–9
    horse mobilization section 135
    Mechanical Transport Committee 138
    reforms 53, 75
    and strategy xxi
War Office (Reconstruction) Committee
    53
war on two fronts
    Bonaparte and 104–5
    Elder Moltke and 106–7
    French assumptions about German
        intentions 117–18
    Schlieffen and 104
warfare, asymmetric 48
Waterloo, Battle of 22–3
    Mont St Jean ridge 356–7
    and Quatre Bras 275
Wavell, FM Lord 105–6, 334
Wellington, Duke of
    Peninsular War 378
    see also Waterloo
Wenninger, Karl von 405
The West Wing xix
Western Front
    effect of failure of Gallipoli on 449
    siege warfare 450–1
Wigram, Maj. Clive 427–8
Wilburg, Herr 151–2
Wilhelm I, king of Prussia 45
    and 'Ems Telegram' 40–1
Wilhelm II, Kaiser 18, 45, 60
    article in *Daily Telegraph* (1908) 148–9
        and n
    authorization of general mobilization
        200–1
    and Belgian resistance 257–8
    bellicosity 182, 183*n*
    and Bismarck 45
    character 172, 176
    'contemptible' remark 260*n*
    cruise to Arctic Circle (1914) 182, 184
    exhortation of Hunnic spirit 413*n*
    expectation of British support for
        France 172
    and First Balkan War 171
    and German navy 143, 144, **145**
    and Lichnowsky 181

and military planning 105
relations with Edward VII 46
and Schlieffen 107
visits to London 58, 154*n*
on Waterloo 23
Weltpolitik policy 18, 45 *and n*
and Willy–Nicky telegrams with Tsar
193, 194, 197
Wilson, Sir Arthur, Admiral of the Fleet
career and character 160–1
reputation for strategy 161–2
secret meeting of CID (Aug. 1911) 155,
157, 159–62
Wilson, Pte George, VC 415
Wilson, Maj.-Gen. Henry 121–39
and Churchill 167
as DMO (from 1910) 128–39
early career and character 121–4
expectations of German mobilization
117*n*
and Foch 127–8, 150, 166
in France 124, 167, 235
and French general staff view of short
war 16
and French plans (1911) 154, 155–6
and Huguet 126–7, 166–7
and Joffre 167, 269, 399
Kitchener's view of 282
and Le Cateau 342, 348–9, 370–1, 379
and Maurice 427*n*
and meeting with Lanrezac 247–8
and misappreciation of German main
effort on right 276, 280, 315–16
and mobilization 196
planning 234; for deployment of BEF
at Maubeuge 12–13, 150, 156–7,
164; at secret meeting of CID
(Aug. 1911) 155–9; size of BEF 156

and n, 163, 205, 227; and supply
of horses 132–8; at war council (5
Aug.) 10–11, 10*n*
preparations for mobilization 149–50
and n; assumption of simultaneous
mobilization with France 204
with Sir John French (16/17 Aug.) 244,
247
Wilson, Woodrow, US President 175
and n, 178*n*
withdrawal in contact, logistics of 326–7
Witte, Lt-Gen. Leon de, Belgian cavalry
division 245*n*
Wright, Capt. Theodore, VC 312 *and n*
Württemberg, General Albrecht, duke of,
German 4th Army 268, 423
Wyatt, LCpl George, VC 354*n*

Xylander, Major Rudolph (Ritter) von
405

Yate, Maj., Yorks LI 367
Yeldham, Capt. 369
Yeomanry 67, 421
Ypres, BEF at 423
Ypres, First Battle of (Oct.–Nov. 1914) xx,
425–6
Ypres, Third Battle of (1917) 460
Yser, river 423

Zehl, General Johan von, VII Corps 284*n*
Zenker, Capt. Hans 182
Zimmerman, Arthur von, German
under-secretary of state 20, 152
Zola, Émile 112*n*
Zuber, Terence 113
on Le Cateau 346–7*n*, 364*n*, 376*n*
on Mons 307*n*, 309*n*, 310–11*n*

Allan Mallinson is a former infantry and cavalry officer, with thirty-five years' service in the British army. He is the author of the popular Matthew Hervey series of historical novels and of *Light Dragoons* – a history of four regiments of British cavalry (one of which he commanded) – as well as the acclaimed *The Making of the British Army*. Besides writing on defence matters for *The Times*, he regularly reviews for *The Times* and the *Spectator*. Allan Mallinson lives on Salisbury Plain in Wiltshire. To find out more, visit: www.allanmallinsonbooks.com